ART OF EMPIRE

The Roman Frescoes and Imperial Cult Chamber in Luxor Temple

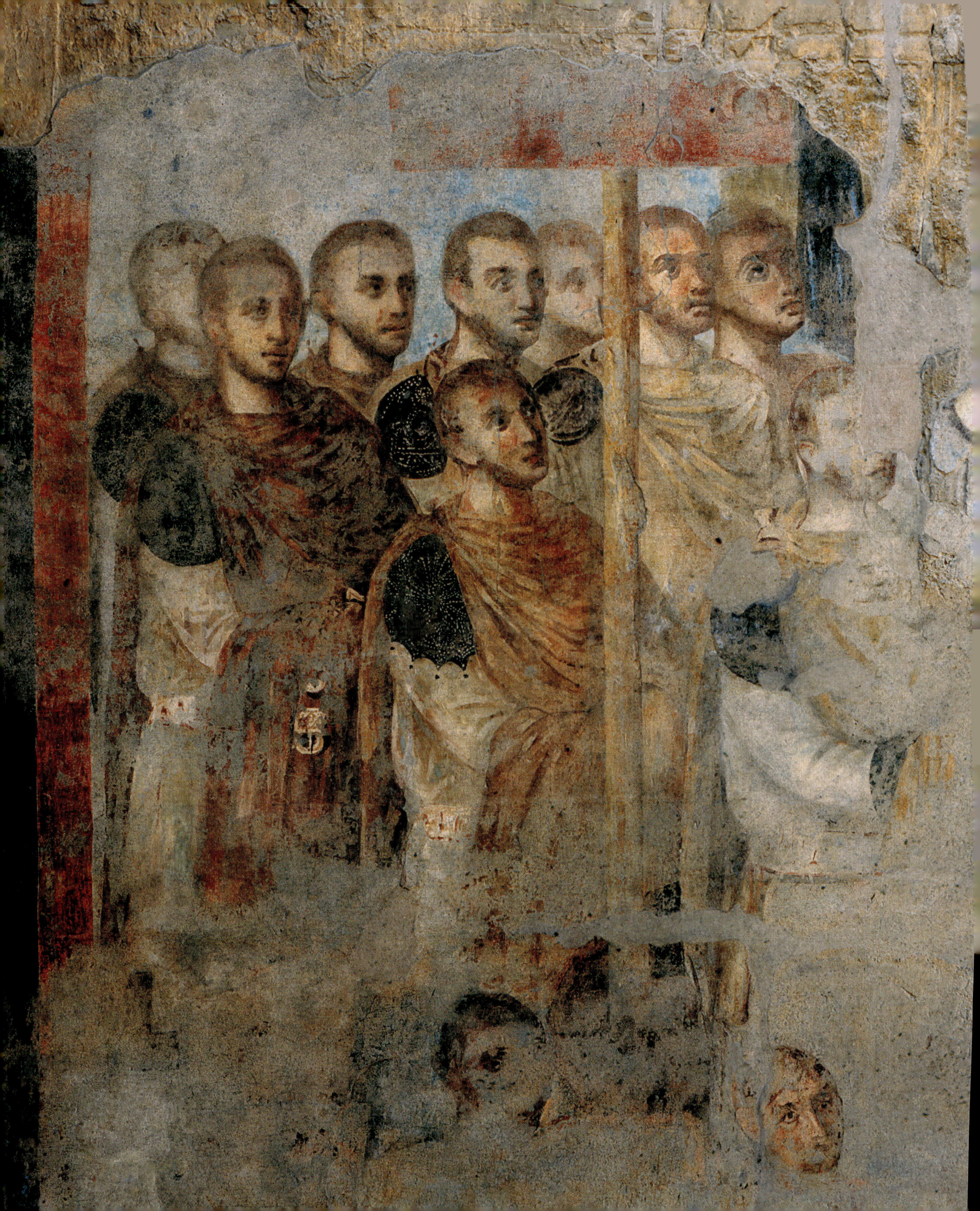

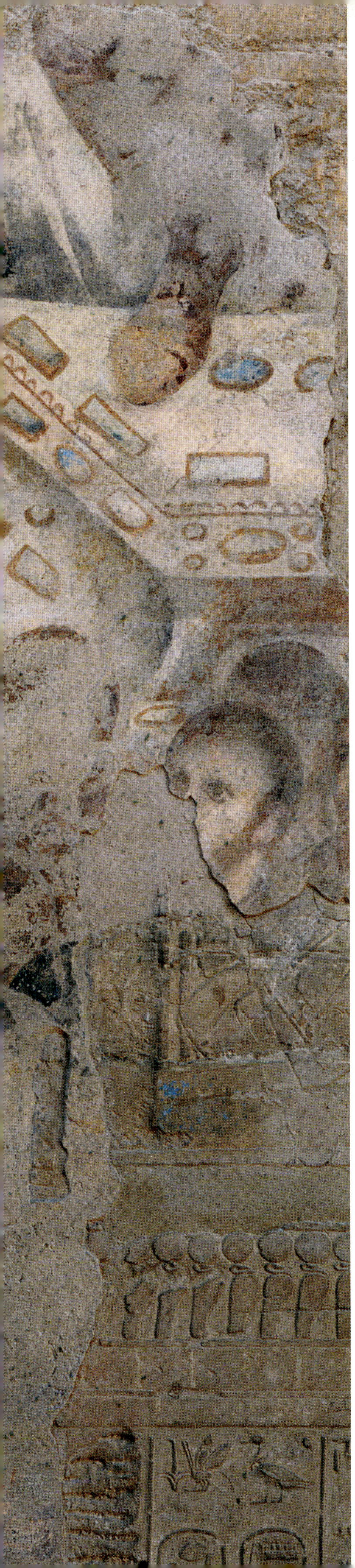

ART OF EMPIRE

The Roman Frescoes and Imperial Cult Chamber in Luxor Temple

Edited by Michael Jones
and Susanna McFadden

American Research Center in Egypt, Inc.
Yale University Press New Haven and London

2 Midan Simon Bolivar, Garden City, Cairo, Egypt 11461
8700 Crownhill Blvd., Suite 507, San Antonio, TX 78209

This publication is made possible by the generous support of the American people through the United States Agency for International Development (USAID). The contents are the responsibility of the authors and do not necessarily reflect the views of USAID or the United States Government.

yalebooks.com/art

Designed by Peter M. Blaiwas, Vern Associates, Inc.
Set in Minion and Marcellus by Brian Hotchkiss
Printed and bound in China

Library of Congress Control Number: 2015932387
ISBN 978-0-300-16912-6

A catalogue record for this book is available from the British Library.

This paper meets the requirements of ANSI/NISO Z39.48-1992
(Permanence of Paper).

10 9 8 7 6 5 4 3 2 1

Jacket illustrations:
(front)
Dignitaries revering the emperor at the east end of the south wall of the imperial cult chamber; detail of figure 6.16.

(back)
View of the imperial cult chamber from the Amenhotep III portico; detail of figure 7.3.

Frontispiece:
Dignitaries express their esteem for an emperor seated above, his foot resting on a jeweled footstool. East end of the south wall of the imperial cult chamber; detail of figure 6.16.

This publication is made possible by the generous support of the American people through the United States Agency for International Development (USAID).

CONTENTS

FOREWORD

This volume presents the work of several scholars, drawn from different fields of expertise. It is prompted by a conservation project undertaken by the American Research Center in Egypt (ARCE) in the Temple of Amun at Luxor, Egypt. This project was carried out in concert with Egypt's Ministry of State for Antiquities (MSA) through a grant from the United States Agency for International Development (USAID). Since the mid-1990s, ARCE has worked with its colleagues in the MSA (formerly the Supreme Council of Antiquities; SCA) and at USAID in the areas of conservation and training to help document, conserve, and preserve Egypt's priceless cultural heritage, a heritage that is of worldwide significance. In its conservation projects, ARCE has worked in virtually all eras of Egypt's long past, from the prehistoric to the Ottoman Period. This project in the high-profile Luxor Temple, one of Egypt's major ancient monuments and a central site for tourism, is entirely in keeping with ARCE's efforts to conserve heritage monuments that might otherwise be lost, to preserve them for future generations, and to present them to a wider audience. Its focus is the remains of the Roman imperial frescoes preserved in a central room of Luxor Temple. These frescoes are the finest Roman paintings preserved in Egypt, and they therefore hold a unique place in the field of Roman art. Before this project was undertaken, they were obscured by surface accretions and damage. Now they have the potential to engage the viewer in a significant moment in the history of the temple that is frequently overlooked. In subject matter, they celebrate the imperial cult of the four rulers (the Tetrarchs) who held sway over the Roman Empire at the time of their creation. In design they represent a school of court painters whose work is otherwise entirely lost.

Between 2005 and 2008, ARCE conducted the comprehensive project to clean, conserve, and document the paintings. The work was carried out by a skilled team of Italian conservators in collaboration with the Epigraphic Survey of the Oriental Institute of the University of Chicago, which has long been involved in documenting the site. When created, the paintings were a focal point of the Roman administrative center and military camp that was based in the Egyptian temple. Though Sir John Gardner Wilkinson recorded the paintings in 1856, the fact that the primary focus of modern visitors and scholars is the temple's pharaonic remains has meant that the Roman paintings have not necessarily received the attention they deserve and, indeed, were long misunderstood by scholars and visitors. Consequently, the project to conserve these exceptional paintings has presented the opportunity to reexamine their historical and art historical importance within the wider context of late Roman Egypt under the emperor Diocletian. In undertaking this reassessment, we are grateful to the scholars and conservators who have contributed their expertise and to all those who have assisted in this effort.

Gerry D. Scott III
Director
American Research Center in Egypt

ACKNOWLEDGMENTS

All who have participated in this project value the encouragement and assistance of numerous friends and colleagues both in Egypt and internationally.

The project would not have been possible without the support of the American people through funding by the United States Agency for International Development (USAID Egypt). We are grateful to Mission Directors Hilda Arellano and Walter North and to Richard Rousseau, Seifallah Hassanein, Anthony Vance, and Sylvia Atalla Hanna. It is also an honor to acknowledge the interest and support of two former U.S. ambassadors to Egypt, Francis Ricciardone and Margaret Scoby, and to thank them for their endorsement of ARCE's work in the field of cultural heritage preservation in Egypt.

We are most grateful for the collegial support we have received from the Ministry of State for Antiquities (MSA) and Supreme Council of Antiquities (SCA). Our thanks go especially to Ministers of Antiquities Dr. Muhammed Ibrahim Ali and Dr. Zahi Hawass and to Sabri Abd al-Aziz, Magdi al-Ghandour, Muhammed Ismail, and all the members of the Permanent Committee of the MSA who have approved the permits for us to undertake the conservation work. Thanks also to Hisham el-Leithy for securing permission to publish the Osirid statue and shroud of Tyras in the Luxor Museum (figures I.8 and 1.6), to Tarek al-Awady and Yasmin el-Shazli at the Egyptian Museum, Cairo, for permission to publish the porphyry bust from Benha (figure 2.3), and to Chris Naunton and Joanne Kyffin at the Egypt Exploration Society for permission to publish the image of the Buchis stela of Diocletian from Armant (figure 1.5).

The Luxor SCA Inspectorate facilitated the work in every way with courtesy and efficiency. We are grateful to Mansour Boraik, former chief inspector of Luxor; Sultan Id, chief inspector of Luxor Temple; and his staff who accompanied the project in the field, in particular Sana' Yussef al-Kahu, Hana' Mussa al-Dassuqi, and Saha Abd al-Latif Abd al-Rahim.

We are also grateful to the staff and board of the American Research Center in Egypt (ARCE), particularly Presidents Emily Teeter, Richard Martin, and Carol Redmount; the director, Dr. Gerry D. Scott III; the publications director, Kathleen Scott, for seeing this book through its various stages to publication; Assistant Director Amira Khattab for managing the bureaucratic procedures necessary to keep the project running; Grant Administrator Janie Abdulaziz for handling the contractual arrangements with the conservation team; and John Shearman, director of ARCE-Luxor, for his constant support for the project, especially during the research stage for the preparation of this book.

Special thanks are due to Jaroslaw Dobrowolski for his invaluable work preparing the images, maps, and diagrams and to Sara Montgomery for translating the original Italian of chapter 5 into English. We are also grateful to Johannes Deckers for allowing us to reprint and build upon his masterful 1979 reconstruction of the Luxor painted program.

The project was carried out in collaboration with the Epigraphic Survey of the Oriental Institute of the University of Chicago, Luxor (Chicago House). Logistical and technical support provided by Chicago House guaranteed the success of the project. We are particularly grateful to the field director, Ray Johnson, and the epigraphers J. Brett McClain and Christian Greco; the conservator Hiroko Kawai; the photographer Yarko Kobylecky, who documented the frescoes before, during, and after conservation; Tina di Cerbo; the librarian Marie

Bryan; the master mason Frank Helmholz and his team; the artist Susan Osgood; and the financial manager Safinaz Ouri.

Thanks are due to Arnaldo and Alessandro Vescovo for their fine photographs of Luxor Temple taken in February 2009, many of which are included here.

For providing access to superb collections of historical photographs of Luxor we are indebted to Chicago House's photographic archives assistant, Ellie Smith, and photographic archives assistant and photographer, Susan Lezon; John Larson, archivist at the Oriental Institute, University of Chicago; Angie Park, archivist and manager of the Special Library Collections at the Brooklyn Museum; Ola Seif, photographic archivist at the American University in Cairo; Jeanette Clough, senior reference librarian at the Research Library of the Getty Conservation Institute, Los Angeles; Jaromír Málek and Cat Warsi at the Griffith Institute, Oxford; Kurt and Maggy Lambelet at Lehnert and Landrock in Cairo; Aboudi's and Gaddis's bookshops in Luxor; and James Kerr of Pump Park Vintage Photography.

We are also grateful to Helen Whitehouse at the Ashmolean Museum, Oxford, for her insightful comments and for drawing our attention to the watercolor by General Sausmarez; to Marta Weiss, curator of photographs at the Victoria and Albert Museum, London; and to Revinda Chahal at the Victoria and Albert Museum for providing the scan of the Sausmarez watercolor and permission to reproduce it here (figure 4.6).

Richard Ovenden, associate director at the Bodleian Library, Oxford, and Eva Oledzka, reference librarian there, facilitated access to and provided scans of John Gardner Wilkinson's 1856 sketchbook (MS Wilkinson Dep. d. 34) and gave permission to reproduce the drawings in the appendix.

It is a pleasure to acknowledge personal friends, mentors, and colleagues who have supported the fieldwork and research associated with this project. Among these are Jere Bacharach, Norbert Baer, Elizabeth Bolman, Edwin Brock, Colin Davies, Richard and Carol Downer, Alaa al-Habashi, Renata Holod, Helen and Jean Jacquet, Mohsen Kamel, Ann Kuttner, Mary Ellen Lane, William Lyster, Stephen Rickerby, C. Brian Rose, Giovanni Ruffini, Peter Sheehan, Tarek Swelim, Jason Thompson, Nicholas Warner, and Kent Weeks. We also thank our colleagues at the Getty Conservation Institute, Los Angeles, Neville Agnew, Martha Demas, Lorinda Wong, Tom Roby, and David Myers, for their hospitality and valuable discussions both in Egypt and at the Getty Center in Los Angeles. Finally, very special appreciation is due to Angela Milward Jones, whose advice, patience, and meticulous editing have resulted in numerous improvements and have moved this book toward completion.

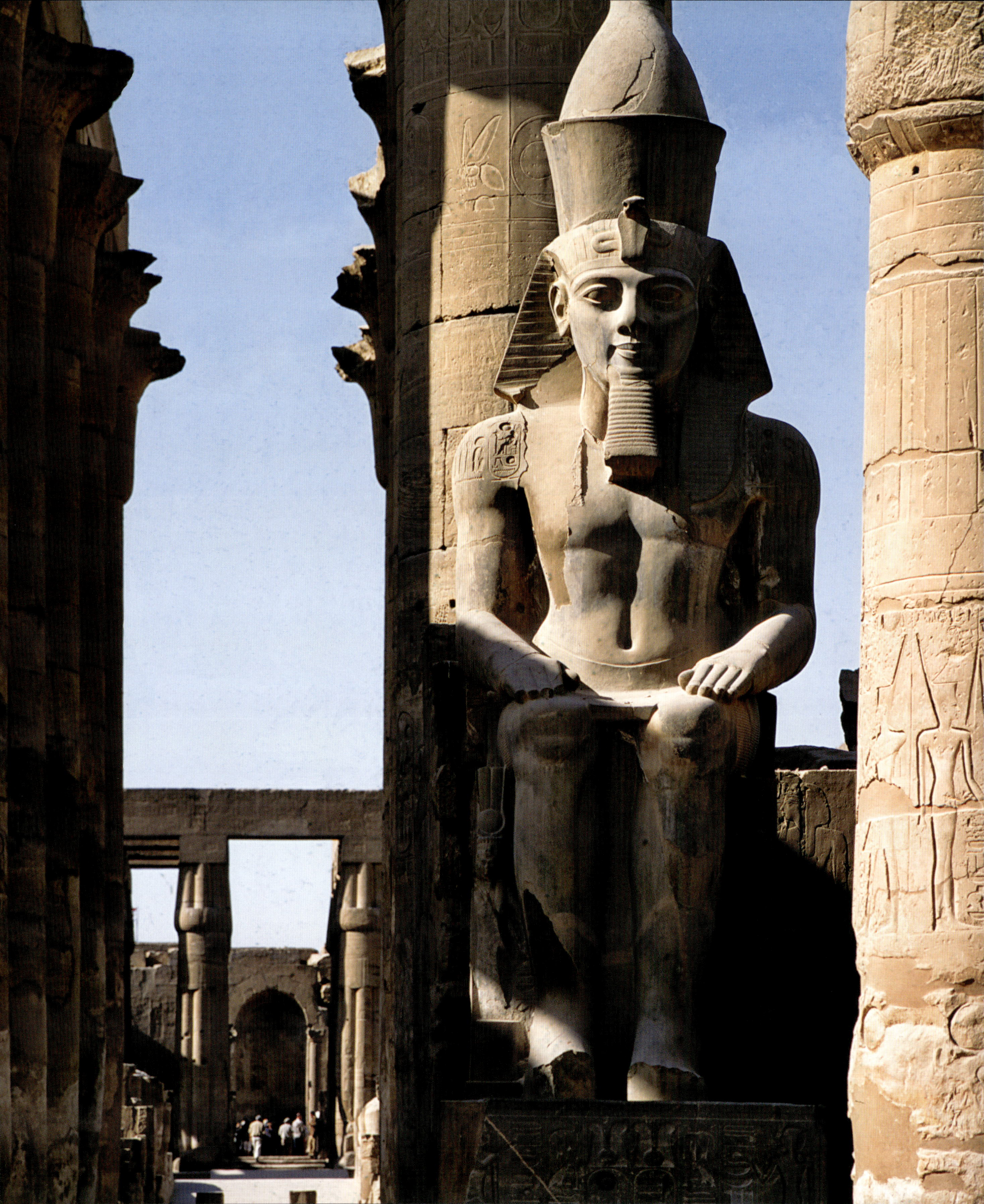

INTRODUCTION

MICHAEL JONES AND SUSANNA McFADDEN

THIS BOOK FOCUSES ON THE IMPERIAL CULT CHAMBER and the remains of the late Roman frescoes that were created in Luxor Temple at a critical moment in the history of Egypt and the Roman Empire.[1] This moment was the turn of the fourth century CE, when the emperor Diocletian's reforms in government, economic, administrative, religious, and military activities were affecting almost every aspect of Roman life. Diocletian (r. 284–305), the creator of the tetrarchic system and primary sovereign of the First Tetrarchy (293–305), had come to Egypt to supervise the military campaign that ended the revolts that had recently threatened to destabilize the country and to manage the reorganization necessary to maintain Roman authority. The surviving frescoes are the most arresting sign of extensive late Roman modifications made to the ancient temple of Amun of Luxor (Thebes) in this era.[2] These included a fortified enclosure constructed around the temple, probably replacing or building on existing walls (see figure 2.1).[3] Colonnaded streets were laid out on both the east and west sides of the temple; monumental tetrastyles (four-columned monuments) were constructed at the crossroads, which reflect at least two stages of embellishment and architectural modifications.[4] At the heart of the temple, the Roman builders converted the room in front of the offering hall—which precedes the rooms in which the image of the god Amun was kept—into an imperial cult chamber by removing the columns, blocking the original doorway leading to the rooms beyond, and creating a niche in its place. They covered the Eighteenth-Dynasty reliefs in this room with plaster and decorated the walls with frescoes in purely Roman style. A canopy supported on four granite columns was placed in front of the painted niche to serve as the centerpiece of the room (figure I.2).

FIGURE I.1
View from the Ramesses II court through the temple to the niche in the imperial cult chamber.

The remains of these frescoes are unmistakable reminders of how the tetrarchic renovations give new meanings to Luxor Temple, past and present. Between 2005 and 2008, they were cleaned and conserved by the American Research Center in Egypt (ARCE) in collaboration with the Egyptian Supreme Council of Antiquities (SCA) and the Epigraphic Survey of the Oriental Institute, University of Chicago (Chicago House), in Luxor. A team of Italian wall painting conservators directed by the late Luigi De Cesaris, Maria Cristina Tomassetti, and Alberto Sucato carried out the work. Funding was provided by the United States Agency for International Development (USAID), granted to ARCE for cultural heritage conservation, and administered as the Egyptian Antiquities Conservation Project.

The frescoes are now in a very fragmentary state, preserved on the ruined temple walls, where they have been exposed and subjected to all the vagaries of weather, human interference, and neglect both in antiquity and since they were discovered 160 years ago, hazards long since recognized as acute for the long-term preservation of archaeological sites (figure I.2).[5] Nevertheless, newly cleaned, they stand out in their pharaonic setting as an exceptional and eye-catching invitation to explore an otherwise overlooked aspect of the temple's history (see the frontispiece). Previous scholarly and popular histories of Luxor Temple have largely relegated the tetrarchic phase to a footnote, owing in part to the misinterpretation of the imperial cult chamber as an early Christian church, first proposed by Edward Lane in the 1820s that persisted in scholarly circles until the mid-twentieth century and lingers still in vernacular memory today (see chapter 4). In the early 1950s the imperial Roman identity was firmly established by Ugo Monneret de Villard, who rediscovered the graphic record of the paintings

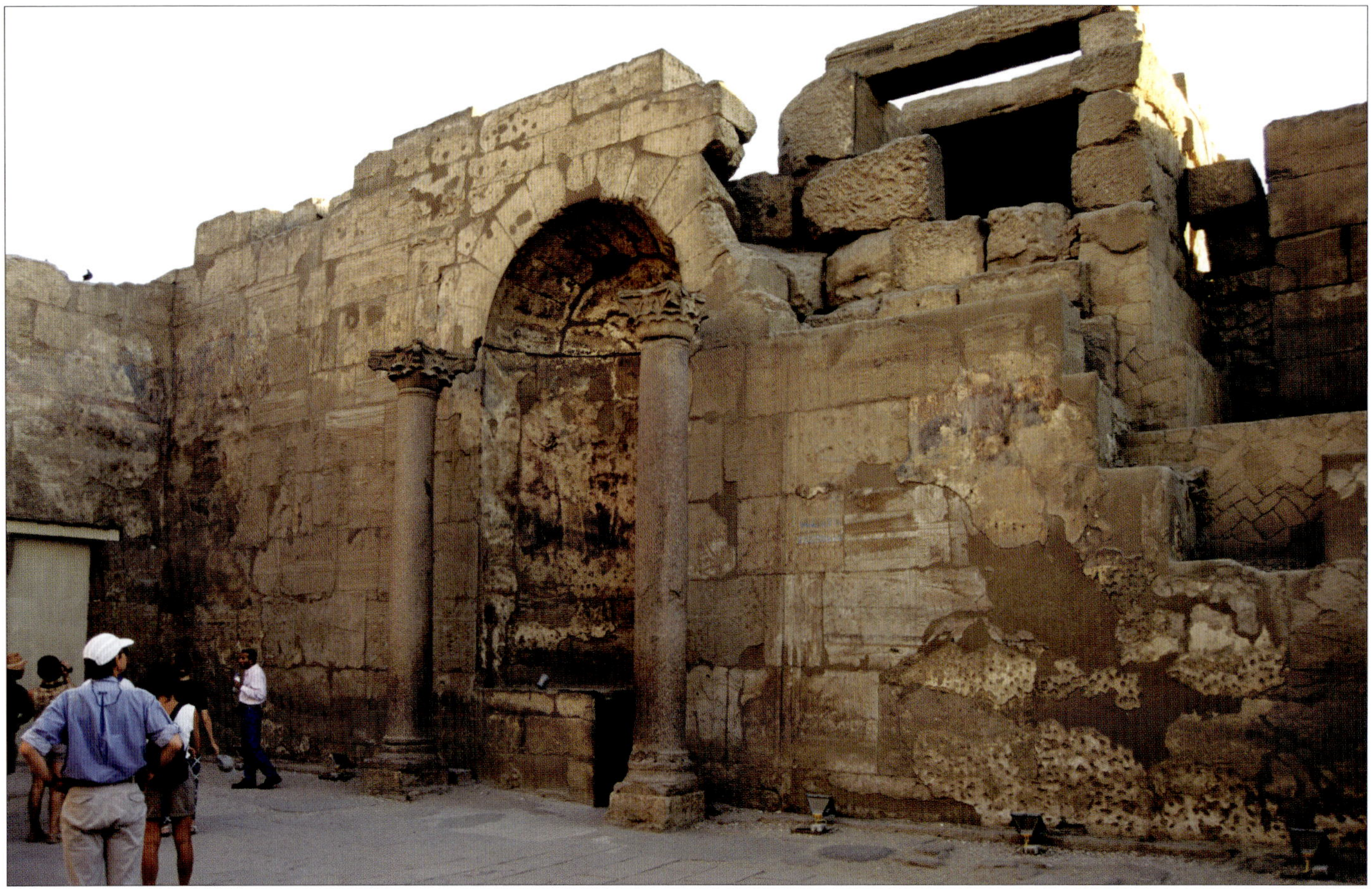

FIGURE I.2
Imperial cult chamber before conservation, 1997.

made by John Gardner Wilkinson in 1856, reproduced in full for the first time in the appendix.[6] Subsequent focused art historical studies of the paintings confirmed their tetrarchic date and improved our understanding of the iconographic program while French excavations in the 1980s refined the plan of the Roman camp.[7] These studies, however, largely treated the frescoes in isolation from the archaeology, architecture, and history of their physical situation. In addition to presenting the results of the 2005–2008 conservation campaigns, therefore, this volume offers a multidisciplinary approach to the Roman frescoes by restoring a synchronic context, spatially and historically, at the same time revealing their significance in the modern cultural construct of Luxor Temple.

The Luxor imperial cult chamber and its frescoes embody a transformation in the structure and expression of Roman imperial authority manifested in the creation of the tetrarchic system of rule initiated by Diocletian in response to the turbulent world over which he had taken command. As a result, the paintings hold a key place in the corpus of late Roman art, both in Egypt and the wider empire. Like much that characterizes the tetrarchic government, the frescoes and the Roman architecture accompanying them are a high-profile innovation in the existing fabric of an ancient institution, in this case Luxor Temple. When they were new, they must have contrasted vividly, as they still do today, with the distinctive pharaonic architecture and the rituals depicted on its walls. Cultural juxtapositions and interconnectedness, as well as the dissociation between material culture and memory, are thus some of the themes explored from a variety of disciplines in this book. Through the cleaning and conservation project on the site and the essays in this book, the frescoes provide an entrée to a wide range of archaeological, historical, art historical, and architectural research (figure I.3).

The temple that survives today dates back to the Late Bronze Age, during the fourteenth and thirteenth centuries BCE, when Eighteenth- and Nineteenth-Dynasty rulers replaced the older shrine of Amun of Luxor with the present buildings. The temple stands where the ancient Egyptians experienced an annual renewal of the divine origin of their ruler's authority and power. This event took place during the Festival of Opet, celebrated at the height of the summer Nile inundation, in which the king's connection with the essence

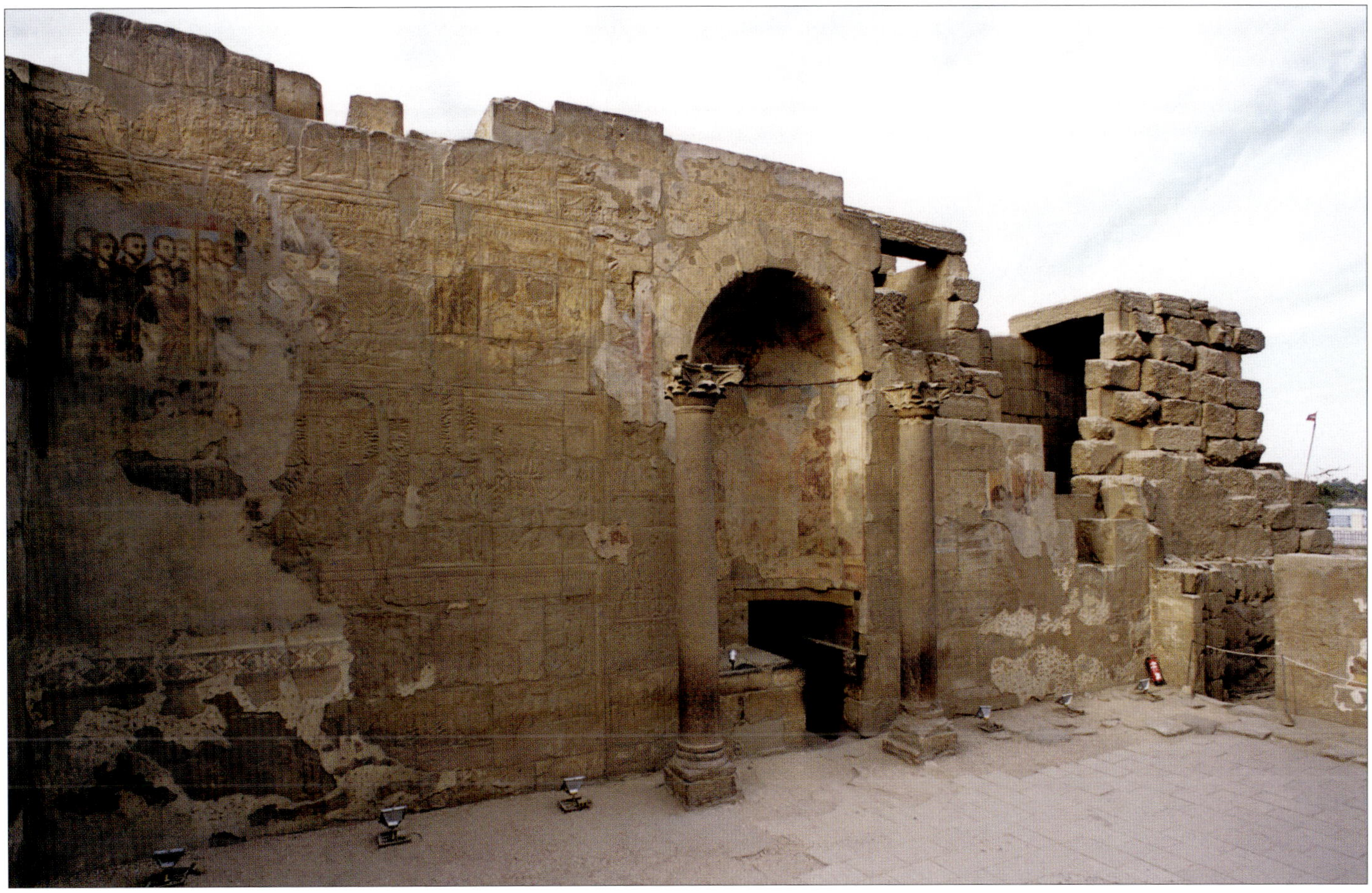

FIGURE I.3
Imperial cult chamber after conservation, 2009.

of kingship, the royal *ka* shared with the lineage of his ancestors, was reaffirmed (see chapter 3).[8] The festival included processions in which the sacred images of Amun-Re, Mut, and Khonsu were taken from Karnak to Luxor and back. Amun-Re and the pharaoh were understood to begin a new annual cycle in their respective roles as god and divine king, and the celebrations culminated in a reenactment of the pharaoh's coronation, in which he received divine authority to rule. Other festivals and processions were held that linked the temples on both sides of the Nile. Thus, Luxor was part of an interconnected mythological and ritual landscape from the second millennium BCE and into the Roman period, in which the origins of divine and kingly power were constantly reaffirmed and perpetuated.[9] Though official patronage for Egyptian religion had dwindled by the end of the third century CE, traditional veneration at local cult sites in the Theban region continued, such as those for Montu at Armant and Medamud, Isis at Medamud and Imhotep, and Amenhotep, son to Hapu, at Deir el-Bahri (see chapter 1), but whether anything was still happening at Luxor at this period remains unknown.

Amenhotep III (r. 1391–1353 BCE)[10] was responsible for constructing the greater part of the present Luxor Temple, including the shrines at the southern end of the complex, the barque shrine room, the offering hall and the room in front of it that would later be turned into the imperial cult chamber under Roman authority, the columned portico before it, and the open, colonnaded court and the colonnade hall in front of that. Tutankhamun and Horemheb (r. 1333–1307 BCE) completed the colonnade hall. Shortly afterward, Ramesses II (r. 1290–1224 BCE) added another court to the front of the temple, replacing whatever was here previously with double rows of columns on four sides, two seated granite colossi and standing granite colossi between the columns. Ramesses II also added the pylons, colossal statues, and a pair of obelisks to create a monumental facade.

Modifications and additional structures are attested from the dedications of rulers and officials over the next fifteen hundred years. For example, Shabako (r. 712–698 BCE) built a colonnaded kiosk that stood in front of the entrance of Ramesses II's pylon; Nectanebo I (r. 380–362 BCE) constructed a monumental gateway at the entrance to his avenue of sphinxes; Alexander the Great dedicated a new barque shrine

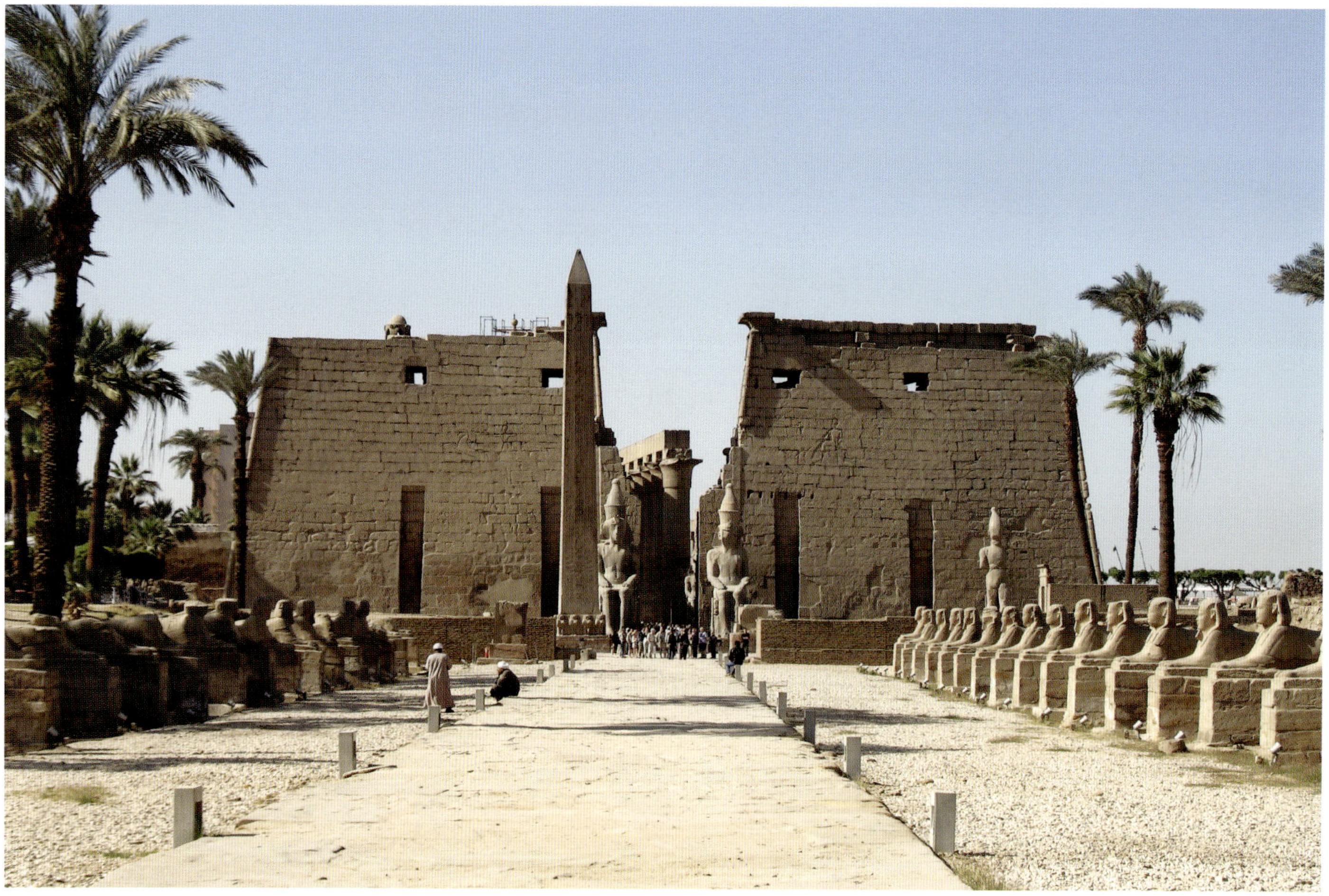

FIGURE I.4
(right) Luxor Temple: pylons, obelisk, statues of Ramesses II and sphinxes of Nectanebo I.

FIGURE I.5
(below) Roman bastion and ruins of the Church of St. Thekla at the northeast corner of the pylon of Ramesses II.

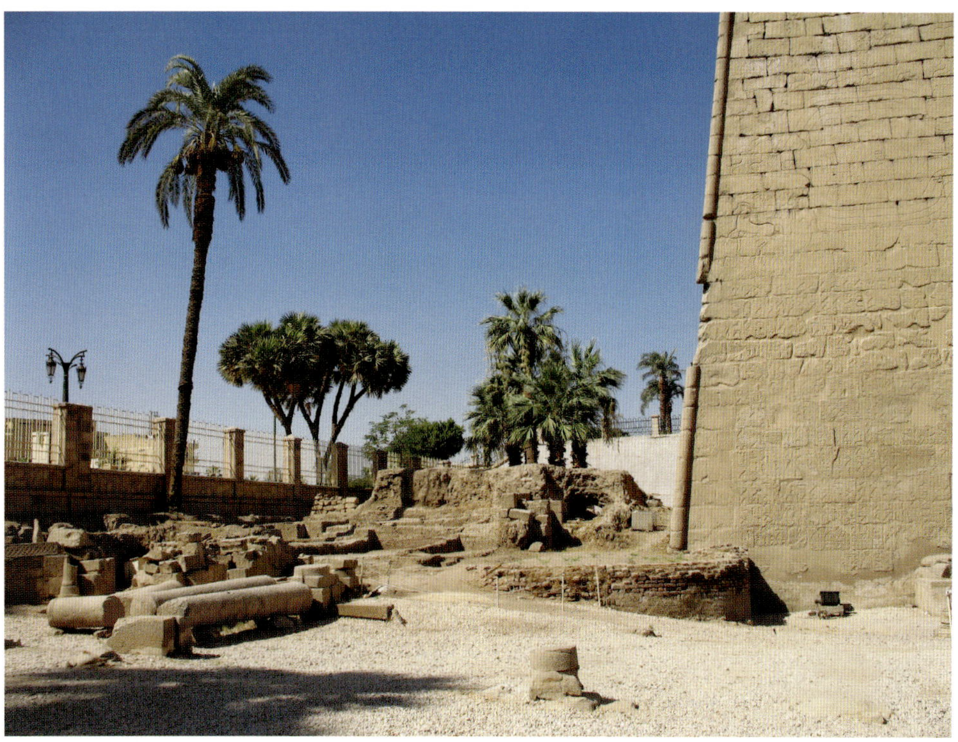

between 332 and 322 BCE in recognition of his "father" Amun, and a shrine for Serapis was rebuilt in the reign of Hadrian (126 CE) in front of the temple (see figure 2.2).[11] Some of these later buildings were subsequently removed, surviving today only as recycled fragments incorporated into later structures, such as the tetrarchic modifications to the temple and its surroundings. For example, elements of the kiosk of Shabako were used to raise the floor of the imperial cult chamber, and blocks from a building of Nectanebo I can be seen in the gateways of the Roman enclosure wall.[12]

When, in the last decade of the third century CE, the Romans selected Luxor Temple to house the imperial cult chamber, the temple facade of Ramesses II would have looked very different from its appearance today. The battle reliefs and statues of Ramesses II would probably still have retained some of their colored paintwork. Two obelisks flanked the entrance, and the colonnaded kiosk of Shabako was probably still standing, leading up to the temple entrance and filling much of the space between the pylons and the gateway of Nectanebo I in the temple enclosure wall. The current impression of a spa-

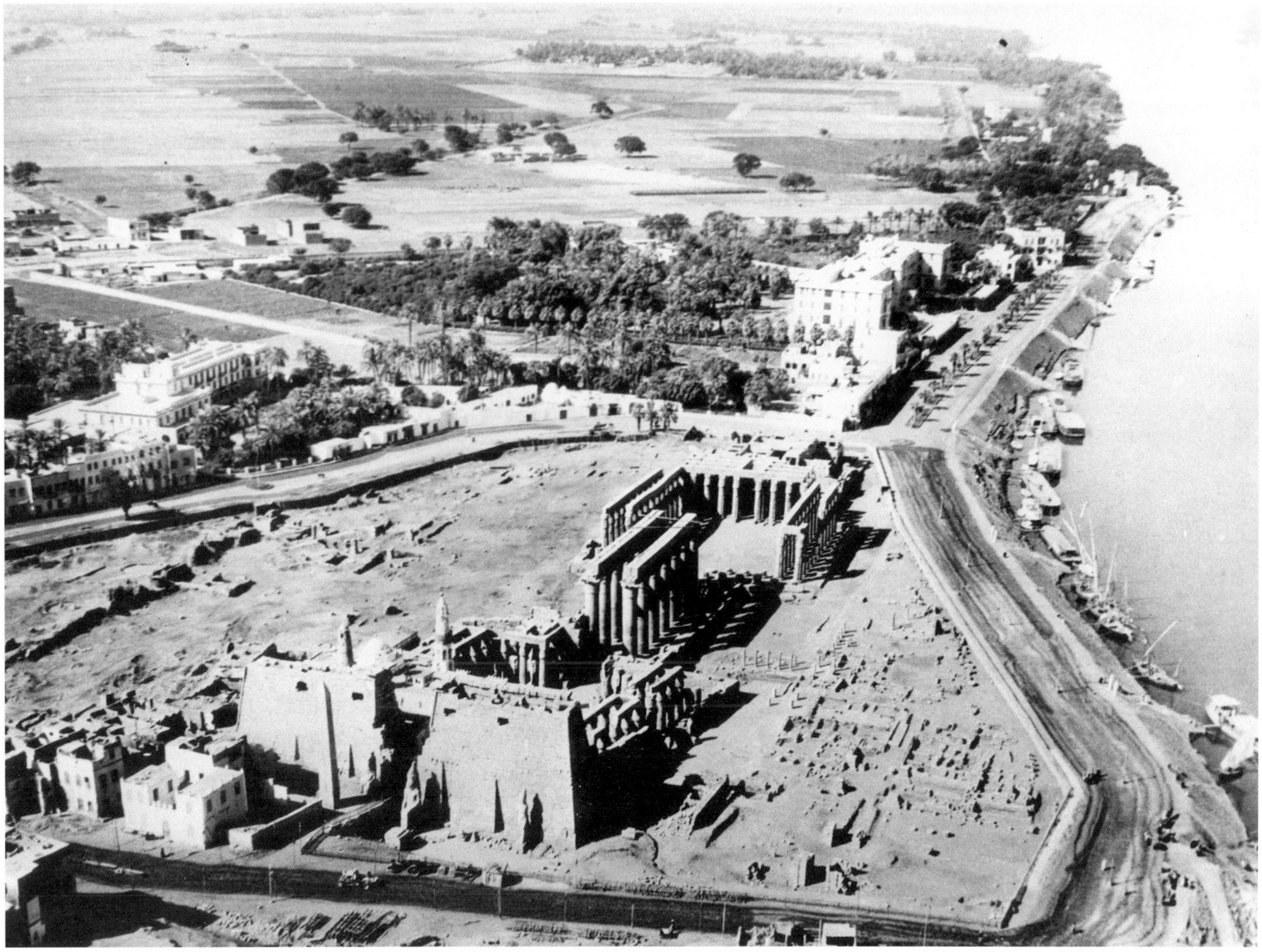

FIGURE I.6
Aerial view of Luxor Temple, looking south, showing the fortification walls (left) and Roman constructions on either side of the temple. The photo is dated 7 July 1937 and captioned, "A Contrast in the Modern and Ancient Glory of Egypt."

cious plaza in front of the temple results from modern clearing that removed every encumbrance to an unhindered view of the pylons (figure I.4). Though we do not know whether the Shabako kiosk removed by the tetrarchic builders was replaced by another structure, the modern spaciousness might reflect the intended Roman view of the facade, in which the battle reliefs would have made a bold statement of military might, redolent with the prowess of the legendary Ramesses II, while other Egyptian symbols such as the obelisks and statues would have reinforced this perception.[13] Seen thus, the imagery of Ramesses II protecting Egypt's security and defeating enemies on the frontiers reflects the principal aims of tetrarchic intervention in Egypt: to subdue rebels, secure the borders against outside forces, and impose a central authority.[14] When the tetrarchic fortifications were added, the facade would have impressed on anyone who saw it the strength of Roman authority endorsed by the ancient traditions rooted in this place.

Roman engineers built around the temple, integrating the existing structure into a new plan. The monumental pylons of Ramesses II at the temple entrance became part of the north wall, and the south wall of the temple marked the southern boundary. Thus, a fortified curtain wall enclosed the temple with quadrangular towers at the corners and U-shaped towers along its sides (figures I.5 and 2.1). Made of mud-brick walls with stone and fired brick gateways, these fortifications enclose an area roughly 268 by 207 meters. The shape echoes that of the contemporary well-preserved fortress at Babylon–Old Cairo; at both fortifications, the wall on the southwest side takes an oblique turn to counter the effect of the Nile current (see figure 1.3).[15]

Within this enclosure, on either side of the ancient temple the Romans constructed intersecting roads with two main thoroughfares, their junctions marked by tetrastyles (figures I.6, I.7, 2.4, and 2.5). Each of the four columns in both tetra-

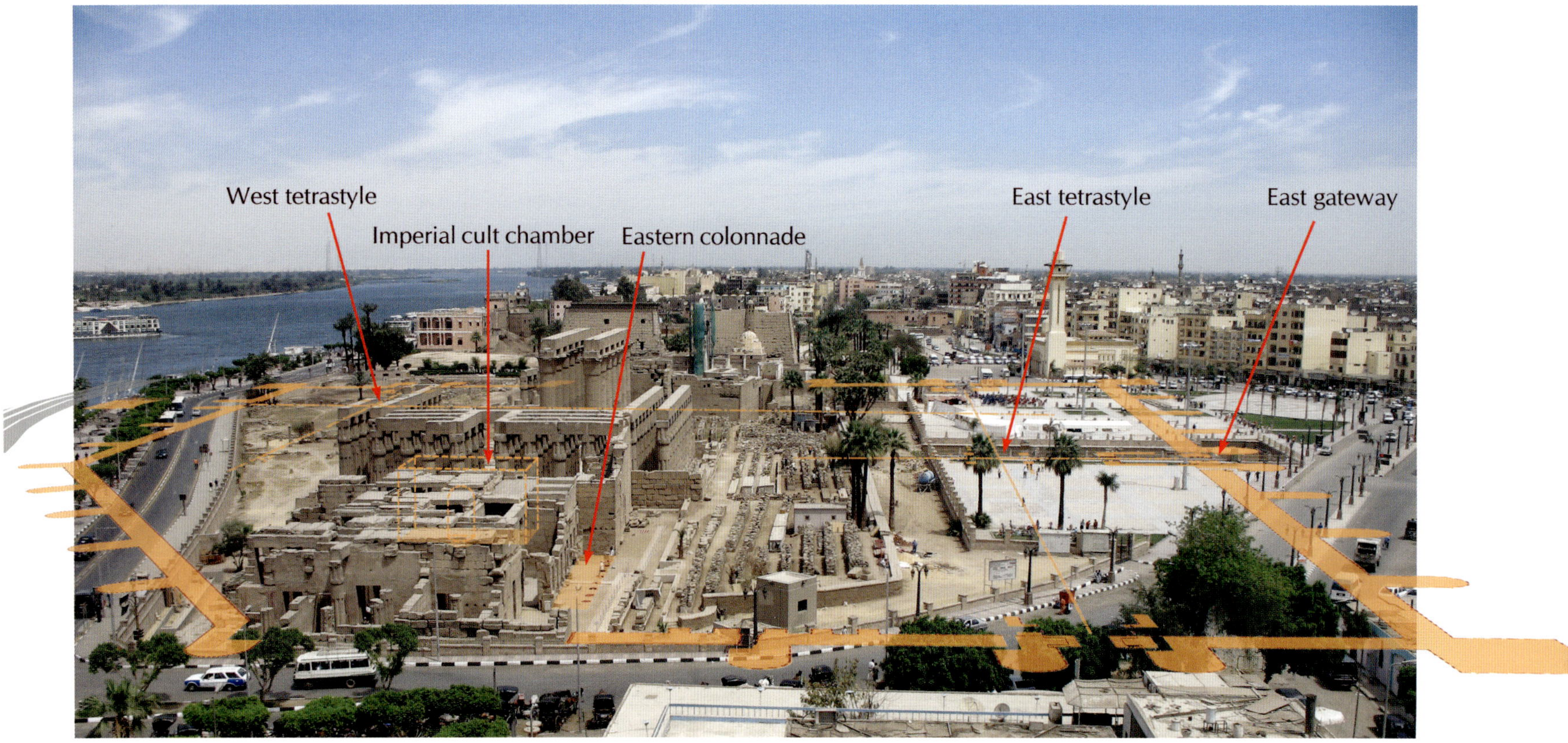

FIGURE I.7
Luxor Temple today, looking north, with a superimposed outline of the Roman fortification walls.

styles was presumably topped with a statue of one of the four rulers of the Tetrarchy in power at the time of its construction, but no fragments of such statues have yet been recognized. Very little now survives of the once well-preserved Roman structures uncovered in the eastern half of the camp during the excavations of the 1930s. Nevertheless, the published plan shows the north-south street with findspots of Egyptian sculpture and earlier Roman hieroglyphic stelae of Tiberius that may have been collected from other parts of the temple and positioned conspicuously along the street and in the entrances.[16] A colossal Osirid statue inscribed for Ramesses II was found in the eastern entrance corridor, which suggests that it was relocated and displayed in the new Roman setting (figure I.8).[17]

The ancient entryway into the temple between the pylons of Ramesses II was also modified, and traces remain where arches and rounded brick piers were constructed to form a Roman-style entrance (see figure 3.19). This leads directly into the first court of Ramesses II, with its double colonnades and standing red granite colossi of the king. The doorway on the right of the court leads to the Nile between the bases of the western tetrastyle. Opposite, a similar eastern doorway leads into an area as yet unexplored archaeologically. To the left is the only stratified building sequence now left of the post-tetrarchic occupation: a stone-built church (all that survives of a complex of late Roman buildings constructed on the axial alignments of the first court) with the mosque of Sheikh Yussef Abu al-Hajjaj al-Uqsuri built on its roof (figure I.9).[18] Ahead, two seated black granite colossi of Ramesses II signal the entrance to the avenue formed by the colonnade hall of Amenhotep III and Tutankhamun, leading across the open court of Amenhotep III and down the central axis of the colonnaded portico, straight toward the niche in the imperial cult chamber (see figure I.1). In antiquity at least four portals would have blocked this view, including the Roman doorway inserted into the southern end of the colonnade hall (see figure 3.20).

The chapters in this book consider the importance of the Luxor frescoes as a superior example of late Roman visual culture preserved in a unique context as well as a critical case study for understanding culture and politics in late antique Egypt. During the conservation project and the subsequent research that contributed to this book, many questions were raised. Among the most critical to any assessment are: What was the reason for the use of Luxor Temple as a military installation and venue for the imperial cult under

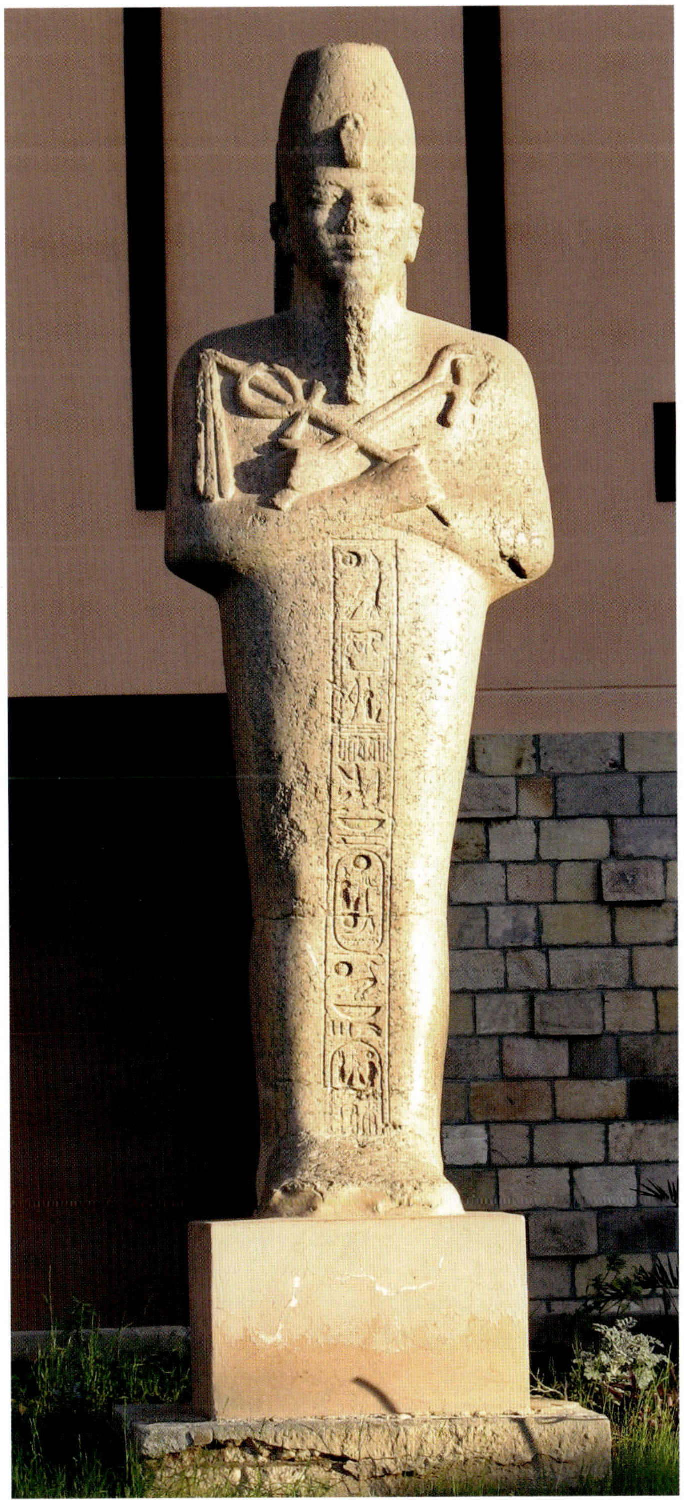

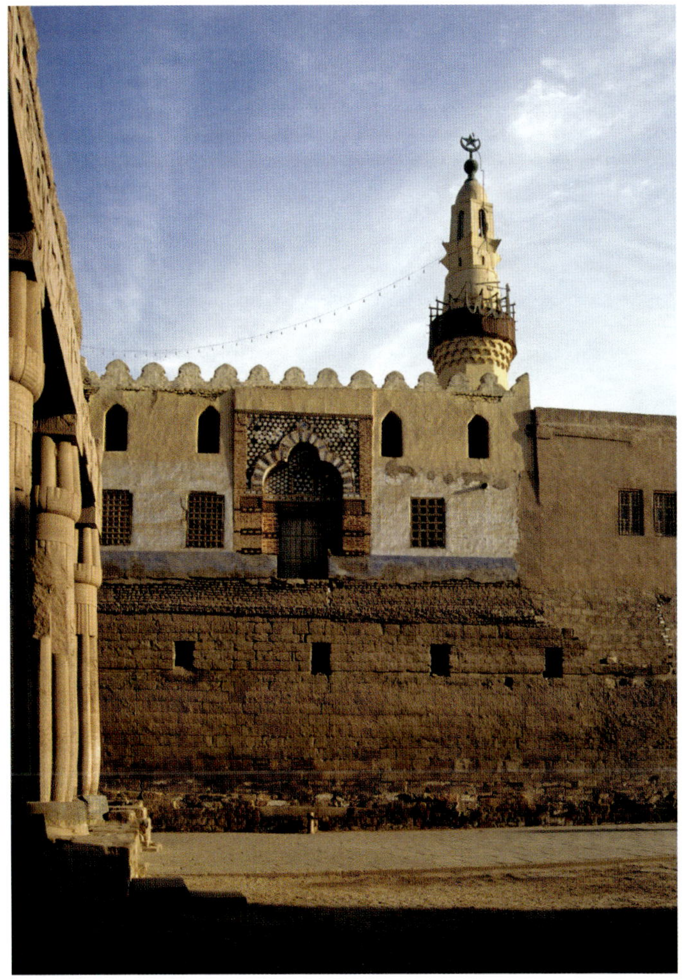

FIGURE I.8
(right) Colossal Osirid statue found in the east gateway to the fort. Luxor Museum.

FIGURE I.9
(far right) Mosque of Yussef Abu al-Hajjaj al-Uqsuri in 1997, built on an earlier church.

the Tetrarchs? What was the relationship between the Roman imperial cult at Luxor and the time-honored tradition of the cyclic renewal of kingship established here? Each has been tackled in different ways in the following chapters, although in many cases definite answers remain elusive and may now be unachievable because of the substantial losses of archaeological evidence that have occurred. Nevertheless, the editors hope that this will not be the last word on the subject and that others will be inspired to build on these present studies and explore the significant material that lies beyond the scope of this book.[19]

Chapter 1 confronts one of the fundamental problems in attempting to assess Thebes during the tetrarchic period: the dearth of direct and well-preserved evidence. Arguing that the tetrarchic reconstruction of Luxor Temple took place in a cultural environment still preserving traditional beliefs and cultic practices, Giovanni Ruffini weaves together the historical narratives of Thebes in the second and third centuries, setting the stage for Diocletian's arrival in Egypt. The literary record and the evidence from burials are shown to indicate a Roman presence and a romanizing influence at Thebes in the first and second centuries CE, but these become scarce in the third century and, with few exceptions, disappear before the tetrarchic period. Even the earlier records never reflect the same range and extent of information preserved on the abundant papyri and ostraca from other contemporary sites in Egypt. Nevertheless, the survival of traditional religious beliefs in the vicinity of Thebes is documented, for example, in a series of graffiti at Deir el-Bahri left by pilgrims from Armant, where veneration of the Buchis Bull survived until the mid-fourth century. At Luxor Temple, however, no such material is preserved, and it is impossible to say for sure whether the tetrarchic alterations took place beside existing rituals or were intended to revive the use of the temple for a purely Roman purpose.

Chapter 2 reassesses the evidence for the date of the Roman paintings and proposes a new appraisal of the frescoes and the accompanying ceremonial architecture erected by the Romans at Luxor vis-à-vis other late Roman-era constructions in Egypt. The frescoes are examined alongside the known historical data for Egypt in this period to explain the identity of the uninscribed emperors painted in the imperial cult chamber niche and thereby connect the paintings specifically to the emperor Diocletian's presence in Egypt some time between 298 and 302 CE. The chapter further suggests that previous authors' assumptions—that the Roman appropriation of Luxor Temple was purely for building a military fort in a temple devoid of cultic use—do not go far enough to explain the meanings of the archaeological remains, especially considering the ancient significance of the temple and the cult of the royal ka. Finally, the chapter considers why Luxor Temple was chosen as the location for this monument to tetrarchic rule and what the architectural features situated in and around the pharaonic temple might represent. The reader is invited to evaluate the renovations to this temple and its surroundings as the legacy of Roman civic building projects at other cities in Egypt whose features survive in the archaeological record or are known today only from literary sources.

Chapter 3 describes the Roman architectural modifications made to the southern part of the temple and assesses the evidence for the survival of the cult of Amun at Luxor at the end of the third century. Through an examination of the surviving traces of Roman reconstruction work in and around the imperial cult chamber, the authors reimagine characteristic Roman features in the form of a trussed roof, classical-style statues erected in the colonnaded approach, and a possible monumental facade on the front of the Amenhotep III portico, which would have been compatible with the entirely Roman style of the frescoes. Other measures, such as the construction of a new entrance to the barque shrine room and sanctuaries of Amun at the southern end of the temple, which were isolated from the rest of the temple by the creation of the Roman niche in the imperial cult chamber, indicate the possibility that these southern rooms retained their sacred use. Moreover, a cachette of pharaonic sculpture discovered in the court of Amenhotep III may suggest that the tetrarchic engineers were obliged to remove the surviving statuary from the sanctuary area of the temple and the chapels on the east side when the latter were dismantled to create the new entrance to the shrine of Amun.

Chapter 4 introduces the archaeological background and conservation processes that have affected the imperial cult chamber and the frescoes, which led ultimately to the compelling conditions that inspired the conservation project. The village (later town) of Luxor and the temple ruins are presented as components of a historical landscape that underwent dramatic and far-reaching changes in the nineteenth and twentieth centuries. By the mid-nineteenth century scholarly interest, combined with collectors' zeal, led to excavations that included the imperial cult chamber and the exposure of the frescoes. Photography, from 1849–1850 to the present, provides a crucial form of documentation in the absence of formal records. The chapter shows how nineteenth-century excavations instantly placed the temple, the imperial cult chamber, and the frescoes in a contemporaneous context by creating access to the site and by influencing how the remains were understood and treated. Simultaneously, they were exposed to a complex array of conservation issues that persisted into the twenty-first century and grew increasingly hazardous, prompting the decision to carry out the project described in detail in chapter 5. The chapter concludes by assessing conditions affecting the preservation of the frescoes, the various options available for cleaning, conservation, and future display, and how the decision was reached to carry out the project.

Chapter 5 is the record of the treatments carried out by the conservators, explaining the methodology and presenting the results of their work on the frescoes, describing how decisions were made concerning levels of intervention, specific details of their approaches to the cleaning and conservation, and the aesthetic presentation of the frescoes in their setting for display to visitors. The composition of the plaster layers and working methods of the ancient painters discerned during the course of the work are described, together with the results of scientific analyses identifying the materials used and how they were applied.

Chapter 6 examines the style and iconography of the newly conserved paintings in the imperial cult chamber and places them in the context of late Roman art in both Egypt and the wider empire. By drawing on a combination of historical sources, such as Wilkinson's watercolors of 1856 (see the appendix), nineteenth-century photographs, Deckers's published drawings and interpretations, and the remains in situ, the frescoes, their arrangement on the walls, and the figural and decorative program are thoroughly described and analyzed both as singular vignettes and as part of a larger, unified program promoting tetrarchic ideology. Despite extensive losses, especially to the north and west walls, one particular theme stands out on the east wall, identifiable from comparanda as an *adventus:* the celebration of the arrival of an emperor or his proxy, which could be in the form of a portrait, accompanied by ceremonial processions and rituals. Together with the iconic and powerful representations of the four Tetrarchs still extant in the niche on the south wall, the painted program overall marks the space of the imperial cult chamber and Luxor Temple with the eternal presence of the Roman emperors and indicates their appropriation and reformulation of the ancient mythology of the temple to fit the propaganda of the tetrarchic regime.

Chapter 7 considers the audience for the Roman paintings and replicates the ancient experience of the images in their pharaonic setting. The dramatic juxtaposition of pharaonic architecture and decoration with the purely Roman iconography of the frescoes in their midst is illustrated by following the route of a visitor through the temple to the imperial cult chamber. The chapter further examines the imperial cult in Egypt and the role of the imperial portrait in the promulgation of ideology throughout the Roman era. As an additional tool of tetrarchic propaganda, the paintings at Luxor, especially the adventus scene, are shown to be a type of visual panegyric (speech of praise) and evidence of the remarkable coherence between the presentation of imperial power in art and literature during late antiquity. This chapter asks whether the intended message embedded in the images would have been intelligible and effectively conveyed to a non-Roman audience. An answer is proposed by contrasting the courtly rites depicted and preserved in the frescoes and the panegyrics with a series of letters complaining about the procuring of supplies for the intended visit of Diocletian from exasperated bureaucrats. The comparison suggests a gulf between the official propaganda of the imperial court and the actual perceptions of the local populace.

The appendix presents facsimiles of the six pages of watercolor sketches made on the spot by John Gardner Wilkinson in January 1856, soon after the imperial cult chamber had been excavated. These are now preserved among Wilkinson's papers at the Bodleian Library, Oxford. They are the only known comprehensive color depictions of the frescoes made before erosion and damage diminished them. When examined beside the earliest photographs (see chapter 4), this archive can be recognized as being of the utmost importance for reconstructing much of what is now lost. Wilkinson's notes, written in his distinctive and sometimes difficult handwriting, are separately illustrated.

The conservation process alters existing conditions forever and offers opportunities for recording and documentation present only at the moment of intervention; the range of data observable during the work can be retrieved and recorded only once. After this moment has passed, the chance of in-depth investigation is over and cannot be repeated. Every conservation project, therefore, over and above the obvious treatment objectives, is a unique and unrepeatable occasion for studying the structure of the object or work of art and those attributes that demonstrate how it was made, how it was used, and how it eventually achieved the condition in which it was found. This leads to research uncovering evidence for the "cultural biography" of the object: the differing and shifting ways in which people have seen, used, reused, and adapted it for new and modern needs.[20] Understanding that the archaeological remains we have today are the result of the value and significance applied by people in the past and how these concepts encapsulate present attitudes is now firmly integrated in heritage studies and conservation practice, so much so that they are the basis of evaluation in the project-planning stages, decision making during implementation, and the accompanying research.[21]

The conservation philosophy employed during this project recognized that the frescoes were specifically made for the place in the temple where they are now preserved, overlying the Eighteenth-Dynasty reliefs. Therefore, no attempt was made to replicate missing sections on the basis of nineteenth-century copies or to hide lacunae, as such interventions would have falsified or obscured existing conditions that express the history of the place. As a historical monument, the temple is a record of all the events and human activities that have influenced its survival and contributed to its present form and appearance, including this most recent conservation project, which, like past interventions, will inevitably influence how future generations will perceive the frescoes and the imperial cult chamber.[22] Considered thus, Luxor Temple is a palimpsest of activities on which the tetrarchic period has made a considerable impression.

When we look at paintings or archaeological ruins, we try to visualize the time when they were active parts of living culture; thus, the fragments we have at present come to

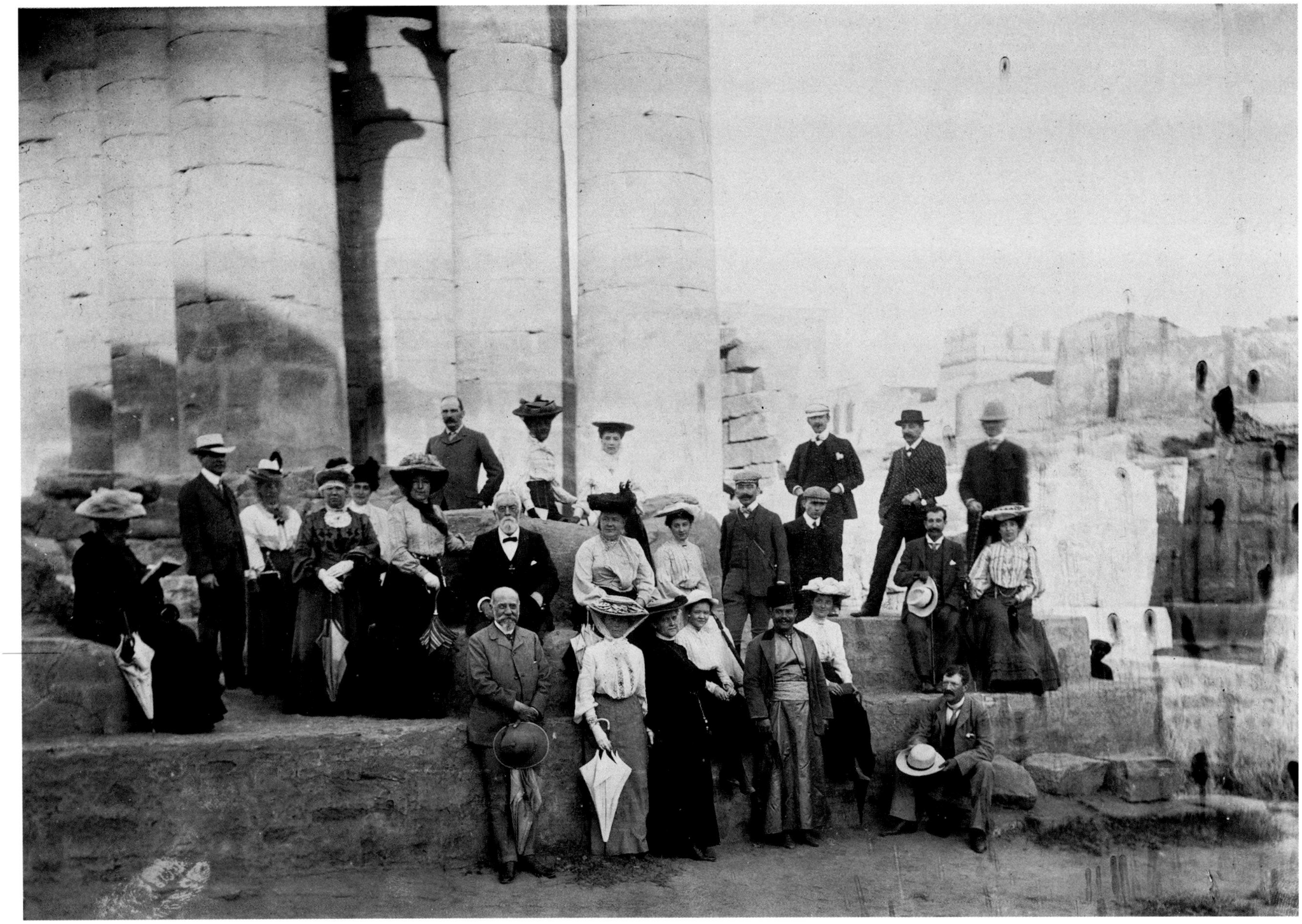

FIGURE I.10
Tourist group at the temple, captioned "Our party at Luxor Dec. 1905."

encapsulate the once complete but irretrievable whole.[23] Looking at Luxor Temple today, displayed as a form of public art in an archaeological park beside the Nile against the modern city, it is very difficult to imagine what the temple and its surroundings might have looked like in antiquity, when they were a closed area with restricted access. Indeed, they have never looked as they do now at any other time in their history, since the temple ruins in their present state, and their present-day setting, were fashioned by modern archaeologists and planners (see figure I.4). As the site has always been part of an evolving landscape both physically and intellectually, and because there has been such a dislocation in our cultural chain,[24] it has been adapted over the past century and a half for a modern society, receiving new meanings that guarantee its preservation in a world very different from that in which it functioned many centuries ago. Since the nineteenth century it has served the needs of scholars and was soon adopted as a commodity in the global tourism marketplace (figure I.10).[25] But, as is true of any exotic commodity, its significance lies not in the fact that it has been adopted but in the way it has been culturally redefined and put to use with new value.[26]

Something similar might be said about what happened at the turn of the fourth century, when the temple and its surroundings were extensively remodeled and assumed new associations. These renovations may have suited military, administrative, and ceremonial purposes that differed con-

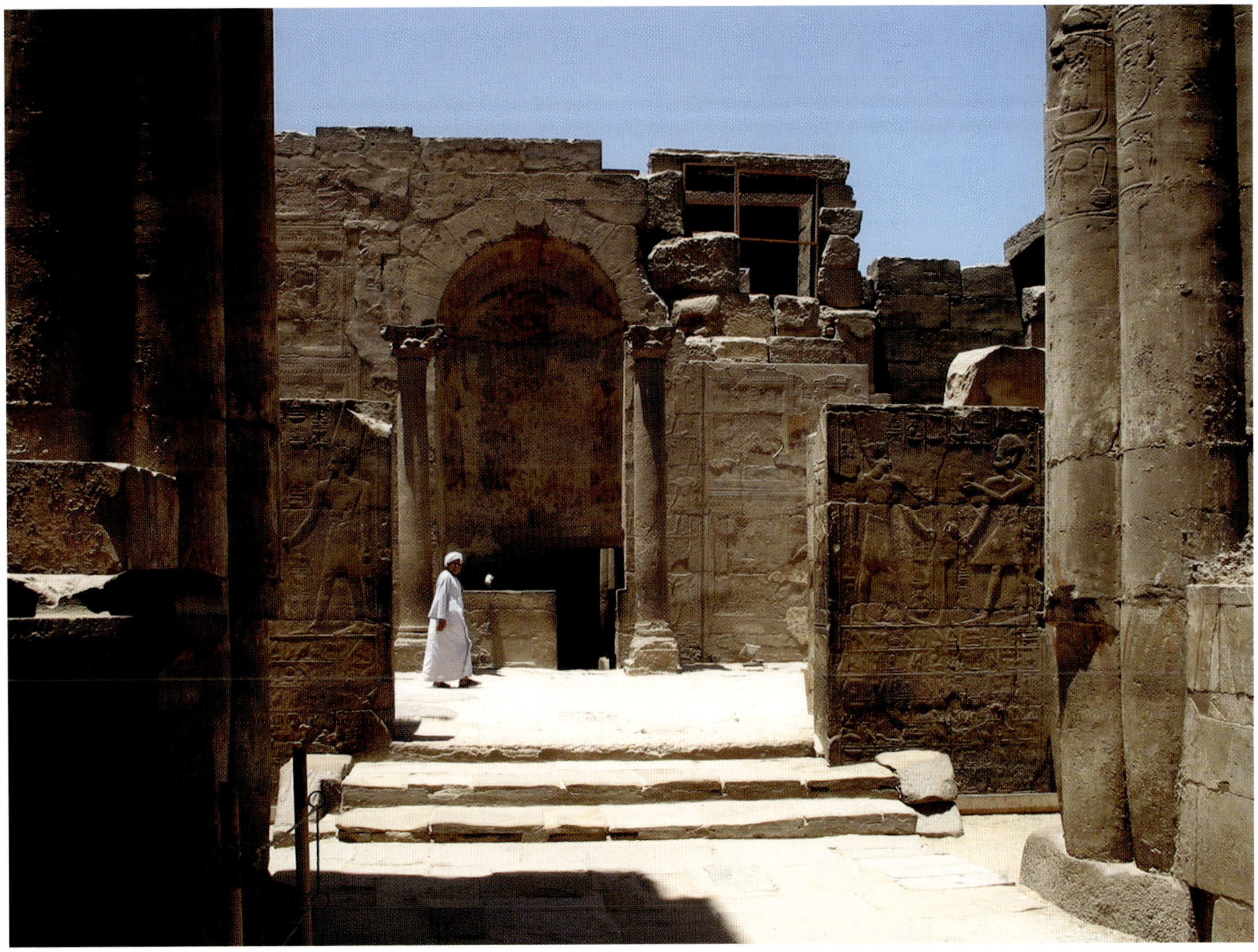

FIGURE I.11
The imperial cult chamber and niche seen from the north.

siderably from the tradition for which it had been built some fifteen hundred years earlier, yet they may also have been intended as a syncretism of contemporary and ancient beliefs. This underlines another theme running through this book: the weaving together of intersecting cultural and chronological threads encapsulated in Luxor Temple. Among them are the indigenous Egyptian culture in which the temple came into being and endured, the Roman adaptations, modern discovery of the temple, the temple with the tetrarchic modifications and frescoes today, and the recent conservation project that is the vehicle for this book.

The significance of the frescoes is also enhanced by the facts that they are part of the architectural ensemble of Luxor Temple, that they are preserved in their original location, and that they define (or redefine) the room in which they were painted. Diocletian himself, or possibly his Caesar in the East, Galerius, may have held court from a throne under the canopy that stood in front of the niche painted with images of himself and his imperial colleagues (figure I.11). Thus, the status of the imperial cult chamber still resonates through the relationship that survives, linking the subject of the frescoes, their place in the heart of Luxor Temple, and a modern audience. Viewing what remains of the frescoes in situ from the same vantage points as the first spectators for whom they were originally painted connects today's viewer with the artists who painted them and the ancient audience for whom they were made. "When you stand in the place of the original, its historical moment is literally there before your eyes."[27]

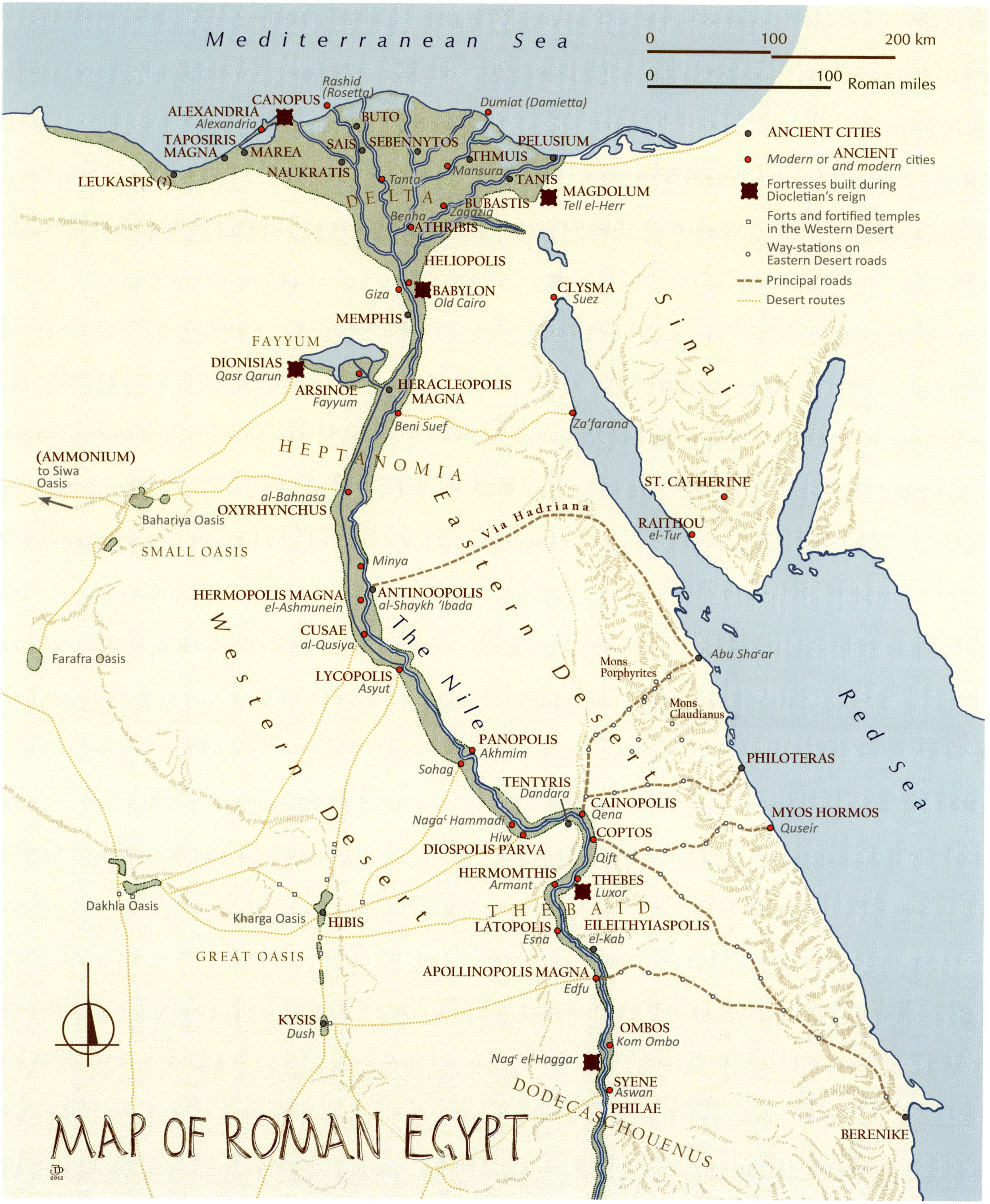
MAP OF ROMAN EGYPT
Mediterranean Sea
0 100 200 km
0 100 Roman miles
ANCIENT CITIES
Modern or ANCIENT and modern cities
Fortresses built during Diocletian's reign
Forts and fortified temples in the Western Desert
Way-stations on Eastern Desert roads
Principal roads
Desert routes
ALEXANDRIA
Alexandria
CANOPUS
Rashid (Rosetta)
BUTO
Dumiat (Damietta)
TAPOSIRIS MAGNA
MAREA
SAIS
SEBENNYTOS
PELUSIUM
THMUIS
Mansura
LEUKASPIS (?)
NAUKRATIS
Tanta
TANIS
MAGDOLUM
Tell el-Herr
DELTA
BUBASTIS
Zagazig
Benha
ATHRIBIS
HELIOPOLIS
Giza
BABYLON
Old Cairo
CLYSMA
Suez
MEMPHIS
FAYYUM
DIONISIAS
Qasr Qarun
ARSINOE
Fayyum
HERACLEOPOLIS MAGNA
Beni Suef
Za'farana
Sinai
(AMMONIUM)
to Siwa Oasis
HEPTANOMIA
ST. CATHERINE
al-Bahnasa
OXYRHYNCHUS
Bahariya Oasis
SMALL OASIS
Via Hadriana
RAITHOU
el-Tur
Eastern Desert
Minya
ANTINOOPOLIS
al-Shaykh 'Ibada
HERMOPOLIS MAGNA
el-Ashmunein
CUSAE
al-Qusiya
Farafra Oasis
Western Desert
The Nile
Abu Sha^car
Mons Porphyrites
LYCOPOLIS
Asyut
Mons Claudianus
Red Sea
PANOPOLIS
Akhmim
Sohag
PHILOTERAS
TENTYRIS
Dandara
CAINOPOLIS
Qena
MYOS HORMOS
Quseir
Nag^c Hammadi
Hiw
COPTOS
Qift
DIOSPOLIS PARVA
HERMOMTHIS
Armant
THEBES
Luxor
Dakhla Oasis
Kharga Oasis
HIBIS
THEBAID
LATOPOLIS
Esna
EILEITHYIASPOLIS
el-Kab
GREAT OASIS
APOLLINOPOLIS MAGNA
Edfu
KYSIS
Dush
OMBOS
Kom Ombo
Nag^c el-Haggar
SYENE
Aswan
PHILAE
DODECASCHOUENUS
BERENIKE
JD 2012

Chapter 1

LATE ROMAN THEBES

Taxes, Tourists, Temples, and Tombs

GIOVANNI RUFFINI

FIGURE 1.1
Map of Roman Egypt.

IN THE LATE THIRD CENTURY, DIOCLETIAN'S ARMY APPROPRIATED Luxor Temple in the midst of a local culture alive and well and still deeply rooted in its indigenous past. This impression is only an educated guess. What we see of local activities in the area around Thebes, however, gives reasonable support to this picture. This chapter therefore surveys the available textual evidence for Theban local culture and behavior to provide a glimpse of the contemporary living world that awaited the arrival of the Roman army in the 290s.[1]

In the summer of 283 Pamonthes, Pekusis, and over a dozen of their colleagues in an unidentified professional guild went to the temple of Deir el-Bahri, across the Nile from the city of Thebes, and left a Greek inscription commemorating their prayers (*proskynemata*) to "the Lords Amenothes [Amenhotep] and Asklepios [Imhotep]."[2] These deified human beings from the distant past, Amenhotep, son of Hapu, and Imhotep, were once relatively modest divine figures, but both appear to have undergone an evolution under Ptolemaic and Roman rule, "which made cosmic gods of them, equal in rank to the great gods of the Egyptian pantheon." Although this inscription is the last at Deir el-Bahri to mention the cult of Amenhotep and Imhotep by name, it is striking evidence of continuity between the beliefs and practices of ancient Egypt, on the one hand, and the living world of Diocletian's late Roman Egypt, on the other.[3]

In the following year, the guild of ironworkers from nearby Hermonthis (Armant) left the first of several more general inscriptions in another niche in the same temple.[4] Their corporate visits would continue for a generation, attested in a series of closely grouped inscriptions in four neighboring niches on the temple's upper terrace. The most complete of their inscriptions dates to December 324, when the association's president and others—including Plenis, son of Pkylis the brewer; Hatres, the association's secretary; and Plenis, the donkey keeper—prayed to "the great god" (Amenhotep may have been meant, but he is not named), and sacrificed a donkey in his honor.[5] These events, recorded by corporation scribes, represent continued interest in a religious site some modern scholars believe to have been abandoned already but still well preserved in the early fourth century.[6] Deir el-Bahri is directly across the Nile from Thebes. Hermonthis, home to the visiting ironworkers, was a separate settlement with important pharaonic roots and its own cult of the god Montu only nineteen kilometers farther south on the west bank (figure 1.2).

These inscriptions document Egyptian religious continuity close to Thebes in the late Roman period. But in other ways, the documentation fails us. The bulk of the textual evidence we will survey comes from the first and second centuries, falling silent through the course of the third. The local elite families and prominent tax collectors populating the landscape in the early Roman period are absent in the period of Diocletian and the Tetrarchy. Thus, parts of our discussion focus on this earlier period as a way to project social and cultural trends in Roman Thebes into the tetrarchic period.

In that period, as the ironworkers were continuing indigenous religious practices on the Theban west bank, a dramatic architectural transformation of Luxor Temple was taking place across the river at Thebes itself, sparked by a generation of unrest at the imperial level, beginning with the death of the Roman Emperor Valerian in 260 CE. During this period, it seems likely that the Thebaid's Roman officials were largely cut off from contact with any central Roman authority by vari-

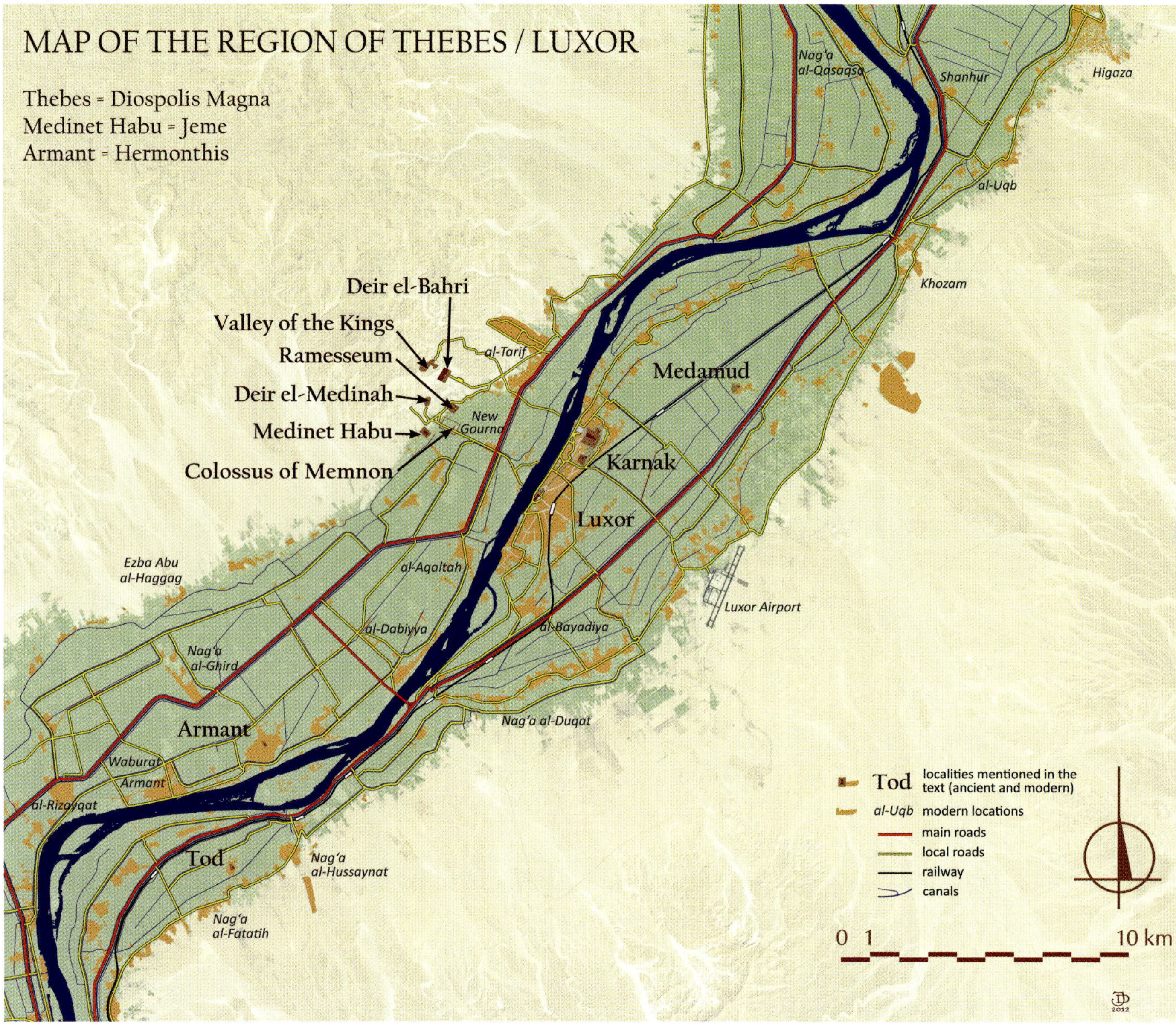

FIGURE 1.2

Map of the Theban region.

ous usurpers.[7] Egypt may have revolted twice before Diocletian's campaign against a rebellion in the late 290s required his personal intervention to secure the province.[8] The sources for these revolts, however, do not speak of Thebes but rather of Alexandria and Coptos (Qift), the military base and commercial hub located forty kilometers to the north of Thebes where the overland trade route from Quseir (Myos Hormos) on the Red Sea coast arrived at the Nile Valley (see figure 1.1).[9] This suggests that Coptos had perhaps eclipsed Thebes in strategic and economic significance in the Roman period.

Indeed, the only contemporary documentary evidence from the Thebaid specifically connected to the revolts of the 290s comes from the Paniskos family archive.[10] The action in that archive took place chiefly at Coptos in 297 or 298, where Paniskos served in some capacity connected to one of the usurper's high-ranking officials, Achilleus. Diocletian's Egyptian itinerary during and after this revolt is relatively well known: Alexandria, Oxyrhynchos (Al-Bahnasa), Panopolis (Akhmim), presumably Thebes, and south to Philae.[11] His actions en route are also relatively well known. He reconstituted the empire's southern frontier;[12] possibly continued his work of reorganizing Egypt's administrative divisions whereby the Thebaid received a new structure and capital at Antinoopolis;[13] arranged Egypt's military units, reducing their size; and feasibly also constructed or augmented forts such as the one that concerns us here, in the Temple of Amun at Thebes.[14]

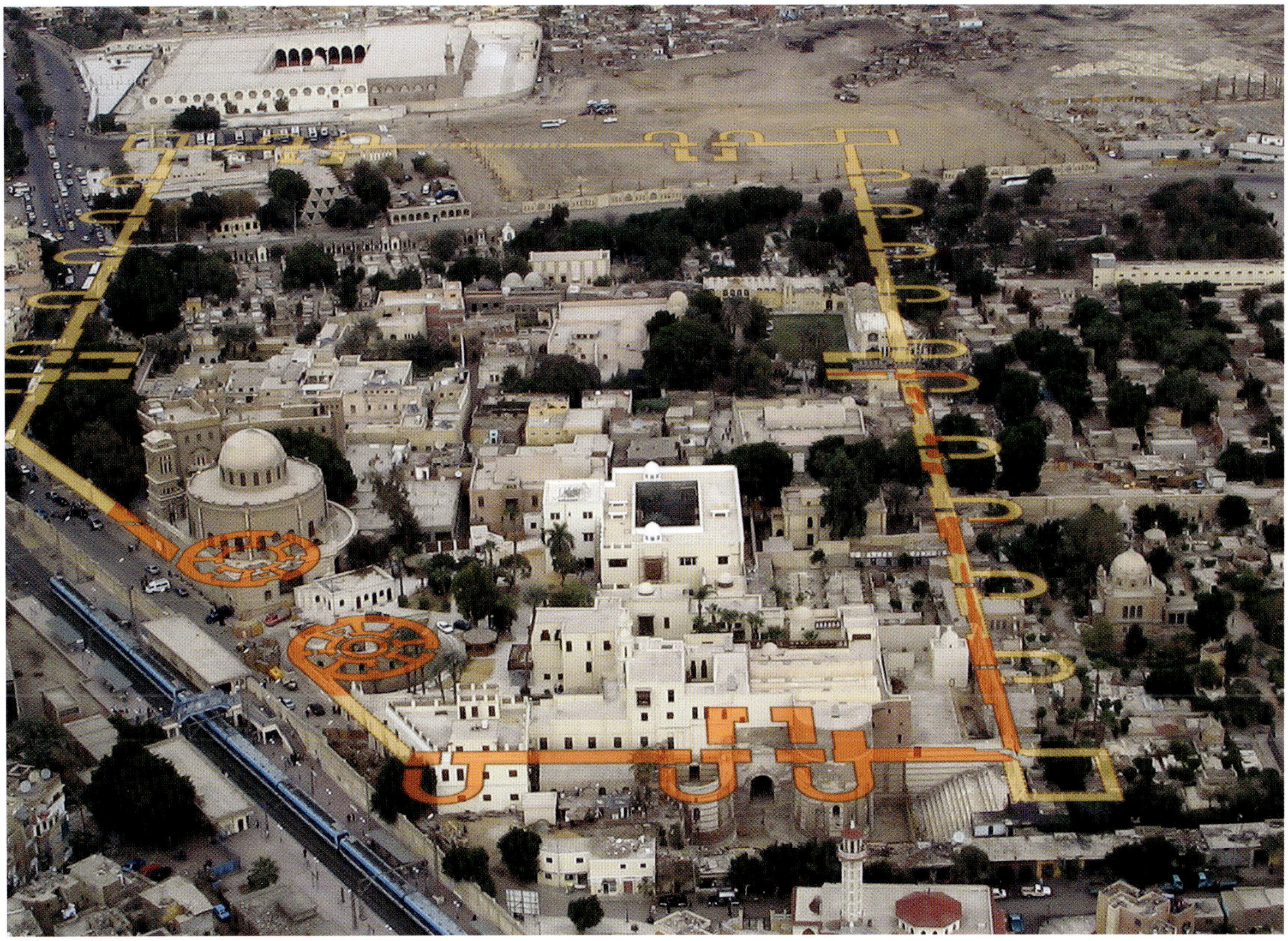

FIGURE 1.3
Aerial photograph of Old Cairo with an outline of fortification walls, 2005.

As is discussed in the following chapter, from the point of view of the surviving textual sources, however, the motivation behind the appropriation of the Temple of Amun at Thebes is unclear, given the area's relative obscurity in the sources compared with Coptos. Certainly the need to assert Roman authority in a rebellious region may have been in play, and economic considerations presumably had a role as well. But Diocletian's other Egyptian forts were built with an eye to their strategic locations, and the value of Thebes from such a perspective is difficult to determine. For example, the fort at Old Cairo commanded the Nile Delta divide and the entrance to the Red Sea canal (figure 1.3).[15] The fort at Nag' el-Hagar, some thirty kilometers north of Aswan, is similar in many ways to Diocletian's fort at Luxor, and "may be understood as part of a . . . fortification system . . . protecting the eastern side of the Nile valley, forming a link between the garrisons of Kom Ombo and Syene."[16] The fort at Qasr Qarun on the western edge of the Fayyum has been dated to Diocletian's reign for the structural similarities it shares with the fort at Luxor as well.[17] What makes the Luxor fort exceptional, however, is the potential symbolic value of the place and the fact that religious activity at the temple might still have lingered in the period leading up to Diocletian's visit, thereby influencing the choice of this site.

It seems doubtful that the ironworkers of Hermonthis on the other side of the Nile could ever have entered Diocletian's mental landscape, although workers like them might well have labored on the Luxor fort. Their continuation of older cult practices as suggested by the epigraphic evidence cited above implies that the local religious culture of the Theban region overall still survived in some form. If we were to look at Thebes through the ironworkers' indigenous eyes, we might glimpse a culture preserving deep historical connections. The tetrarchic appropriation of Luxor Temple thus seems less the desecration of a corpse than the creative romanization of a still living cultural landscape.[18]

Modern scholars, however, have not always seen late Roman Luxor in this light. Looking at Thebes through the lens of Greco-Roman culture and the Roman state, scholars have discerned a ghost town abandoned by the tourists of earlier centuries, leaving only the Roman tax structure, collecting from an ever more impoverished population. Indeed, historians of the twentieth century were unrelenting in their pessimism, which stemmed partly from the inadequacy of the available source material. The vast majority of written remains from this region in the Roman period focus on taxation, thereby providing only limited insights into questions of social and cultural history.[19] Previous generations of scholars have perhaps drawn too many conclusions from this silence. Thebes is presented as a backwater, doomed never to return to its former heights, its temples and priesthoods in a slow, inexorable decline, its funerary culture decadent, technically and artistically bereft, its people few, impoverished, and poorly hellenized, suffering under an "increased and ever-increasing fiscal oppression."[20]

Such historiography arises from several discrete scholarly dialogues, about demography, travel, funerary and religious practices, and other issues, that fail to provide a composite picture. The alliterative subtitle of this chapter—taxes, tourists, temples, and tombs—is therefore a snapshot of the late Roman Thebes that has been distorted in that inexact historiography by the surviving evidence. Such distortion is long-standing; millennia of evolving monumental pharaonic religious and funerary architecture reflecting an ancient and continuous cultural tradition had made Thebes a site renowned throughout the classical world. The Roman visitors who made their way there were often disappointed by what they found, the contrast between the glories of "Homeric Thebes" and its crumbling remains too pronounced to miss.

The physical remains of that pharaonic tradition dominate our view, much as they dominated the view of Greeks and Romans looking south up the Nile. The many graffiti and inscriptions revealing Greco-Roman tourist and pilgrim interest in Thebes do little to reveal the local Thebans themselves. The ostraca do much better in this regard, but they still show the native Egyptians primarily through the lens of the Roman state, as both taxpayers and tax collectors. Missing are the treasure troves of documentary papyri that illuminate so many aspects of daily life in other parts of Roman Egypt.

No systematic reappraisal of this earlier image of a waning culture has yet appeared in studies of Roman Thebes, although many segments of the picture have been challenged recently. Some scholars have drawn attention to a resurgence of local cult practices at the end of the third century. Graffiti by pagan pilgrims, previously just as likely to earn scorn for the errancy of their Greek grammar, are now receiving reconsideration for the evidence they give for a "real emotional investment in the environment" on the part of visitors to the religious sites of the Egyptian gods most revered at Thebes.[21] Roman-era funerary practices in the Theban area, once criticized by modern scholars for callous reuse of old tombs and impoverished accompanying grave goods, are also being reevaluated as "practical" and "potent" solutions to the problems posed by centuries of burial in the region.[22] Finally, the many mundane tax documents surviving from the area, long understudied because of their repetitive nature, highlight the interesting social and ethnic tensions to be found in the Roman bureaucracy at Thebes.

These individual reappraisals do not portray a unified image of social life in the Theban area; this is just not possible given the extant evidence. But they do at least give us snapshots with which to assemble a new picture. The following discussions focus on evidence from the first and second centuries CE, predating the tetrarchic era by generations, even centuries. By the tetrarchic era, the bulk of the written evidence for Roman Thebes has simply run dry, and that absence tells us precious little. It is unclear whether this silence is a result of inadequate preservation or simply that texts from this period never existed. Compounding the problem is the fact that much of the Roman city of Thebes now lies buried under modern Luxor, and substantial parts were destroyed without record when the settlement in and around the temple was cleared in the nineteenth and twentieth centuries (figure 1.4; see also chapter 4). Evidence from the hinterlands of the city must stand in for what is lost from its center. In looking at the earlier evidence, we must therefore acknowledge the risk of anachronism, but those sources may at least suggest that the late Roman installation of the imperial cult chamber in Luxor Temple was not so much an appropriation of an abandoned cult center but an attempt to romanize a functioning one.

TAXES AND THE PRESENCE OF THE STATE

Ample evidence survives for the Roman state's mechanisms of economic control over Egypt generally and the Thebaid specifically, feeding the traditional view that Roman authority negatively affected the life of the average Egyptian. Naphtali Lewis wrote of the "increased and ever-increasing fiscal oppression which the Roman domination brought for the Egyptian people."[23] If Roman taxation in Egypt was oppressive,

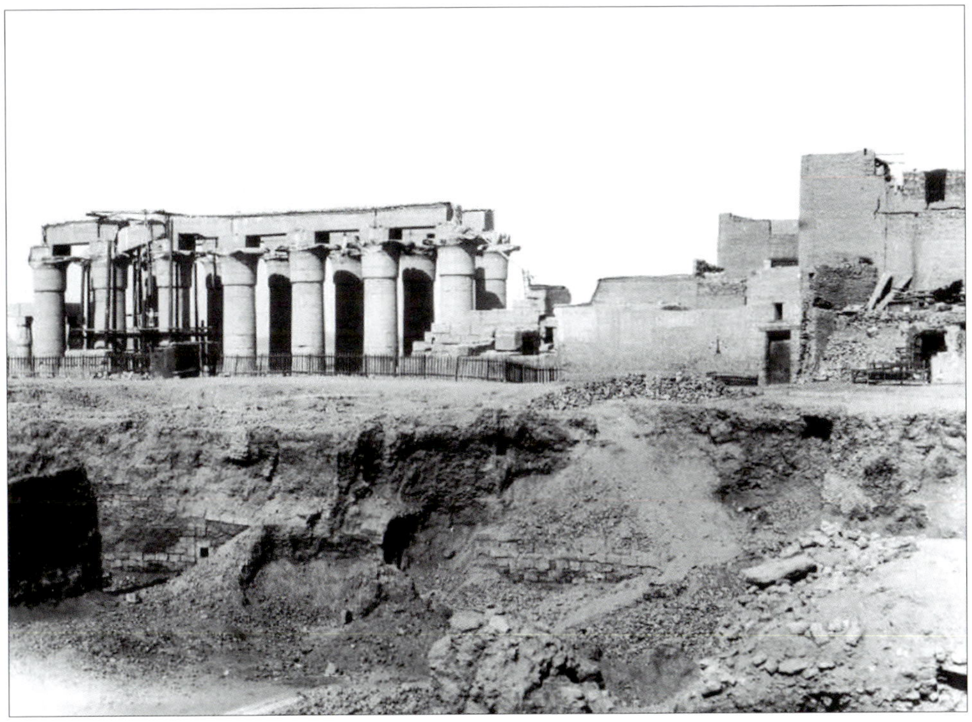

FIGURE 1.4
Excavation of the Roman settlement on the east side of the temple, 20 May 1933.

some Egyptians were active agents in that oppression. Tax records from early Roman Thebes reveal many tax collectors with Egyptian theophoric names, a rough but reliable indicator of involvement by ethnic Egyptians. Evidence elsewhere in this survey demonstrates religious cross-fertilization between Egyptians and Romans in the Theban area, and it shows the local Egyptian elite cultivating contacts with the wider Roman world. The Roman state's employment of local Theban tax collectors and the integration of those Egyptians into the Roman state apparatus would have furthered these processes. Demotic ostraca recording payments of money taxes from Thebes and nearby Hermonthis in the first and second centuries CE include collectors with strikingly Egyptian names: Snachomneus, Psenchonsis, and the particularly Theban name Pamonthes, for example.[24] Nor is this phenomenon simply a symptom of the language of the text: tax collectors with names of Egyptian etymological derivation appear in texts written in both Egyptian and Greek. The collectors in Roman Thebes included a reasonable share of men with Greek names: Kleon, Soter, and Apollonios, for instance.[25] But the collectors drafting the Greek receipts also bore such Egyptian names as Petosiris, Psansnos, and, again, Pamonthes.[26]

In short, surviving evidence shows that the Roman state apparatus touched the lives of the average Egyptian through the mediation of other Egyptian tax collectors by means of a system of considerable complexity. All this is part of the process that turned Egypt into one of what Keith Hopkins once described as Rome's "tax-exporting provinces," producing wealth never meant for local consumption but designed to feed Rome's central state apparatus and the armies stationed at its more volatile frontier zones.[27] The fiscal and political instability of the third century presumably disrupted the continuity of this process, but not before many generations of Theban elite had been accustomed to interaction with Rome's fiscal organization.

ONOMASTICS AND IDENTITY

Evidence from personal names elucidates how Theban natives were necessary participants in Roman state systems. As noted above, the Egyptian onomastic presence in ostraca documenting tax collection is quite clear. The same phenomenon appears in the textual record for the localized military presence at Thebes. Surviving evidence attests to village-level police forces receiving orders from local military officers, particularly in the late second and third centuries.[28] Willy Clarysse argued that second-century ostraca from a disparate series of collections were, on prosopographical grounds, likely to be from a single find, which related to a Roman military unit stationed near Thebes, at an unknown place that was probably in the eastern desert. He pointed to the recurrence in these ostraca of "typically Theban personal names" and the frequent use of the Montu element, which is "virtually non-existent" elsewhere.[29] All this contrasts sharply with the evidence for Rome's military presence at the strategic city of Coptos, some forty kilometers north of Thebes, which had a decidedly international flavor.[30] Coptos received attention and interprovincial military expenditures from the authorities not afforded in this period to more provincial Thebes.

As the Theban military ostraca make clear, there was a complex intermingling of the civilian and military in the day-to-day business of these units. This is particularly true of the military management of the civilian *skopeloi* or *skopelarioi* (watchtower guards).[31] These skopeloi were apparently smaller units, staffed by a "non-hellenized stratum."[32] The editors of one list of such guards noted that "almost all of the names are Egyptian, and there is no-one [on the list] who has neither an Egyptian name nor an Egyptian patronymic."[33]

Local name choices provide further information about the Theban people, giving the impression of considerable localizing tendencies. The editors of the Theban tax ostraca held in the Royal Ontario Museum note that in those ostraca, "Names characteristic of Lower Egypt, or the names peculiar to Elephantine upriver, rarely if ever appear at Thebes, and few peculiarly Theban names can be found elsewhere. This was a peasant population, tied to the land, and few moved from the land which they, their fathers, and their grandfathers before them farmed."[34] Adam Łajtar's 2006 study of Deir el-Bahri analyzes the names of several hundred visitors to that temple from the second century BCE to the second century CE, as recorded in just over three hundred graffiti and dipinti.[35] Though the social status of these visitors is hard to determine, as occupations typically went unrecorded, Egyptian names are more common than Greek among these visitors.

Predictably, theophoric names with the Montu element are the most common. Montu, a warrior god portrayed with a falcon head or as a bull, was a patron of Thebes and popular in the region. At Medamud, eight kilometers northeast of Karnak, renovations to the temple of Montu continued into the second century, including decoration from the reigns of Trajan and Antoninus Pius.[36] The cult of Montu was also celebrated at Hermonthis, home of the ironworkers we met earlier. Burials of Buchis bulls, sacred to Montu of Hermonthis, continued well into the mid-fourth century, a further indication of continuity in local cults of the region (figure 1.5).[37] Willy Clarysse's study, already mentioned, drew attention to such names as Pamonthes, Nechmonthes, and Phthoumonthes, and those based on Buchis. He argued that the rarity of such Theban theophoric elements in personal names outside the Theban area could make the presence of such names in unprovenanced texts proof of their Theban origin.[38]

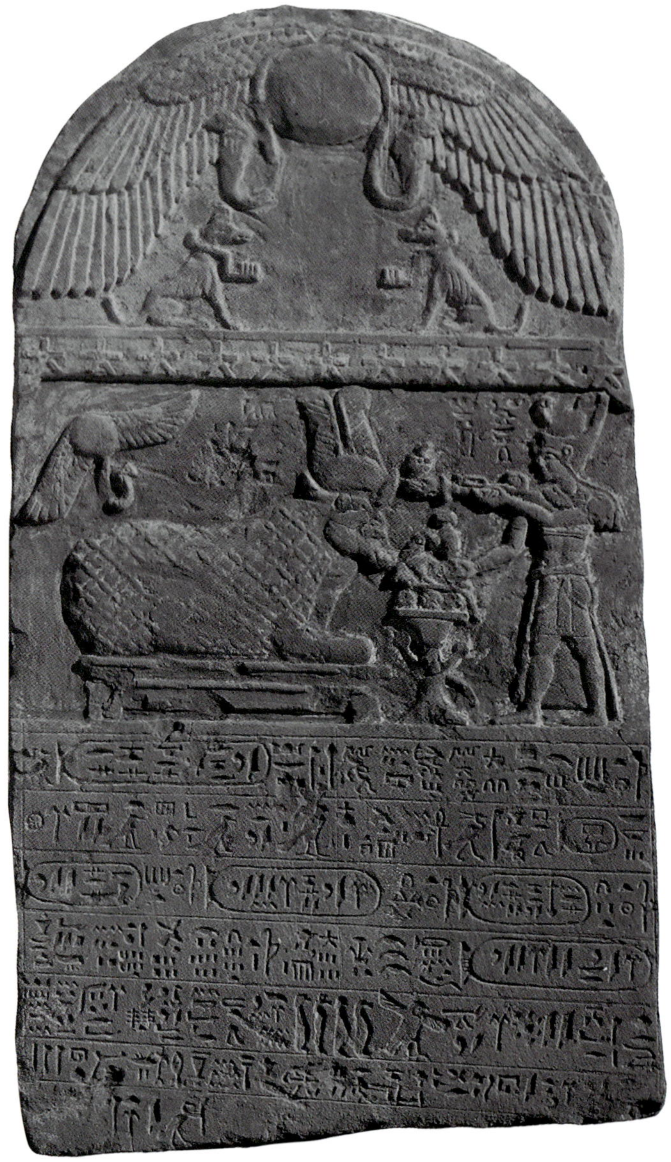

FIGURE 1.5
Buchis bull stela of 295 CE, naming Diocletian, Galerius, and Maximian. From the Bucheum, Armant.

The sociological implications of localizing naming practices are not obvious.[39] Bataille long ago came to visualize the population of the Theban area as including a Greek colony and natives, somewhat but not profoundly hellenized, on the basis in part of the evidence of the Roman-era inscriptions added to the Colossus of Memnon (discussed below).[40] Indeed, most of the graffiti from Deir el-Bahri were written in Greek, though Bataille proclaimed, "But what Greek!"[41] Onomastic evidence, however, leaves an impression counter to Bataille's linguistic elitism. Personal names from the Theban evidence show localizing trends: many Theban names appear usually, and sometimes only, in the Theban region and nowhere else in Egypt. Assuming that our limited evidence is at all representative of the bulk of the original source material, which one might assume is lost, this suggests a lack of population mobility, either into or out of the area. It equally suggests an indigenous population at least partially immune to hellenizing influences, as it preserved names that represented the most visible form of its members' native identity. Perhaps, then, the question of hellenization in Thebes is a false one, and comments about the region's poor Greek grammar are equally undeserved. The inhabitants of Roman Thebes were probably not judging themselves by modern scholarly standards of classical achievement, by which they could have been fairly painted as living in a backwater; they were, if their naming practices tell us anything, more likely living the traditions and practices of their own ancestors at a regional level.

DEMOGRAPHY

Nonetheless, Bataille's grim picture of Greco-Roman Thebes and its surroundings, in studies now over half a century old, continues to influence more recent historiography.[42] Much of his impression stemmed from the sharp contrasts he saw between Greco-Roman Thebes and the same region during the preceding Ptolemaic era. Thebes remained a great demographic, economic, and religious center in the Ptolemaic period.[43] Its status, however, took a beating in the final generations of Ptolemaic rule. According to Pausanias, when Ptolemy IX Soter II returned to Egypt in the 80s BCE, Thebes rose in revolt and was destroyed in the third year of its resistance.[44] The record of this destruction complements another reason for the impression of decline in the Theban region, the abrupt decrease in documentation. Starting in the first century BCE, the previous wealth of papyri available for the region disappears and ostraca become our only meaningful source of documentary evidence.[45] But a decline in the amount of written data really tells us nothing: the Fayyum and Oxyrhynchos, where the first centuries CE produced a resurgence in the amount of extant papyri, are pleasing anomalies; the silence of Thebes is much more typical.[46]

To an earlier generation of scholars, Bataille's impression of a region and a people in decline received some statistical support from the Theban tax ostraca. Just as striking are the figures more recent scholars have derived from the *dekaneia* lists, which appear to indicate that the population of the Theban region was relatively small.[47] These lists, found on 158 ostraca from the area, are nothing but names and were designed to record adult males assigned to guard specific locations; they were organized by quarters or neighborhoods, roughly some fifteen districts, in the Theban region. Family members often appear together on these lists, sometimes dominating them. Some of the individuals in question are specifically known from Theban money and grain tax receipts. This evidence, which dwindles to a halt by the mid-third century, does not cover the tetrarchic period. Nonetheless, the evidence from the dekaneia system paints a picture of Thebes as relatively underpopulated; this picture is unlikely to have changed much by the end of the third century.

Under the dekaneia system, "surveillance became another corvée, in which the population was systematically catalogued and rotated through guard duty over a period of time."[48] Using the dekaneia lists then available to him, one modern scholar determined that 5,400 men formed "a significant fraction, but certainly not the totality, of the adult male population of the Theban region."[49] But how significant is this fraction? Using standard demographic ratios between the number of adult males and the rest of a population, this figure probably suggests a total of some 18,400 men, women, and children.[50] If as many as half of the adult males did no surveillance duty, perhaps for reasons of status or other forms of privilege, a rough estimate might give a total population for the Theban region of just under 40,000 men, women, and children. But this is an arbitrary estimate: if the dekaneia lists represent a smaller percentage, then the Theban population could have been much larger.

If the documentary evidence gives the impression of a relatively small population, it may nonetheless have been growing in some parts. This held true across the Nile on the west bank, where the town of Jeme (at Medinet Habu) (see figure 1.2) has provided us with so much evidence from the pharaonic period through late antiquity.[51] In the late New Kingdom and Third Intermediate period that settlement administered the Theban funerary cults and royal tombs. Subsequently, during the Late and Ptolemaic periods, the town went through a decline but recovered in the Roman period, when new houses were built, together with new walls, kilns, and a bathhouse, which gave the impression of revitalization, although the excavator noted, "We do not know whether this occurred systematically and by governmental order or whether the peasants from the surrounding villages, driven by necessity, sought protection behind the easily reconstructible walls of the old town." These activities occurred in many cases "no earlier than the third or fourth century after Christ."[52] This period of growth coincides with other signs of resurgent activity on the Theban west bank, as is clear from the discussion of Deir el-Bahri below.

TOURISTS

When Romans imagined southern Egypt, Thebes loomed large in their mind's eye. To no small degree, this was a symptom of a good classical education rather than an indicator of the importance of the site in their own times. No less an authority than Homer had praised Egyptian Thebes, where "treasures in greatest store are laid up in men's houses . . . a city of one hundred gates."[53] Generations of prominent Roman literary and political figures made their way up the Nile to Thebes. The image of Roman Thebes as a town notable only for the visible remains of its pharaonic past stemmed primarily from the literary and epigraphic records of their journeys.[54]

If Strabo is at all typical, reliance on Homeric preconceptions might have filled many of these Roman-era tourists with disappointment. Strabo accompanied Aelius Gallus, the prefect of Egypt from 26 to 24 BCE, and in his description of the visit he quotes book 9 of the *Iliad* twice before noting that only traces of the city's former grandeur are still visible, Cambyses having allegedly mutilated most of the temples. Thebes is, in his words "now only a collection of villages."[55] His silence on the temples at Luxor and Karnak may be a symptom of his inability as an outsider to gain access to these temples or equally a symptom of his inability to tie them to any figures of Greco-Roman history or myth. Strengthening for readers both ancient and modern the impression of Thebes as a ghost town, Strabo is impressed only by the royal tombs on the west bank, which "are marvelously constructed, and are a spectacle worth seeing."[56]

Just as impressive to other visitors of the Theban region, if not more so, was the so-called Colossus of Memnon, one of a pair of monumental statues of Amenhotep III that Greco-Roman visitors identified with the Trojan hero Memnon. Part of the attraction of this statue, while it lasted, was the mysterious humming or harp-twanging sound it often made at sunrise. Strabo, Tacitus, Pliny, Pausanias, and Philostratus all report this phenomenon.[57] Sixty-one inscriptions in Greek, forty-five in Latin, and one in both Greek and Latin were carved on the statue by visitors to memorialize their presence.[58] If Egyptians paid any attention to the site at all, they saw no need to commemorate it in their own language; clearly, this part of our written record shows us the region from the point of view of outsiders or of Egyptians adopting a Greco-Roman identity. Dated inscriptions range from 20 to 205 CE.[59] It has been suggested that the undated inscriptions belong to a later period. Earlier generations of scholars, having Jerome's fourth-century testimony that the statue ultimately fell silent, and believing the latest text on the statue to date to 196, attributed a "restoration" to Septimius Severus, who visited the site in 199.[60] Given that the site remained a tourist destination until at least 205, if not later in the third century, responsibility for the restoration is now simply a matter of conjecture.[61]

Many of the inscriptions were not idle scratches but lengthy literary enterprises. Such epigraphic "tattooing" was so popular that it continued until virtually all reachable space on the statue was covered with inscriptions. If tourism to the site ultimately tapered off, it tells us less about the local population and its interests in the region than about travel preferences among the Mediterranean's Greco-Roman elite. That elite may well have had their travel options drastically narrowed in the economic and political uncertainty immediately before the accession of Diocletian in 284 CE.

TEMPLES AND RELIGIOUS LIFE

Too much focus on Theban religious sites as tourist destinations can take attention from the still considerable draw these sites retained for other reasons. Ian Rutherford notes that travel to religious sites in Greco-Roman Egypt took place for various reasons: tourism, casual visits, scientific enquiry, religious piety.[62] Pilgrimage to the area had an international character: Bataille long ago pointed out that pilgrims came from Greece, Asia Minor, Syria, Spain, even Gaul. But the attractions Thebes held for traveling pious outsiders did not survive into late antiquity. Inscriptions found in the Valley of the Kings show that pilgrimage activity fell between the end of the first and the end of the third centuries. This was true not simply of the international traveler. The majority of visitors' inscriptions were made by Theban locals or Greek-speaking Egyptians, and these inscriptions also disappear in the same period.[63] It is possible that a silent majority of visitors were nonliterate, but we have no way to track their presence in these sites and no way to tell whether their pilgrimage practices varied considerably from those of their more visibly literate exemplars.

If pilgrim interest in Theban religious sites was strong through the third century, it is not obvious that traditional religious institutions fared quite so well. We know that Thebes remained a center of magical activity in the Greco-Roman period.[64] One author, however, has noted the "striking dearth of [textual] evidence [for example, inscriptions or graffiti] for priests or cults of the Egyptian gods at Thebes after the mid-second century."[65] A recent study of Theban clergy in the Roman period notes this lack of documentary evidence as well: the author collects a few Greek and demotic texts that find Theban priests active in tax collection but little else.[66] Indeed, for some time, a focus on decline in local cults and priesthoods in the early Roman period was standard in the historiography. Again, for Bataille the impression was strengthened by contrast with the image of Thebes in the Hellenistic period, which presents evidence of more intense religious activity.[67] But Bataille cautioned against viewing apparent religious decadence in isolation, and he saw a close relationship between the decline of local religious institutions and the decline of the local economic situation. In his view, the residents of Roman Thebes were not less pious, simply poorer.[68]

Adam Łajtar's recent work on Deir el-Bahri is a rich case study that allows us to reassess religious practices in the area of Thebes during the tetrarchic period. Cultic activity at shrines of Amenhotep, son of Hapu, and Imhotep at Deir el-Bahri came in two waves, the first wave hitting its peak in the first and second centuries CE, and the second wave in late antiquity.[69] Three hundred twenty-five painted or scratched inscriptions survive from this period, including several left by families visiting as a group.[70] In the year 112, for instance, "Phatres son of Phatres and his wife Kelis together with a daughter while feasting in the sacred precinct" wrote that they made offerings to Amenhotep and Imhotep "together with those who love us and are loved by us." In keeping with the tradition of tourism by Roman officials in this period, a strategos named Celer visited in the early second century and left his mark there as well.[71] The last of these inscriptions with an exact date is from 162; after the end of the second century, no more inscriptions are found for more than one hundred years. Cultic activity requiring pious dedications written on the walls at this site seems simply to have stopped until late antiquity.

All indications suggest that though these sites remained active from the second century BCE to the second century CE, they were chiefly local in their importance. Visitors' names are both Greek and Egyptian, but mostly the latter, and there is a clearly local Theban overtone.[72] In other words, if Deir el-Bahri is any indication, activity at west bank sites was not just the tourism suggestive of a dead museum town. The visitors at Deir el-Bahri were mainly Egyptians, the presence of an oil worker and a donkey keeper giving the "impression that they belonged to the lower strata of Egyptian society of the period under consideration and were simply peasants and craftsmen." The apparent predominance of local rather than long-distance travel gives the impression that "this was a small cult place of local importance," the site perhaps most frequently of casual family visits to family graves, a "folk sanctuary with a cult of predominantly festive character."[73]

Recorded cultic activity at Deir el-Bahri ceased for unknown reasons at the end of the second century, but it was resurgent for a fifty-year period starting in about 280 CE, documented in the form of visitors' inscriptions.[74] The most important group of texts was left by the aforementioned corporation of Hermonthite ironworkers, spanning 283–334, through the services of Hatres, son of Horion, their professional scribe. The imagery in these texts is highly evocative: donkey sacrifices to neutralize the threat from the underworld, banquets and overnight temple stays, a dramatic preservation of ancient Egyptian culture. Several of these inscriptions date to the start of the Egyptian month of Tybi. Their editor has suggested that they were a culminating part of the celebration of the triumph of the Egyptian god Horus over his enemies in the feast of Choiak, the month just before Tybi.[75]

If the impression from the west bank is one of local, and at times even resurgent, Egyptian religious devotion in the late third century, the situation at Luxor Temple is less clear. Early publications included twenty-one Greek inscriptions, the majority of which were judged to be from the Roman era on palaeographical and linguistic grounds.[76] A more recent collection of fifty-three Greek and Latin inscriptions from Luxor Temple includes that earlier material.[77] Some of these inscriptions, typically *proskynemata* to Amun, the temple's chief god, were carved by men with Greek names such as Neon, son of Apollonios, and Dioskoras, who made *proskynema* in 126.[78]

These inscriptions, which frequently have some form of the phrase "I came to Diospolis," do not suggest a local population. One late Ptolemaic proskynema, for example, from the Eighteenth-Dynasty chapel of Khonsu, in the first court of Luxor Temple, was carved by a certain Heron, son of Amonios, from the Arsinoite nome.[79] Riad pointed out that the majority of these inscriptions were made in the Egyptian month of Pauni (May–June), which suggests that this level of pilgrimage to Luxor Temple coincided with some continuation of the pharaonic-era Feast of the Valley.[80] The apparent participation of non-Egyptians is a sign of the religious cross-fertilization so typical of Greco-Roman Egypt. Similarly, the participation of nonlocals suggests that at least some strata of Theban religious culture were integrated with the wider Egyptian world.

FUNERARY CULTURE AND THE THEBAN ELITE

Just as scholars now tend to see Theban religious life in the Roman period as more vibrant and personal than previous generations of historians imagined, a similar reassessment has begun in the field of funerary practices.[81] In Bataille's view, the local tendency in this period toward reuse of New Kingdom tombs in preference to building new ones was further evidence for local impoverishment and decadence.[82] Modern scholars tend more toward finding positive interpretations for the material remains. The Roman period in Egypt is now seen as a time of changing attitudes toward what mattered most in burial. A considerable number of Roman-period burials on the west bank, including a catacomb with at least sixty Roman mummies, all reuse previously constructed tombs without regard for the actual burial context. This is part of a larger trend apparent from as early as the end of the second millennium BCE that inclined burial practices away from the tomb goods and monuments associated with elaborate burial assemblages. In this trend, the body of the deceased itself becomes the focus, "an elaborately wrapped and decorated burial in microcosm."[83]

Twenty-six mummy masks from Deir el-Bahri dating from about 220–270 show both adaptation and continuity in their decoration style, and they also exhibit great care in the preparation of the bodies for burial.[84] Noting that third-century burials at Deir el-Bahri "incorporated funerary goods that were up to several hundred years old at the time," one modern scholar argues against the traditional historiographical view that these practices were "abhorrent

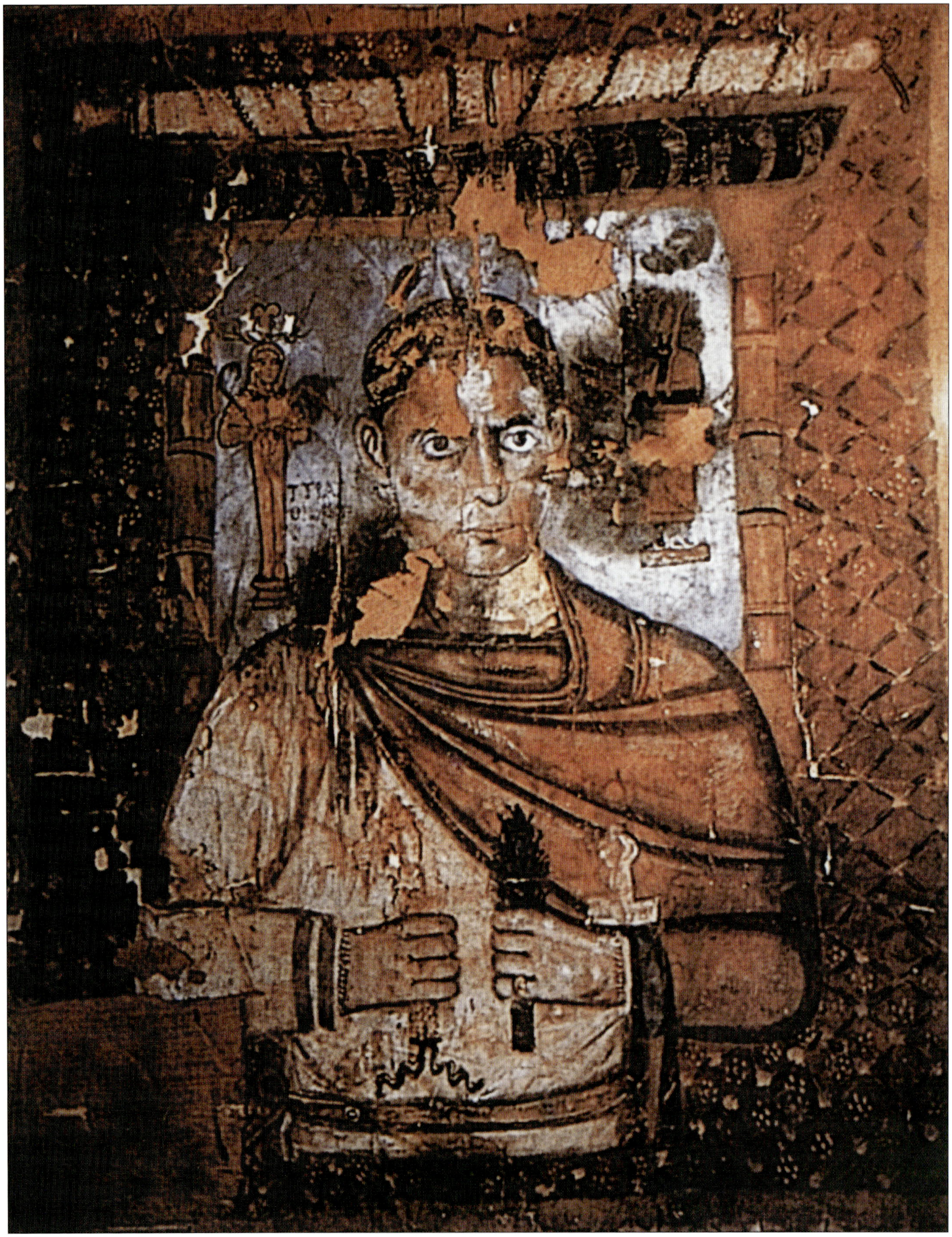

FIGURE 1.6
Shroud of a soldier named Tyras. Late second or early third century CE. Painted Linen. L: 88.5 cm. W: 70.5 cm. Luxor Museum.

and impoverished," preferring to see them instead as "practical . . . and . . . potent" solutions to funerary crowding and an expression of a long-practiced participation in the hallowedness of old funerary sites.[85]

Occasionally the textual finds at these funerary sites are so detailed that entire families emerge, giving us rare glimpses into the lives and identities of the people of Roman Thebes. One case in particular suggests that the local Theban elite was in some cases the product of considerable multicultural intermingling. Nineteenth-century excavations at an unrecorded site on the west bank of Thebes produced the coffin and epitaph of Soter, son of Cornelius Pollius, who was described as an archon of Thebes.[86] Other Greek, hieroglyphic, and demotic epitaphs from the same find mention ten other members of Soter's family, spanning the second half of the first and the first half of the second centuries CE. A recent study described this as a "noble family . . . probably of Greek origin, the members of which adopted Egyptian funerary beliefs and rituals. Some of them had Greek, others Egyptian names, some used both Egyptian and Greek forms."[87]

The Pebos family, buried in Theban Tomb 1407/House C3 at Deir el-Medinah, gives us another glimpse of a family of the Theban elite in the Roman period.[88] This family lived later than the Soter family as shown by several of their funeral texts dated on palaeographical grounds to the early third century. As Montserrat and Meskell put it, there is "strong circumstantial evidence that this was a local family who had achieved . . . prominence." Pebos and another member of the family both held the title of temple caretaker of the great Serapis, an Alexandrian priestly title "often held by Roman citizens who also held other major civic titles such as *gymnasiarch, exegetes,* member of the *boule* or even member of the Museion."[89] The Pebos and Soter families may have been exceptional, but they indicate that to some small degree, Theban local elite had ties to Alexandria and the wider Roman world.

The families of Soter and Pebos are both from the Roman period, from the first two centuries into the early third century, and thus predate the tetrarchic presence at Thebes. A soldier named Tyras comes to us from the same period; his shroud, painted with his portrait, shows him armed with a sword and wearing a military tunic, standing between images of Anubis and Osiris (figure 1.6).[90] No comparable picture of the local Theban elite emerges from later in the third century—no reference to a Soter or Pebos hiring the Hermonthite ironworkers, for instance—and it is not known how the local upper classes reacted to the Roman imperial presence in Thebes in the late 290s.

In the decades after Diocletian's visit to Egypt, Thebes continued to be a high-profile destination for prominent Roman officials.[91] But the epigraphic record of their visits makes it clear that neither the curiosity of a tourist nor the piety of a pilgrim was the chief motive at stake. Aurelius Reginus, *praeses* (regional governor) of the Thebaid around 300/302; Valerius Euethius, *rationalis Aegypti* (treasurer) in 302–304; and Aurelius Maximinus, *dux Aegypti Thebaidos utrarumque Libyarum* (duke of Egypt and the Thebais and both Libyas) in 308/310 dedicated a series of Latin inscriptions at Luxor Temple dating from their years in office.[92] Maximinus dedicated an inscription to Licinius, "the promoter of dutiful conduct, the extinguisher of barbarian populations."[93] Euethius, also known from papyri from Oxyrhynchos and Hermopolis, dedicated an inscription to Constantius, "to your spirit and majesty."[94] These are the marks of a new age and a reminder to any rebel that the emperor of Rome was always close at hand.

CONCLUSION

Earlier scholarship may have imagined Diocletian finding a museum town whose local nobilities were impoverished nobodies, but the topical and chronological coverage of the evidence makes painting a full picture impossible. The funerary remains show continuity of practice through the third century, but they give no clear snapshots of local elite families any later than the early third century. Though Christianity was clearly growing in importance in Egypt generally during the period of the Tetrarchy, we see no particular evidence of this trend at Luxor. The ostraca reveal a ubiquitous state presence in the form of taxation and the military in the first and second centuries CE, but they give us no way to trace this presence through the period of Diocletian. Indeed, the documentary evidence sheds no light on what was happening at Thebes itself during this period. Perhaps Diocletian shared Strabo's disappointment in Thebes as nothing but a collection of villages and thought to remake or reinvigorate the villages according to his own vision. Still, those villages and other sites nearby were healthy enough to produce resurgent cultic activity through the reign of Diocletian and beyond. The guild of Hermonthite ironworkers, with their donkey sacrifices and overnight temple visits, may have been precisely the type of people Diocletian aimed to impress with his military construction, precisely the people he wanted to remind of Rome's constant imperial presence in this new era.

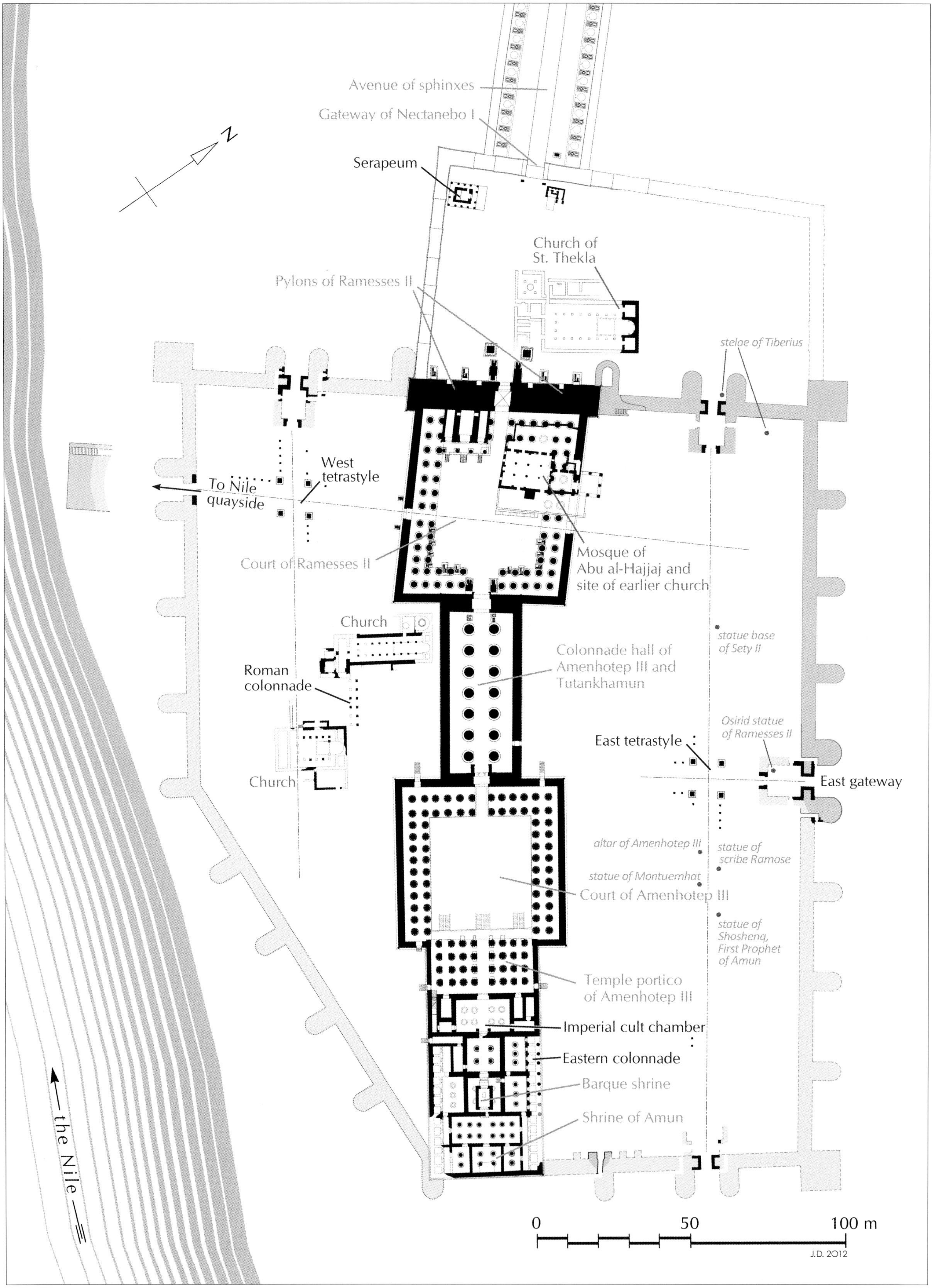

Avenue of sphinxes
Gateway of Nectanebo I
N
Serapeum
Church of
St. Thekla
Pylons of Ramesses II
stelae of Tiberius
West
tetrastyle
To Nile
quayside
Court of Ramesses II
Mosque of
Abu al-Hajjaj and
site of earlier church
Church
statue base
of Sety II
Roman
colonnade
Colonnade hall of
Amenhotep III and
Tutankhamun
Osirid statue
of Ramesses II
East tetrastyle
Church
East gateway
altar of Amenhotep III
statue of
scribe Ramose
statue of Montuemhat
Court of Amenhotep III
statue of
Shoshenq,
First Prophet
of Amun
Temple portico
of Amenhotep III
Imperial cult chamber
Eastern colonnade
Barque shrine
Shrine of Amun
the Nile
0
50
100 m
J.D. 2012

Chapter 2

DATING THE LUXOR CAMP AND THE POLITICS OF BUILDING IN THE TETRARCHIC ERA

SUSANNA McFADDEN

EARLIER STUDIES OF LUXOR TEMPLE AND THE CITY OF Thebes have wrestled with two fundamental questions: Why did the Roman authorities at the very end of the third century CE appropriate a seemingly derelict pharaonic temple for military use, and to what extent was this appropriation in keeping with Roman imperial policy in the larger empire? Precise answers remain elusive because the frescoes in the imperial cult chamber, the most visually arresting aspect of this activity, have been discussed previously only as a complement to the insufficient epigraphic materials rather than as the principal source of evidence for tetrarchic activities at Luxor. These questions are addressed anew in this chapter by looking at late Roman Thebes through an interpretive lens that privileges visual and material culture rather than simply the textual sources—acknowledging, of course, that such an exercise is by nature speculative. By considering the impact of the Roman paintings and concomitant decorative architectural embellishments such as the tetrastyles as primary evidence, however, it is possible to achieve a more nuanced impression of late antique Luxor and tetrarchic building policies as a whole. Indeed, I would argue that the visual and archaeological evidence from the tetrarchic era suggests that the Roman alterations and additions, rather than simply representing the pragmatic appropriation of a ready-made architectural shell, instead capitalized on the ancient pharaonic significance of Luxor Temple to bolster the impression of Roman authority.

THE DATE OF THE ROMAN FORT

This book assumes, as do earlier studies, that the reconfiguring of Luxor Temple as the spine of a military camp, and the placement of the Roman paintings at its center, took place during the First Tetrarchy of Diocletian (293–305) (figure 2.1).[1] More specifically, it is argued that plans for the renovations and the paintings were set in motion during one of Diocletian's two personal visits to Egypt between 297/298 and 301/302. This dating, for the fort and for the paintings, is conjectural, but it is the most plausible given the existing epigraphic and stylistic evidence related to the tetrastyles and paintings surveyed briefly below—what can be considered the more ceremonial aspects of the late Roman renovations to the temple and the main focus of this essay.[2]

A smattering of circumstantial evidence from the second century indicates a possible Roman military presence at Thebes, possibly implying that some of the practical architectural renovations to the temple were begun in an earlier century.[3] A Latin inscription from the reign of Antoninus Pius (r. 138–161), supposedly found in the temple "near the entry of the great court" (probably the court of Amenhotep III) records building work by the *Cohors Augusta Equitata*.[4] Furthermore, a fragmentary Latin inscription from Luxor Temple (now lost), published by H. Riad, refers to the *Cohors II Thracum* and a person named Ulpius Primanius, prefect of Egypt (between 195/196) during the reign of Septimius Severus (r. 193–211).[5] We know from other evidence that this cohort was stationed near Thebes around 200, but not necessarily at Luxor Temple.[6] Finally, second-century ostraca from the vicinity of Thebes record deliveries of straw to heat baths at a military camp that is interpreted as being at Luxor Temple.[7]

In contrast to this scanty record of a Roman military presence in the second century, there exists more concrete evidence for Roman patronage of a cultic nature at the site in the form of a small Greco-Roman-style Serapeum still

FIGURE 2.1
Plan of Luxor Temple showing Roman fortifications.

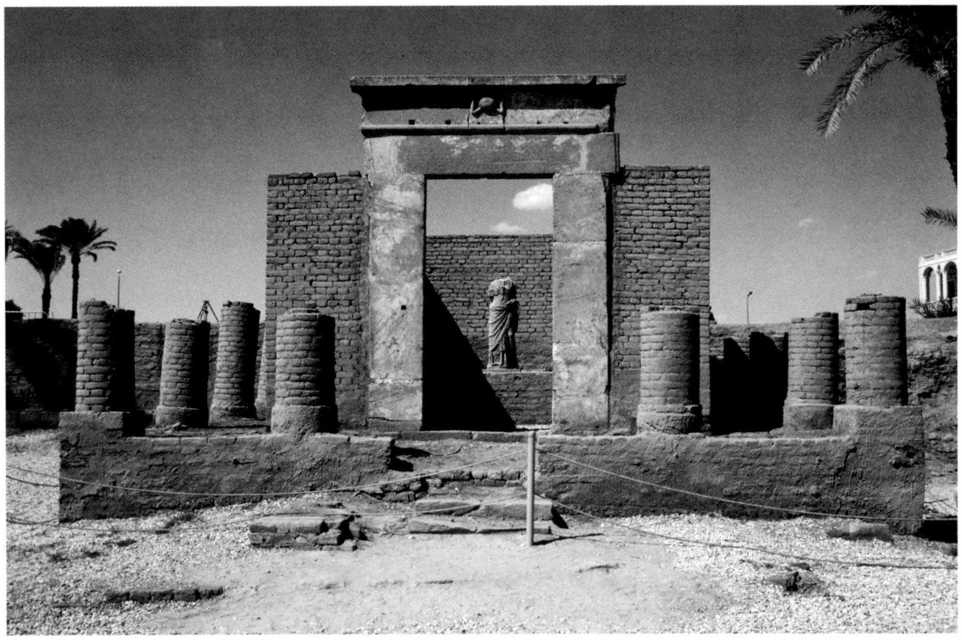

FIGURE 2.2
Restored shrine of Serapis (Serapeum) in front of Luxor Temple.

extant in the forecourt of Luxor Temple, within the enclosure walls renovated by the Emperor Tiberius (figure 2.2).[8] This temple, dedicated on 26 January 126 by one Gaius Julius Antonius, an ex-decurion and *neokoros* of the Serapis cult, signals a Roman imperial presence of sorts in that its consecration date coincides with that of the annual celebration of the Emperor Hadrian's *dies natalis* (birthday). Its construction is probably also connected to a visit to Thebes in the same year by the prefect of Egypt at the time, Titus Flavius Tatianus, recorded by an inscription on the Colossus of Memnon.[9] The small size of this shrine and its position outside the main sanctuary were previously interpreted as evidence for the decline of traditional Theban cults, but these attributes have recently been reassessed instead as a sign of deference to the chief deity of Luxor Temple and hence an indication of the Amun cult's continued activity, at least in the second century.[10]

This small temple aside, securely datable physical remains at Luxor Temple pointing to comprehensive Roman renovations do not exist before the late third century. While some of the architectural interventions described in chapter 3 might be traces of earlier military work, the Roman paintings in the imperial cult chamber cannot belong to a pre-tetrarchic occupation. Their style and iconography, discussed in detail in chapter 6, are wholly correct for imperial art of the late third and early fourth centuries. Considering their central position in the Roman reconfiguration of the temple, it is reasonable to assume that a major campaign of renovations should belong to the same moment as the execution of the paintings. Furthermore, the subject matter of the paintings supports the historical context of these elaborations. The images preserved on the south and east walls refer to an *adventus* (see chapter 7), a ceremony celebrating an imperial visit; hence it is reasonable to speculate that the images were prepared just before, or in commemoration of, such an event.

Ancient sources record at least three imperial visits to Egypt in the last decade of the third and first decade of the fourth centuries, although not to Thebes specifically.[11] The first documented visit of a Tetrarch to Egypt is that of Diocletian's junior colleague (Caesar) Galerius, who in 293 came to put down a rebellion centered at the important military and commercial center of Coptos (Qift), forty kilometers north of Luxor (figure 2.3).[12] For this victory, Galerius received the titles *Aegyptiacus maximus* and *Thebaicus maximus,* but this titulature appeared only, it seems, after he was promoted Augustus in 305.[13] Though no text refers explicitly to Galerius's presence in Thebes, a fragmentary inscription found in the vicinity of Luxor Temple is tenuously dated to 293, the year of Galerius's visit to Egypt.[14] This inscription refers to the *legio II Flavia Constantia,* a legion that, according to the fifth-century *Notitia Dignitatum,* was stationed at Thebes and might have been one of two legions named after the Caesars of the First Tetrarchy.[15] On the strength of this inscription it has been suggested that the renovations to Luxor Temple began under the aegis of Galerius, specifically to house this unit.[16] If this were correct, one might speculate that in 293 Galerius put into motion plans for an elaborate scheme of ceremonial embellishments to the fort, such as the imperial cult chamber, its paintings, and the tetrastyles. Such plans are not impossible to imagine, especially given Galerius's later decorative proclivities in other parts of the empire; the style of the paintings is certainly comparable to that of other works of art attributed to the court of Galerius (see figure 7.5).[17] But given the retroactive application of titulature celebrating the 293 victory, the importance of Galerius's military endeavors in Egypt might have been recognized only later.[18] By extension, the need to commemorate this victory with elaborate decorations such as the frescoes would not have become manifest until later.

Moreover, though the paintings might have been conceived by Galerius during a visit to Upper Egypt in 293, the iconography of the images, in particular the visual references to the god Jupiter (see chapter 6), indicates that they were ultimately not for him but that they pay particular tribute to the most senior of the Tetrarchs, Diocletian. Could Galerius, acting as a subordinate to Diocletian, have ordered the creation of an imperial cult chamber at Luxor Temple deco-

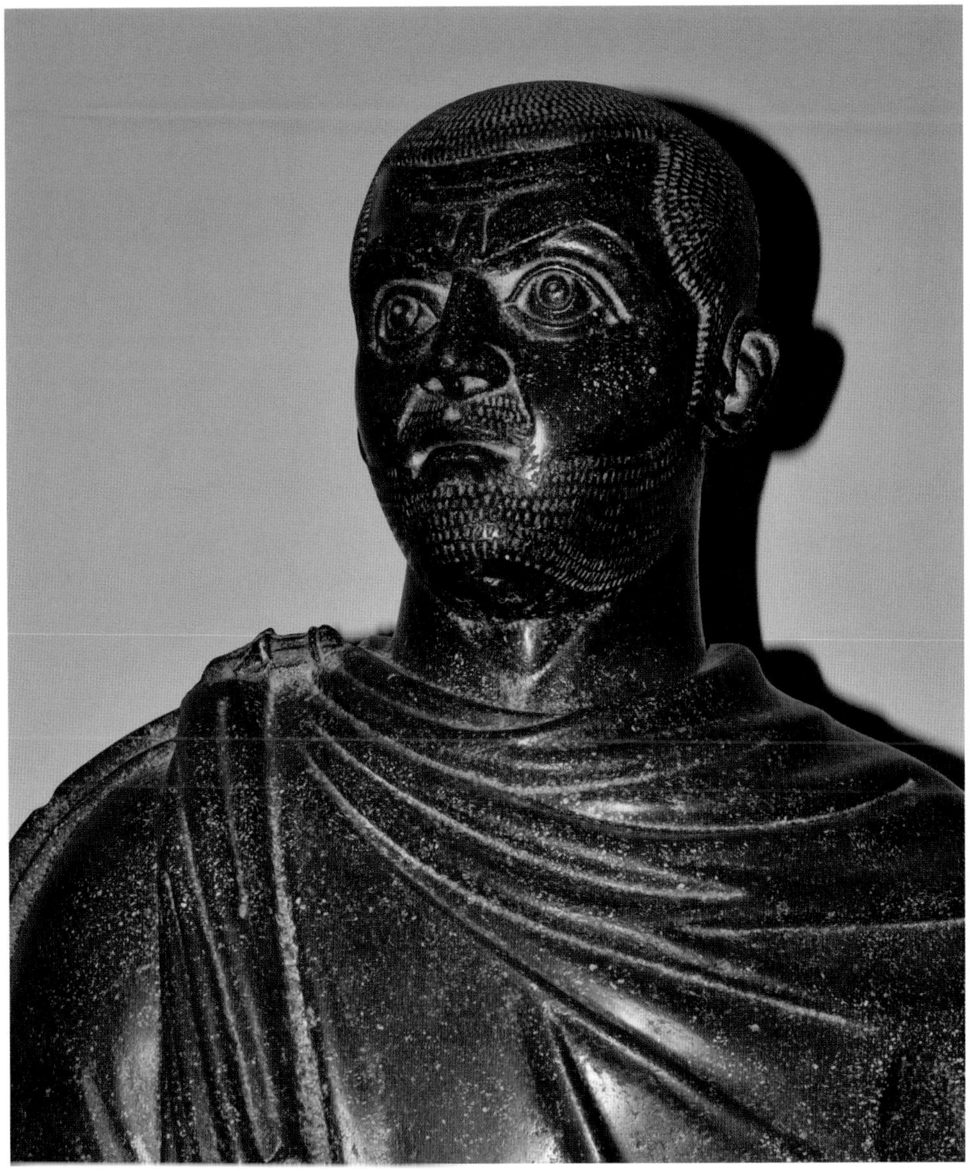

FIGURE 2.3
Porphyry bust, probably Galerius, from Benha (Tell Atrib), Egyptian Museum, Cairo.

rated with the appropriate iconography promoting *concordia* and Diocletian as an avatar of Jupiter? It is certainly possible, but the iconography of the images seems tied to the celebration of an imperial visit (either actual or virtual), and thus it is more reasonable to assume that an image program celebrating the primacy of Diocletian might actually commemorate the specific actions of Diocletian in Egypt, rather than those of a subordinate. But in the aftermath of the revolt in 293, there is no evidence to suggest that Diocletian himself intended an inspection of Egypt. It is not until another uprising at Alexandria in 297 that Diocletian felt obliged to visit Egypt personally.

Sources detailing this second imperial visit to the province of Egypt in late antiquity provide a more comprehensive narrative about the senior Augustus's movements than is available for Galerius's visit. The fourth-century *Breviarum* of Eutropius records how the rebellion that broke out in Alexandria in 297 was so intense that Diocletian, the senior Augustus of the newly established Tetrarchy, had to intervene himself.[19] This major revolt, the second in a decade, was led by the Alexandrian usurper Lucius Domitius Domitianus and lasted almost a year. After a prolonged siege, Diocletian finally recovered Alexandria in the spring of 298, after which he traveled to Philae to refortify and reorganize the southern frontier of Egypt.[20] From a few other fragmentary sources, historians have deduced that Diocletian spent almost a year in Egypt, his legions in tow, supervising a major military reorganization of the province.[21] It is presumed that during this restructuring, the *legio III Diocletiana* came to be stationed permanently at Thebes—as recorded retrospectively in the fifth-century *Notitia Dignitatum*—and it was for this military community that Luxor Temple was decorated with the elaborate murals discussed in this book.

Unfortunately, no direct evidence attesting to Roman activity in Thebes during the spring of 298 exists, nor is there any direct evidence that Diocletian ever stepped foot in the city. Instead, the first epigraphic records of Roman building works are the commemorative inscriptions from the western tetrastyle, dated to 301/302, which honors the four rulers of the First Tetrarchy (figure 2.4).[22] This date does not correspond to Diocletian's first visit, but several sources speak of a possible second visit to Egypt by Diocletian in March 302.[23] Although these texts note his presence only in Alexandria, it is possible that just before his Alexandrian appearance in the sources he revisited Upper Egypt, during which time the western tetrastyle was commissioned.[24] Alternatively, the monument could have been erected in anticipation of a visit that never came to fruition, or it could be seen to represent the final touches to a construction campaign that began in 298. While these inscriptions cannot be read as evidence for the physical presence of any or all of the four Tetrarchs, such honorifics constituted the symbolic presence of the contemporary rulers, and they were an essential element of any commemorative monument. Whether Diocletian ever stepped foot in Luxor Temple was beside the point; the inscriptions replicated his presence at the moment of erection and in perpetuity.

Complicating the matter of dating the paintings are several blocks now in the Luxor Temple block yard that bear Latin inscriptions and postdate Diocletian's second visit but that lack clear provenances. For example, two fragments of statue bases

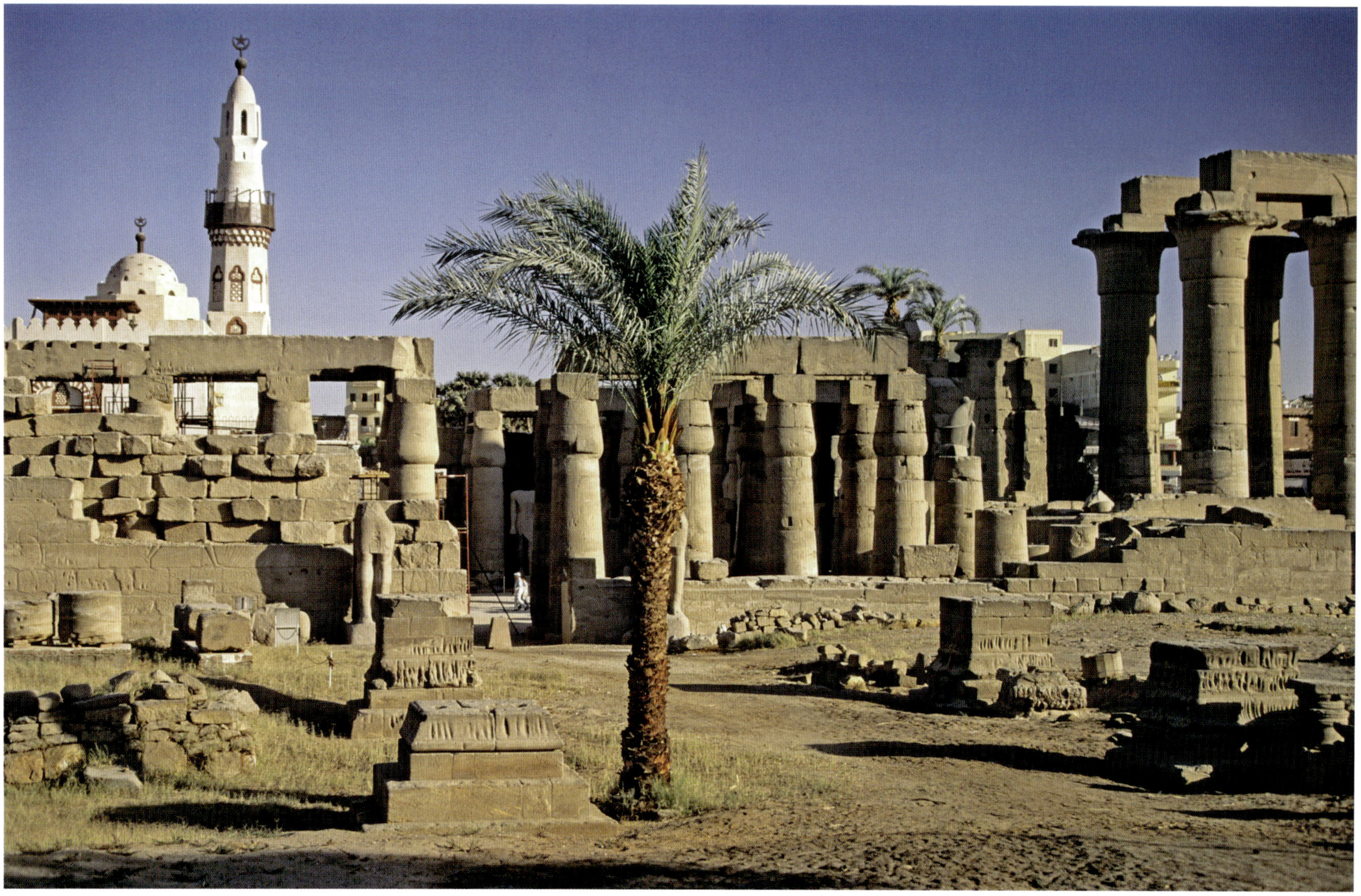

FIGURE 2.4
Remains of the western tetrastyle, looking east toward the Ramesses II court.

dedicated to the two junior Tetrarchs of the First Tetrarchy, Galerius and Constantius Chlorus, probably date to between 303 and 305.[25] Moreover, the eastern tetrastyle, dedicated to the emperors of a later Tetrarchy, composed of Galerius and Licinius (Augusti), Maximinus Daia, and Constantine (Caesars), is dated between 308 and 310 (figure 2.5).[26] Finally, a Thracian who held the office of *dux* named Valerius Rometalca dedicated at least three statues to the emperor Constantine. Although a fragment of the base of one of these is in the block yard and the whereabouts of another is currently unknown, the third base remains in situ in the Amenhotep III portico in front of the imperial cult chamber and provides at least some sense of the original context for such statues (figure 2.6).[27]

These Constantinian inscriptions should be dated after 310, when imperial authorities in the East recognized Constantine as Augustus in the West. Their *terminus ante quem* is normally given as 324, just before Constantine's defeat of Licinius in September of that year, because of the appearance of the title *invictus*. Dedicatory inscriptions postdating Constantine's victory, which attest to Constantine's new role as sole leader of the empire, usually use the title *victor* instead of *invictus*.[28] This chronology, however, is not without problems. If the bases were to date to before 324, when Licinius was still Augustus of the East (and, hence, controlled Egypt), it would seem unusual or perhaps even subversive for a *dux* of Egypt to commission not one but three statues to Constantine when Constantine held no official authority in Egypt before Licinius's downfall.[29] Given this, the statues logically should be dated *after* September 324 or, more precisely, immediately after Licinius's defeat, when Constantine's official titulature was still in flux, which would account for the use of the title *invictus*.

Against this varied epigraphic background, ranging between 293 and 325, how can the execution of the paintings be linked so certainly to Diocletian and not to some later iteration of the Tetrarchy? The damaged faces of the four Tetrarchs in the niche of the imperial cult chamber make portrait comparisons impossible, yet this imagery, the centerpiece

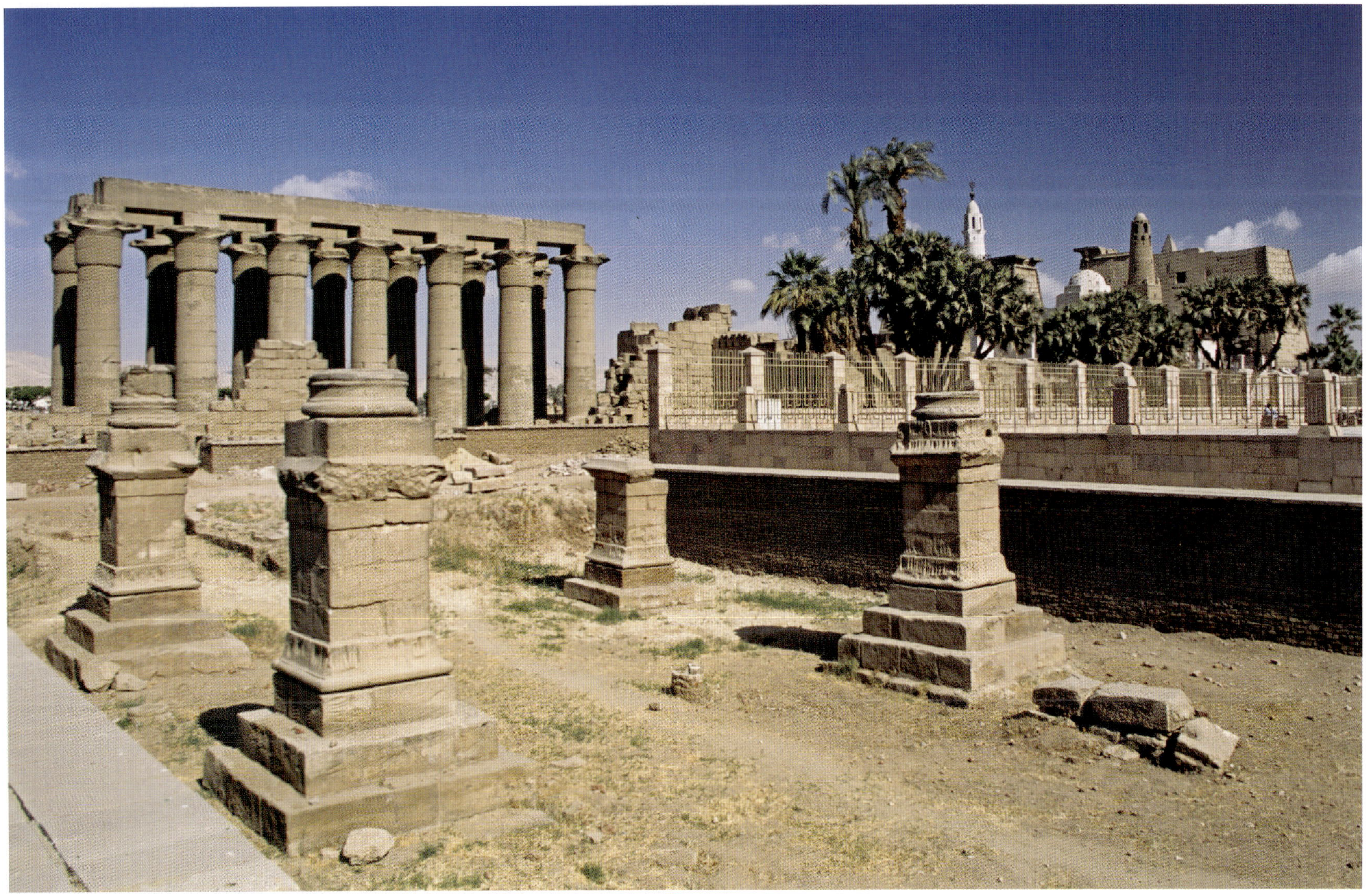

FIGURE 2.5
Remains of the eastern tetrastyle, looking northwest.

of the composition, as noted above, specifically emphasizes Jupiter, thus anchoring the composition to Diocletian (see chapter 6). Moreover, the subsidiary images on the south and east walls depict an adventus, the ceremony that accompanied an imperial visit, such as those we know Diocletian made to Egypt between 297/298 or 301/302.

One last piece of potentially complicating evidence is what appears to be a *damnatio memoriae* of the emperor pictured second from right (west) in the niche of the imperial cult chamber. The image has been almost completely rubbed away in an effort to remove the top layer of the fresco, an operation less violent and more time-consuming than the wholesale chipping away of the plaster detailing the Tetrarchs' faces, which also occurred in antiquity, probably the result of iconoclasm. Distinct from iconoclasm, damnatio memoriae, literally "damnation of memory," is the modern term for what was an official and time-honored method of asserting dominance over a political foe in the Roman world—the systematic mutilation or transformation of a name or image. A damnatio memoriae was often declared through imperial edicts, and we see the results of such edicts in the material record; names are erased from inscriptions, sculptures are recut to represent a new ruler, and figures are eliminated from group portraits (see figure 6.2). The effect is essentially a visual reminder to viewers that they must forget the person so damned.[30] Because of the international scope of these edicts, it should be a simple matter to identify the defaced figure at Luxor through comparison with the textual records. But there are two possible candidates for this treatment in the time frame under consideration here.

According to Lactantius, Constantine decreed a damnatio memoriae against Maximian, Augustus of the First Tetrarchy, sometime between the forced suicide of Maximian in 310 and the death of Diocletian on 3 December 311.[31] The official reason is not known, but it probably reflects Constantine's ongoing conflict with Maximian's son Maxentius for primacy in the West.[32] By 317/318, however, this damnatio had been rescinded

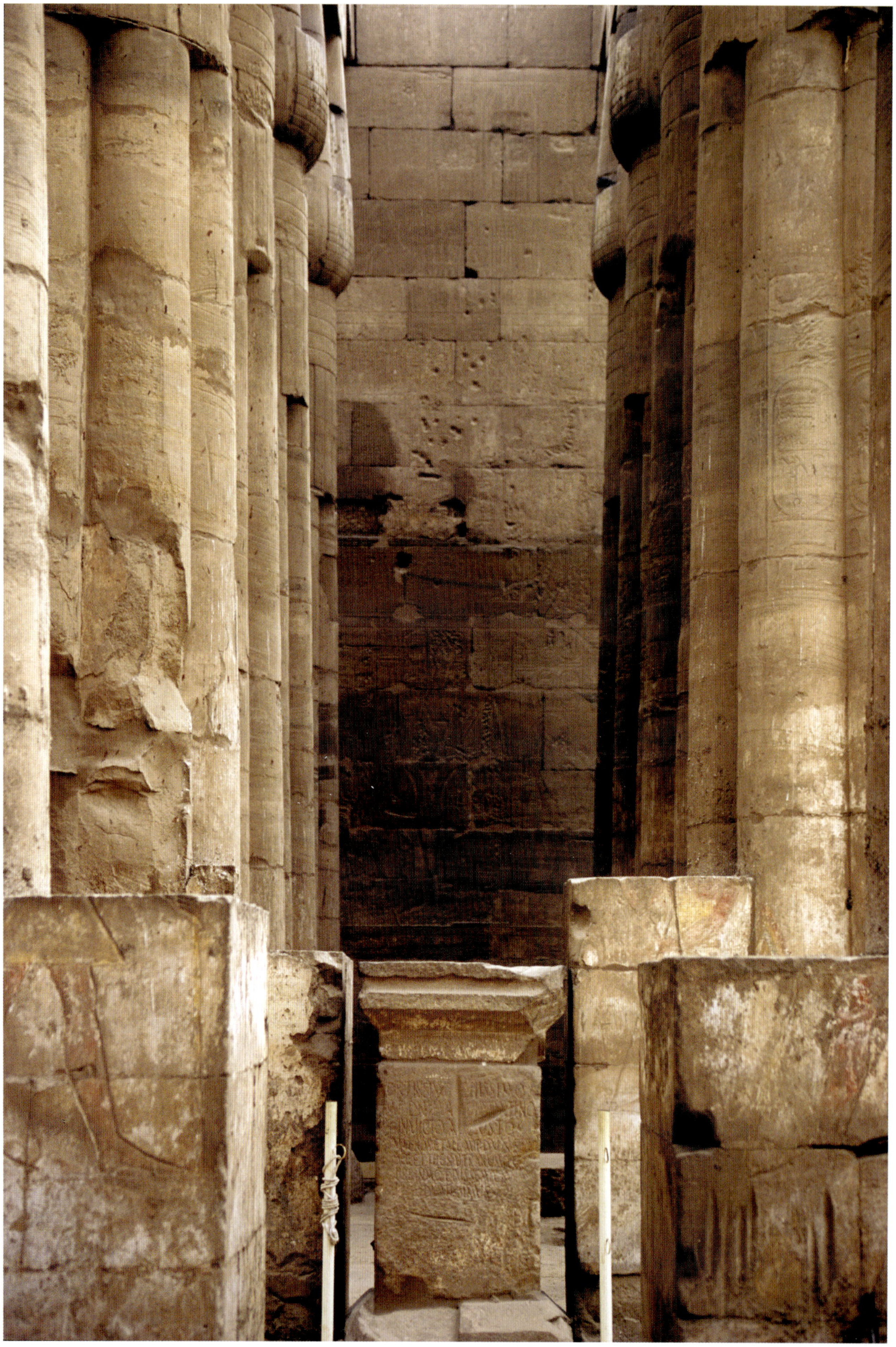

FIGURE 2.6
Statue base with inscription dedicated to the emperor Constantine in situ in the portico of Amenhotep III, ca. 310–325.

and Maximian's reputation rehabilitated, as evidenced by coins proclaiming Maximian *divus*.[33]

The second damnatio was issued against Maximinus Daia, probably sometime after his defeat by Licinius and his death at Tarsus in the summer of 313. Eusebius writes vividly about Maximinus's public disgrace and the subsequent violent destruction of his painted portraits and statues.[34] Since Maximinus Daia is also named on the eastern tetrastyle at Luxor, it has been suggested that it is perhaps his image that was defaced and not Maximian's and that the paintings, having been executed at the same time as the erection of the eastern tetrastyle, between 308 and 309, depict the Tetrarchy presumably named there, that of Galerius, Licinius, Maximinus Daia, and Constantine.[35]

This theory suffers from too many assumed premises. Had the damnatio been intended for Maximinus Daia, then the wrong figure was erased. Tetrarchic artistic convention dictated that when illustrating all four emperors together, the senior Augusti were generally placed in the middle, flanked by the Caesars (for example, see figure 7.5, second register)—so the erased figure must have held the rank of Augustus at the time of the damnatio.[36] If the paintings had depicted the Tetrarchy named on the eastern tetrastyle, then the image of Maximinus Daia would have been placed either on the right or the left flank of the group. He would not have been one of the central figures, since between 308 and 310, Maximinus Daia was still Caesar and hence technically subordinate. Since the images are not identified with inscriptions, and tetrarchic portraiture rejects verisimilitude, it is possible that whoever carried out the damnatio simply made a mistake. But this argument assumes that contemporary viewers were as underprivileged in their information as are modern scholars about who was who on the wall.

The likelier candidate for the identity of the defaced figure is thus the Augustus Maximian of the First Tetrarchy. Unfortunately, additional clues in Egypt are lacking to attest to systematic erasures of Maximian's name or image in other official circumstances. Even the inscription on the western tetrastyle at Luxor Temple, which should have celebrated Maximian's name, is lost, so it cannot corroborate the evidence from the frescoes. There are, nevertheless, indications from other provinces that Maximian's public image was removed from display, so the erasure at Luxor is not necessarily a unique occurrence.[37]

This hypothesis of course has its own difficulties. The most pressing question is that if Egypt was within the purview of Licinius at the time of Maximian's disgrace, why was it politically expedient that Licinius ensure his rival Constantine's wishes were carried out? Again, in the absence of additional textual sources, we cannot reconstruct the specific sequence of events or precise motivations. But it is clear that at some point in antiquity the image of a senior Augustus was systematically erased; the figure was not attacked violently, which would be indicative of iconoclasm; rather, the top layer of plaster was stripped off by abrading the surface so that details of the painting applied dry (*a secco*) to the fresco would be erased, effectively removing the figure's identity, while the base layer of the figure remained visible in the *intonaco* layer. Such an operation makes sense only in the context of a damnatio memoriae, and the most credible interpretation identifies Maximian as the focus of this damnatio, thus lending additional credence to the association of the Luxor paintings with the First Tetrarchy. It is reasonable to assert, then, that at some point between 312 and 317 an imperial edict ordering the erasure of Maximian's image was carried out at Luxor. Even more thought-provoking is the fact that the figure was never restored, signifying that at Thebes the rehabilitation of Maximian's reputation was either never communicated or thought necessary by the ruling authorities in Egypt at that time.

Though the exact nature of the power dynamics resulting in the erasure of this single image cannot be reconstructed, and while a precise date for the execution of the paintings and construction of the camp remains unattainable, the visual evidence alone should speak loudly about the identity of the figures depicted in the paintings. Given this, in spite of the confusing sequence of dates relating to Roman building activities at Luxor Temple provided by the inscriptions discussed above, the likeliest scenario, at least in terms of the inception of the paintings, is that they were conceived, with the imperial cult chamber, sometime just before Diocletian's first visit to Upper Egypt in 298 or perhaps in anticipation of a second visit in late 301 or early 302. The primacy of Diocletian in the visual program and the triumphalist nature of its theme (detailed in chapter 6) affirm in particular a connection with the reason for Diocletian's first visit to Egypt—the revolt against Roman rule beginning in 297, the effects of which had lasting repercussions. Though the rebellion was short-lived, the administrative reforms imposed by Diocletian as a consequence were not; these reforms were one means by which the presence of imperial authority reverberated long after the emperor himself departed the province. The tetrarchic embellishments to Luxor Temple can be seen as yet another means of asserting such a presence, a measure made all the more potent by the specific location chosen for such honors.

WHY THEBES?

Presuming, then, that the late Roman paintings at the heart of this book came to occupy an imperial cult chamber at the center of Luxor Temple during a comprehensive renovation of the site by the Roman army of Diocletian, the question remains: Why was Luxor Temple chosen to receive such elaborations? Unfortunately, the textual sources of the era tell us very little about what the Roman army was doing in Luxor in particular in the first place. This is not to say that Diocletian's reasons for taking his army to Egypt are opaque. Rather, the specific actions of his army in Thebes are not recorded. The legion's general presence in the Thebaid is well attested in the Panopolis papyri and the *Notitia Dignitatum,* but no corroborating epigraphic or papyrological evidence explicitly stating its occupation of Luxor Temple in the late third to early fourth century has been found.[38] The inscriptions on the tetrastyles honoring two different Tetrarchies date discrete episodes of Roman architectural additions to Luxor Temple, but there is nothing explicitly militaristic in their tone.[39] Individuals with the titles *praeses* (west tetrastyle) and *dux* (east tetrastyle) are named as the agents of the dedications to the emperors, the former being a civil title while the latter is military, but no reference is made to any military unit.[40]

Without the physical evidence of the Roman modifications to Luxor Temple, late Roman Luxor would have been absent entirely from the story of Diocletian in Egypt. The dearth of textual evidence pertaining to Luxor in late antiquity thus accounts for a somewhat unbalanced picture of the importance of the city in modern histories of the era, as was discussed in chapter 1.[41] Thebes had once been a grand ceremonial city during the New Kingdom, so much so that Homer in book 9 of the *Iliad* saw fit to preserve the memory of this greatness by describing Thebes as the "hundred-gated city."[42] It was the seat of the cult of Amun, who, through royal patronage during the New Kingdom, became the highest god of the Egyptian pantheon, and therefore the city had special significance to Egyptian religious life.[43] Though it had ceased to be the political and administrative center of Upper Egypt by the time of the Ptolemies, Hellenistic rulers at first continued to support the cult of Amun at Thebes, as they did for the deities of all the major cities throughout Egypt.[44] Several revolts centered at Thebes against Ptolemaic rule in the second and first centuries BCE put an end to this munificence, and the city was treated harshly in retribution, according to later accounts, such as that of Pausanias in the second century CE.[45] As a result, by the advent of Roman rule, Thebes had become a "quiet provincial town" that was popular with tourists.[46] But if this was indeed the status of the city, why would Diocletian choose such a place to base his legions and construct an important shrine to the imperial cult within the walls of a supposedly defunct temple?

The nature of the debate over the status of the city of Thebes in the Roman period hinges on the question of whether these ancient sanctuaries were still functioning by the time of the tetrarchic modifications to Luxor Temple.[47] Whereas epigraphic evidence at these temples (or lack thereof after the second century) has traditionally been interpreted as an abandonment of the extensive temple bureaucracies that had been in place since the New Kingdom, it seems clear that traditional religious rituals and practices still continued on a local or regional level in contexts such as the domestic and the funerary, as described in chapter 1. That such practices continued in the temples themselves, admittedly in a pared-down fashion, is attested in a number of localities, including Luxor Temple.[48] Yet most modern histories of late antique Egypt explain the appropriation of Luxor Temple by the Romans as a simple matter of reuse "for military purposes," a rationale that suggests a pressing need to construct the fort quickly and efficiently, hence the appropriation of the preexisting, readily available shell of Luxor Temple.[49]

This no-nonsense explanation seems only part of the story. Even if Luxor Temple was completely abandoned by the end of the third century, its skeleton does not lend itself practically for adaptation as a military base. Certainly, the agency for construction initially belonged with the Roman army, but what kind of military purposes were intended for the site? Luxor Temple cannot be thought of as a Roman fort in the traditional sense because the sole purpose of the Roman modifications to Luxor Temple could not simply have been defense and the maintenance of order—the city of Thebes, as far as we can tell from the surviving sources, had not been involved in either of the revolts of the 290s.

In fact, if we think about the decision to construct a military compound at Thebes solely in terms of military strategy, the choice of site seems strange. Other tetrarchic-era military constructions in Egypt, such as Tell el-Herr (*Magdolum*) in the eastern Delta/Sinai, Qasr Qarun (*Dionysias*) in the Fayyum, Babylon in Old Cairo (see figure 1.3), Nag al-Hagar near Aswan, and Abu Shaar on the Red Sea, among others, were clearly designed to refortify the borders and revivify a Roman military presence in light of late third-century revolts, and they thus tended to be located along strategic transportation routes (see figure 1.1).[50] Although the Luxor camp shares certain architectural characteristics with these forts (square or rectangular layout, projecting U-shaped towers), it does not generally present a perfect typological comparison. For example, Abu Shaar and Qasr Qarun (*Dionysias*) are often cited as parallels to the Luxor fort because within their fortified enclosures can also be found *sacella* (small shrines) dedicated to the cult of the military standards (*signa*), which are prominently and centrally situated within the camps, as is the imperial cult chamber at Luxor.[51] The fact that the imperial cult chamber at Luxor was constructed within an already existing sacred complex, however, makes for a contrast rather than comparison. Furthermore, while there is evidence of painted plaster being employed for decoration in late Roman forts in other parts of the empire, frescoes of the same quality and quantity as found in the Luxor imperial cult chamber have not been detected in any other military installations of the era, or, indeed, of any era.[52] Given this, the Luxor chamber's elaborate decorations appear to amplify the room's—and indeed by extension the whole camp's—ceremonial function. The Luxor cult chamber was not simply a shrine to the legionary standards, and this distinctiveness, discussed in chapter 7, marks the site as unique in Egypt.[53] Overall, there are as many contrasts between the Luxor camp and other tetrarchic-era forts in Egypt as there are similarities. While other *forts* were constructed on top of preexisting military architecture (Tell el-Herr/Magdolum), or de novo along caravan routes (Qasr Qarun/Dionysias and Abu Shaar), or on the edge of tetrarchic-era frontiers (Nag al-Hagar), the city of Thebes appears not to have had any clear geographical relevance in the administration of Roman Egypt.[54]

All this further fuels the question, Why create such a sophisticated visual environment as that of the imperial cult chamber inside Luxor Temple if the whole complex was to be used, as is suggested elsewhere, simply as a place to billet the Roman army? The answer lies in the specific symbolic meaning of the pharaonic temple and the Romans' desire to harness that meaning for their own political agenda. Luxor Temple was a monumental complex already almost two millennia old at the end of the third century. Built during the Eighteenth and Nineteenth Dynasties of the New Kingdom, the temple was dedicated to the Theban triad, Amun, his consort, Mut, and their son, Khonsu. It was also a place strongly associated with the cult of the deified Egyptian king, and this association probably endured far longer than the pharaohs who built it. Luxor Temple seems to have functioned as the mythological and theological power base of the reigning monarchs from the New Kingdom onward.[55] Indeed, we know that even up to the fourth century BCE and the advent of the Greco-Roman period, the symbolic power of the place was recognized. Though he himself never visited Upper Egypt, Alexander the Great, for example, the self-proclaimed son of Zeus-Ammon, ordered the renovation of the temple's barque shrine, its walls redecorated to show Alexander as pharaoh.[56]

The extent to which Luxor Temple continued to function as a potent nexus of authority by the time of Diocletian is still debated. Six centuries after Alexander, the appropriation of this temple for "secular" use—its conversion into an army camp—is often cited as glaring evidence that the Egyptian cult was no longer active at Thebes.[57] Yet the specific way in which the Romans appropriated the temple's existing architecture makes no sense if we presume the place had no symbolic significance. As noted above, the visual and archaeological evidence instead suggests that the Roman constructions at Luxor reflect a continued acknowledgment of the place's power.

The specific architectural embellishments, detailed in chapter 3, are highly suggestive in this respect. The engineers of the Luxor camp incorporated the enormous pharaonic temple of Amun into the Roman fortification (see figure 2.1). Rather than demolish the pharaonic structure or simply choose another, unoccupied location, Roman engineers built around the temple, integrating the already existing infrastructure into their camp.[58] The temple ran from one end of the fort to the other, as would the *cardo* or *via principalis* in any other traditional grid plan (see figure 3.1), and yet this north-south thoroughfare did not facilitate traffic circulation within the camp; rather, it funneled all traffic toward the imperial cult chamber and the paintings within it at the southern end of the temple. This was a ceremonial route (described in more detail in chapter 7), not a practical one, and such restructuring of an extant site points to an agenda beyond expediency.

The Roman modifications seem even more exceptional when we consider the fact that the atypical incorporation of the pharaonic monument into the Roman fort essentially separated what we presume were the functional areas of the camp. North-south and east-west thoroughfares further sectioned off each autonomous side of the camp, and at the junctions of these crossroads were placed the aforementioned tetrastyles. These tetrastyles in particular mark the site as something other than a simple legionary fort. Similar honorific monuments are found in numerous cities throughout the Roman Empire, though tetrastyles seem to have been especially popular in Egypt starting in the second century.[59] Ancient sources make reference to examples at Arsinoe,

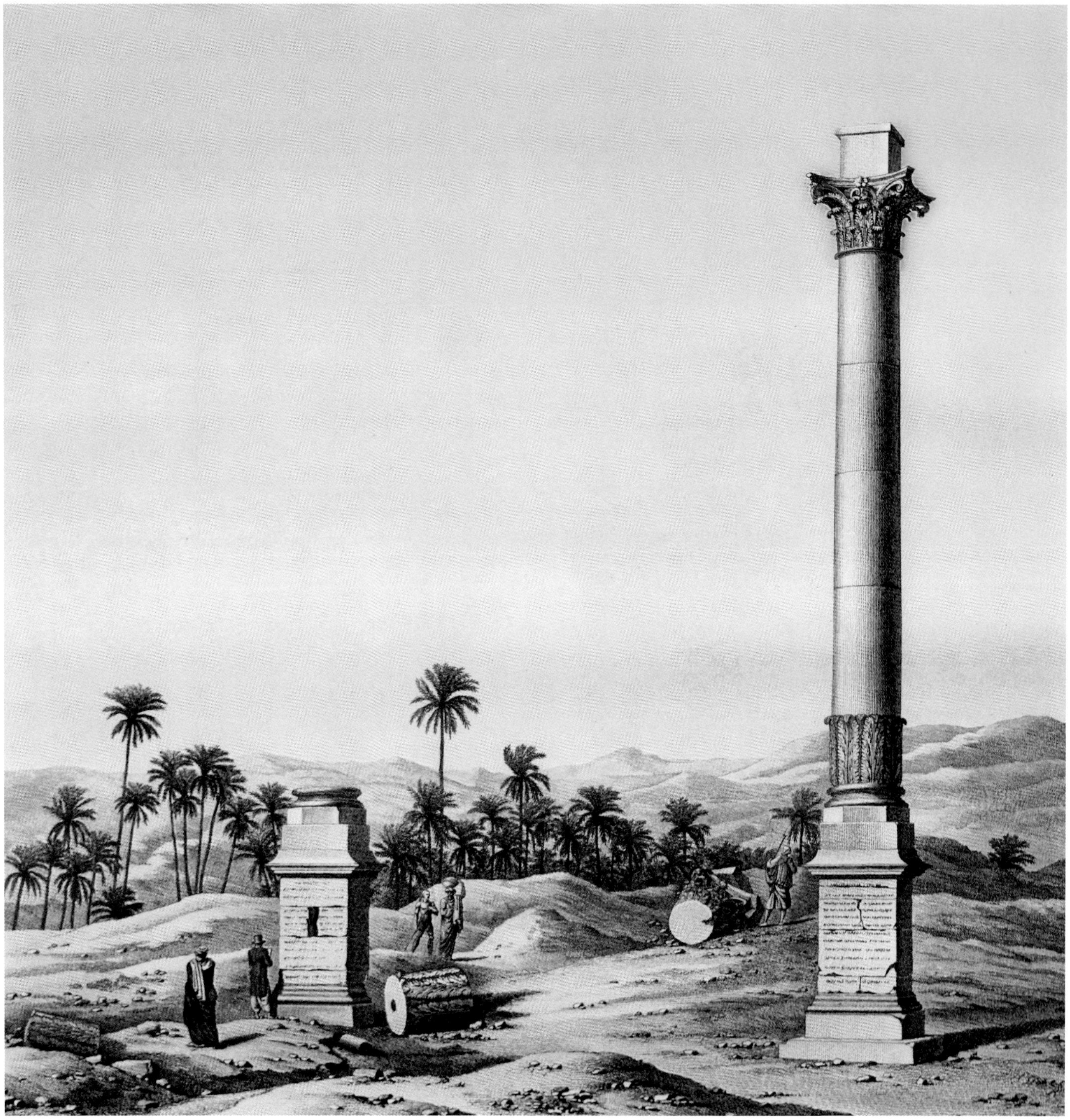

FIGURE 2.7
1798 drawing of the Antinoopolis tetrastyle from the *Description de l'Égypte, Antiquités,* vol. 4, pl. 59, 1798.

Oxyrhynchos, and Antinoopolis and to three different tetrastyles along the main east-west road of Hermopolis Magna.[60] The closest of these in terms of chronology and form to Luxor's tetrastyles, including the acanthus design at the bases of the columns, seems to be the monument at Antinoopolis (known best from drawings predating its destruction in about 1830), dated by an inscription to the reign of Severus Alexander (225–235 CE) (figures 2.7 and 2.8).[61]

At Luxor, the four column bases of the western tetrastyle honored the four emperors reigning at the time of its construction in late 301 or early 302—the senior emperors (Augusti) Diocletian and Maximian and the two junior

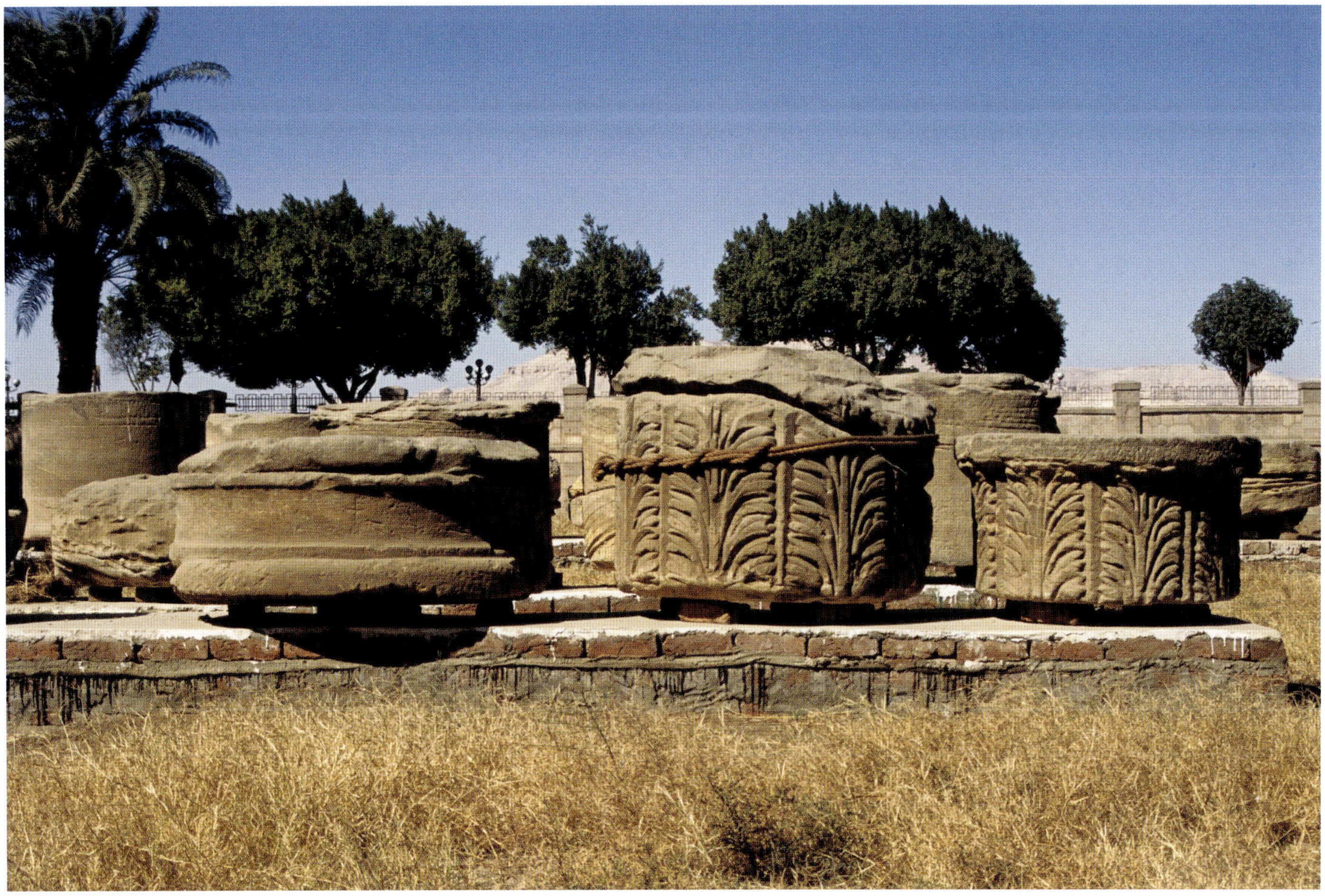

FIGURE 2.8
Column drums from the western tetrastyle, decorated with acanthus leaves.

emperors (Caesars) Galerius and Constantius Chlorus (see figures 2.4 and 2.1). Interestingly, the slightly smaller eastern tetrastyle is positioned asymmetrically in relation to the central camp axis created by the temple and is not contemporaneous with its western counterpart (see figures 2.5 and 2.1). As noted above, the inscriptions on its column bases are dedicated to a later Tetrarchy of Licinius and Galerius (Augusti), and Constantine and Maximinus Daia (Caesars), thus dating its construction to between 308 and 310. These monuments therefore represent discrete moments of construction rather than a single commemorative endeavor in which the tetrastyles mark the beginning and end of a long building campaign focused on Luxor Temple. Their independent construction and the fact that their inscriptions signal the symbolic presence of the emperors rather than the Roman legions further indicate a use pattern for Luxor Temple distinctive from other Diocletianic forts.[63]

Given that the physical modifications to Luxor Temple under Roman occupation seem to suit ceremonial rather than practical military purposes, it is perhaps more useful to analyze the Roman restructuring of Luxor Temple outside a purely martial function. Instead, the site can be considered alongside patterns of Roman urbanization in Egypt, especially those that take coherent form in the second century.[64] The fort at Luxor seems to exhibit the characteristics of a city center with its own "armature," to use William MacDonald's term for the monuments that make up the fundamental building blocks of Roman imperial urbanism: colonnaded streets, piazzas, gates, and archways.[65] Such monuments expressed directional and spatial unity and provided a framework for civic, public activity, and they were characterized by the fluidity with which one was able to move through them.[66] Though elements of Roman armatures are evident in a variety of forms in other Late Roman forts in Egypt,[67] the monuments added by the Romans to Luxor Temple and its immediate surroundings can be related particularly to several cities in Upper Egypt that were given a classical veneer in the second century. The systematic employment of Roman-style architecture in numerous Egyptian towns up and down the Nile Valley in the second century (as opposed to building in the Egyptian style) is attested in the papyrological record, but unfortunately the physical remains of such building campaigns are far less numerous.[68] Those sites at which archaeological traces of Roman armatures can be detected in the Thebaid include Oxyrhynchos, Hermopolis Magna, and Antinoopolis.[69]

The Roman remains of Hermopolis Magna are currently the best understood of this group. Although it was already an important city at the start of the Ptolemaic period, much of the extant architecture in situ today dates to the second century CE, during which time the city center was given a Roman facade (that is, a facade that was distinct from the already hellenized infrastructures developed by the Ptolemies). The most notable redistribution of space occurred around the main Ptolemaic sanctuary to Thoth/Hermes, one of the great syncretic gods that became popular with the arrival of the Greeks.[70] In the second century the enclosure wall of this sanctuary was actually cut down in places to create a large piazza that was then connected to a tetrastyle at the crossroads of two main colonnaded streets.[71] These Antonine-era modifications included the construction of a building that has been labeled a *komasterion,* a basilica-like edifice where sacred processions assembled, to the east of the tetrastyle.[72] Presumably this assembly place was the starting point for processional ceremonies of all kinds that headed to the sanctuary of Thoth to the north, for example, but perhaps also to an imperial cult sanctuary, the existence of which is also known from the papyri.[73]

As Hermopolis Magna attests, it is clear that in many cities in Egypt the Romans spared no expense on public infrastructure designed to facilitate civic (and processional) ceremony, a practice that continued into late antiquity.[74] The modifications made to Luxor Temple at the turn of the fourth century can be seen as the legacy of such initiatives. Roman engineers not only built a quasi-military installation but also sought to remake the cityscape of the southern part of Thebes into a ceremonial center honoring the Roman emperor in both divine and human forms. The characterization of Thebes in late antiquity as a "quiet provincial town" is owing in part to the lack of evidence regarding its role in the larger Egyptian economy and administration, but it also may stem from the fact that Thebes had no city center according to the principles of Roman planning; hence, in earlier studies of the site, the modifications to Luxor Temple were not considered in terms of civic euergetism.[75] Textual evidence suggests that the main residential area of Greco-Roman Thebes was Diospolis Magna, around the main complex of the Amun cult at Karnak.[76] Whether this settlement extended southward all the way to Luxor Temple, or whether there was a separate enclave serving the "southern sanctuary," as Luxor Temple was known in hieroglyphic texts, is unclear, but it does seem that Luxor Temple traditionally occupied a subordinate position, at least in administrative terms, since it did not have its own priests and was serviced instead from Karnak.[77] Given this hierarchy, it is thought-provoking that the Romans chose to embellish Luxor Temple instead of Karnak with ceremonial architecture appropriate to a civic center.

The choice of Luxor Temple has previously been explained in practical terms—as a nonfunctioning structure that was therefore easily appropriated. But the visual and archaeological evidence of the paintings, coupled with the tetrastyles, complicates this explanation. One could instead consider these embellishments as evidence that Luxor Temple's distinctive symbolic connection to the ideology of divine kingship still resonated in late antiquity and was particularly appealing to promoters of tetrarchic ideology, which prompted the Romans to mark the site with their own armature to capitalize on the site's history. The iconography of the imperial cult chamber celebrating the divine authority of the Roman emperors (detailed in chapters 6 and 7) is highly appropriate to such an agenda.

It could of course be merely coincidental that a Roman space designed to venerate both the divine and human aspects of the Roman emperor was placed in the heart of a temple previously used for the veneration of the pharaoh in his human and divine aspects. As discussed in chapter 1, modern scholars are able only to glimpse the living world of late antique Thebes through disjointed snapshots of evidence. It is impossible to recover through texts the social memories of local Thebans, or conquering Romans for that matter, at the moment of the tetrarchic appropriation of Luxor Temple, and hence it is difficult to reconstruct exactly what the inhabitants of Luxor in late antiquity might have remembered about Luxor Temple's specific pharaonic theological significance.

Recent studies on the relationship between monuments and "social memory" and the ways in which material remains can be fruitfully mined for indications of shared remembrances, however, allow us at least to consider the possibility that the memory of Luxor Temple's previous significance influenced the reuse of the temple in the Roman period.[78] The reconfiguration of civic and sacred spaces to conjure specific memories of the past and thus harness that symbolism for the present, as can be seen to have occurred at Luxor Temple in the tetrarchic era, is a process not without precedent in the Roman world. Recent studies of Roman Greece in particular have highlighted the sophisticated ways in which the Romans rearranged important civic monuments and landscapes with an acute awareness of past meanings, which sometimes resulted in local audiences becoming complicit in the reframing of those meanings for the present. As Susan Alcock has demonstrated for the Athenian agora under Roman rule, to name just one example, the memory of an idealized classical Greek past was localized in particular monuments and spaces and reembedded into a new material framework to enhance the authority of Roman rule.[79] Investigations of social memory and its effects therefore are best anchored in studies of the physical setting of remembrance. Indeed, monuments often become the nucleus around which people reinvent the past and affect designs for the future.[80]

For Egypt, these processes are less clear because we have no contemporary accounts of the experience of sacred sites, such as we have for Roman Greece in the High Empire. In particular, Pausanias's *Guide to Greece* describes the major Panhellenic sanctuaries as well as minor cult spaces as they existed in the second century CE from the point of view of a Greek pilgrim living in a Roman world. Scholars have deduced from reading Pausanias that elite travelers in the Roman era found inspiration in and sought connections to the ancient cults of classical Greece to better understand their identity within the Roman Empire.[81] Given the evidence for Greek and Roman pilgrimage to Thebes, discussed in chapter 1, it is not so unreasonable to imagine that the engineers who repurposed Luxor Temple for use by the Roman imperial army were similarly aware of the potential for such connectivity between the Roman present and the pharaonic past.

In support of the idea that the architectural and artistic additions to Luxor Temple indicate an acknowledgment on the part of the Romans of the site's symbolic importance, it should be noted that the process detected at Luxor, whereby an indigenous cult space was integrated into a Roman fort, was not a unique phenomenon in the tetrarchic era or limited to Egypt. On the eastern border of the empire, the sacred precinct of Allat-Minerva at Palmyra, established in the first century BCE, was, like Luxor Temple, incorporated into a Diocletianic fort constructed in the late third or early fourth century (see figure 3.3).[82] The Palmyrene temple's *temenos* walls were altered to accommodate the military installation, but the actual building housing the cult statue of Allat-Minerva seems to have survived among the barracks through the fourth century.[83]

In conclusion, while we cannot pinpoint exactly how people understood and used these spaces sacred to deities of local origin (the Temple of Amun and the Temple of Allat-Minerva), the very fact of their survival within their new Roman contexts is significant evidence for an engagement on the part of the Roman military, and by extension the emperors, with the practice of memory politics in late antiquity.[84]

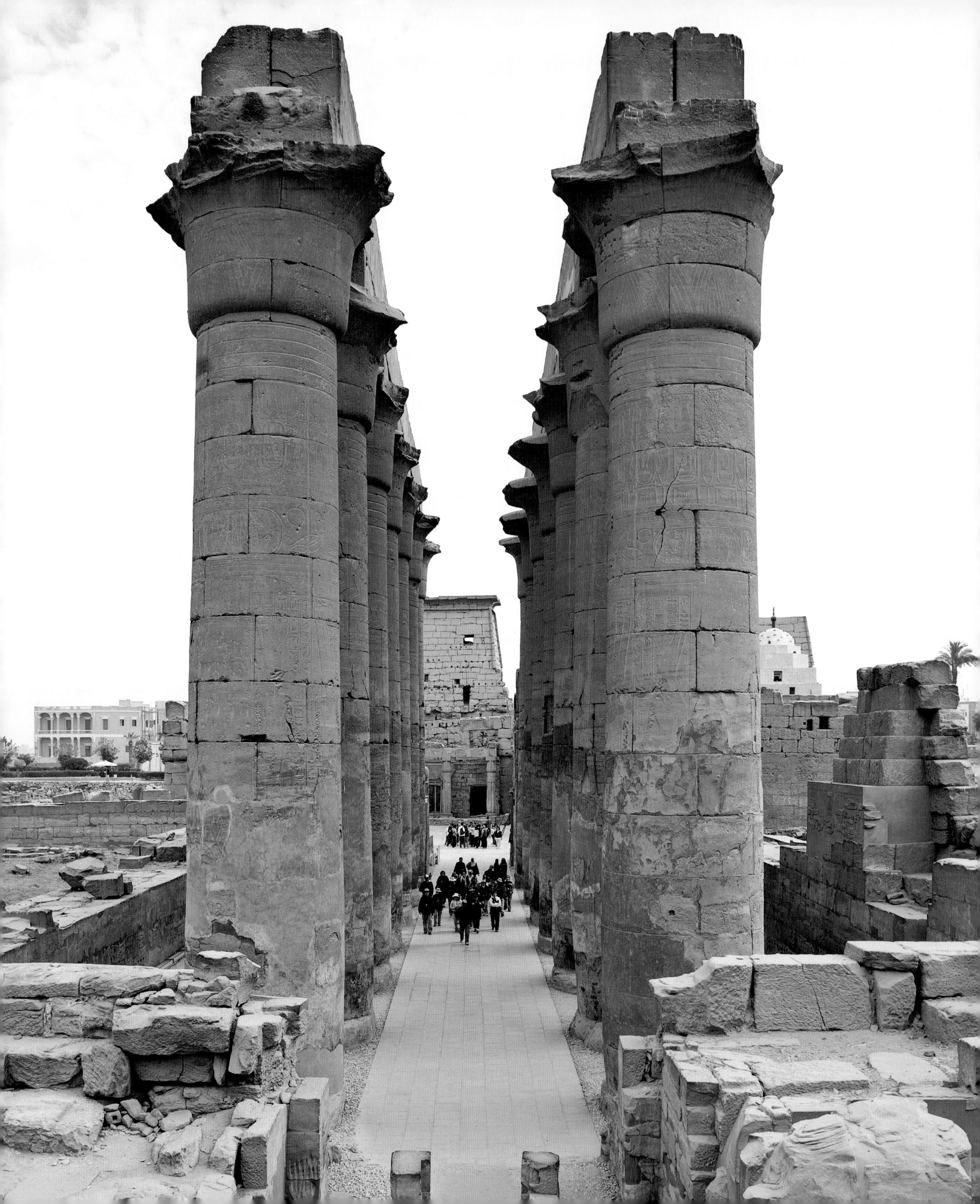

Chapter 3

THE TETRARCHIC ARCHITECTURAL RENOVATION OF LUXOR TEMPLE

Context, Significance, and the Amun Cult

JAMES B. HEIDEL AND W. RAYMOND JOHNSON

FIGURE 3.1
View looking north into the colonnade of Amenhotep III and Tutankhamun, showing Roman doorjambs inserted between the colonnade and Amenhotep III court.

THE ARCHITECTURAL MODIFICATION OF LUXOR TEMPLE into a Roman military installation and imperial cult center by Diocletian and the Tetrarchy is an extraordinary chapter in the later history of the already ancient complex. Trying to understand the intent behind the modifications is a challenge for several reasons: the parallel architectural material is limited;[1] the temple proper was cleared before scientific archaeology was developed in Egypt; and most of the Roman levels around the temple remain unexcavated. Still, architectural clues abound that shed light on the monument at the moment the imperial cult chamber was frescoed in the decades bracketing the turn of the fourth century. Several possible models of intent will be examined in this chapter, with the understanding that this is not the final word on the subject but only the beginning of a new conversation.[2] The analysis will begin with a brief discussion of select comparanda that relate to the architectural organization of the tetrarchic renovation of Luxor Temple. It will continue with a detailed discussion of the architectural reconstruction of the imperial cult chamber itself and the rooms that adjoin it (the immediate architectural context of the frescoes), and the main-axis approach. Finally, the issue of the possible political or theological significance of the modifications, particularly in relation to the Amun cult, will be examined. Throughout this discussion the text will differentiate between elements of the reconstruction that are based on evidence remaining at the site and elements that are in some measure hypothetical in their form but nonetheless necessary to constitute what the Romans would have seen as a fully formed narrative architectural ensemble. All references to Roman modifications to the temple, unless otherwise specified, refer to those of the tetrarchic phase.

COMPARANDA

The Roman fortification at Luxor was laid out around the temple, the buildings on an orthogonal plan. The temple itself was integrated into this design as the main north-south axis running through the whole complex, so that it effectively divided the fortified enclosure into two halves, one on the east and the other on the west, beside the Nile. It was surrounded by defensive walls regularly punctuated by gates and towers that were connected by straight arterial streets lined with colonnades. Monumental tetrastyles were erected where the main streets intersected on both the east and west sides. The colonnades in the Luxor Temple complex are shown in Lacau's plan of 1934,[3] and a few remaining bases are visible in situ, one south of the temple's east tetrastyle and a few north of the west tetrastyle. The bases and capitals are of limestone, and the column shafts are baked brick coated in stucco (figure 3.2). At the heart of the temple, one of the original Eighteenth-Dynasty rooms was converted into the imperial cult chamber, which corresponds with the position in contemporary Roman fortifications of the central *principia* (headquarters building) at the back of a large, colonnaded court with an axial approach. Two sites in the Eastern Empire roughly contemporaneous with the tetrarchic renovations of Luxor Temple that illustrate this pattern are the legionary fortress at El-Lejjun in Jordan (figure 3.3, left) and the fortified site at Palmyra in Syria (figure 3.3 right). Though individual camps were often of divergent forms, sometimes based on local conditions, there are also many correspondences that can be tied to features at Luxor and that have informed our present reconstruction of the Romans' work at the site. The camp

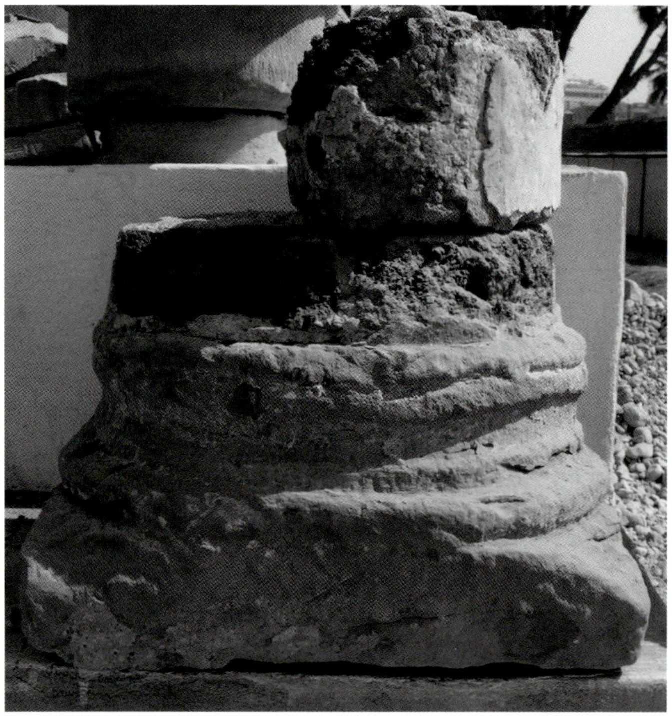

FIGURE 3.2
(right) Base and partial shaft of a column from street colonnades displayed in the Luxor Temple open-air museum.

at Palmyra is particularly germane, as it is a tetrarchic-period fortification attached to a preexisting sacred site.

THE IMPERIAL CULT CHAMBER

In Luxor Temple, the imperial cult chamber and Amun sanctuary behind it occupy the position in a standard Roman fortification plan that would normally contain the principia, or headquarters, of the legion.[4] It is widely accepted that before the tetrarchic interventions at Luxor Temple, this room (01, figures 3.4 and 3.13),[5] constructed during the reign of Amenhotep III (Eighteenth Dynasty), was the sanctuary of the divine pharaoh. The room measures 17.50 meters east-west and 10.56 meters north-south. On the basis of the arrangement of columns in the adjacent rooms around it, we can conclude that eight papyrus-bundle columns in this chamber originally supported abaci, sandstone architraves, and flat sandstone roof blocks, all removed during the tetrarchic renovation. The stone was possibly reused for new constructions in and around the precinct, such as the fortification gate

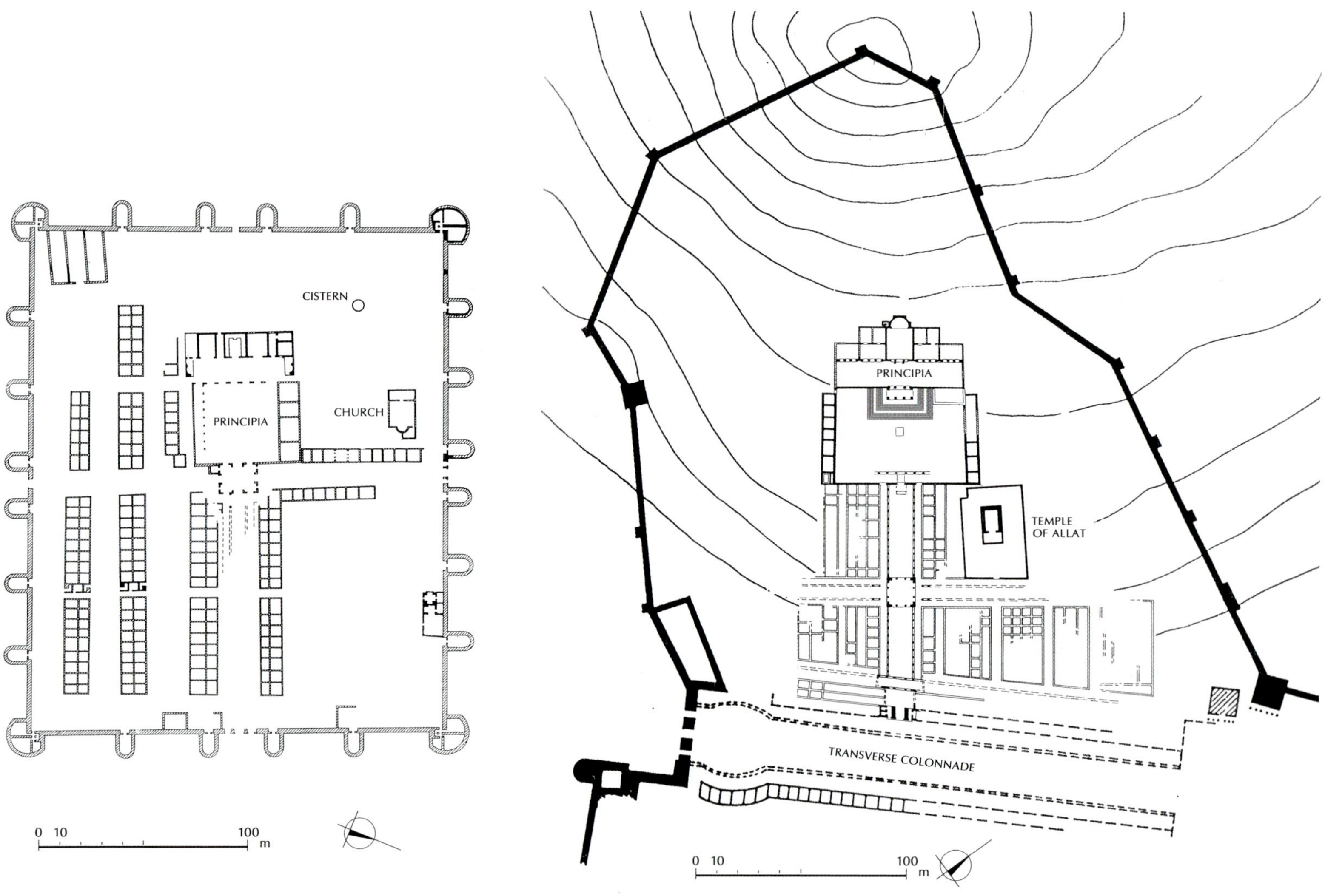

FIGURE 3.3
(below) *Left:* plan of the Roman camp at El-Lejjun, Jordan. *Right:* plan of the Roman camp at Palmyra, Syria, showing the fortification walls, principia, and approach.

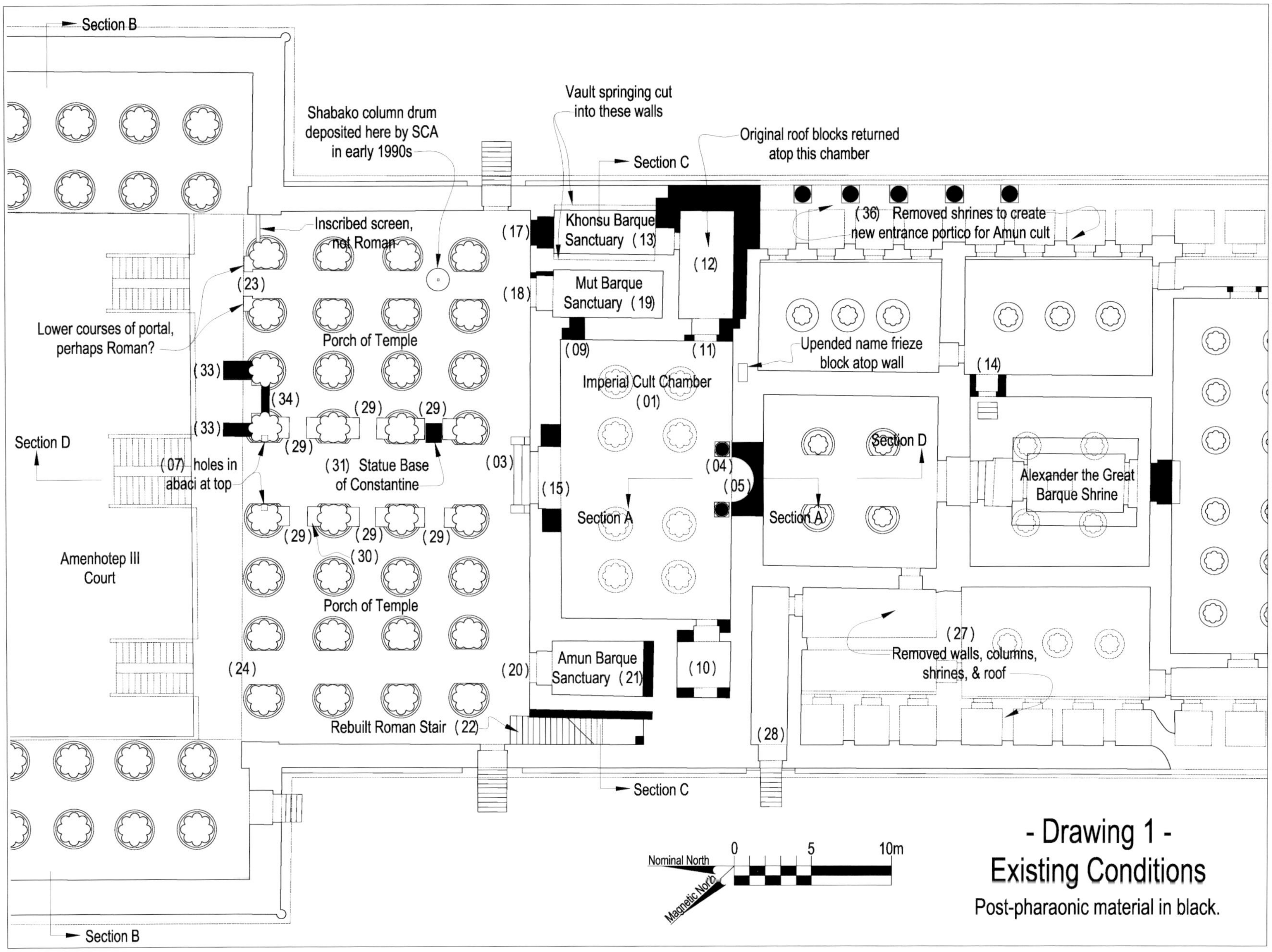

FIGURE 3.4
Drawing 1. Existing conditions at Luxor Temple.

towers and the riverside quay, which all display reused material. The Romans raised the floor of the imperial cult chamber above its pharaonic level (02) by about half a meter with red granite blocks and column drums from a kiosk of the pharaoh Shabako (Twenty-fifth Dynasty) that probably stood north of the Ramesses II pylon (Nineteenth Dynasty), which was dismantled at this time.[6] See figures 3.10, 3.12, and 3.13, where the floor-level change is visible. This maneuver both raised the chamber's floor and efficiently cleared the area north of the Ramesses II pylon.

A short flight of three steps (03) was installed at the chamber's north entrance doors, of which the best preserved element is the east stringer, or triangular block, at the steps' end (figure 3.5). The floor was possibly finished with a setting bed of mortar into which may have been set an *opus sectile* floor of "commodity stones" such as granite and porphyry, or the floor of the chamber may have been a simple pattern of stone rectangles.

Preserved in situ, flanking the chamber's niche, are two of the four granite columns that would have supported a dais canopy (04). These two columns are visible standing in the earliest known photographs of the chamber (see figures 4.9 and 4.11). The columns frame a large arcuated niche (05), the construction of which blocked up the Amenhotep III–period door that gave access to the shrines in the south part of the temple. The construction of this niche is securely dated to

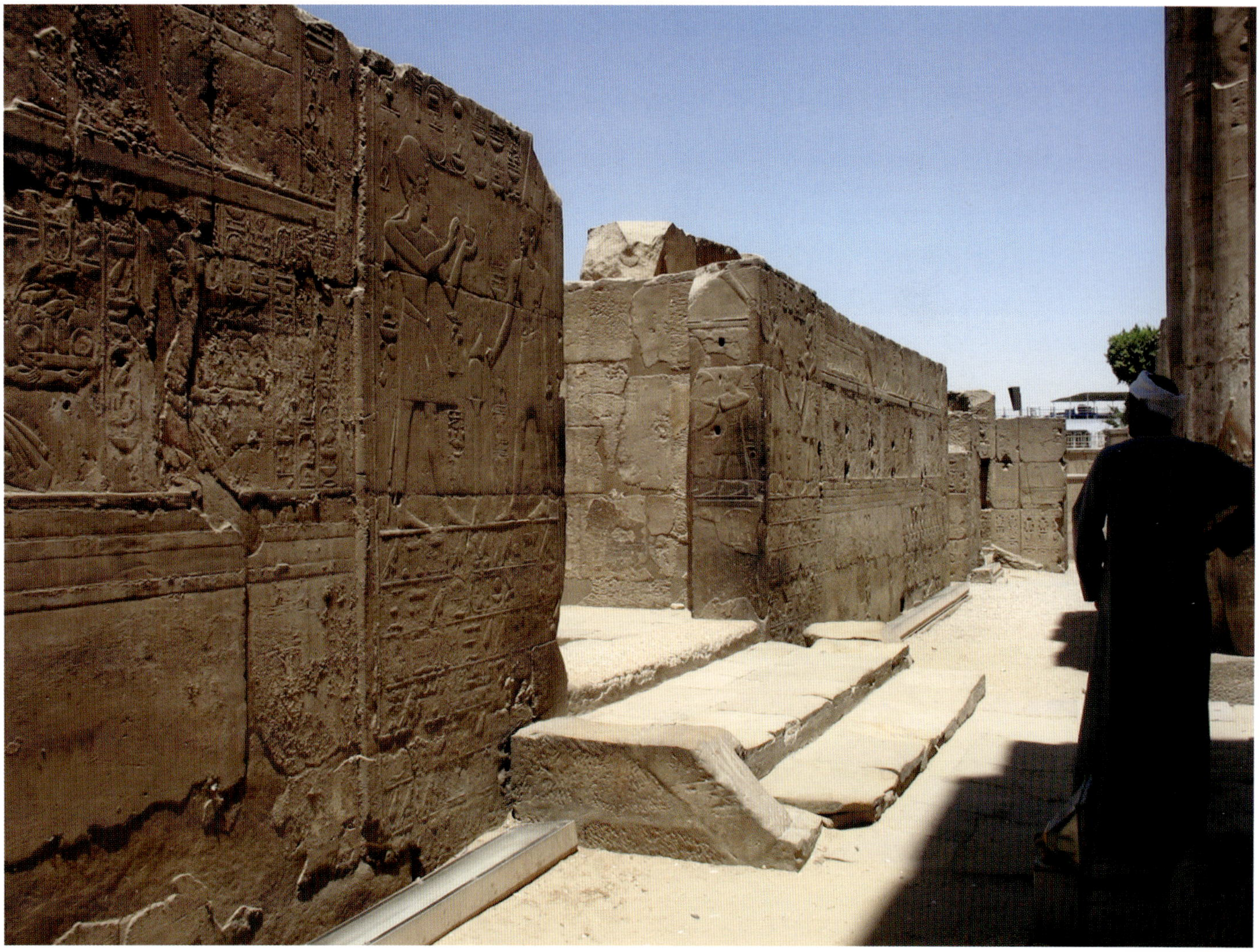

FIGURE 3.5
Steps at the entrance to the imperial cult chamber.

the Roman period, since it employs voussoirs (wedge-shaped stones) to create a true arch and half dome, rather than the corbel false-vault technique commonly used to create arched stone masonry in Egypt before the Roman conquest.[7] The upper part of the stone wall above the niche was rebuilt as well, and none of the blocks in the niche or above shows any signs of pre-Roman carved decoration on their north-facing sides. Some Amenhotep III–period reliefs are visible within accessible spaces inside the wall and on the wall's south face. On the wall's north face, to the upper left of the niche, is a chiseling scar where the cavetto cornice of the Amenhotep III door was removed. All this was covered by the frescoes that are now missing from this area. The niche was painted with a dado surmounted by four human figures, possibly a floating bust of Jupiter, an eagle, and a bejeweled wreath as part of the imperial cult chamber project (see chapter 6). The bottom of the niche was about 1.5 meters above the new floor level, forming a shelf made of reused sandstone ashlars. A slot along its upper front lip with holes cut into the sidewalls of the niche was made to receive a wood railing (06).

The columns standing in situ before the niche have shafts and bases of red granite and Corinthian capitals of a flattened proportion made of large-grained limestone (figure 3.6). The plinths of the bases (their lowermost, square parts) are raised up on stone platforms. The platforms provide the height of the dais on which the columns stood above the floor of the chamber. At a height of 26 centimeters, this dais is on the short side, but its height is corroborated by the fresco remains on the adjoining wall to the east, which show the foot of a seated figure on a similarly short bejeweled dais. The canopy borne atop the dais ensemble would have been roughly square in plan. No trace of the two additional columns that supported the canopy remains in the chamber. One additional matching capital (matching order, same size, same stone, same odd pro-

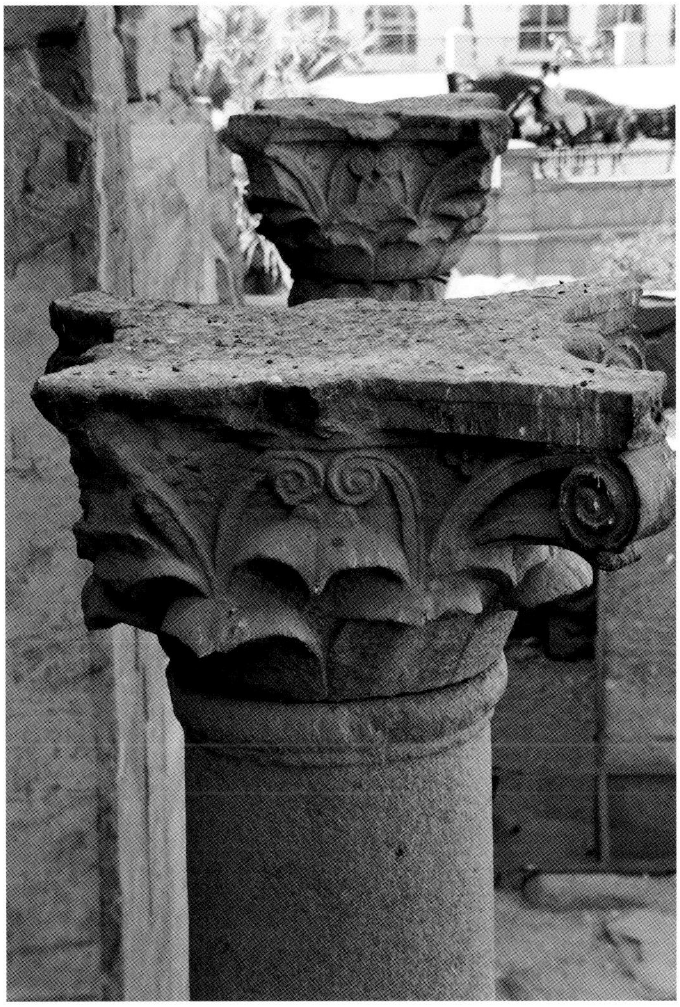

FIGURE 3.6
Capital of the eastern granite column flanking the niche.

portions) and at least two red granite shafts of the correct size, however, have been located west of the temple.[8]

Because still-visible J-shaped slots were cut into the lowest voussoirs of the apse semi-dome immediately adjacent to the in situ capitals (see figure 4.11), it is possible to conclude that the columns carried a wood-and-plaster canopy. The slots have recently been filled with mortar, which makes them harder to discern, but they could only have allowed the assembled pieces of a wood architrave seated atop each column capital to anchor into the stone wall for stability. The J-shaped slots on either side of the niche are mirror images of each other; the shorter vertical is toward the center of the niche. The tall vertical slots on the outside, therefore, provide the full-size height of the vertical architrave band around the exterior of the canopy. The shorter vertical slots on the inside would have been the same height as the outside ones if the canopy had flat, horizontally trabeated (beamed) architraves. The fact that they are shorter suggests that the underside of the canopy was vaulted. Only vaulting would allow a view of the eagle clutching the jeweled wreath painted in the niche's semi-dome beyond.

For this essay's reconstruction of the imperial cult chamber, Deckers's drawing of the canopy in front of the niche in the imperial cult chamber (see figure 6.20) has been reworked, and his drawings of the paintings incorporated into the architectural reconstruction drawings. The surviving column capitals are of the Corinthian order, so it follows that the architrave, frieze, and cornice featured elements of the Corinthian order as well, though whether the canopy would have been constructed of stone or a lighter material such as wood or plaster is impossible to determine.[9] Principles of expression used in stone architecture in the Roman world commonly reappear as imitations in lighter forms such as wood, plaster, or even in fantastical painted representations. If the canopy was actually built of stone, it would have required a counterweight (a statue or an architectural element) to act as a buttress atop the cornice above the columns; otherwise, the resolution of structural forces in the arches would have pushed the columns outward and caused the whole ensemble to collapse. Even if the form of the canopy was translated into wood, the Roman designers would still have maintained the counterweight element; that is to say that the tectonic language of an arcuated canopy requires a counterweight device above the columns, even if that language is fiction when rendered in wood.

The broken pediment device used in the reconstruction drawings at the canopy corners thus occupied a location where a visual counterweight was necessary for the architectural composition. The broken pediment device appears in Roman stone architecture in the early imperial period and is most famously seen on the mid-third-century Arch of Septimius Severus at Leptis Magna. In another North African example, it appears as part of segmental (curved) pediments on the so-called Arch of Trajan at ancient Thamugadi (modern Timgad, Algeria). The use of the broken pediment device in the canopy above the dais in the Luxor Temple imperial cult chamber, while conjectural, is logical for the period and the status of the sanctuary.

The Amenhotep III stone columns and roof in the imperial cult chamber were probably replaced with a new roof in the Roman style. Because no fragments of vaulting have been found, this probably took the form of the standard wooden-truss roof, a system of wood members joined to form a rigid triangular shape designed to span larger widths than possible with simple beams (08). With a span of about eleven meters, the Luxor Temple imperial cult chamber posed no challenge for Roman engineers who routinely used wood trusses to span chambers of twenty-five meters and even thirty meters wide.[10] Because the frescoes program suggests that the height of the cult chamber was considerably greater than that of the chambers around it, a raised clerestory with a band of windows in the room's upper walls above the roofline of the surrounding rooms, standard in Egyptian and Roman architecture, might have provided light.[11]

The undersides of the trusses may also have been finished with *lacunaria* (coffers), such as those found at the roughly contemporary Trier basilica (Basilica of Constantine), or, though it is less likely, may have been left open—as may have been the case with the basilica that Marcus Vitruvius Pollio built at Fanum.[12] As for the roof surface, one might expect *tegulae,* the ubiquitous terra-cotta Roman pan tiles, fragments of which are found in abundance throughout the Mediterranean world. These are absent from archaeological sites in Upper Egypt, however, and no trace of them has been found at Luxor Temple. Lead remains were observed in the past in debris near the Luxor Temple sanctuary, perhaps remnants of roofing from Roman structures. One possible parallel, the roof of the church in St. Catherine's Monastery in Sinai, preserves original trusses that were set in place between 548 and 564, as their inscriptions indicate.[13] Though now mostly covered with modern corrugated galvanized metal sheets, the original roof surface was lead sheets on wood decking. The lead roofing on top of the apse is still exposed where it was mounted onto battens laid directly over the granite vaulting stones.[14]

ROOMS ADJACENT TO THE IMPERIAL CULT CHAMBER

Three doors lead from the imperial cult chamber in Luxor Temple. The door in the west wall of the imperial cult chamber leads to a single room (10), shown in figure 3.4, the walls of which are preserved to a height of about three meters. Even though the floor of this room does not appear to have been raised to the same level as that of the imperial cult chamber, it was clearly fitted out as a shrine: a niche was created in the room's west wall in alignment with the door. At both the west wall and the door, ashlars were added to create the niche and accompanying alignment. Though the niche and the door align, they are both off-center in the room. Where there are not clearly reused blocks, the walls are blank stone with thick, white plaster visible in multiple locations. Since some of the ashlars feature pharaonic decoration upside down, the walls must have been completely plastered, though no trace of decoration survives. The door (11) in the east wall of the imperial cult chamber leads to a small suite of two rooms whose walls are preserved to their full height (12) (13). Their floors have not been raised with stone, so there was either a platform wood floor or steps down into this area from the cult chamber. The architectural organization of these two rooms is casual; their layout and architectural elements do not share the linear alignments and formal organization typical of the more sophisticated design the Romans employed in the adjoining rooms or in other fortified camps. This suggests that they were secure storage rooms for items used in the cult chamber itself (rather than shrines or formal spaces) as well as a "backstage" area from which functionaries could appear or to which they might retire. Unlike the small west shrine (10), whose upper walls are not preserved, these two rooms had ceilings that were quite tall. The room immediately adjacent to the imperial cult chamber (12) received the most construction work of any extant part of Luxor Temple in the post-Pharaonic period, presumably during the late Roman renovations associated with construction of the imperial cult chamber itself. After its roof blocks were removed, its entire south and east walls and part of its north wall were dismantled to the ground before being reconstructed with sandstone ashlars to its original height, and its original roof blocks were carefully returned to their positions. Both the inside and outside of these three walls are composed of large sandstone blocks, and the occasional block with pharaonic decoration is turned sideways or upside down. In addition, there are clear ragged, but mated, joints where these reconstructed walls join the original Amenhotep III walls. A "foot graffito"[15] is visible atop the remaining roof block, and half of a cutout for a funnel-shaped light well is visible in its side.[16] The facts that the foot graffito is on top of the block and that the light-well cutout is right side up indicate that the roof blocks were reinstalled right side up after the walls supporting them were reerected. As the room does not seem to have been redesigned differently from its pharaonic form, one possible explanation for this work is that the rebuilding was repair work for a subsiding corner. The small room (13) beyond it has mostly smooth walls with a few Amenhotep III scenes carved on its otherwise blank stone surfaces. None of the walls in this room seems to have been covered with plaster. This chamber was originally the barque sanctuary of Khonsu, and a doorway in its north wall leading under the temple porch or portico was blocked up with sandstone ashlars. An off-center niche may have been intended high up in the door blocking, but the ashlars are now mutilated to the point that no finished surfaces are visible.

Though the first room (12) of the suite had its original roof blocks carefully returned to their original position, that is not the case in the adjoining room (13) to the north. The north room had its roof removed (even though its walls were not dismantled) and had ledges cut high in its long ashlar walls (on the east and west sides; see figure 3.4) to support a vault springing. This vault must have been completed in baked brick, but no trace of it survives. A barrel vault springing from these ledges would allow a load-bearing platform at the same height as the replaced roof blocks in the adjacent room. A slot was cut in the ceiling wall juncture centered above the door in the south wall to admit light to this room from the south.

THE APPROACH TO THE IMPERIAL CULT CHAMBER

Upon exiting the imperial cult chamber through the entrance in the center of its north wall (15) and descending the three steps (03), one stands in the portico of the temple at the south end of the court of Amenhotep III. This entrance doorway was extensively rebuilt with reused pharaonic ashlars that made up the east and west jambs of the south side of the doorway, but great care was taken to leave the exterior Amenhotep III door-casing scenes on the north side in place (see figure 3.5). This means the door preserved its original Amenhotep III Egyptian-style vignettes on the north side of both jambs and probably its original Amenhotep III cornice and torus molding on the north side even after the Roman work was finished. The rebuilt interior recessed jambs (for door panels) suggest that the Roman renovation also included two door leaves.[17] On the inside, the rebuilt jambs incorporating reused upside-down pharaonic blocks were covered with frescoed plaster. In contrast to the Egyptian raised-door casing on the exterior (north side), there is no casing preserved in the blocks remaining on the interior side of the jambs (see figure 6.10).

The wall that contains the monumental doorway into the imperial cult chamber also contains, east to west, the blocked door (17) in association with the room (13) that originally led to the barque sanctuary of Khonsu, a repaired door (18) entering the preserved Mut barque sanctuary (19), the door to the imperial cult chamber (15), the door (20) to the preserved Amun barque sanctuary (21), and finally a small doorway with a stair (22) that led to the roof. The Amun barque sanctuary (21) is oddly refitted, for though the side walls, east and west, preserve their original Amenhotep III reliefs, the focal south wall has received a new ashlar veneer with a smooth face. There is no trace of paint or plaster on this smooth stone wall and no sign of the scoring that marks the usual preparation of a substrate for the application of plaster. Nonetheless, the shrine is in a pendant position to the just-mentioned Mut barque sanctuary (19) to the east. Each of these two shrines (19; 21) is centered at the south end of an enfilade (an axial arrangement of two flanking rows, producing a focal vista) of Amenhotep III portico columns by which it must have been approached, and the Mut barque sanctuary (19) even preserves blocks of a portal (23) at the facade of the portico carved with Amenhotep III cartouches on both sides. The original height of this portal can be judged from the keyed cuts for the portal's cornice in the columns above the in situ blocks. The portals are a late pharaonic addition; the cartouches are poorly cut, and the blocks of the portals partly cover cartouches of Ramesses IV on the columns, inscribed long after Amenhotep III's death. The Amun barque sanctuary (21), to the west, has no portal blocks preserved, but it is shown (24) in the drawings as a pendant to that of Mut. The height of the Mut barque sanctuary is certain, since the Amenhotep III decoration is preserved on three walls all the way to the top of the name frieze that marked the juncture of the wall with the (now missing) ceiling.

THE ROOF AREA

The stair (22) located to the west of the Amun barque sanctuary has had its entire east wall rebuilt in small sandstone ashlars bearing reused earlier reliefs. It was also rebuilt partly in baked brick, as is clear from an area of brick and mortar still in situ for the stair's underpinning at the top of the preserved wall height, about 2.4 meters above the portico's floor level. The entrance steps do not begin inside the stair's doorway but spill out of it, the last few steps sticking out onto the temple portico. This feature is not evidence of Roman rebuilding, since the Ramesses IV cartouche name frieze, in the dado flanking the steps (see figure 3.7) to the west, step up with the first few steps and are not masked by them, which indicates that the lowest steps were in place when the name frieze was carved. Nonetheless, the rebuilt east wall, together with the lumps of in situ baked brick, indicates that the stair was rebuilt at least once as part of the Romans' work. This would argue that the Romans' design scheme required regular access to the roof (for security in particular), and the aforementioned load-bearing roof atop the storage chambers (12; 13) east of the imperial cult chamber reinforces this assertion.

THE TEMPLE PORTICO AND CENTRAL AXIS

In addition to the side aisles leading to the barque sanctuaries of Mut (19) and Amun (21), the central axis leading to the entrance to the imperial cult chamber beneath the portico gives us substantial clues about its final form. Here were a series of six broken-lintel portals (29) built in the late

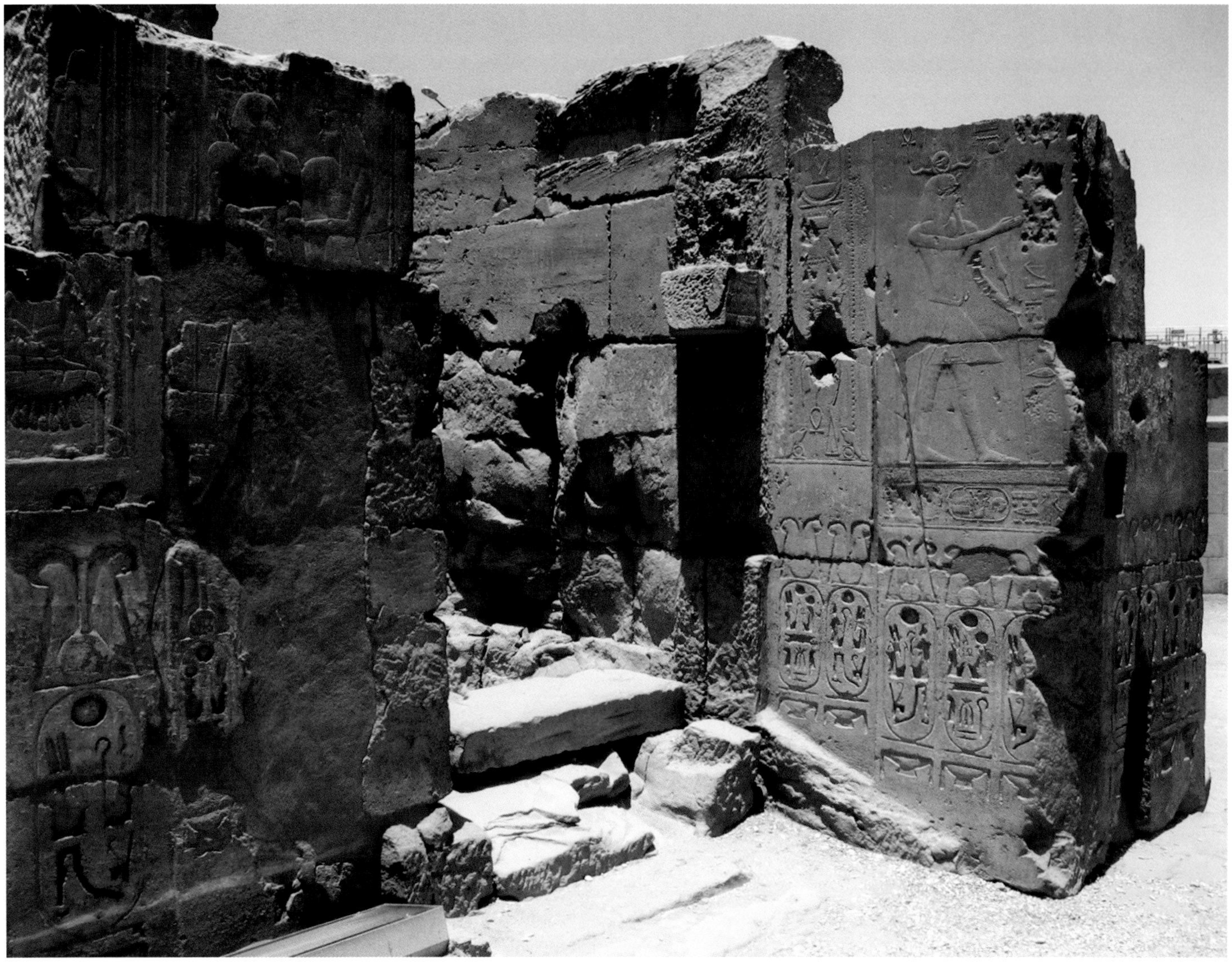

FIGURE 3.7
Stair (22) with Ramesses IV name frieze.

pharaonic period between the columns flanking the central axis.[18] The Romans kept these six portals in place; the lower courses of all six are still present. (See figure 3.13.) On the west side (at location 30—shown in figure 3.4) there are two helpful fragments (not in situ) resting atop the in situ lowest portal courses. One is a cavetto cornice fragment, the back side of which has been cut in a concave radius matching the radius of the adjacent lobe of the papyrus bundle column against which it was set. The other is an end fragment of a broken lintel preserving its cut-out lower corner and relief carving on the reveal. These two fragments indicate that the portals were the broken-lintel type and allowed the reconstruction of their likely size and proportion. The radiused back of the cornice block makes their association with these doorways certain.

Within the opening of the southeast portal on the main axis, one statue base (31), dedicated to Constantine, remains in situ (see figure 2.6). Scattered fragments of several other statue bases of this series survive. Therefore, the other five portals (29) almost surely contained statue bases honoring different men, in size and material comparable to the one remaining of Constantine. All six were probably surmounted by life-size metal, possibly bronze, statues, as is evident by the holes in the upper surface of the Constantine base that indicate the position of the statue's two feet. Stone sculptures required a rectangular support for stability and a rectangular cut in any raised base, something the tensile strength of bronze did not require. Life-size statues are suggested both by the distance between the foot scars and because, as figure 3.13 shows, a life-size height (here restored at 1.8 meters) is the maximum the projected height of the portals would comfortably permit. The bases and statues were fitted into the preexisting portals, as can be seen in figure 3.13, and the portals and the lower reaches of the portico columns between them were covered with a thick layer of plaster and whitewashed; no painted decoration survives. Thus, the central axial approach to the imperial cult chamber was shifted toward a mingling of the Egyptian idiom and a canonical Roman style at least at eye level as a prelude to the Roman style of the interior of the imperial cult chamber. Looking up along this axis, the visitor would still have found the top halves of Amenhotep III's papyrus bundle columns visible, along with the architraves covered in Eighteenth-Dynasty hieroglyphic inscriptions and the Amenhotep III vignettes on both sides of door (15) leading into the imperial cult chamber. There is no evidence that any of this was blocked from view.

Since this axial approach to the entrance to the imperial cult chamber was classicized at the viewer's eye level, the tetrarchic Romans may also have chosen to add a classical element to the ceiling between the central row of columns to prepare the visitor for the completely classical space to be found in the chamber. The Amenhotep III architraves of the temple portico are all preserved in situ today, except for the two that connected the north wall of the imperial cult chamber with columns of the portico on the central axis and the four at the west edge of the portico where the exterior wall is mostly gone. In figure 3.8 (drawing 2b) dashed lines denote the architrave scheme; missing ones are noted. The architraves along the central axis run north and south; no architraves cross the central axis, save one at the portico facade, which is also still in situ. The architraves of the side aisles all run east-west. If the Romans removed the central axis roof blocks, they would probably have heightened this central axial emphasis with a classicizing element to cap the Romanizing features of the axis discussed above. The drawings reconstruct a hypothetical classical feature in this location to emphasize the central axis, a coffered wood and stucco barrel vault (32) of a style found in earlier parallel material.[19]

THE TEMPLE PORTICO FACADE

Evidence suggests that the facade of the temple portico itself was also romanized as part of the tetrarchic program. The pharaonic facade of the temple portico was extremely uniform with the other three sides of the court, for which it formed the south boundary. The temple portico, built first, and the other three sides of the court have the same height platform and the same size columns, architraves, and cornice.

The remains of two small platforms (33) composed of reused blocks (some from the Middle Kingdom) immediately in front of the two Amenhotep III facade columns east of the central axis provide possible evidence of the Roman reworking of this part of the court. These are alternately cut into the Amenhotep III column bases or cut around them. The platforms are preserved to a height of forty centimeters (east platform) and seventy centimeters (west platform). They have been called statue bases,[20] but the usual location for statues on a Roman temple portico facade is between the columns, and thus under shelter, rather than in front of the columns. In fact, between the two Amenhotep III facade columns immediately east of the center axis, there are the remains of a third platform of reused blocks (34) preserved to a height of seventy centimeters, more suitable to a larger-than-life-size classical-style sculpture. The fact that the platforms are Roman constructions of reused materials endorses this interpretation and supports the removal of all pharaonic sculpture from the portico during the tetrarchic alterations.

The drawings present a structural solution for the two platforms (33) to the north of the Amenhotep III columns that is consistent with parallel imperial building projects of the same period, such as those at Palmyra. It reconstructs the two platforms as supports for two of the columns of a four-columned classical portico (35). A four-columned portico is consistent with design elsewhere in the empire during this period and provides a compelling model for the facade of Luxor Temple's imperial cult chamber. But because of its location in a provincial outpost such as Luxor, it would probably have been made of less costly materials than were similar forms in Rome's capital or other political centers. As the barrel vault above the temple portico would most probably have been made of wood and plaster, so the pediment—the triangular part of the portico—would also have been made of wood and plaster and could have been attached to the barrel vault system, which would have stabilized the whole ensemble. The columns supporting the pediment would have been made, like other Roman columns throughout the temple precinct, of stuccoed brick.[21] As figure 3.11 demonstrates, this portico would have delivered a powerful Roman-style hierarchy and narrative flow to the architecture of the court at Luxor Temple; it would have prepared visitors for the classical interior beyond and informed them of the Roman authority embodied in the space within.

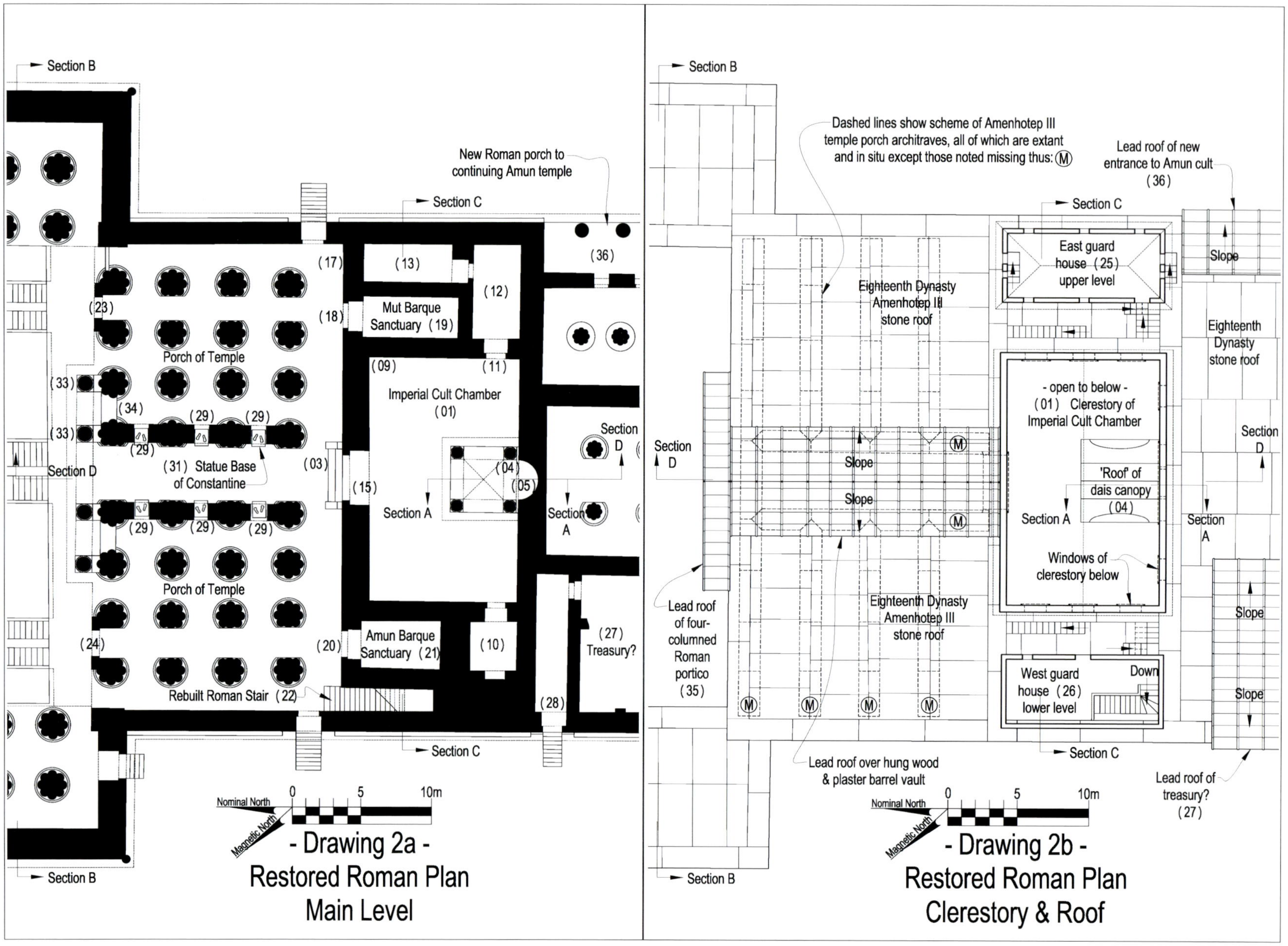

FIGURE 3.8

Drawing 2a (left): restored plan, main level. Drawing 2b (right): restored Roman plan, clerestory and roof.

ROMAN INTERVENTIONS AT LUXOR TEMPLE AND THE AMUN-RE CULT

It has generally been assumed that by the time the Luxor Temple precinct was adapted for use as a military fortress under Diocletian, Egyptian cult practices at the site had ceased.[22] But the cleaning of the imperial cult frescoes and the reassessment of the frescoes' architectural context require the issue of the Amun cult to be revisited. Luxor Temple was founded as the birthplace of the state god Amun-Re at the inauguration of the god's cult in Thebes (ancient Waset) in the early Middle Kingdom (ca. 2000 BCE).[23] It was only one part of Amun-Re's vast domain in Thebes, which also included Karnak Temple, the memorial temples of "millions of years" on the west bank, and the small Amun Temple at Medinet Habu. Luxor Temple was the site of the god's annual regeneration and rebirth through the medium of the king during the great Opet Festival, celebrated annually at the height of the Nile inundation. Both god and king were reborn and relegitimized in the process.[24]

The imperial cult chamber represents a significant departure from the standard Roman practice of cultic monument building in Egypt. From the time that Octavian (Augustus Caesar) seized control of Egypt in 29 BCE, Roman emperors continued the tradition of Alexander the Great and his successors, the Ptolemies, by embellishing Egypt's ancient temple complexes with new monuments, in stone and mud brick, dedicated to the local gods in the Egyptian style.[25] At Luxor

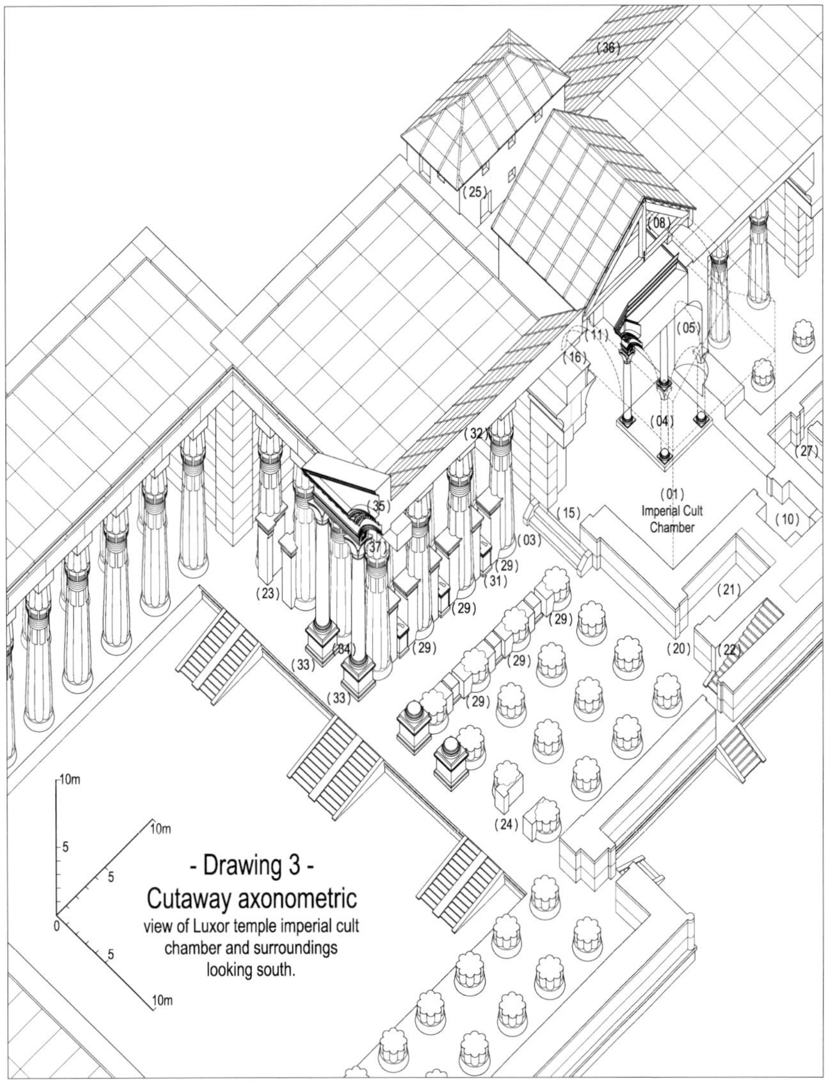

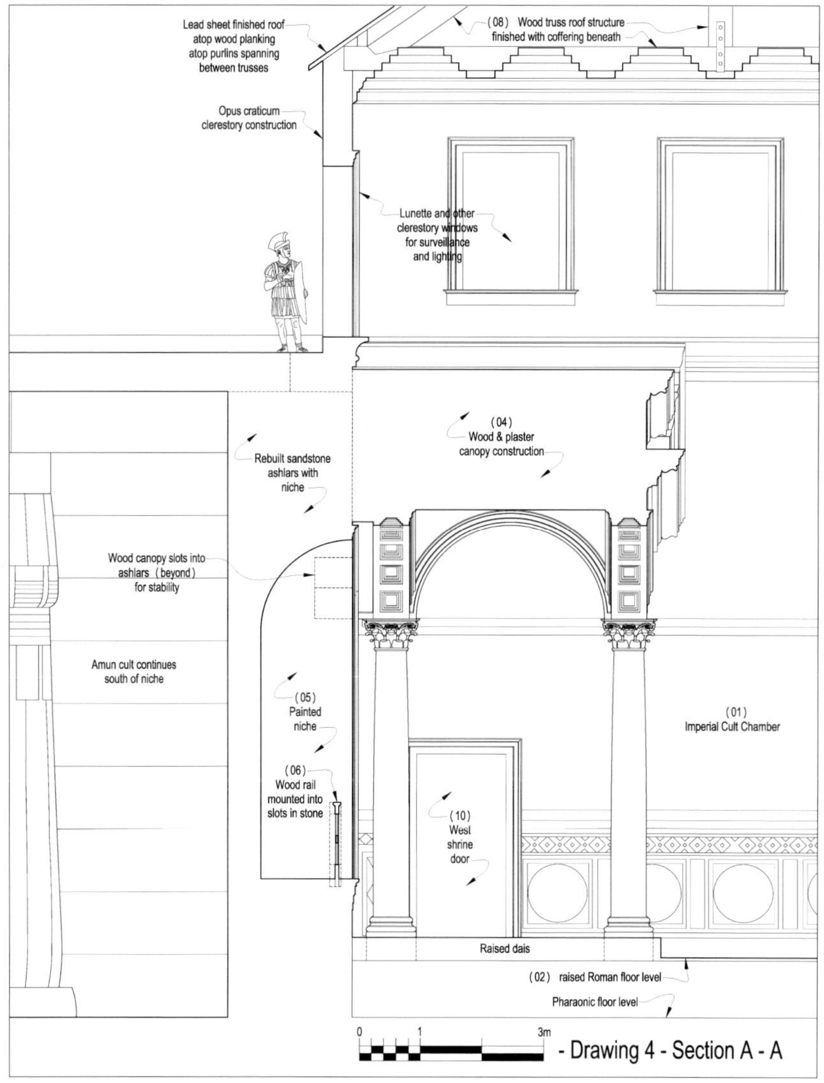

FIGURE 3.9
(left) Drawing 3: cutaway axonometric view of the imperial cult chamber and surroundings, looking south.

FIGURE 3.10
(right) Drawing 4: section A–A.

Temple, the room originally dedicated to the cult of the pharaoh was adapted as the Roman imperial cult chamber under the Tetrarchy. This act updated the state worship of the ruler, while—intentionally or not—still celebrating his traditional association with the creator god–sun god Amun-Re, Ammon, the Egyptian Jupiter,[26] whose sanctuary lay just beyond. In this instance, however, the cult of the ruler was presented not in the Egyptian style but in a Roman one. The pharaonic reliefs of Amenhotep III in the chamber were plastered over and frescoed with images of the emperors and their entourages in the Roman style. Not only was the whole room rebuilt to reflect a purely Roman visual culture entirely in the classical tradition, but the raised floor and blocking of the doorway leading to the god's shrine with a niche turned this room into a new sanctuary at the end of the processional route through the temple. In essence, a purely Roman temple was inserted into the very center of one of the most venerated sanctuaries in Egypt, while leaving Amun's sanctuary at the back untouched.

Several aspects of the Roman elaboration to Luxor Temple may indicate that the Amun cult, or at least the memory of the Amun cult, was still active in some form in late antiquity. In 1989 a deposit of statues possibly related to the tetrarchic renovation was found. In the process of boring holes to test the salinity of the groundwater, the Egyptian Antiquities Organization (EAO)[27] hit stone about half a meter below the ground surface in the middle of the court on its western side.[28] The EAO excavated the area and found a slab of granodiorite covering a group of statues, all carefully buried (figure 3.14).[29] The centerpiece of the group was a life-size, quartzite striding statue of Amenhotep III standing on a sledge and wearing the double crown of Upper and Lower Egypt.[30] It lay on its right side, facing west, head to the north, and was encircled by the other statues, all of granodiorite: a small, kneeling

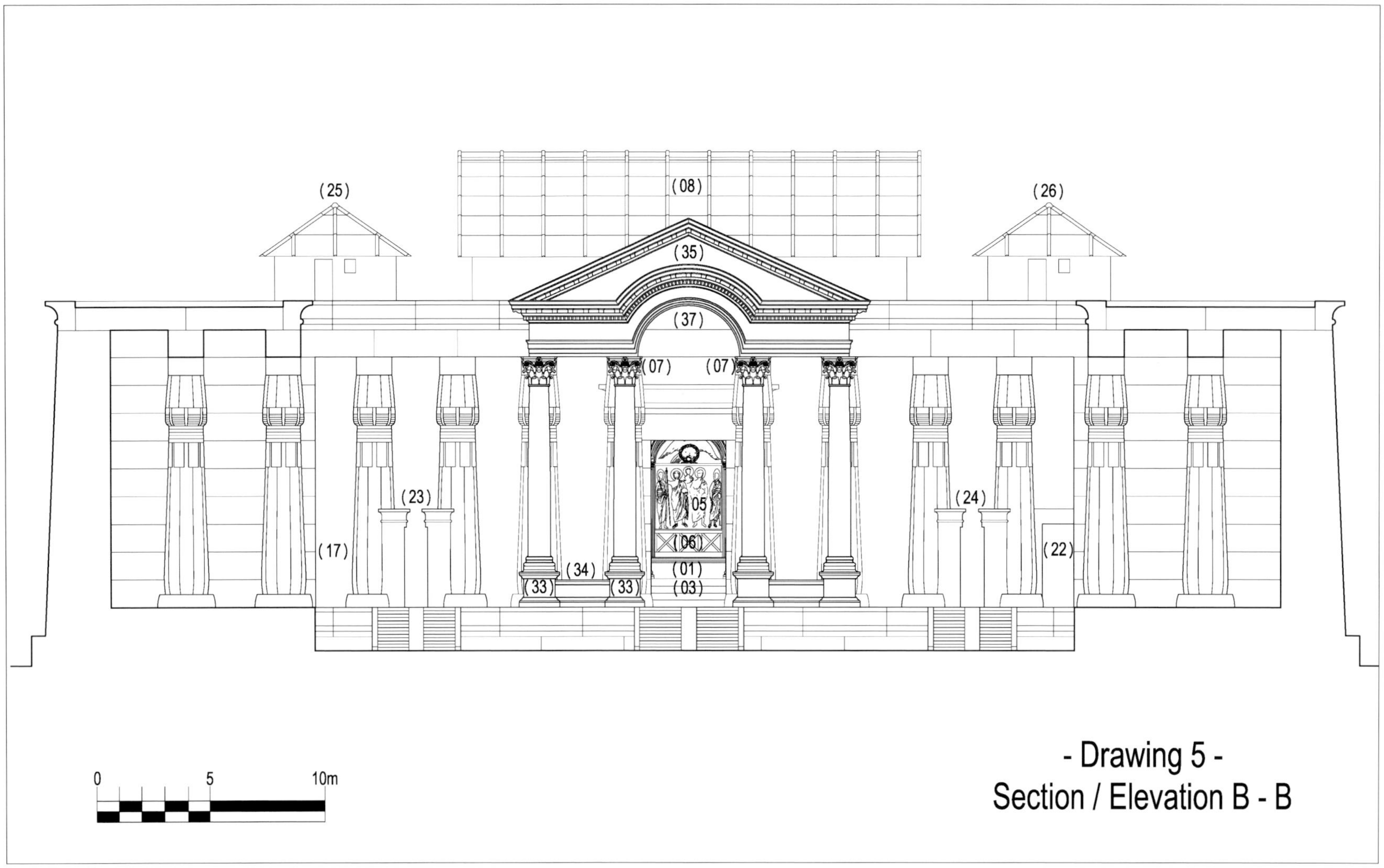

FIGURE 3.11
(top) Drawing 5: section/ elevation B–B

Opposite page:
FIGURE 3.12
(top) Drawing 6: section C–C.

FIGURE 3.13
(bottom) Drawing 7: section D–D.

statue of Horemheb holding round *nu* jars; a seated statue of the creator god Atum (inscribed for Horemheb); a seated figure of the goddess Iwnet;[31] and a seated statue of the goddess Hathor.[32] The inscriptions on the thrones of the goddesses indicate that both statues were commissioned by Amenhotep III for the sanctuary of Luxor Temple.[33] The slab of granodiorite that had been used to cover the statues in the pit was the base of the Horemheb and Atum pair. Originally the two statues were set into its upper surface facing each other. Traces of gilded gesso that still survived on the matte surface of the kilt of the king indicate that this group had been gilded, and the deity statues as well.[34]

The position of the statues indicates a careful burial, and a special reverence was displayed toward the quartzite cult statue of the deified Amenhotep III.[35] After the removal of this group by the excavators, a second deposit of twenty more statues was discovered beneath the first layer, upright but resting diagonally against each other, carefully arranged in rows in a pit three meters below the present ground surface. These statues are of both royalty and deities, and they date from the mid-Eighteenth Dynasty through the Ptolemaic period. The only statue displaying a lack of care in its burial was found beneath the second layer: a large, late Eighteenth-Dynasty indurated limestone dyad of Amun and Mut, found upside down.[36]

At the eastern side of the burial pit the excavators found late Roman pottery shards and intact amphorae.[37] It is probable that the gilded, seated statues of Hathor and Iwnet were from two of the twenty-four sanctuaries arranged around the central sanctuary of Amun of Luxor Temple.[38] Each sanctuary would have had a raised area for a single statue. The southernmost of these sanctuaries on the eastern and western sides of the temple were dismantled during the Roman renovation of the temple at the time of the installation of the imperial cult chamber, and it is possible that the sanctuaries of the two goddesses were among them.

The sandstone gates of the mud-brick Diocletianic fortification wall surrounding Luxor Temple were constructed of reused blocks quarried from these sanctuaries and other monuments around the temple (see figure 3.15). Gates on the northern end of the fortress were constructed from elements

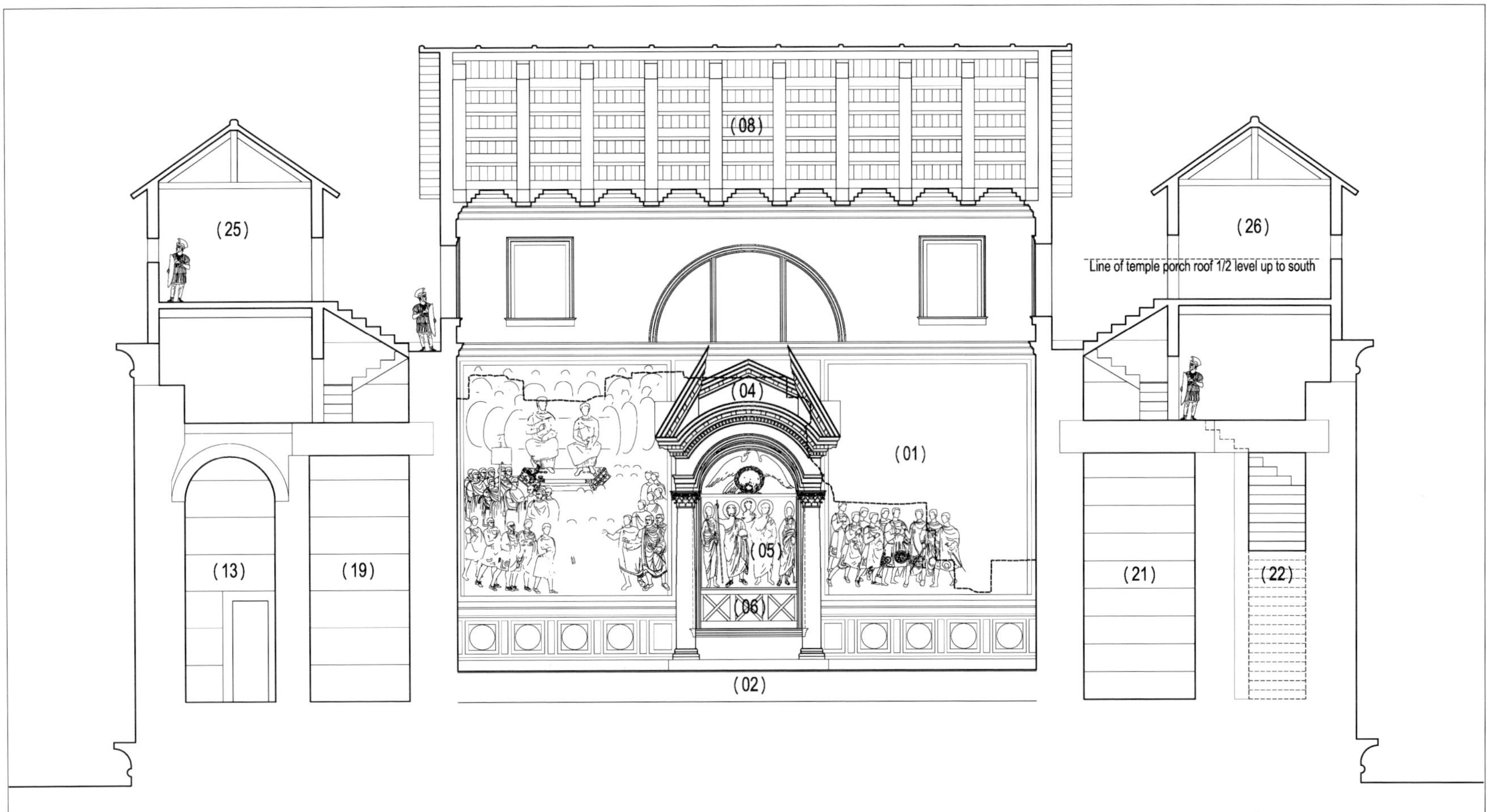

- Drawing 6 -
Section C - C

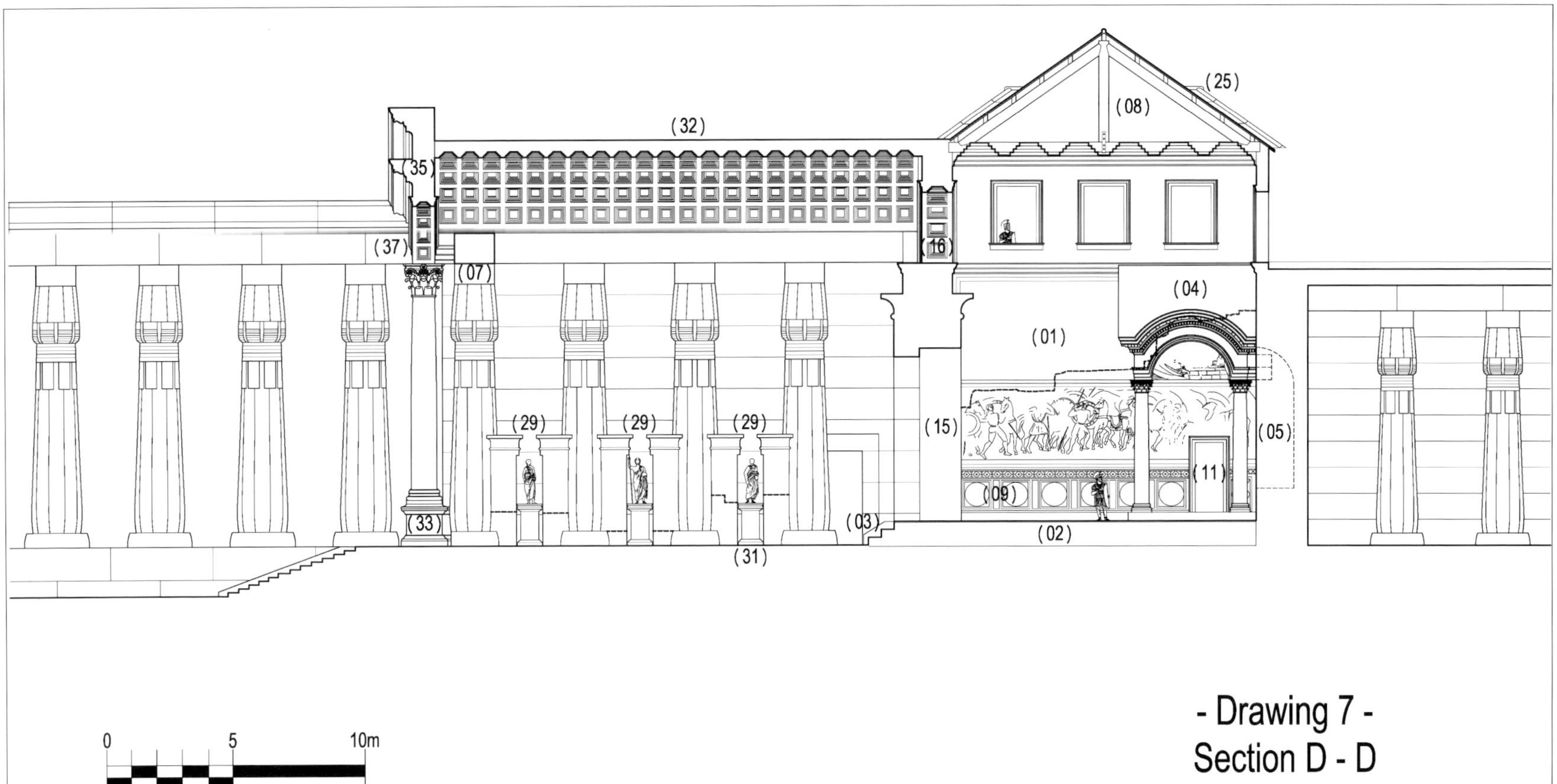

- Drawing 7 -
Section D - D

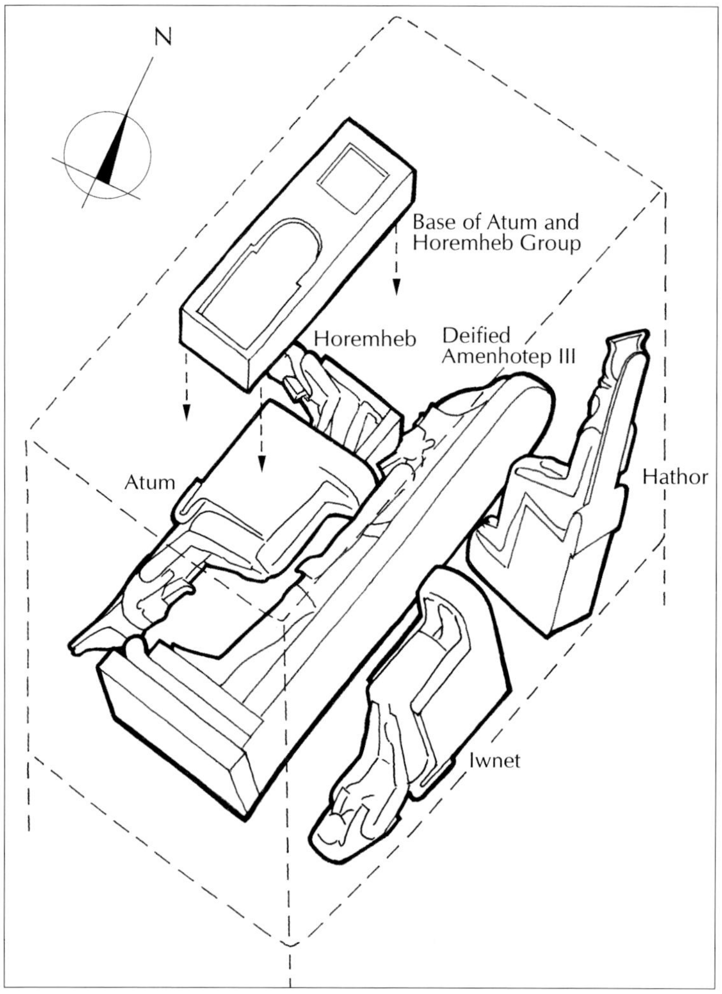

FIGURE 3.14
Drawing of the upper layer of the cache of statues in the Amenhotep III court, as found; after published and unpublished photographs of Mohamed El-Saghir.

of the kiosk of Shabako from north of the Ramesses II pylon (also used to raise the floor of the imperial cult chamber), as well as a sandstone gateway of Nectanebo I farther to the north, which marked the southern terminus of the great sphinx avenue linking Luxor and Karnak temples. The eastern and southern tetrarchic gates appear to have been constructed of sandstone quarried mostly from the Luxor Temple sanctuary area, eastern and western walls, and the side walls of the sanctuaries within. The texts and compositions on these blocks clearly show that the sanctuaries were originally carved in raised relief by Amenhotep III with offering scenes to the various deities therein. The exteriors of the eastern, western, and southern walls were left blank by Amenhotep III, but later they were inscribed with two to three registers of offerings scenes of Ramesses III in deeply sunken relief. Both sets of carved scenes are found reused in the east gate and southeast gate on blocks depicting Amenhotep III making an offering to a goddess wearing Hathor's horned disk, which may be from the sanctuary of Hathor; the Hathor statue found in the cache may have come from this very sanctuary.[39] Because of the number of sanctuaries on each side of the temple proper—fourteen on each—it appears that

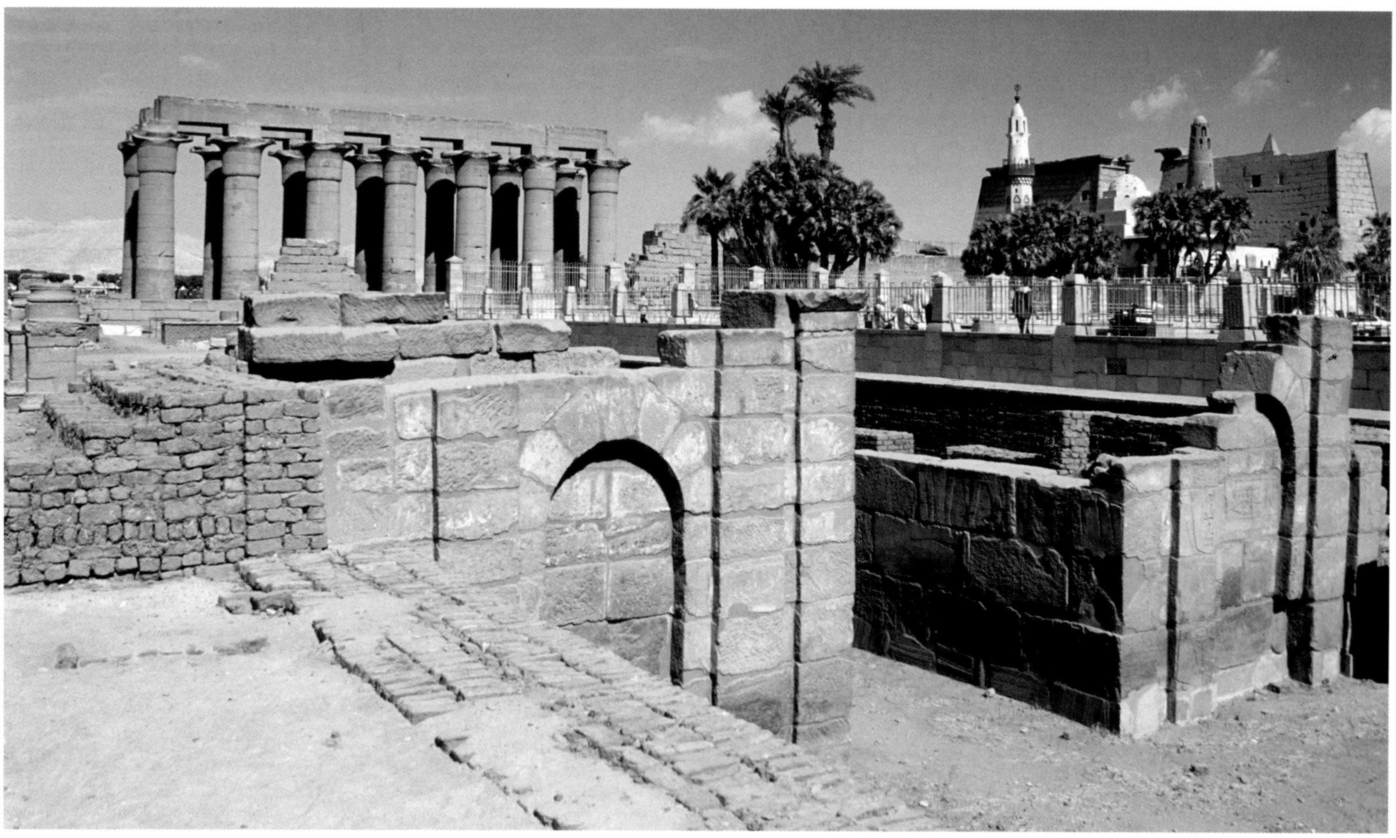

FIGURE 3.15
The east gateway.

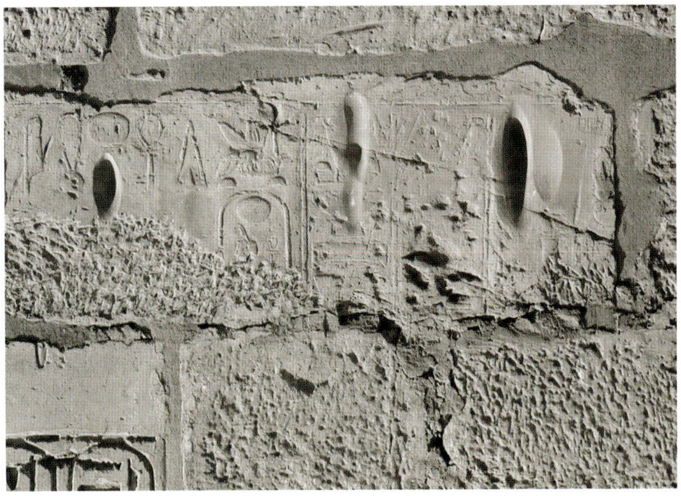

FIGURE 3.16
Reused block of Amenhotep III in the northern anta of the east gateway with traces of the name of the goddess Mut in the column to the right of the cartouche.

the major gods of northern and southern Egypt had shrines and statues here; blocks from the sanctuaries of Atum, Nut, and Mut were also found among the reused masonry of the Roman-built southern and northern antae (figure 3.16).[40]

While it is possible that the statues were removed from their sanctuaries before the tetrarchic modifications to the sanctuary area, another possibility is that the sculpture was deposited when the sanctuaries were dismantled. The lack of pharaonic sculpture exclusively in the areas used in the imperial cult (the dismantled sanctuaries, the Amenhotep III court, the corridor through the colonnaded portico, and the sanctuary of the king or imperial cult chamber) suggests that these sculptures might have been removed from those areas as part of the tetrarchic program. The reverential burial of the statues might even be interpreted as evidence for the survival of the pharaonic cult at the time of the Tetrarchy. A seated Anubis statue now in Copenhagen (figure 3.17), of the same scale and style and with the same matte finish, also inscribed by Amenhotep III for Luxor Temple, indicates by its state of preservation that the cache of sculptures found in 1989 may not have been the only deposit.[41]

In addition, a text preserving the story of the Martyrium of Chanatomus, Sophronius, and Dalcina hints at the continuation of the Amun cult at Luxor Temple shortly after the tetrarchic conversion. The text describes a gathering of people in the temple who make offerings both to the "divine idols" and to the genius of Caesar, suggesting that the imperial cult still shared space with other deities, of which Amun is the most likely candidate.[42]

Another piece of evidence attesting to the survival of the Amun cult in some form is a Greek graffito in a tabula ansata inscribed just inside the entrance of the colonnade hall by the Roman army surgeon Ptollion (figure 3.18). Translated, the text reads, "I, Ptollion, doctor of the cohort for the second

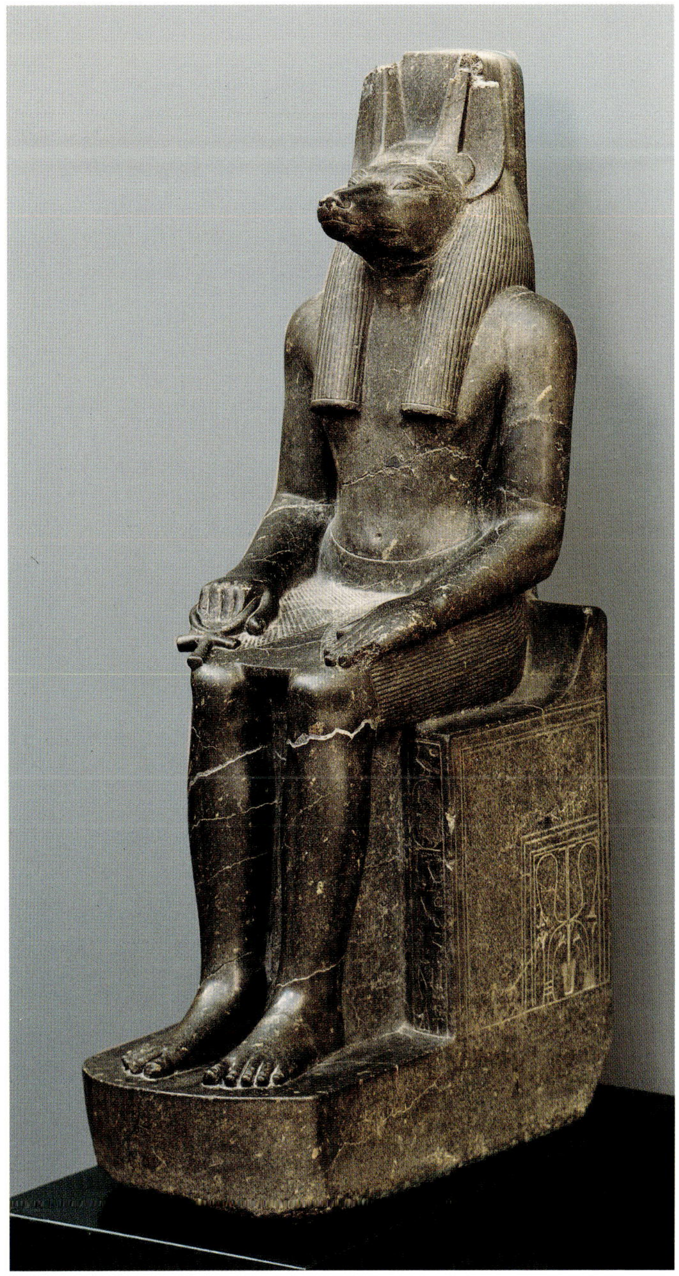

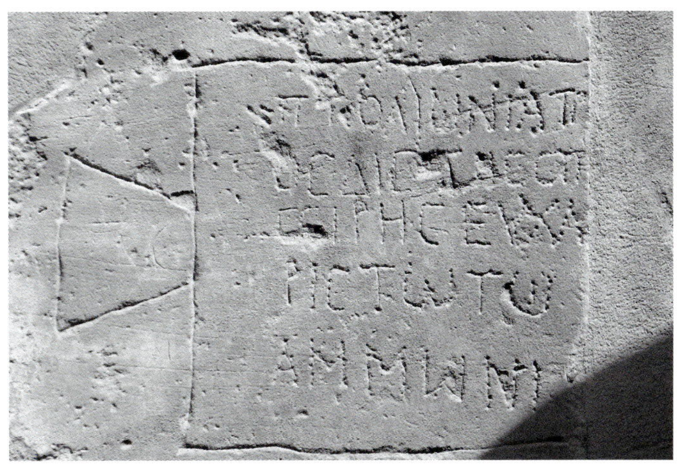

Right column:

FIGURE 3.17
(top) Seated Anubis statue, Ny Carlsberg Glyptotek.

FIGURE 3.18
(bottom) Greek graffito of the Roman army surgeon Ptollion invoking Amun.

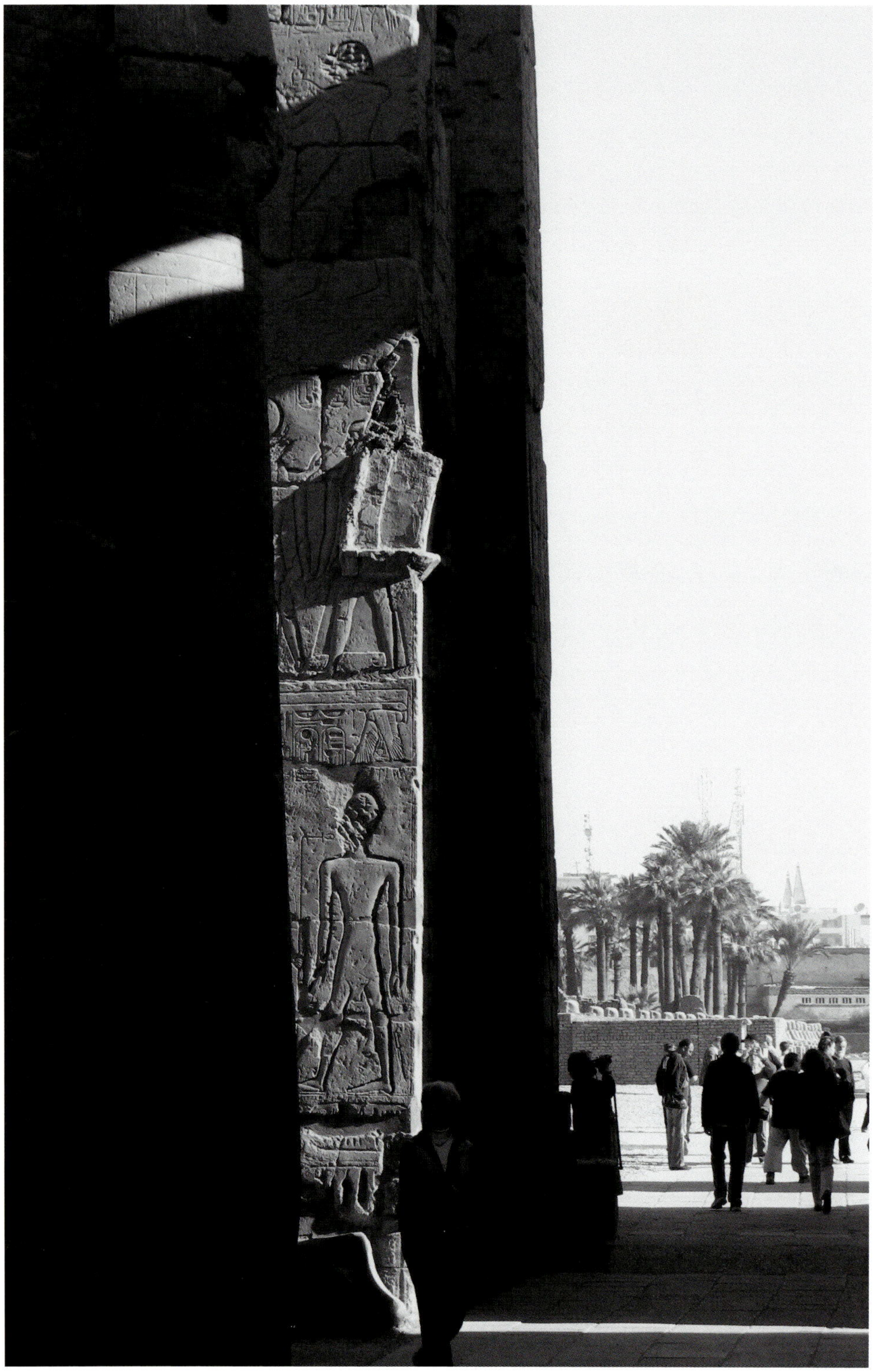

FIGURE 3.19
The springing of the Roman arch inserted into reliefs of Ramesses II in the southwest jamb of the first pylon.

time, thank Ammon." Though we have no way of determining the precise date of this inscription, or if Ptollion served in the cohort stationed within the Luxor camp at the beginning of the fourth century, the possibility that it might indicate a fourth-century soldier still venerating Amun/Ammon cannot be excluded.[43]

ROMAN MODIFICATIONS TO THE TEMPLE FABRIC: OVERVIEW AND SUMMARY

The Approach to the Imperial Cult Precinct

The approach to the sanctuary of the imperial cult began at the pylons of Ramesses II, the monumental northern entrance to the Roman camp (see figure I.4), with its colossal statuary and obelisks. The pylon doorway was given new front doorjambs and a groined, brick arch in the Roman style, but it is not clear whether this was added to the existing structure to romanize the great entrance to the fortress or to repair the earthquake-damaged entryway (figure 3.19).[44] Whatever the case may be, the renovated approach was a fusion of pharaonic and Roman architectural traditions, as Roman structures were built into the pharaonic masonry.

There is no evidence for any Roman modifications to the first court of Ramesses II.[45] Late antique structures found in the northwestern and southern quadrants of the court, which were removed in the 1980s, were made up primarily of Akhenaten talatat blocks quarried from the second, ninth, and tenth pylons at Karnak and were brought to Luxor Temple for reuse after the time of the Tetrarchy.[46] The eastern and western gates, adjacent to the main northern pylon entryway, opened onto side streets to the east and west within the camp. The road beyond the western gate led through the monumental four-columned tetrastyle to the riverside gate and quay and was the main approach from the Nile. The remains of the western tetrastyle indicate that it was considerably larger than its counterpart on the eastern side of the complex, perhaps because of its greater visibility from the river.[47]

Immediately beyond the first court, the great colonnade hall of Amenhotep III and Tutankhamun was given a new roof, perhaps as part of the renovation program of the temple at the time of the Tetrarchy, but also perhaps earlier. That the repair involved Roman-style vaulting, the emplacement for which is visible on the western architrave, western side, is all we can say with certainty.[48] Dowel holes along the edges of the colossal papyrus-umbel capitals, broken when the stone roof blocks came down on them, indicate repair of the edges with new stone or plaster as well. The large southern portal at the end of the hall that led to the Amenhotep III court beyond was modified and given a much smaller, more secure doorway, the lower courses of which are still in situ (see figures 3.1 and 3.20).[49] A new, larger door was cut through the eastern wall of the colonnade hall at the southern end and appears to have been made to be the new exit for the hall, directing traffic away from the main axis and around to the east of the temple.

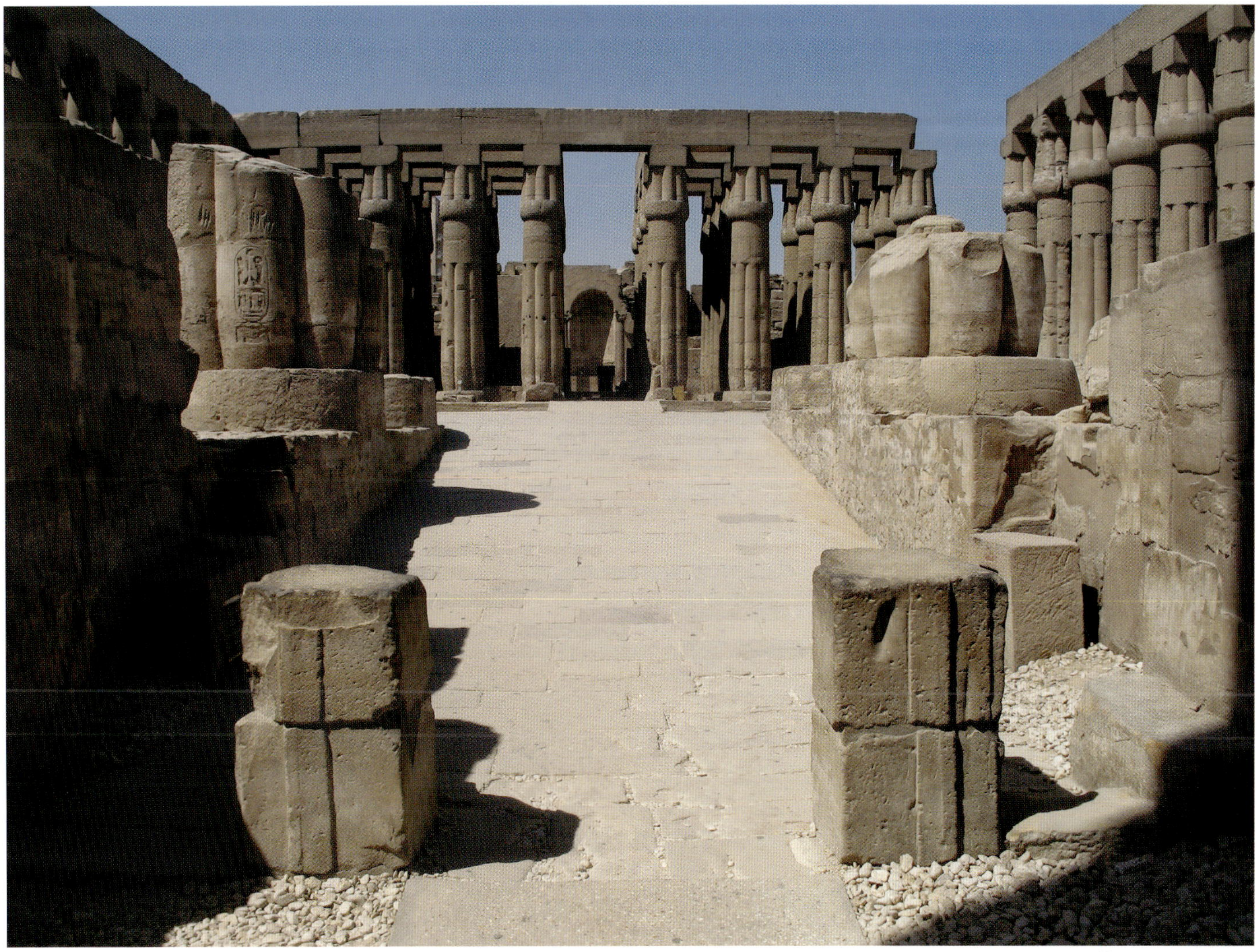

FIGURE 3.20
Roman doorjambs inserted into southern portal of the colonnade of Amenhotep III and Tutankhamun, looking south.

This eastward detour, as well as the removal of all pharaonic sculpture from the Amenhotep III court and the imperial cult chamber, suggests a new segregation of these areas to rededicate the center of the temple as the precinct of the imperial cult. Pharaonic sculpture was allowed to remain in the front areas of the temple, the first court, and outside the pylons of Ramesses II.

The Revised Approach to the Amun Cult

The rededication of the king's sanctuary for the imperial cult would have necessitated a redirection of religious processions along a new processional road if the Amun cult was still functioning in the sanctuary area now closed off by the niche in the imperial cult chamber. A mud-brick arch emplacement on the southeasternmost exterior corner of the Amenhotep III court might indicate the possible existence of a processional way along the eastern side of both courts in a straight line (figure 3.21). This route would have led to an open court to the east of the Luxor Temple sanctuary. The eastern sandstone wall of the temple and the fourteen chapels along the inside were dismantled for the creation of a new, eight-columned portico entryway from the east into the main sanctuary area (the eastern colonnade) (figure 3.22). The colonnade of stuccoed-brick columns (four of which partly survive) was bookended by two carefully built antae (pilasters), the northernmost of which still stands to its original height and keys into the rebuilt chambers immediately to the east of the imperial cult sanctuary, which makes the colonnade and the imperial cult modifications contemporary. The southern anta was completely dismantled at an unknown later date, although some of the blocks used for its construction can be seen in the block yard open-air museum, where loose blocks from the temple collected during excavations are displayed immediately in front of the colonnade. The original eastern doorway to the sanctuary was reworked into a Roman-style entrance topped by a "true arch" (figure 3.23), immediately

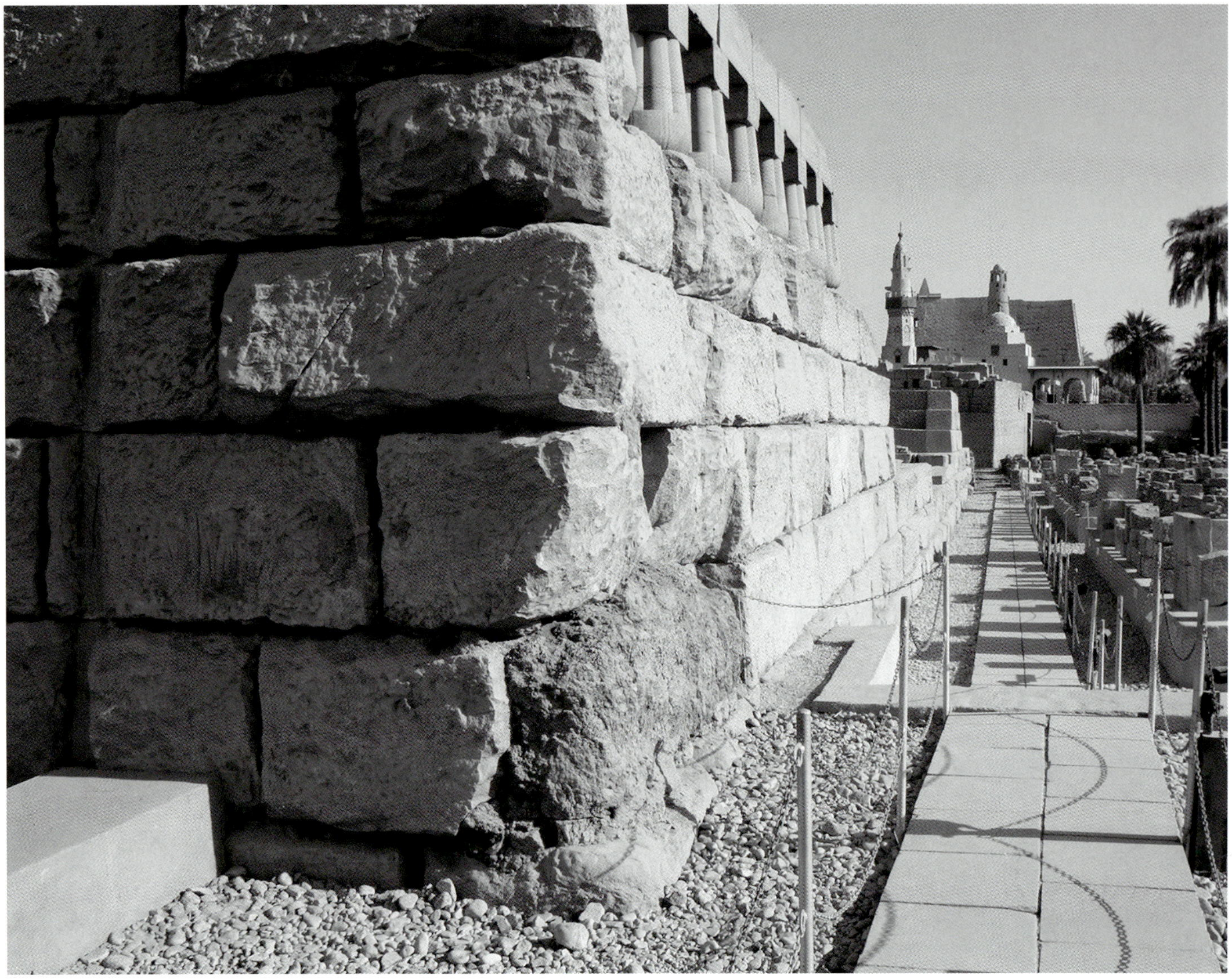

FIGURE 3.21
Fragment of a mud-brick arch at the outer southeast corner of the Amenhotep III court.

past which lay the barque sanctuary of Amun of Karnak; this had been rebuilt by Alexander the Great, who replaced the four columns of the hall with a freestanding sanctuary that now supports the roof. The back wall of the sanctuary room on the south was originally the location of a false door that mystically communicated with the sanctuary of Amun of Luxor Temple behind the solid wall. In Alexander's time, his barque sanctuary was open at both north and south sides, and this wall was opened up into a real doorway (in the Greek style) that allowed access to the sanctuaries beyond (figure 3.24).[50] In the only obvious Roman reworking of the barque sanctuary, this doorway was blocked up and returned to its solid-wall state. By blocking up the door, the Romans—whether intentionally or not—restored the wall's original function as a symbolic, not literal, entryway to Amun-Re of Luxor Temple's Holy of Holies.

The new eastern colonnade may have been flat-roofed or perhaps featured a pediment in its middle section, giving the new entrance to the barque sanctuary of Amun the appearance of a Roman-style temple.[51] A similar situation is to be found at the site of Antinoopolis, where the front of the temple of Miwer built under Ramesses II was given a similar Roman-style portico-and-anta facade when Hadrian rededicated the site as the cult city of the deified Osiris-Antinous.[52] The new, updated tetrarchic entryway to the Luxor Temple sanctuary could be interpreted as another indication of the continued veneration of the cult within.

THE IMPERIAL CULT CHAMBER: CONCLUSION

The location of the imperial cult chamber in the room that originally had been dedicated to the cult of the Egyptian pharaoh, located directly in front of the cultic area originally

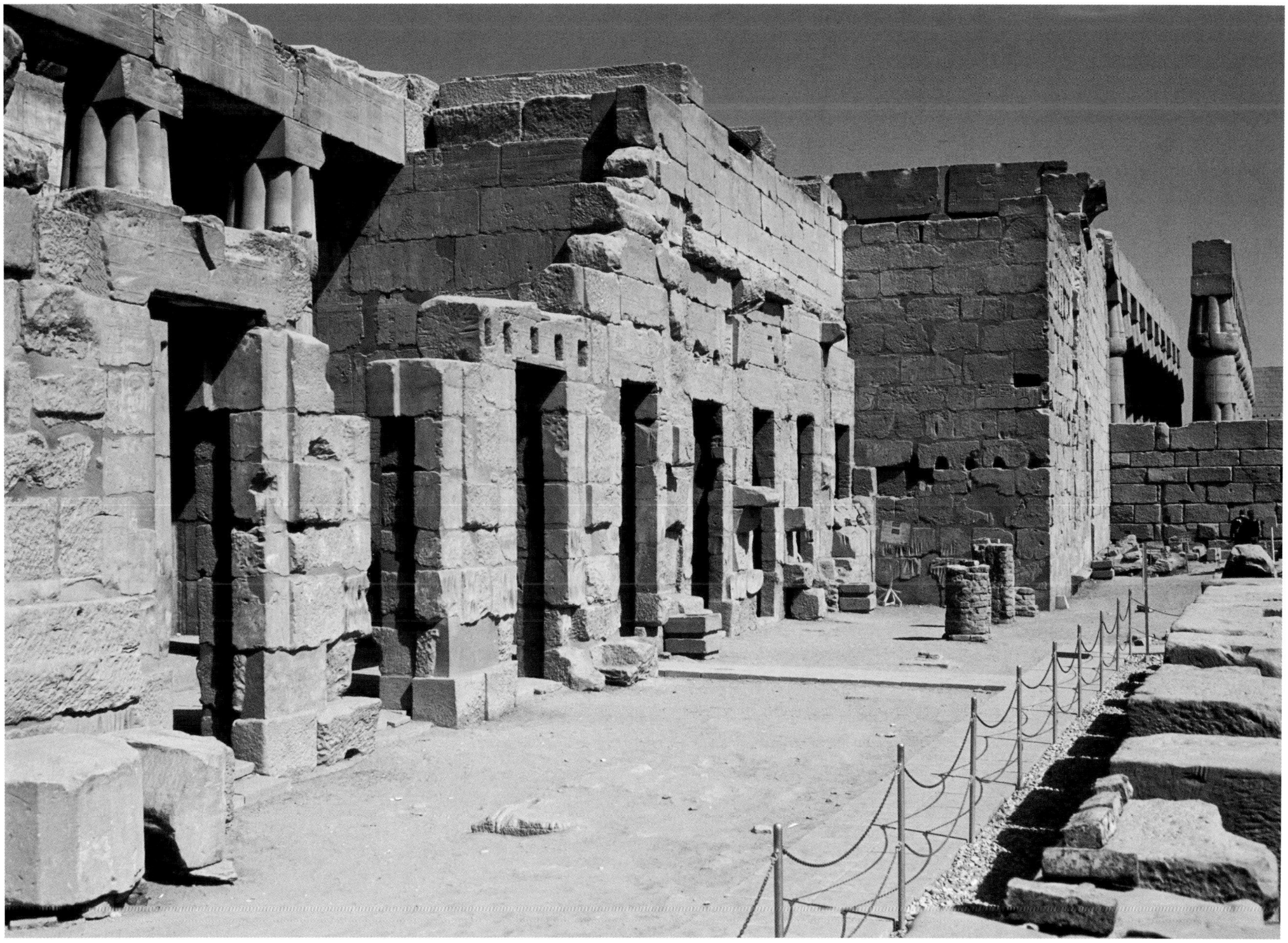

FIGURE 3.22
Remains of the Roman colonnade on the eastern side of the sanctuary area.

dedicated to Amun-Re, whether by design or not, echoes the pharaonic program at Luxor Temple. The Egyptian pharaoh participated in the rejuvenation rituals of Amun-Re, his "father," during the Opet Festival each year, when Amun of Karnak journeyed back to Luxor Temple, the place of his original birth, to reunite with Amun of Luxor Temple and be reborn. At the culmination of the ritual, the king and Amun of Karnak symbolically communicated through the false door of the barque sanctuary with Amun of Luxor Temple in his sanctuary on the other side. Both god and king were rejuvenated in the process, and Amun-Re returned to Karnak youthful and renewed. From the king's chamber the pharaoh was presented to the populace gathered in the great papyrus-columned court beyond, and the king's coronation ritual was reenacted. The culmination of the king's first coronation also took place here, when he united with Amun-Re during the Opet ritual and was thenceforth Amun's son and thus the legitimate ruler of Egypt.[53]

Of course, the architectural and other evidence can be interpreted in directly opposite ways. The careful segregation of the imperial cult chamber and the Amun sanctuary beyond, with its new entryway, could be interpreted as an indication that the Amun cult at Luxor Temple was still functioning at the time of the Tetrarchy. But the tetrarchic modifications to the very fabric of the temple itself could also be interpreted as evidence that cultic activity there had

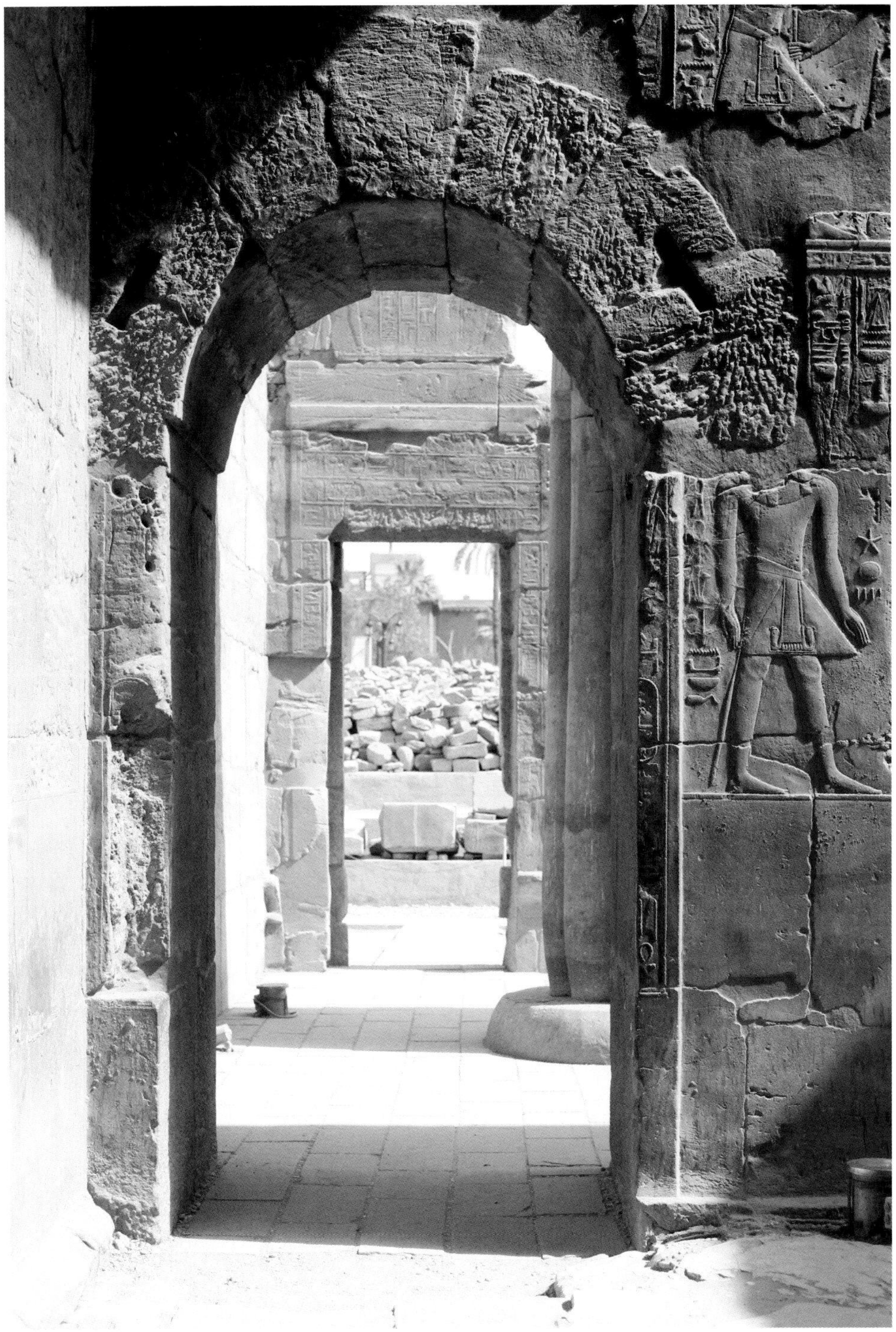

FIGURE 3.23
Original Eighteenth-Dynasty doorway reworked with a "true arch," looking east from the barque sanctuary.

ceased by that time. Elsewhere, inscriptions from the time of the emperor Decius (ca. 248–251) at Esna Temple, the last known for that site, indicate normal cultic activity near Thebes before the time of Diocletian and the Tetrarchy.[54] There are no monuments that can be linked directly with the Tetrarchy within the Karnak precinct, but third-century pottery and coins of Diocletian recently found in a Roman bath complex outside of the entryway to Karnak indicate a settlement with a Roman civic building at the site during the tetrarchic period.[55] Excavations conducted along the Karnak embankment by the SCA during the past few years have revealed a series of bath complexes from the Ptolemaic period into the late Roman period that still respect the boundaries of the sacred complex.[56] The next firmly dated material at Karnak is from the time of the emperor Constantine, who removed two obelisks from the precinct for his new capital at Constantinople and whose men dismantled part of the southeastern enclosure wall and created a ramp to the Nile in order to do so.[57] Excavation of a Constantine-period Roman villa, located between the eighth and ninth pylons along the north-south axis of the sacred avenue that led to the temple of Mut and joined the processional route to Luxor Temple, revealed that the villa was built immediately east of the road, which suggests that the road was still functioning.[58] The last known stela from the Bucheum at nearby Armant dates to the later reign of Constantius II, 337–361, which indicates pagan cultic activity parallel to Christianity at least until that time in the Theban area.[59] There is no evidence for any quarrying of the Karnak Temple complex for building stone until the post-tetrarchic period.[60] The tetrarchic modifications and interventions at Luxor Temple used absolutely no building material quarried from Karnak.

When the king's chamber at Luxor Temple was converted into the imperial cult chamber, the main axis doorway leading from it to the temple sanctuary was blocked and turned into a large, round-topped niche, the sacred focus of the imperial cult. The niche was painted with frescoes of the four Tetrarchs below a huge Roman eagle, a purely Roman composition, yet one that reflects the earlier, pharaonic program (see figure 7.1). Floating between the heads of the two central painted Tetrarch figures was a portrait bust of a fifth figure that might have been a representation of Jupiter wearing a laurel wreath.[61] If this was Jupiter, the position of the god's head in the center of the composition gives the impression that he is looking out from the sanctuary beyond. The iconography and setting could be seen as reinforcing the association of Jupiter with Amun/Ammon. In the program of the pharaonic reliefs concealed by the imperial frescoes in this room, Amun emerges from his sanctuary beyond to bless Amenhotep III and put the divine stamp of legitimacy on his rule, which reinforces Bell's suggestion that "the Romans' selection of this part of the temple for the worship of the divine emperors was

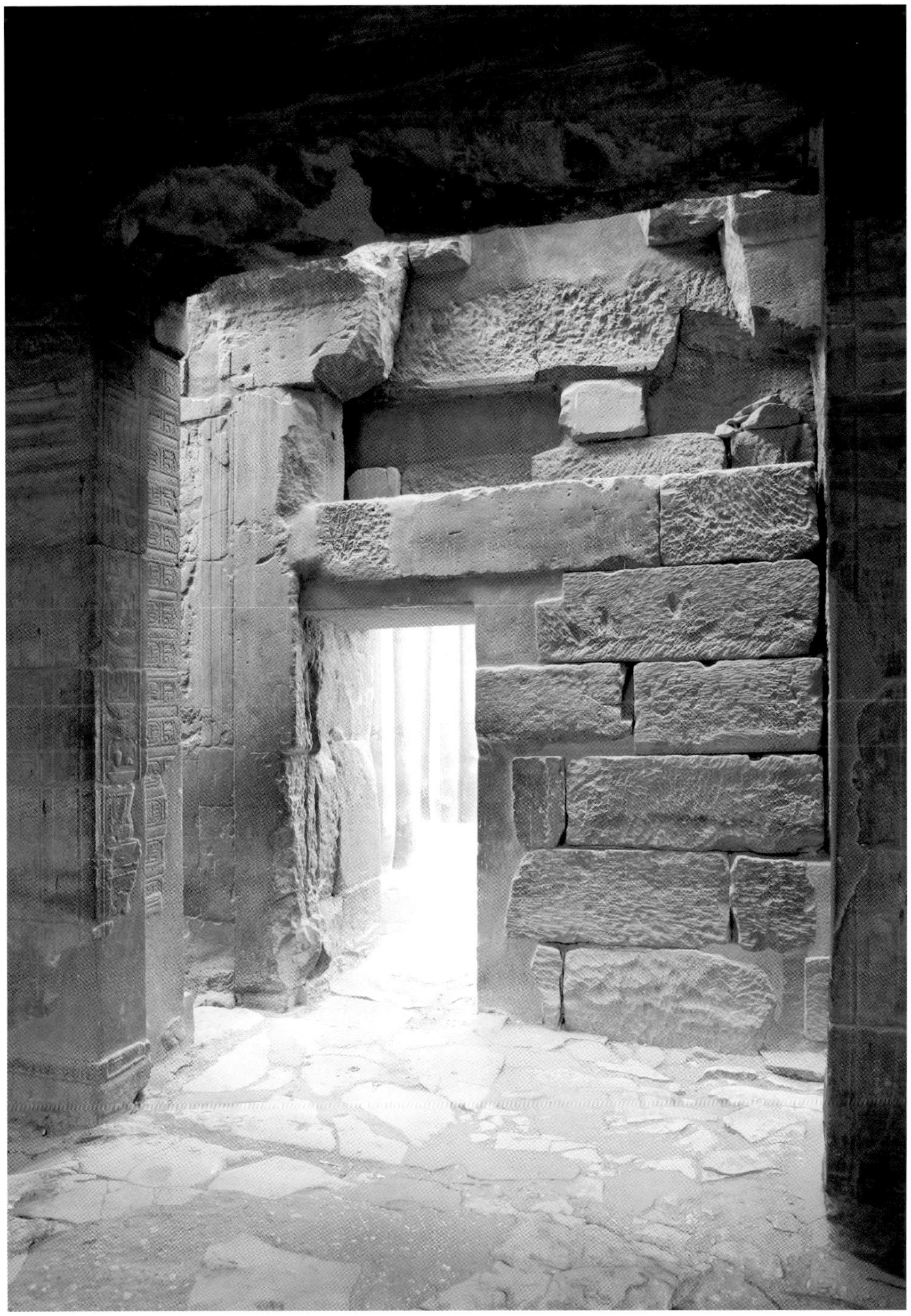

FIGURE 3.24
Roman blocking of the Hellenistic doorway that replaced the original false door in the south wall of the barque sanctuary. The present opening was made in 1954.

surely deliberate, motivated by awareness of the 1500-year-long tradition with the cult of the divine king."[62]

Before the tetrarchic renovations to Luxor Temple, Diocletian had suppressed a very serious revolt in Egypt and reaffirmed his rule. Probably not coincidentally, with the subsequent transformation of Luxor Temple, the experience of a visitor arriving along the central axis was designed to be a narrative journey through successive zones of an increasingly classicized architectural vocabulary, beginning with completely Egyptian elements to the north and culminating in the completely classicized space of the interior of the Roman imperial cult chamber. This must have demonstrated clearly to even the most reluctant viewer that a government with the power to effect such a radical change in the very center of one of the most important temples in Egypt must hold absolute authority over the country and its citizens. The apparent deference given to the Amun-Re sanctuary behind the imperial cult sanctuary could be interpreted as a message that, in László Tőrők's words, "the Roman rulers [the Tetrarchs] are legitimate successors of Egypt's ancient kings, and their Egyptian regency is built upon Egypt's timeless traditions and sanctity."[63]

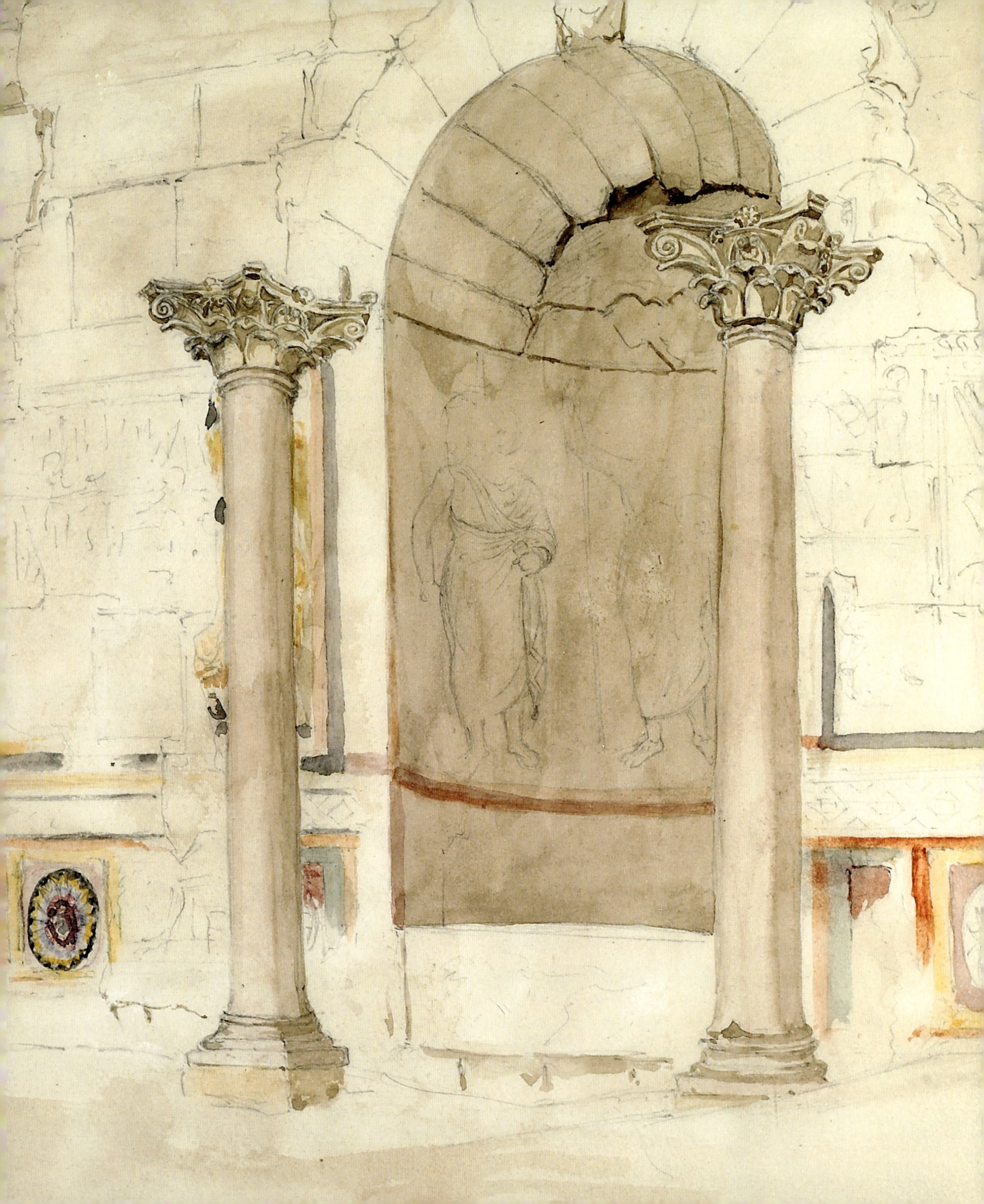

Chapter 4

FROM RUINS IN A LANDSCAPE TO A MONUMENT ON DISPLAY

A Conservation History of the Imperial Cult Chamber and Its Paintings

MICHAEL JONES

THE TRANSFORMATIVE PROCESSES THAT HAVE AFFECTED Luxor Temple and its surroundings have inevitably affected the Roman imperial cult chamber, whose conservation history is inseparably linked to the destiny of the temple. The frescoes that form the central theme of this book, and that undoubtedly originally covered all the interior mural surfaces of the room, have always relied for their survival on the supporting walls. As the temple fell out of use and became a ruin, changes began that ultimately led to the condition in which the frescoes were found when the room was excavated in the nineteenth century. The purpose of this chapter is to reconstruct an archaeological and conservation history of the imperial cult chamber and its painted interior by tracing the fortunes of the temple as a whole from its abandonment to modern times.

The sources for this study are limited and sporadic. There are no systematic archaeological reports, but, nonetheless, written and pictorial records of Luxor have survived, beginning in the seventeenth century with the brief accounts of early visitors and growing more abundant and explicit during the nineteenth and twentieth centuries (figure 4.1). They include antiquarians' written accounts, sketches and engravings, maps, watercolors, drawings, photographs, and, not least, the remains at the site itself. The intense interest in Luxor as a tourist destination from the mid-nineteenth century to the present means that it is one of the most thoroughly documented historical towns and archaeological sites in Egypt, although the record is erratic and incomplete.

Pictorial records of all kinds are by far the most informative sources, augmented shortly after the invention of photography by the first photographs, of which some rare daguerreotypes have survived.[1] After improved photographic methods arrived in Egypt in 1849, the record proliferated, at first mainly to present Egypt to a European audience and later to meet the demand for souvenirs and postcards for the growing number of tourists. In addition to charting the changing perception of the ruins and their contemporary value, photographers coincidentally documented the building boom in and around the temple as Luxor grew from a small village into a thriving international tourist town. Well-known buildings constructed during this period, such as the French House, constructed on the roof of the southern rooms in 1815 and demolished in 1885, and the house of Mustafa Agha, built between 1851 and 1855 and removed in 1889, chronicle the development of the town as they appear and later disappear from the record. The photographs emphasize the affiliation of photography, tourism, and scholarly research and reveal the ways in which the European and American discovery of ancient Thebes affected Luxor and its surroundings in the nineteenth century.[2] By documenting the temple before, during, and after the nineteenth- and twentieth-century excavations that disengaged it from its historical setting, the photographs show forcefully how the ruins, once excavated, were irreversibly changed to become part of the present.[3]

The archival evidence shows that the fortunes of the imperial cult chamber can be divided conveniently into three phases, preceded by the long, undocumented silent years of late antiquity and the premodern period. The first documented phase began in the seventeenth and eighteenth centuries, when Europeans arriving at Luxor observed the remains of the temple in the landscape with a reduced yet enduring settlement around the Shrine of Sheikh Yussef

FIGURE 4.1
Detail of the niche from Wilkinson's watercolor of the imperial cult chamber, page 26r.

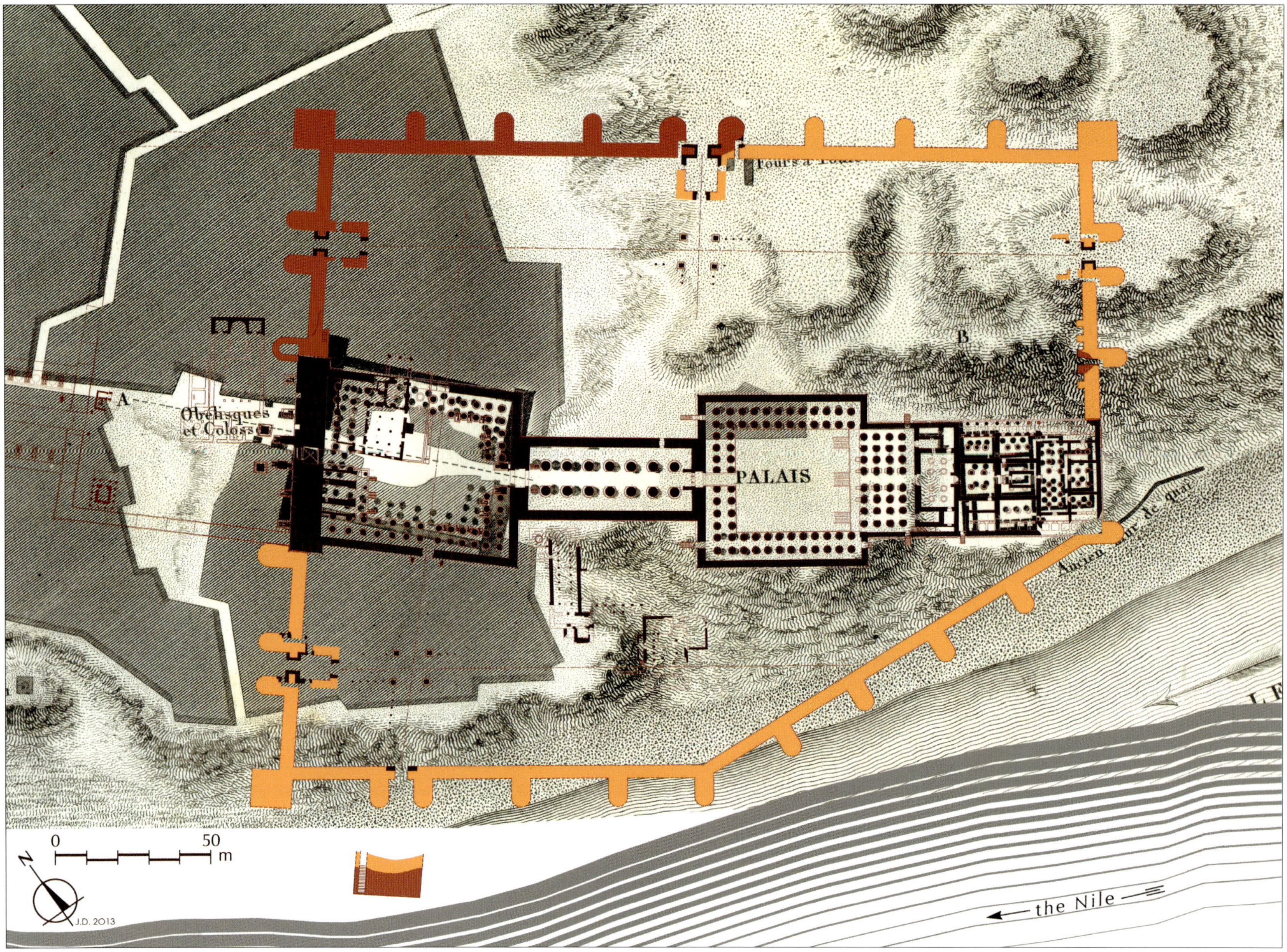

FIGURE 4.2
Napoleonic plan of Luxor and Luxor Temple showing the extent of the ruin mounds and contemporary settlement overlain with the remains extant today (*dark red*) and the outline of the Roman fort showing archaeologically verified fortifications (*light red*) and inferred walls (*yellow*).

Abu al-Hajjaj at the northern end of the temple ruins (figure 4.2).[4] The second phase began in the 1850s, when the imperial cult chamber was excavated to floor level and made accessible. As far as can be determined, it was the first part of the temple to be excavated, and the earliest accurate documentation of it dates from this time. The final phase began when the Antiquities Service cleared the room again as part of the complete exposure of Luxor Temple from 1885 to 1894 and continues until the present. It is characterized by the modern scholarly rediscovery of the temple and by increased conservation risks associated especially with the late twentieth-century population growth and the promotion of Luxor as an international mass tourism destination.

AN ARCHAEOLOGICAL LANDSCAPE IN THEBES

The transformation from a functioning temple to a ruin in an archaeological landscape began in the late Roman period, when the temple lost its primary function and a church and other structures were built in the first court of Ramesses II.[5] In the imperial cult chamber, ancient vandalism was probably responsible for damage inflicted on selected areas, such as the faces of the emperor figures painted in the niche. The roof timbers were undoubtedly taken away for reuse, leaving the room exposed to the elements. The greatest loss, however, occurred when the upper parts of the walls were demolished and reduced to their present heights. A large part of the paintings thus perished with the building itself long before records

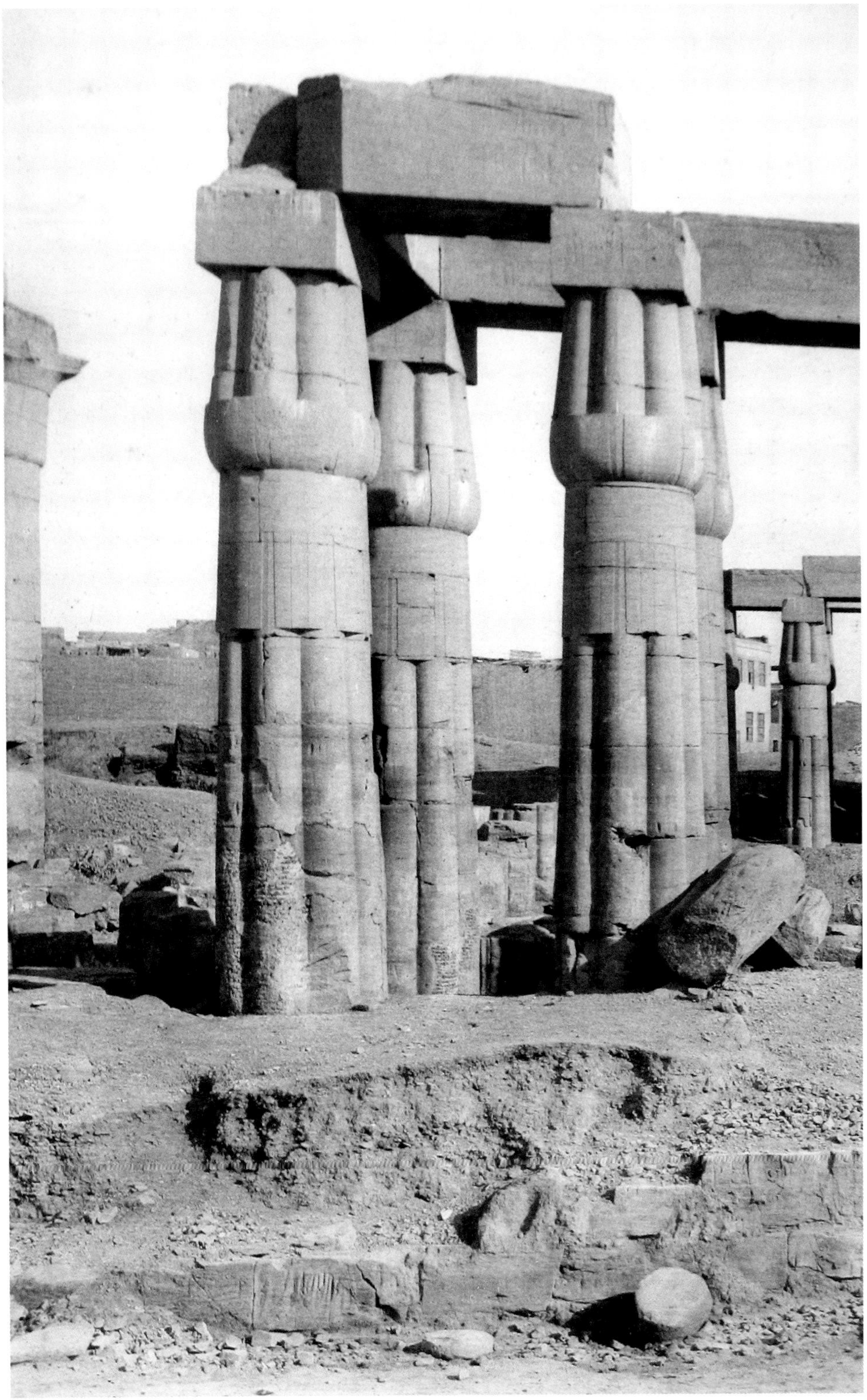

FIGURE 4.3
Northwest corner of the court of Amenhotep III during clearance, showing layers of stone chippings from the destruction of the temple walls.

began to be made. Erosion would have set in and continued while the room was filling with the debris that, paradoxically, also protected the surviving frescoes in their neglected state by preventing further exposure and access. The ruined temple at that point stood at the heart of a substantial settlement that continued to rise in elevation, surrounding and partly filling the huge colonnades and porticos and eventually covering the truncated remains of walls and columns, thereby leaving higher, upstanding sections protruding aboveground. This settlement was later abandoned and reduced to mounds, forming an archaeological tell in and around the temple ruins. Archaeological evidence that might have elaborated on the formation and eventual decline of the settlement was lost when large-scale clearance works removed the tell in the nineteenth and twentieth centuries. Nevertheless, photographs taken during the clearance, showing stone chippings at the lowest levels, suggest that extensive demolition of the temple began soon after it fell out of use, which contributed to the early accumulation of debris around the walls and columns (figure 4.3).

When the first European travelers arrived at Luxor, they encountered an archaeological landscape in which ancient remains were spread across the Nile Valley flood plain on both sides of the river.[6] Francis Norden and Richard Pococke, who visited Luxor on their separate journeys in the winter of 1737–1738, provide the earliest glimpses.[7] Norden shows three views of the "antiquités superbes à Luxxor" with Luxor village on the mounds at the northern end of the temple. Norden's records also include measured sketches clearly based on observations made at the site.[8] A plan deduced from the standing remains visible aboveground correctly shows the bent axis of the temple, although in the published version the temple axis is straight and other details omitted or changed.[9] Norden's field drawings show the area of the imperial cult chamber as a narrow transverse room with no internal features and omit the side rooms to the east and west. The niche is mistakenly positioned in the center of the north wall, facing into the portico of Amenhotep III. In the published drawings an open doorway replaces the niche (figure 4.4).

Details in Norden's and Pococke's drawings and those of the Napoleonic expedition of some sixty years later can be compared to give an assessment of the general condition of the imperial cult chamber at the time.[10] Both Pococke and the engineers of the Napoleonic expedition of 1798–1799 attempted imaginative reconstructions of the buried parts.[11] Pococke's plan shows the wall outlines of the eastern and western side rooms as if they were complete, but the west side is clearly copied from what he could see of the eastern rooms. The doorway leading from the imperial cult chamber into the east side room is not shown, indicating that it was probably buried below ground level. The absence of detail in Norden's drawings and Pococke's mistaken reconstruction of the west side point to a considerable depth of archaeological deposit filling the imperial cult chamber that had buried the whole of that side of the temple. Neither of them shows either of the two granite columns in front of the niche, sug-

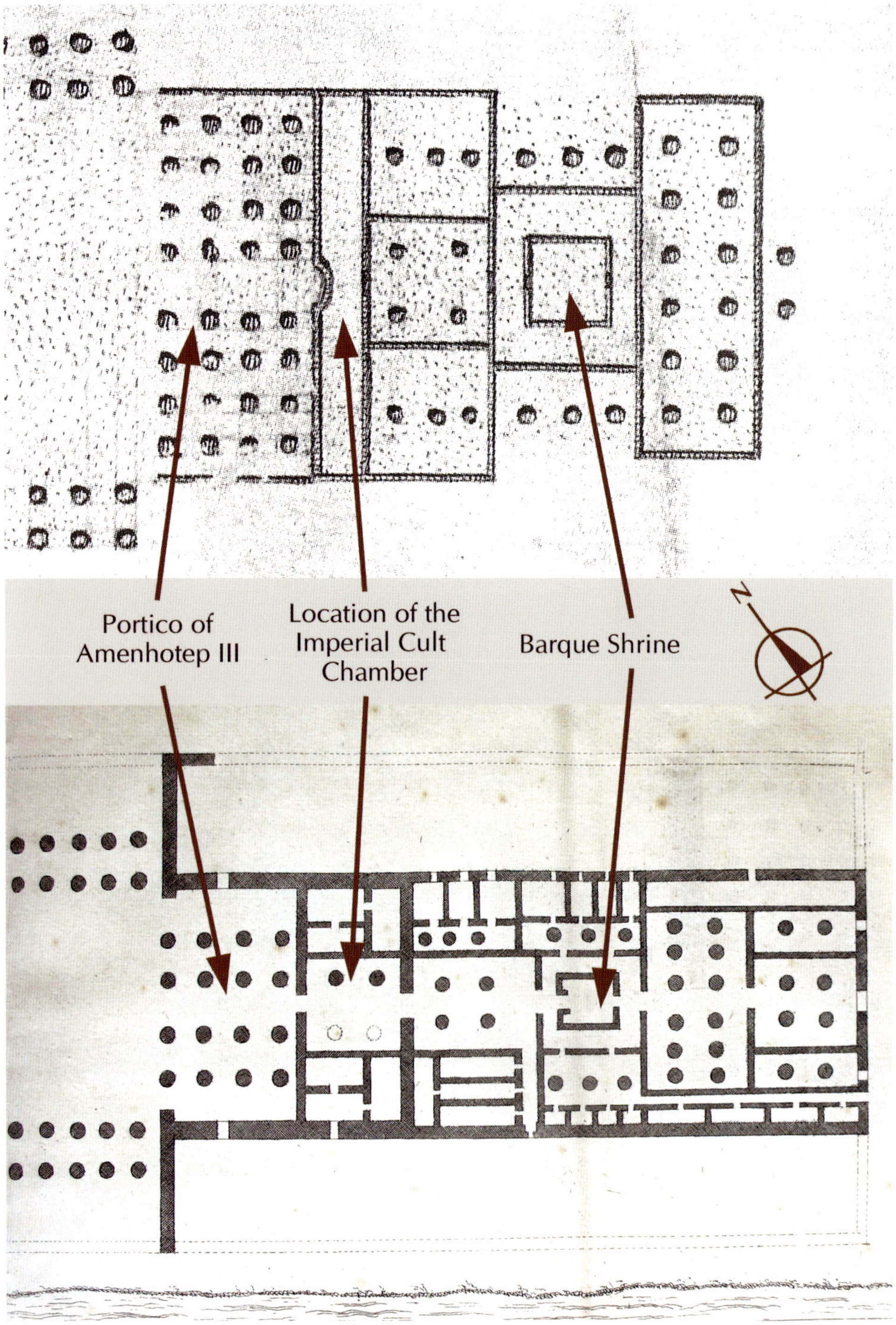

FIGURE 4.4
Plans of the southern end of Luxor Temple: upper based on F. Norden; lower based on R. Pococke.

gesting that these too were covered by debris. Pococke's narrative supports this interpretation with a description of a restricted view of the top of the niche from one side and the top of the blocked doorway seen from inside the hall beyond: "I observed a door here with a straight top within; but without it was cut in an arch, something like the shell of a niche, which might first give the thought for the arch in Egypt."[12] Pococke's ground plan shows the doorway in place of the niche, which, supported by his description, indicates how little was visible below the arch of the niche or of the blocking in the chamber behind it. Pococke also reconstructed the buried parts showing walls and side rooms around the barque shrine and sanctuaries omitted by Norden. By comparison, however, Norden's field sketch plan can claim to be a more reliable general guide to existing conditions in the eighteenth century, despite the wrongly placed niche.

The Napoleonic topographic map of Luxor and views of 1798–1799 support the inferences drawn from Norden's and Pococke's drawings and adds further details (figure 4.5).[13] These drawings show how little conditions had changed in the intervening years; the temple is engulfed by mounds, mostly abandoned, and the contemporary village of Luxor is situated in the first court of Ramesses II and in the area immediately to the north. Debris is shown filling the imperial cult chamber, apparently covering all the interior of this and the adjacent rooms, apart from the outlines of two of the eastern side chambers and the southern end of the east wall, where it is preserved to its fullest height. The shape of the room is not defined on the plan; only the south wall is shown as continuous, indicating that the walls we now know to define the north, east, and west sides were concealed below ground level. The niche is shown but without the two columns in front of it, indicating that they were still buried. As the center of the arch over the niche is seven meters above the present floor level, Pococke's description and the Napoleonic survey drawing together denote an accumulation of between six and seven meters of archaeological material against the east and south walls of the imperial cult chamber in the eighteenth century.[14] Such a deep deposit could have been formed from collapsed roofing material, possibly mudbrick vaulting that had fallen into the room as the upper sections of the building were being demolished. The debris was higher on the east side and sloped downward across the room to the west where it was still deep enough to cover the truncated northern and western walls.

The Napoleonic engineers deduced that the semi-dome visible to them above the level of the fill was the top of a niche, not a doorway (see the elevation in figure 4.5). Their reconstruction drawing shows the base of the niche at floor level, whereas it is actually 1.25 meters above the pavement level of the room. No digging would have been required to imagine such a feature here, and this reconstruction implies that the blocking of the original door was visible as such on the reverse. The French engineer Pascal Coste made a similar plan of Luxor Temple in 1821, probably based on the published Napoleonic survey.[15] Like all early surveyors, Coste was hampered where remains lay buried below the contempo-

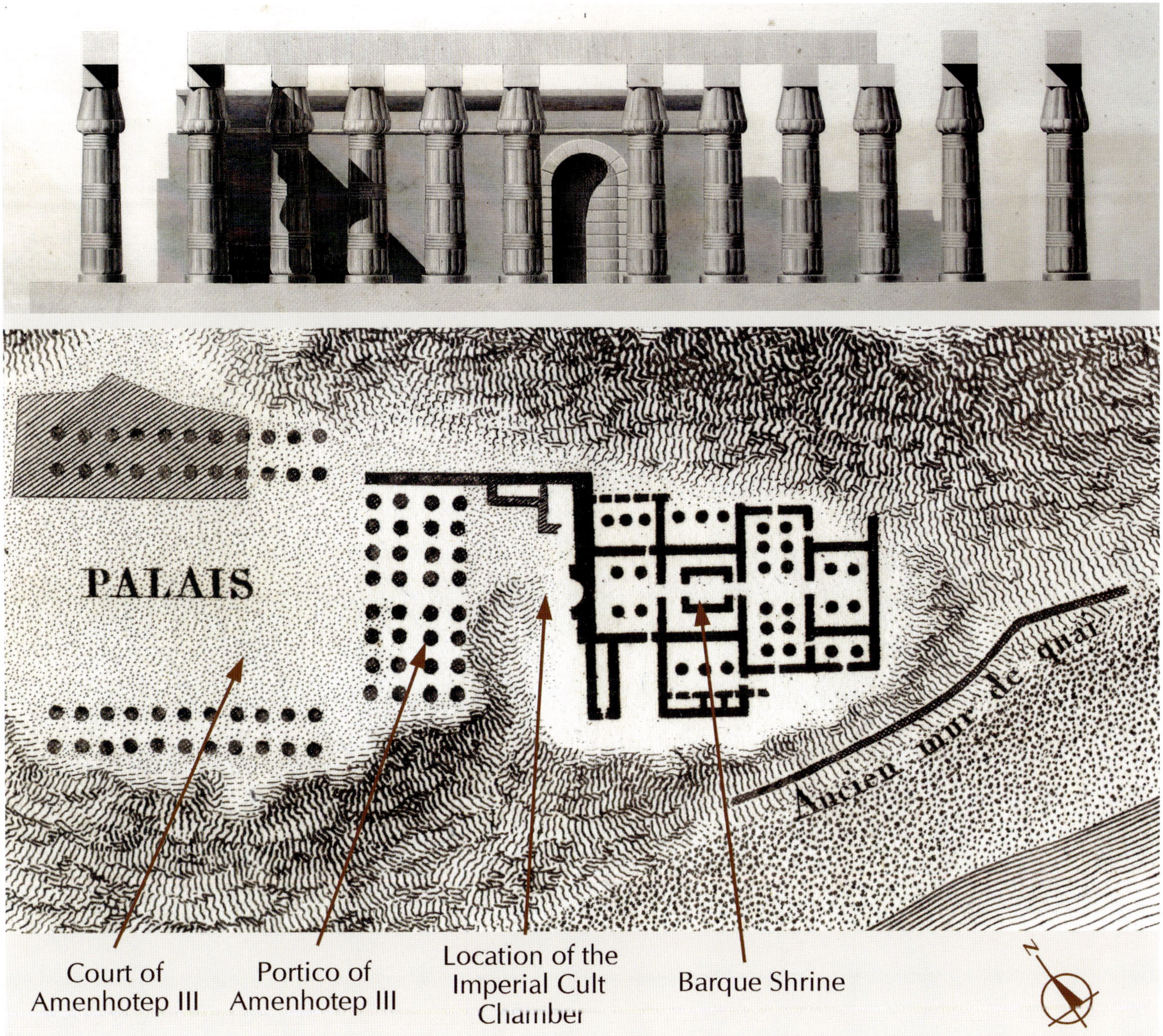

FIGURE 4.5
Composite image of Luxor Temple in 1798–1799 using drawings from the *Description de l'Égypte.* Upper: reconstructed elevation of the portico of Amenhotep III and the niche; *Antiquités* vol. 3, pl. 9. Lower: plan detail of Luxor Temple in 1798–1799; *Antiquités* vol. 3, pl. 1.

rary ground surface. In his plan, the imperial cult chamber remains undefined apart from its southern and eastern walls and a rough outline of the three eastern side rooms, shown without doorways. The niche is not shown, but Coste substituted an open doorway, probably intending the original plan of the temple.[16]

After the defeat of Napoleon in 1815, nationalist rivalry between the English and the French influenced the drive to acquire antiquities for private collections and museums abroad that resulted in devastation at many sites. Some of the earliest Egyptologists, including Edward Lane, Robert Hay, and John Gardner Wilkinson, respected the value of monuments in their actual settings, and Hay and Wilkinson especially spent lengthy periods at Thebes aware that accurate documentation was a form of preservation.[17] Lane was at Luxor in 1827 working for Hay and saw the temple just as the critical changes of the nineteenth century were beginning.[18] His methodical description of the temple in its actual condition adds considerably to the preceding records and is augmented by carefully observed drawings that avoid the imaginative reconstructions of earlier visitors.[19] These belong to a new kind of scholarship that links the eighteenth-century antiquarians with the earliest photographers, who were to arrive less than a quarter century later.

Lane's description of the imperial cult chamber is quoted here in full: "Behind it [the portico of Amenhotep III] there appears to have been an open space, with small side-chambers. From this place, a central door led to one of the principal chambers of the innermost part of the temple: but it has been closed up with masonry by some early Christians, who have made, in its place, an arched niche, apparently for their altar."[20] He mentions neither the granite columns in front of the niche nor the frescoes.

An almost contemporary description by Hay provides further information and another interpretation of the niche.[21] Having described the court and portico of Amenhotep III, Hay goes directly to the south wall of the imperial cult chamber: "The door entering into the next chamber is filled up with an arch made by the Greeks for their altar forming a circular headed nich [*sic*] on which remains of their painting is to be seen. It, moreover, faces a person standing at the table at lunch who looks to the West end. It is well and strongly built with a small proportion of plaster. On the NW is part of a granite column standing."[22] This is the first mention of the frescoes and the first indication that one of the granite columns, the western column, was now visible, implying that some digging had taken place. The "person standing at the table" is not immediately identifiable. Hay lost interest in his Egyptian archive after returning to Scotland, but Lane remained active in contemporary Egyptian research, and it was Lane's identification of the niche, although ultimately recognized as a mistake, that was to influence scholarly interpretations and popular opinion during the nineteenth and twentieth centuries.

Both Lane and Hay produced drawings of the southern and eastern sides of the temple, showing the house built in 1815 (the French House) on the roof of the barque shrine and adjacent rooms. Within a few years, a cluster of houses or annexes to the original house had developed around this part of the temple.[23] All these new buildings had appeared since the Napoleonic expedition of 1798–1799 and seem to have been the catalyst for a rapid housing development at this end of the temple that grew and eventually connected with the simultaneously expanding village around the Mosque of Abu al-Hajjaj to the north. The French House and the subsequent development around it must have introduced risks into the ecological balance around this part of the temple, including the usual human factors such as indifference to the surroundings, waste disposal, and an inevitable increase in vermin, insects, and other wildlife. Lane described the barque shrine room as a "receptacle for filth" and hints at the associated conservation risk. An annex on the north side of the house stood directly on the southern wall of the imperial cult chamber, where several coats of yellow, discolored wash on the upper courses of the temple walls, partly obscuring Roman plaster and paint layers, were probably applied when the outside walls of the house above were painted down to the top of the debris filling the imperial cult chamber (see figure 4.24 and the discussion in chapter 5).[24]

The plan of Luxor Temple made by the Prussian Expedition of 1844–1845, led by Richard Lepsius, illustrates how the mounds of archaeological material throughout the temple restricted access, obliging surveyors to rely on informed guesswork for their reconstruction drawings.[25] It shows the imperial cult chamber with debris covering all of the west side and the north wall, as well as the north end of the east wall. The eastern side rooms are shown but without their internal doorways, whose lintels must have been below the fill, whereas the western side rooms are omitted altogether. Only the southeast corner, where the walls stand to their maximum preserved heights, is indicated as certain. Lepsius's documentation is the last to show the imperial cult chamber in this condition.

THE IMPERIAL CULT CHAMBER EXCAVATED

At some time during the decade following the Prussian Expedition, the imperial cult chamber was excavated to floor level. The first confirmation is a watercolor by George de Sausmarez, dated 2 March 1855 and entitled "Excavated Roman Hall in an Egyptian Temple. Luxor. Thebes" (figure 4.6).[26] The title reveals that Sausmarez, who was not involved with the English Egyptological set of the time, was probably unaware of the Christian interpretation proposed by Lane and already published by Wilkinson.[27] Sausmarez's vantage point was near the northeast corner of the imperial cult chamber on the mounds still filling the portico of Amenhotep III. The sketch is framed on the left by the southeast corner of the room and includes the niche with the two granite columns in front of it, and it takes in a short length of the wall west of the niche. The entrance to the east side rooms is sketched in pencil near the left edge. The ground level is close to the base of the wall and seems to slope upward out of the picture to the right, as though some debris remained there. The frescoes are shown in bold colors, particularly the well-preserved lowest register of the imitation *opus sectile* panels. Two of the emperors in the niche are shown, and extensive traces of paintings on the wall to the east (left) of the niche are divided by a large lacuna that exposes the stone masonry under the Roman plaster. Immediately west (right) of the niche, a damaged section disturbs the frescoes, and part of the standing figure is visible just beyond at the right edge of the sketch. Sausmarez's watercolor gives

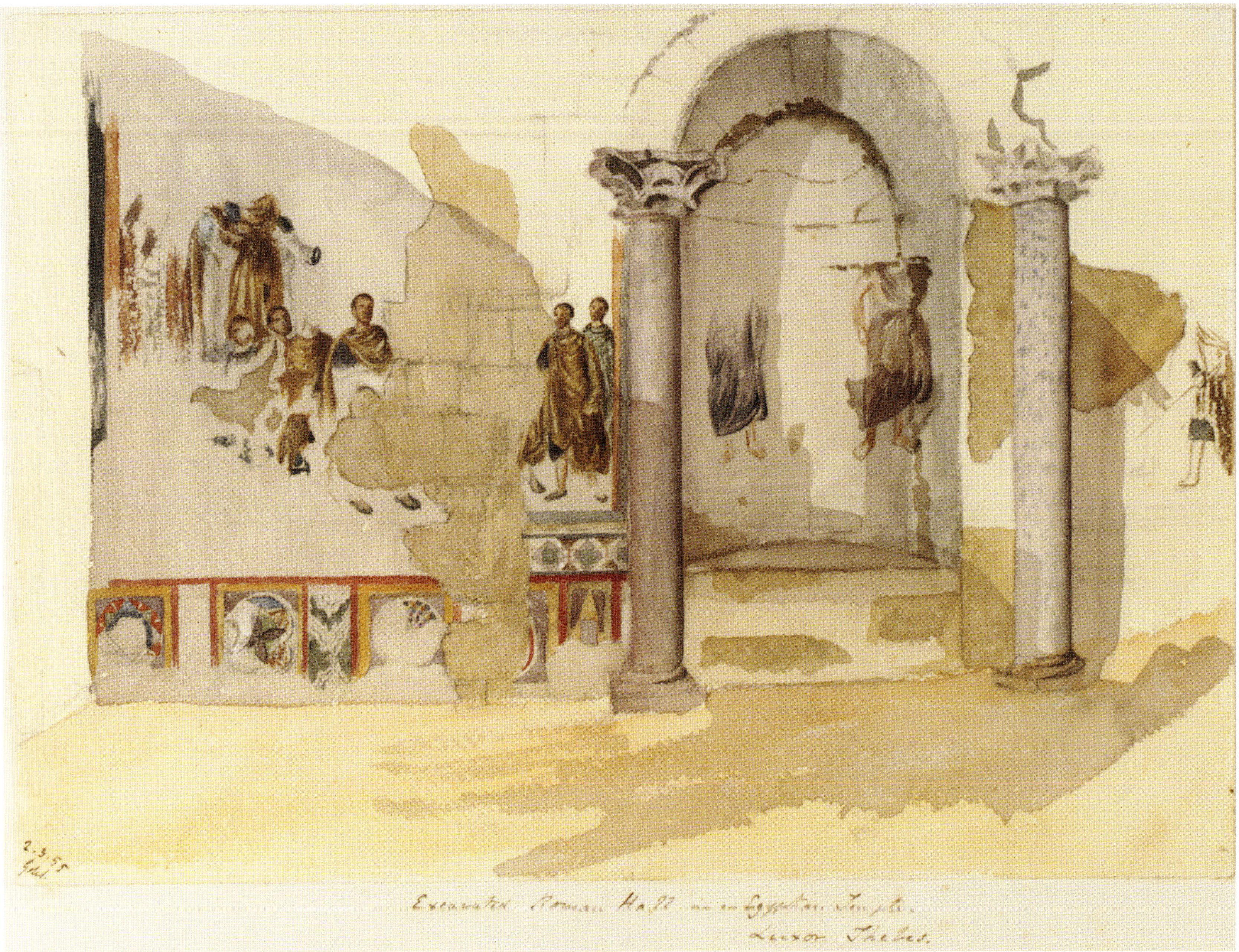

FIGURE 4.6
Watercolor by George de Sausmarez of the niche and south wall of the imperial cult chamber.

an impression of fresh colors suggestive of the brightness of recently uncovered paintings.

Less than a year later, in January 1856, John Gardner Wilkinson was in Luxor on his last journey through Egypt. His watercolor and pencil sketches of the imperial cult chamber and its frescoes are now well known and form the definitive record, showing their state of preservation in the mid-nineteenth century, very soon after they were first excavated. (Wilkinson's sketches are reproduced in full in the appendix.) The panoramic view from inside the northwest corner of the room shows the interior fully exposed (see figure A.1). The western granite column appears to have debris around its base, as Sausmarez also suggested, and no paving slabs are shown, as if the floor was still not completely uncovered. Mounds of debris fill the portico of Amenhotep III, sloping toward the top of the north wall and spilling through the entrance. A house built on the mounds is sketched faintly in outline above the east wall. Wilkinson famously depicts the well-preserved scene of soldiers and horses on the east wall, even managing in the small format of his sketchbook to convey some of the energy he sensed in this large and dynamic painting. Two of the emperor figures are drawn in pencil in the niche. The decorative panels forming the lower dados are brightly painted, corroborating the impression given by Sausmarez. The capitals on the two granite columns are drawn in exquisite detail (see figure 4.1). Wilkinson's sketches create contexts for

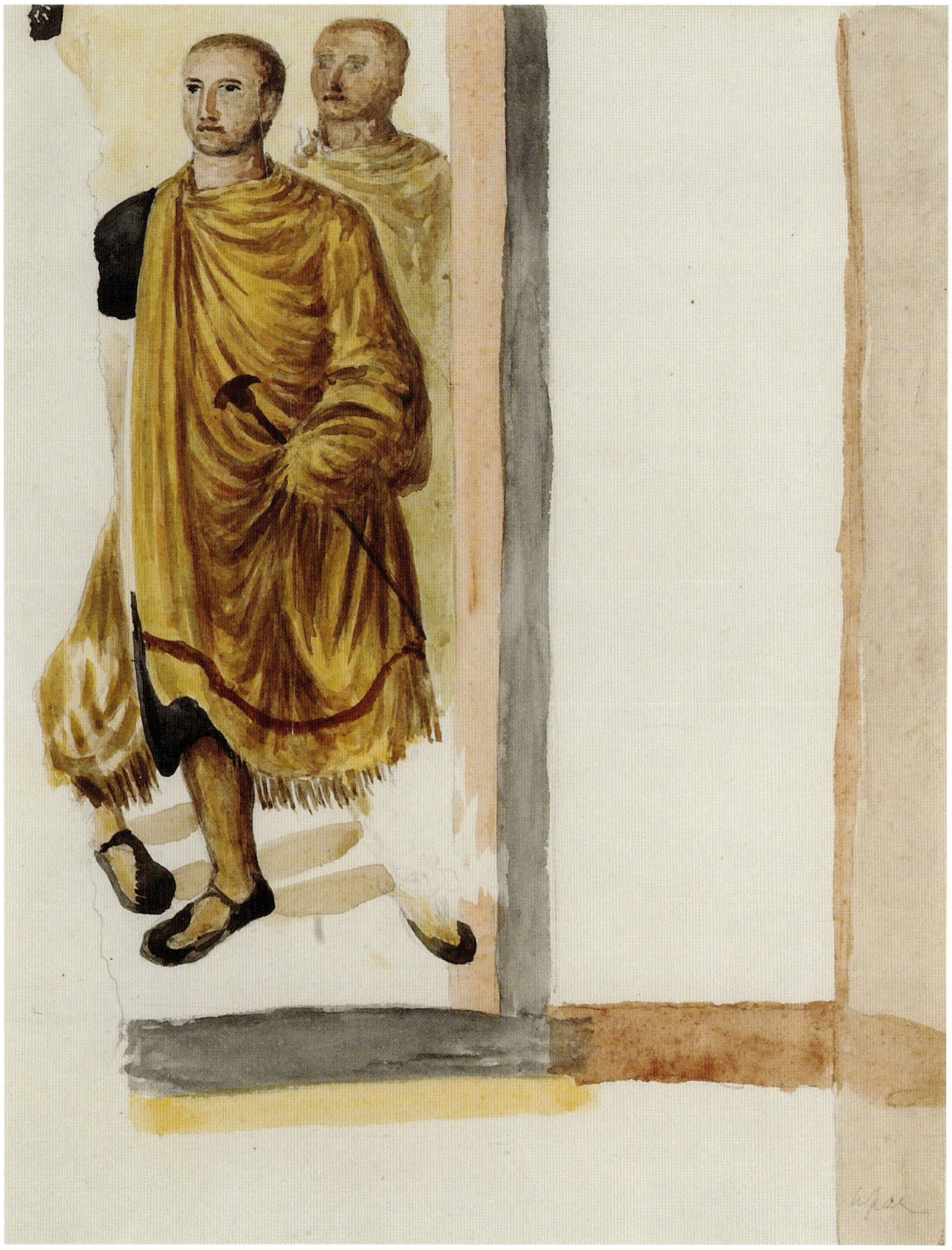

FIGURE 4.7
East of the niche; two figures now lost. Detail from Wilkinson's sketchbook, page 27r.

the room itself and the fragmentary fresco groups and show accurately their state of preservation soon after they were first uncovered. His details of both figural images and decorative motifs painted on the north, east, and south walls are a unique record of sections that have since disappeared. Among these are groups of figures on the south wall to the west of the niche, now badly damaged; figures east of the niche now lost (figures 4.7 and A.2); and the legs and feet on both parts of the north wall, now also lost (see figure A.2, lower), the now badly abraded east wall scene, and most of the imitation opus sectile dado patterns.

Wilkinson wrote various notes beside the sketches, recording insights about dating the frescoes and providing clues for when the room was excavated (see figure A.7). Two notes under the panorama of the imperial cult chamber are particularly informative. At first Wilkinson seems to assume the Christian origin proposed by Lane and already accepted and published by himself: "the chamber with niche added by Romans of the 400 or the 600," presumably meaning the fifth or seventh century. Beside this he added a qualification: "If the name of Diocletian is in the i[nscri]ptions they are older."[28] This note seems to refer to another written in ink on the page opposite the colored sketch of the two figures immediately left (east) of the niche, stating that "M. Monier [*sic*] told Mr. Harris that the name of 'Diocletian' was written on the chariot wheels in this fresco."

M. "Monier" is almost certainly Victor Gustave Maunier, a French photographer and antiquities dealer who also served as unofficial French consul in Luxor and oversaw Auguste Mariette's excavations at Denderah, Thebes, and Edfu in his absence.[29] He spent the winters in Luxor, staying in the French House, where the young Heinrich Karl Brugsch visited him in 1853–1854, an encounter that yielded a colorful description in his memoirs.[30] Maunier had obtained a permit from the Khedive Abbas I to excavate in Luxor Temple, and, mentioning Maunier's work, the French photographic periodical *La Lumière* for 1 April 1854 reported: "Authorized by the government to excavate part of these ruins [Luxor Temple] to obtain a more pleasing view, our skilled and learned compatriot has discovered frescoes and copper ornaments of the greatest beauty."[31] This probably refers to an excavation, apparently otherwise unrecorded, in the imperial cult chamber that led to the discovery of the frescoes by Maunier in the winter of 1853–1854. The date would correspond with the timing of the announcement in *La Lumière,* with Sausmarez's watercolor of 1855 and his title "excavated Roman hall," and with Wilkinson's attention to it in 1856, no doubt expecting the early church that he had noted during his earlier years with Lane in Luxor.[32] Unfortunately, no more is known about the copper ornaments reportedly found by Maunier or whether they were related to the imperial cult chamber.

The enigmatic reference to the name of Diocletian on a chariot wheel cannot be verified and, though Wilkinson does not say he saw the name of Diocletian himself, he took the mention seriously enough to include two notes on it. Nevertheless, Wilkinson did not record a chariot in the frescoes, and there is no evidence that either a chariot or the wheels of one had survived among the figures painted to the east of the niche, to which Wilkinson may have related

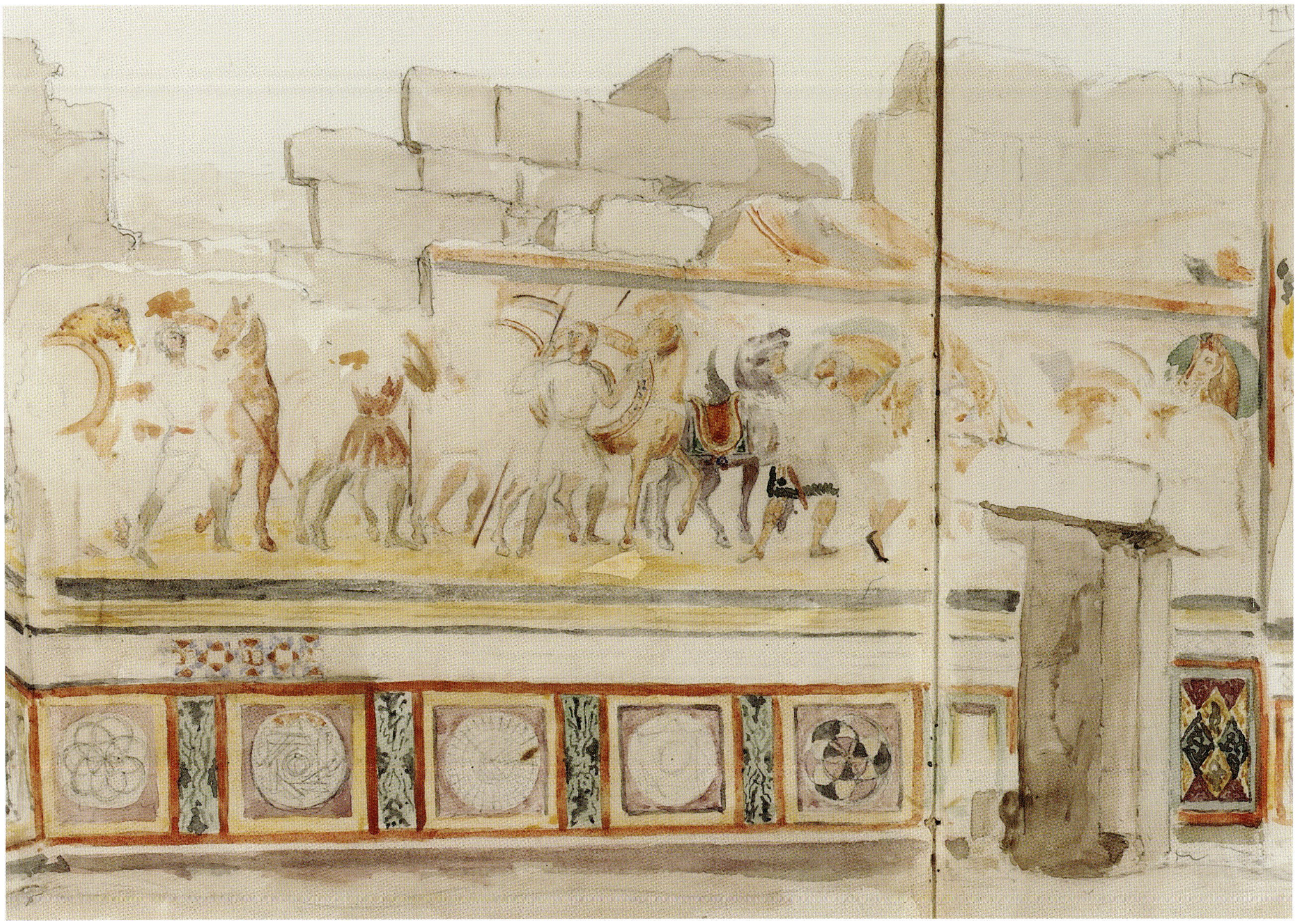

FIGURE 4.8
East wall; horses and soldiers. Detail from Wilkinson's sketchbook, page 25v.

his note, or among the soldiers and horses on the east wall (figures 4.8 and A.1, upper). No other description mentions Diocletian's name, and no trace of it came to light when the paintings were cleaned between 2005 and 2008, during the conservation project. Nevertheless, it is hard to imagine why Wilkinson's informants should have invented an inscription naming Diocletian in particular when the figures painted in the niche had not been identified as specifically tetrarchic, even if some recognized them as "Roman." The inscriptions on the eastern and western tetrastyles that would later assign the Roman alterations to the age of the Tetrarchs were still unexcavated in the archaeological tell around the temple. The consensus, at least among Wilkinson's English-speaking circle, was that the niche and paintings were the remains of a church.

A contemporary visitor was the American William Prime, who was in Luxor during the winter of 1855–1856. He described the imperial cult chamber: "One of the rooms, now open to the sky, was used in early times by the Christians as a chapel for the worship of Christ, and around it are the remains of their paintings on plaster, which covered and preserved the hieroglyphics on the stone walls. . . . And while early Christians defaced and destroyed much which they regarded as idolatrous and profane, they have preserved much else by covering it with plaster and mud, which being now removed leaves the sculptures as fresh and clear as they were a thousand years ago."[33] It could be construed that even as soon as they had been discovered, the frescoes were being removed without record to reveal the pharaonic reliefs behind, in which case the chariot wheels and the emperor's name may have been among the early casualties.[34]

Wilkinson went to Egypt on this tour to record Christian monuments. The sketchbook containing the imperial cult chamber also preserves drawings of the Red and White Monastery churches near Sohag and churches near Naqada, which he had visited on his way to Luxor.[35] In his earlier account of Luxor Temple, he describes the imperial cult chamber, observing that the door leading to the sanctuary "was closed by the Christians, who cut the niche of their altar in its place."[36] His initial fifth- or seventh-century dating in the 1856 sketchbook note supports this view, and another note in the sketchbook relates the designs in the imitation opus sectile dado to "mosaics of apses—catacombs" and may thus also relate to an assumed Christian connection. But the notes about Diocletian show that Wilkinson was prepared to question this identification. His sketchbook, however, was to remain unpublished and virtually forgotten until almost a century later, when Monneret de Villard discovered it and published an authoritative interpretation of the imperial cult chamber that finally established its tetrarchic origin.[37] Thus, although Wilkinson's notes cast doubt on the Christian interpretation, his suggestion of an earlier, imperial Roman date seems to have made no impression on the contemporary and later response to the imperial cult chamber and the frescoes.

Sausmarez's amateur watercolor contrasts strikingly with Wilkinson's detailed annotated drawings, yet it is ironic that both of these, the first records of the room known to have been made following its excavation, remained unavailable to scholars for so long afterward. Having been one of the pioneer Egyptologists while living at Thebes with Lane, Hay, Bonomi, Burton, and others during the 1820s and 1830s, Wilkinson drifted away from the developing field of nineteenth-century Egyptology in his later years.[38] Nevertheless, his contribution was not entirely lost. Murray's first handbook for travelers to Egypt, published in 1847, and in later editions, was written mostly by Wilkinson and preserves his insights into the identity of the imperial cult chamber. The 1873 edition states:

> Between this part [the sanctuary] and the great columnar hall is one of the old chambers, measuring 34 ft. 6 by 57 ft. 1, with a semi circular niche. The walls are covered in frescos of late Roman time; and it was evidently a court of law with the usual tribunal, in which are painted three figures larger than life wearing the toga and sandals. The centre one holds a staff or scepter (scipio) in the right hand and a globe in the left; and near him was some object now defaced. The other two figures have each a scroll in one hand. On the walls to the right and left are the traces of figures, which are interesting from their costume; and on the side-wall to the E. are several soldiers with their horses, drawn with great spirit. The colors are much damaged by exposure, and the frescos can hardly be distinguished. They probably date after the age of Constantine. The costumes are remarkable; and some of the men wear embroidered upper garments, tight hose, and laced boots, or shoes tied over the instep [see figure A.4]. The false wainscot, or dado, below is richly colored in imitation of porphyry and other stones incrusted in patterns, and is better preserved than the frescos of the upper part, where the old gods of Egypt in bas-relief have outlived the paintings that once concealed them. There appear to be traces of a small cross at one side of the tribune, and the figures have a nimbus round their heads, but without any of the character of Christian saints. Nor was the nimbus confined to saints by the early Christians.[39]

Like the name of Diocletian on chariot wheels, the "small cross" cannot be substantiated. A cross in a rectangular frame is drawn in pencil beside the left shoulder of Wilkinson's sketch of the emperor figure on the right (west) of the group in the niche, but the feature is more likely to represent a *signum* (see figure A.5). Georg Ebers, in his description of the imperial cult chamber, mentions Greek inscriptions "which have been found near them [the paintings]"; Friedrich Wilhelm von Bissing, referring to Ebers and to Wilkinson's text in *Murray's Handbook*, mentions Greek texts and the "traces of a small cross painted at one side of the tribune," doubtless referring to the design noted by Wilkinson inside the right edge of the niche.[40] The references to Greek texts are vague, and none has been documented. They might have been Coptic graffiti, in which case the name of Diocletian could have been part of a date in the Coptic "Era of Diocletian."[41] A date written thus occurs in a medieval graffito in the Red Monastery church near Sohag.[42]

By the time Sausmarez and Wilkinson were in Luxor in the mid-1850s, Maxime du Camp (in Luxor 1849–1851), Félix Teynard (1851–1852), John Shaw Smith (1851–1852), Robert Murray (1852–1853), and John Beasly Greene (1853 and 1855) had made the first photographic prints of Luxor Temple.

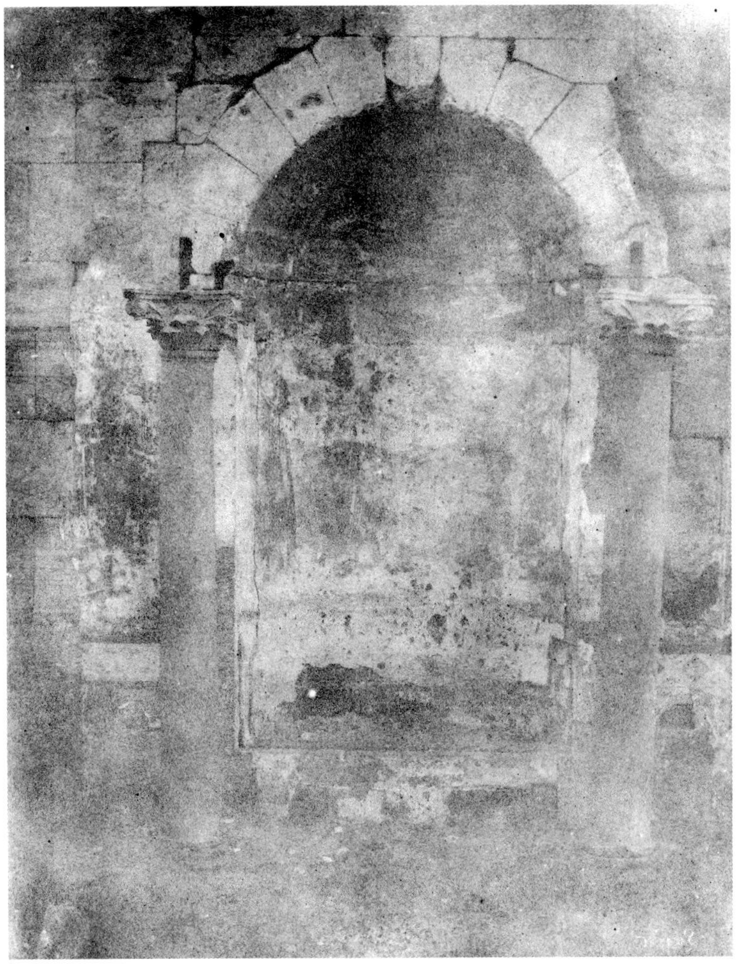

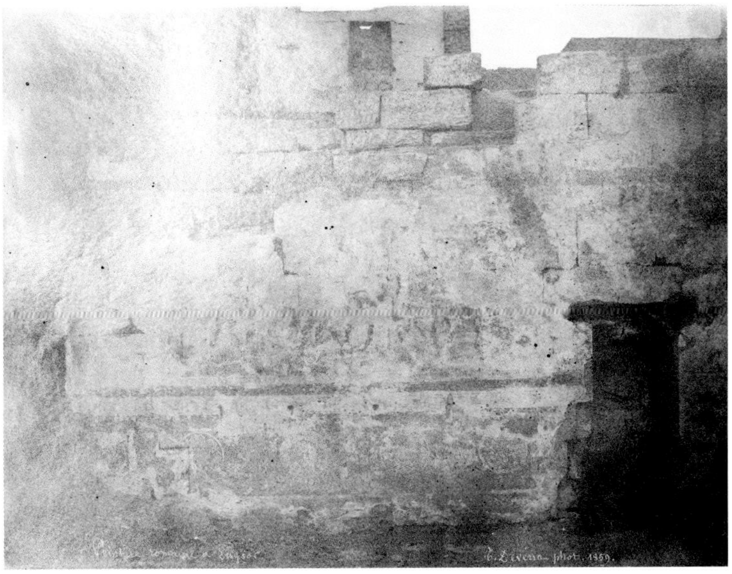

FIGURE 4.9
(top) Devéria's photograph of the niche, 1859.

FIGURE 4.10
(bottom) Devéria's photograph of the east wall, 1859.

Greene had also excavated at Medinet Habu and carried out the first photographically recorded archaeological work there.[43] Among them they created an extraordinarily valuable archive of images documenting Thebes, both east and west, in the mid-nineteenth century. Inadvertently, they were also recording the transition that was changing Luxor from traditional village into tourist town. Yet, for all that Luxor Temple was so avidly photographed, the early photographers recorded an exasperatingly limited range of views. Until the late 1880s, when the interior of the temple was cleared and made accessible, almost all photographs of the temple were taken from the outside.[44] Among the numerous mid- and later nineteenth-century photographs, very few have been found of the imperial cult chamber. The earliest known are two photographs by Théodule Devéria taken in 1859.[45] The image of the niche and granite columns was taken from the mounds outside the north entrance. It shows the paintings of the emperors in the niche and the room excavated to floor level at the bases of the columns (figure 4.9). The other photograph shows the whole of the east wall down to floor level with the doorway leading into the eastern side rooms at the right of the picture (figure 4.10). The paintings of soldiers and horses are visible together with well-preserved sections of the imitation opus sectile below. At the top of the photograph, just behind the east wall, houses built on the high mounds appear, as they do in Wilkinson's sketch. Both these photographs confirm the conditions shown in Sausmarez's and Wilkinson's watercolors, although erosion of the paintings is also clear, particularly on the east wall, as Wilkinson noted in *Murray's Handbook*. They also highlight how the watercolors and photographs complement one another by combining the objectivity of the camera with color details that photographs could not yet convey.

Two slightly later photographs show the niche and granite columns with some of the adjacent wall surfaces. Part of the French House is visible at the top above the niche. Neither image can be dated precisely, although one, if not both, was taken by Antonio Beato and therefore after 1862, when he opened his studio in Luxor, but before 1885, when the French House was removed (figure 4.11).[46] The condition of the frescoes close to the niche confirms Sausmarez's and Wilkinson's watercolors. Roughly one meter of debris, however, had accumulated nearly to the top of the platform below the niche since Devéria photographed it in 1859. One of these images was later reworked into an engraving, embellished with local color by adding a "native" and his donkey; it appeared as a plate in a popular series of volumes entitled *Picturesque Palestine, Sinai and Egypt* and as a postcard (figure 4.12).[47]

An engraving by Bernhard Fiedler, who was in Luxor in 1854–1855 and again in 1865–1866, offers a further mid-century glimpse and corroborates the evidence cited above.[48] The whole of the imperial cult chamber is seen from the west, framed by the columns of the Amenhotep III portico on the left; the outlines of the still-buried western side rooms are in the foreground, and the south wall with the niche is to

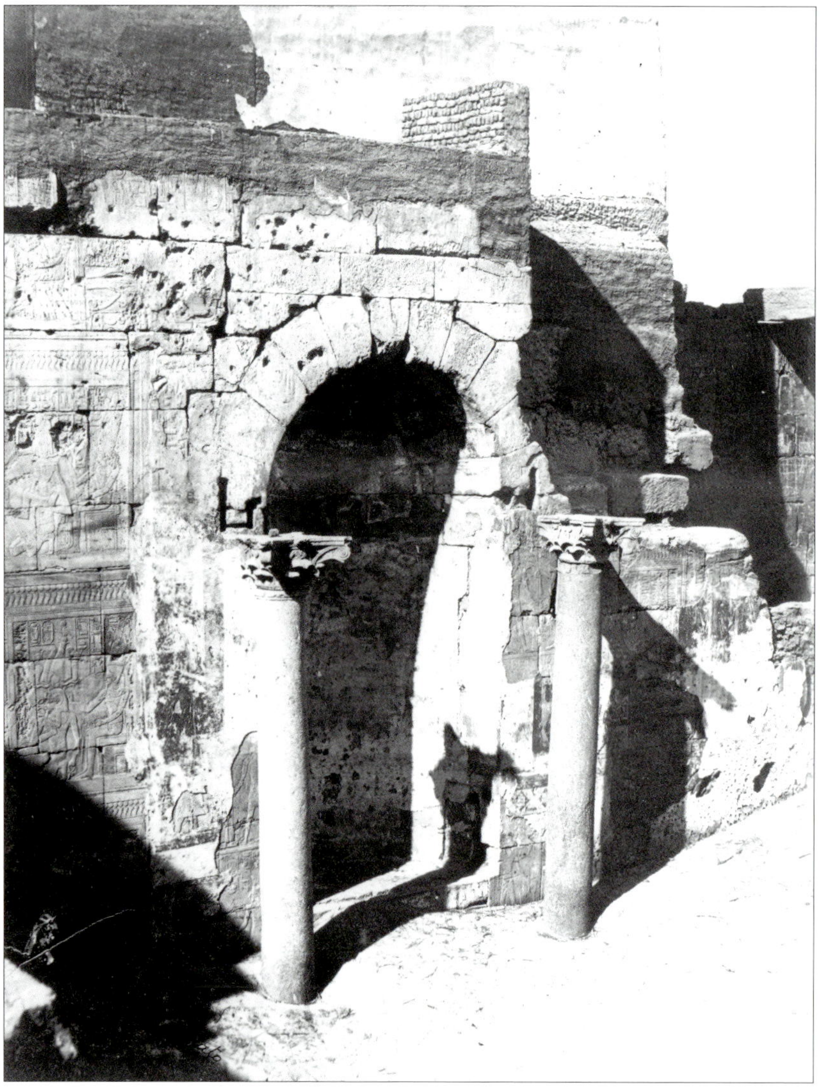

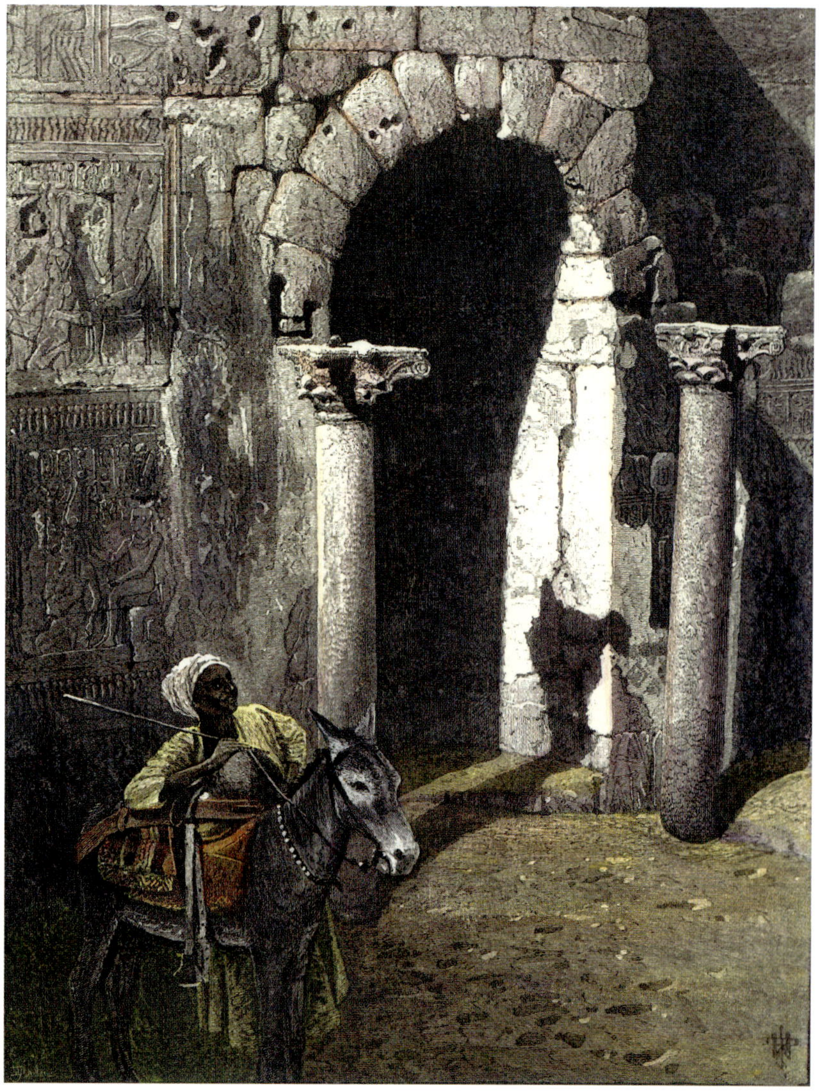

FIGURE 4.11
(left) Photograph of the niche by Antonio Beato, ca. 1880.

FIGURE 4.12
(right) Colored engraving by William Jay Dana after Antonio Beato's photograph of the niche.

the right (figure 4.13). The north, east, and south walls; the niche; and the two granite columns are all visible, cleared to floor level, perhaps indicating a date during Fiedler's first visit in the 1850s, before the room had started to fill again. The impression is of a pit excavated in the heart of the temple. Debris partly fills the colonnades of the Amenhotep III portico, at the upper right over the niche is the wall of the French House, and above and behind the east wall is the house shown in the earlier images. Unlike Wilkinson's general view, Fiedler's drawing shows all four sides of the imperial cult chamber, thereby enlarging the scope of the available documentation and illustrating how much of the north and west walls had already been lost before the accumulating debris had attained its final level.

Fiedler's drawing is the only nineteenth-century image yet found showing the imperial cult chamber in the context of its immediate surroundings, which makes it especially important. But despite Fiedler's accurate portrayal of the architecture, he was not so precise with his rendering of the paintings. Artistic license is obvious where he replaced the soldiers and horses on the east wall with the four emperor figures from the niche, including the partly erased figure second from the right, all trimmed to fit the sloping upper edge of the wall. The imitation opus sectile dado is reduced to an impressionistic and fanciful sketch of patterns in three registers. Fiedler combined the romantic and the documentary in the spirit of the Orientalist genre, but his work is still a significant record of the condition of the site in the mid-nineteenth century. It shows the open room surrounded by the mounds, pigeon towers, and houses that still filled the temple as it would have appeared to a visitor standing on the mounds against the western side of

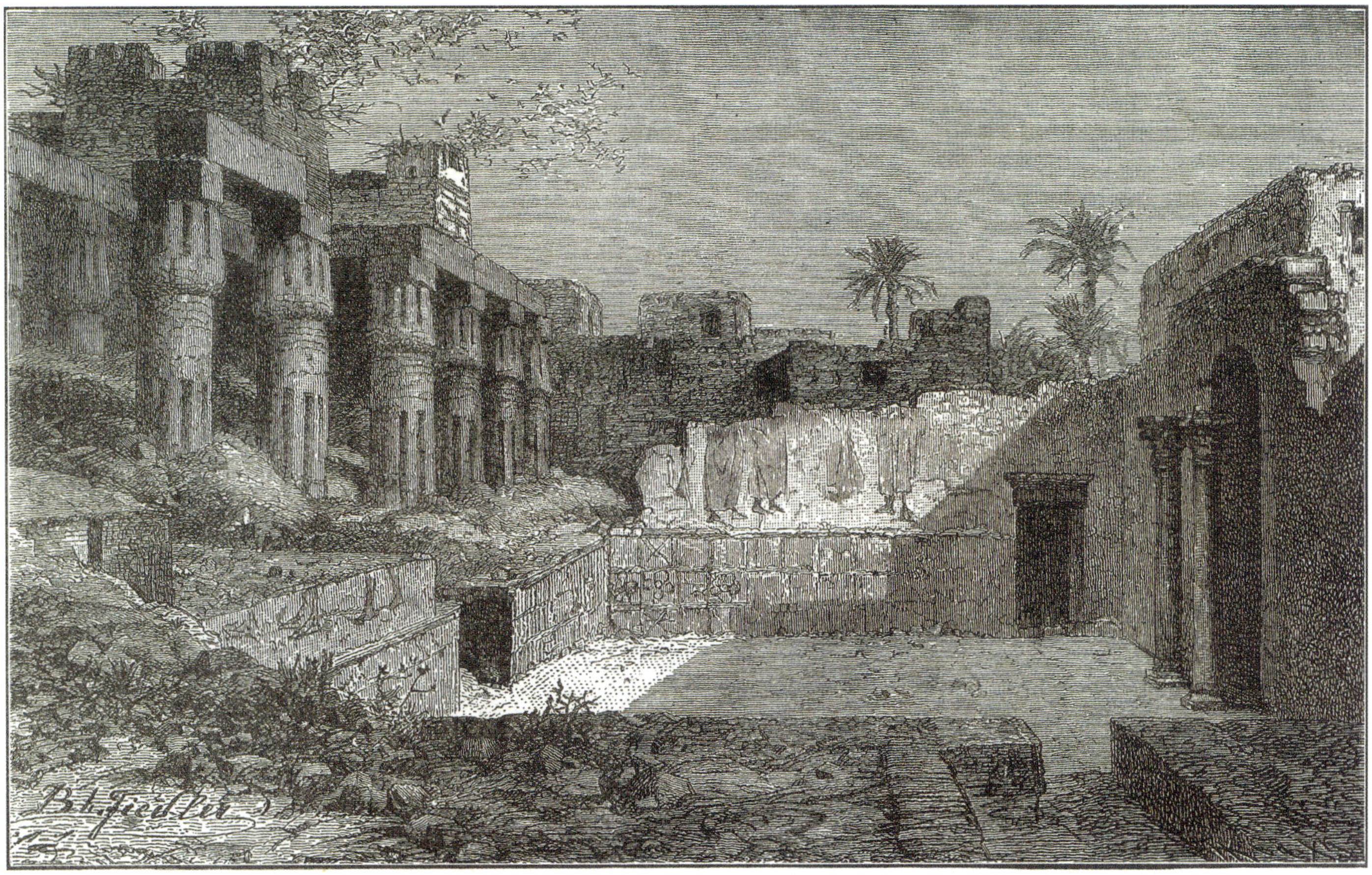

REMAINS OF CHRISTIAN CHURCH IN THE TEMPLE AT LUXOR.

FIGURE 4.13
Engraving after a drawing by Bernhard Fiedler of the imperial cult chamber, seen from the west.

the temple and looking in before the rest of the temple was cleared around it.[49]

Photographers, unlike artists, found it hard to romanticize and edit, although figures were posed and views selected for their effect, often emphasizing exotic and picturesque aspects of what others saw as impoverished and squalid. From its beginnings, photography connected with archaeology. John Beasly Greene's excavations at Medinet Habu in 1853 were the first to be photographically documented, and the imperial cult chamber at Luxor was almost certainly excavated by the photographer Maunier in 1853–1854. Apart from the works of Sausmarez, Wilkinson, and Fiedler, the most comprehensive record of this phase in the history of Luxor, the temple, and the imperial cult chamber is the enormous visual record produced by photographers and the engravings made from their works for postcards and book and magazine illustrations. As the town overwhelmed the temple, their work incidentally documented a conservation issue of enormous magnitude. This important and early example of "conservation through documentation" forms a primary reference source as, by the end of the nineteenth century, a large portion of the archaeological landscape that had been familiar to every visitor and had formed the background of community life for generations would be eliminated from the cultural geography of Luxor, and the chief record is in the surviving photographs. Clearing the temple and the surrounding area from 1885 onward, initiated by scholars and supported by the authorities, continued through the twentieth century with direct consequences for how the temple has been perceived, displayed, and conserved.

A MONUMENT ON DISPLAY

The rapid growth of Luxor over the next twenty-five years resulted in the temple becoming progressively more inaccessible, overwhelmed by the daily activities of the inhabitants. New houses reoccupied the ancient settlement mounds in and around the temple where they were safely elevated above the level of the annual Nile flood. Day-to-day activities threatened the fabric of the temple. Rubbish dumping and constructions abutting the architecture endangered the ancient structures (figure 4.14). In Daressy's words, the local people had turned the temple into "*un réceptacle d'ordures,*"

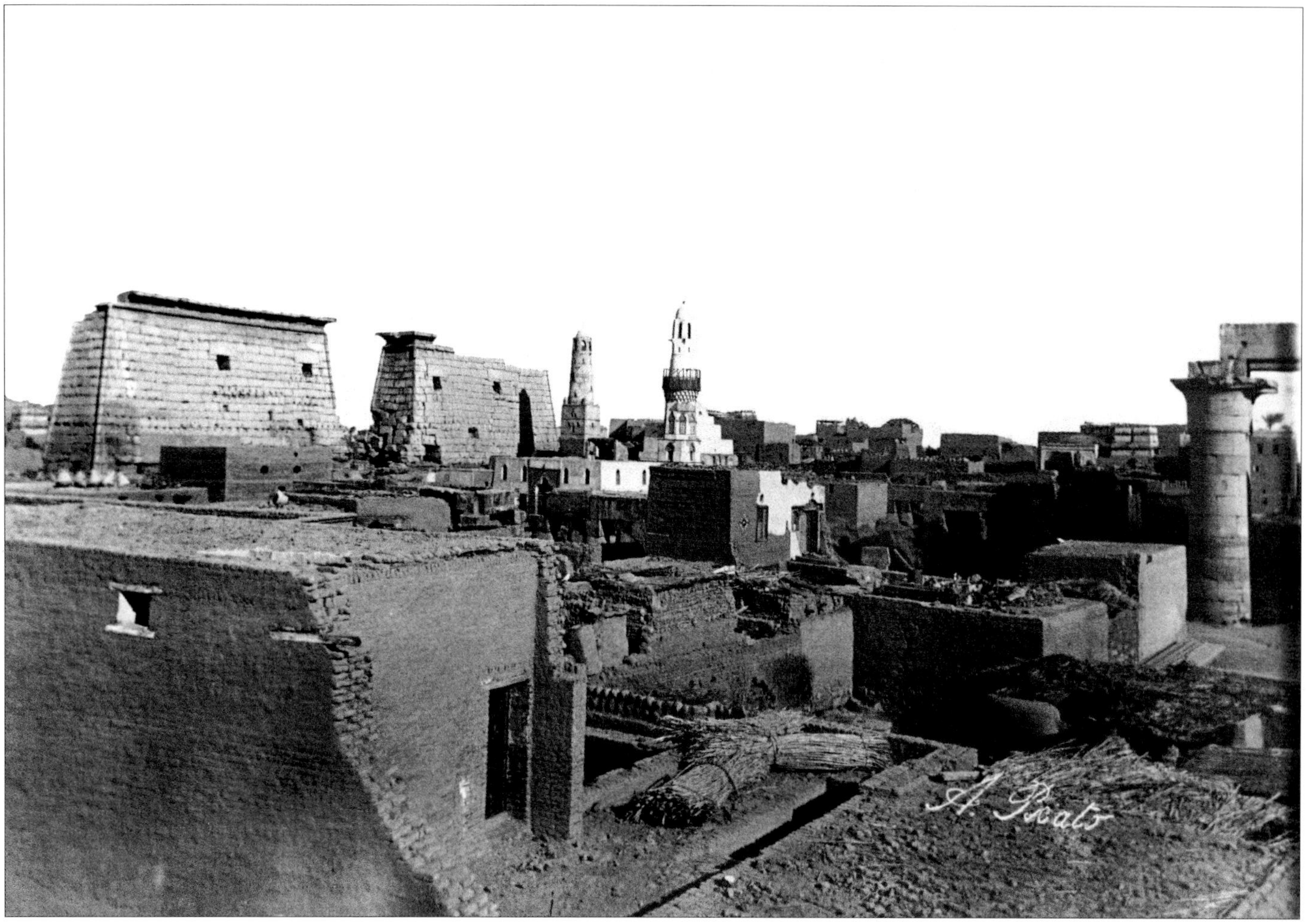

FIGURE 4.14
Luxor Temple and the town ca. 1880, photographed by Antonio Beato.

echoing Lane's comment of 1827 about the interior of the barque shrine room.[50] Amelia Edwards, writing in 1873–1874, was even more graphic: "All the sordid routine . . . was going on amid winding alleys that masked the colonnades and defaced the inscriptions of the Pharaohs. To trace the plan of this part of the building was then impossible."[51] By the 1870s modern Luxor had come into being, and the town, the ancient settlement, and the temple ruins were inseparable. They coexisted in a living archaeological landscape in which the physical remains of the past and the active present encompassed the interests of local people, foreign settlers, and visitors from enormously differing backgrounds. The "trophies of science" and "spoils of history"[52] were connected to a developing interest in accurate recording and documentation by and for interested people, some of whom came to see for themselves, and many more who were content to be armchair enthusiasts. Scholars and informed visitors alike realized that the preservation of the temple was jeopardized by the activities of the inhabitants and by uncontrolled admission for visitors, many of whom were callous enough to want to carve off their own souvenirs or otherwise deface the walls.[53] The buried parts of Luxor temple represented an immense archive of hidden information, and the expansion of the town restricted access to more than just the remains above ground (figure 4.15).

In 1881 Gaston Maspero, director of the Antiquities Service, formulated a plan to be enacted by the Ministry of Public Works to reveal the temple "in its actual state."[54] Excavations began on 5 January 1885. After a hiatus caused by local resistance to enforced property sequestration and demolition, work resumed the following year when the Antiquities Service allowed farmers to take the *sebakh* (organic deposits filling the temple) to spread as compost on their fields and simultaneously to expedite the clearance at minimal cost.[55] By 1894 the interior of the temple had been cleared down to a ground surface that corresponded to the New Kingdom pavements. In the same year Daressy wrote that "the clearance of the temple of Luxor is now finished, save for the north-east part still occupied by the Mosque of Abu al-Hajjaj."[56] But as soon as the archaeological tell was removed, the temple was flooded

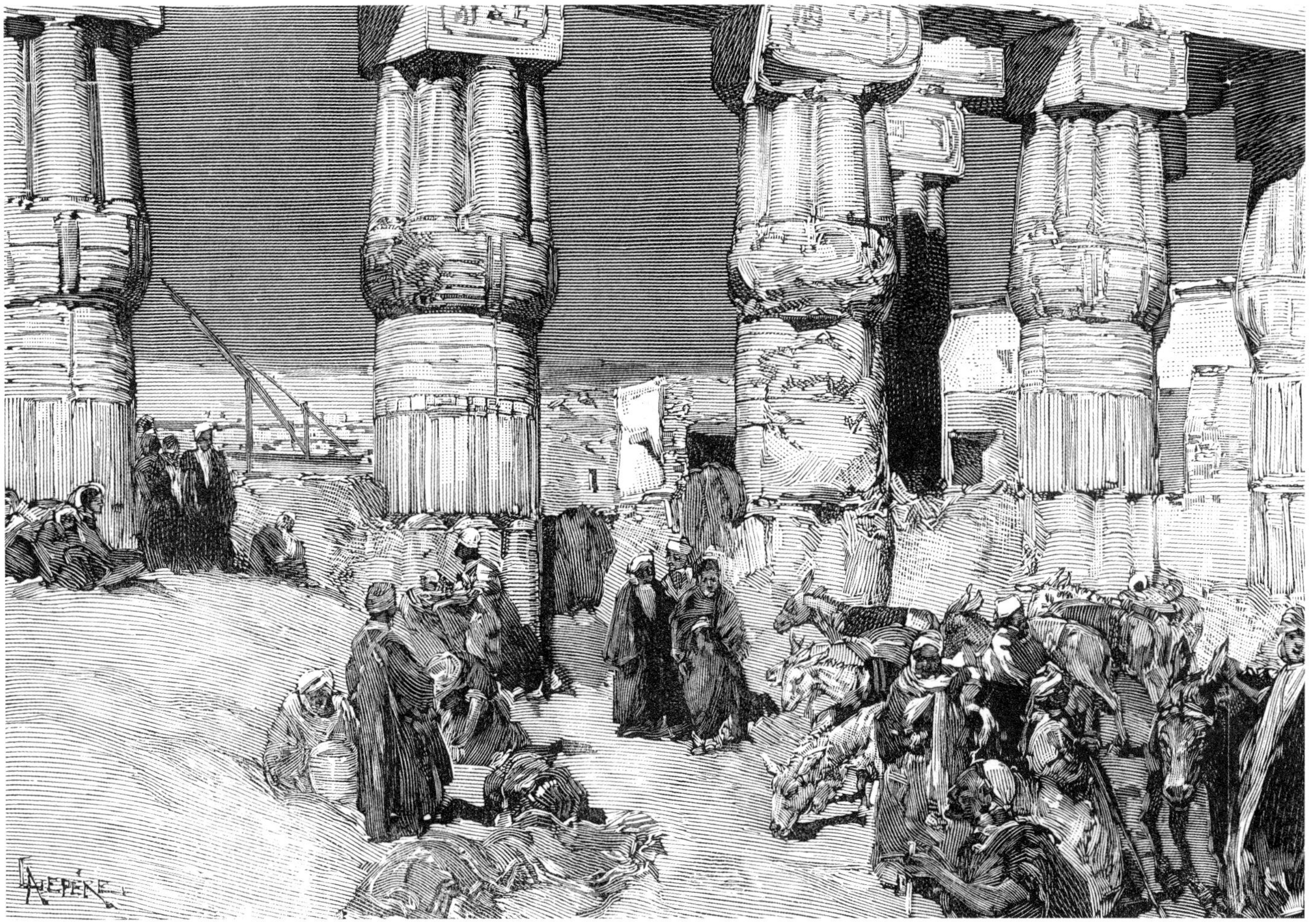

FIGURE 4.15
The police station and government storehouses in 1884. Detail from *Le Monde Illustré,* 1885, by Auguste-Louis Lepère, after a photograph by Antonio Beato.

by the summer inundation of the Nile (figure 4.16). Daressy explained that it was necessary to let the water wash the salt efflorescence from the newly exposed stone masonry, clearly describing a serious conservation issue instigated by the clearance of the surrounding mounds.[57] Soon afterward, further clearances to the west of the temple on the Nile side removed houses and archaeological deposits as far as the riverbank. An embankment was formed with the debris to isolate the temple from the river, creating the Nile Corniche to form the edge of the site, but annual summer flooding of the temple continued well into the twentieth century.

The decision to remove the modern town and underlying settlement remains from the temple area resulted in a spectacular instance of "heritage cleansing," as the community was cleared away from the site for academic and touristic interests. It served political and colonial agendas that were not articulated as such at the time; they have since been recognized and examined and described in detail in the context of the modern application of this approach to heritage management in the Luxor area.[58] Maspero and his contemporaries justified the scheme as a much-needed conservation measure to save the temple from further damage by the local inhabitants living among the ruins and to make it available to tourists and scholars. Even after the first clearance phase, the temple was still overlooked by the houses of the townspeople (figure 4.17). Rubbish dumping persisted as the excavated temple was turned into a useful refuse pit by people who had been hostile to the sequestration and demolition of houses among the temple ruins. Further work to protect the temple from accumulating refuse was necessary in 1905–1906.[59]

Even though the imperial cult chamber had been excavated some thirty-five years previously, it had partly refilled with debris almost a meter deep in front of the niche, as shown in the pre-1885 photograph (see figure 4.11). Grébaut, in his summary of the work of clearing the southern part of the temple, specifically mentions that "the large hall converted into a chapel by the Copts, to the north of the sanctuary, was cleared to the ancient floor."[60] This can mean only the imperial cult chamber. He continues, "Four new rooms converted into sacristies by the first Christians came to light

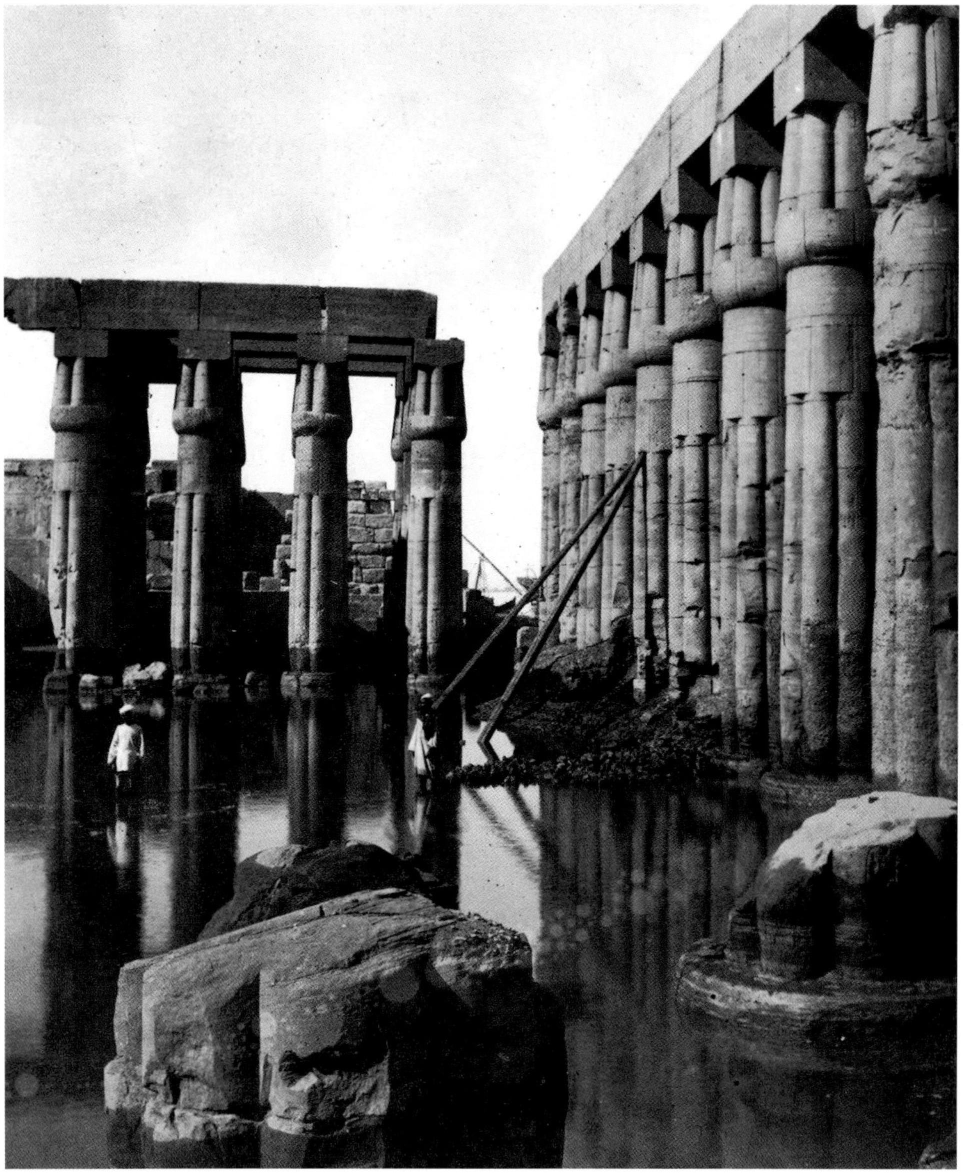

FIGURE 4.16
Amenhotep III court during the annual inundation, looking toward the imperial cult chamber. Photo by Antonio Beato, ca. 1900.

under the mounds," referring to the three eastern side rooms and the western side room left uncleared in the 1850s. This corresponds to the conditions shown by Bernhard Fiedler in figure 4.13.[61] The columned portico of Amenhotep III in front of the imperial cult chamber was also cleared at this time, and the statue base of Constantine, identified as an altar "inscribed in barbarous Latin," was found in situ where it still stands today, on the east side of the central axis between the two columns closest to the entrance of the imperial cult chamber (see figure 2.6).[62]

As early as the 1890s Daressy lamented the poor condition of the Roman wall paintings, adding, "These frescoes seem to have been highly accomplished and would have provided a good example of Roman art in decline."[63] Later, in 1917 and 1920, Legrain and Daressy noted that the paintings were in such poor condition that it was hard to recognize the subjects depicted.[64] Daressy suggested that the paintings had been affected by the sebakh that filled the room and by exposure to bad weather, adding, however, "All hope of knowing what they were should not be abandoned because Bouriant had made tracings soon after they were uncovered."[65] Urbain Bouriant was active at Luxor Temple in the 1890s, but, unfortunately, these tracings have not been found. Sausmarez's and Wilkinson's watercolors of the 1850s, with their bold colors and clearly defined figures and designs, show how the lower sections of the paintings were better preserved than the upper zones immediately after they were first uncovered, which implies, contrary to Daressy's suggestion, that the filling material had not been especially destructive and had probably served to protect the wall surfaces while they were still buried. Subsequent exposure to sunlight, the annual Nile inundation, and the weather are more plausible reasons for deterioration.

The worsening condition of the paintings at this time is hard to follow exactly from the sporadic and rather casual observations made by visitors. For example, Michel Jullien[66] mentions noticeable deterioration between his two visits in 1896 and 1901.[67] Johann Georg records von Bissing's reminiscence of how, as a boy of eight years old, he had been taken to Luxor and had seen the frescoes "still completely intact."[68] This would have been in 1880, over twenty-five years after Maunier's excavation of the imperial cult chamber and just before Maspero's clearance. Von Bissing's memory cannot have served him too well, since Wilkinson's copies show substantial losses in 1856 and Devéria's photographs of 1859 show erosion near the upper edge of the east wall frescoes. Despite the obvious damage, however, the impressive scene of horses and soldiers was well preserved when Wilkinson copied it, and enough might have remained to make a lasting impression on von Bissing as a boy.

For the Egyptologists working at Luxor at the time, the Roman plaster layers and paintings hindered complete access to the original Amenhotep III reliefs. Albert Gayet, who was engaged in copying and translating the pharaonic reliefs and texts, wanted access to the walls behind the Roman plaster. It was reasoned that these later frescoes, like the superimposed archaeological layers that had obscured the temple, could be justly removed; he is clear about his attempts to cut the Roman plaster off the walls to reveal the concealed reliefs as part of the ongoing works in the temple in the 1880s and 1890s. Referring to the imperial cult chamber, which he called "the first vestibule," Gayet states that it was "transformed by the Copts into a chapel, most of the decoration has disappeared under superimposed layers of

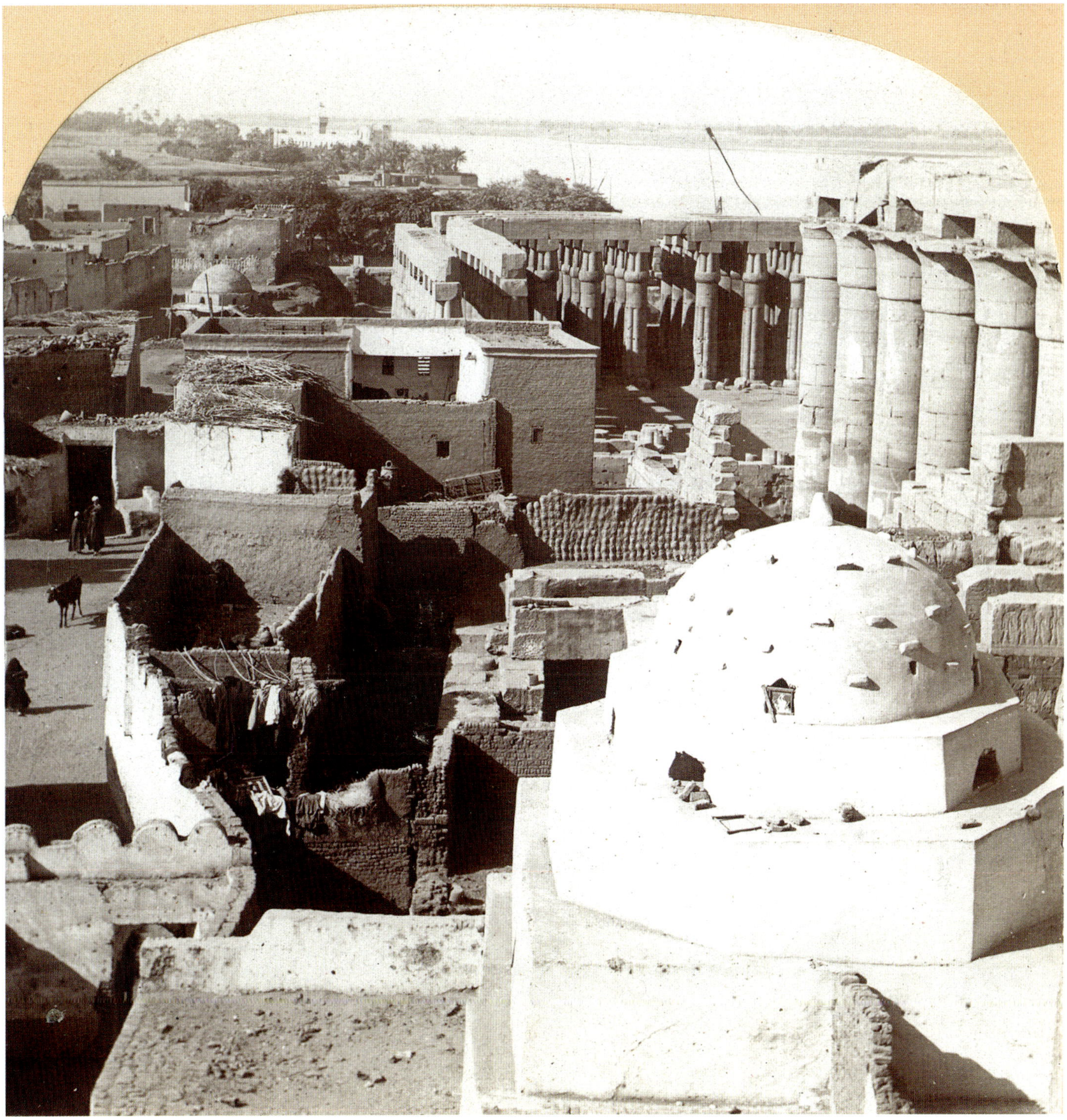

FIGURE 4.17
View south across Luxor Temple from the top of the east tower of the Ramesses II pylon, 1899.

paintings; it is only by causing these to fall off that one can come to distinguish those scenes that formerly decorated the walls."[69] Fortunately for the survival of the remaining frescoes, the underlying masonry was frequently found in an abraded condition where little or no trace of the Eighteenth-Dynasty reliefs was preserved. The work of removing the Roman plaster was halted, but the effects of this "excavation" on the walls can be seen today in the form of large, straight-edged, roughly rectangular lacunae cut out of the Roman plaster. Other areas of the Roman plaster, particularly sections of the imitation opus sectile borders below the figurative scenes and the once well-preserved standing figures on either side of the niche, were removed. The opus sectile patterns and their supporting plaster layers on the lower parts of the walls were undoubtedly also affected by the flooding that followed the clearance of the temple. The photograph of the niche taken before final clearance shows that frescoes recorded by Wilkinson and partly by Sausmarez on either side of the niche were still preserved in situ (see figures 4.6 and 4.7). By the time Beato photographed the music troupe

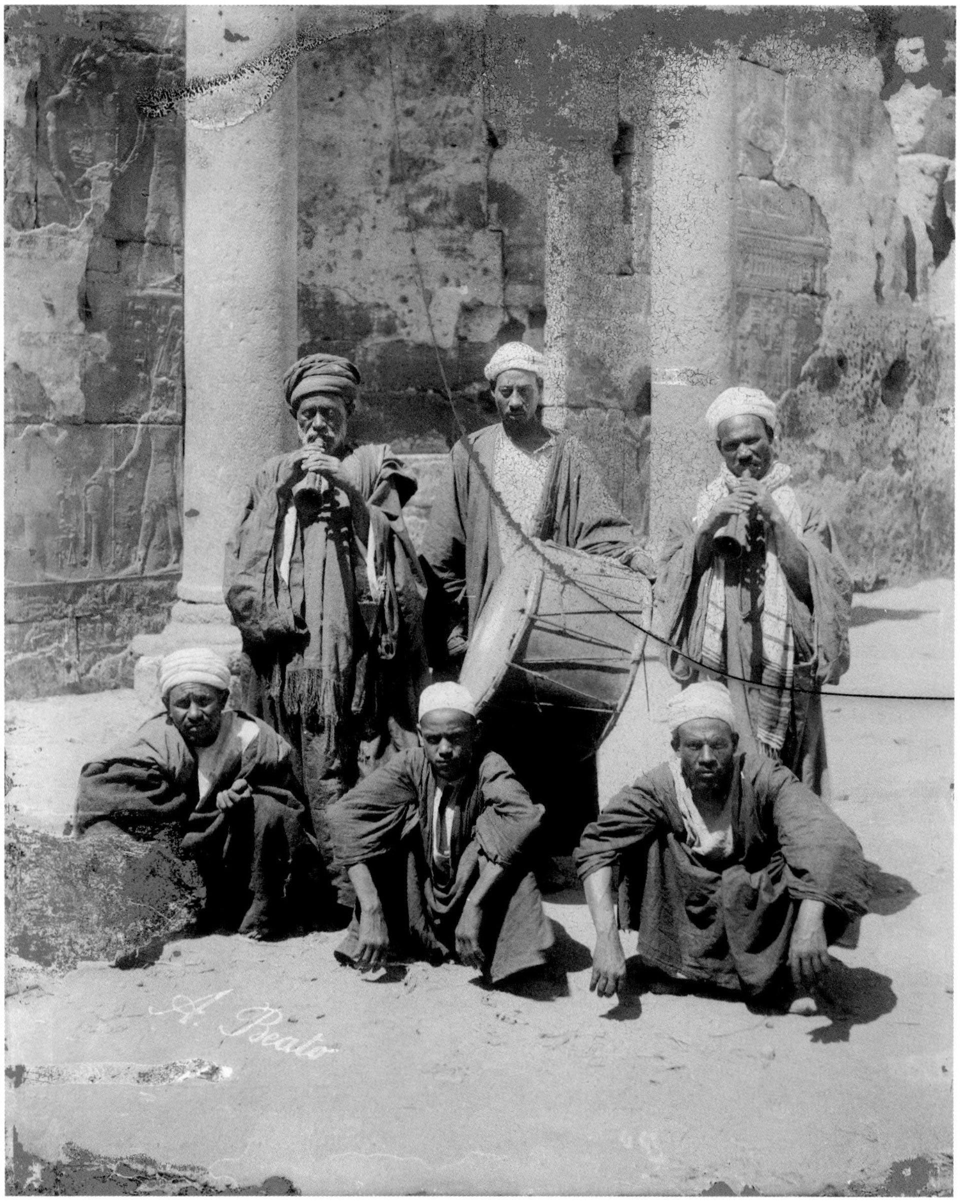

FIGURE 4.18
Musical troupe posed in front of the niche of the imperial cult chamber, photographed by Antonio Beato, ca. 1900.

in front of the niche, some time between the reclearance of the imperial cult chamber in 1887 and his death in 1906, extensive losses had occurred in these areas too (figure 4.18). It is impossible to be sure that all the post-clearance damage to the Roman plaster layers was caused in order to gain access to the underlying reliefs in the work described by Gayet, but most of it probably was, judging by the chronology of the photographs.[70] Michel Jullien's comment that the paintings had noticeably deteriorated between his two visits could refer to his impressions before and after they had been partially removed. None of the detached fragments has been recovered nor any suggestion found that they were saved. Bouriant's tracings mentioned by Daressy might have been intended as the documentation phase preceding a planned scheme to remove the Roman plaster layers, but, as mentioned above, they have not been found.

By the last decade of the nineteenth century, both scholarly opinion and travelers' guidebooks had mostly discarded previous suggestions that the niche, the two granite columns, and the wall paintings were associated with imperial Roman ceremonials. The early Christian origin was generally assumed and persisted even long after the real identification of the remains had been established. In the 1892 edition of Baedeker's *Egypt,* readers were informed: "The ancient entrance to the sanctuary-chambers has here been altered into a kind of apsidal recess, bounded on the right and left by two granite Corinthian columns. The court in front of this was used as a church in later Christian times, and the fine ancient sculptures were covered with lime and gaudily painted in the early Christian style."[71] By 1907 the eleventh edition of *Murray's Handbook Egypt,* "thoroughly revised and brought up to date with numerous additions and revisions" by H. R. Hall, had adopted the Christian interpretation. Most tour guides today still describe the imperial cult chamber to their clients as a church.[72] Well-documented alterations at some pharaonic temples for churches, such as Medinet Habu, Philae, and Wadi al-Sabua, reinforced this explanation, especially since no other example of a temple adapted in the Roman style for Roman imperial use was known (figure 4.19).

Somers Clarke included the imperial cult chamber in his survey of Christian monuments in the Nile Valley and deplored the removal of the painted plaster to reveal the pharaonic reliefs, apparently unaware of Bouriant's tracings as he complained about the failure to document the paintings before their removal.[73] Legrain refers to "a chamber preceding the sanctuary of Amon . . . transformed into a chapel and a niche fitted into the doorway. Two columns made of rose granite, with hard sandstone [*sic*] composite capitals, decorate the doorjambs, and the old pharaonic reliefs that covered the walls are hidden under a render on which an unknown artist painted large frescoes of which we cannot determine the subject today."[74] Daressy describes the imperial cult chamber as the "Coptic church in the temple" and suggests that the niche that divided the temple into two parts was constructed to stop "those who remained faithful to the ancient religion" from accessing the shrine of Amun, adding, "In this case, one could suppose that the establishing of this niche dates back to the first moment of triumphant Christianity."[75]

The most detailed elaboration of the imagined Christian construct is the work of von Bissing, describing the paintings and tentatively identifying some of the subjects.[76] To von Biss-

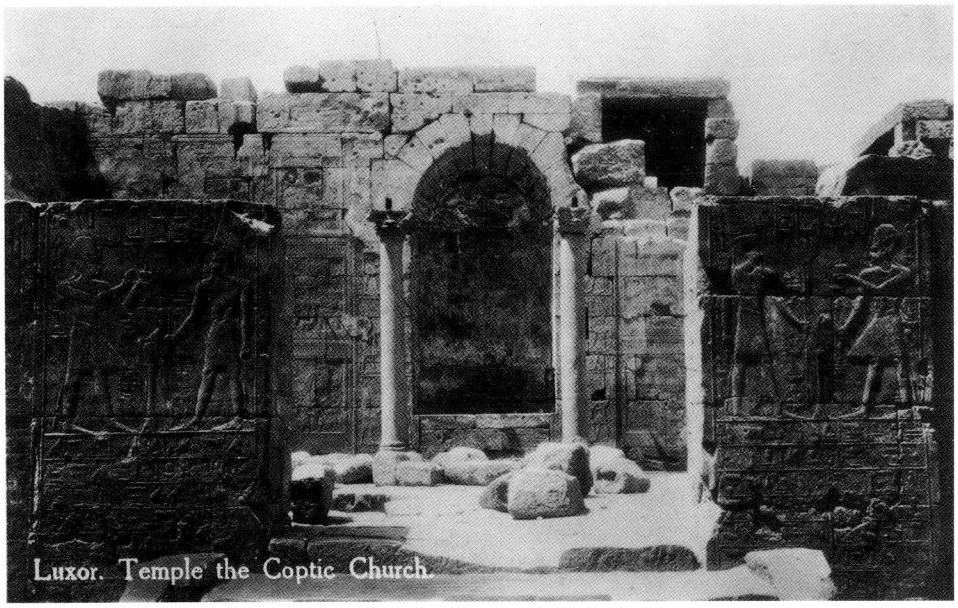

FIGURE 4.19
Postcard of the niche in the imperial cult chamber, from a photograph of 1934.

ing, the horses and soldiers on the east wall suggested the biblical account of the Crossing of the Red Sea (see figure 4.8). In the niche he was tempted to see an image of John the Baptist with Zakaria and Elizabeth and possibly the Virgin Mary, while rejecting Johann Georg's proposal for an Ascension scene here. To date the frescoes, von Bissing compared wall paintings found at the Monastery of Apa Jeremias at Saqqara and the Monastery of Apa Apollo at Bawit,[77] but he admitted that the Luxor paintings are closer in appearance to "Fayyum portraits."[78] Rather than concluding that they might be something other than Christian paintings, he suggested that "it is an antique tradition of the mid-imperial era which lives on here."[79] Notwithstanding his mistaken interpretations, von Bissing was the first to describe the imperial cult chamber coherently as an architectural unit with its adapted architecture and frescoes. His description is important, particularly in the absence of other sources, because it clarifies the condition of the paintings in the 1920s on the basis of his own observations and earlier accounts. The worsening visibility of the frescoes could partly explain von Bissing's errors, although his personal religious faith doubtless influenced what he saw, a view that had been endorsed by scholarly consensus for decades since the clearance of the temple.[80] By fashioning a Christian identity for the whole imperial cult chamber, respected scholars of the nineteenth and twentieth centuries had not only fabricated a spurious monument within the history of the temple but also invented a fictional example of early Christian art in Egypt. This fact illustrates how poorly studied were late antique wall paintings at that time: no reasonable parallels from actual churches could be cited in support of the proposed subjects in the Luxor frescoes. It was not until the importance of the inscriptions on the tetrastyles naming the Tetrarchs had been realized that a more accurate identification was proposed.

Clearance work west and east of the temple uncovered the column bases of the two tetrastyles, in 1916 and 1933, respectively, inscribed for two different iterations of the Tetrarchy (figure 4.20 and also see figures 2.4 and 2.5). Loose blocks bearing Latin inscriptions were also discovered that complemented those in situ on the tetrastyle bases. Together these finds connected the site to a major tetrarchic building phase. Pierre Lacau published these Latin texts in 1934, concluding that there was absolutely no reason for assuming an early Christian church in the converted room because on the surviving plaster "there is neither a single symbol nor a single figure that one can truly say is Christian." After describing the figures painted in the niche, Lacau asked, "Is it not possible to suggest the four emperors? I leave the task of clarifying this point to others. It is a study to be resumed."[81] By the middle of the twentieth century, Lacau's observations were receiving serious attention, although a reluctance to abandon the Christian identification altogether led to a mingling of the two interpretations. William Stevenson Smith, in a digest of excavations carried out at Luxor in 1950, mentions that column drums of Shabako had been found "used to pave the first vestibule of the sanctuary at the south end of the temple in Roman times when the flooring was raised and the building used first as a kind of imperial chamber and later as a Christian church."[82]

Daressy had already noted that the raised floor incorporated reused column drums, but he mistakenly interpreted them as pieces of the dismantled columns that had once stood in the room itself.[83] Several informative and hitherto unpublished photographs show that the imperial cult chamber floor had already been partly excavated in 1934, coinciding with the removal of ancient settlement remains from the east side of the temple (figure 4.21). Some of the granite and sandstone blocks were moved but, despite the scale of the work, its high visibility at the time, and ultimately its irreversibility, this intrusion into the imperial cult chamber floor went virtually undocumented, apart from a few coincidental photographs. These show displaced, rectangular blocks, some leaning against the eastern section of the north wall and, at the bottom of one of these images, a cavity where blocks have been removed. Stone chippings and loose, sandy soil heaped against the inside face of the north wall to the left of the entrance must have come from the excavation. Photographs also reveal that granite blocks to the east and west of the reused Shabako column drums were among the pieces taken up. This is cor-

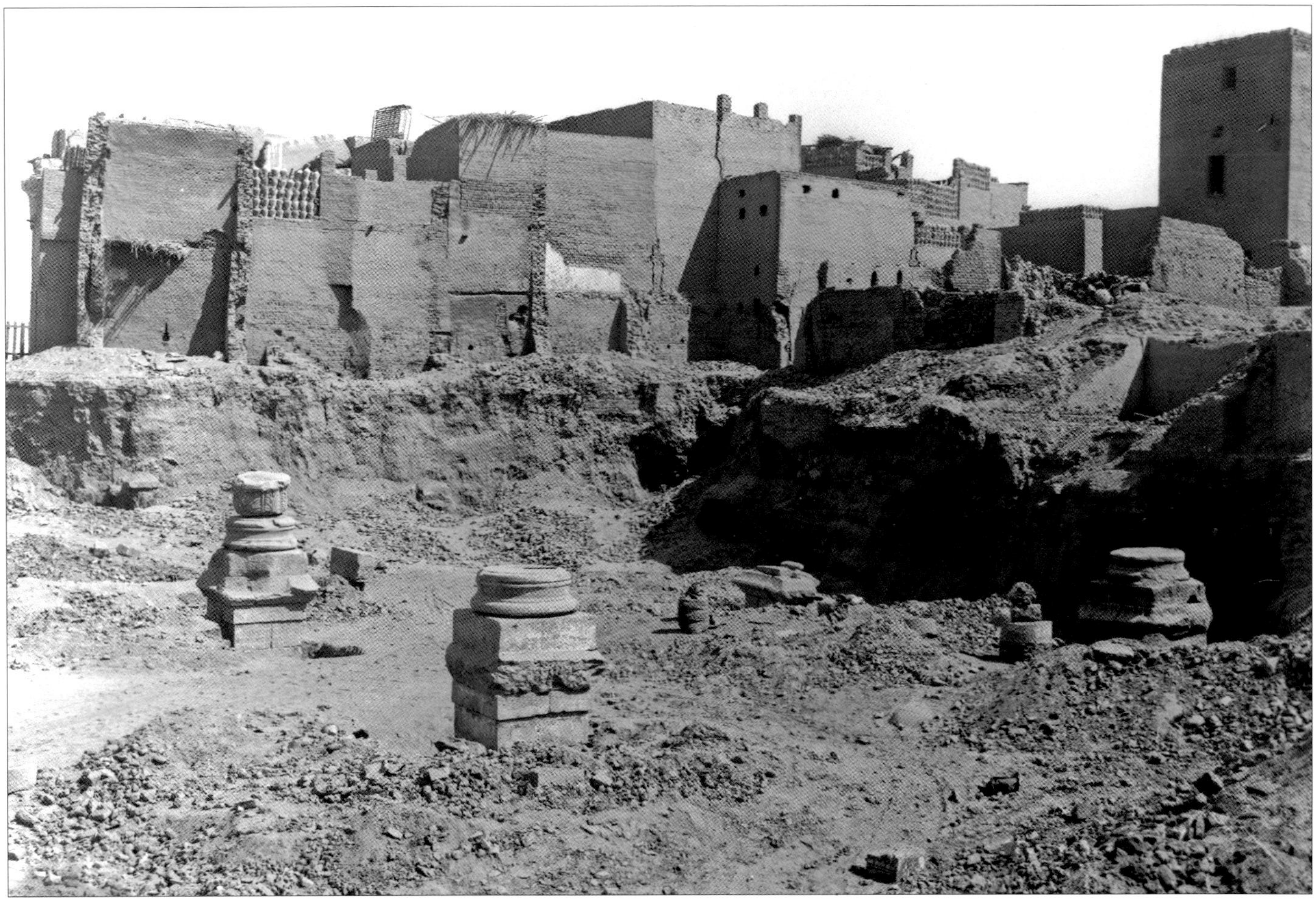

FIGURE 4.20
Excavation of the eastern tetrastyle in 1933.

roborated by two more photographs, one of them made into a contemporary postcard entitled "Luxor. Temple the Coptic Church," in which the distinctive granite blocks with rounded edges are lying on the intact floor in the center of the room (see figure 4.19). The excavation in 1934 was the most intrusive interference since the removal of Roman plaster and paintings from the walls in the 1890s. Its purpose is not known unless it was simply to look for buried inscribed material or to investigate the underlying original pharaonic floor. It is impossible to estimate how many of the floor blocks were taken up, how far this excavation extended into the room, or whether the pavement blocks were replaced in the same configuration as the original. A photograph of the imperial cult chamber taken through the entrance in the north wall, dated 1947, shows the floor reinstated.[84]

It was not until 1950, when the spaces between the column drums were cleaned out to reveal the inscriptions, that the masonry used to raise the floor of the imperial cult chamber was properly identified and documented as reused column drums, bases and capitals, and intercolumnar blocks, all identifiable as fragments of a dismantled kiosk of Shabako.[85] These pieces were concentrated in the central area of the room, while the eastern and western sections of the raised floor were filled with red granite blocks, which Jean Leclant suggested were from the pavement of the same kiosk.[86] Leclant is especially valuable as an eyewitness to an otherwise unpublished excavation. A photograph that he took at the time shows the pavement with the reused Shabako column drums and other recycled masonry in situ.[87] Cleaning the surfaces and spaces between the column drums and adjacent blocks, however, had removed all the packing material between the blocks and eradicated any remaining traces of the Roman floor laid over this foundation, so that it is impossible to know whether the floor of the room was a simple plaster layer, constructed of stone slabs, or a more elaborate inlaid or painted finish.[88] The photograph also shows the bases of both granite columns in front of the niche standing on the reused column drums rather than set into them, which indicates that the reused masonry was a foundation layer used to raise the floor level, not the finished floor surface, which would have been ten to fifteen centimeters higher. Some twenty years later, Deckers published photographs showing the condition of the floor after examining it to check for evidence of another pair of columns that would indicate the presence of a canopy.[89]

A more drastic intrusion into the historical fabric took place in 1996–1997, irreversibly altering the condition and

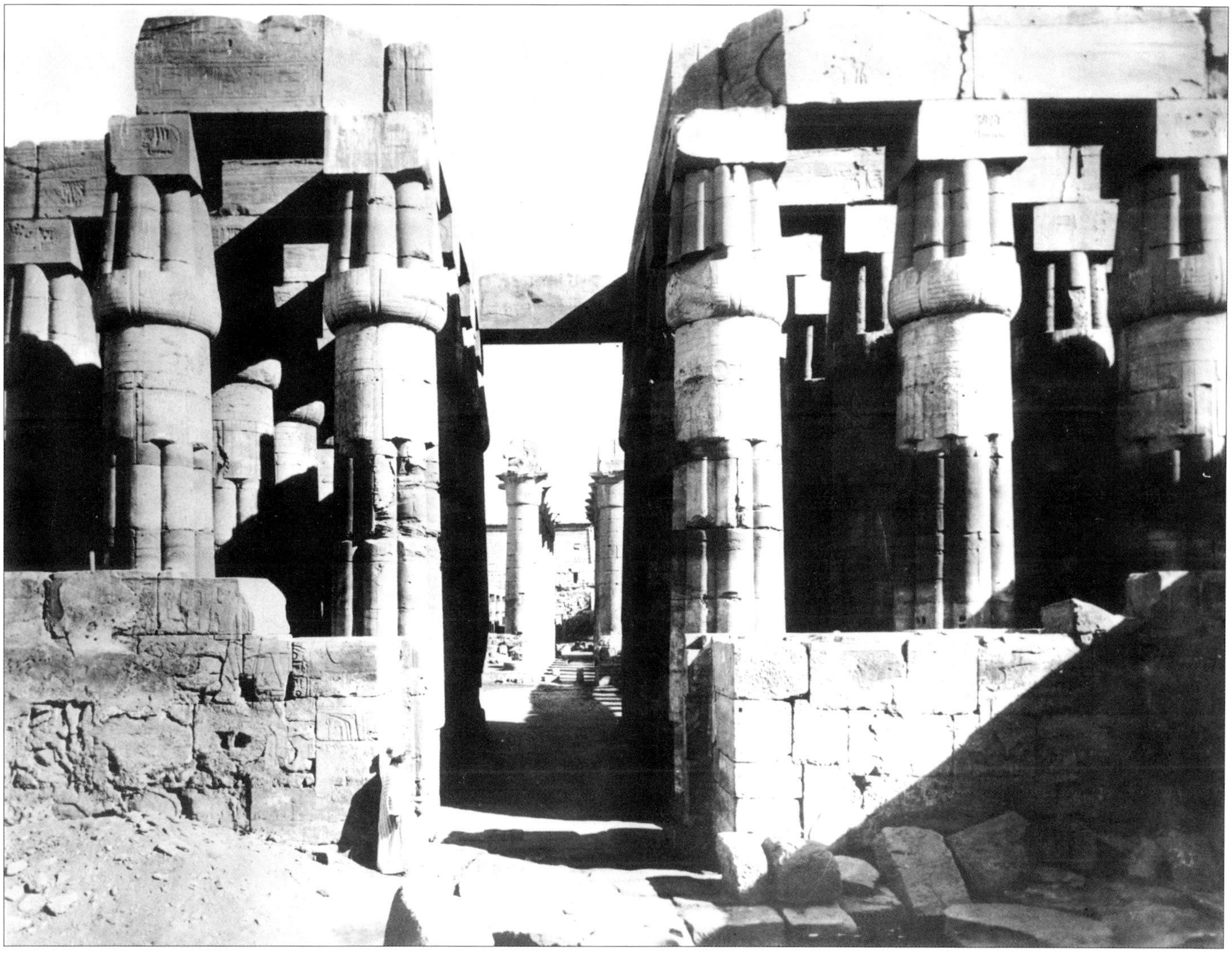

FIGURE 4.21
North wall of the imperial cult chamber, showing displaced floor foundations during the 1934 excavation, dated 11 October 1934.

character of the floor (figure 4.22). All the reused column drums inscribed for Shabako were removed to the block storage yards on the east side of the temple. The original Eighteenth-Dynasty pavement blocks were found to be in situ and well preserved under the protective layer of Roman masonry. The cavity created was subsequently filled with modern stone paving set slightly lower than the granite blocks remaining in place. Photographs taken at the time show the void in the center of the room where the reused Shabako elements had been located.[90] Today, gravel fills the parts where stones were not replaced.

Concerns were being raised in the mid-1990s about the observable effects of groundwater in the temple foundations and salt damage on the lower courses of stonework, which prompted investigations into subsurface conditions. Whether there was evidence of this sort to justify removing the Roman floor is not known. It is more likely that this measure was carried out because of the increasing erosion caused by the sudden rise in the number of tourists walking on the Roman pavement, introducing a risk that needed to be addressed. In response, the endangered parts were removed and the cavity left in the floor filled with modern slabs; the granite blocks on either side were either left alone or in some instances reset. They appear today mostly as shown in Leclant's published photograph. By destroying the Roman construction and replacing it with a modern pavement that does not reflect the distinctive scheme of the Roman reused masonry, however, the original condition was altered irreversibly. A more sensitive solution for preserving the ancient remains would have been reburial of the Roman pavement by installing a modern floor above it. Such a treatment would have protected the original and restored the floor level to that of the finished Roman floor surface, which had once covered the foundations containing the reused Shabako column drums.

Another major modification occurred in 1954, when a doorway was cut through the niche into the offering hall and barque shrine beyond, creating direct access for the first time since the Roman conversion (figure 4.23).[91] Two sandstone blocks with traces of Amenhotep III relief now lying on the

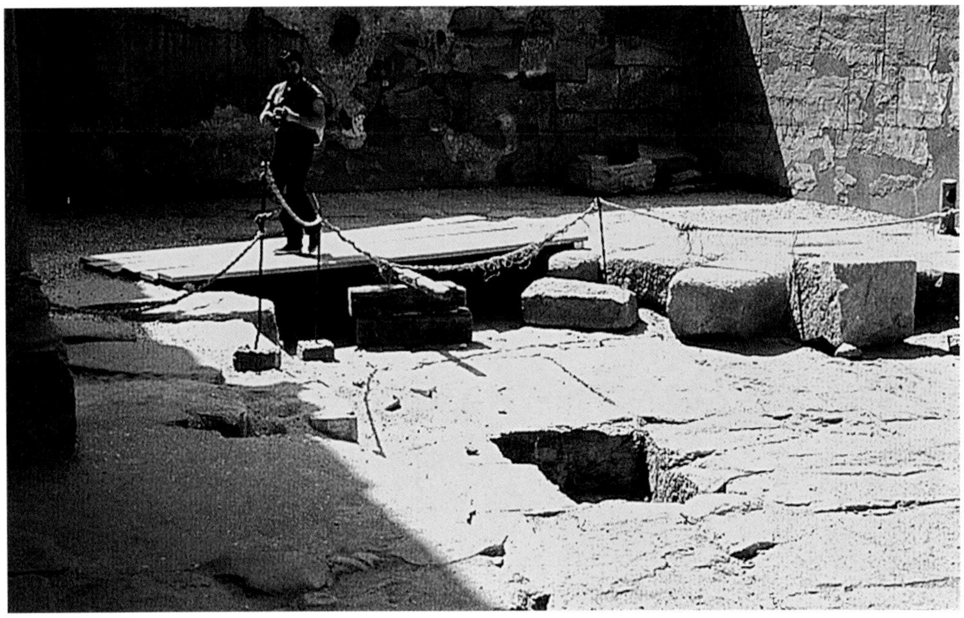

FIGURE 4.22
Excavation of the floor of the imperial cult chamber in 1996–1997.

pavement in the northeast corner of the room seem to be the only pieces removed from the Roman construction of the niche that survive. One piece, carved into an arc matching the curve of the niche, surely derives from the lower course of stonework in the niche. The other may once have been in the wall, forming the platform below the niche.[92]

The new doorway changed both the visual effect and the intention of the niche, destroying its structural integrity while obscuring its originally intended purpose. Initially constructed as a new focus of veneration, the niche now no longer acts as the focal point of the temple or conveys the architectural statement and purpose of the temple in its last phase of cultic use. The doorway, however, was doubtless justified as a partial restoration of what is known to have been the ancient temple builders' original design by reconnecting the two parts of the temple physically divided by the Roman niche—a compromise to reinstate an aspect of older authenticity while simultaneously preserving the later phases of the building. To some degree it fulfilled on the spot what Pococke, Norden, Lepsius, and others had attempted theoretically in their plans. All these operations in the floor and the niche were invasive procedures involving inappropriate restoration, destruction of original fabric, and extensive renewal with modern materials.[93] Today, removing the floor and cutting through the niche would be considered disrespectful to the monument's unique character and to the complexity of the temple's history, but now, almost sixty years later, most visitors and scholars are unaware that the doorway is a modern feature.[94] It has become an accepted part of the structure, integrated as yet another layer of history in the evolution of the site.

Scholarly perception of the imperial cult chamber advanced considerably in 1953, when Monneret de Villard accepted the challenge "to answer the questions so clearly posed by Lacau."[95] He published Wilkinson's watercolors for the first time, using them, together with an extensive description of the site itself, to establish the real significance of the adaptations as a shrine dedicated to the cult of Diocletian and his co-rulers of the Tetrarchy. His review of earlier writers dismantled the Christian construct once and for all.[96] Two photographs published by Monneret de Villard are important for showing the condition of the room in the middle of the twentieth century, especially the worn state of the Roman steps in front of the northern entrance.[97] He refers to Wilkinson's note about the name of Diocletian, accepting that an inscription recording the emperor's name might once have been among the paintings, although he found no trace of it.[98] He also notes Ebers's enigmatic comment mentioning "a few fragments of Greek inscription which have been found near them [the paintings]."[99]

The state of the frescoes in the middle decades of the twentieth century was such that they could be described as "the almost obliterated frescoes at the Temple of the Imperial Cult at Luxor."[100] Their significance was by this time well established, and this understandably increased their value for the academic study of Roman art, but the surviving fragments on the walls were difficult to see (figure 4.24). A turning point came with the work of Deckers and his team and of Kalavrezou-Maxeiner in the early 1970s.[101] Decker's team found the plaster layers in some areas very fragile and even detaching from the walls around cracks and edges of lacunae. Their work included the first detailed condition assessment that documented the state of conservation and a description of the techniques used to create the plaster layers and paintings, going beyond the merely visual impressions that characterize earlier observations. It also involved the first known protective conservation measures and cleaning aimed at providing greater visibility to the obscured paintings, albeit only temporarily, for copyists and art historians. Deckers incorporated a report by Meyer-Graft, the first documented conservation intervention in the history of the frescoes, into his comprehensive published survey of the imperial cult chamber. It summarizes observations and remedial steps taken to secure the paintings where they were found to be at risk.[102]

The paintings in the lower borders (imitation opus sectile dado) were cleaned using mechanical means to remove dust, spiders' webs, and soiling caused by bird

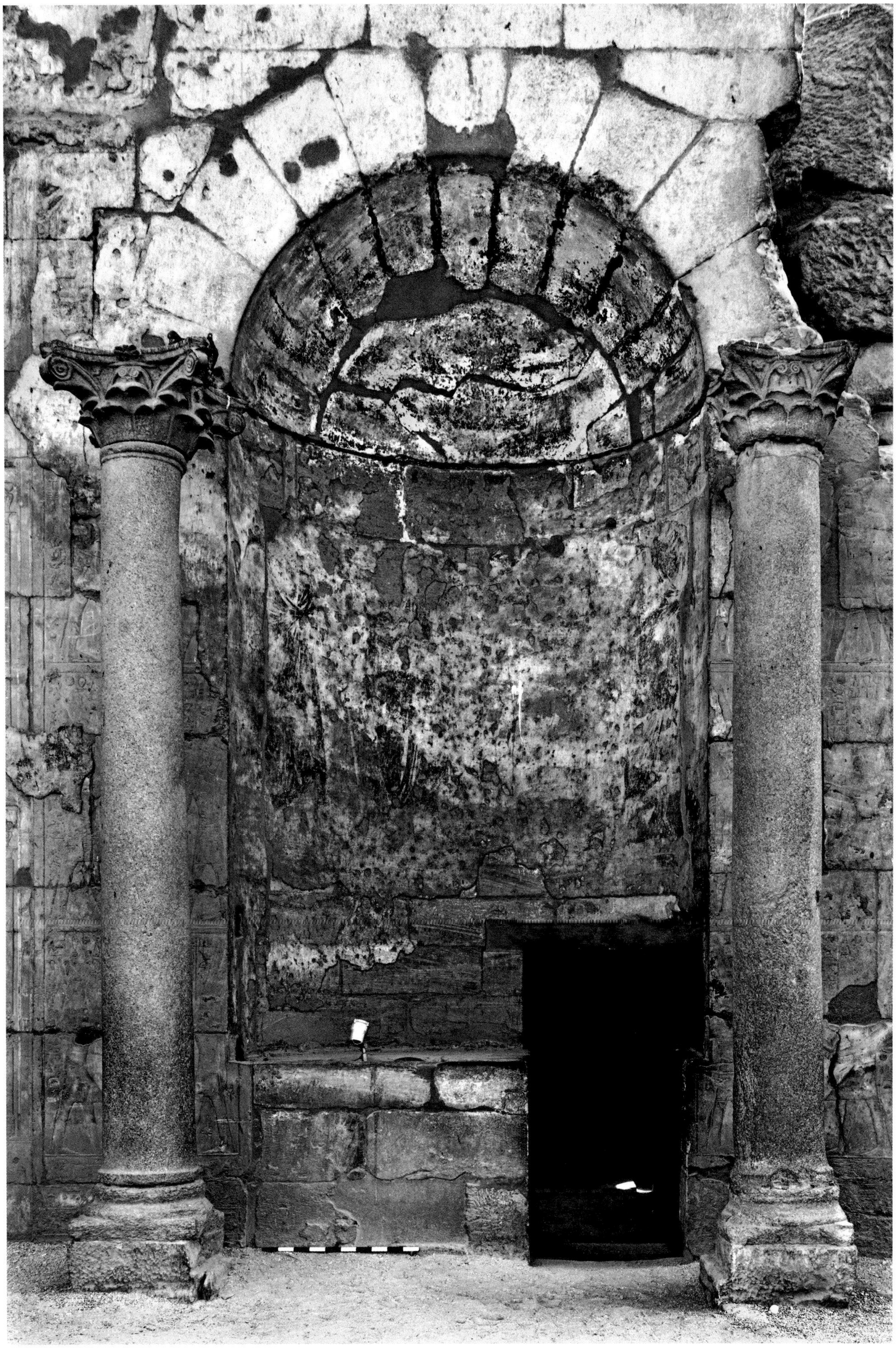

FIGURE 4.23
South wall niche in 2005: existing conditions before conservation.

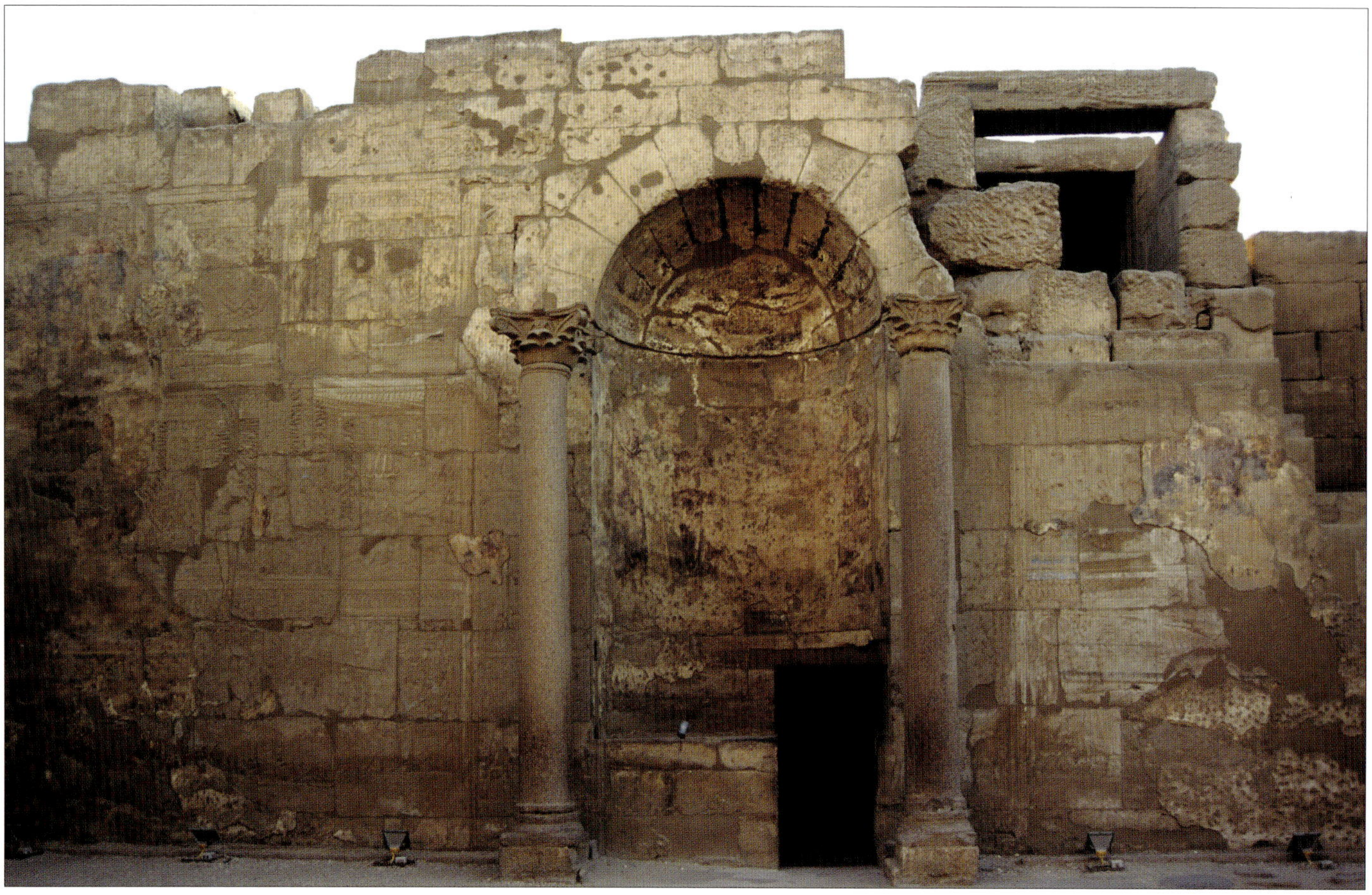

FIGURE 4.24
South wall in 1998: before conservation.

droppings. The figurative paintings were cleaned with scalpels and paintbrushes. A lime layer that overlay parts of the paintings on the south and east walls (Deckers's Walls A and B, respectively) had to be removed with scalpels, and in this way it was possible to expose especially well-preserved sections. This may be the same as the yellow wash noticed above the niche on the south wall (see figure 4.24; see also the discussion in chapter 5). Meyer-Graft also noticed the "crackling and peeling formation" that he suspected might indicate the use of casein as a binding agent in the paint. The edges of particularly well-preserved paintings on the south wall were protected with plaster made from Nile mud mixed with chopped straw. (The same modern mud plaster mixture was also found applied to parts of the painted surface on the western section of the north wall in 2005.) Meyer-Graft describes how the paintings were moistened using an intermediary layer of tissue, onto which the solvent was applied so that it did not directly touch the paint layer; thus, the methods used did not damage the paintings or threaten their continued survival. Through the use of moisture, the color could be sufficiently enhanced and, because a slow-drying moistening agent was applied, large areas of the painted surfaces remained moist long enough for the archaeological investigation to take place. He also remarked that the paintings remained seriously threatened and "only a thorough restoration can ensure their future preservation."[103]

Though the paintings have been much admired since the nineteenth century for the quality of the artists' workmanship,[104] recognition of their value as extraordinary survivors of imperial Roman art of this type and period is thanks mainly to the results of these researches.[105] Deckers and Kalavrezou-Maxeiner recognized the full potential of the frescoes as primary sources for artistic and political aspects of Roman imperial statecraft and the influence of Egyptian heritage on Diocletian's reframing of the role of the emperor. Deckers's holistic presentation of the imperial cult chamber placed it in the context of modern archaeological research for the first time and eventually led to the conservation project of 2005–2008.[106]

Throughout the twentieth century, repairs to damaged masonry often went unrecorded, but their impact can be evaluated by comparing earlier photographs with modern conditions. For example, the worn steps in front of the northern entrance shown in an early photograph published by Legrain[107] have been repaired several times with new sandstone pieces set in modern cement, an inevitable and recurring maintenance task (see figure 3.5). The holes in the

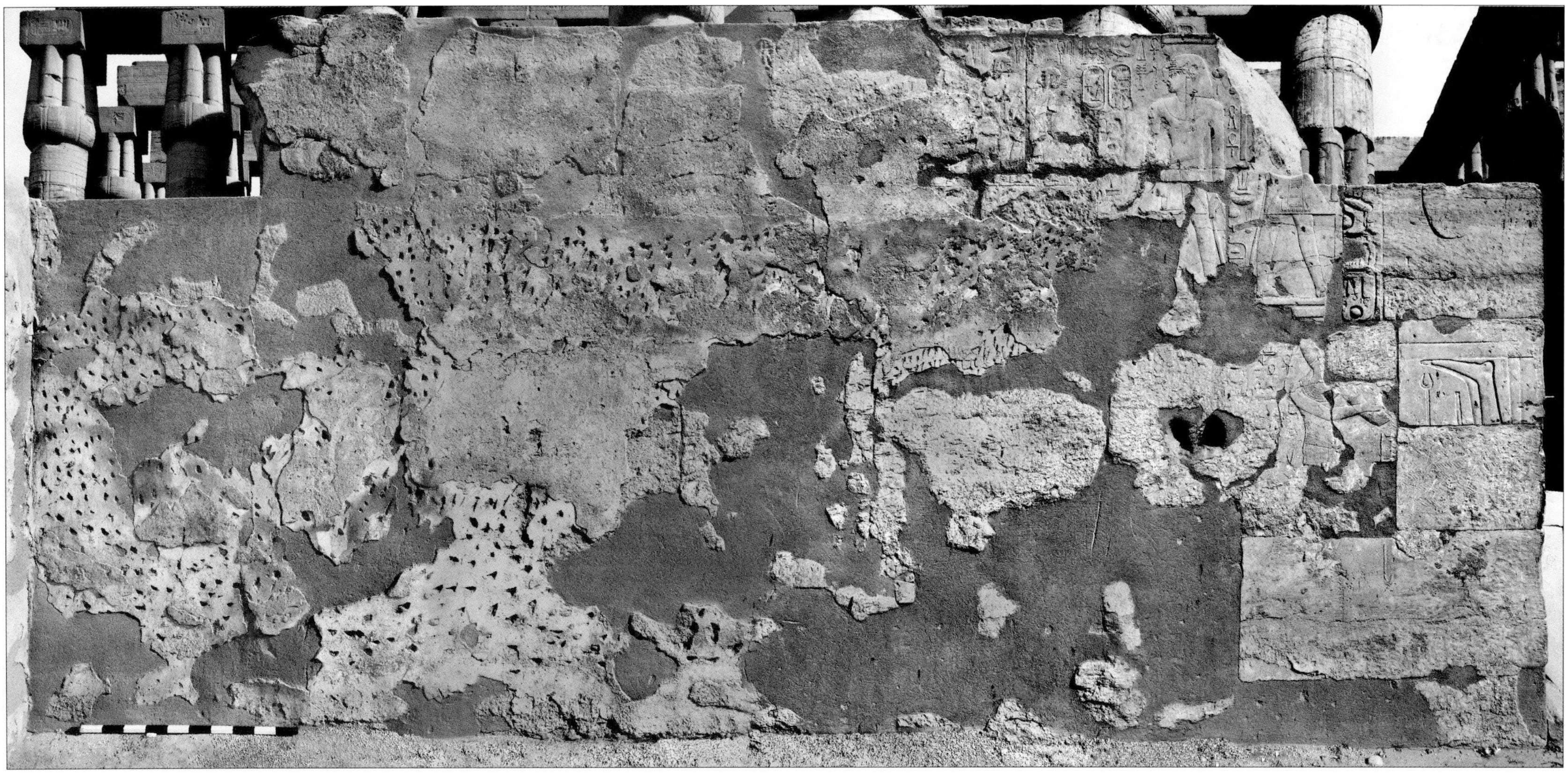

FIGURE 4.25
North wall west of the entrance in 2005: existing conditions before conservation.

wall above the niche have been filled; spalling cavities in the sandstone walls have been repointed; the upper blocks on the east wall have been moved and reset in some places, probably on several occasions. The effects of these repairs are particularly clear on the east and the north walls, where serious erosion can be seen in early twentieth-century photographs (compare figure 4.21, before repairs, with figures 4.25 and 4.26).

The last thirty years of the twentieth century were another period of growth in tourist numbers, in housing and hotel construction, and in the population of Luxor.[108] Cruise boats on the Nile grew in size and numbers, as did their emissions and vibrations. Moorings remained in their traditional location close to the temple, later spreading along the riverbank toward Karnak and eventually occupying much of the east bank of the Nile. Commensurate with the rise in the number of boats and their clients was the increase in vehicle traffic, particularly motor coaches, to carry tourists between their hotels and boats and the monuments and sites. Population growth, more vehicle traffic, poorly considered infrastructure in the vicinity of the temple, and a vastly enlarged town with numerous new hotels all contributed to higher groundwater, a rise in atmospheric pollution and humidity, and an increase in insects, bats, and birds roosting on the temple walls. Intensified visitor numbers in the temple caused abrasion and soiling on the lower sections of the walls and painted surfaces. Though reliable statistics are not available, the damaging effects of these conditions on air quality are observable, and vibrations from traffic can be felt.[109] Additional stress was introduced when, in the 1980s, the gardens formerly covering the sloping Nile embankment were replaced by a continuous concrete riverwalk designed to accommodate new and bigger cruise boats and to contain shops and restaurants. The effect was to reduce evaporation of subsurface moisture and to seal groundwater under the temple. Subsequently, dampness and salt efflorescence on the ground surface and walls and their damaging effects on the stonework of the temple grew increasingly evident. Thus, by the end of the twentieth century the temple was in an increasingly unstable and deteriorating environment.[110]

A preliminary investigation was carried out in November 2005 to determine whether the frescoes in their present condition and environment merited conservation treatment. This was accompanied by a series of orthographic photographs showing the extent of the surviving Roman plaster on the Eighteenth-Dynasty masonry (figures 4.23, 4.25–4.27). The aim was to ascertain the state of conservation of the paintings and the supporting plaster layers, to examine the execution techniques, and to carry out cleaning tests to develop a suitable conservation methodology (see chapter 6). A number of issues were addressed, including whether cleaning the paintings would expose them to

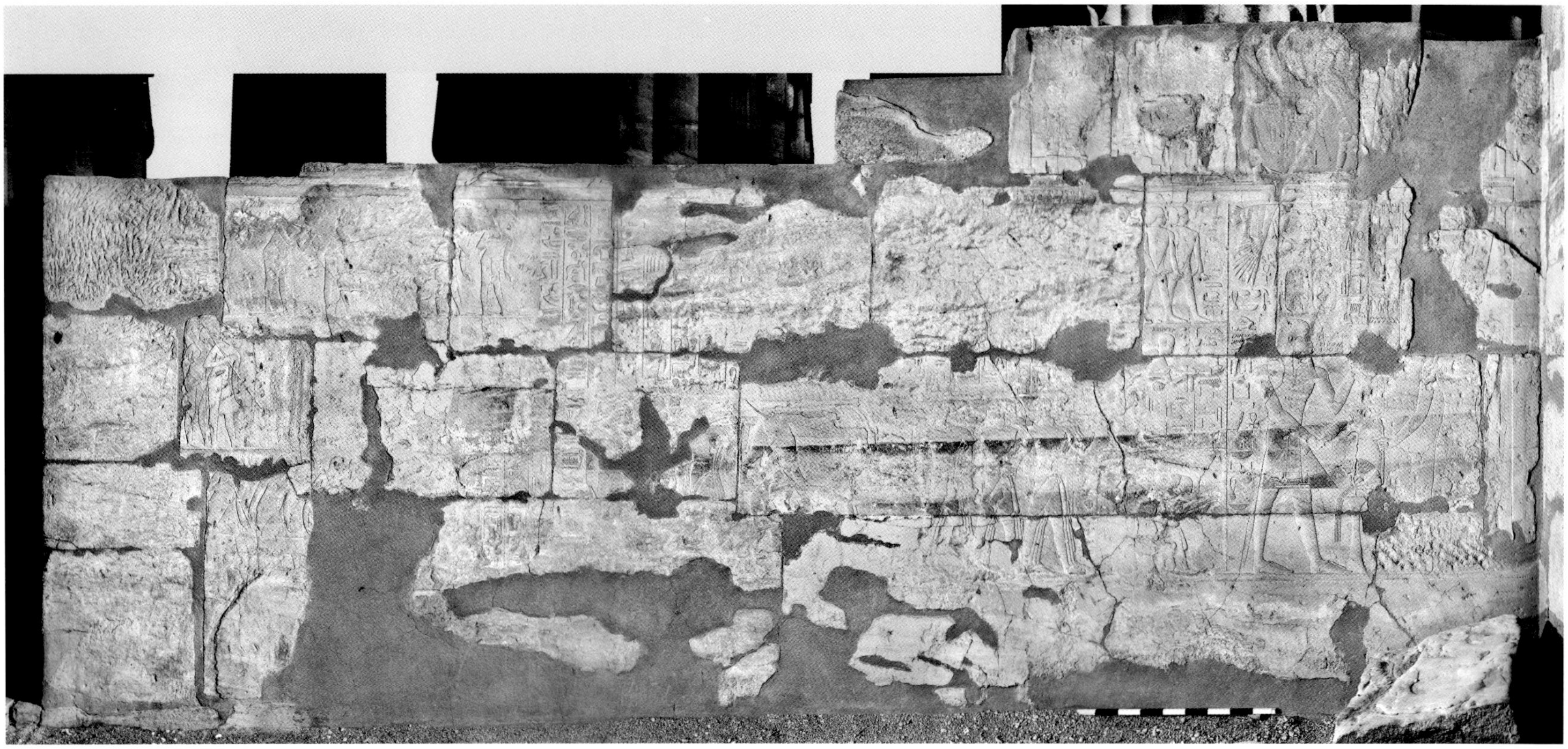

FIGURE 4.26
(above) North wall east of the entrance in 2005: existing conditions before conservation.

FIGURE 4.27
East wall in 2005: existing conditions before conservation.

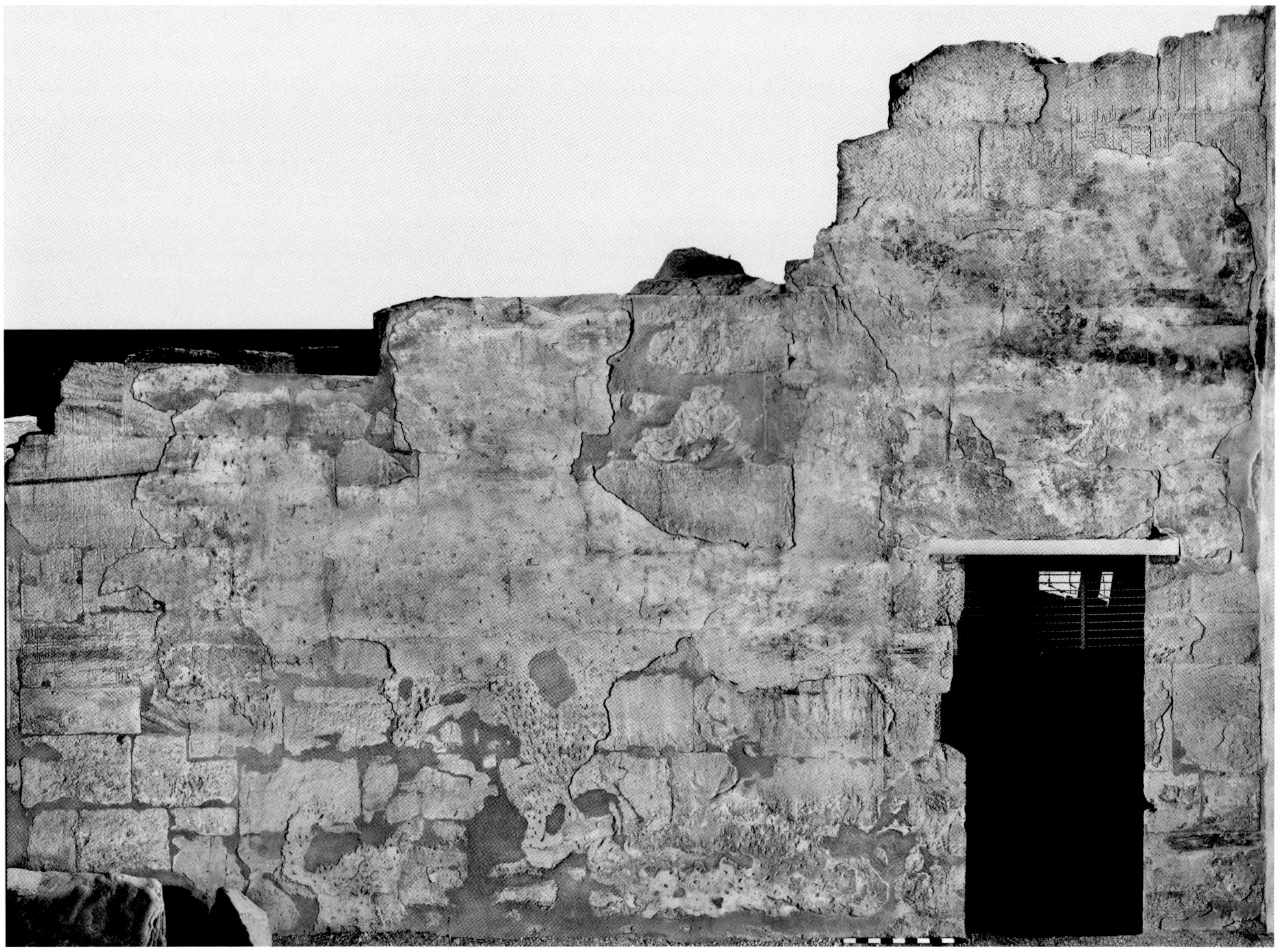

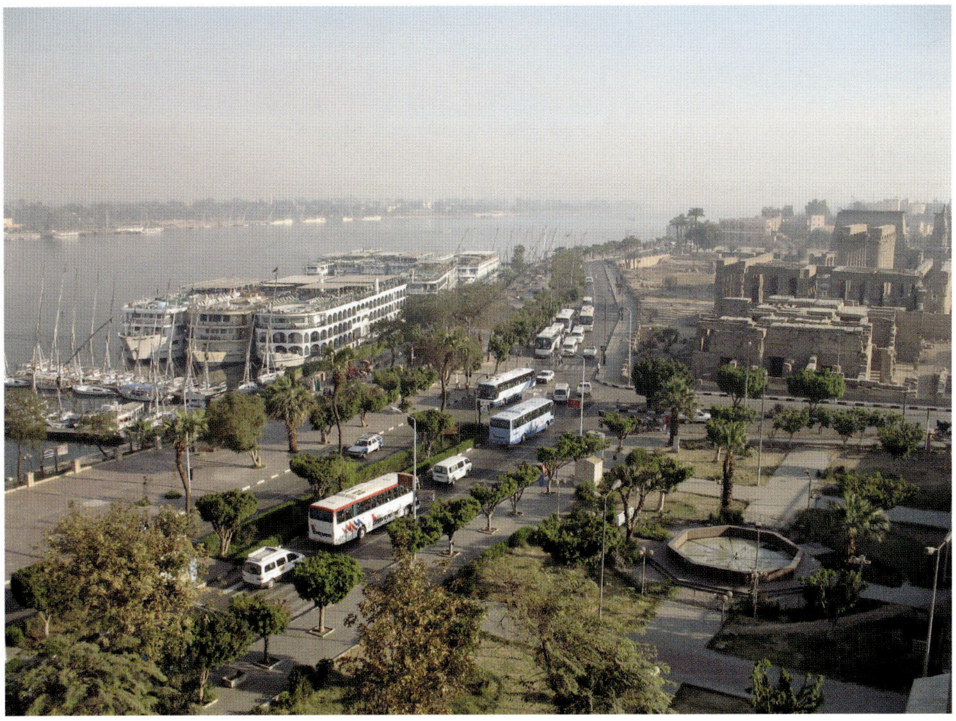

FIGURE 4.28
Atmospheric pollution over Luxor Temple in 2005.

greater risks and hasten their ultimate destruction in the prevailing conditions. In that case, another option considered was to make a comprehensive photographic record of the frescoes and then leave them in situ as they were without further treatment.

Another approach proposed evaluating, cleaning, and consolidating the remains of the frescoes in situ, accompanied by comprehensive documentation, followed by removal of the paintings for display and presentation in a controlled environment. A suitable venue considered was Luxor Museum, where they might form part of a specially constructed exhibition on Roman Luxor and the tetrarchic reconfiguration of the temple. This would have added an archaeological component to the fieldwork requiring full documentation of the removal process, followed by conservation, recording, and protection of the Eighteenth-Dynasty reliefs on the walls underlying the Roman plaster layers. This approach was rejected for both ethical and technical reasons.[111] Although they are palimpsests obscuring earlier aspects of the history of the temple, as Gayet recognized over a century ago, the Roman frescoes are now acknowledged as an important part of the temple, integrally associated with its development both physically and culturally. They encapsulate a reimaging through imperial patronage of the politico-religious functions of the Amun cult in its final moments and are a unique witness to Diocletian's restructuring of Roman authority whereby Thebes and Egypt were connected to the greater Roman world. Removal would compromise this history by marring the authenticity of context present in the frescoes while risking injury to the fabric of the walls. Gayet remarked how his attempts to remove the Roman plaster were curtailed owing to the fragile state of the supporting masonry. This was a clear warning that such an approach today might jeopardize both the Roman plaster and paint layers and the reliefs where they are still covered and protected by the later plaster.

The fourth option was to clean the frescoes in situ accompanied by comprehensive graphic and photographic documentation before further deterioration could take place. Cleaning the original images would not only enhance their visibility but also create both physical and intellectual access to a major resource for art historians, historians, and archaeologists and allow visitors to appreciate an overlooked yet potentially striking and informative aspect of the temple. Such a project would provide important new information about a significant but neglected phase in the life of the temple. It would help disengage the paintings from previous misconceptions, such as the Christian interpretation, still alive sixty years after being refuted by Monneret de Villard. It was decided, on the basis of observations made during the preliminary investigation, that this option—cleaning, recording, and documentation in situ followed by publication—was the most practicable solution for the problems facing the frescoes in their modern environment (figure 4.28).

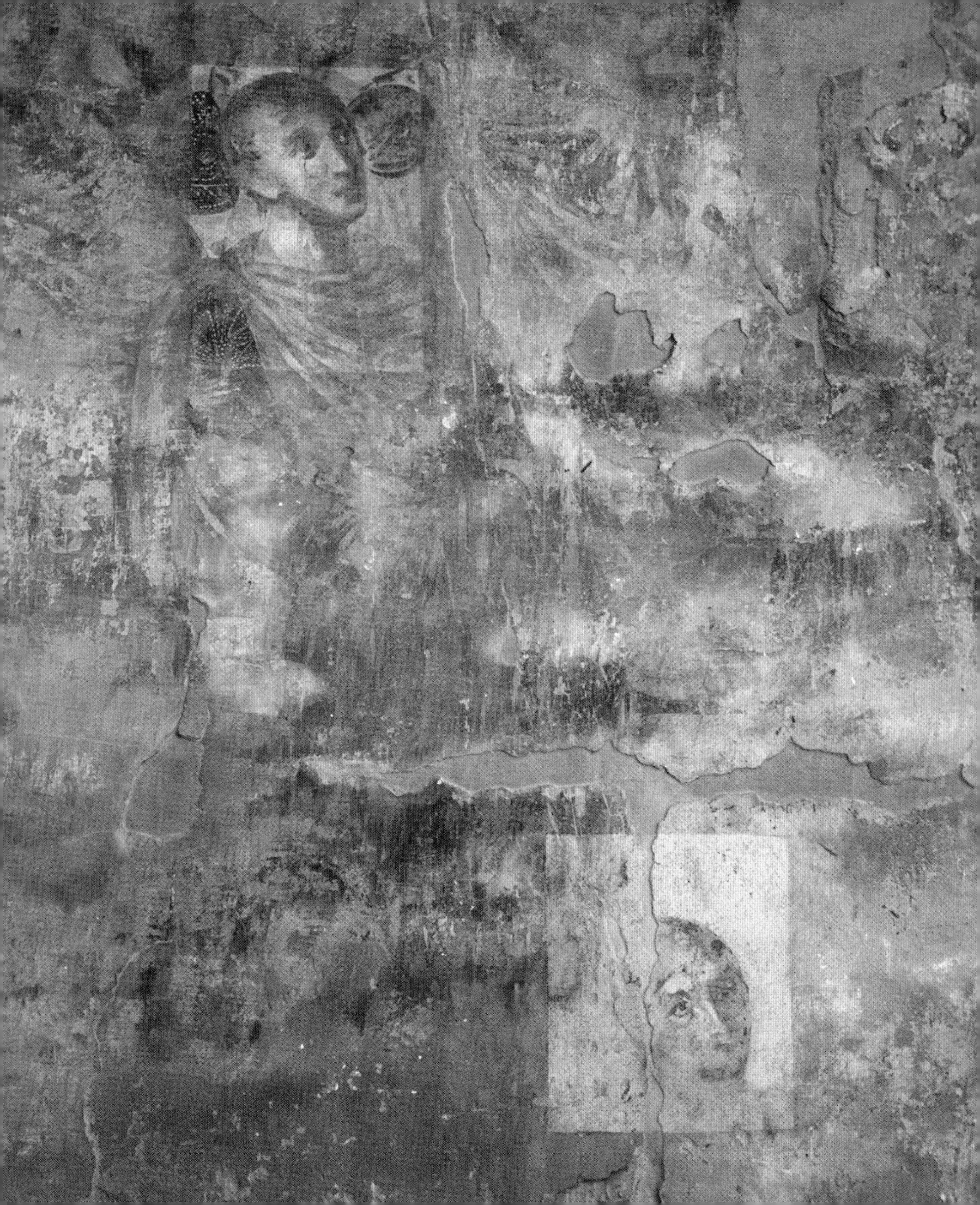

Chapter 5

CONSERVATION OF THE FRAGMENTS OF ROMAN WALL PAINTINGS IN THE IMPERIAL CULT CHAMBER OF LUXOR TEMPLE

LUIGI DE CESARIS, ALBERTO SUCATO, AND EMILIANO RICCHI
Translated by Sara Montgomery

INTRODUCTION

Luigi De Cesaris

THE SURVIVING FRAGMENTS OF ROMAN WALL PAINTING in the imperial cult chamber of Luxor Temple were conserved over a four-year period from 2005 to 2008. The work was planned and directed by the conservators Luigi De Cesaris and Alberto Sucato, with the assistance of a team of professional conservators managed on-site by Maria Cristina Tomassetti. The first site visit and preliminary investigations took place in 2005; the aim was to analyze the state of preservation of the paintings and carry out an initial study of the causes of deterioration affecting the wall paintings. The project was completed in four conservation seasons, each lasting approximately two months and employing a team of eight conservators.[1]

Our approach in the planning phase of the work on the Roman frescoes that celebrate the imperial cult and the emperor's *adventus* ceremony had to take into consideration the significance of their location in the room that, before its transformation into the imperial cult chamber, had been at the heart of the ancient temple dedicated to the cult of Amun. The paintings represent a striking example of the way in which Rome was superimposed on ancient Egypt in the heart of Thebes, which led us to reject our initial ideas about removing the fragments, conserving them in a laboratory, and placing them in a museum to avoid their further exposure to the atmospheric agents that have been the principal cause of their deterioration. Removing the fragments, possibly the only surviving example of Roman frescoes in Egypt, would have disconnected them from their original context, thereby reducing a great part of their significance. In the same way, the removal of the paintings would have deprived the temple of a very important witness to its history. Conservation in situ meant that these magnificent and unique paintings can be enjoyed in their original surroundings, with all their historical and symbolic significance intact.

The first short season of preliminary surveys and conservation work took place in November 2005 and concentrated on the south wall to the east of the central niche, where the Tetrarchs are depicted. The frescoes were in an extremely patchy state, the result of the loss of extensive areas of plaster; the paint layer was also very patchy and, where present, was flaking off and affected by various kinds of deposits that rendered many details almost indecipherable (figure 5.2). The main aim of this first season was to carry out a close analysis of the state of the masonry and the preparatory and paint layers together with a preliminary study of the previous and present causes of the deterioration of the frescoes. A portable vertical microscope was used to carry out an in-depth analysis of the materials. These investigations were followed by a series of localized micro-test cleanings to make soluble the dirt and substances overlying the paintings.

On the basis of the data collected during this first phase of study, three larger test cleanings, measuring approximately fifty by forty centimeters, were carried out near the southeast corner of the south wall (figure 5.1). The three areas were chosen to verify the effectiveness of the conservation methods and to obtain an initial idea of the aesthetic effect of the completed restoration project. At the end of this short season the project plan and methodology were produced, together with an initial estimate of the time and number of conservators required to complete the conservation work.

FIGURE 5.1
South wall, east side: two cleaning tests carried out in 2005.

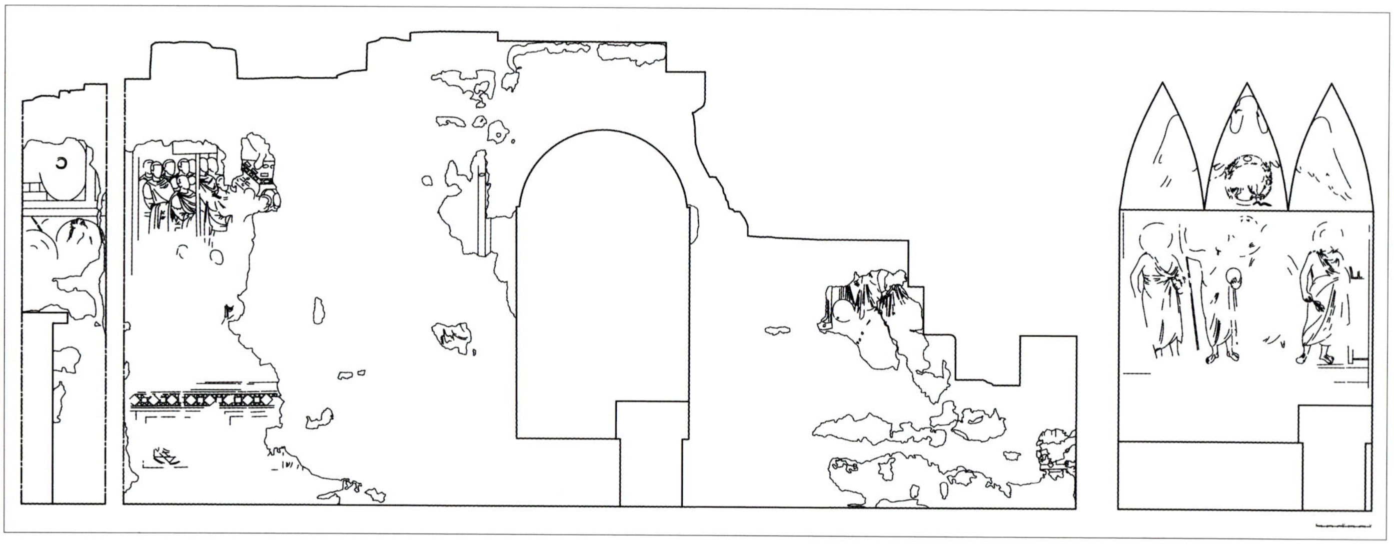

FIGURE 5.2
South wall conservation record: east side and niche showing extant plaster and paint layers.

ORIGINAL EXECUTION TECHNIQUES

Luigi De Cesaris

Masonry and Preparatory Layers

The walls of the imperial cult chamber are built of sandstone blocks bearing reliefs and inscriptions of Amenhotep III. The Romans altered the structure of the south wall and the doorways to the side rooms. The rectangular monumental doorway in the center of the south wall was closed with blocks taken from elsewhere and altered to create the apsidal section of the niche. Inside the niche, only the lateral blocks were left in situ, reworked, and made concave.[2] Whether worked in situ or removed, reworked, and replaced, the blocks bear clear signs of the *subbia* chisel, stoneworker's hammer, and various toothed tools (figure 5.3). Deep holes made by a bow drill are also visible.

Inside the semi-dome, there are four rectangular holes bored in a symmetrical arrangement. These were housings for the props that shored up the vault while it was being built. Once the semi-dome was completed and the scaffolding removed, the holes were filled with plaster. Observation of the wall paintings, particularly near the southeast corner, makes it clear that they once extended upward for another tier, which shows that the walls were originally much higher than they are today.[3]

It seems possible that the plaster was first applied at the top of the walls where they met the roof and continued groundward; the same is probably true of the paint layer. Given the poor state of preservation of the plaster, only one *pontata* line,[4] at approximately 2.5 meters above ground level, has been identified, although it is possible that there

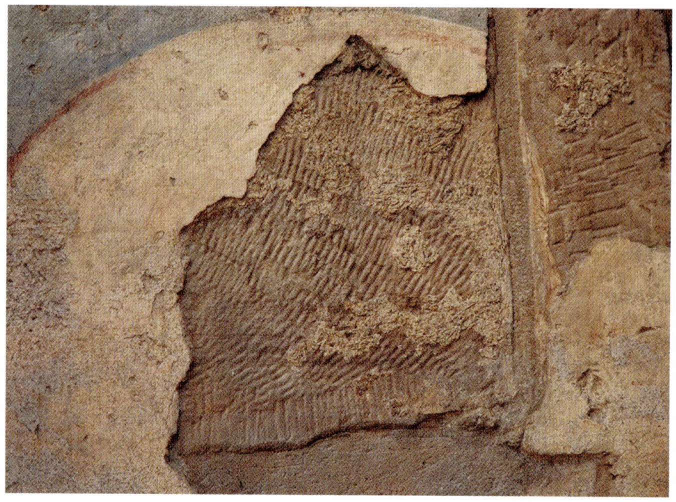

FIGURE 5.3
South wall niche, first figure on the left: stone blocks bearing the marks of chisels and toothed tools.

was another one above the fragments surviving today that divided the composition into two tiers. Inside the niche, two areas of plaster application can be seen, one in the semi-dome and the second lower down, separated horizontally by a small, raised seam.

The stratigraphy of the preparatory layers is as follows. The first rough coat of plaster, or *arriccio,* was applied directly to the masonry to level the uneven surface of the reliefs and the irregularities in the stonework; for this reason the preparatory layer varies in thickness, as the masonry was already in a poor state of preservation by the time the Roman plaster was applied. On the inside of the niche, however, where the newly reused stone was smoothed in readiness for receiving the plaster, the preparatory layer is uniform in thickness. Here the plaster even assumes the appearance of a very thin wash, proof of the extreme care with which the stone had been worked. The plaster contains

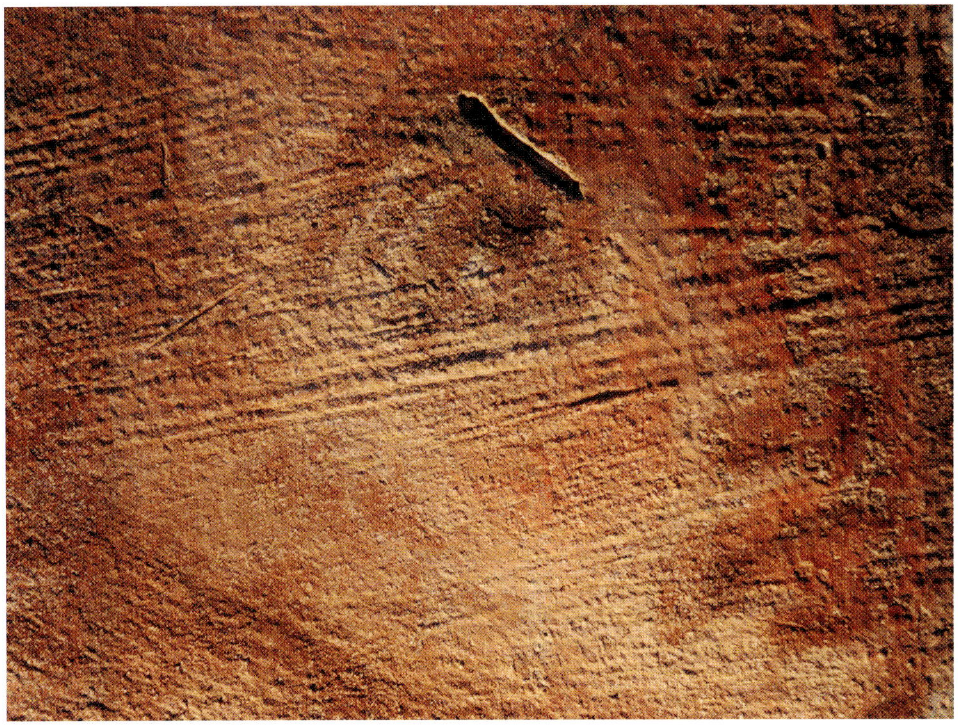

FIGURE 5.4
South wall, east side: face of a dignitary photographed under raking light to show impressions of brush strokes.

a considerable quantity of straw and a small amount of sand, and lime was used as a binder (see figure 5.23).[5] The use of straw, especially in a hot, dry climate, is connected with the need to prolong drying times as much as possible by keeping the plaster damp and elastic and preventing it from cracking so that the fresco technique can be used on very large areas of plaster applied at one time.

A second layer of plaster, the *intonaco,* approximately 3–5 millimeters thick and composed only of lime and sand, was applied on top of the purposely rough arriccio. The surface of the intonaco, intended to receive the paint layer, is not especially smooth, however. It was primed with a very thin layer of lime applied with large brushes, the bristles of which have left clear marks and loosened small grains of sand from the substrate. These features are consistent with the swift, impressionistic style in which the figures were painted (figure 5.4). The wall paintings belong to the late imperial period, when interest in illusionism decreased, "the aesthetic reason for polishing was taken away," and Roman painting underwent a rapid simplification of technique.[6] Quite unlike the elaborate preparations advocated by Vitruvius, renderings were generally reduced to two layers, losing in the process the compactness characteristic of the classical era. The rough-and-ready nature of the material and working methods should be measured on a new aesthetic scale.

A third coat of plaster, probably applied when work on the paintings in the upper part of the chamber had already begun, can be seen in the lower part of the room, some 2.5 meters from the ground.[7] Before this third layer was applied, deep pick holes were made all over the surface of the second layer to provide a good bond (see figure 5.14).[8] The composition of the third layer of plaster is similar to that of the second layer. It was probably applied so that the surface could be highly polished, since it was to be painted with imitation polychrome marble *opus sectile* that was intended to shine like real

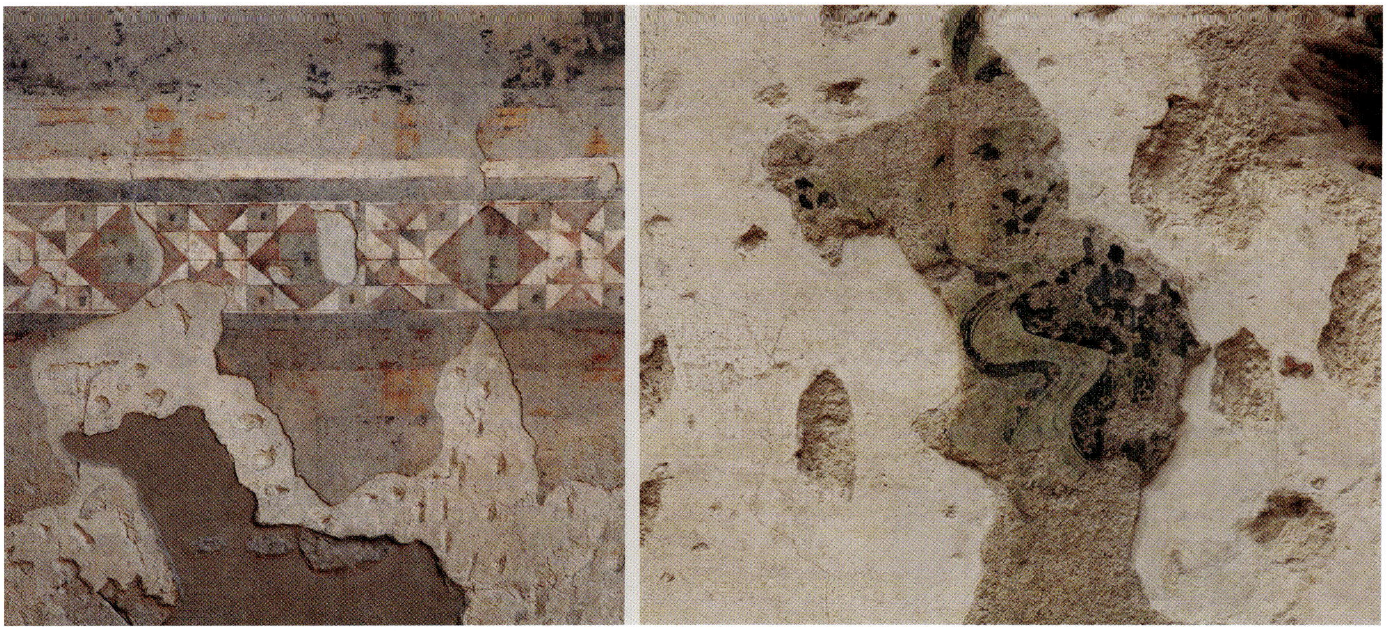

FIGURE 5.5
Left: south wall, detail of an imitation opus sectile panel painted over an underlying layer extensively marked with pick holes. *Right:* east wall, fragment of an opus sectile panel imitating green marble.

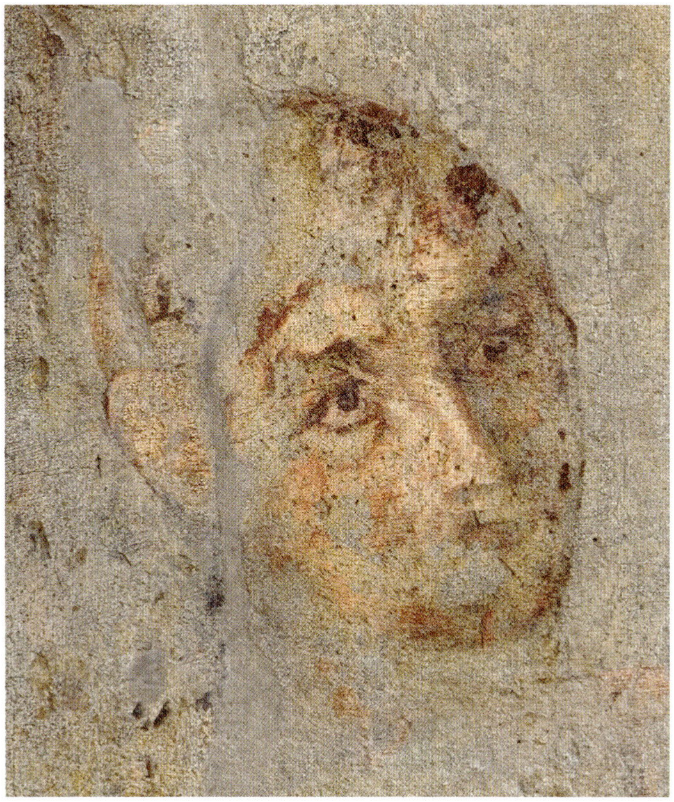

FIGURE 5.6
(left) South wall, east end: detail of a face showing preparatory drawing in red pigment.

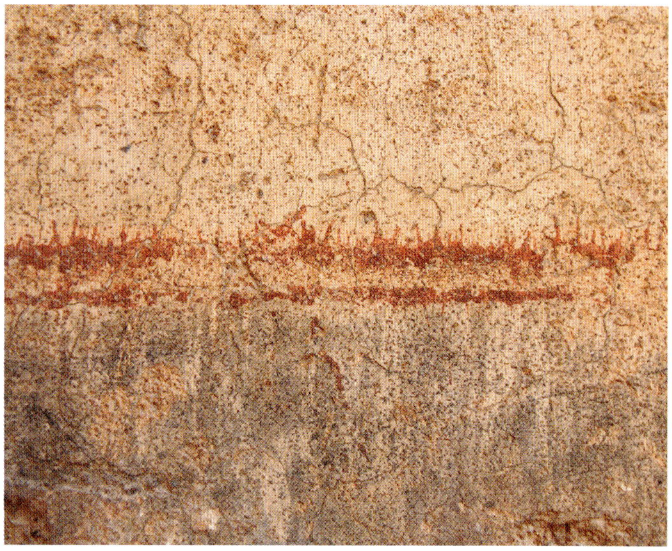

FIGURE 5.7
(right) South wall, east end: preliminary drawing showing straight lines using the builder's cord technique.

Opposite page:
FIGURE 5.8
(left) South wall crowd scene, details of robes: the epaulettes are painted with dots of bianco sangiovanni representing embroidery, and the belt buckle is painted with bianco sangiovanni and yellow ocher.

FIGURE 5.9
(right) South wall niche: imprint of the laurel branch held by the emperor Constantius Chlorus, originally painted in secco.

marble cladding (figure 5.5). It is also possible that the reason for applying a third layer was purely technical: the plaster may already have dried out and become unsuitable for painting, thus requiring the artist to cover it with a new layer.

Paint Layer

On the basis of preliminary analyses carried out during the first site visit and closer inspection during the course of the conservation work, we were able to confirm that the paintings were executed using the fresco technique, in which pigments are applied to damp, fresh lime plaster. The extensive background areas and broad impressionistic brushstrokes reflect the vast expanses of surface that had to be covered and the time constraints on the execution of the work. Despite the poor state of preservation of the paintings, the naturalistic skills of the artists are evident. Their masterful use of shading and highlighting creates an extremely three-dimensional impression, clearly the work of highly skilled and superior artists (see figure 6.1).

During the planning phase of the composition the artists executed a preparatory freehand drawing using a brush and a red-earth pigment. This is a fairly rough design, although in some places the artists lingered over the definition of certain details (figure 5.6). For the preliminary drawing of the geometrical imitation marble panels, however, they used the "builder's cord" technique, whereby a cord is soaked in paint and stretched close to the wall; once the two ends are anchored, the cord is plucked away from the wall and released, spattering paint onto the wall in a straight line (figure 5.7).

In the best preserved areas of painting, cleaning revealed detailed finishing touches, such as the intricate embroidery that decorates the robes of the imperial dignitaries, the highlighting of the eyes, and other details such as belt buckles that are painted in heavy brushstrokes loaded with color and the lime-white pigment known as *bianco sangiovanni* (figure 5.8). The palette includes natural pigments such as green earth, red ocher, yellow ocher, and yellow jarosite as well as artificial black, white, and blue.[9] We discovered that for most of the painting, the artists applied only a single layer of color, and for certain details we have been able to identify localized original finishing touches painted in *secco,* where the pigment was applied after the plaster had dried. When color is applied to dry plaster, the pigment is mixed with a binder, generally of an organic nature, so that it adheres to the substrate. Details painted using this technique are fragile and tend to become detached and fall off when exposed to adverse environmental conditions. A clear example of this is the laurel branch in the hand of Constantius Chlorus that has left an imprint on the underlying fresco, although the detail itself has been lost (figure 5.9). It appears that the green and blue pigments were also applied in secco.

The brushstrokes of the fresco work still appear quite thick, particularly within the niche, which has helped pro-

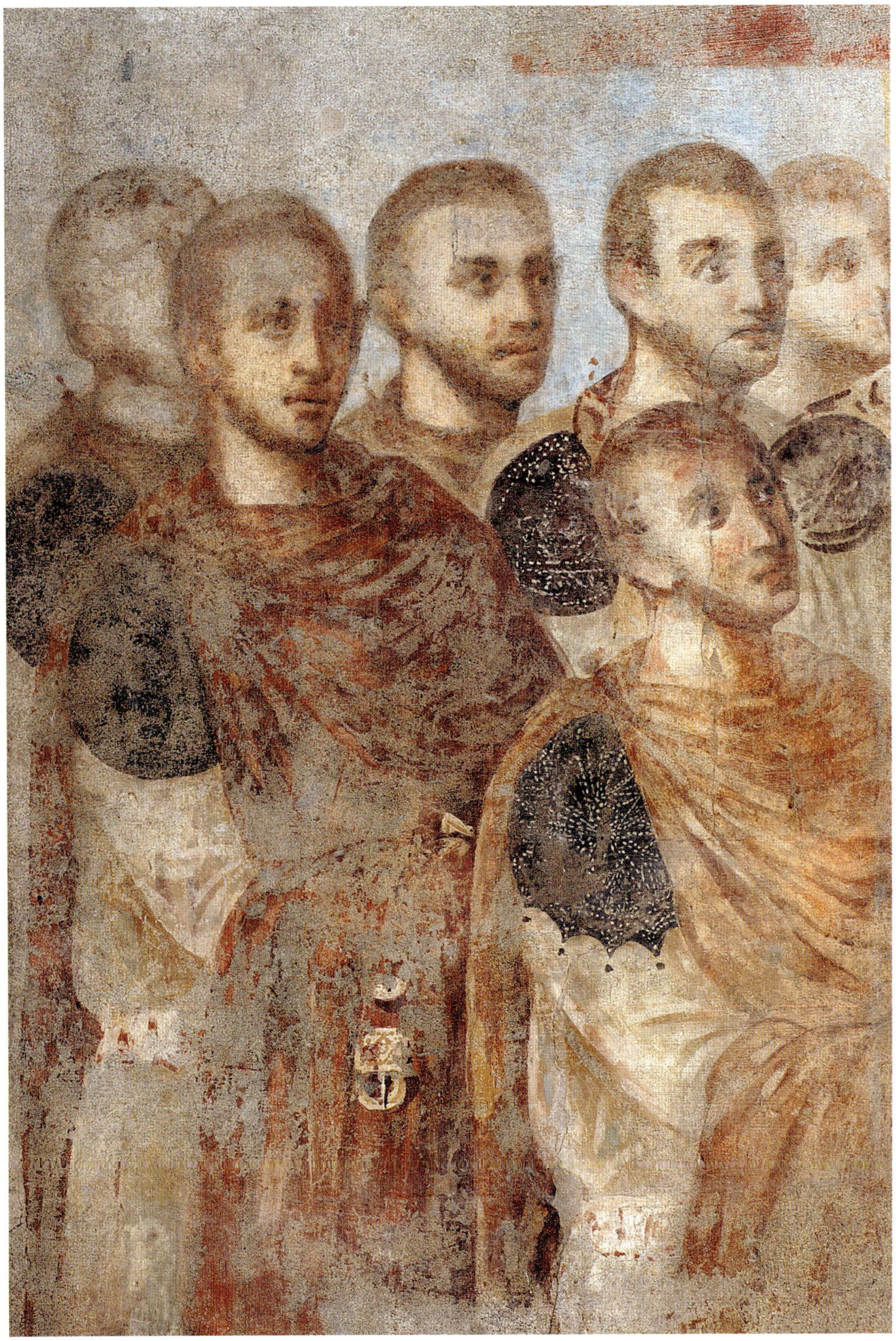

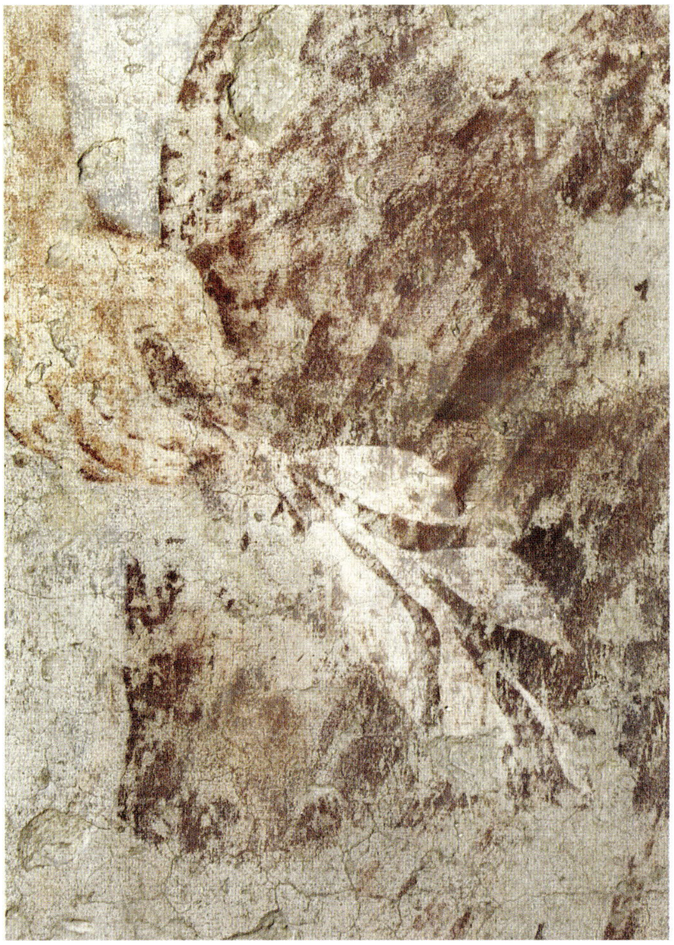

tect the paintings. The imposing figures of the four emperors were intended to appear especially three-dimensional and solid. The clear-cut dark shadows cast by their bodies stand out against the ground that is rendered in swift brushstrokes that shade from green to yellow. Higher up, the blue background to the four figures makes use of the Roman technique of superimposing color on a dark base to make the Egyptian blue appear more intense.[10] Here the artists made effective use of the *cangiantismo* technique of painting textiles using two contrasting colors (rather than darker and lighter tones of the same color) to create an effect that imitates "shot" fabrics.[11] Despite the advanced state of deterioration of the painting, the effect can still be seen on Diocletian's mantle where blue combined with a purple background gives an especially plastic appearance to the drapery (figure 5.10).

The artists blended different pigments to render the colors and nuances required to imitate the marble paneling of the opus sectile. Porphyry is imitated by a combination of two different reds, the darker background is obtained by mixing a red ocher with black, and the pink inclusions in the marble are painted in the same ocher mixed with lime white. Egyptian frit was applied in secco to render the blue and green veining of marble. Given the extremely patchy nature of the paintings in this area, only certain types of marble are recognizable, but comparison with Wilkinson's watercolors, painted in the nineteenth century when the

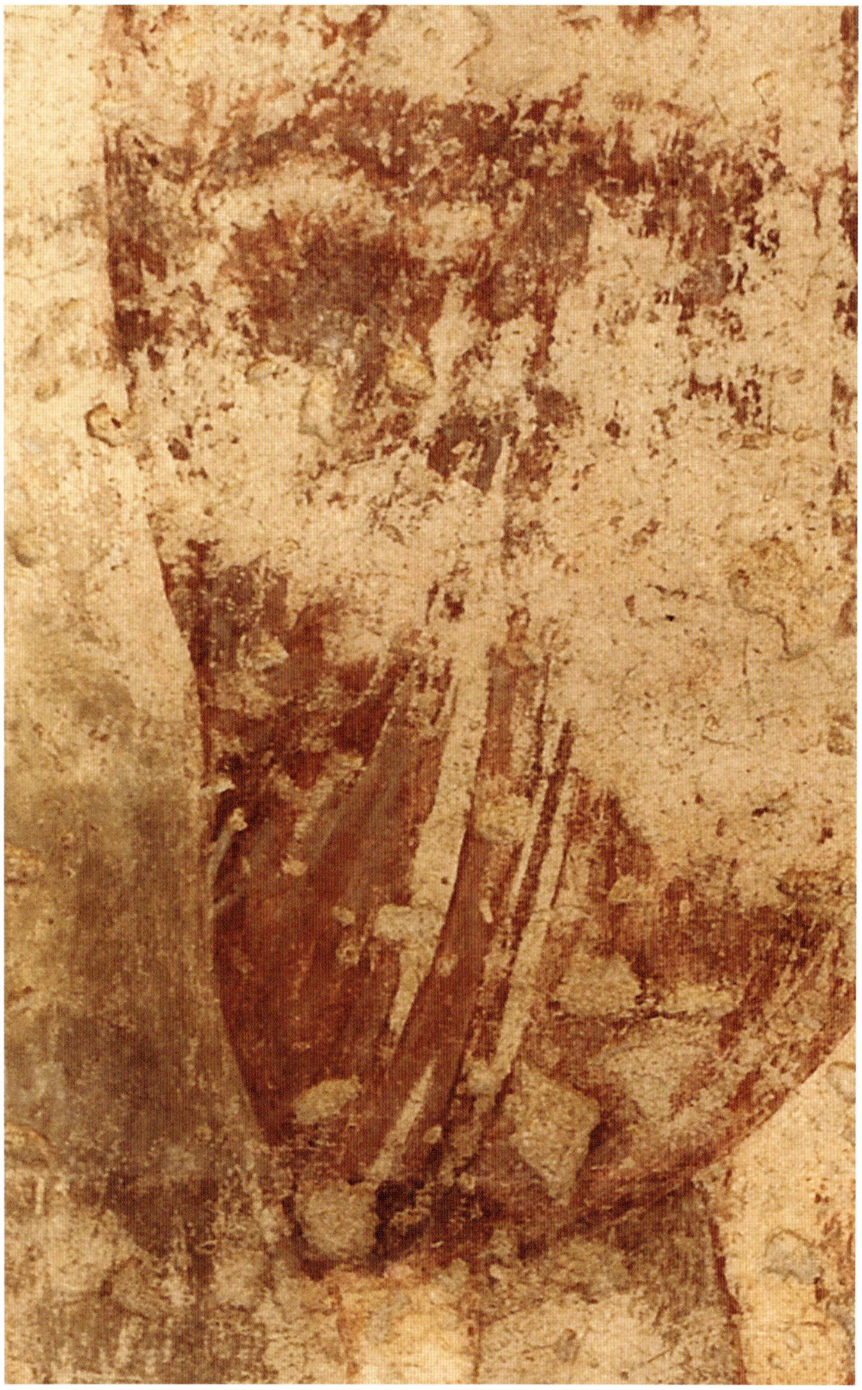

FIGURE 5.10
South wall niche: detail of Diocletian's cloak showing the effect of the cangiantismo technique of blue on a purple background, which gives the appearance of "shot" fabric.

paint layer was better preserved, has allowed us to reconstruct the layout of the composition and suggest the main types of stone that the artists imitated (see figure A.4 left). The band of opus sectile is made up of alternating square and rectangular panels. The former contain elaborate circular compositions, no two of which are alike. The entire band is contained within a double red frame. Among the different types of marble depicted are giallo antico (*marmor numidicum*); rosso antico (*marmor taenarium*); verde antico (*marmor thessalicum* or *marmor atracium*); and cipollino (*marmor carystium*), as well as porphyry.

EXISTING CONDITIONS AND CONSERVATION TREATMENT

Alberto Sucato

Existing Conditions

Anyone entering the imperial cult chamber from the north is immediately struck by the extremely fragmentary state of the frescoes. Before conservation, the surviving fragments were obscured by a thick deposit that rendered them almost indecipherable (figure 5.11).[12] During the preliminary study phase, earlier causes of deterioration were analyzed together with those still affecting the frescoes and associated with historically recent phenomena, such as the deposition of oily particulate matter caused by urban pollution. This study was greatly assisted by Wilkinson's watercolors, which depict the frescoes shortly after their excavation and therefore enable us to compare their state of preservation in 1856 with their current condition (see the appendix and chapter 4). The results of this comparison have allowed us to formulate precise theories about the causes, progress, and speed of the deterioration process.

Natural and environmental factors and direct or indirect human activities are the two main causes of deterioration. The main factor that negatively affected the condition of the paintings is undoubtedly prolonged exposure to the elements following the loss of the roof. As a direct consequence of these new conditions and the chamber's sudden exposure to the weather, sand-bearing desert winds abraded the surface of the frescoes and deposited particulate matter. Heating of the surface by solar radiation caused the paint layer and underlying plaster to expand unevenly. This triggered detachment between layers, cracking of the masonry, and the alteration and loss of delicate finishing touches to the paintings added in secco. The effect of rare but sometimes heavy rain should not be underestimated. Rain wets and weakens the paint layer so that it becomes detached from the plaster, and tiny fragments are lost. Finally, bird droppings deposited by the numerous colonies of swallows, sparrows, and pigeons living in the temple have caused and continue to cause localized rising and "tearing" of the paint layer.

The nearby Nile, which flooded the area annually until 1964, was and still is one of the main causes of the deterioration of the paintings, as it generates a great deal of atmospheric water vapor that causes condensation, particularly at dawn. The moisture exchange between the masonry and the atmosphere and the migration of soluble salts cause saline efflorescence and incrustations on the surface as well as subsurface

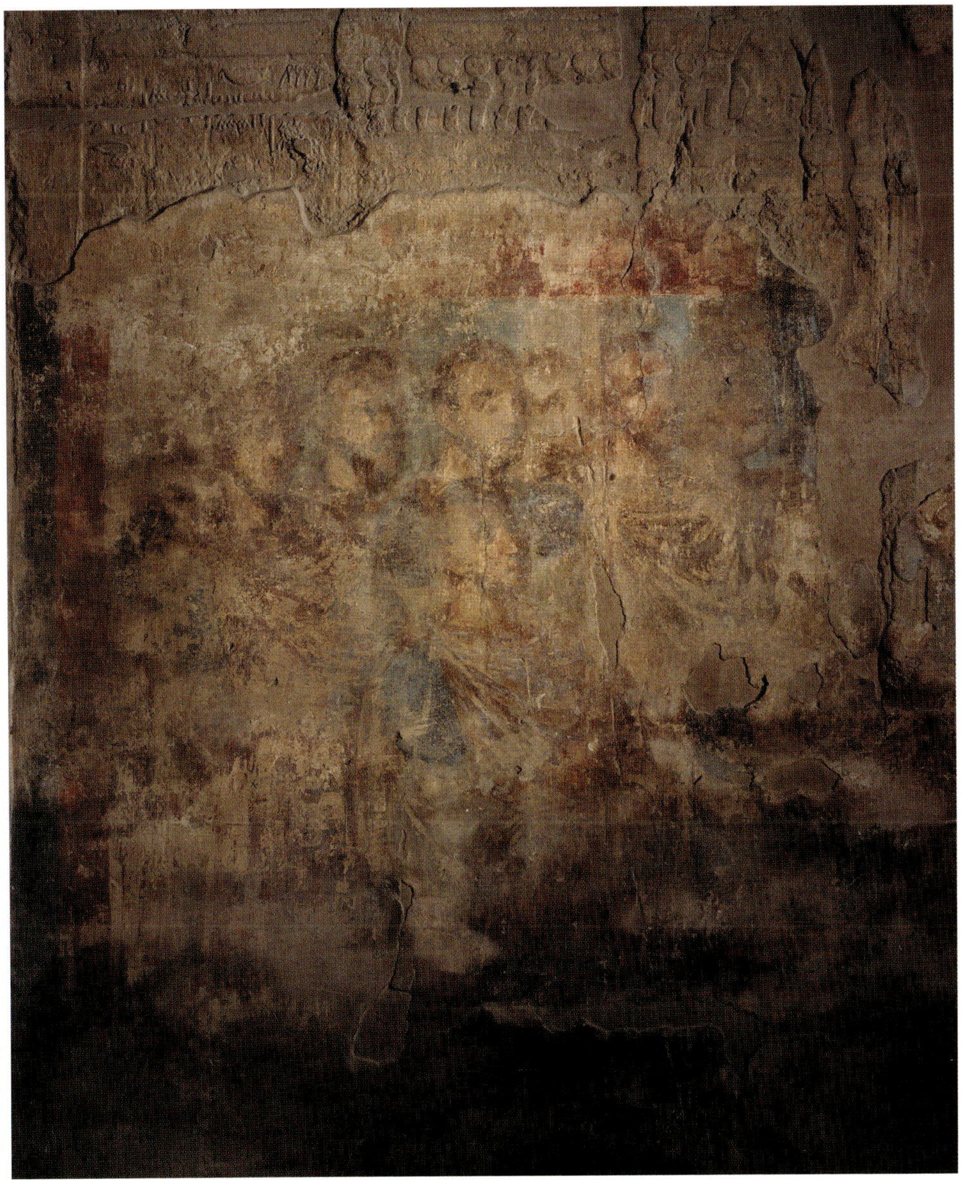

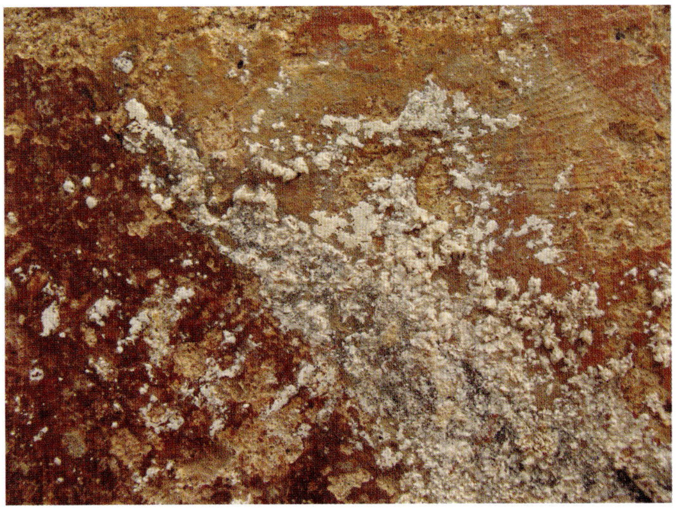

efflorescence where the salt crystallizes between the layers of paint and plaster, causing them to detach and fall off (figures 5.12 and 5.13). In Wilkinson's watercolors the lower part of the walls appears to be in good condition. It is possible that as a result of the excavation of the room, the balance that had been achieved in the flow of moisture between the subsoil and the masonry was suddenly upset, reactivating the movement of soluble salts and contributing to the destruction of the lower areas of the frescoes (figure 5.14). Annual flooding in the post-clearance period also undoubtedly damaged the lower painted registers, as suggested in chapter 4.

Human intervention has also seriously altered and damaged the frescoes. The image of the emperor second from right was obliterated in an act of *damnatio memoriae* (discussed in chapter 2) by abrading the surface of the top layer of paint. The yellow base layer, which extends beyond the

FIGURE 5.11
(above, left) South wall, east corner, before conservation.

FIGURE 5.12
(above, right) West wall: thick layer of crystallized soluble salts on the fresco surface.

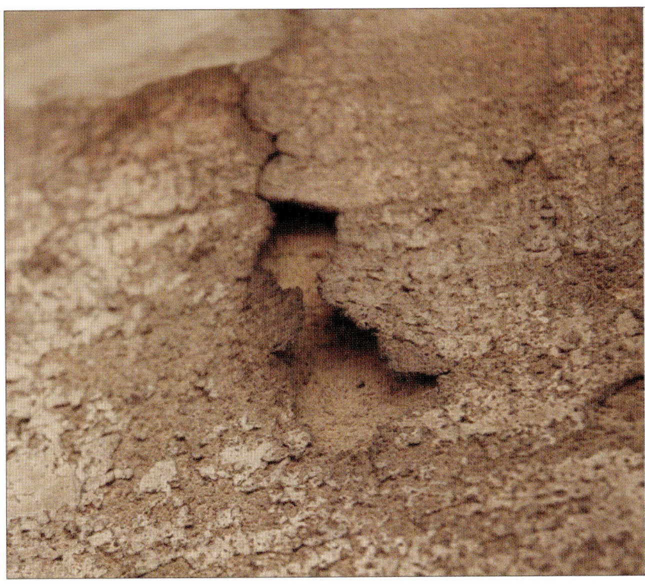

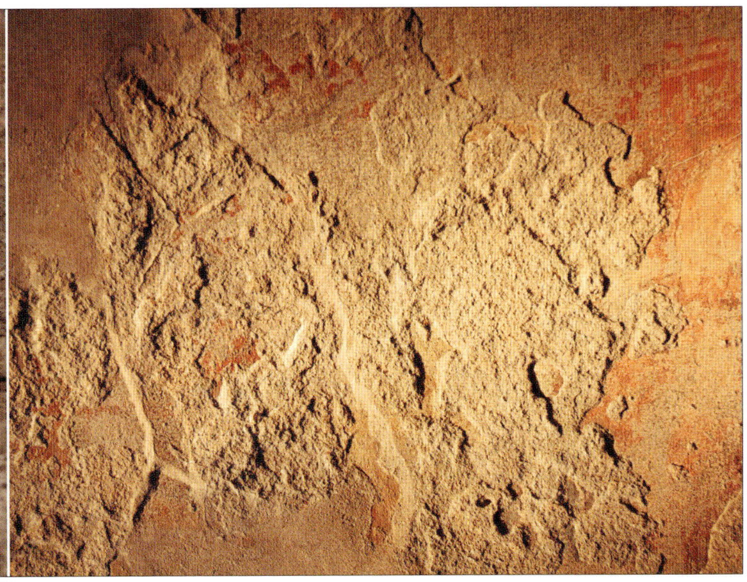

FIGURE 5.13
West wall: details of plaster with surfaces lifted (left) and detached (right) because of salt crystallization.

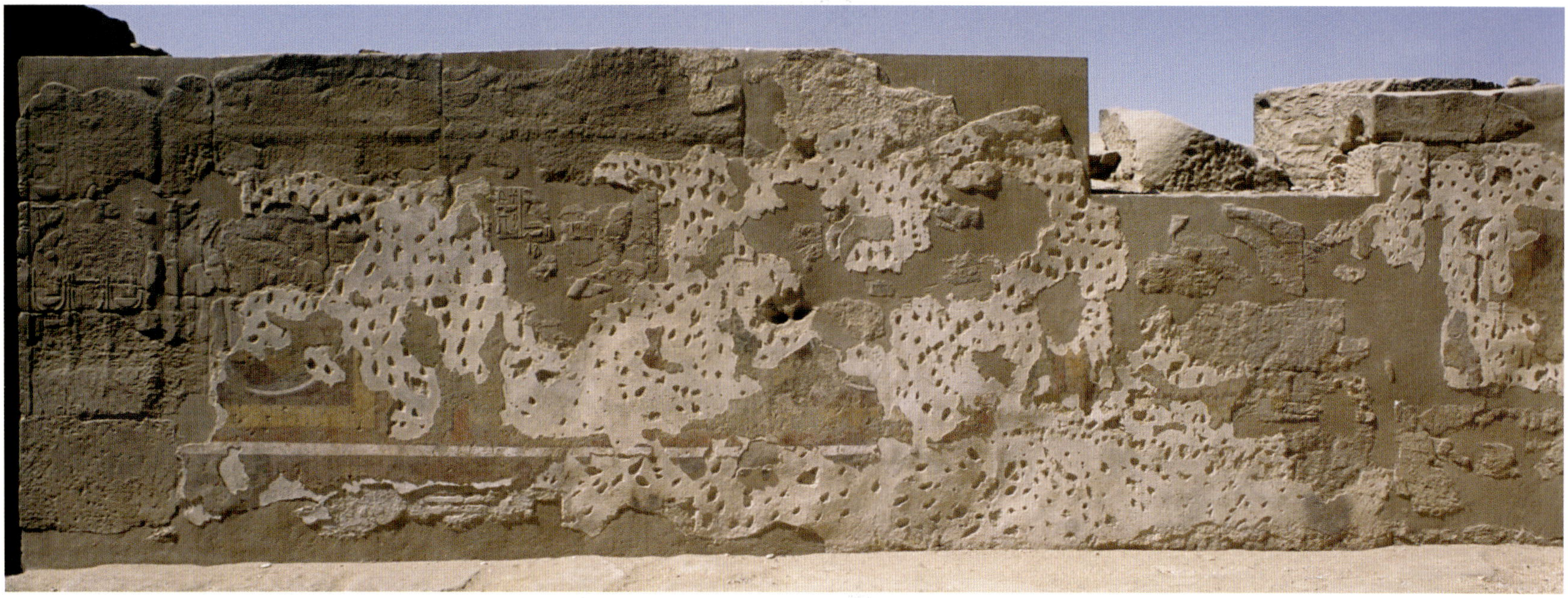

FIGURE 5.14
(above) West wall after conservation, showing damage to the lower parts of the fresco.

profile of the head to form the tetrarch's halo, has remained intact, however (figure 5.15). Even more serious damage was caused to the images of the other three emperors inside the apse at different times and for different reasons. The faces of the three emperors Constantius Chlorus, Galerius, and Diocletian were vandalized by someone's hacking out an entire section of plaster (figure 5.16).

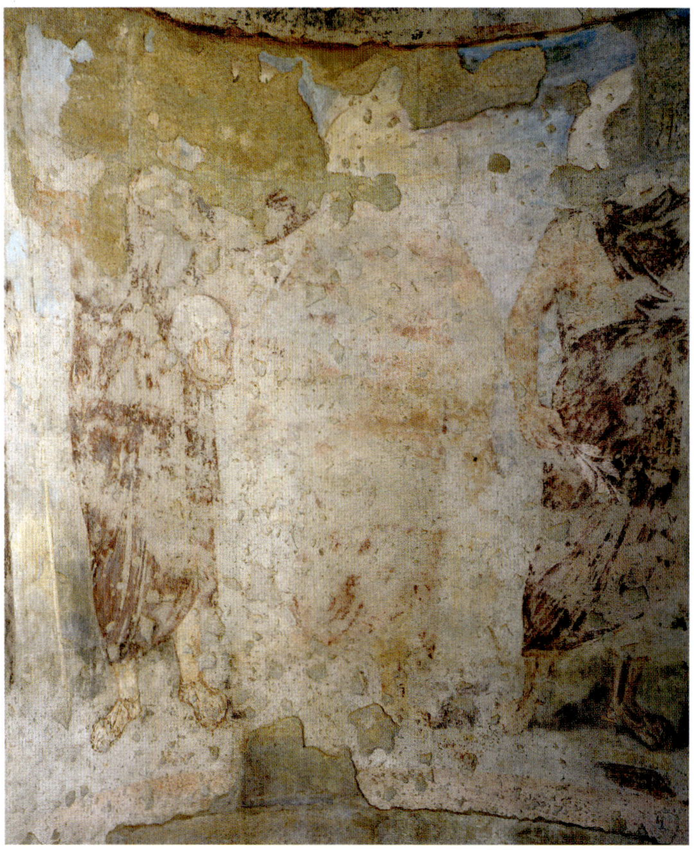

FIGURE 5.15
The heavily abraded figure in the niche.

The presence of extensive rectangular lacunae in the plaster on the east wall is clear evidence of the removal of plaster in the recent past, as described in chapter 4. At various times after the partial burying of the chamber, those portions of the walls above the fill were adapted for living purposes. This exposed the paintings to further damage, including the application of gypsum-based washes (see figure 4.24).[13] Wilkinson's watercolors (see the appendix) make it possible to identify where these were applied, as he did not reproduce the faces of the dignitaries at the left corner of the south wall since at that time they were still concealed beneath a layer of wash (figure 5.17).

Previous Conservation Interventions

The most recent human intervention affecting the frescoes is previous conservation work. This is extremely hard to quantify; indeed, the only campaign that can be dated with any certainty took place in the early 1970s.[14] It may have been at this time, or more probably during an earlier campaign, that a consolidating and brightening agent based on plant gum was applied.[15] In the absence of cleaning before its application, the substance effectively fixed the dirt on the painted surface. This layer, which is heavily blackened and oxidized as a result of continuous exposure to the sun and the elements, has also undergone considerable contraction, causing a dense and extensive network of cracks to form on the paint layer (figure 5.18). Repairs to the gaps in the stonework of the walls and ribbon pointing of the edges of the surviving fresco fragments, both carried out using lime mortar, can be attributed to more recent restoration campaigns carried out by the SCA (see figures 4.25 and 4.26).

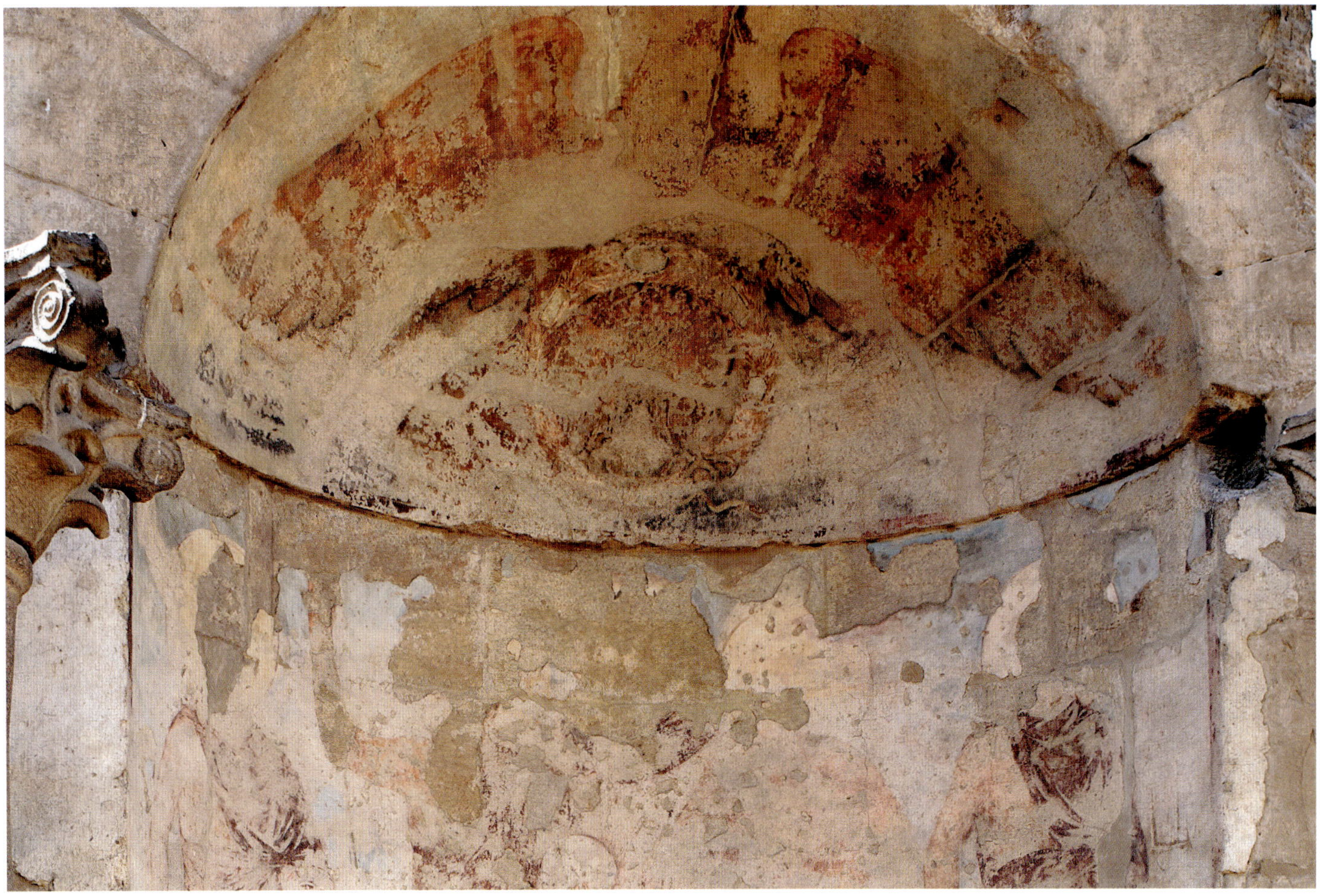

FIGURE 5.16
South wall: upper part of the niche, showing destroyed faces of the emperors.

FIGURE 5.17
South wall conservation record: orange indicates the extent of gypsum-based wash obscuring the frescoes and green the filling of cavities.

Present Conservation Treatment

The project took a total of six months of work, carried out by eight conservators. The campaigns took place in the fall of each year and each lasted two months. During the first campaign (2006), work was carried out on the east side of the south wall and a small part of the east wall. The second campaign (2007) addressed the niche in the center of the south wall, the painted fragments on the west side, and part of the lower tier of the same wall. During the third and final campaign (2008), the east wall was completed, together with the few surviving fragments of imitation opus sectile decoration on the west wall.

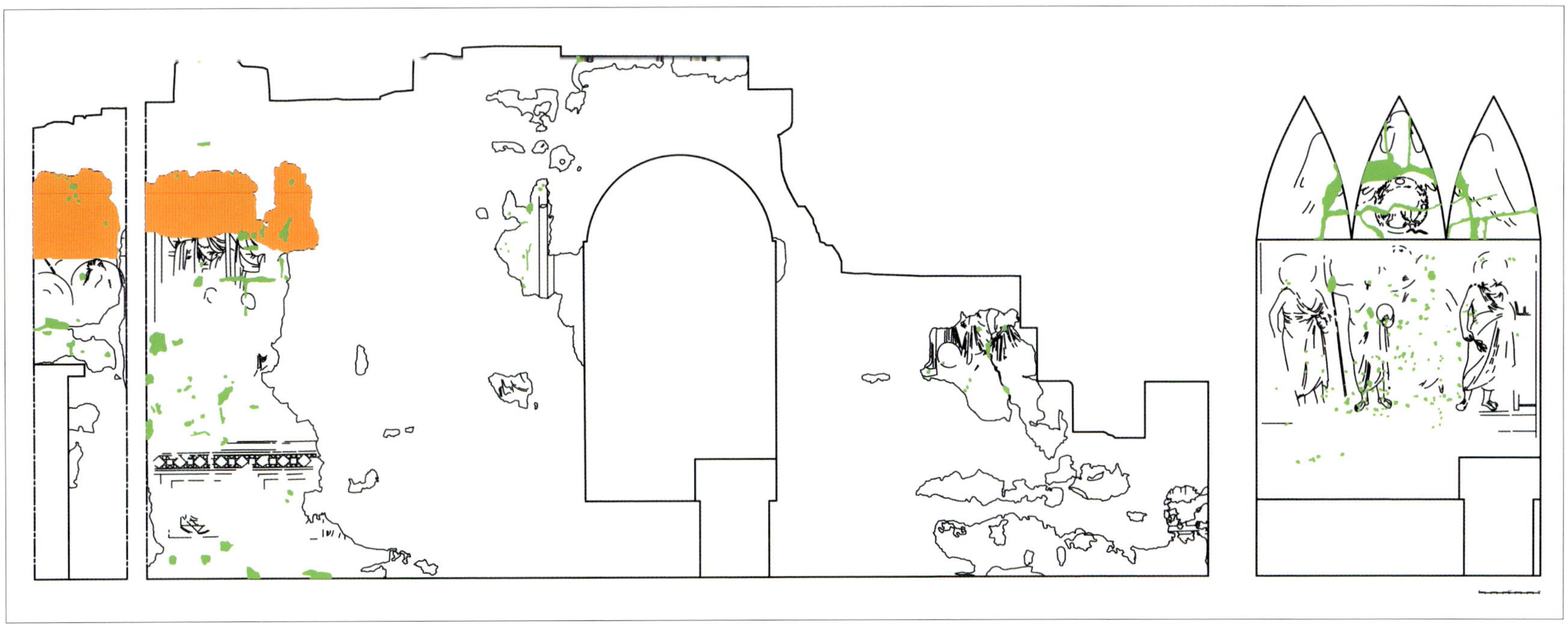

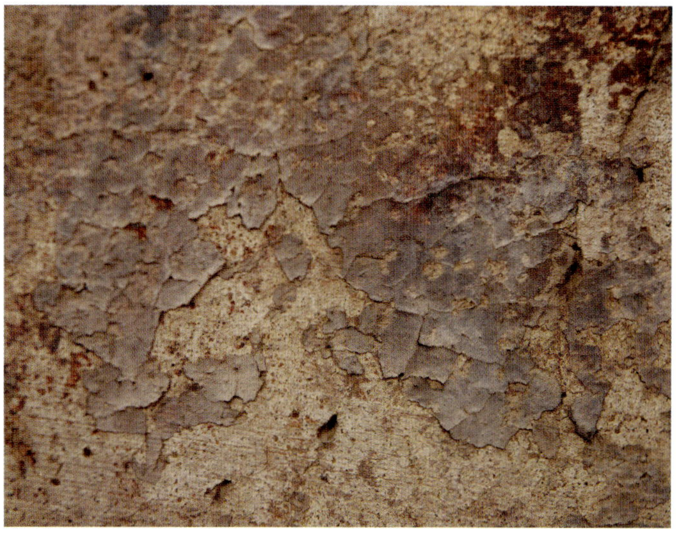

FIGURE 5.18
Detail showing how the paint layer has risen and cracked because of the deterioration of a fixative applied during previous restoration work.

The first step was to remove all the dust from the surfaces of the paintings, the Eighteenth-Dynasty reliefs, and the tops of the walls using soft bristle brushes. At the same time, all the fragments of plaster and paint layer that were in immediate danger of falling off were secured and consolidated (figure 5.19). This was done in two ways: the larger and more seriously detached fragments were secured with strips of Japanese paper fixed with a 15 percent solution of acrylic resin, and smaller flakes of plaster or paint layer were consolidated by directly injecting them with an acrylic resin emulsion using a fine syringe.

Clumsy pointing applied by earlier conservators around the edges of the plaster partially obscured the painted decoration and was removed mechanically with micro-scalpels and chisels. Mortar used to repair gaps and fill the spaces between the stone blocks was left in place because it was still fulfilling its intended purpose and was compatible with the original material. Repairs to the plaster were carried out using a mortar similar in composition and grain size to the original (two parts powdered sandstone, one part yellow sand, and one part slaked lime). Inside the niche, the extensive pick marks were partially filled to minimize the accumulation of particulate matter in the holes and to increase the legibility of the painting. Areas of plaster were consolidated by means of injections of liquid hydraulic mortar similar in composition to the original plaster. Before this, some pointing was carried out along the edges of the fragments to prevent the liquid mortar from leaking out.

The frescoes were cleaned with a solution of inorganic salts (ammonium carbonate) dissolved in water (sixty grams per liter) applied to the surfaces using a cellulose fiber compress. A cellulose ether (hydroxymethylcellulose) was added to the solution owing to its ability to keep water at the interface between the compress and paint layer, thereby preventing moisture from soaking the plaster. Contact times, developed on a case-by-case basis depending on the state of preservation and the painting technique used in each of the areas treated, varied from ten to twenty minutes. Once the compress was

FIGURE 5.19
Conservation record: loss of the plaster layer and lack of adhesion. Magenta indicates larger, seriously detached areas and blue the smaller detached areas of the plaster and paint layer.

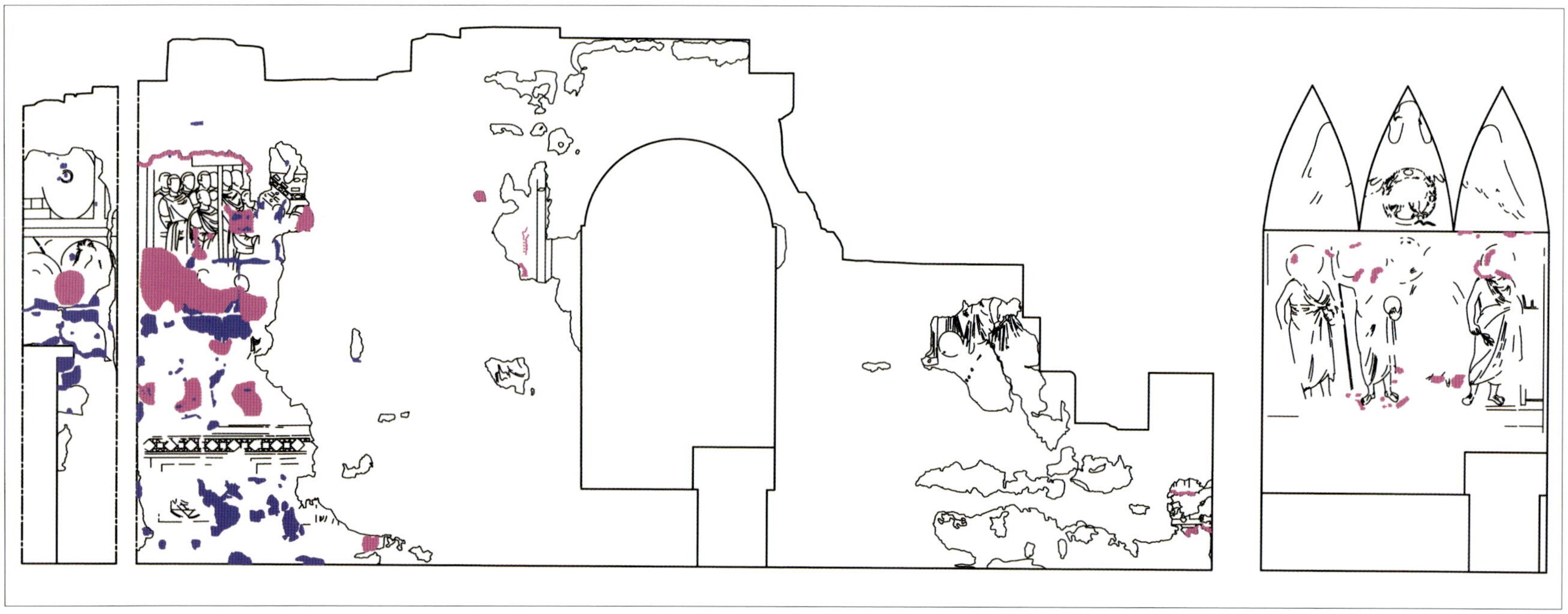

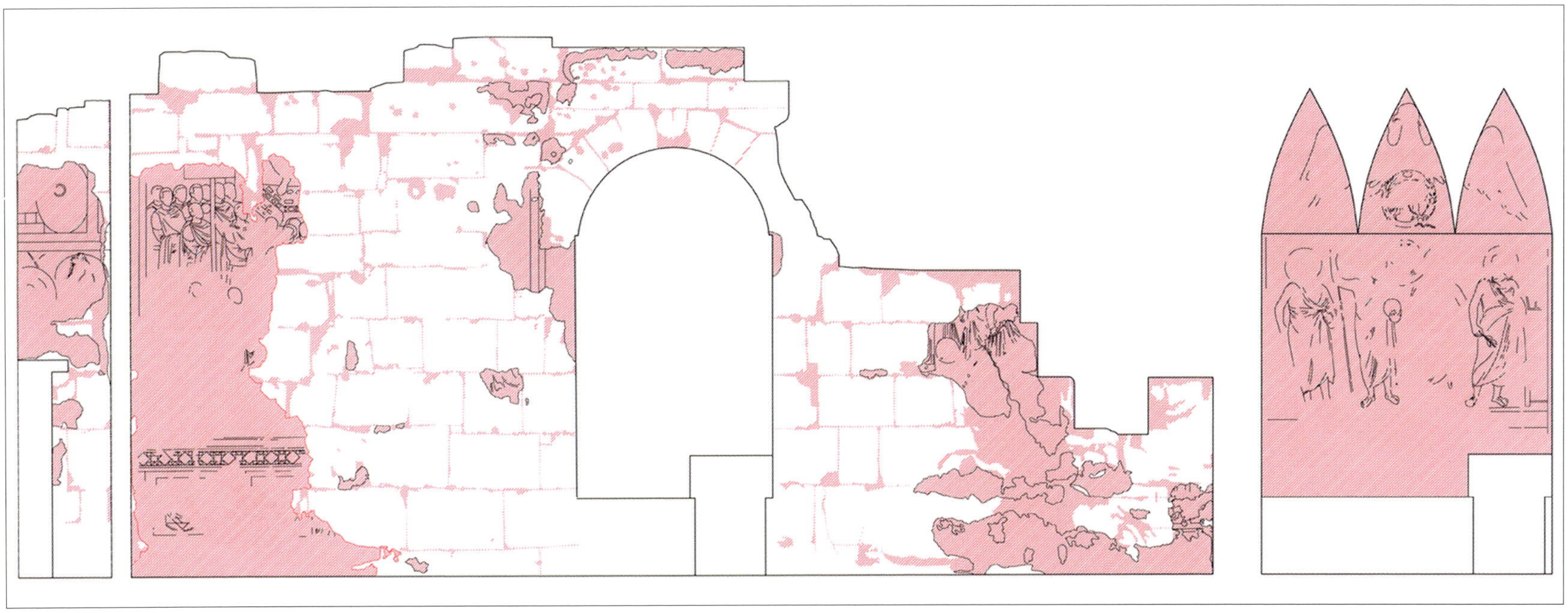

FIGURE 5.20
Conservation record: area cleaned (in pink), southeast corner, south wall, and niche.

removed, residual dirt, salt deposits, and substances that had been applied to the surface were carefully removed with bristle brushes and natural sponges. A compress of Japanese paper and distilled water was then applied to the painted surface to remove soluble salt residues. This method of cleaning softened the stubborn deposits on the surface that concealed artistic details, such as the beak of the eagle in the apse, and allowed them to be removed. Finer details and finishing touches applied in secco were cleaned with the same solution applied on Japanese paper for a contact time of seven minutes. After the paper was removed, any deposits were gently sponged away (figure 5.20).

On the lower part of the west wall, which was decorated with imitation opus sectile patterns, a thick and continuous layer of saline efflorescence was removed mechanically using chisels, fine fiberglass pens, and an electric micro-drill. In places where the paint layer had become seriously weakened and powdery owing to the deterioration of the binder, it was consolidated using a 1 percent solution of acrylic resin in an organic solvent.[16]

The final step was to increase the legibility of the frescoes by subtly deepening the light tone of the widespread gaps in the paint layer that made it hard to discern figurative details and geometric decorative motifs amid areas of surface loss and other damage. Specially stable and reversible watercolors were used to give a balanced patina to the areas where the background plaster had been noticeably lightened by the cleaning operations, appearing as gray tones in figure 5.8.

SCIENTIFIC INVESTIGATIONS AND ANALYSES

Emiliano Ricchi

The conservation of the paintings in the imperial cult chamber of Luxor Temple provided an opportunity to study in situ the aesthetics, materials, and techniques of Roman wall paintings of the tetrarchic period. By taking a series of observations and related investigations carried out during the course of the work as a starting point, a methodological model could be applied to the paintings. This meant that, at a later stage, we could develop a more targeted and comprehensive program of scientific diagnostic investigations, most of which were also carried out in situ.

The removal of layers of dirt and substances applied during previous maintenance and restoration work, such as varnish and repointing, enabled us to discover and assess the characteristics of the materials and working methods employed on the painted surfaces and to formulate an initial assessment of the pigments used. The unpainted areas of plaster and the preparatory layers visible through the many deep holes in the plaster were also carefully examined.

The preparation of plaster for the conservators to use in pointing work and repairs enabled us to study in depth the composition of Roman plaster types. The types of plaster we prepared imitated the originals as closely as possible in composition and compatibility, grain size, and color. This re-creation of ancient plaster types, based on research into materials and traditional local techniques, allowed us to carry out a comparative study that generated important information

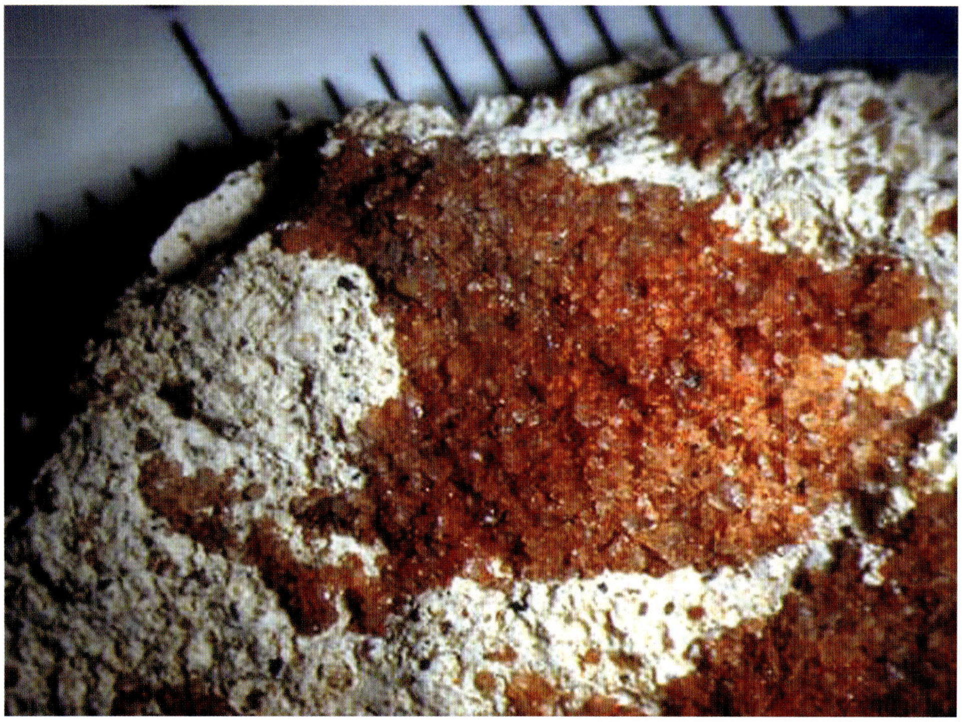

FIGURE 5.21
Macrophotograph of the internal face of a plaster sample with reddish-brown fragments of Nubian sandstone.

about the mineralogical characteristics and geological provenances of the raw materials. It also kept the number of microsamples of the original materials to a minimum.[17]

From its earliest stages, the project proceeded on the basis of interdisciplinary collaboration among scientists, architects, art historians, and conservators. The information collected during the course of the work was enhanced by a targeted program of analytical investigations, carried out mostly in situ by the geologist Domenico Poggi, whose analyses provided scientific backing for most of the information presented in this section of the chapter. His invaluable work enabled us to identify the stone used in the masonry of the temple, the stratigraphic sequence, and the nature of the various plaster and paint layers. Through the analysis it was also possible to identify and isolate the areas treated with modern materials during previous interventions in order to reconstruct the chronological sequence of the various phases of execution.

The samples collected were examined under a stereomicroscope, and some were selected for further, more detailed analysis. Subsequently, the most representative were subjected to

- thin-section microstratigraphic analysis together with microchemical and histochemical tests
- microchemical and mineralogical optical observations to identify pigments
- microchemical tests aimed at classifying the binders and fixative-preservatives
- chemical and mineralogical analysis using infrared spectrophotometry (Fourier Transform Infrared Spectroscopy, FT-IR).

The results of the main analyses of the various materials are shown below. These proved to be an indispensable aid to the completion of the study of working methods and state of preservation presented earlier in this chapter.

Masonry Supporting the Frescoes

Stereomicroscopic analysis of stone samples from the masonry taken from the base of the arriccio layer identified the lithotype as Nubian sandstone. Dispersions of hematite and limonite in the stone account for its characteristic reddish-brown color (figure 5.21).[18] By studying the samples collected, we were able to identify the characteristics of the preparatory double layer of lime-based render that is typical of fresco wall paintings.

The Plaster Layers

The arriccio was created by applying a render of lime, siliceous sand (largely quartzitic in composition), and plant fibers (figures 5.22 and 5.23). The last comprised mostly chopped straw, added because of its excellent moisture-retaining properties and ability to help the render adhere to the sandstone wall surface and prevent the formation of cracks during the drying phase. The fibrous material gives structure and solidity to this preparatory layer, applied in a single coat to even out irregularities in the masonry, as described in the section above on working methods.

The render reproduced on-site during the conservation work to repair gaps in the arriccio provided the opportunity for an accurate reconstruction of the process used to prepare straw for inclusion in the plaster. The fiber was roughly ground up using rudimentary hand mills to crush the stalks. The resulting fragments were subsequently sorted according to size by sieving. Before being added to the render, the vegetable fiber had to be thoroughly washed under running water to remove all traces of the coloring substances that otherwise would have dyed the plaster a permanent deep, bright yellow.[19] The layer of intonaco is a render between 1.5 and 2.5 centimeters thick, comprising lime and siliceous sand of the quartzitic type found in the desert around Luxor (figure 5.22, upper).

The undersides of certain plaster fragments among the samples typically have a smooth surface sometimes dis-

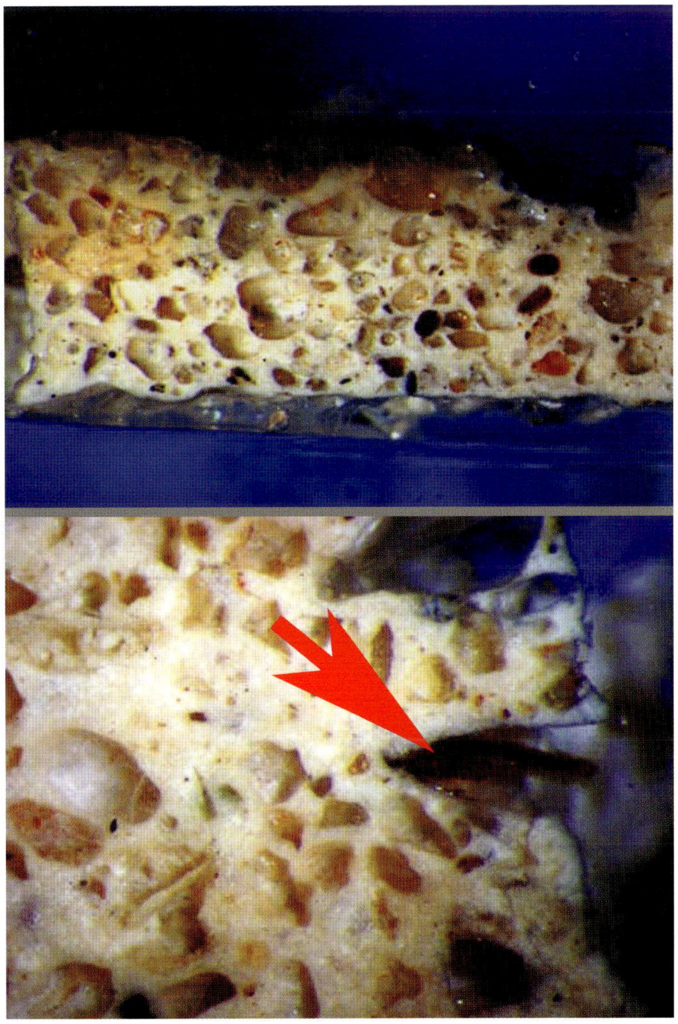

FIGURE 5.22
(right) Thin-section microstratigraphic analysis in reflected light of a sample of arriccio (upper approximately ×16), and the final layer of plaster, the intonaco (lower, approximately ×26), showing the similarities in the composition of both. Plant fiber is indicated by the red arrow.

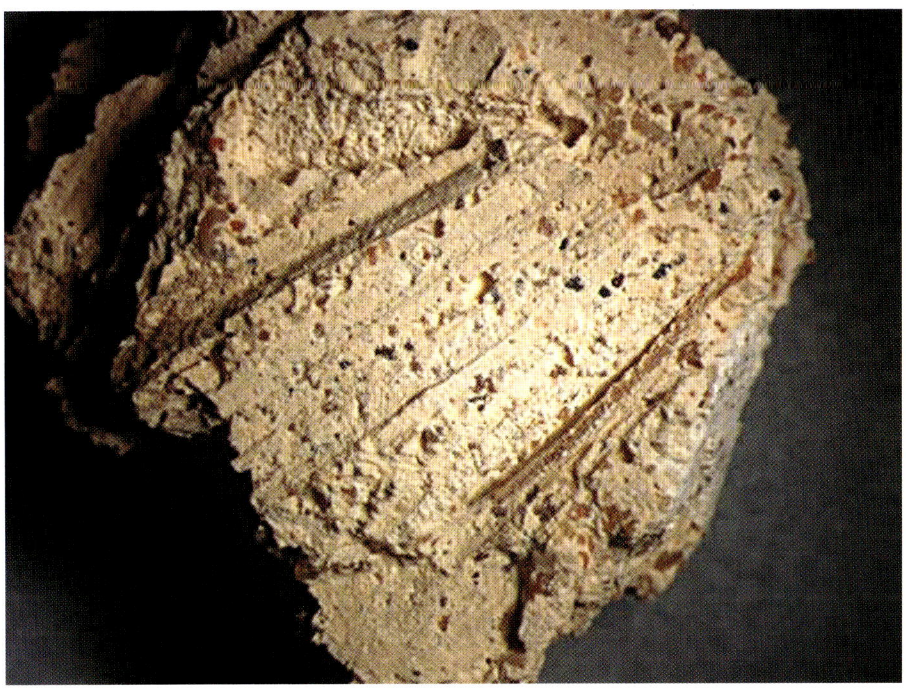

FIGURE 5.23
(below) Stereomicroscope image of the arriccio, showing plant fibers (approximately ×7).

tinguished by a thin, whitish application of lime, probably applied as a primer and painted directly onto the arriccio with a brush. None of the samples collected contained a fragment comprising both the arriccio layer and the overlying intonaco plaster, which showed that adhesion between the two preparatory layers was poor. The surface of the plaster is generally smooth and well finished, bearing the signs of careful working with level and trowel.

The Paint Layer

The paint layer is made up of a single more-or-less dense coat of pigment applied in fresco to this surface and compatible with the basicity of the damp plaster. As explained in the section on working methods, certain pigments applied in secco are instead dissolved in an organic binder. The process of painting vast areas of wet plaster applied, as in this case, in pontate often means that the render has had a long time to dry out before color is applied to it, especially in the last areas to be painted. This difficulty, in our case doubtless exacerbated by the weather conditions in Luxor, was usually resolved using the Roman technique of carefully pressing the plaster with the flat of a trowel before painting to bring a certain amount of lime to the surface. A number of samples that seem to be representative of the working methods used for all the samples examined display in cross section a thin, whitish layer covering the lime and sand plaster (figure 5.24, layer 1b). This could be the accumulation of lime at the surface caused by the smoothing process just described, or it could be that the paint was primed with a wash of grainy-textured lime that retains the imprint of the brush used to apply it, as described in the section on working methods.

Observation of cross sections and data obtained from the FT-IR analyses and the microchemical and histochemical tests reveal the presence of calcium carbonate in a great many painted areas. The presence of this substance may indicate the use of a certain amount of highly diluted whitewash for dissolving pigments and helping the paint layer adhere to the plaster as it dried; however, it is more likely to be connected with the use of a white pigment that did not function as a binder and was obtained by crushing lumps of desiccated lime.

In two samples that were examined in stratigraphic section (figures 5.24 and 5.26), the presence of Egyptian blue in the paint layer seems to confirm that this pigment was dissolved in an organic binder before application. The green paint on the shield behind the horse on the east wall (figure 5.25, lower register) comprises a base of hematite red (Fe_2O_3) applied to wet

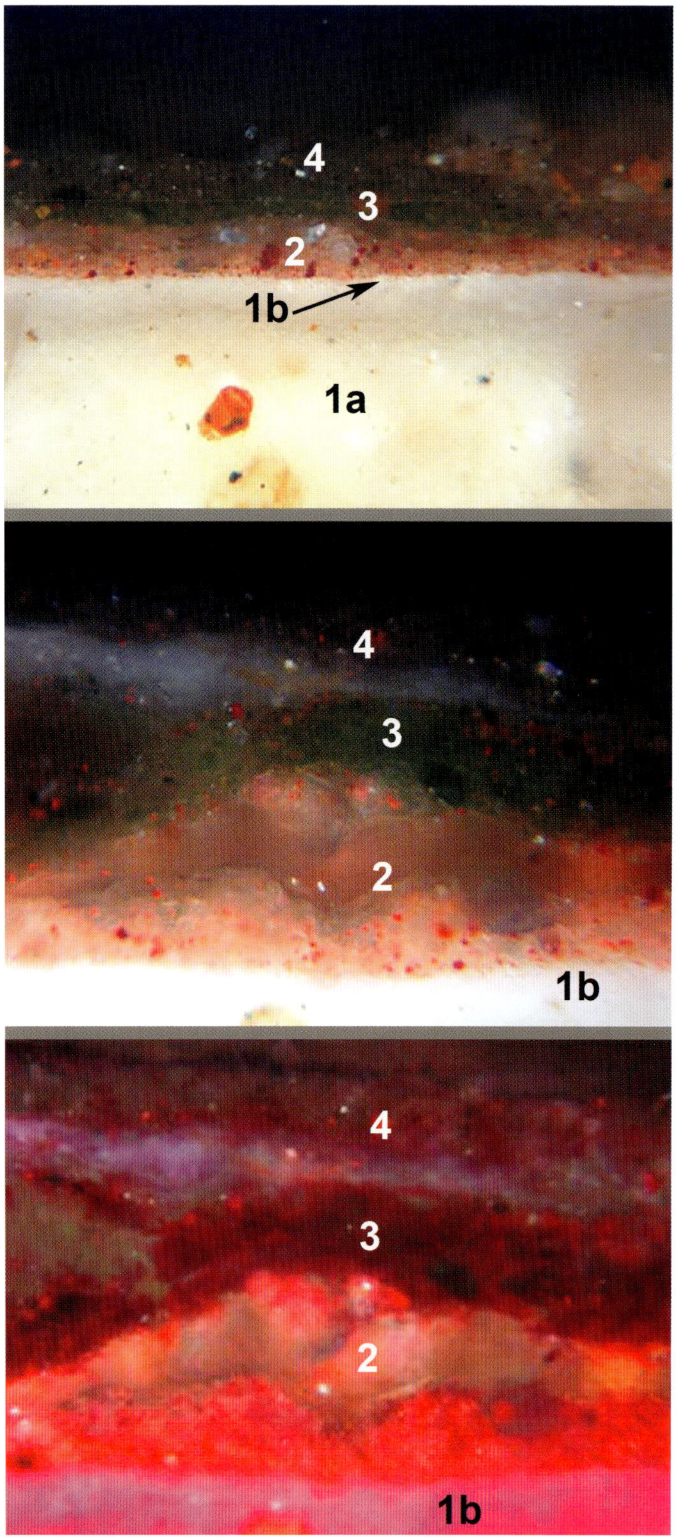

FIGURE 5.24
Thin-section microstratigraphic analysis in reflected light of a sample of green paint on the shield behind the horse (see figure 5.25) showing the structure. Upper: approximately ×200, showing layers—(1a) siliceous sand and lime plaster; (1b) thin, whitish layer, probably a surface accumulation of lime caused by smoothing the plaster; (2) hematite red base (Fe_2O_3) applied to wet plaster; (3) green paint colored with green earth, green Egyptian frit, and the rare Egyptian blue; (4) substances such as fixatives and protective coating applied to the painted surface during previous conservation work and areas of repainting. Center: approximately ×500, showing the same layers. Lower: the same sample, tested with a fuchsine reagent, confirming the presence of a protein-based binder used to apply the third layer of green pigment.

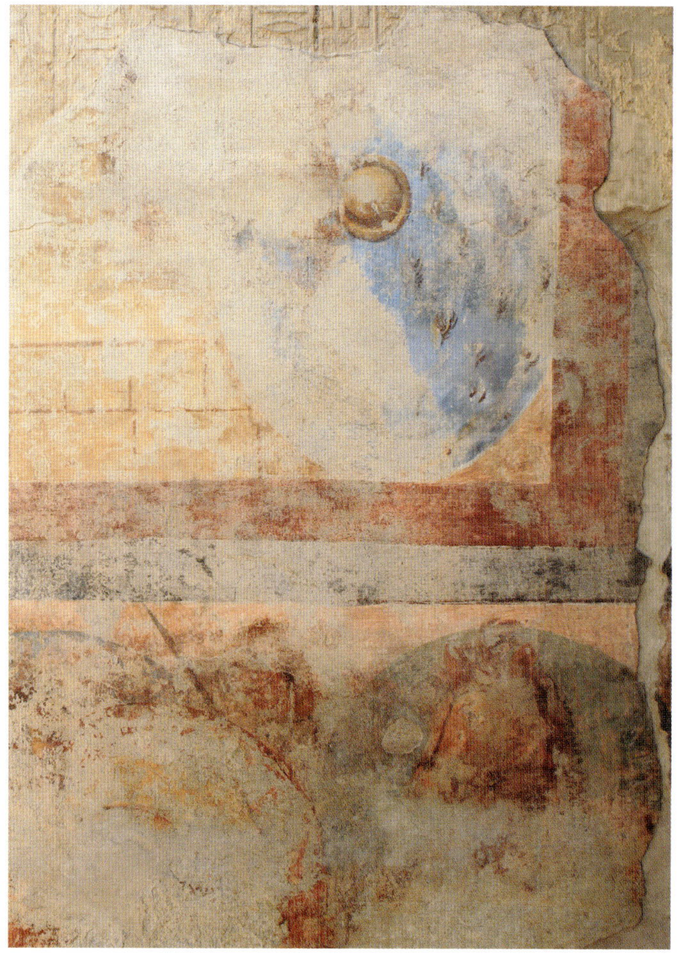

FIGURE 5.25
(right) Southeast corner of the east wall: a shield painted with Egyptian blue (above) and a horse's head in front of a green shield (below).

plaster covered by a layer of green comprising green earth, a little green Egyptian frit, and occasional Egyptian blue (figure 5.24, layers 2 and 3).[20] Testing with a fuchsine reagent confirmed the presence of a protein binder (figure 5.24, lower). The blue shield on the same wall is painted exclusively in Egyptian blue (figure 5.25, upper register). The near absence of calcite in the mixture indicates that it was applied in secco technique in a protein-based tempera. The microchemical and histochemical tests carried out, however, were unable to identify the nature of the binder used, probably owing to the extreme alteration and mineralization into oxalates of the binder itself, assisted by the presence of copper in the blue cuprorivaite-based pigment ($CaCuSi_4O_{10}$). The pigment was subjected to mineralogical optical analysis under a transmitted light–polarizing microscope and FT-IR spectrum analysis (figure 5.26, lower right).

Traces of Earlier Conservation Work

The microstratigraphic analyses, microchemical and histochemical tests, and FT-IR spectroscopy also clarified the nature of the washes and layers of gray-brown deposits, all of which can be attributed to earlier maintenance or conservation work. The ivory-colored wash was found to be made up of lime, gypsum, and animal glue, possibly lightly tinted with earth pigments and affected by ancient deposits of atmospheric particulate matter. This layer is often covered by a brown film also composed of an adhesive or protective substance based on gum arabic (see figure 5.24, layer 4).[21] In all the samples, the gray-brown layer overlies the paint layer or the base layers (plaster layers and wash). The analyses suggest that this layer may be connected to relatively recent repainting work carried out as a maintenance measure using gypsum, a small amount of charcoal, earth pigments, and protein-based binders.

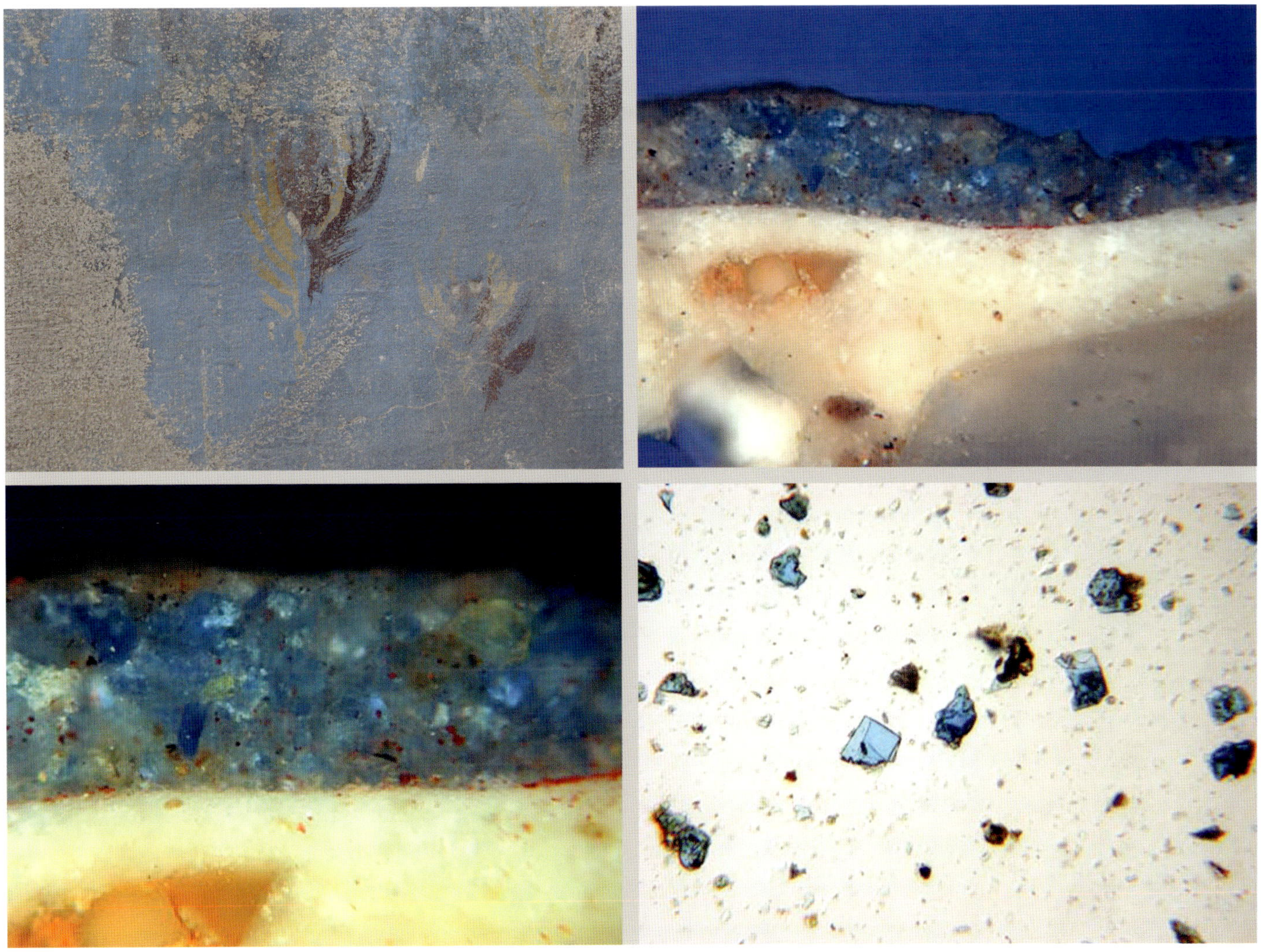

FIGURE 5.26
Thin-section microstratigraphic analysis in reflected light of a sample of blue paint from the shield (see figure 5.25). Upper left: detail of the thick layer of blue pigment based on Egyptian blue. Upper right: approximately ×100. Lower left: approximately ×200. Lower right: mineralogical and microchemical optical analysis by a transmitted light-polarizing microscope, showing grains of Egyptian blue, typically varying from light to dark blue in color, and the presence of prismatic inclusions; approximately ×250.

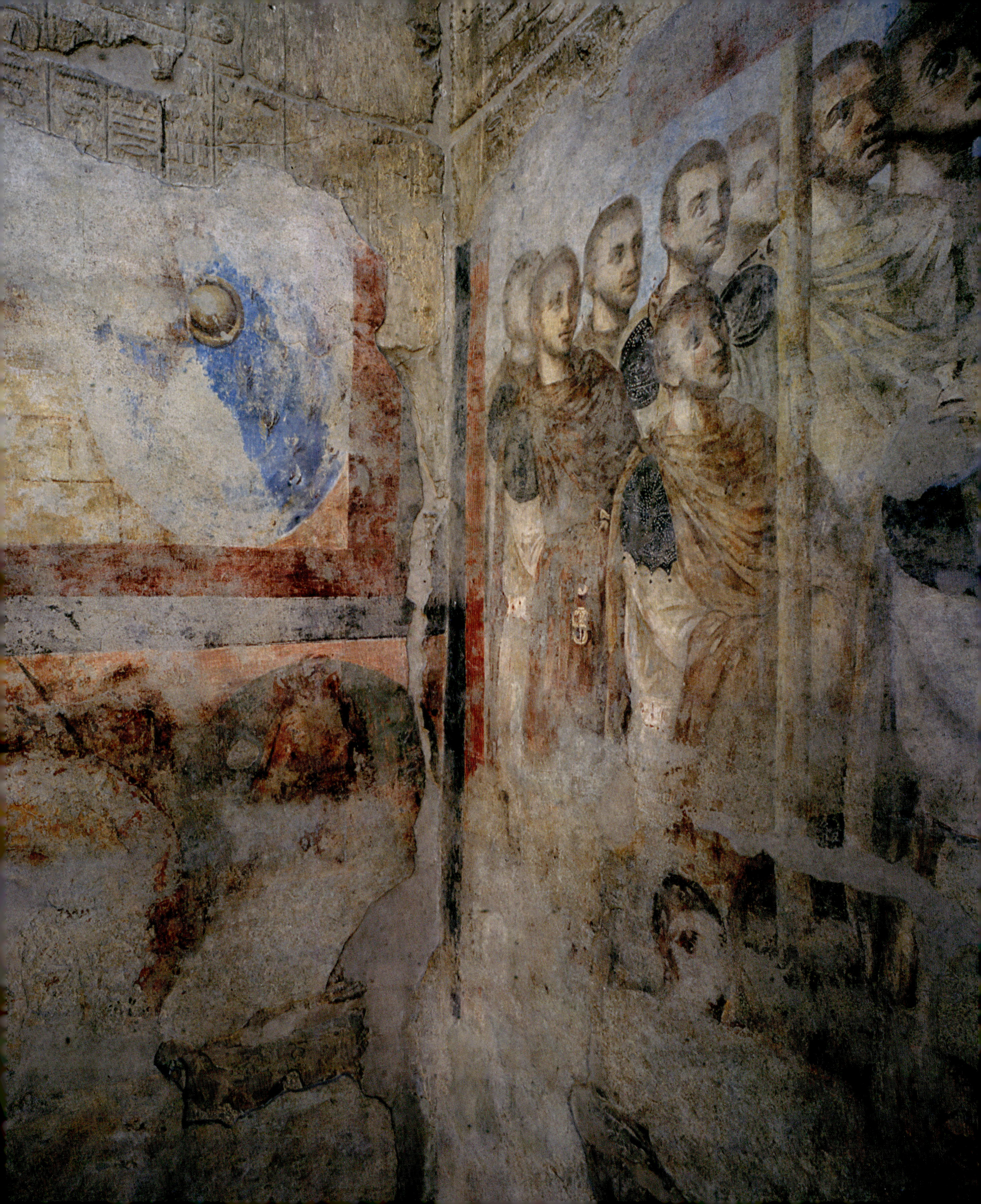

Chapter 6

THE LUXOR TEMPLE PAINTINGS IN CONTEXT

Roman Visual Culture in Late Antiquity

SUSANNA McFADDEN

CATEGORIZING THE LATE ROMAN PAINTINGS IN LUXOR Temple is a complex undertaking. On the one hand, they are classic examples of late Roman state art. In their style and iconography they could be found anywhere in the empire and be recognized as such. On the other hand, they are exceptional as the only extant monumental paintings of any kind from the tetrarchic era and the sole remaining high-quality *buon fresco* in Roman Egypt.[1] Therefore, the paintings are extremely important as some of the few surviving representations of a decorative medium that was widely used in antiquity.[2] They are also the best preserved examples (in any medium) of a decorative program from a site related to the imperial cult, and in this way they must also stand in for a larger body of lost examples. To fully understand the paintings' polysemic significance, therefore, it is necessary to examine them from multiple methodological perspectives. This chapter discusses the paintings first in purely art historical terms. Building on the work of several important studies of the paintings in the 1970s, the style and iconography of the images are examined in a manner permitting visualization of the original program of the painted room as well as situation of these paintings within a larger chronology of Roman art.[3] Chapter 7 then follows with an examination of the typology and function of the room in which the images were placed, the so-called imperial cult chamber, considering the historical implication of such a site being situated in the unusual architectural context of Luxor Temple, as well as the importance of the Luxor paintings in the wider framework of late Roman culture. The overarching questions guiding these micro-studies are: What were the intentions of Roman image makers at Luxor in the late third and early fourth centuries, and how did the images facilitate the aims of imperial policy? What message did the Romans wish to communicate by placing frescoes in the heart of a pharaonic temple, and to what extent can we evaluate the success of this endeavor?

STYLISTIC OVERVIEW

While the multiple scenes that form the painted program of the imperial cult chamber are unified in subject—simply put, together they are a triumphalist homage to the majesty of the Tetrarchy—the constituent parts of the program are not necessarily unified in terms of style and composition. The division of wall space into decorative zones (registers) is not the same on all four walls, and the compositions within each decorative zone do not exhibit a homogeneous visual language.[4] These inconsistencies do not simply suggest different artistic hands, although a team undoubtedly painted the frescoes. Rather, the stylistic differences between the east wall scenes and those of the south wall, for example, are symptomatic of late antique aesthetic preferences and are typical of state-sponsored art of this period.[5] It was not unusual in late antiquity for Roman artists, in all media, to deliberately juxtapose naturalistic compositions with more symbolic, stylized scenes in programs related to the imperial court in order to signal a shift in thematic content.[6]

In addition to this stylistic variability, the compositional format of the room is not consistent across all four walls. It is possible to deduce from Wilkinson's drawings and the fragments in situ that the east, north, and, probably, west walls were divided into at least three horizontal registers of decoration. A fourth register on these walls is not out of the realm of possibility, if the height of the Roman ceiling was equal to or greater than that of the original pharaonic space, as hypoth-

FIGURE 6.1
Southeast corner and south wall viewed from an oblique angle, illustrating the illusionism of the crowd scene and the naturalism of the figures' facial features.

esized in chapter 3. The upper edge of the lowest band of decoration is approximately 2.2 meters above the present floor, slightly above eye level, and is the same height across these three surfaces. It is ornamental, painted to resemble marble inlay, a technique known as *opus sectile.* In contrast, while the lowest register of decoration on the south wall is still above eye level and of the same design, the frieze is approximately 15 centimeters lower in height than the geometric frieze on the other walls of the room, causing a visual disjuncture at the southeast corner (and probably also the southwest), where the east wall opus sectile register meets its counterpart on the south wall (see figure A.1). This discrepancy in the height of the painted opus sectile is probably deliberate—designed to draw special attention to the figural compositions above. The lower register of opus sectile "carries" the middle figural registers, the most important in terms of decorative hierarchy, and at Luxor it is especially necessary to mark a conceptual distinction between the subject matter of the east wall's middle register and that of the south wall. This is accomplished not only by a lack of symmetry in the size of the decorative registers but also by the inclusion of visual framing devices; bold, vertical outlines of red and black enclose the edges of the south wall composition, sectioning it off from the other scenes that surround it. Presumably every individual episode in the Luxor program was similarly framed. The overall effect is such that each illustrated panel has an internal narrative and compositional coherency, but it is also just one panel in a larger story. Traces of these framing lines are still visible in the southeast corner, vertically delineating the south wall composition from that of the east wall, as well as horizontally dividing the east wall narrative register from the one above it (figure 6.1).

The visual disjuncture between the middle registers of the east and south walls is emphasized not only in terms of format but by the style of the compositions as well. On the east wall the second register of decoration contains naturalistically rendered figures engaged in a procession. Wilkinson recorded traces on the north wall indicating a similar parade there also. These scenes range horizontally across the space of the wall and have a narrative quality whereby the figures appear to inhabit and interact with one another in a realistic spatial setting. In contrast, the composition of the south wall's figural register, with the niche in the center, is hieratic in scale and "out of time" in terms of thematic content. The scenes depicted there are symbolic and eternal in concept rather than narrative. The south wall's middle band of figural decoration is also much larger and higher overall than those of the east and, presumably at one time, the west and north walls.[7] The figures are arrayed vertically and stacked against the picture plane, so that they do not appear to reside in a realistic, three-dimensional spatial setting.

Notably, the kinds of formal variations evident in the frescoes at Luxor occur completely within the confines of a classical visual vocabulary, a factor that is quite unusual in comparison to other extant paintings from Roman Egypt, which often combine Egyptian and Roman visual languages in a single composition. This synthesis is especially evident in the funerary realm, which has yielded the largest corpus of painted remains from the era of Ptolemaic and Roman rule.[8] The third-century painted linen shroud inscribed in Greek for a soldier named Tyras is a good illustration of this amalgamation of styles (see figure 1.6). Combined in this one image are two different modes of representing the human body—the naturalistic and the conceptual.[9] Tyras wears a contemporary Roman soldier's garment and gazes outward, as if to confront the viewer. His features and clothing give the impression of volume and corporeality, both characteristic of a Greco-Roman visual vocabulary not seen in Egypt before the Ptolemies. In contrast, Tyras stands in an unrealistic setting before a stylized niche decorated with tiny statuettes of Osiris and Anubis on either side of his head. These are represented as linear, two-dimensional figures in the Egyptian manner and connect Tyras to traditional Egyptian cult practices.[10] Such stylistic elements, individually associated with distinctive cultural polities, thus mingle to create a new visual vocabulary typifying the complex cultural and ethnic demographics of Roman Egypt.[11]

Such mingling of styles, which makes it difficult to determine the ethnic identity of subjects like Tyras, is a phenomenon that did not extend in the Roman period to state-sponsored art. In the realm of power, and particularly in the representation of the Roman ruler, Egyptian stylistic conventions for representing the human figure were generally adopted completely or not at all.[12] For example, in the early empire, Roman emperors represented in the temples of Upper Egypt were illustrated as pharaohs, and their names were inscribed in hieroglyphs.[13] By the third century this practice seems to have been largely abandoned.[14] Instead, surviving images of the later Roman emperors were rendered according to classical conventions, exemplified by the famous dynastic tondo of Septimius Severus and his family discovered in the Fayyum, the only painted, portable imperial image to have survived antiquity (figure 6.2). Yet in spite of the decidedly Greco-Roman style of this tondo, it is also an Egyptian product. It has been argued that the image of Septimius Severus resembles depictions of the god Serapis, which would affirm the emperor's connection to the synthetic cults of Greco-

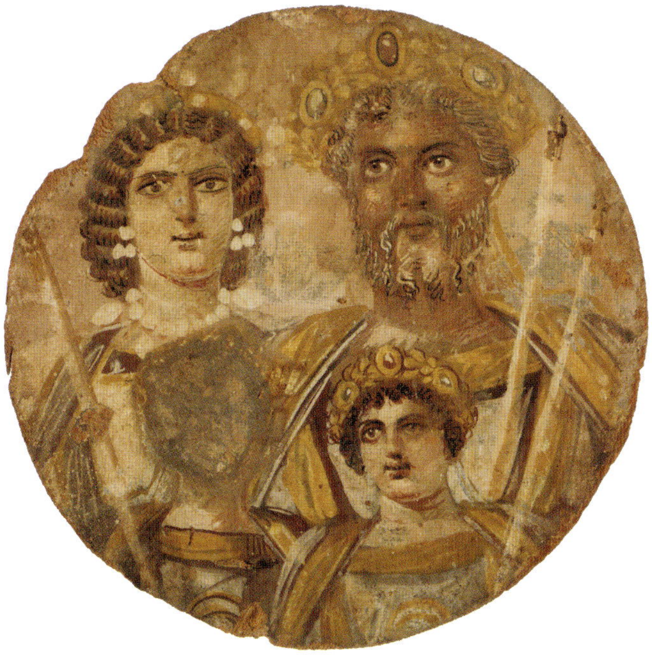

FIGURE 6.2
Painted tondo of Septimius Severus, his wife, Julia Domna, and their children, Caracalla and Geta (erased in antiquity), from Egypt, ca. 200, tempera on wood, Antikensammlung, Staatlich Museen, Berlin.

Roman Egypt.[15] In addition, the technique with which the painting is rendered may be linked to contemporary workshops in the Fayyum producing mummy portraits.[16]

The Luxor paintings, on the other hand, in their style and technique stand apart from both contemporary non-elite and imperial painting practices in Egypt. It is likely that the artists of the Luxor program were not local but, rather, itinerant artisans directly associated with the imperial court or the army. And though it is probable that frescoes of the same quality and appearance once existed in the cosmopolitan context of Alexandria, no evidence of this material has been found.[17] Were we to consider the iconography of the Luxor paintings alone, without their pharaonic architectural frame, there would be nothing identifiable in their content connecting them to Egypt.

In short, the imperial cult chamber at Luxor Temple was a wholly Roman visual environment. Every surface of the walls would have been decorated with colorful paintings, so riotous in color and diverse in content that the specific subject matter and organization of each scene might not have been immediately evident to a visitor upon first entering the space. And yet, there is no question about the most important decorative zone in the room—the south wall. The gaze of a visitor entering the space today is immediately drawn to the four larger-than-life-size figures of the Tetrarchs situated in the south wall niche, directly opposite the entrance to the room (figure 6.3). This

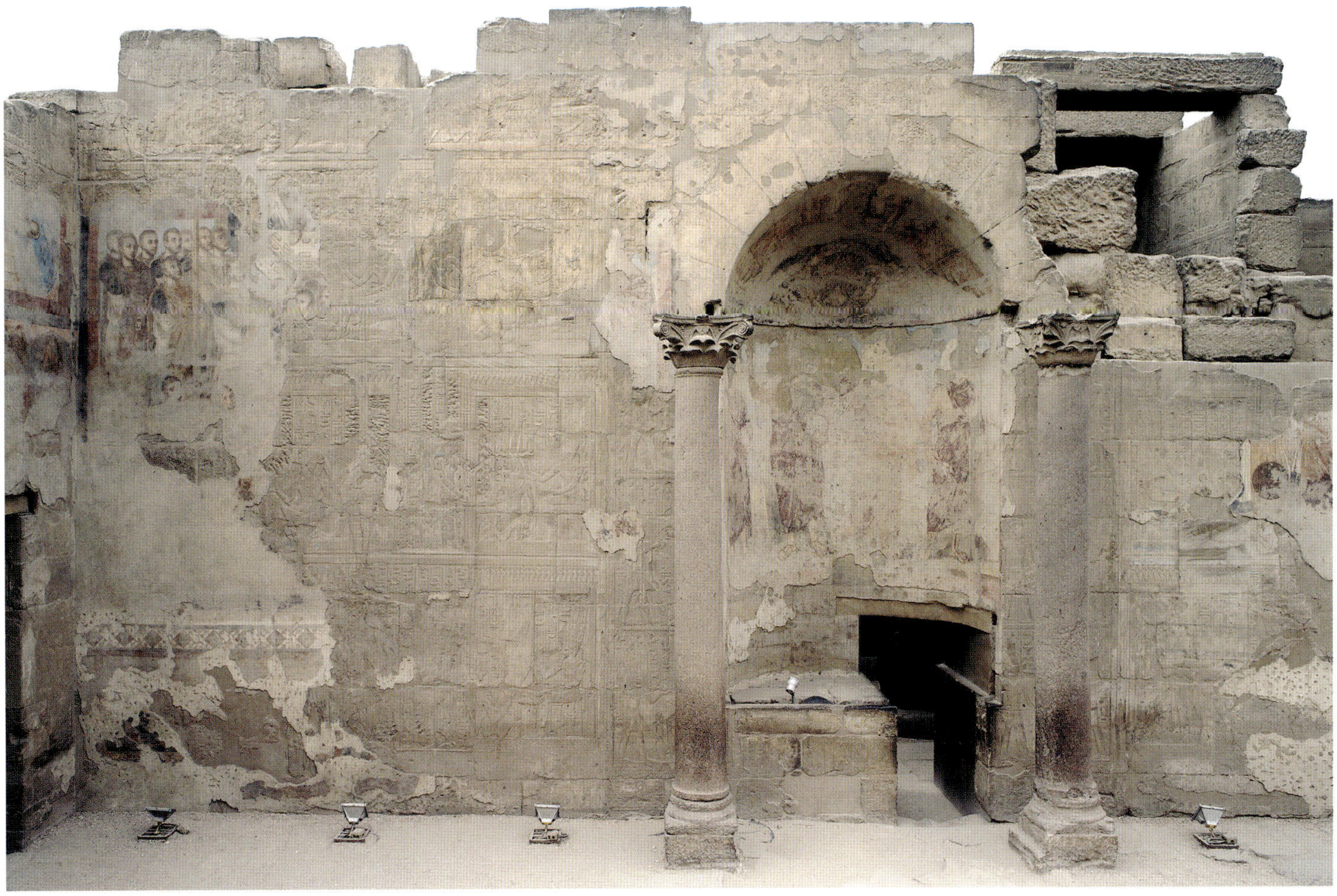

FIGURE 6.3
South wall, east side, and the niche.

sightline is certainly the most important one in the room, and we will return to it, as the primary figural zone of decoration on the south wall, in more detail later. For the moment, however, a description of what survives of the subsidiary mural decorations is in order, using the nineteenth-century documentation of the room along with the evidence of the recently cleaned frescoes.

EAST, NORTH, AND WEST WALLS

When Wilkinson sketched the imperial cult chamber, the most complete and legible section of Roman plaster was that of the east wall, where three registers of decoration are still discernible. The bottom register depicts a geometric pattern of imitation opus sectile, and the middle register contains a figural composition; the subject matter of the topmost register is difficult to determine because of the state of the plaster, both in the nineteenth century and today (figure 6.4). This section of plaster is now so badly degraded overall that, in spite of the recent conservation, only traces of the dynamic composition recorded by Wilkinson survive. It is, however, enough to affirm the relative accuracy of his 1856 watercolors, at least in relation to the middle, and most important, register of decoration (figure 6.5).

The episode represented in this register takes place within an illusionistically rendered space (see figures A.1, A.6 right, and 4.8). Men and horses stand on a mustard-yellow ground line of a color that is not unlike the color of the beaten earth in and around Luxor Temple, which suggests perhaps that the viewer is meant to draw a visual parallel between the real space in which he or she stands and the fictive episode depicted. The paintings can thus be understood to illustrate the type of ceremonial procession that might have taken place in real life in the space of the temple. Adding to the illusion-

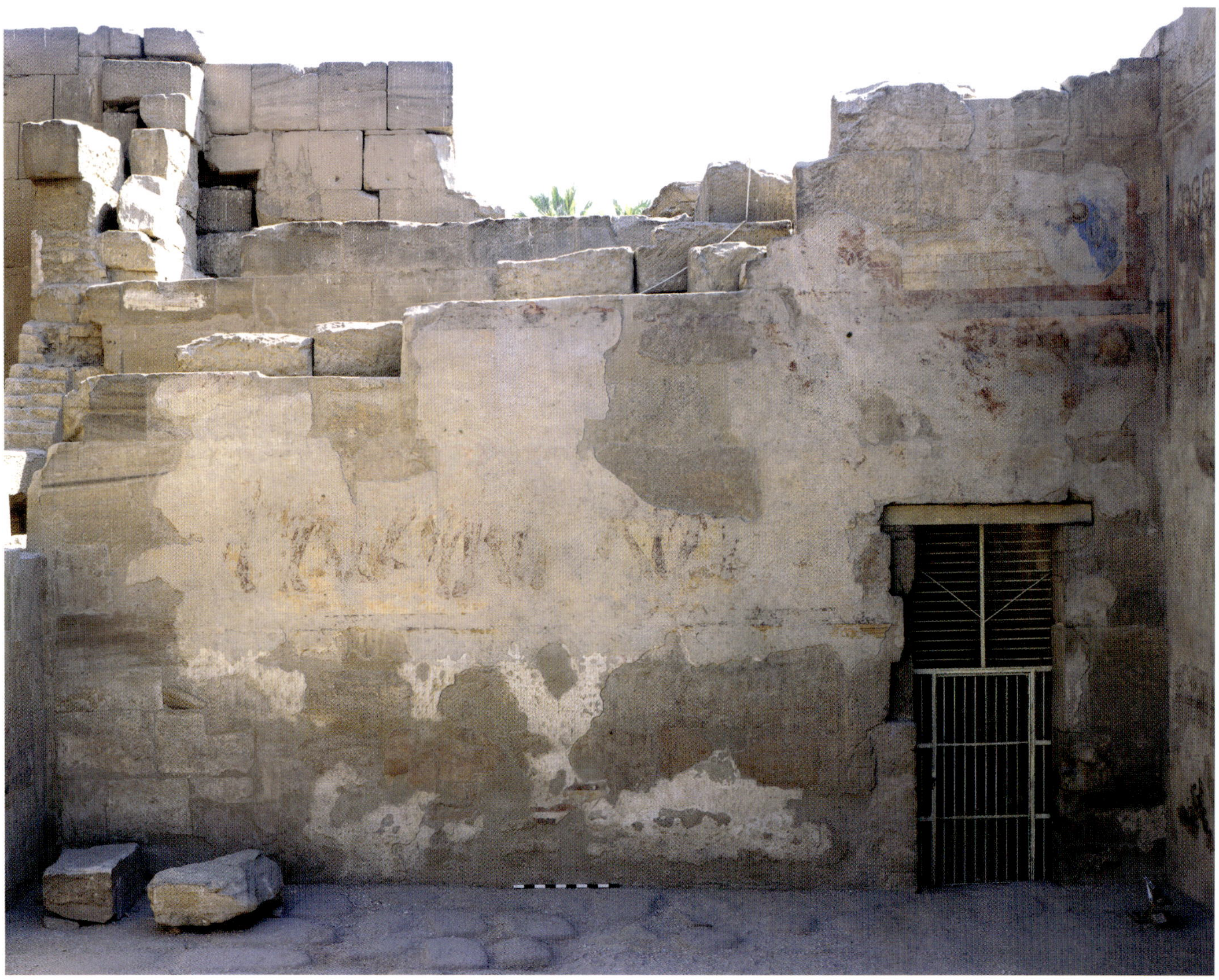

FIGURE 6.4
East wall.

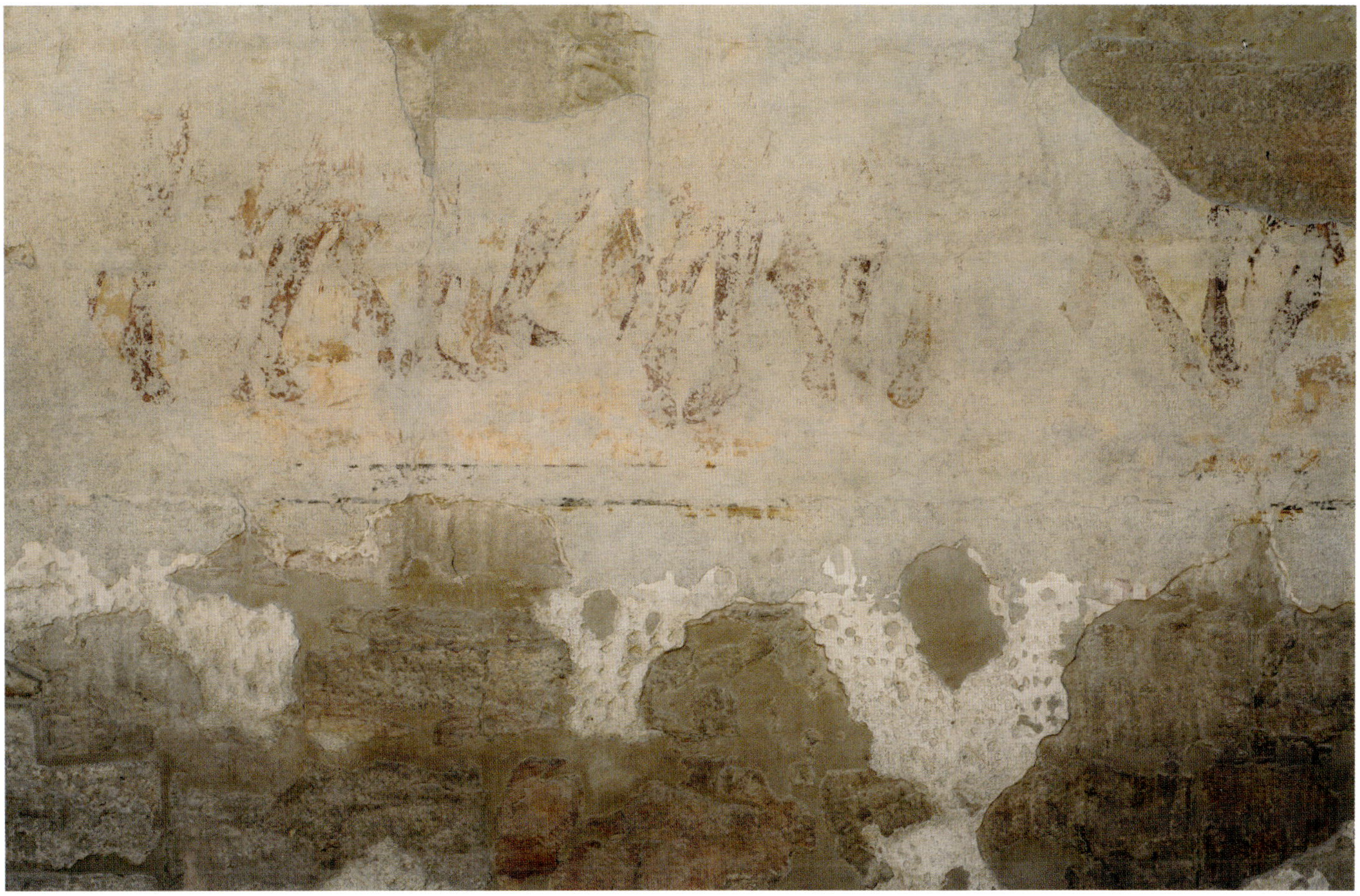

FIGURE 6.5
East wall detail: overlapping feet of soldiers and horses in procession.

ism of the scene and its impression of movement, the painted figures cast shadows on the sandstone-yellow ground as if illuminated from behind and to their right. The artists have further suggested recession into space by overlapping the figures and rendering them in three-quarter profiles. The direction of the procession southward (toward the right from the point of view of the spectator) is clearly suggested by the stance of the soldiers, a convention for representing bodies in motion; they bend their left legs at the knee, angle their left feet toward the south wall, and lean their bodies in that same direction. Though the figures are moving in concert to the south, however, other aspects of their poses are individualized. The figure in the middle of Wilkinson's east wall overview, for example, looks backward, as if to chat with the person behind him in line, while the soldier on the right edge of the scene gazes up at his horse, whose body is angled toward the viewer and is foreshortened accordingly. This soldier appears to be struggling to keep his horse in rank, as would be normal in a real-life procession of soldiers and their mounts. Indeed, all the horses and figures are dynamically rendered, especially the lively pose of the man on the right side of Wilkinson's detail (figure 6.6), who is turning his back on the viewer in order to grab the reins of his black horse.

The recent cleaning of the plaster has revealed another dynamic vignette on the far right side of the register, just above the door leading into a subsidiary chamber (figures 6.7 and 5.25). There we see the twisting head of a brown horse glancing over its right shoulder at a cluster of other horses and figures holding shields and spears. The position of the horse's head and that of the barely visible rider recall images of rearing horses at the front of the *adventus* procession on the Arch of Galerius (see figure 7.5). Here perhaps is the leader of the parade, mounted to distinguish his rank from those of the other figures, who walk beside their horses.[18] Interactive vignettes of this kind within the east wall composition make the kinetic energy of the procession palpable and convey an overall impression of spontaneity.

The figures are identifiable as soldiers by their lances and shields, and one can discern from Wilkinson's detail that the man struggling to control the black horse has a scabbard hanging from his waist. Each soldier also wears the close-cropped hairstyle typical of the tetrarchic era. They are not decked out in typical battle attire, however. They do not wear helmets or cuirasses, which one would expect if this episode depicted a martial procession, as many other Roman commemorative monuments do, such as the Column of Marcus Aurelius in Rome (figure 6.8). Instead, the men wear ceremonial attire: short, embroidered tunics belted at the waist of a type often found in Egypt in the archaeological and artistic record.[19] On the east wall, the

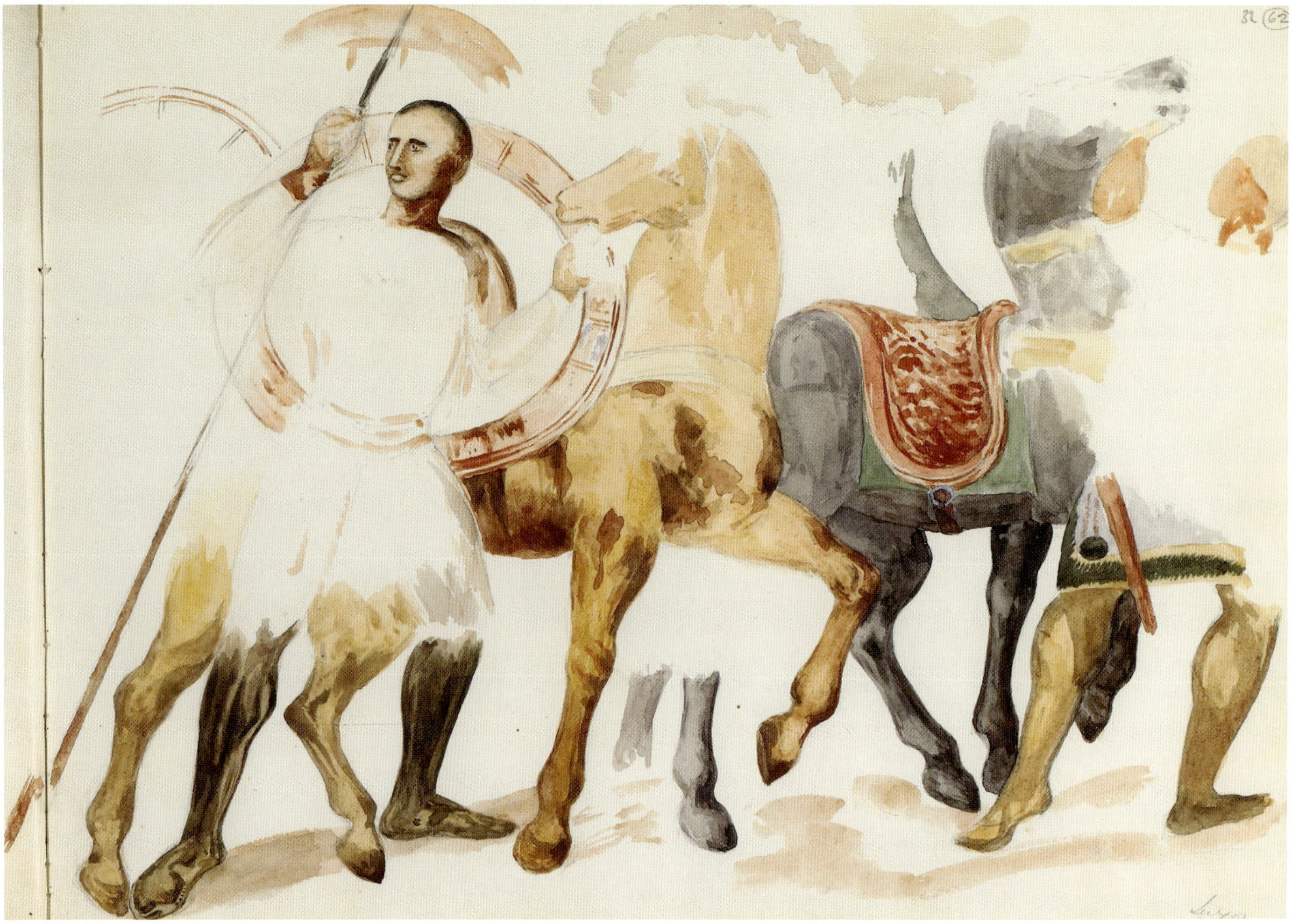

FIGURE 6.6
Detail of soldiers and horses from Wilkinson's sketchbook, page 31r.

best example of this garment is seen in Wilkinson's detail in which the white tunic of the figure trying to control his horse is decorated with a small *orbiculus* and is hemmed with a *clavus,* or possibly a fringed border. Such embroidered tunics are generally thought to have an eastern origin,[20] but in late antiquity they were common throughout the empire and signaled, if not high rank, then at least status above that of a lowly foot soldier.[21] It is possible that these soldiers also wore leggings (*toubia*). The dark-brown hue used for the legs of the figure on the left of Wilkinson's detail suggests as much, but Wilkinson's watercolors are too impressionistic to tell for sure.

Above this procession of soldiers on the east wall are fragments of another register of decoration. Wilkinson's panorama of the east side of the imperial cult chamber (see figure A.1) is the only nineteenth-century graphic record we have of this section of plaster, and he interprets the remains indistinctly, having seen what he thought was a loop of drapery. Study of this section by Johannes Deckers in the 1970s and the recent conservation work, however, have revealed several clues suggesting that this third register contained a more complex vignette, one that might even have been figural. The section of plaster remaining in situ constitutes the bottom right corner of the register's composition. It depicts two red-ocher cylindrical objects to the left of three courses of yellow masonry (see figure 6.7). A blue shield with a bronze boss, decorated with a motif resembling feathery flower buds, rests against the exterior of the masonry on the other side. Elaborate shields of this kind were common in the Roman army, usually denoting the legion or cohort to which the soldier carrying it belonged. Such accouterments were also displayed as legionary insignia, as attested by the illustrated pages of the *Notitia Dignitatum,* a list of civil and military offices in the late Roman world made some time after the Theodosian division of the empire in 395, but surviving only in fifteenth-century copies (figure 6.9).[22] The shield pattern for the *Tertia Diocletiana Thebaeorum* (= legio III Diocletiana) is illustrated on a page containing the shield patterns of units under the command of the *Magister*

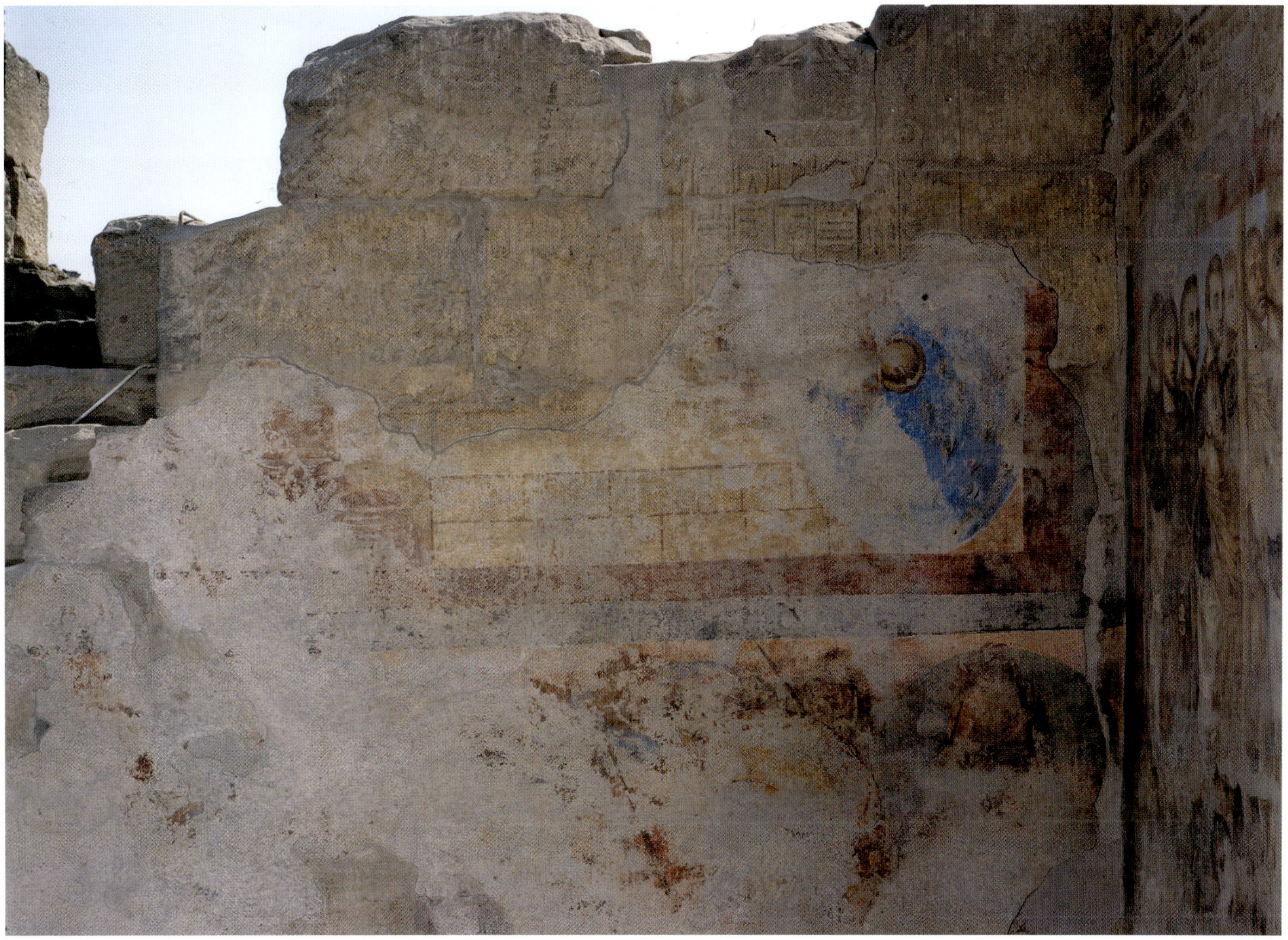

FIGURE 6.7
East wall, south end: detail of the blue shield resting against masonry and the rearing horses in the register below.

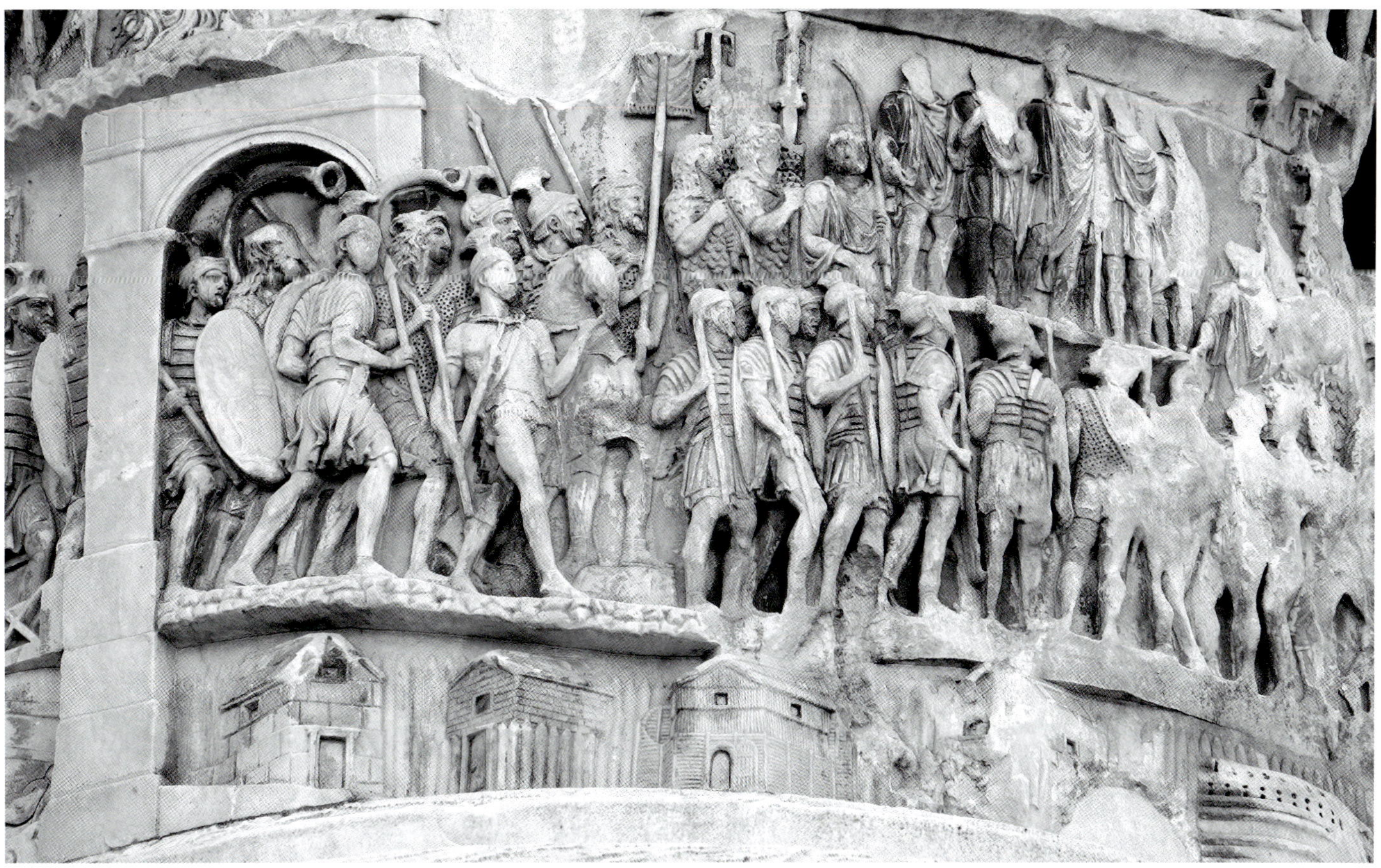

FIGURE 6.8
Column of Marcus Aurelius, Rome, ca. 180–192; Roman soldiers campaigning in Germany.

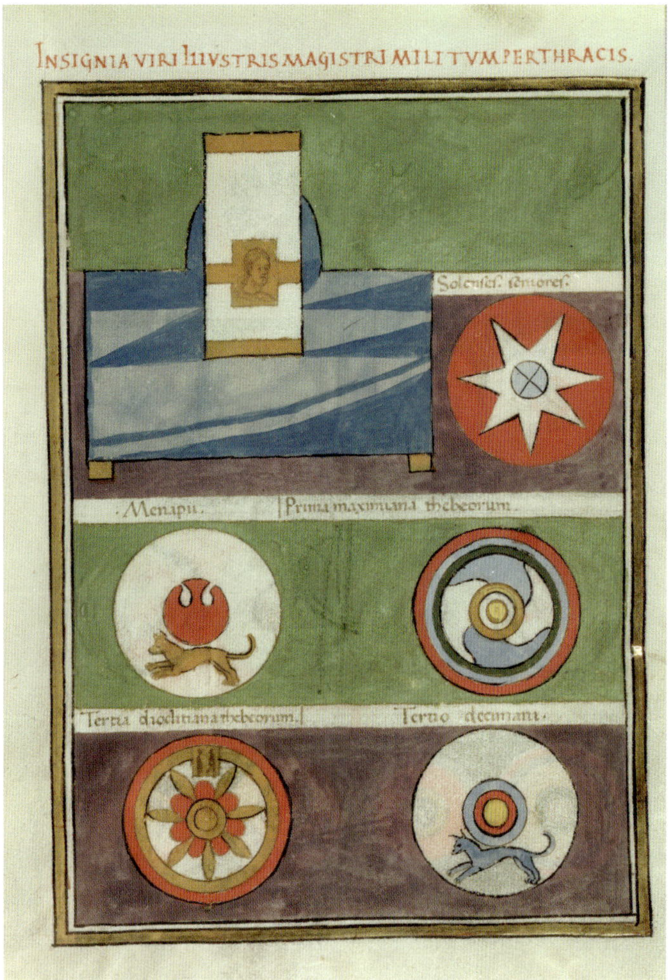

FIGURE 6.9
Insignia of the Magister Militum per Thracis. Page from the *Notitia Dignitatum.* Fifteenth-century copy of a ca. fifth-century manuscript. Bodleian Library, Oxford.

Militum per Thracias ("Master of the Soldiers in Thrace"). Neither this shield pattern nor that of another Egyptian unit on the same page, the *Prima Maximiana Thebaeorum,* resembles the pattern of the in situ blue shield, but this does not necessarily preclude the idea that the blue shield represents the insignia of the legion stationed at Luxor.

Unfortunately, so little survives of the larger scene in which the shield appears that any reconstruction is purely hypothetical. Given extant parallels, however, it is reasonable to speculate that the courses of masonry still visible in the fresco are just part of a larger structure such as a gateway, an architectural element often included in depictions of imperial processions like the one pictured in the adventus scene from the Arch of Galerius mentioned above (see figure 7.5). The left side of the masonry seems to curve around the smaller of the two cylindrical objects, as if to indicate a recess in the wall, or perhaps an open doorway. The base of the other, larger object seems to be decorated with motifs that could be interpreted as the tips of acanthus fronds, suggesting the base of a column such as those of the west tetrastyle at Luxor (see figure 2.8). If this section of masonry was indeed a gate, with columns decorating its entrance and the insignia of the legion on its exterior, perhaps what was once pictured was the ultimate destination of the procession depicted below, the gates of the Luxor fort itself.

Though the complete subject of the east wall's third register must remain a mystery, we can deduce at least that the viewer is meant to understand that the second register of figural decoration is a continuation of a similar procession depicted at the same height on the north wall of the room. Unfortunately, just small patches of the preparatory plaster layer (*arriccio*) remain on this wall, where once there was imitation opus sectile at the level of the first register of decoration (figure 6.10). In the nineteenth century, however, traces of several feet from the figural register were still visible above the opus sectile on both sides of the entrance, as recorded in Wilkinson's panorama of the east side of the room (see figure A.1). From this drawing it is apparent that the virtual procession divided into two parts at the entryway in the north wall of the room. The remaining figure on the easternmost side of the north entry wall, sketched in detail by Wilkinson on page 27r of his notebook, angles his feet eastward toward the figures in the east wall procession, which suggests continuity between the action depicted on the northeast side of the north wall and that on the east wall.

In contrast, the five feet on the west side of the north wall in the panorama are angled away from the east wall procession. Wilkinson included a detail of these feet (probably representing two figures and the foot of another) on page 28v, which confirms the directionality of this side of the composition and also provides further information about the figures' identities (see figure A.4 left). These individuals wear black shoes that can be identified as *campagia,* part of everyday military attire in the tetrarchic era.[23] Hence, it seems that this part of the wall also depicted a procession of soldiers, but in this case moving westward toward the middle register of the west wall, which perhaps once contained a figural composition pendant to that of the east.[24]

While Wilkinson's page 28v thus serves to clarify certain aspects of the north wall's figural register, the other vignettes on this notebook page, details of the opus sectile decorations, are not as easy to place back on the walls (see figure A.4 left). The primary pattern of opus sectile encircling the walls of the room, as gleaned from Wilkinson's panorama of the east side of the room, George de Sausmarez's view of the south wall (see figure 4.6), and Théodule Devéria's 1859 photographs of the east and south walls (see figures 4.9 and 4.10), consists of a series of alternating square and rectangular panels of imitation marble designs, above which runs a frieze of smaller geometric patterns. Monneret de Villard fittingly calls this miniature frieze "almost cosmatesque in its effect."[25] The larger square panels contain roundels of varying design and color, while the rectangular panels are monolithic and painted in patterns of green and white to suggest the veins of *verde antico* or *verde cipollino* marble (see figure 5.5). An additional watercolor published by von Bissing in 1926 illustrates the western end of the north wall, a section that Wilkinson does not appear to have recorded and that is now almost completely devoid of paint (figure 6.11).[26] Von Bissing's drawing illustrates an interruption in the rhythm of alternating rectangular and square designs, because the first rectangular panel at the northwest side of this wall is slightly wider than the others. Instead of imitation green marble, this panel contains a purple rectangle (probably imitating porphyry) inlaid with a yellow lozenge (*giallo antico*), itself inlaid with another purple square. Deckers's 1979 drawing of the in situ plaster confirms the correspondence of von Bissing's watercolor with the northwest edge of the north wall (figure 6.12), but unfortunately no trace of the *intonaco* remains today.

Notably, Wilkinson's panorama illustrates several other instances of distinctively proportioned rectangular panels. He draws two on either side of a door on the east wall, and his watercolor hints at two others flanking the niche on the south wall. Devéria's photograph of the south wall clearly shows sections of the opus sectile register still in situ on either side of the niche, though any specific decorative motifs besides the cosmatesque border are difficult to make out. Curiously, Sausmarez

FIGURE 6.10
North wall of the imperial cult chamber looking north: the entrance is in the center, and columns of the portico of Amenhotep III lie beyond.

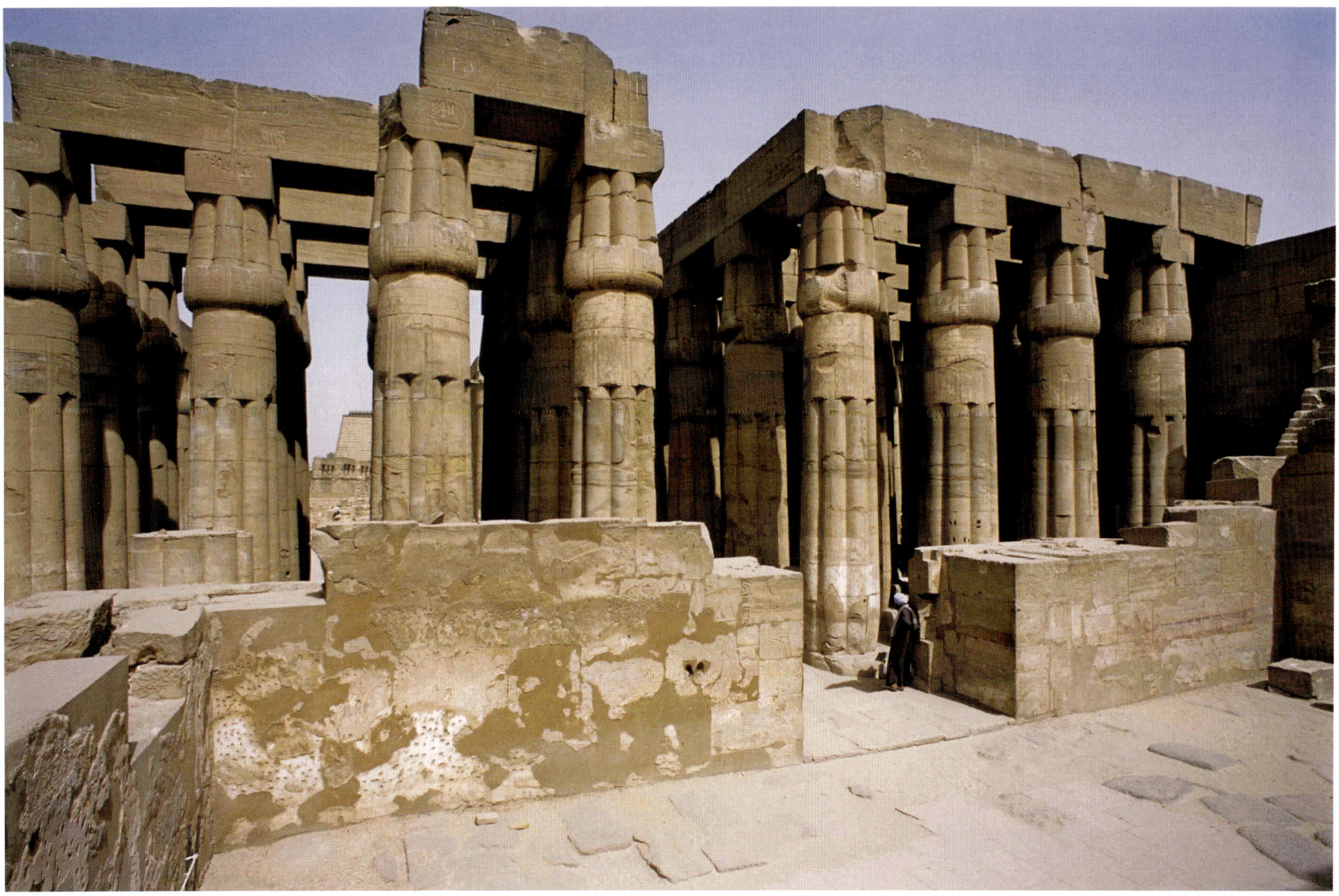

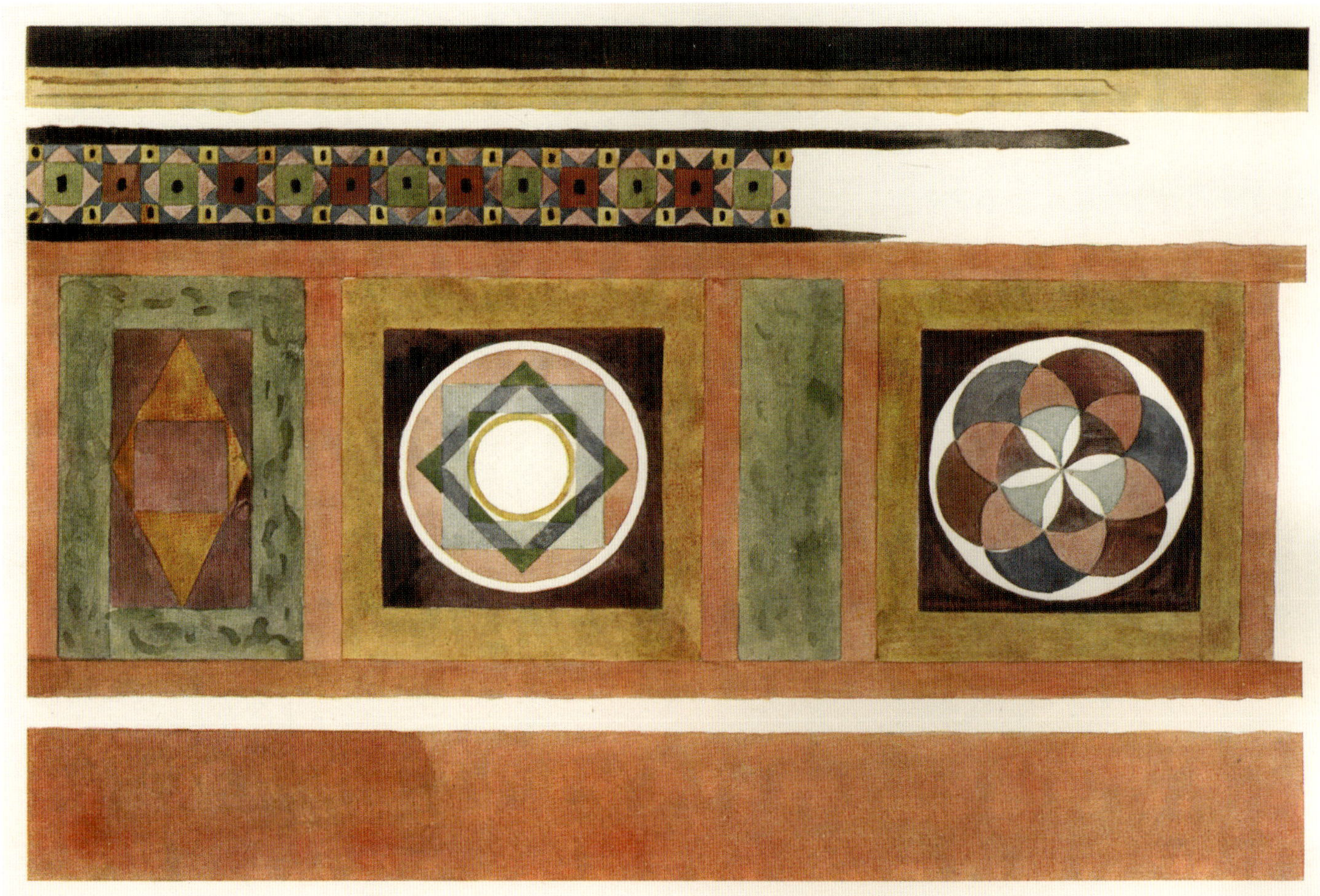

FIGURE 6.11
Von Bissing's watercolor of the imitation opus sectile panels on the west end of the north wall. Von Bissing 1926, facing page 188.

(see figure 4.6) also draws a distinctive rectangular panel on the east (left) side of the niche, almost identical in design to the one illustrated by von Bissing, but, unlike Wilkinson, he does not include its twin on the opposite side of the niche.

The in situ evidence for the design of the opus sectile register does not help resolve these inconsistencies. Only a few large patches of the arriccio layer and a few small segments of color representing the intonaco layer still survive. For example, one can still see the cosmatesque motif on the south wall and fragments of a square panel containing a six-lobed interlocking circle motif and two patches of the imitation verde cippolino on the west wall (figures 6.13 and 6.14). Unfortunately, the evidence regarding the opus sectile register provided by Wilkinson's page 28v (see figure A.4 left) does not clarify this matter any further. On this sketchbook page Wilkinson has copied in color and in two rows various opus sectile roundel designs such as interlocking circles (six-lobed as well as quadrilobed), interlaced squares forming interior octagons, stylized rosettes, and a pattern of radiating triangles, but most are rendered without their accompanying frames. A close look at these patterns reveals a correspondence between the top row of the page 28v roundels and the opus sectile designs sketched in pencil by Wilkinson in his east wall panorama (see figure A.1), as well as some of the patterns still visible in Devéria's photograph of the same wall (see figure 4.9).[27]

The three roundels in the bottom row are harder to relocate. Two of them bear a resemblance to the first two panels of opus sectile on the south wall (moving east to west) drawn by both Wilkinson and Sausmarez. The design of the only remaining roundel preserved in situ on the south wall (figure 6.13) corresponds nicely with the first roundel of the second row on page 28v. But the design third from bottom left on the page matches neither Wilkinson's nor Sausmarez's design third from left on the south wall (a design not recorded elsewhere). So in the case of page 28v, it seems that Wilkinson did not draw the opus sectile patterns in a sequence meant to correspond with their sequence on the walls. Instead, the roundel third from left on the bottom row of page 28v belongs on the west side of the niche; it matches the design Wilkinson sketched lightly in pencil in that area of the south wall on page 26r.

In addition to the page 28v drawings, there is one other drawing related to the geometric register on page 26v of

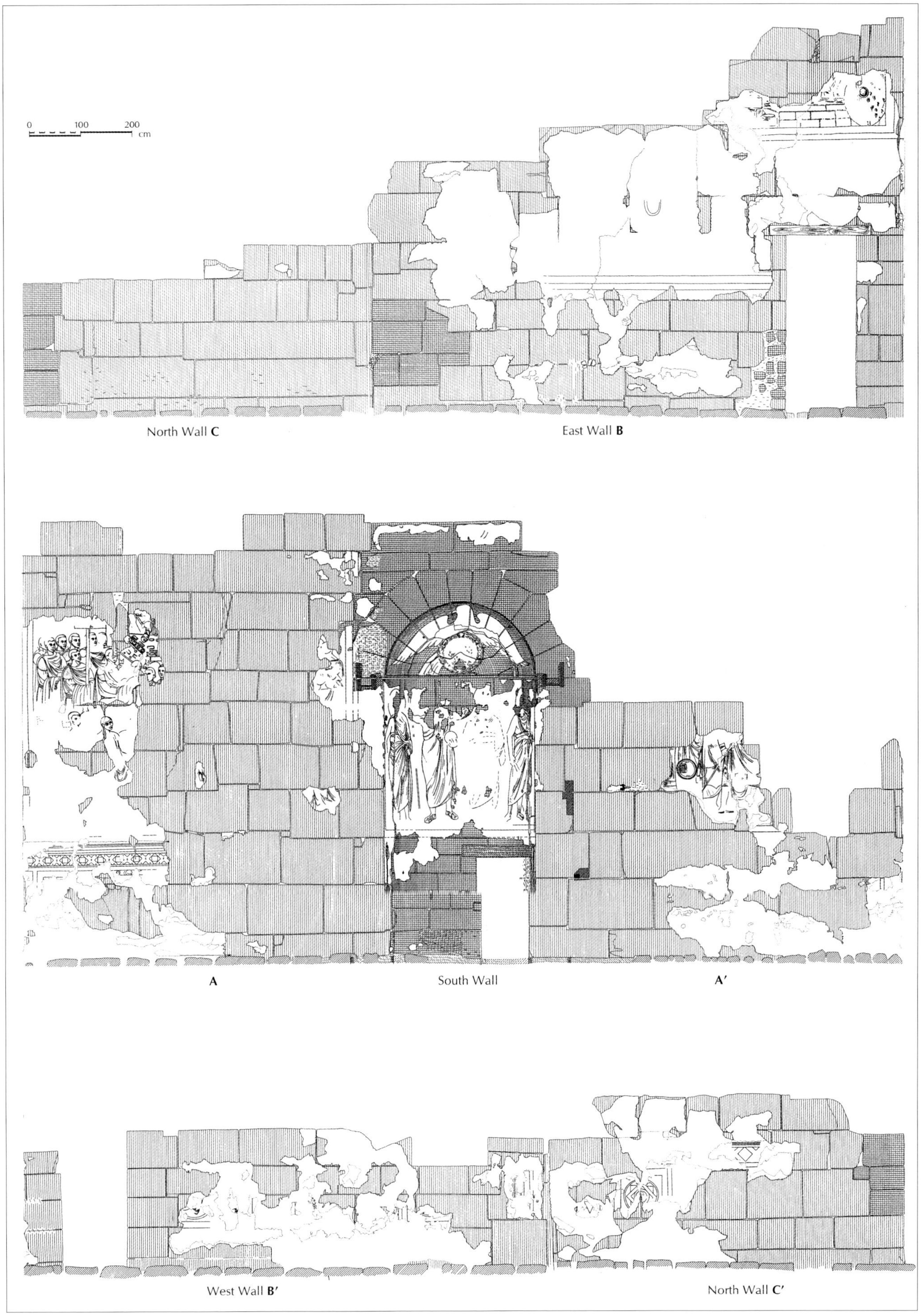

FIGURE 6.12
Drawings of the Roman plaster layers on the south and west walls extant in 1979; after Deckers 1979, fig. 33.

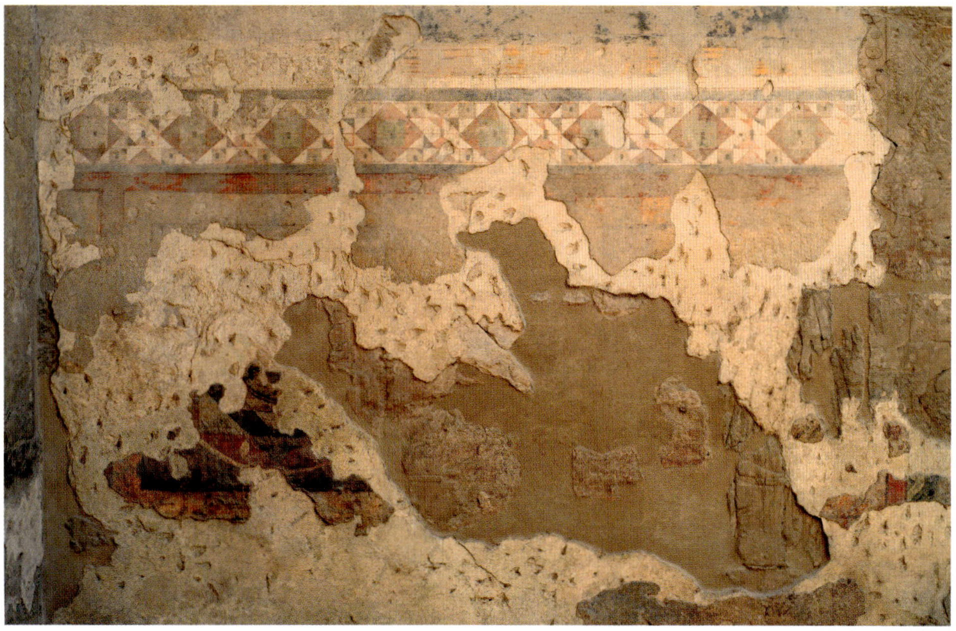

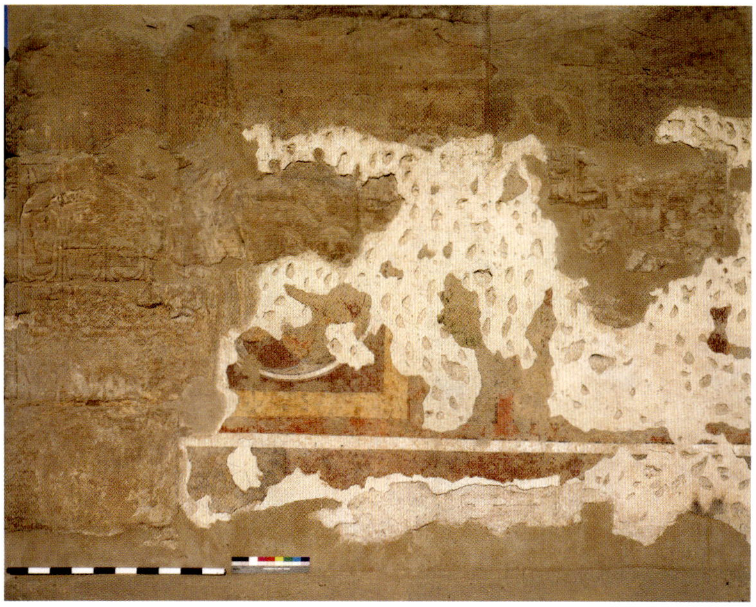

FIGURE 6.13
(top) South wall, east end: detail of the imitation opus sectile register.

FIGURE 6.14
West wall, south end: detail of the imitation opus sectile register.

Wilkinson's notebook. This page is mostly blank, save for a pencil sketch in the upper left corner depicting a roundel with a six-lobed interlaced circle design and a small section of the cosmatesque frieze (see figure A.2 left). The recent conservation has revealed a section of plaster on the west wall that can be connected to this pencil drawing, and which also resembles the first (from left) roundel on page 28v. The drawing and the in situ fragment share the same color scheme and pattern—six interlocking circles placed inside a square with a yellow border and purple background (see figure 6.14). If the roundel from page 28v is a representation of what Wilkinson saw on the east wall, then its recurrence on the west wall suggests that the artists of the site replicated roundel designs throughout the room. Whether these patterns were repeated systematically or there is a particular reason for the reuse of specific motifs instead of others, we will, unfortunately, never know, owing to the state of the plaster. At the very least we can say that the geometric registers at Luxor attest to a taste for trompe l'oeil effects and chromatic variety on the part of late antique patrons, artists, and viewers. All the opus sectile patterns would have produced sophisticated optical effects in which colors and shapes move back and forth between foreground and background, achieving a sensation much in tune with contemporary decorative trends throughout the late empire.[28]

Marble opus sectile revetment was commonly employed on the walls and floors of prestigious imperial building projects such as basilicas and bath complexes in the high empire, though the technique itself is far older.[29] Real opus sectile is also found in the homes of wealthy citizens throughout the empire, so its use was not limited to public congregational spaces. But in the context of an imperial setting, the dizzying carpet and wall revetment of multicolored panels signified a map of the territory the empire commanded. Each color of stone inlay represented a far-off quarry—yellow *giallo antico* from North Africa, *verde antico* from Greece, porphyry from Egypt, and so on—that took considerable expense to maintain and exploit.[30] Hence, only the wealthiest in the empire could afford the materials for genuine opus sectile decoration. When funds were unavailable for actual marble, the technique was instead imitated in paint, and thus fictive forms of opus sectile decoration also became common throughout the empire in a variety of contexts, especially in late antiquity.[31]

Was it because of economic factors that the artists at Luxor did not employ actual marble for the opus sectile register? Since the initiative for decorating the space presumably came from the highest administrative authority in Egypt, it may seem at first logical that real opus sectile should have been used instead of paint, as no expense would have been spared for an imperial cult chamber-cum-reception room. It is also possible, however, that the ornamentation of this particular room needed to be accomplished posthaste, if we imagine the commissioning of the decorations in anticipation of a visit by Diocletian and his entourage in either 298 or 302. One reason for the use of paint instead of marble therefore might simply have been expediency rather than expense. If a convenient supply of marble was not readily available nearby, rather than wait for the marble to be imported (along with the artisans who specialized in the opus sectile technique), it was decided to decorate the whole room with fresco instead.

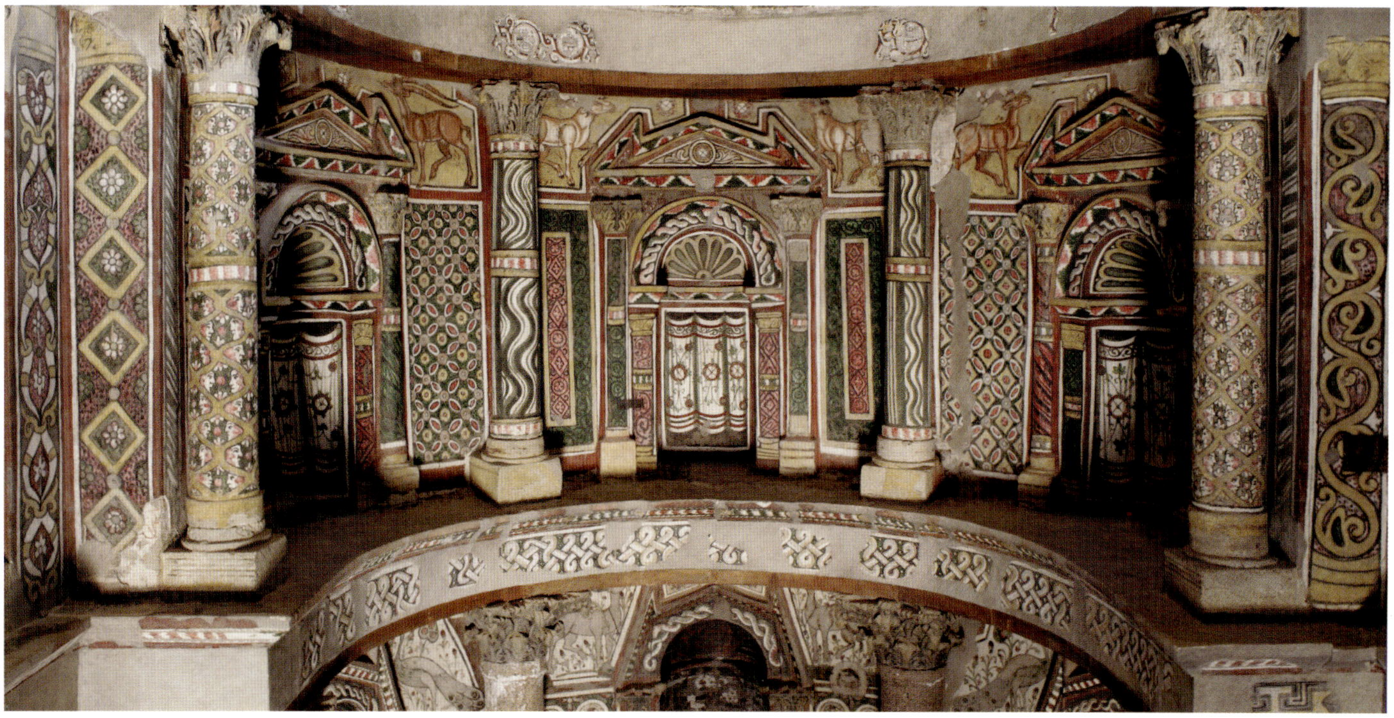

FIGURE 6.15
Red Monastery church, Sohag, wall paintings in the east apse, ca. sixth century.

But it is also possible that the decision to employ trompe l'oeil effects in the decoration of the Luxor imperial cult chamber had nothing to do with practical concerns. In antiquity, the use of painted opus sectile was not always simply a means of imitating more expensive materials. Rather, Roman artists and viewers of all classes took much delight in the interplay between artifice and reality that was made possible only through the medium of painting. Roman artists often used the two-dimensional surface of a wall to fool the eye into seeing stone, textiles, or three-dimensional architecture instead of two-dimensional plaster in a long tradition going back to the first Pompeian masonry style popular in the second and first centuries BCE.[32] By late antiquity, fictive media came to mingle with their actual counterparts in riotous decorative programs that combined surface patterns and polychromy in an aesthetic sometimes called the Jeweled Style.[33] Indeed, this taste for illusory surface decorations, which took root in the late antique period, became an important element of early Byzantine aesthetics. Recent conservation work at the Red Monastery church near Sohag, for example, has revealed a later stage in the evolution of the sophisticated polychromatic decorative style evident at Luxor. There, not only does painting imitate marble, but painted motifs mimicking molded stucco and textiles cover both the two-dimensional surface of the wall and the three-dimensional surfaces of columns, pilaster capitals, and niche apron (figure 6.15). The visual effect is a dazzling array of color and pattern that dissolve the solidity of the wall surface.[34]

Clearly, the Luxor opus sectile register was impressive in the complexity of its design and scale; the top of the register is more than two meters above the present floor level. Yet the figural compositions above, containing vignettes related to imperial ceremony and triumph, would have been even more so. Despite the missing plaster, we can be fairly certain that the procession depicted on the east and north walls (and probably the west) of the Luxor chamber had a particular association with an imperial rite, the adventus, or arrival of the emperor. The virtual performance of this event was regularly depicted on public monuments in the Roman Empire starting in the second century CE, when the programmatic content of Roman state art became increasingly formulaic in terms of representing the actions of the emperor.[35] Though the specific occasion for a monument's construction might vary (commemorating a military campaign or an anniversary), the emperor's participation in these events was illustrated according to prescribed visual tropes not necessarily specific to time and place. These tropes were designed to highlight the emperor's virtues by showing actions expected of an ideal emperor: addressing his troops (*adlocutio*), making a sacrifice or conducting a purification ritual (*lustratio*), giving generous monetary gifts to his subjects (*liberalitas*), being merciful to his enemies (*clementia*), or departing or entering a city with much pomp and circumstance (*profectio* and *adventus*).[36]

These scenes were never illustrated alone, and indeed at Luxor it is likely that the east wall adventus was just one facet of a multilayered program celebrating the virtues and deeds of the Tetrarchs. Nevertheless, the adventus is particularly important at Luxor because the motif is broadly linked to themes of victory, and it is thus relevant especially to Diocletian's activities in Egypt.[37] An adventus was a celebration that in concept commemorated the arrival of the emperor into a city, but in reality was an occasion intertwined with the martial aspects of imperial rule. As I discuss in chapter 7, the ceremony might even have been performed in the space of Luxor Temple in Diocletian's honor after his army had quelled the rebellion that brought him to Egypt. The painted representation of this historical event on the walls both preserved this honor for eternity and served as a constant reminder that Diocletian's presence in Egypt was a consequence of rebellion. The specific locus of the painted adventus in Luxor Temple in turn might also have reinforced the theme of victory by granting legitimacy to Diocletian's rule through the temple's long association with divine kingship. The architectural context of the Roman imperial cult chamber and its paintings thus adds an additional layer of meaning to an otherwise standard late-Roman artistic composition.[38]

Before turning to the primary decorative zone in the chamber, one last fragment of information pertaining to the west wall must be mentioned. Wilkinson's small pencil sketch of the opus sectile design on page 26v of his notebook (see figure A.2) is the only surviving record of the west wall plaster, because much of this wall is missing today, and it was probably missing in the nineteenth century as well.[39] Page 26v, however, contains a cryptic clue that has previously been interpreted as an allusion to the contrary. The page is almost blank; the exceptions are the aforementioned opus sectile panel, a small sketch of the imperial cult chamber's dimensions in the lower left corner of the page, and a note at the bottom of the page that says, "Mr. Monier told Mr. Harris that the name of 'Diocletian' was on one of the chariot wheels in this fresco."[40] This is a curious statement because a chariot or chariot wheel is not illustrated in any of Wilkinson's other drawings of the room, nor is there any trace of one today, so it has been presumed that this page was left blank, perhaps as a placeholder for a drawing of the west wall that Wilkinson never got around to making.

It is tempting therefore to speculate that an image of Diocletian in a chariot once did exist on the west wall.[41] Indeed, it was just such an assumption that previously divided opinion about the overall symmetry of the composition. Unquestionably, the emperors depicted in the niche of the south wall are the centerpieces of the program, but the extent to which the format and iconography of the subsidiary scenes were visually and conceptually balanced on either side of the niche is more difficult to reconstruct. Deckers, for example, argued (rightly, in my opinion) that the east and west figural registers are decorative units visually separate from the south wall composition (though programmatically linked, as in an early church decoration). The east and west walls would probably have mirrored each other and illustrated a procession of Roman soldiers and dignitaries that started on either side of the main door on the north side of the room and ended at the southwest and southeast corners of the room (understood to be virtually converging on the niche and the representations of the Tetrarchs, to whom the soldiers would pay homage).[42] Ioli Kalavrezou-Maxeiner, on the other hand, contended that the south wall composition depicted a continuation of the east and west wall processions and further suggested that these processions were not in fact symmetrically arranged around the niche or of equal length but, rather, met at a now missing depiction of Diocletian on the west wall.[43] Certainly such a visual topos—the emperor in a chariot—is perfectly aligned thematically with the images of procession on the east and north walls. And if the figural registers of these walls make up part of an imperial adventus, then we might expect to see an image of the emperor in a chariot somewhere in the composition, as we do, for example, in the adventus scenes of the Arches of Galerius and Constantine (see figures 7.5 and 7.6). Unfortunately, Wilkinson's enigmatic statement on page 26v is simply insufficient to allow a placement of such a scene on the west wall, especially since all evidence suggests that the west wall's figural registers had already been destroyed in Wilkinson's day.[44]

THE SOUTH WALL

The aesthetic character of the south wall figural zone is a striking contrast to the dynamic and naturalistic scenes decorating the east, north, and west walls of the imperial cult chamber (see figure 6.3). Unconstrained by the horizontal registers that make up the format of the subsidiary walls, the visual field of the south wall stretches across approximately ninety-three square meters of the wall's surface, to a height of more than seven meters, and is punctuated in the middle by the niche containing larger-than-life-size images of the Tetrarchs. Deckers fittingly calls this south wall composition a triptych, referring to the way

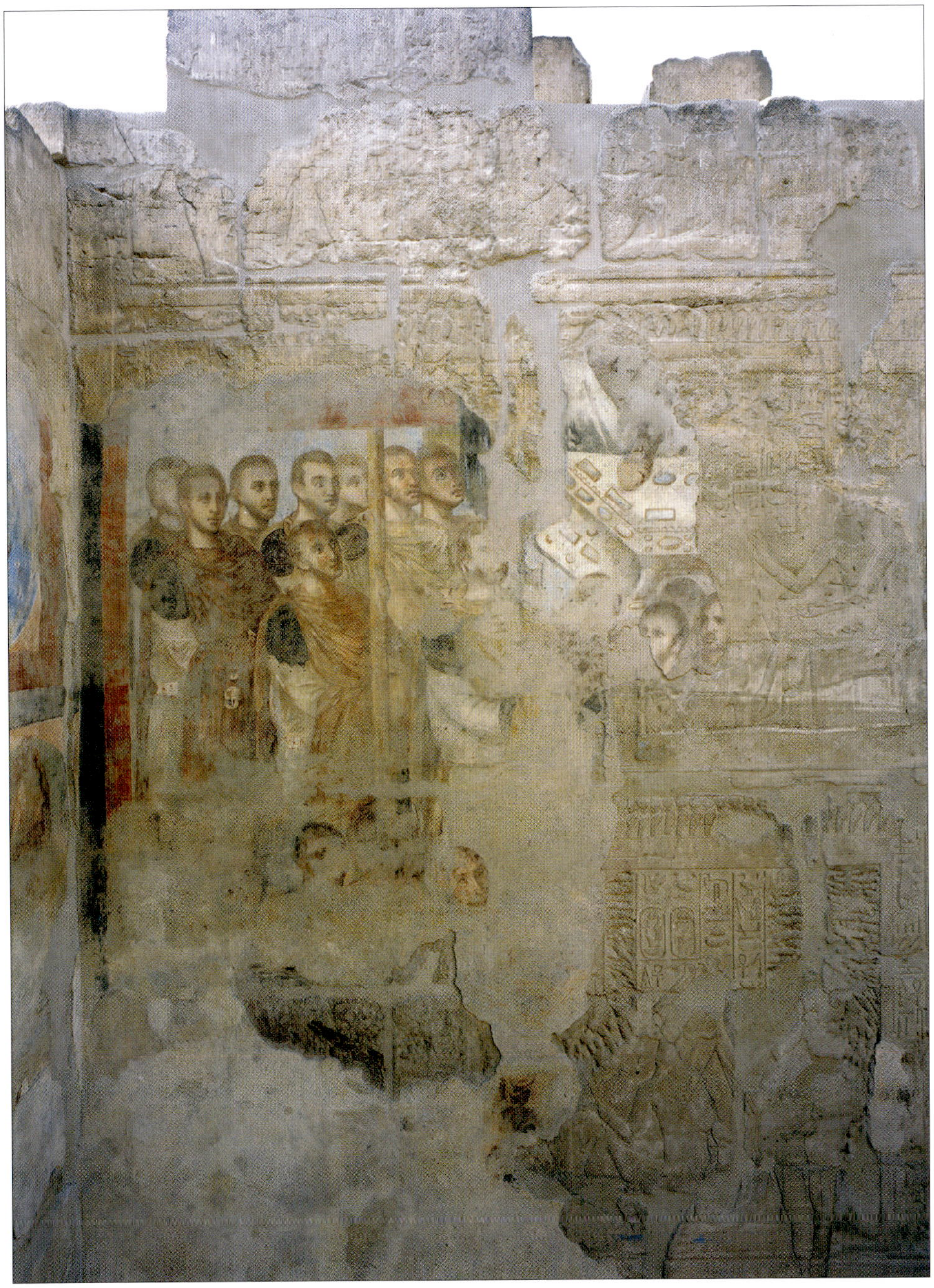

FIGURE 6.16
South wall, east side: dignitaries gathered around the emperor, whose foot is visible on a bejeweled footstool in the center.

in which the scenes on either side of the niche (the "wings" of the triptych) frame and emphasize the significance of the central vignette but have independent content of their own.[45]

The best preserved section of the south wall today is the large swath of fresco in the southeast corner of the room, where we see a scene of well-dressed Roman dignitaries paying homage to an enthroned figure (figure 6.16). Their prestige is signaled by the richness of their clothing and further accented by their hieratic mode of representation. As was the convention for depicting persons of high status in the late empire, the organization of figures lacks the spontaneity of the soldiers in the procession, and their movements are not fixed in a laterally defined, natural space.[46] This segment of in situ plaster can be matched with a section on Wilkinson's notebook page 30r (see figure A.5 right), though the concordance is not perfect. The left-hand side of this page is labeled "Luxor (left of apse)," and it illustrates an indeterminate spatial setting containing eight figures aligned in two diagonal rows plus the foot of a ninth figure somewhat detached from the group. All the figures are rendered in three-quarter profile and are oriented in the same direction, westward toward the niche. This directionality is accentuated by the fact that they also extend their draped hands and arms westward. The individuals in the top row wear red-ocher cloaks of high office (*paludamenta*) fastened at their right shoulders with *fibulae*.[47] Underneath their cloaks they are clothed in white tunics (*paragaudae*) cinched with bejeweled belts and decorated with shoulder patches (*segmenta* or *orbiculi*) that would, in life, have been ornately embroidered with white (or possibly gold) thread.[48] The recent cleaning of the plaster has allowed for a better glimpse of the intricacies of these embroidery patterns, realized through the application of white pigment in a staccato pattern (see figure 5.8). Each segmentum is unique and in life would have been carefully curated by the wearer, repeatedly removed from old, worn garments and resewn onto new.[49]

Wilkinson drew the two rows of figures stacked so that the heads in the front row are level with the hips of those in the row above. This alignment suggests recession into space symbolically rather than naturalistically. All told, the way in which these figures mimic each other in pose gives the overall impression of tessellation, like a geometric pattern. Such a rhythmic configuration is typical of late antique compositions that emphasize order and hierarchy over realism. This mode of representation is commonly considered to be Byzantine or medieval in character, but recent studies of Roman art reveal that, in political contexts, artists regularly and deliberately employed a symbolic visual language rather than a naturalistic one long before the early middle ages.[50] Starting in the second century especially, frontal, static compositions illustrating the Roman emperor and his entourage became more frequent, prefiguring the symbolic visual language used for the depiction of saints and other holy figures. The representation of power, therefore, in both the classical and early Christian world necessitated a visual language that was, in its essence, otherworldly.[51]

The bottom row of figures on page 30r (see figure A.5 right) consists of four men and the foot of a fifth, which Wilkinson has annotated, "This foot should be rather lower." Wilkinson sketched this section a second time in pencil on

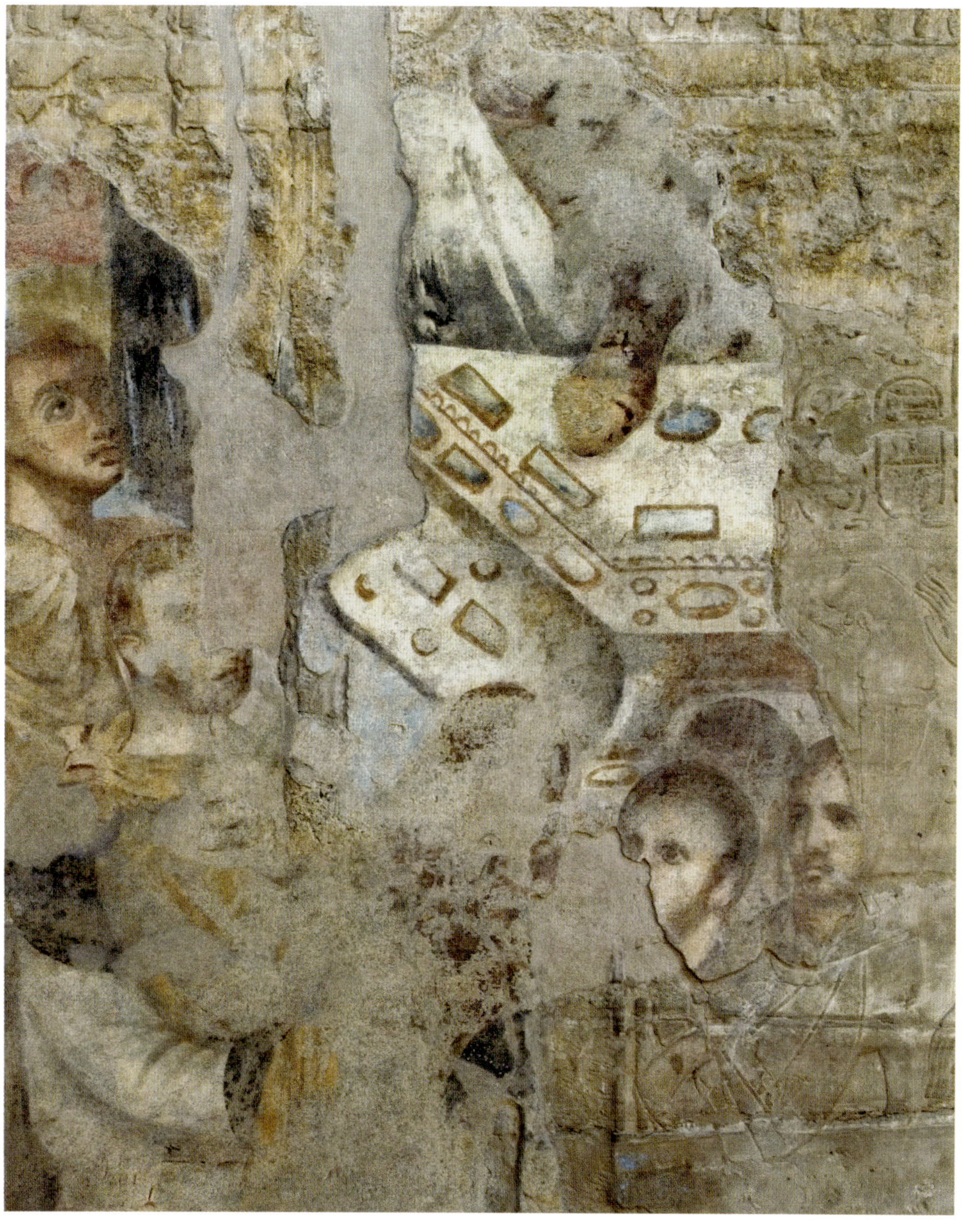

FIGURE 6.17
South wall, east side: detail of the bejeweled footstool.

the adjacent page 29v, probably to correct the mistakes in scale he discerned in his earlier drawing. For example, in the pencil sketch, the foot of the fifth figure has been placed more in line with the other figures in the group, and Wilkinson has written "probable position" under the figure second from left. Of this bottom row of figures illustrated in Wilkinson's watercolor, only the face of one (bottom row, third from left), a small section of his robe, and the outline of the head of another figure are visible today (see figures 5.6 and 6.16).

The figures corresponding to the upper row in Wilkinson's sketchbook page 30r are much better preserved, but here the nineteenth-century graphic record diverges from the extant frescoes. In a curious reversal of expectations, some sections of the scene that are visible in situ today are missing from both Wilkinson's rendition and Sausmarez's watercolor of the south wall. For example, of the upper row of figures depicted on page 30r, Wilkinson illustrates only the necks and torsos of three figures and the shoulder of a fourth, which suggests that the plaster above this section was not legible in the nineteenth century. That this was indeed the case even in the mid-twentieth century is confirmed by Monneret de Villard, who describes these figures as headless in his seminal article that established the Roman rather than Christian identity of the frescoes.[52] It was not until Deckers's careful study of the paintings and the concomitant conservation efforts of Reinhard Meyer-Graft in the 1970s that a complete assessment of this section of in situ fragments could be made, whereupon the upper edges of this vignette were cleaned of a layer of lime that obscured the extant frescoes beneath (see chapter 4).[53] This action revealed the missing heads of Wilkinson's figures, in addition to evidence for another row of figures above and to the right of the originally recorded group, bringing the number of individuals who can be reconstructed in this crowd scene to seventeen. Yet another figure emerged during the conservation work documented in chapter 5, bringing the total number to eighteen.

It was also at the time of Deckers's study that the most important element of the composition of the east "wing" of the south wall triptych was revealed. Just to the west of this crowd scene is a fragment of plaster depicting the corner of a bejeweled footstool (*suppedaneum*) on which rests the purple-shod foot of an individual who is most certainly an emperor (figure 6.17). This image can be reconstructed as an enthroned ruler presiding over his subjects in a tableau of imperial pageantry. Similar depictions appear often in the late empire across media, and they vary less in style than in terms of the particular virtue the image was intended to emphasize.[54] Notable later parallels to the suppedaneum depicted at Luxor are found in a manuscript page from the Codex-Calendar of 354 depicting the emperor Constantius II (see figure 7.8) and a silver commemorative dish from Spain known as the Missorium of Theodosius, which celebrates the *decennalia* (ten-year anniversary) of the emperor Theodosius I in 387 or 388 (see figure 7.9).[55]

The page from the Codex-Calendar illustrates the haloed and ornately dressed emperor sitting in a curtained niche with his foot on a bejeweled suppedaneum, arrayed in sanctified splendor. He wears a diadem, holds a scepter, and drops coins from his right hand in a gesture of *sparsio* or *liberalitas* (imperial benefaction).[56] Conspicuously, the recipients of the emperor's generosity are not pictured. Instead, the emperor's beneficence is referenced generically, to highlight the generous nature of an ideal ruler isolated from his subjects by his divine majesty. Similarly, the Missorium of Theodosius

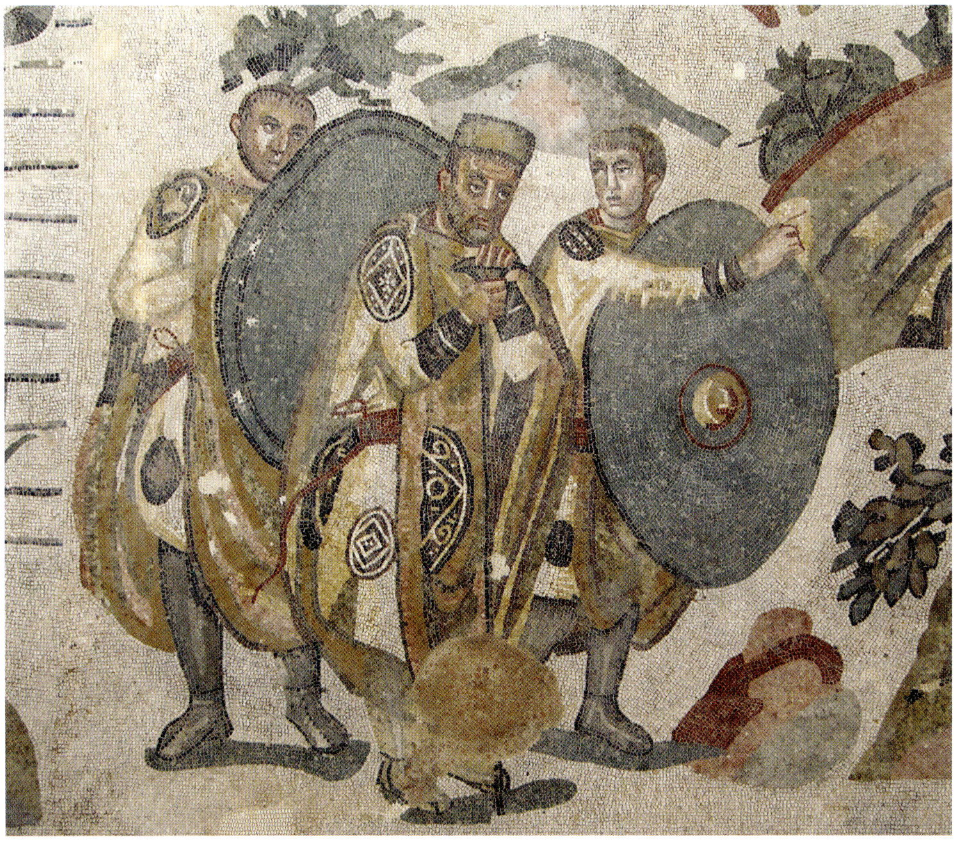

FIGURE 6.18
The villa of Piazza Armerina, Sicily, detail of the Great Hunt mosaic, ca. fourth century.

emphasizes the splendid segregation of the emperor, in spite of the other figures sharing the composition.

In each of these parallels, the figure of the emperor resides beneath a schematic portico that visually frames the emperor and sets him apart from the ordinary world and the actions of his subjects. In the case of the Missorium, Theodosius sits beneath an arcuated lintel, which further emphasizes the semidivinity of the figure below.[57] Though no evidence of a similar architectural frame is found in the paintings at Luxor, a section of dark-hued plaster behind and just to the viewer's left of the suppedaneum looks like the bottom edge of a curtain (see figures 6.16 and 6.17). One could reconstruct this drapery as hanging down from above the throne, but swept aside to reveal the emperor, as in the page from the Codex-Calendar of 354. It is likely therefore that the enthroned Tetrarch was distanced visually from his subjects who surround him in this section of the wall. The segregation of the imperial image carries over into the niche of the south wall, where actual architecture, the *ciborium* situated in front of the niche, visually provided the real equivalent of the virtual frame depicted in the Missorium and the manuscript page.

These images of the emperor, as well as those of the emperors at Luxor Temple, were illustrations not of reality, but of how the late Roman state wished its rulers to be perceived. Ammianus Marcellinus famously describes the emperor Constantius II as similarly remote and statuelike during an adventus ceremony in Rome in 357 CE, attesting to the close affinity between images and text in late antiquity (see chapter 7).[58] Whether they were *actually* perceived as sacred and splendid is, unfortunately, difficult to reconstruct in the absence of a record of contemporary responses to the images. That such a visual topos, however, was at times effective at least can be deduced by the way in which scenes of enthroned, isolated, and numinous figures were adapted almost seamlessly into the iconographic vocabulary of early Christianity.[59]

Additional evidence pertaining to the composition of the east wing of the south wall triptych is provided by Wilkinson's notebook page 27r. On the left-hand side of the page, two figures are illustrated, as well as the embroidered shoulder patch of another and the foot of a fourth (see figures 4.7 and A.2 right). The individuals are framed on their left (viewer's right) by red and black lines similar to those delineating the borders of other figural vignettes in the room. Wilkinson annotated "apse" in the shaded space just to the right of this border, confirming that these figures belong immediately east of the niche.[60] The figures are also discernible in several early photographs of the apse (see figures 4.9 and 4.11); thus, it is clear that this section of plaster once depicted another cluster of dignitaries in three-quarter profile, though in this case their bodies are oriented eastward, away from the niche. These men are richly dressed, the figure in the foreground of Wilkinson's drawing especially so. The black embroidery on the edge of this man's tunic peeks out from under his golden-brown *sagum,* and his cloak is bordered with a reddish-purple stripe as well as a fringe (a motif also discernible on the cloak of the fragmentary figure to his right).[61] These may be an indication of a particular rank, which could be further suggested by the *baculus* in the veiled left hand of the foreground figure. Batons of this type were a sign of distinction and an attribute of authority.[62] Elaborately dressed officials carrying the baculus are represented in other late Roman artworks, such as the Great Hunt Mosaic from Piazza Armerina in Sicily (figure 6.18). Several figures in the Great Hunt scene are additionally notable because their attire closely resembles the costumes in the Luxor paintings. In the mosaics, the gentleman holding the baculus, for example, wears a cloak decorated with an elaborately embroidered orbiculus; at one time he was thought to be the Tetrarch Maximian, though this attribution is much debated, as is the date of the villa.[63] The baculus is also pictured in the hands of a togate figure leading a *suovetaurelia* procession on a sculpted relief almost contemporary with the Luxor paintings, known as the Decennalia Base, in the Roman

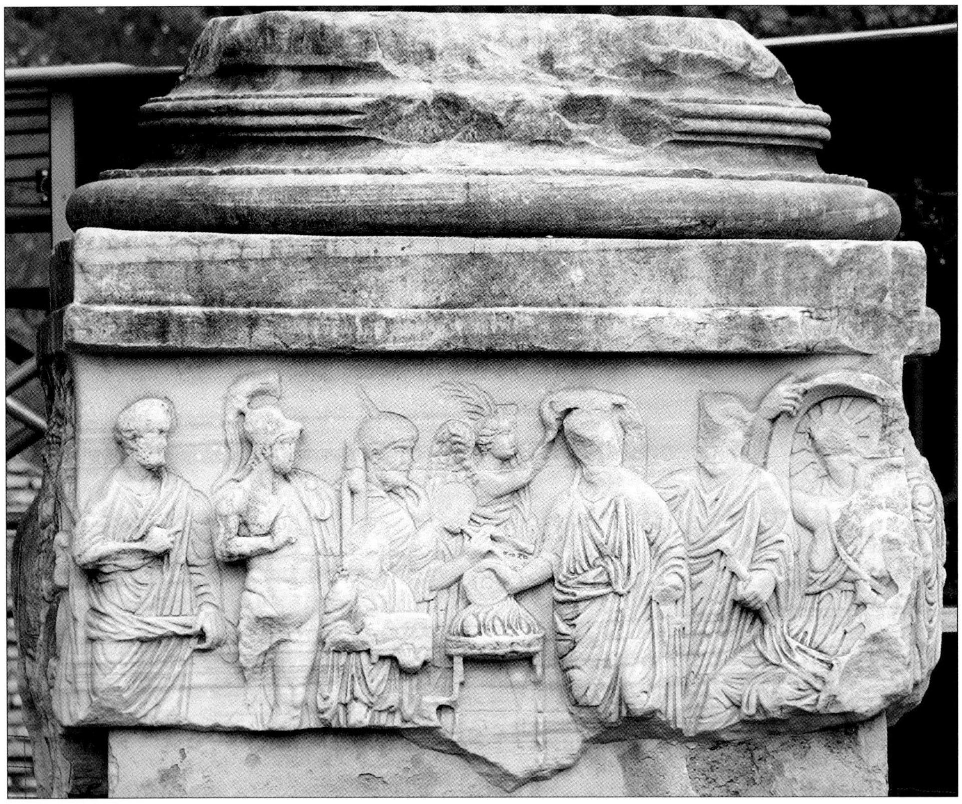

FIGURE 6.19
Sacrifice scene from the sole surviving base of the five-columned Decennalia monument erected in the Roman Forum, Rome, ca. 303.

Forum. This was once part of a five-columned installation celebrating collectively the twentieth anniversary of Diocletian's accession (*vicennalia*) and the tenth anniversary (*decennalia*) of the Tetrarchy, in 303 (figure 6.19).[64]

The figures from page 27r occupy the same level in the south wall composition as the first row of figures from pages 29v and 30r (see figure A.5). Presumably, the lacuna between them also contained individuals now lost, and we can imagine a scene with two clusters, one moving in from the east, the other from the west, meeting in the middle. From Wilkinson's drawings, we can see not only the direction in which the figures move but also the slight upward angle of their gaze directed toward the emperor enthroned above them. Given their physical location on the south wall, the fragmentary remains of the suppedaneum and the figure enthroned on it thus represent the focal point of the southeast wing of the south wall triptych, as Deckers so carefully reconstructs (figure 6.20). All the other figures within the composition encircle and frame the throne while residing in a somewhat unnatural physical space; the second and third row of figures closer to the throne, for example, would have appeared as if floating above the earth, though it seems as if the first row at least was anchored to a rudimentary ground line. That the figures were symmetrically or heraldically arranged around the throne in this way is confirmed by a section of plaster just to the east of the niche but above the level of the in situ ciborium capital. The torso and head of another male figure clad in a red-brown paludamentum face west. They are now legible again after conservation, as are minute traces of what must have been several additional figures clustered together in a manner similar to that depicted in the better preserved crowd scene on the other side of the throne, directly to the east (figure 6.21). This small section of plaster is indiscernible in the nineteenth-century record, and previously only Deckers appears to have made note of it in his reconstruction drawing.

The figures encircling the throne are not clustered aimlessly. Several of them have their hands veiled (*manus velatae*) to create a barrier between themselves, the objects they carry, and the sacred person of the emperor.[65] The performances of manus velatae and *proskynesis* (prostrating oneself in the presence of the emperor, *adoratio* in Latin) were acts of humility that became permanent fixtures in late-imperial ceremonies under Diocletian.[66] Such acts marked the emperor's authority as distinct from that of a normal mortal, and they reinforced his unapproachable and superhuman quality.[67] The picturing of such obeisance was further adapted in the realm of Christian art, as evidenced by one of the earliest examples of mosaic apse decorations in Rome, in which Saint Peter's hands are veiled so that he can receive the keys touched by Christ (figure 6.22).[68] At Luxor we can discern that the dignitary second from left in the upper row of the crowd scene appears to be offering to the emperor, with covered hands, a belt decorated with a gold buckle (see figures 5.8 and 6.1).[69] One figure in the bottom row probably also carried a standard from which hung a cloth banner called a *vexillum,* itself a sacred object.[70] The names of the legion and of the emperor(s) it served usually appeared on such banners.[71] The bottom edge of the vexillum is still visible just above the heads of the top row of figures in the crowd scene, along with the suggestion of a horseshoe-shaped letter or symbol in the lower right corner of the cloth (see figure 6.17).

Although there is no explicit evidence for it, Deckers added a second enthroned figure to the tableau in his imagined reconstruction, and, by extension, one can envision a similar pair of enthroned figures on the south wall, west of the niche. This is certainly a reasonable hypothesis in light of contemporary, or near contemporary, tetrarchic monuments. Though it is not unusual to find a single Tetrarch as the focus of a particular vignette in a larger visual program celebrating the power of the Tetrarchy, the type of scene in which one of the four emperors appears alone usually represents an action carried out in mundane time. For example, on what is today the south face of the Decennalia Base in Rome, only one of the four Tetrarchs, probably the Caesar Galerius, is illustrated making a sacrifice, a rite that was carried out for a specific

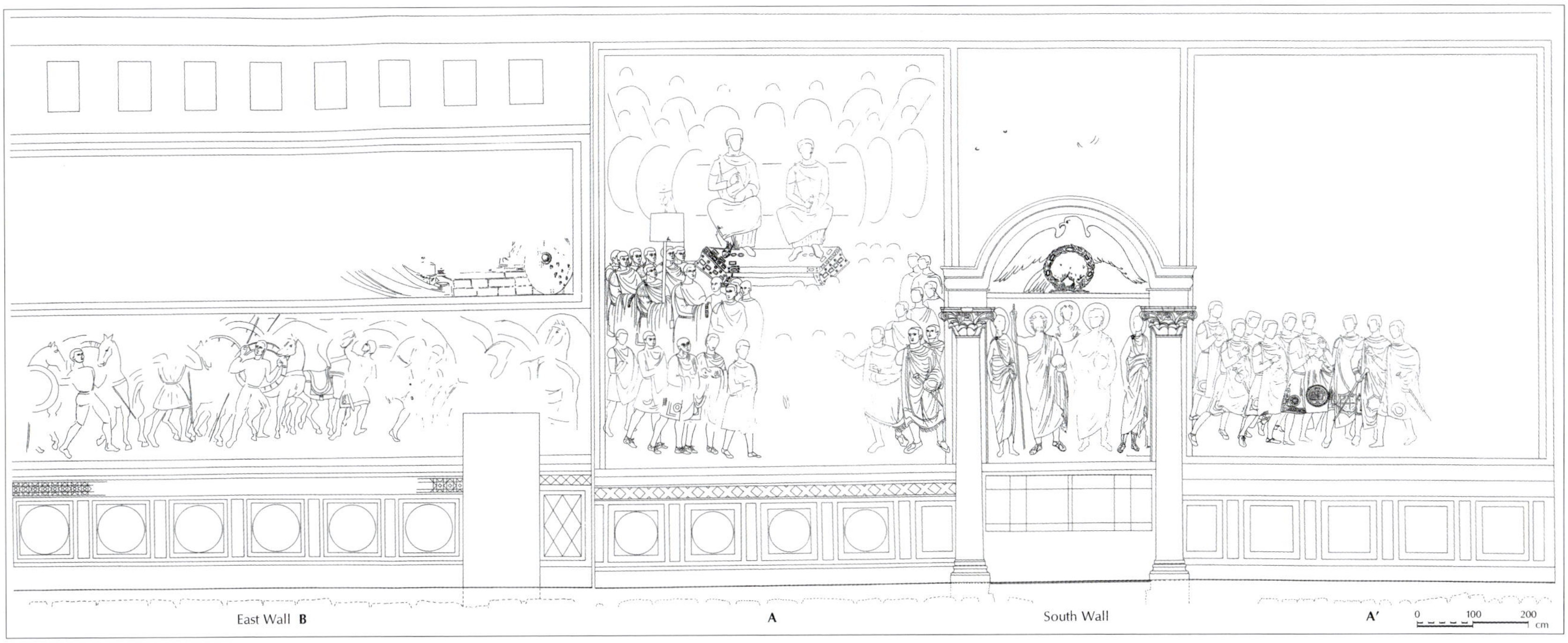

FIGURE 6.20
(above) Reconstruction of the painted program in the imperial cult chamber, after Deckers 1979, fig. 34.

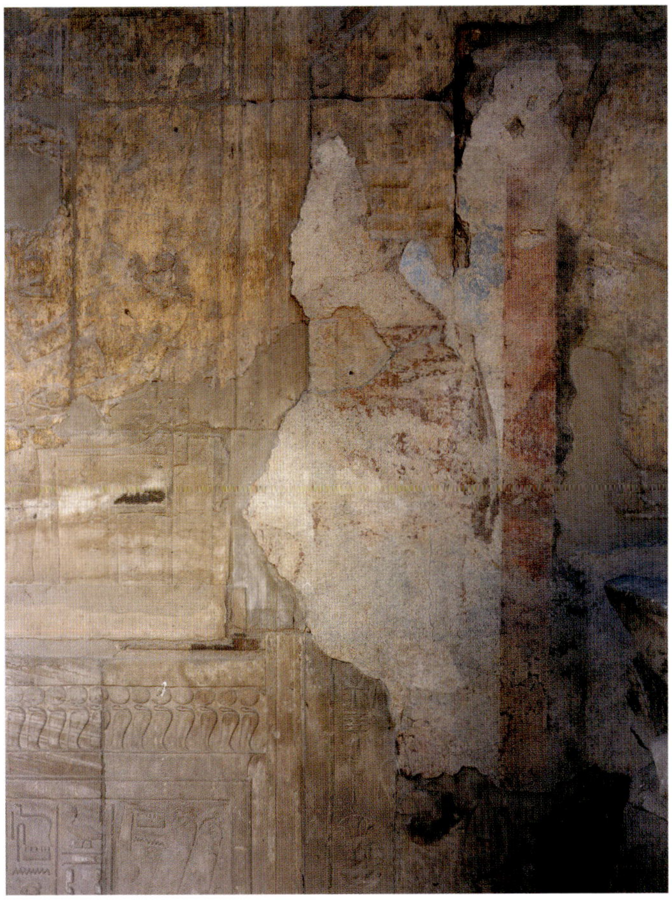

FIGURE 6.21
South wall, east side: detail of figures east of the niche.

event, in this case that of the tenth anniversary of the Tetrarchy (see figure 6.19).[72] Perhaps the most directly comparable example of the manipulation of style and theme evident in the Luxor image program, however, is that of a near contemporary monument, the Arch of Galerius, erected circa 305 in Thessaloniki, a city used by Galerius as one of the empire's provincial capitals (see figure 7.5).[73] As is the case in the Luxor paintings, the monument promotes the particular importance of the subject to whom this monument is dedicated (in this case the Caesar Galerius, at Luxor the Augustus Diocletian) while simultaneously promulgating the ideology of *concordia,* or consensus, of the Tetrarchs.

For example, on the north face of the arch's southwest pier, the best preserved and most often cited section of the arch's sculptures, one can still see four registers of sculpted relief, each depicting a different "stock theme" of Roman imperial art. The top or fourth register illustrates the *profectio* (departure) and subsequent adventus (arrival) of the emperor Galerius, and the row below shows Galerius locked in battle with a barbarian foe (here the Sasanian Persian King Narses)—both actual, if embellished, historical events. The second register, on the other hand, displays Galerius's imperial *pietas* (piety) and loyalty toward his fellow co-emperors by depicting all four Tetrarchs in a static enthronement tableau.[74] The emperors are understood here to reside in an otherworldly realm, and the hieratic and schematic scene is a deliberate visual contrast to the style of the registers above. In the late empire, therefore, the topos of the emperor enthroned became an iconic image, symbolic of the eternal and all-encompassing authority of the emperor. Although we have evidence for only one enthroned Tetrarch at Luxor, it is most plausible that originally all four would have been pictured to emphasize the ideology of shared authority.

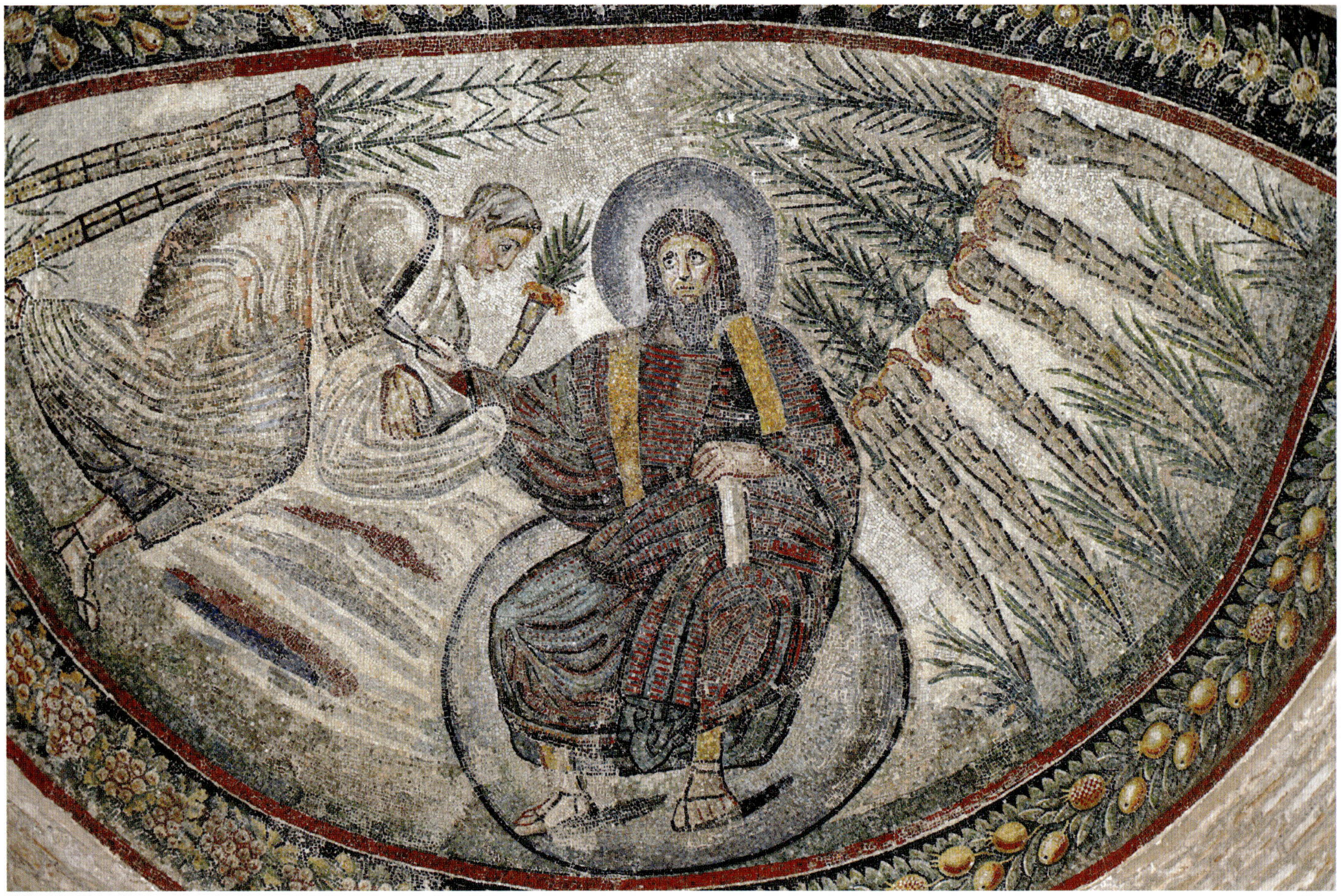

FIGURE 6.22
Mausoleum of Santa Costanza, Rome, apse mosaic, ca. 350; Saint Peter with veiled hands receives the keys to the Kingdom of Heaven from Christ.

It is thus also probable that the composition of the west wing of the south wall triptych mirrored that of the eastern wing, though confirmation is impossible owing to the current state of the plaster and the relative dearth of nineteenth-century documentation. It was not even until the 1970s that Wilkinson's drawing stretching across notebook pages 27v–28r was securely associated with the in situ plaster on the wall west of the niche, because much of what was visible in Wilkinson's day had already been removed in the 1890s, as described in chapter 4; missing in particular is the plaster that corresponds to page 27v (see figure A.3 left).[75]

Wilkinson's watercolor illustrates the lower halves of at least seven figures, of which only three remain. They would have been placed in the figural composition directly to the west of the niche and just above the opus sectile register.[76] As he did in the drawing on page 27r (see figure A.2 right), Wilkinson has set the figures within a black frame that delineates the boundaries of the figural composition. The lost figures shown on page 27v of Wilkinson's notebook are represented from an oblique angle, moving in a westerly direction away from the niche. The legs of these figures cast shadows on the ground, as if the light is coming from behind their right shoulders, which is consistent with the light source represented on the east wall. Like those of the other well-dressed dignitaries from the east side of the niche, the hems of these figures' tunics are decorated with elaborately stitched clavi and orbiculi, and they wear paludamenta in shades of yellow and red ocher decorated with large, embroidered segmenta. The embroidery patterns on the cloaks worn by the three figures on the far right of Wilkinson's page 28r are still visible in situ and attest to the richness of their costumes (figures 6.23 and 6.24).

The figure on the far right of the preserved plaster and of Wilkinson's drawing is noteworthy as another baculus holder (figure 6.24). Given the way he holds his staff, he appears to be positioned in a more static pose than the other figures on the south wall. He is rendered as if facing outward toward the viewer rather than in the more typical three-quarter profile. At first glance, Wilkinson's version of the dignitary's pose is actually quite awkward; the figure's feet are drawn in two-dimensional profile while his torso is *en face,* much like the Egyptian convention for representing the human figure. But this awkwardness is probably due to Wilkinson's misreading of the badly preserved intonaco layer in this section of the composi-

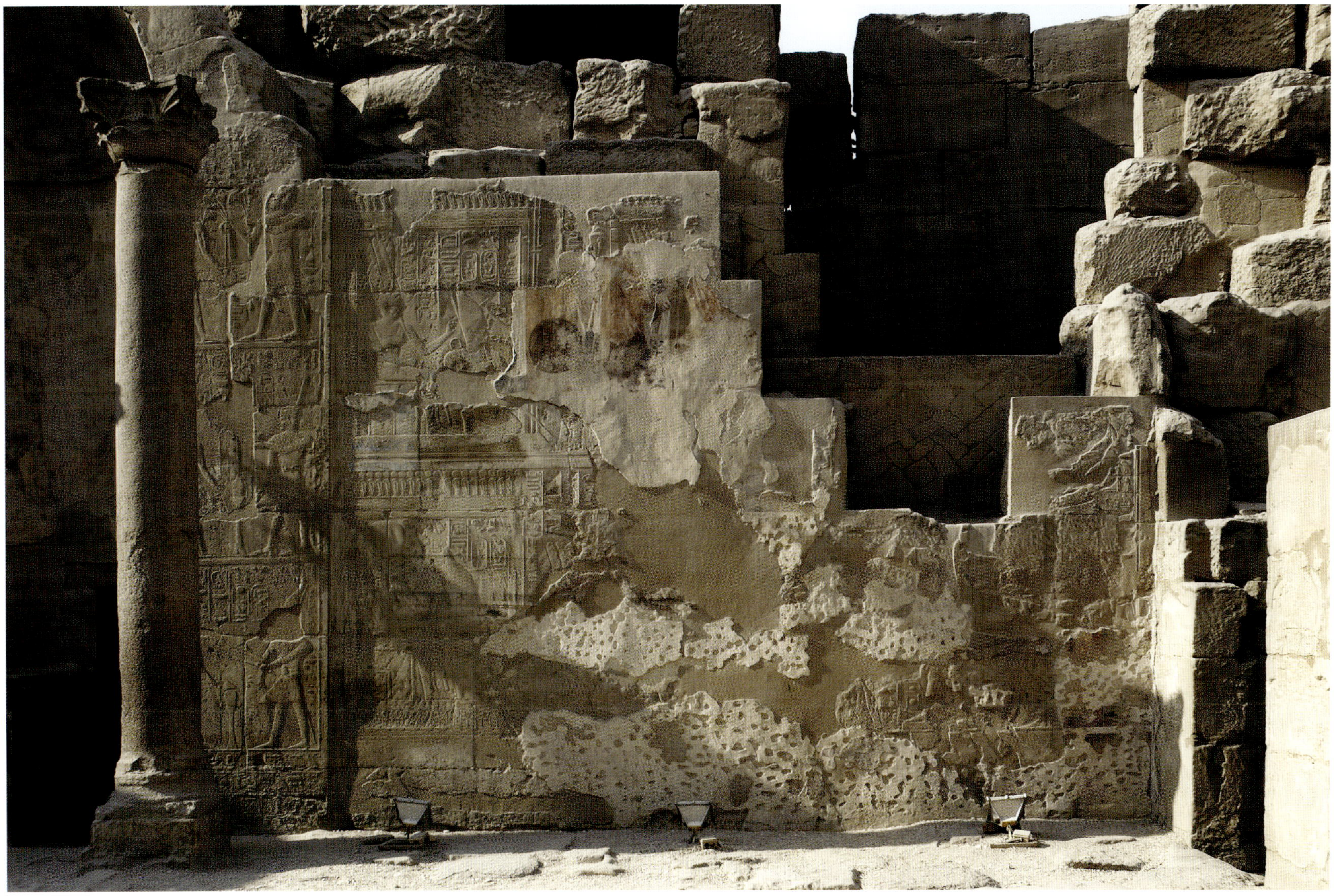

FIGURE 6.23
(above) South wall, west of the niche.

FIGURE 6.24
(right) South wall, west of the niche: detail of extant figures.

tion. Where he saw the feet of only a single figure, it makes more sense, given the way the figures are pressed together in this scene to give the impression of depth, that what was originally pictured was the foreshortened feet of two overlapping figures. The apparent gracelessness of the figure on the far right today is not in keeping with the artistic proficiency demonstrated in other sections of the paintings. While it is common to find stylized, linear forms juxtaposed with more naturalistically rendered figures in late Roman compositions, it is certainly not typical to find these distinctive stylistic features combined in the representation of a single individual.

On the basis of the pictorial conventions discussed above, the torso of this figure facing outward suggests that he is of a higher status than those illustrated in lateral motion. The same can be said of the figure depicted just to his right. The recent cleaning of this section of plaster permits a better reading of this second figure's stance; he too appears *en face,* with his right arm raised, as if gesturing toward the scene of the enthroned emperors possibly depicted above. The stasis

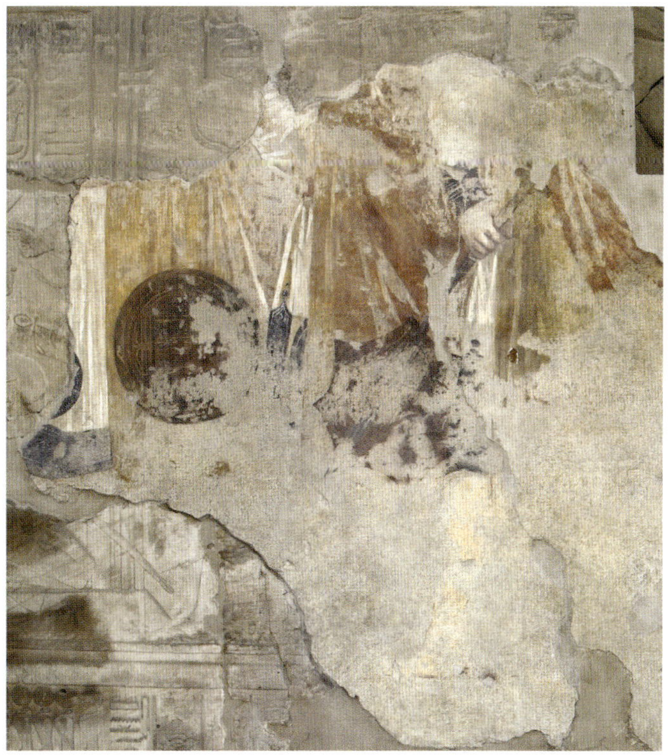

of these two figures also makes sense, given their location within the composition as a whole. If the south wall west of the niche was indeed a mirror image of the tableau on the east side, then the figures facing out at the viewer roughly corresponded to the bottom center of the west wing's image field, just below the vignette of the enthroned emperors. As is true of the southeast triptych wing, one can imagine that this composition depicted several rows of well-dressed dignitaries cascading around the thrones of the Tetrarchs from both east and west and that the figures facing the viewer represent the point at which the rows meet.

While one cannot describe the south wall scene as realistic in terms of its spatial setting, certain internal details revealed by the recent conservation suggest that the south wall triptych wings overall are far more dynamic than suggested by the nineteenth-century graphic record. Visually, the iconic image of the emperors enthroned at Luxor complements in concept the magisterial display of co-rule in the central niche.[77] But the figures surrounding the throne, in contrast, are decidedly human. For example, the uppermost row of six figures revealed in the 1970s seems to be only about a head's width above those below, giving the impression of a spontaneously formed, closely knit crowd rather than the hierarchically layered figures suggested by Wilkinson. Moreover, for those figures whose faces survive, individuality is asserted in the careful articulation of bone structure reflecting sculptural practices, an impression that would have been even more apparent from the original viewing angle below, when the artists' ingenious attention to shading would have brought the figures to life (see figure 6.1). The high degree of individuality in the facial features of these men suggests that the images were intended to be portraits, perhaps of particular personages within Diocletian's entourage (see figure 7.10). The inclusion of portraiture in a setting that, in modern art historical literature, is otherwise deemed a conventional hieratic and nonnaturalistic scene might suggest instead that tetrarchic art was far more varied in style than previously assumed.

In past studies of late Roman art, the Luxor frescoes are generally relegated to purely stylistic discussions rather than consideration of them in their unique Egyptian context.[78] The composition of the south wall particularly is cited as an illustration of the increasingly formalized depictions of imperial ceremony in late antiquity, and it is categorized alongside the better known sculptural depictions of the Tetrarchs as evidence of a fundamental turn away from naturalism in the art of the imperial court during the late third century.[79] Most scholars today attribute this stylistic shift in the tetrarchic era to a political agenda; the need for the four co-emperors to appear in complete agreement was so paramount that the figures' individuality was downplayed to highlight instead their similitude, understood as a pictorial embodiment of the concept of concordia (consensus or accord). There is also still a tendency in nonacademic circles, however, to attribute this stylistic development to decline. The third century of the Roman Empire was tumultuous indeed, and the artistic output of the period, especially during the latter half of the century, tends often to be dismissed as low quality in comparison to that of earlier eras. Since the recent cleaning of the plaster has exposed paintings of exceedingly high quality and elements that can be considered quite naturalistic, this pejorative assessment of the arts of the late empire can be even further discredited.

THE TETRARCHS IN THE NICHE

In contrast to the overall complexity of the south wall triptych wings, the iconography of the niche at the center of the composition is a simplified tableau of imperial majesty and the focus of the elaborate program decorating the imperial cult chamber. Wilkinson did not make a complete sketch of the scene, but he included a drawing of the Tetrarch on the westernmost edge of the niche in his detailed watercolor of the crowd scene (page 30r), and the two Tetrarchs from the eastern side of the niche appear on page 29r (see figures A.4 right and A.5 right). These drawings are a fairly accurate record of the in situ plaster, with the few exceptions discussed below.

The painted images of the four front-facing, larger-than-life-size Tetrarchs are not simply imperial portraits of the reigning emperors, but images that signal the presence of divine beings. They reside in a semicircular apselike space constructed specially for the chamber by the Romans as a means of synthesizing two ideological traditions—Egyptian and Roman—within Luxor Temple. Though an apse is an architectural feature more commonly associated in late antiquity with early Christian spaces and frequently decorated with the image of Christ to create a liturgical focal point, the connection among apses, *exedrae,* and sacred images is far older. In the pre-Christian world the apse was a feature used to shelter cult statues in which the presence of the divine being resided, or it served to frame the living emperor (or his image) during imperial audiences.[80] At Luxor these two functions were probably combined in the space of the imperial cult chamber (see chapter 7), but the creation of the niche in this particular spot within the temple served the additional pur-

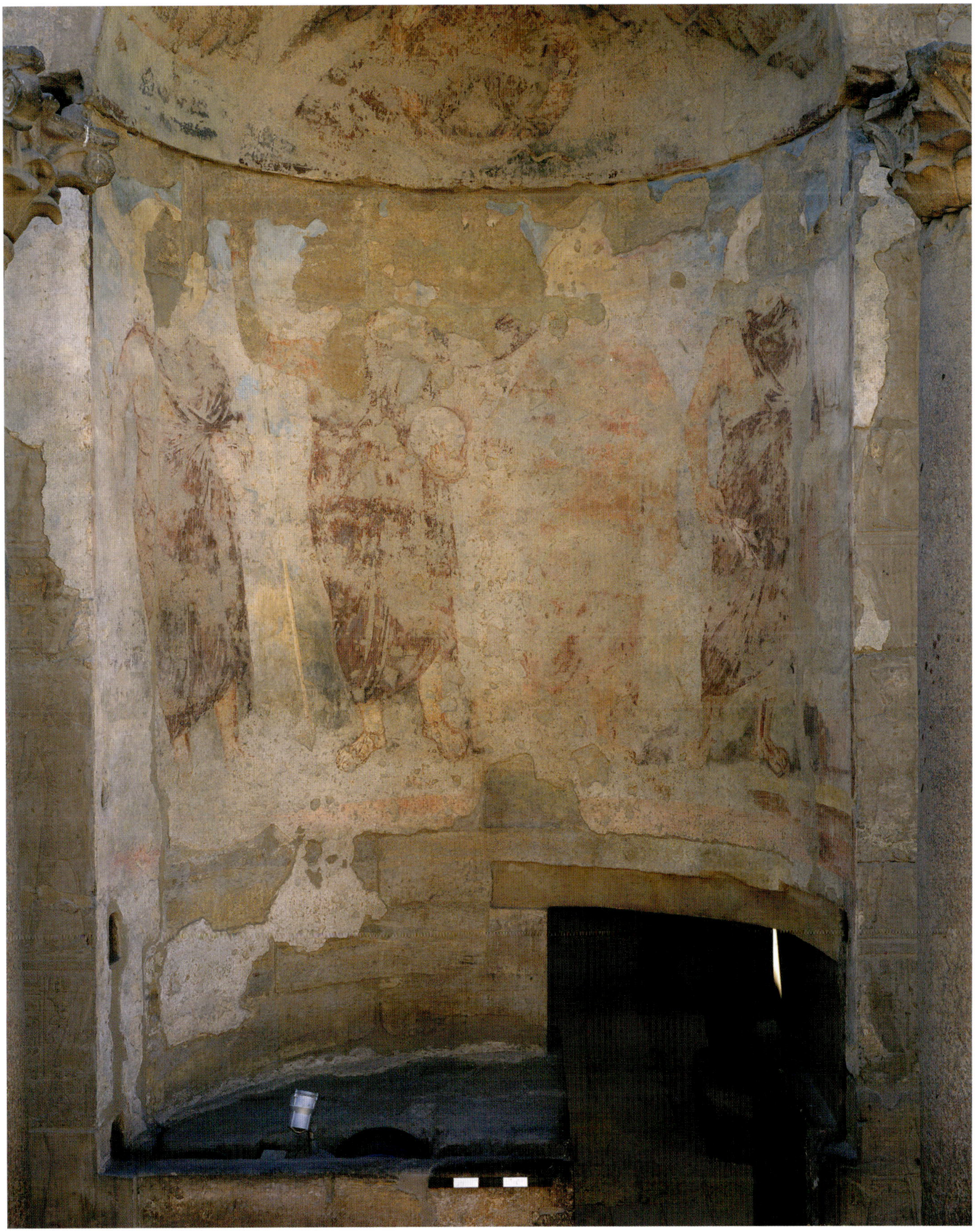

FIGURE 6.25
South wall niche: the four Tetrarchs.

pose of capitalizing on whatever lingering associations the site might have had with the king-making authority of the temple's pharaonic patron deity, Amun.

The room that became the imperial cult chamber during the Tetrarchy was in pharaonic times the first in a series of halls that made up the temple's inner sanctum. Immediately upon entry, visitors (exclusively priests in the Egyptian cult, because the unpurified were never allowed into this part of the temple) were confronted with a large doorway on the opposite, southern wall that led into another hall, which led to the barque shrine, where the image-bearing boat was kept, and finally ended in the holiest chamber of all, the sanctuary of Amun. This first room was therefore a liminal space, marked as important by its inaccessibility to the general public, yet it was not a room in which the presence of the deity resided permanently. It was, however, a space where a visitor physically realized the transition from secular to sacred space, by moving through it, or at least seeing through it, toward the gods (or rather, the statues of the gods in the inner sanctuary). The choice of this room as the focus of Roman modifications to Luxor Temple seems therefore a particularly powerful political statement. By the Romans' blocking the southern doorway of this room, which once led to the pharaonic inner sanctum, and filling it instead with images of the Roman emperors, the reconfigured room simultaneously usurped access to the pharaonic god and was reconstituted as a space in which the Roman emperors, represented by their painted presence, underwent a divine transformation. Diocletian especially, illustrated with the attributes of Jupiter, the Roman avatar of Amun, was not only presented as the divine ruler of Egypt but also as the arbiter of legitimate temporal power.

Given the symbolic importance of the niche in the temple, the images of the Tetrarchs within had to be visually distinct from the paintings in the rest of the room, and since the recent cleaning the dramatic effect of the larger-than-life-size figures is even more apparent (figure 6.25). The four nimbate figures, dressed in imperial purple mantles, stand in a nebulous space, even less distinct than the triptych wing tableaux on either side of the niche. Their sandal-clad feet rest on an ill-defined ground against a sky-blue background; there are no distinguishing features of landscape or dress to suggest time, place, or event. Above them all, in the semi-dome of the niche, hovers an eagle holding a bejeweled *corona* (crown). The two central figures are the Augusti, Diocletian and Maximian, whose authority over the flanking junior emperors, Constantius Chlorus and Galerius, is emphasized optically. The figures of the two Caesars are several centimeters smaller than the Augusti, and their bodies appear attenuated in comparison to the two senior Tetrarchs because of the curvature of the niche and their positions on the edges of the composition. The third figure from the left is conspicuously and deliberately erased, supporting his identification as Maximian, who was officially subjected to a *damnatio memoriae* under Constantine some time between 310 and 317 (discussed in chapter 2).[81] Further damage was inflicted on the paintings in antiquity when the faces of all four figures, as well as the head of a figure in a painted *imago clipeus* (portrait medallion) between the Augusti, were deliberately gouged away, possibly the result of early Christian iconoclasm.

The four Tetrarchs in the niche were probably intended to appear identical at first glance. On a superficial level, all imperial imagery of the tetrarchic era is united by an iconography of concordia, or consensus among the emperors, expressed through the similitude of the imperial bodies.[82] When illustrated together, the individual likenesses of the emperors are downplayed to the point of almost complete homogeneity, an expression of shared power on which the Tetrarchy formed by Diocletian was based. This reorganization of the imperial government was conceived to resolve what historians call the "crisis of the third century," in which the central authority of the imperial bureaucracy became increasingly unstable.[83] Concluding that the empire was too big to be ruled by one man, in 293 Diocletian appointed Maximian co-emperor in the West, while he himself continued to rule in the East. The two Augusti, Diocletian and Maximian, then each adopted a junior emperor or Caesar, Galerius in the East and Constantius in the West, to act as their respective helpers and, eventually, their designated heirs.

In reality the four emperors were rarely in the same place simultaneously, but their public images illustrated their equal presence presiding over a united empire (*patrimonium indivisum*). The most famous example of tetrarchic similitude is the porphyry statue group now embedded in the walls of the Basilica of Saint Mark in Venice (figure 6.26).[84] Originally part of a columnar commemorative monument in Constantinople, the Venice sculptures group the Tetrarchs into two pairs; each senior Augustus is shown embracing his appointed Caesar. All four of the static and stylized figures are the same size and wear identical military dress. No distinction is made among them, with the exception of one subtle detail—the older Augusti wear close-cropped beards, whereas the Caesars are clean-shaven. None of these portraits could be mistaken for actual likenesses of the emperors, but they all share common features that are replicated in many media across the empire, such as piercing stares, short-cropped hair, furrowed eyebrows, square jaws, and thick necks.[85] Despite the damage to the faces of the Luxor Tetrarchs, therefore, it is likely that they would have expressed a similar aesthetic given the uniformity of extant tetrarchic group portraits, even considering that the tech-

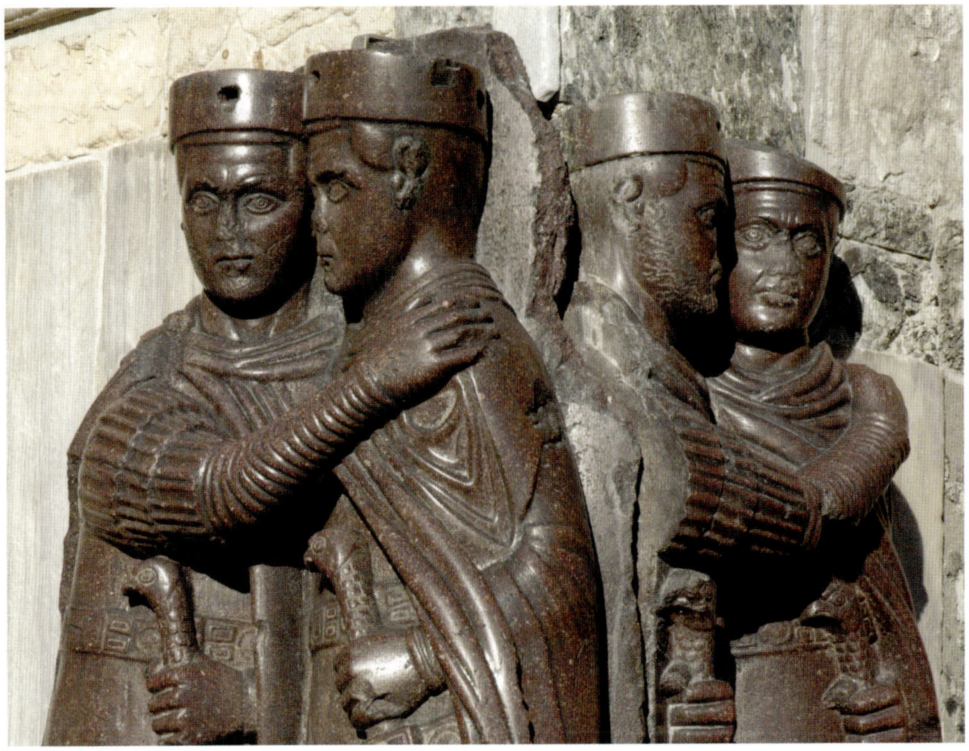

FIGURE 6.26
Porphyry statues of the Tetrarchs, ca. 300; originally from Constantinople, now embedded in the southwest corner of Saint Mark's Basilica, Venice.

nique of painting would have allowed for a slightly greater degree of plasticity in the rendering of facial features than is possible with sculpted porphyry. At the same time, however, to a viewer educated in a Roman visual vocabulary, there are secondary elements of the paintings that mark each figure as distinct, especially the figure of Diocletian, which hints at a more complex political agenda than simply concordia.

A hallmark of the aesthetic changes occurring in Roman art of the third century is the overhaul of the imperial image (discussed above), in which the sovereign is presented as majestic, remote, and semi-divine instead of a man one could relate to, perhaps in an attempt to promote an image of stability in the face of the political turmoil besetting the empire. Both the Luxor paintings and the porphyry Tetrarchs are examples of this trend. But the Tetrarchs in particular further blurred the boundaries between their human selves and their divine associates by adopting *signa* that conveyed their special connection to their chosen namesakes.[86] Diocletian thus appended "Jovius" ("belonging to Jupiter") to his title, and Maximian claimed "Herculius" ("belonging to Hercules").[87] Though these naming conventions were not outright claims of divinity, they amounted to assertions of divine agency, and the titles appear in inscriptions, panegyrics, and some medallions after 286.[88] Interestingly, whereas the alliance of Diocletian and Maximian with their patron deities is pictured especially in the numismatic record, the iconography of the coins never goes so far as to depict Diocletian and Maximian *as* Jupiter and Hercules, respectively.[89] Only a few medallions allude to the conflation of man and god, but these seem to have been in limited circulation in military contexts, so the extent to which the emperor was understood to be an avatar of his divine counterpart in other media is unclear.[90]

Generally in the Roman world, image makers shied away from representing living emperors as divine, even in the decorations of imperial cult temples.[91] Representations of the deceased emperor's *apotheosis* are more common; only after death was it proper for a Roman emperor to become a god. For example, in the apse of the western portico of the Temple of Hercules at Sabratha (186 CE or later), one of the few other surviving examples of painted decoration from a space associated with the imperial cult, the already deceased Marcus Aurelius is depicted being carried to heaven on the back of an eagle.[92] The iconography of the Luxor Tetrarchs in the niche stands apart from this tradition, and it may be the sole surviving example of an image in which the elision between the living emperor Diocletian and Jupiter is overtly suggested, a manifestation perhaps made tolerable only because of the specific symbolism of the site in which the image was placed—a temple associated with the role of Amun, the Egyptian avatar of Jupiter, as a source of divine kingship.[93]

It is because of Diocletian's special connection to Jupiter, then, that we can be reasonably certain that the most visually prominent figure second from left in the niche (Wilkinson page 29r; see figure A.4 right) is in fact the Emperor Diocletian and not one of the other Tetrarchs. This figure holds a spear in his right hand and a *globus* in his left (figure 6.27). Since the early Roman Empire, these objects were understood in Roman iconography to be unmistakable attributes of universal authority bestowed by Jupiter on the reigning sovereign.[94] But the globus and scepter were also attributes of Jupiter himself, an iconographical tradition that has even deeper roots in classical history.[95] In the corpus of tetrarchic images, especially the numismatic record, both Augusti and even the Caesars are illustrated at times holding these objects, emphasizing their equal power over the cosmos.[96] But the fact that only one of the four figures in the niche is shown with the globus and the scepter, despite the contemporary widespread employment of such attributes in other contexts depicting all four emperors, suggests a visual hierarchy. In the context of Luxor Temple, these objects in particular emphasize the relationship between Diocletian and his divine *comes* (companion) Jupiter, an association that was promoted in all media in the tetrarchic era.[97] In comparison, the other figures,

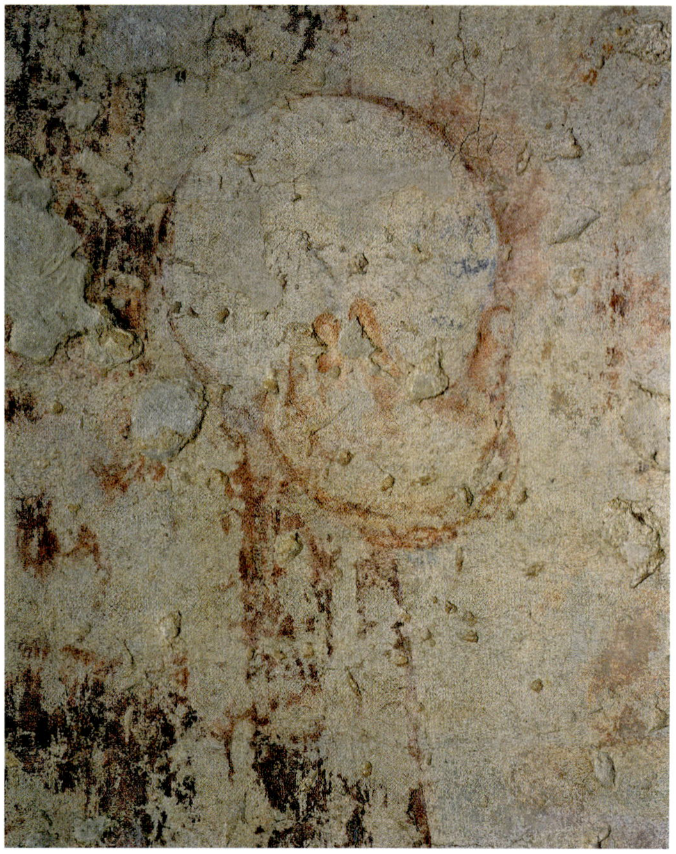

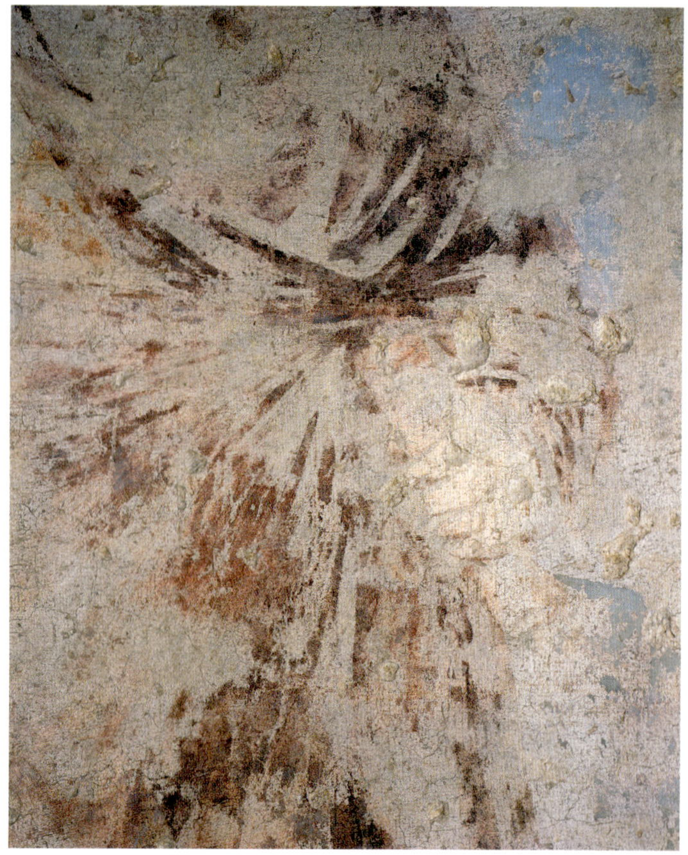

FIGURE 6.27
(left) South wall niche: detail of the globus.

FIGURE 6.28
(right) South wall niche: detail of the rotulus.

though nimbate and majestically proportioned, are not visually linked to a specific deity in the Roman pantheon. The figure to Diocletian's right (Galerius) carries a *rotulus* (scroll) in his left hand (figure 6.28), a symbol of authority but not necessarily the attribute of a particular divinity. The figure to the viewer's right of the erased Maximian holds a laurel branch in his right hand, a detail newly revealed in the recent conservation work (see figures 5.9 and 6.31). In this case the leaves can be understood as a generic symbol of victory.[98]

Furthermore, imagery related to Jupiter is not limited to the figure of Diocletian. Directly above the four Tetrarchs in the semi-dome is the representation of an eagle with wings spread wide (figure 6.29). The eagle is a zoomorphic manifestation of Jupiter, particularly revered by the Roman army, for which the eagle standard, or *aquila,* was the most important ensign of each legion. The eagle grasps in its talons a gilded and bejeweled corona made of oak, a tree sacred to Jupiter. This crown is of a type popular in the late empire; a similar version is worn by Septimius Severus in one of the only other surviving paintings of the Roman emperor known to come from Egypt (see figure 6.2). Though the painting of the eagle is much faded today, one can still see traces of individual feathers, which suggests that it had a lifelike appearance in its original condition. One can imagine that in antiquity, in the low light of the chamber, speckled with sunlight or flickering torchlight, the eagle would seem to be in mid-flight, swooping down from the heavens to crown the victorious Tetrarchs.

Additionally, at the center of the image field between Diocletian and Maximian is an imago clipeus that probably illustrated an *en face* bust of Jupiter, though all that is left today are the tips of his laurel crown and a few traces of the figure's purple mantle (see figure 6.25).[99] The image of Jupiter appears as the fifth and most prominent figure in another tetrarchic portrait constellation in Rome, that of the aforementioned five-columned Decennalia monument that stood behind the rostrum in the Roman Forum and of which the Decennalia Base is the only surviving piece. As we know from a representation of this monument on the northeast face of the Arch of Constantine, a statue of Jupiter with scepter and globus topped the middle and highest of the columns, while statues of the four emperors in identical poses topped the flanking columns, two on either side of Jupiter (figure 6.30). The placement of this monument in the Roman Forum was particularly symbolic, as the site was the millennium-old epicenter of the city, considered the *caput mundi* ("capital of the world"). The Decennalia monument thus promoted the ideology of an empire governed by all four emperors, whose authority was presided over by Jupiter, visually manifest in the statue atop the central column and bolstered by the authority emanating

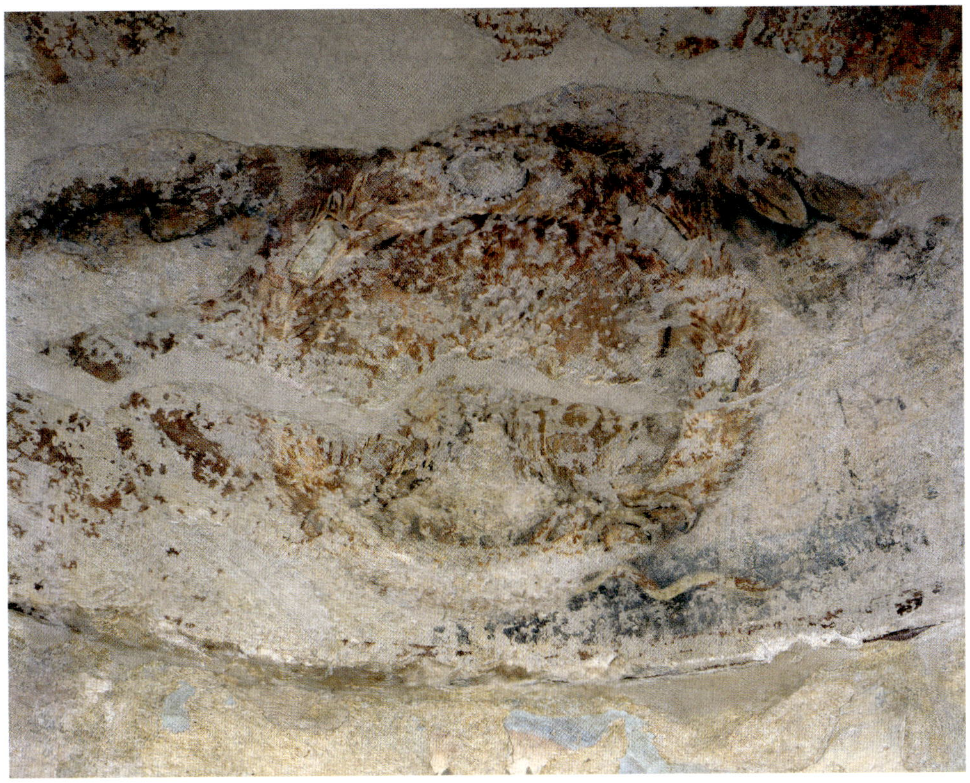

FIGURE 6.29
South wall niche: detail of the semi-dome and the eagle holding a wreath in its talons.

from the most sacred temple of the Jupiter cult, within sight, above on the Capitoline Hill.

At Luxor, however, the figures of the Tetrarchs are more prominent visually than the central portrait bust, the image of Diocletian especially so. He is the only one of the four emperors to strike a distinctive pose—his right arm is raised above his head to grasp the scepter, whereas the arms of the three others are at their sides, including Maximian, whose silhouette is still discernible in spite of the damage to the paint layer. The image of Diocletian manifest as Jupiter thus takes precedence visually over the portrait bust in the central tondo, almost an inversion of the visual hierarchy exhibited in the Decennalia monument. The unusually overt visual declaration of divinity at Luxor is probably due to the particular symbolic association of Luxor Temple with divine kingship. Diocletian appears in the niche as a god, having become one with Jupiter-Amun, who also presides over the epiphanic moment—the visitor's encounter with the divine emperors—in both zoomorphic and anthropomorphic form.

That the niche imagery is a representation of what Deckers calls a theophany (appearance of a god) is further confirmed by the fact that the Tetrarchs appear to be naked beneath their purple mantles.[100] Additionally, the figure of Diocletian is especially singled out by the unusual configuration of his paludamentum. Unlike the other two extant figures whose cloaks are clasped over their right shoulders with bejeweled pins, Diocletian is portrayed with his right shoulder completely bare to emphasize the graceful curve of his raised arm grasping his scepter. Nudity is more regularly associated with the representations of gods in public settings, and it is rare to find the emperor in such a state of undress, although heroic nudity is often employed in more intimate settings to imply divine association. Indeed, the Tetrarchs are more commonly represented in military attire or at the very least with a tunic beneath their paludamenta or togas.

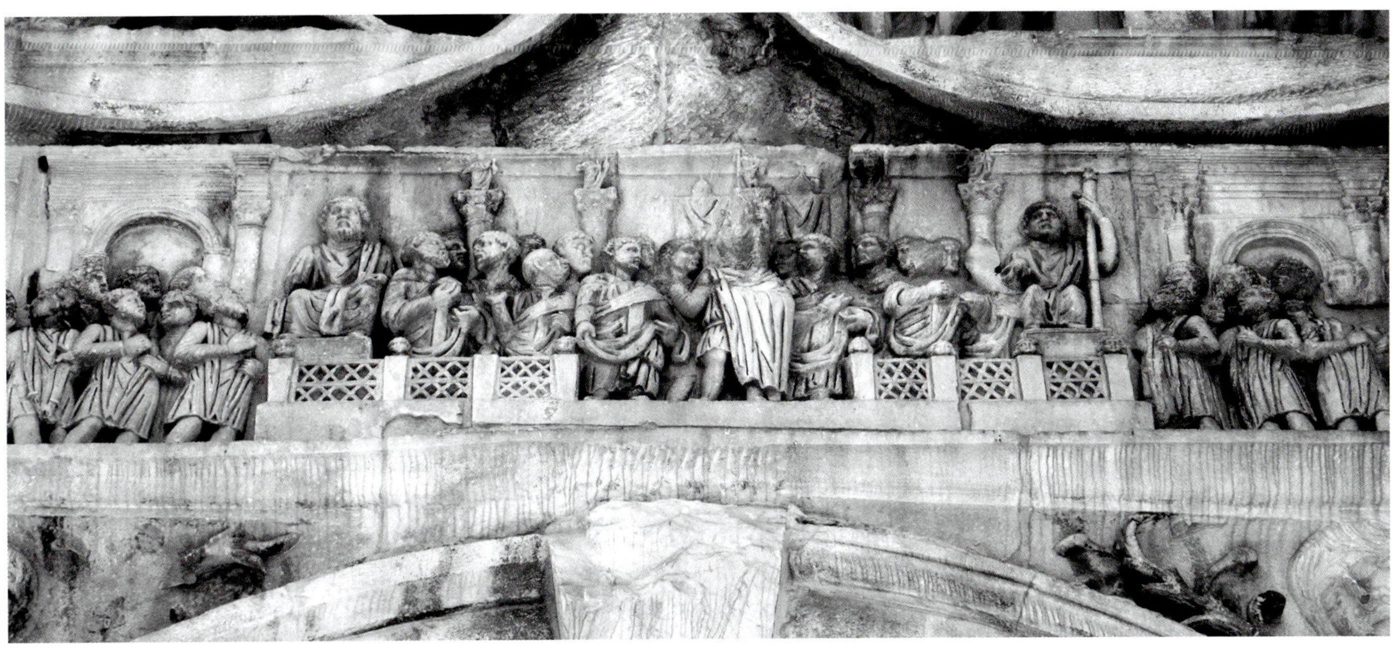

FIGURE 6.30
North face of the Arch of Constantine, Rome, ca. 315; the five columns of the Decennalia monument are visible behind the rostrum as Constantine addresses a crowd in the Roman Forum.

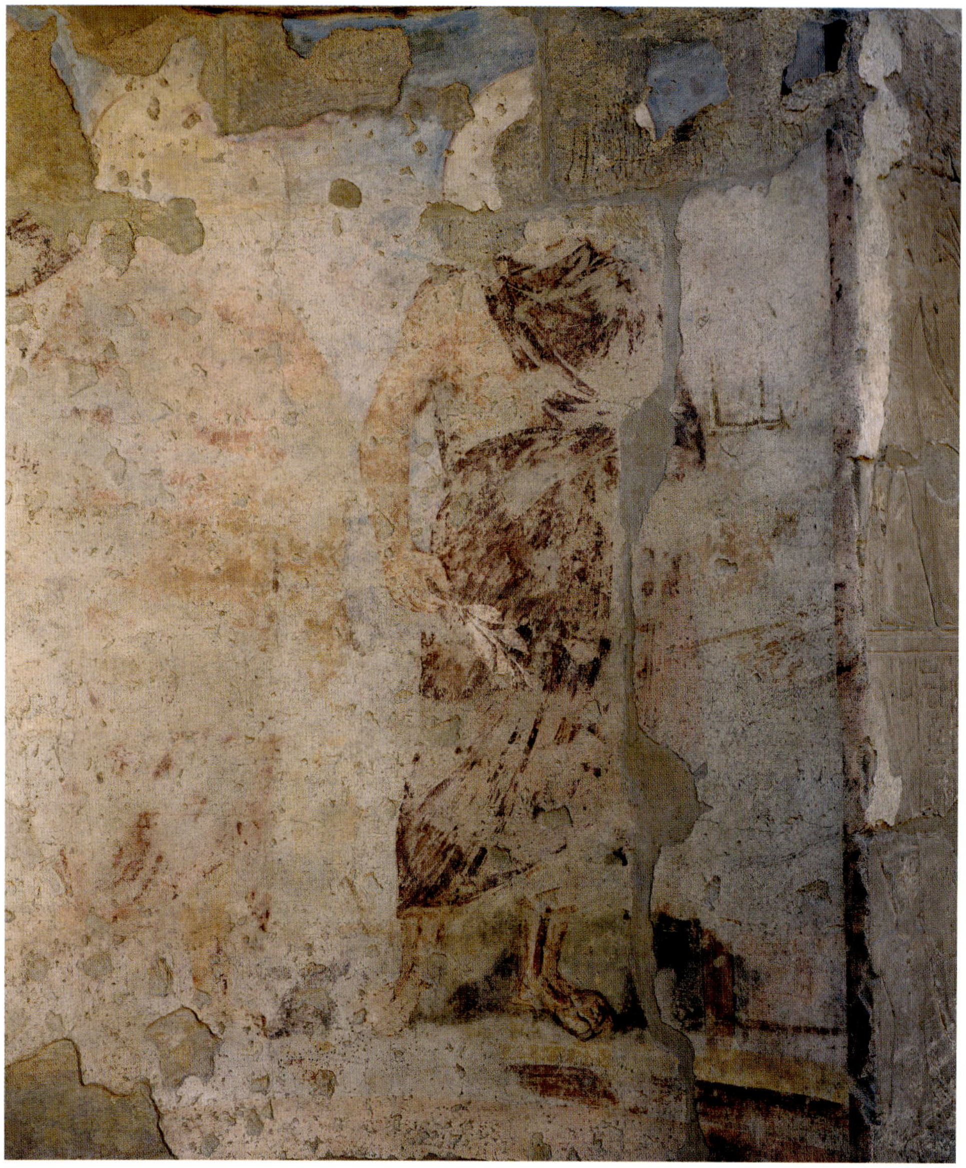

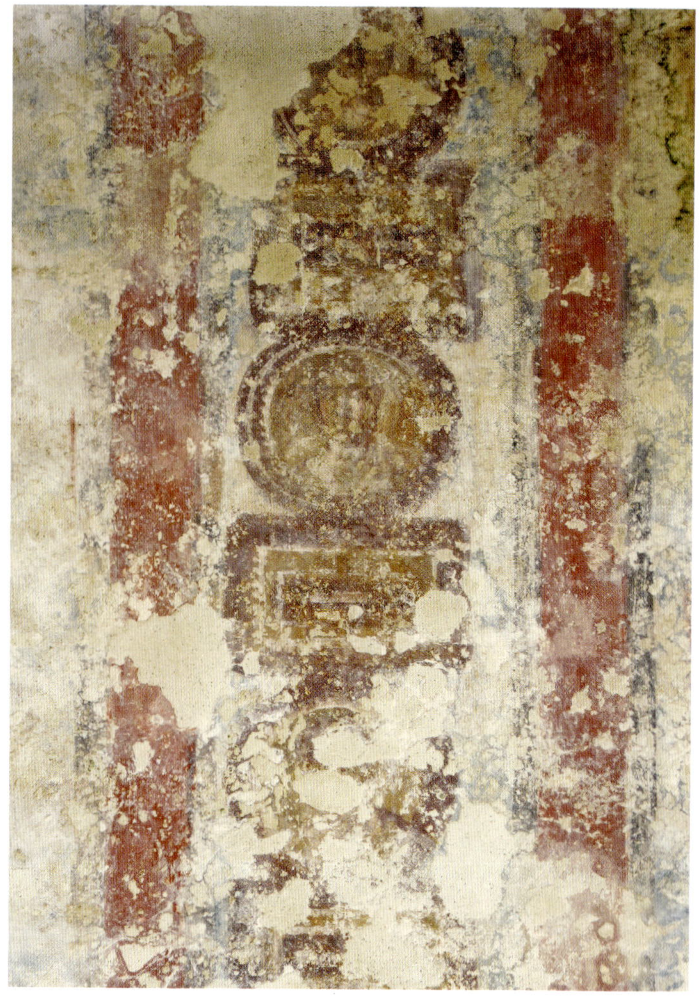

FIGURE 6.31
(above left) South wall niche, west side: figure of a Tetrarch with traces of paint that might once have depicted a signum beside his left shoulder.

FIGURE 6.32
(above right) The villa of Piazza Armerina, Sicily, exterior facade of the entry courtyard, ca. fourth century; painted plaster depicting a signum with images of the Roman emperors.

The golden halos encircling the heads of the four figures are also unusual. Before its widespread assimilation into Christian image vocabularies as a sign of holiness and divinity, the halo or *nimbus* was used for representations of solar gods and apotheosized emperors, and it was probably adapted into Roman art from the east sometime in the early empire.[101] A variation of the halo, the radiate crown or nimbus, was more popular in the third and early fourth centuries for representations of the living emperor and, like the divine nomenclature adopted by Diocletian and Maximian, probably signaled the emperor's special connection to Apollo or Sol Invictus rather than the emperor's outright divinity.[102]

The solid disk of light, on the other hand, was not regularly used as an imperial attribute until the Constantinian era, though it shows up around the heads of the Tetrarchs on several medallions that date to the turn of the fourth century, and the symbol is alluded to in a panegyric dated to 289.[103] The Tetrarchs at Luxor may therefore represent one of the first extant examples of the disk nimbus's employment in a monumental, ceremonial context, and its use in lieu of radiate halos might have had particular connotations with tetrarchic ideology that remain elusive in light of present evidence.[104]

After the Luxor paintings, the disk nimbus is found encircling the heads of Constantine and his father on two reworked Hadrianic reliefs from the Arch of Constantine depicting a boar hunt and a sacrifice to Apollo and Hercules, respectively.[105] It is also used on a series of coins minted in commemoration of Constantine's victory over Maxentius in 312.[106] The halo in these contexts is usually interpreted not as direct attributes of the solar gods Sol Invictus or Apollo but rather as a sign that Constantine shared, somewhat ambiguously, the sun god's divine radiance.[107] Perhaps a similar generic rather than specific association with "divine light" was intended at Luxor.

The use of the halos at Luxor therefore indicates that though some aspects of the style and iconography of the Luxor frescoes are in keeping with time-honored Roman artistic traditions, other aspects are rather innovative for the time and seem more in keeping with Christian iconographical conventions that become common in later eras.[108] For example, whereas Greek and Roman cult statues were normally three-dimensional, at Luxor for the first time we see the two-dimensional images of the divine emperors honored as objects of a cult, not long before the Christians adopted two-dimensional images for the representation of holy figures.[109]

Given that the nimbus is such a common feature in the iconography of Christian art, it is understandable that the figures in the niche came to be misidentified as saints in the nineteenth century. Although Wilkinson himself doubted his earlier Christian identification of the reuse of the room, he interpreted an emblem painted beside the Tetrarch on the west side of the niche as a cross (Wilkinson's notebook page 30r; see figure A.5 right).[110] Today no such symbol is apparent, though traces remain of a design in a square or rectangular frame in this part of the niche (figure 6.31). A candidate more likely than a cross is a *signum,* perhaps displaying the *imagines* of the emperors, like the contemporary painted version found on the exterior wall of the gates of the Piazza Armerina (figure 6.32). Another possibility is that it illustrated the standard of the Luxor legion, itself an object of cult in the space of the imperial cult chamber.

At the time of the imperial cult chamber's design, Diocletian's vehement anti-Christian sentiments would have precluded the appearance of any Christian symbolism within the space of the painted chamber.[111] It is not impossible that the image of a cross was added later, after Christianity had made significant inroads in Egypt, but there is currently no evidence that this space was ever used as a church.[112] Though several churches were eventually built within the walls of the Roman fort in the fifth and sixth centuries, it is notable that they were mostly constructed outside of the walls of Luxor Temple proper. The only exception is the church underneath the current mosque of Abu al-Hajjaj in the Ramesses II court. It seems, therefore, as if the most sacred area of the temple, the sanctuary of Amun (later the imperial cult chamber), was avoided in the early Byzantine period as if in acknowledgment of a symbolic association not easily subsumed by Christianity.[113]

In summation, the temple of Amun at Luxor was a place where the human and divine natures of the king were reaffirmed in ritual action—in pharaonic times certainly and perhaps also in the Roman era—as evidenced by the paintings placed in the heart of the temple. In spite of the Luxor frescoes being wholly Roman in appearance, situated in their Egyptian architectural context, they take on a meaning quite distinct from those of other tetrarchic group portraits. In late antiquity the emperor could be represented as a man with divine characteristics or, posthumously, as a god, but rarely, if ever, were the human and divine combined so directly as in the Luxor niche.

CONCLUSION

Stylistically the Luxor painting cycle as a whole is both hieratic and illusionistic, encompassing the entire repertoire of artistic tropes used by the Romans in this period, and embracing a polysemic conception of the imperial image. Though the hieratic mode of representation on the south wall is meant to illustrate the divine emperor in an otherworldly space (symbolic representation), the illusionistic mode of the east wall procession (a narrative) showed the entourage of the emperor participating in a human ceremony and existing in real space and time. Although the images of the emperors on the south wall are otherworldly and aloof on their pedestals and in the niche, the other figures in the east wing of the triptych appear quite human and even individual in appearance, aspects that have become even more evident now that the paintings have been cleaned.

Furthermore, the Roman paintings' themes of triumph and divine kingship fit nicely in concept into the ancient pharaonic context of Luxor Temple; without these images, the Luxor fort seems a strange architectural conglomeration, and its military purpose is not immediately understood in relation to contemporary comparanda in the rest of Egypt (on this, see chapter 2). One could even consider the adoption of preexisting sacred architecture for military purposes at Luxor as a direct inversion of the process more commonly seen in late antique Egypt: the Christianization of late Roman secular buildings such as military forts.[114] The most conclusive evidence, therefore, that the Luxor camp was part of a more significant political agenda than a mere military outpost lies in the subject matter of the Roman paintings at the heart of the temple. The placement of fundamentally "Roman" images within the pharaonic temple, a place long remembered as the symbolic nucleus of kingly authority, is by no means an arbitrary choice. Juxtaposed with the urban armature of what was understood in Egypt to represent a romanized city (see chapter 2), the late third-century modifications represent an act of appropriation that simultaneously evokes and negates previous traditions. In other words, the appropriation of a temple dedicated in pharaonic times to the cult of the divine king provided a visual juxtaposition of traditions that invites comparison of the Roman present with the Egyptian past. The intentions behind the Roman revitalization of this site speak to a hope for complicity between past and present, Egyptian and Roman, art and experience. But whereas such an assemblage presented a coherent message of imperial power comprehensible to cosmopolitan Roman audiences in the tetrarchic period, it is uncertain whether this propagandistic visual language would have been intelligible in a setting such as Luxor, where there was an equally strong history of local visual idioms. The issue of intention versus reception is explored in the following chapter.

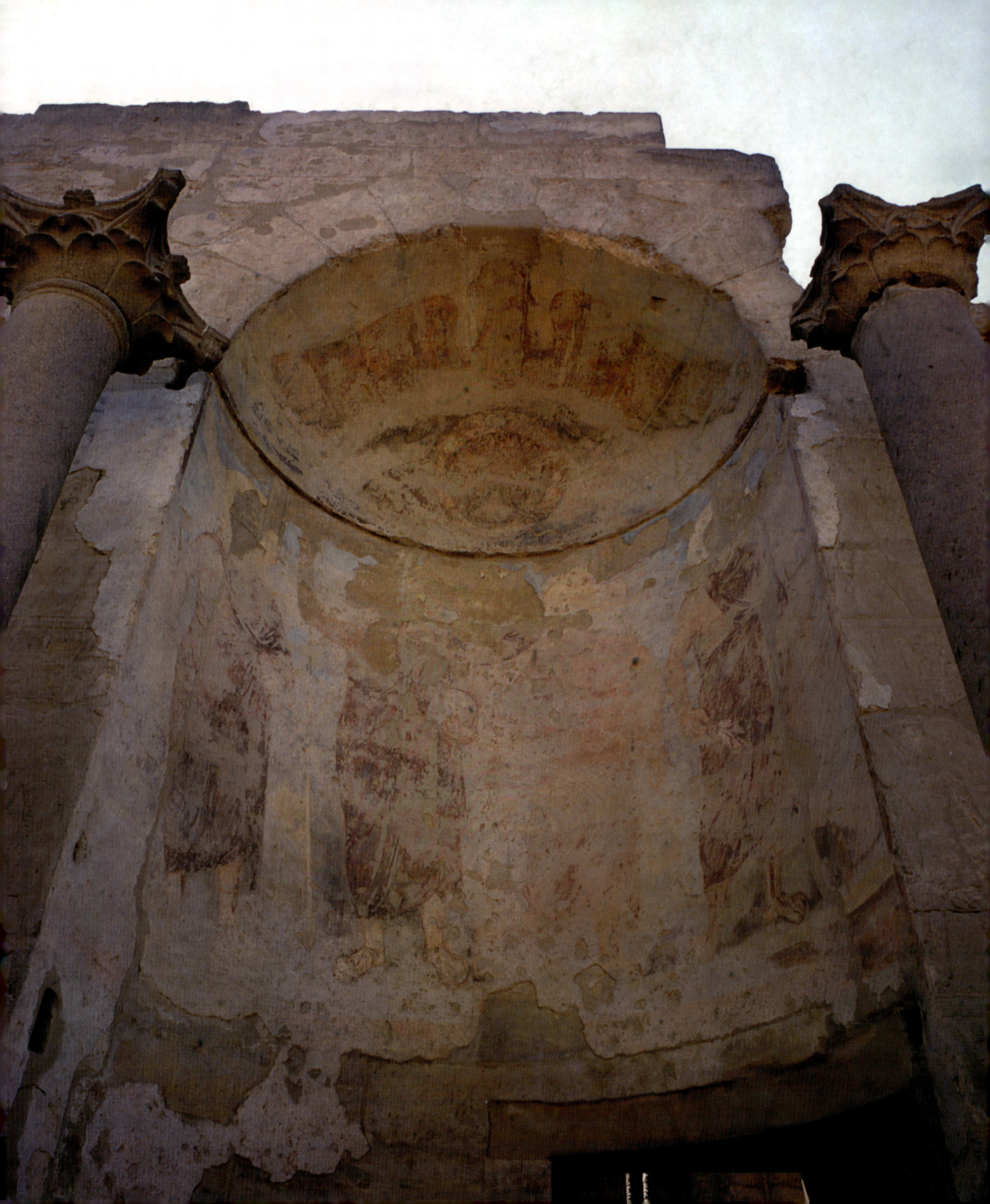

Chapter 7

PICTURING POWER IN LATE ROMAN EGYPT

The Imperial Cult, Imperial Portraits, and a Visual Panegyric for Diocletian

SUSANNA McFADDEN

FIGURE 7.1
View of the Tetrarchs and the eagle in the semi-dome as if standing directly in front of the niche.

WHEN DIOCLETIAN'S ARMY APPROPRIATED LUXOR TEMPLE at the end of the third century, the pharaonic complex was already ancient in the eyes of the Romans. Despite the site's antiquity, however, the particulars of the Roman renovations suggest that the memory of the temple's function as a sacred space dedicated to the cult of the Egyptian king was still alive and well. Diocletian's annexation of the site therefore represents a significant act of symbolic appropriation, the most potent aspect of which was the conversion of a room at the heart of the pharaonic sanctuary into a shrine for the legionary standards and a chamber dedicated to the imperial cult.

The imperial cult chamber at Luxor and its frescoes constitute evidence of a Roman ritual environment imposed on an even older pharaonic one. Similar visual programs so revealing of Roman imperial propaganda rarely survive, making Luxor an extremely important site for studying the way in which the meaning of an image is conveyed through the physical experience of the viewer as much as through the iconography of the images.[1] At sites connected with sacred images in the Roman world, artists and architects often deliberately manipulated the placement of images or objects within monuments to guide a viewer's initial encounter with the most important images in the space or to influence the peripatetic reading of image programs in a specific sequence.[2] The Roman paintings in Luxor, for example, were placed in the temple as the climax of a dramatic processional path laid out through the temple proper. Just as in popular parlance "all roads lead to Rome," in Luxor Temple all ritual paths and viewers' sightlines were directed toward the imperial cult chamber and the focal point of the entire composition, the ciborium and painted niche on the south wall in which one finds representations of the four Tetrarchs.

Though Luxor Temple may have functioned as a military encampment in the Roman era, because of these ritual pathways it was also very much a sacred space, activated by the visitor's encounter with the images of the Roman emperors in the imperial cult chamber. How this encounter was programmed, the significance of the chamber in which the encounter took place, and why those particular images were considered so powerful are discussed in this chapter.

THE IMPERIAL CULT IN EGYPT

The painted image program in Luxor Temple most probably came into being through a fiat from the imperial court rather than as a local civic initiative. The iconography, therefore, reveals a great deal about the tetrarchic ideological agenda in Egypt. But the intended message promoted by the frescoes about the nature of Roman rule vis-à-vis Egyptian concepts of divine kingship was triggered only in the space of the site-specific architectural frame of Luxor Temple. Therefore, the site is both international and local in scope, and it is likely that the message encoded in the painted program was received in different ways depending on the status and ethnic identity of the viewer. The culminating moment of any viewer's experience was the final encounter with the images of the Roman emperors in the imperial cult chamber, and it was the viewer's comprehension of the nature of the imperial image and the purpose of the imperial cult itself that ultimately affected the overall success or failure of the experience.

Much scholarship has been devoted to questions about the overall uniformity of the imperial cult and whether, given the significant local variations in a number of areas of the empire, we can really speak of an empirewide phenomenon.[3] What we call the imperial cult in fact encompasses two concomitant phenomena: worship of the dead emperor and veneration of the living ruler. The consensus is that though institutionalized veneration of the Roman emperor began under Augustus in the first century BCE, during the subsequent four centuries no singular set of practices developed that could be deemed *the* imperial cult, nor did the emperor necessarily need to be divine in order to receive such honors.[4] In the Western Empire only the deceased emperor was revered as a god (*divus*) and the living emperor sought honors only as a mortal (yet was still the son of a god, *divi filius*), but in the Eastern Empire these distinctions were blurred.[5] To complicate matters more, by the third century worship of the living emperor seemed to supplant that of the divi, or deceased emperors, in most parts of the empire.[6] This perhaps accounts in part for the rise of a discourse in Christian literature about the dangers of idolatry.

Regardless of the era, while the focus of the cult in all parts of the empire was always the person of the emperor in some form, how each community chose to express its devotion to the emperor was at the discretion of the individual city and province.[7] This variability of practice allowed the emperor to assume identities—living or deceased (or both), human or divine (or both)—nuanced to meet the needs of individual communities, yet at the same time it created an overarching bond of loyalty to a generic ideal of "emperor" that linked communities empirewide.[8] Clifford Ando fittingly labels this acceptance of an imperial ideal *consensus,* arguing that it accounted for the empire's *longue durée.* Critical to maintaining this consensus was the representation of imperial power and the sanctity of the imperial image.

In this context of emperor worship, imperial portraits came to be understood as an embodiment of the emperor's *genius* or *numen* (sacred guiding spirit).[9] In this way the living emperor could be made present in many places at once. This proxy power of the imperial image depended on a certain degree of recognizability; consistency in appearance of the imperial likeness was assured by the circulation of portrait models, disseminated from Rome or, in the later Roman Empire, from the various regional capitals.[10] But within such practices, consistency in type mattered more than fidelity to the actual appearance of the emperor. And the power of the imperial image relied on the fact that the viewer believed in the existence of a real prototype.[11] That the image of the emperor was understood to communicate his presence was thus a potent tool of imperial ideology, which endured even into the Christian era, when the question of the divinity of the emperor was no longer an active issue.[12]

In late antiquity especially, literary evidence attests to the widespread dissemination of the imperial portrait and also to a certain extent the reception of these portraits by local communities.[13] Ceremonies such as the *adventus,* to be discussed below, a rite that in concept demonstrated the loyalty of the emperor's subjects, could be celebrated for the arrival of the imperial image as well as for the person of the emperor himself.[14] The question remains, though, whether the ancient Roman viewer really believed that the emperor (and thus his image) was divine. As the previous chapter discussed, the images of the Tetrarchs in the niche at Luxor, especially that of Diocletian, exhibit an iconographic conflation of human and divine characteristics. Whether the ancient viewer actually considered the person of the emperor as both man and god simultaneously, or even allowed for the idea that the Roman emperor could be a god at all, is more difficult to reconstruct, especially since modern conceptions of "God" in the Judeo-Christian sense may not correspond with pre-Christian Roman beliefs. In antiquity, divinity was less an absolute concept and more a distinction of status between beings.[15] The living emperor, in relation to other worshippers, certainly had divine status, and the degree to which he was understood as equal to or lesser than other deities depended on the local context in which the cult was practiced.[16] Such pragmatic and polyvalent distinctions have led some scholars to dismiss the imperial cult as fundamentally sociopolitical in nature and to construct parallels between modern movements like nationalism and the imperial cult in antiquity. On the surface such a comparison seems apt. Our textual sources regarding the imperial cult are filled not with theological discussions on the nature of the emperor's godhead but with processions, sacrifices, temples, and images.[17]

On the other hand, there is no doubt that there was a widespread conviction that the ruler was something *like* a god. His divine power was a very real and present force, regarded by his subjects as the guarantor of their *salus,* or physical well-being. To secure this well-being, it was necessary to carry out the demands of cult in the same way they were carried out for other gods. But it was also necessary to sacrifice to the living human emperor, since the ruler could secure the health of his subjects only if he himself was secure.[18] This notion of reciprocity was paramount. Put simply, "If I (the supplicant) carry out the rites which you (the emperor or the god) are due (sacrifice, libations, and so on), then I will expect my petition to be heard and granted in some way."

To define the imperial cult as a "religion" in the modern sense, delineated by the dictates of the great Abrahamic faiths, is therefore misleading. Neither Greek nor Latin had any pre-Christian term for "religion" as we understand the word today. Instead, *religio* meant something more along the lines of reverence or conscientiousness and diligence toward superiors, most often, but not exclusively, the gods.[19] Pre-Christian religions were for this reason more concerned with observances than faith, and they were defined by actions of discourse, such as sacrifice, prayer, and other forms of establishing and constructing dialogues between humans and "another world," the substance of which could be perceived in different ways by different peoples.[20] Such other worlds were distinct in some way from the everyday sphere of existence in which men and women functioned. We typically assume these other worlds to be realms of gods or God, but in late antiquity the world of the imperial court certainly occupied a status akin to that of another world, hence the sanctity of an imperial audience hall, or a space in which the image of the emperor resided in lieu of the emperor's actual presence, as at Luxor.

It is thus more useful to think of Greco-Roman religion within a framework devised by anthropologists, rather than theologians, where the intersection and overlap of the sociopolitical world with the world of the gods was neither a problem nor a contradiction.[21] Emperor worship instead took many shapes, and the degree to which the emperor was considered divine varied. As a result, portraits of the emperor in antiquity elicited a range of responses. Some viewers rationally understood the images as simply artificial and symbolic representations of the emperor, but the notion that the portrait of the emperor was an actual manifestation of the ruler was also deeply embedded in imperial society.[22] Imperial portraits acted as public talismans, and they were revered in a variety of animated ways (petitioned, tended, garlanded, carried in procession, asked for asylum or protection); these responses are well documented, especially in Egypt.[23] Imperial images could elicit decidedly negative responses as well; the act of *damnatio memoriae* would not have packed such a symbolic punch were it not for a tacit understanding on the part of the ancient viewer that the imperial image embodied presence and power.

It is against this background that we examine the particular forms of the Roman imperial cult in Egypt to appreciate how the Luxor imperial cult chamber worked as both an evocation of and a departure from tradition.[24] At the time of the Roman annexation of Egypt in 30 or 29 BCE, there already existed a living, omnipresent tradition of sacralizing royal power.[25] Official Egyptian religion was essentially collective and cultic in nature even before the advent of the Romans, so for Egyptians the imperial cult's conflation of sociopolitical concerns with the "other world" described above would have seemed inherently familiar.[26] In contrast, many empirewide cults of the Roman era, especially popular and exotic mystery religions such as those of Isis, Mithras, and even Christianity at first, thrived on a radical separation of these two realms.[27] Under the Ptolemies, ruler worship had been institutionalized and disseminated from Alexandria. The extent to which the Roman form of ruler worship perpetuated Ptolemaic and older pharaonic traditions is still debated, as is the issue of who the primary patrons of the imperial cult in Egypt might have been.[28] Was the Roman imperial cult a state-sponsored initiative directed from Rome, or was it a purely local phenomenon?[29] The answer, for both the early and late empire, lies somewhere in between, for veneration of the emperor in Egypt took multiple forms, as did the types of spaces that were considered loci of imperial cult, but in all cases the role of the imperial image was paramount.

Archaeological and textual evidence attests two basic types of spaces associated with the imperial image in the Greco-Roman cities of Egypt. On the one hand, there were buildings constructed specifically for the veneration of the emperor, known as *kaisareia, sebastaia,* and *hadrianeia.*[30] The most famous of these buildings was the great Kaisareion of Alexandria, begun under the Ptolemies and claimed by Augustus after his conquest.[31] There were, however, multiple such buildings throughout the province; texts record examples in major metropolitan cities such as Antinoopolis, Arsinoe, Hermopolis Magna, Oxyrhynchos, Elephantine, Lykopolis, and Philadelphia.[32] These buildings were linked with Roman authority from their inception, and they seem to have acted, in addition to being a place for the veneration of the imperial office, as the central place of administration within the respective *nomes* from the second century onward.[33] We learn from papyri, for example, that the images of the emperor within the Kaisareia of Egypt acted as arbiters of legal disputes.[34] Unfortunately, there is little information to confirm the physical form of these temples in the cities, though it is assumed they used a classical architectural language heavily influenced by similar structures in the Greek east.

Notable exceptions to this rule, however, are found at two major Egyptian cult sanctuaries, Philae and Karnak, where small imperial cult shrines were constructed in the form of traditional Roman podium temples, an uncommon typology in the eastern Mediterranean and also a deliberate stylistic contrast with respect to the larger Egyptian cult spaces to which they were appended.[35] These temples date to the first century CE and their dedication was probably a direct imperial initiative under Augustus, though they remained in use throughout the imperial period. At Philae in particular it seems as if the association of the space with the Roman emperor was reaffirmed when Diocletian constructed a monumental arch to create a new entrance at the northern end of the island.[36]

On the other hand, emperor worship was not limited to buildings exclusively associated with the emperor and civic administration. The presence of imperial images in temples dedicated to other gods of the Greco-Roman pantheon is also well attested, and in such spaces the emperor "shared" honors with the primary deity.[37] The best example of this is the temple of Jupiter Capitolinus at Arsinoe in the Fayyum, a building well known from texts but poorly understood archaeologically.[38] This temple is of particular interest because it is the only known example in Egypt of a temple dedicated to an exclusively Roman iteration of the highest god of the Roman pantheon, as opposed to other hybrid avatars of Zeus-Jupiter that are decidedly Hellenistic or Egyptian in character, like the cult of Zeus-Ammon based at Siwa.[39] This suggests that at the cult's inception (unfortunately, its foundation date is unknown), the patron had a particular interest in orienting the temple rites specifically toward the city of Rome, linking the town to a concept of empire greater than its provincial status. Or, alternatively, as was the case at Luxor, the cult might have been founded on an initiative from outside Egypt issued directly from the imperial court.

A papyrus fragment from a cache of papyri recording the expenditures of the temple at Arsinoe over roughly eight months in 214 and 215 furnishes several arresting details: first, that the majority of the festivals celebrated over the course of the year concerned the Severan imperial household; second, that the images of the emperor were venerated alongside that of other gods within the temple, including Jupiter and Souchos,[40] the crocodile god for whom the town of Arsinoe was originally named (Crocodilopolis); and finally, that the images of the gods (and presumably therefore the image of the emperor) participated directly in religious processions.[41] This last function of images in ancient cult is especially noteworthy, as it attests to the performative nature of ancient cult practices, especially those related to the arrival of important personages, in this case the praetorian prefect of Egypt. The text records that a statue of a god (*xoanon*), presumably a representation of Jupiter Capitolinus, was carried out to meet the official in a ceremony known as *komasia*.[42] But another papyrus from the same era makes reference specifically to imperial busts of Caracalla, his mother, Julia Domna, and his divine father (that is, deceased), Septimius Severus, being carried out during ritual processions by an official known as the *komastes protomon* (loosely, "carrier or celebrant of the busts").[43] This same papyrus also lists the property of several temples in the metropolis of Oxyrhynchos and the surrounding countryside. Representations (*eikonidia*) of the emperor and his family are the first items to be recorded for each temple, perhaps signaling their importance in the hierarchy of the temple sanctuary.[44]

The ceremony of carrying out the image of the gods, along with the ritual appearance of the image of the king, had deep roots in pharaonic ritual practice. The Greco-Roman variation in Egypt, the komasia, can also be linked to the Roman version of this event, the imperial celebration known as the adventus. In all three iterations, images become the focal point of a rite centered on the ideology of communal consensus. The moment of encounter between the ritual participants and the normally unseen and remote gods and rulers allowed the laity, who could not access the inner sanctuaries of Egyptian temples, where the cult statues were housed, to become directly involved in the ritual affirmation of their place and the place of the gods in the hierarchy of Egyptian society.[45]

The presence of the Roman emperor was also felt in temples dedicated to the traditional Egyptian cults where his image served as pharaoh in temple reliefs, rendered in Egyptian style and identified by hieroglyphic inscriptions. This is not Roman imperial cult per se, but the format perpetuates the king's official role as the high priest of every cult and the intercessor between the human and divine realms.[46] Continued patronage of the traditional temples through the representation of the ruler from Ptolemaic to Roman times consequently probably did serve to illustrate acceptance by the Romans of Egyptian religion while also legitimizing the importance of the Roman imperial image.[47]

The imperial cult chamber at Luxor and its decorations are therefore unique in the corpus of known buildings related to emperor worship in Egypt. The architectural elaborations carried out by Diocletian's army at Luxor did not create a freestanding temple using a classical architectural idiom, as seems to have been the norm for imperial cult spaces in the major cities of Egypt. Nor was the imperial cult chamber appended to traditional Egyptian cult complexes such as the Roman-style shrines to the imperial cult at Karnak and Philae. And finally, we cannot call the Luxor imperial cult chamber simply a legionary *sacellum* (small shrine) dedicated to the veneration of the military standards, a type of space also intertwined with emperor worship across the empire and found in several Diocletianic forts along the Egyptian *limes* (fortified frontier), because the elaborate iconography of the Roman paintings discussed in chapter 6 indicates an intended message more complex than military honors. At the same time, however, the presence of the imperial image, and the implicit rites of procession required at Luxor in order to encounter the imperial image, is very much in keeping with standard religious praxis in Egypt for rituals connected with the institution of kingship and the cycle of festivals throughout the country.

DIOCLETIAN'S AUDIENCE AND THE VIEWING EXPERIENCE

Luxor Temple's pharaonic architectural skeleton provides a visual complement to the imperial cult chamber's function as a space in which ordinary citizens of the empire reaffirmed their loyalty to the Roman emperor by paying homage to his image, understood as an embodiment of his actual, physical presence. There is no better evidence for the congruence of Egyptian and Roman cult practices than the programmed access routes set up for the visitor to the temple by the architects of the tetrarchic fort. These were ritual pathways in which the viewer progressed through numerous physical encounters with images of the pharaoh as well as the primary deity of the Egyptian pantheon, Amun, before reaching the Roman chamber.

The extent to which the symbolic potency of each tradition, Roman or Egyptian, was effectively conveyed at Luxor Temple probably depended on the identities of the images' audiences and the nature of particular audiences' access to the images in the temple. These variables are impossible to reconstruct with certainty for fourth-century Thebes and the Roman camp, but one can attempt to reimagine the original experience of walking through the temple, the effects of which would certainly have been moderated by status, ethnic origin, and religious practices. It is safe to assume that Luxor Temple functioned as some sort of military garrison, so presumably the main audience for the imperial cult chamber would have been Roman soldiers. Military personnel probably first entered Luxor Temple proper from the west, rather than through the original pharaonic portals on the north side of the temple. Disembarking from a ship on the Nile, or entering the northwest gates, they would head toward the main east-west thoroughfare leading from the Nile quay, marked by a tetrastyle at its midpoint (see figure 2.4).

The Latin dedicatory inscriptions are on the north and south faces of this tetrastyle's columns' bases, a fact that confirms the importance of this east-west flow of processional traffic, as a visitor can see the inscriptions only while moving along the road in an east-west direction between the columns. In contrast, the inscriptions on the eastern tetrastyle (see figure 2.5) were placed on the east and west faces of the columns' bases, so they were most visible when a visitor was moving in a north-south direction, parallel to the temple. This suggests that the eastern honorific columns marked the crossroads of arteries intended to direct visitors toward the southeast exterior of the temple, where the Romans made extensive modifications to the rooms behind the imperial cult chamber (see figure 3.22).[48] The language of these inscriptions is Latin, suggesting these routes within the camp were for a privileged, nonlocal military audience.[49]

Returning to the western tetrastyle, the street leads into the first court of the temple through a large portal in the west wall flanked by monumental standing statues of Ramesses II, still in situ today (see figure 2.4). The dramatic contrast in style between the statues and the classical tetrastyle just meters away would have been apparent. The ancient statues with their imposing and static majesty looked directly out at the columns honoring the four Tetrarchs, whose statues on top of the columns towered over their pharaonic predecessors. The west wall portal, leading directly into the court of Ramesses II, probably became the primary route into the temple for the Romans because of its proximity to the river and also because it was accessed from the interior of the camp. As a result, this entrance to the court of Ramesses II became to a certain degree the more privileged access point, since only those who were allowed inside the camp fortifications could use it.

This raises a question: Who were these Roman soldiers? Since Roman legions were made up of soldiers from all over the empire who may have identified, ethnically, religiously, and culturally with the region of their origin while at the same participating in the *idea* of a Roman polity, the ethnographic label "Roman" is potentially tricky.[50] Though archaeological data gathered at other military garrisons throughout the empire have provided evidence about the social practices of Roman soldiers, no such revealing details have been uncovered at Luxor. The only specific indication we have of anything in the way of religious devotion on the part of a Roman soldier specifically, beyond the existence of the imperial cult chamber, is a Greek graffito in the colonnade hall of Amenhotep III and Tutankhamun, recording a dedication made to "Ammon" by a legionary physician (see figure 3.18). The inscription suggests the survival of some sort of Egyptian cult practice at Luxor at the time of the Roman army encampment, but it reveals nothing about how either the Roman soldiers or the local population understood the intricacies of the cult. At the very least, however, all Roman soldiers, regardless of their ethnic origins or religious practices, would have been educated in the visual trappings of the Roman army, including images of the emperor. And they could not have failed to notice the theatrical juxtaposition of Roman and Egyptian visual languages within the main transit arteries of the camp.

Such juxtapositions also dictated the aesthetics of the northern processional entryway into the temple proper through the temple pylons. This monumental entrance, also flanked by colossal statues of the pharaoh Ramesses II and two obelisks (see figure I.4), gave access to Luxor Temple directly, since the northern perimeter wall of the Roman camp abutted the pylons of the pharaonic temple. Whoever had right of entry here could visit the temple and the imperial cult chamber without first having to proceed through the newly built sectors of the Roman camp. Thus, this north-south access route was perhaps reserved for Egyptian dignitaries, or for more ceremonial occasions. Like the western portal, this entry allowed visitors into the court of Ramesses II, which is aligned obliquely to the earlier Eighteenth-Dynasty structures beyond. The Romans added brick arches that may have supported a dome to the passageway between the pylons (see figure 3.19). This architectural feature had the effect of narrowing a visitor's initial view into the temple proper and reducing the overall monumentality of the original entrance into the temple. It also added to the mystery of the encounter for first-time visitors because the direct approach to the imperial cult chamber inside the temple becomes clear only upon standing in the court of Ramesses II. Here is yet another example of how the modifications made to Luxor Temple by the Romans seem to be aimed at directing access and visitors' sightlines, measures that, in turn, influenced the overall experience of a visit to the site.[51]

Once inside the court of Ramesses II, whether entering from the west or the north, the visitor's view led straight to the imperial cult chamber, the focal point of the Roman modifications to the pharaonic complex (see figure I.1). The niche and the images of the Tetrarchs within are 165 meters distant, yet today they are visible directly to the south. No doubt privilege and the occasion determined who might have beheld this view in antiquity. This axial sightline was interrupted by strategically placed curtains and doors, indications of which survive in the form of slots and bolt holes for wooden fittings at the entrances to the imperial cult chamber, the portico of Amenhotep III, and both ends of the Amenhotep III and Tutankhamun colonnade hall.

In the next stage of a visitor's journey, a unifying visual theme begins to pervade the ritual path leading to the chamber of the imperial cult—that of the presence of the divine ruler. A visitor leaving the court of Ramesses II at its south end would have met another pair of massive black granite statues of Ramesses II enthroned flanking the entrance to the colonnade hall of Amenhotep III and Tutankhamun (figure I.1). These statues, like those outside the Ramesses II pylon, were cult statues of the king and embodiments of the royal *ka*.[52] The hieroglyphic inscription on the colossus to the left of the entrance into the colonnade hall describes the king (and hence the statue) as "living, renewed, and rejuvenated," and the inscription on the statue to the right further describes the king as "the living royal ka."[53] A distinctive coherence between art and text in the pharaonic decorative program of Luxor Temple has allowed Egyptologists to interpret the Nineteenth-Dynasty elements as honoring the cult of the divine king or, more precisely, the cult of the royal ka, an aspect of divine kingship that linked the pharaoh with the gods, especially the god Amun, and with all his royal predecessors.[54] While the royal ka is somewhat distinct from the classical notion of the soul, broadly speaking the similarities between the ka and the concept of the Roman *genius* have been noted.[55] In fact, the royal ka was considered the eternal and divine aspect of kingship, and, as such, it was separable to a certain extent from the reigning king's physical body. Such beliefs were manifest in the veneration of statues representing the living ka of the king, and in the enactment of elaborate rituals involving tribute to and the processional display of these statues. While the intricacies of this theology are not likely to have been comprehended by the average soldier of the Roman army in late antiquity, and the precise meaning of the hieroglyphic inscriptions on the bases of the ka statues may have been legible to only a few Egyptian priests and antiquarian Roman scholars in this era, the monumental presence of these colossi at the most significant portals of the temple would at least have had broad apotropaic value or, in semiotic terms, have been a sign of pharaonic majesty.[56]

After passing the monumental ka statues of Ramesses II, the visitor would move into the colonnade hall of Amenhotep III and Tutankhamun. This colonnade was a long entrance hall consisting of seven pairs of enormous columns with papyrus capitals, one on each side of the main processional route through the temple (see figure 3.1). Unlike the

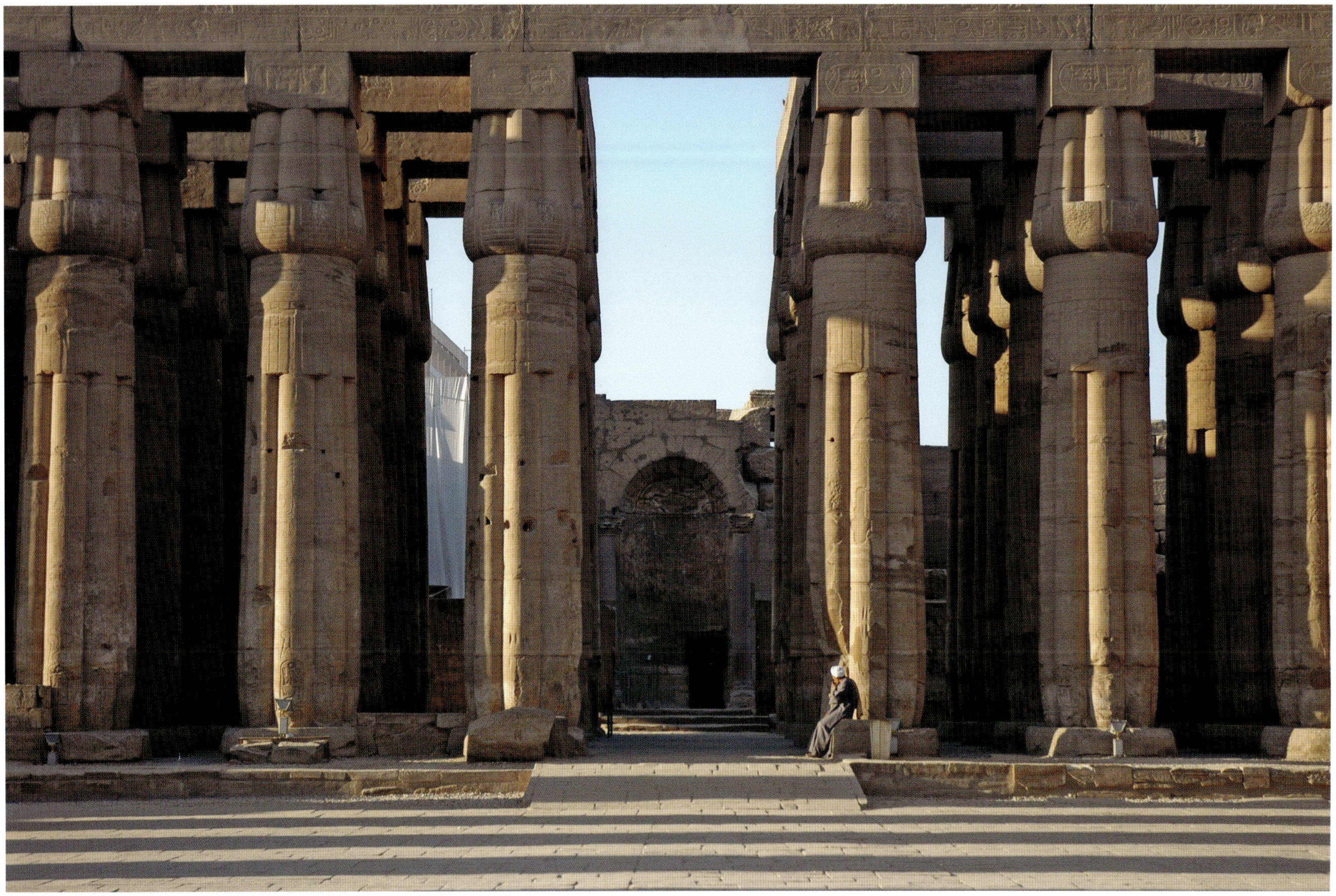

FIGURE 7.2
View of the niche from the court of Amenhotep III, looking south through the columned portico of Amenhotep III.

Ramesses II court, this colonnaded passageway would have been roofed, and its interior walls, visible from the main pathway between the columns, were decorated with reliefs depicting scenes from the Festival of Opet, including the journey of the cult statues of Amun, his divine consort, Mut, and their son, Khonsu, towed up the Nile from Karnak Temple to Luxor.[57] Both the reliefs and the columns of the hall would have been painted with a rich palette of colors typical of Egyptian decoration, earthy reds, bright greens, and blues the color of the sky and lapis lazuli. It is easy to imagine the dramatic effects of such decoration in the hall's low, flickering torchlight, although the state of preservation of these reliefs during the Roman period is not known. Today, much of the masonry is missing and the roof is gone. As a result, the bright sunlight has bleached the stone reliefs to a pale yellow, and the sacral aura of the passageway is muted but not entirely diffused. But a better state of preservation can at least be assumed for the Roman period. Whether or not the Roman visitor understood the meaning of the reliefs, at the very least all visitors must certainly have recognized the ceremoniousness of the colonnade's design, leading the visitor south directly into the spectacular open-air court of Amenhotep III.

The transition from the colonnade hall of Amenhotep III and Tutankhamun to the vast court must have been dramatic in ancient times. The bright sunlight of the court presented a blinding contrast to the darker interior of the enclosed colonnade. The floor level rises upon one's ascending the ramp into the court, and the eyes of Roman visitors would have been drawn once again toward the entrance to the imperial cult chamber on the other side of the piazza (figure 7.2). From this vantage point they might have noticed another dramatic juxtaposition of traditions at the south end of the courtyard. As speculated in chapter 3, the visitor could have seen a monumental classical porch appended to the columned portico of Amenhotep III or, as previous scholars have speculated, four monumental statues of the Tetrarchs, two on either side of the entrance to the central passageway of the portico. The bases for these statues (or perhaps the column bases of the Roman porch, according to Heidel in chapter 3) were found during nineteenth-century excavations; the two inner bases of red granite suggest that they supported figures of the Augusti, whereas the two outer bases, made of limestone blocks, might have been for figures of the Caesars.[58] It is equally plausible, however, that these blocks supported pharaonic statuary, perhaps figures akin to the standing statues of Ramesses II in the first court.

Imagining for a moment that the statues were tetrarchic, they almost certainly would have been made of bronze or carved from porphyry, a type of stone intimately tied to the imperial court at this time and into the Byzantine period. Reserved solely for imperial representation or use, porphyry was found in only one place in the world, Mons Porphyrites, in Egypt's Eastern Desert. By the time of the Tetrarchy, the industrial effort put into the quarrying of this stone had reached an unprecedented height, as attested by the numerous surviving examples of porphyry statuary from the tetrarchic era.[59] Diocletian himself was said to have a particular fascination with the stone, and he put a great deal of effort into refortifying the important trade route between the Red Sea and the Nile, created expressly because of the porphyry trade.[60] The main military fort at the Red Sea end of this route, today known as Abu Shaar, was built or renovated between 309 and 311 CE, indicating perhaps the reigning emperor's particular interest in maintaining the industry even after Diocletian's abdication.[61] The stone was difficult to cut and model, a fact that perhaps accounts in part for the unique stylization of tetrarchic portraits. A particularly monumental example of a porphyry statue of an enthroned emperor from Egypt, today in the Greco-Roman Museum in Alexandria, was found near the crossing of the ancient Via Canopica in 1870.[62] This figure, as well as the bust of Galerius from Athribis (Tell Atrib–Benha) in the Egyptian Museum (see figure 2.3) and the Venice Tetrarchs (see figure 6.26), gives us at least some idea of the aesthetic effect of this stone.

Envisioning porphyry statuary in the court of Amenhotep III is appealing; the purple hue of the monumental Tetrarchs would have stood out against the yellow gold of the pharaonic sandstone pillars, while at the same time the stylized and regal aesthetic of the porphyry portraits would have recalled the equally static and monumental statues of the pharaonic kings that the Romans left standing in other parts of the temple. Regardless of whether visitors understood the nuances of the pharaonic statues' specific identifications, they would not have missed the implicit comparison.

A similar visual comparison would have been generated even if pharaonic statues instead of tetrarchic ones flanked the entrance to the portico of Amenhotep III. The visitor needed only to move farther south into the portico and passageway leading to the imperial cult chamber to find it lined with Roman-style sculptures, in this case probably made of bronze (see chapter 3); for this aspect of the decorations at least we have secure epigraphic evidence, discussed in chapter 2 and below. Once again, the Roman modifications to Luxor Temple seem uniquely suited to provide a sense of both continuity and innovation in their specific, local context of the temple. And regardless of how we reconstruct the facade of the Amenhotep III portico, as a classical porch or as a constellation of four monumental statues, both cases produce a dramatic juxtaposition of visual traditions, much like the one a visitor encountered in the first stage of the journey, from the Roman camp into the court of Ramesses II.

The final step in the progression toward the imperial cult chamber brings the visitor into the Amenhotep III portico of the pharaonic temple's inner sanctuary. This hall of thirty-two monumental columns, evenly placed throughout the room, was designed in pharaonic times to create a route through the mythological landscape of the temple toward the barque shrines of Amun, Mut, and Khonsu and to the main sanctuary in the center. The Roman modifications to the central aisle changed this arrangement and created a single direct approach. The intercolumnar portals were blocked on both sides with statues of the Roman emperors, and the eroded lower parts of the columns were plastered to create a smooth wall that effectively lined the avenue between the columns (figure 7.3). Once again, visual juxtapositions of traditions abound in this space. While visitors moved through the central corridor flanked by statues in Roman style, by simply looking up at the lotus bud column capitals, and straight ahead at the reliefs decorating the exterior wall of the imperial cult chamber, they were firmly reminded of the idiomatic Egyptian surroundings. No trace of plaster can be found on the outer face of the imperial cult chamber's north wall, which suggests that, unlike what happened in the interior of the room, the reliefs of Amenhotep III that face into the portico and the approach between the columns may not have been obscured by the Romans. These reliefs, especially those flanking the entrance on either side of the steps inserted by

Opposite page:
FIGURE 7.3
View of the imperial cult chamber from the Amenhotep III portico; the statue base of Constantine is on the left side of this axial approach.

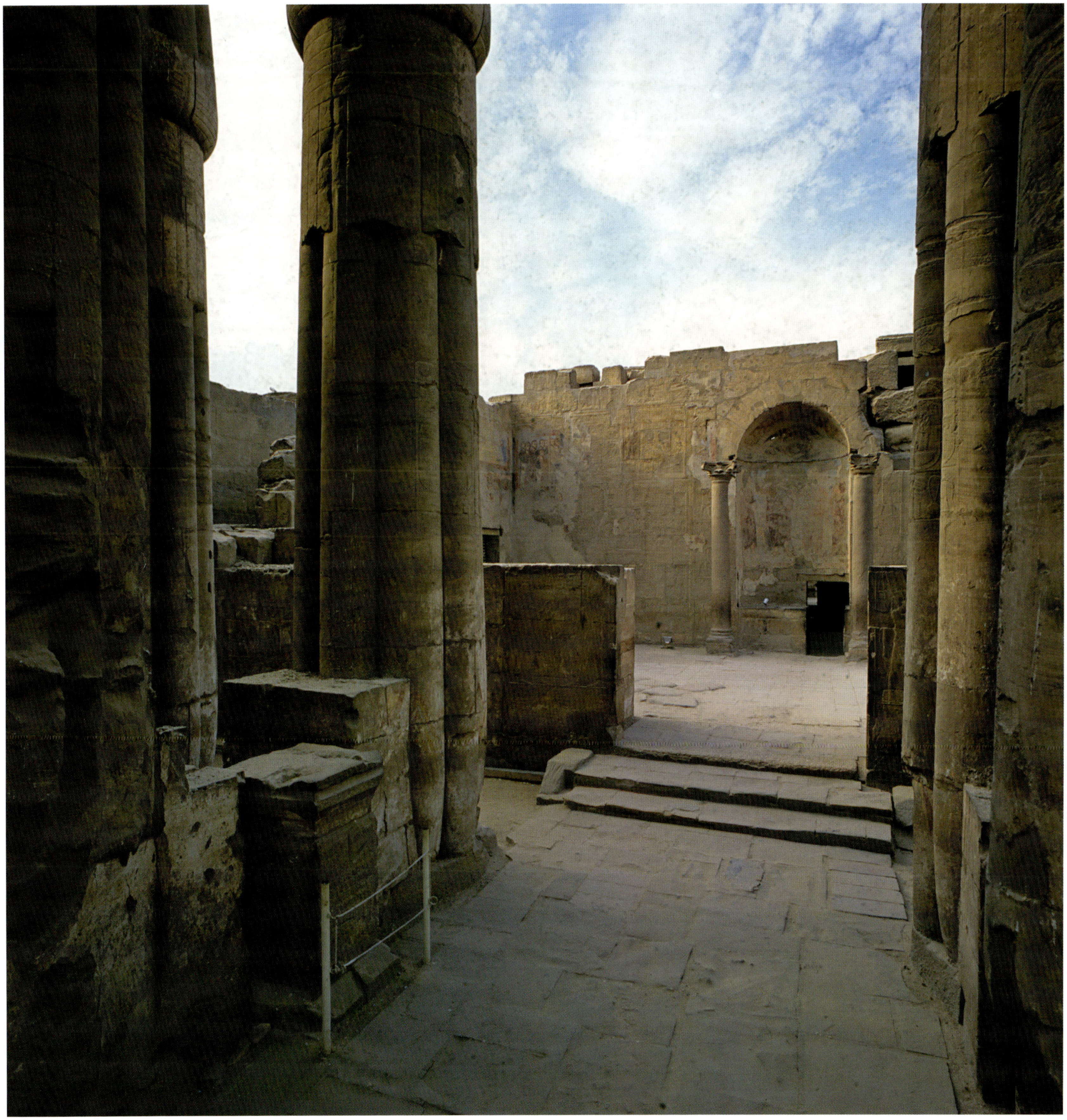

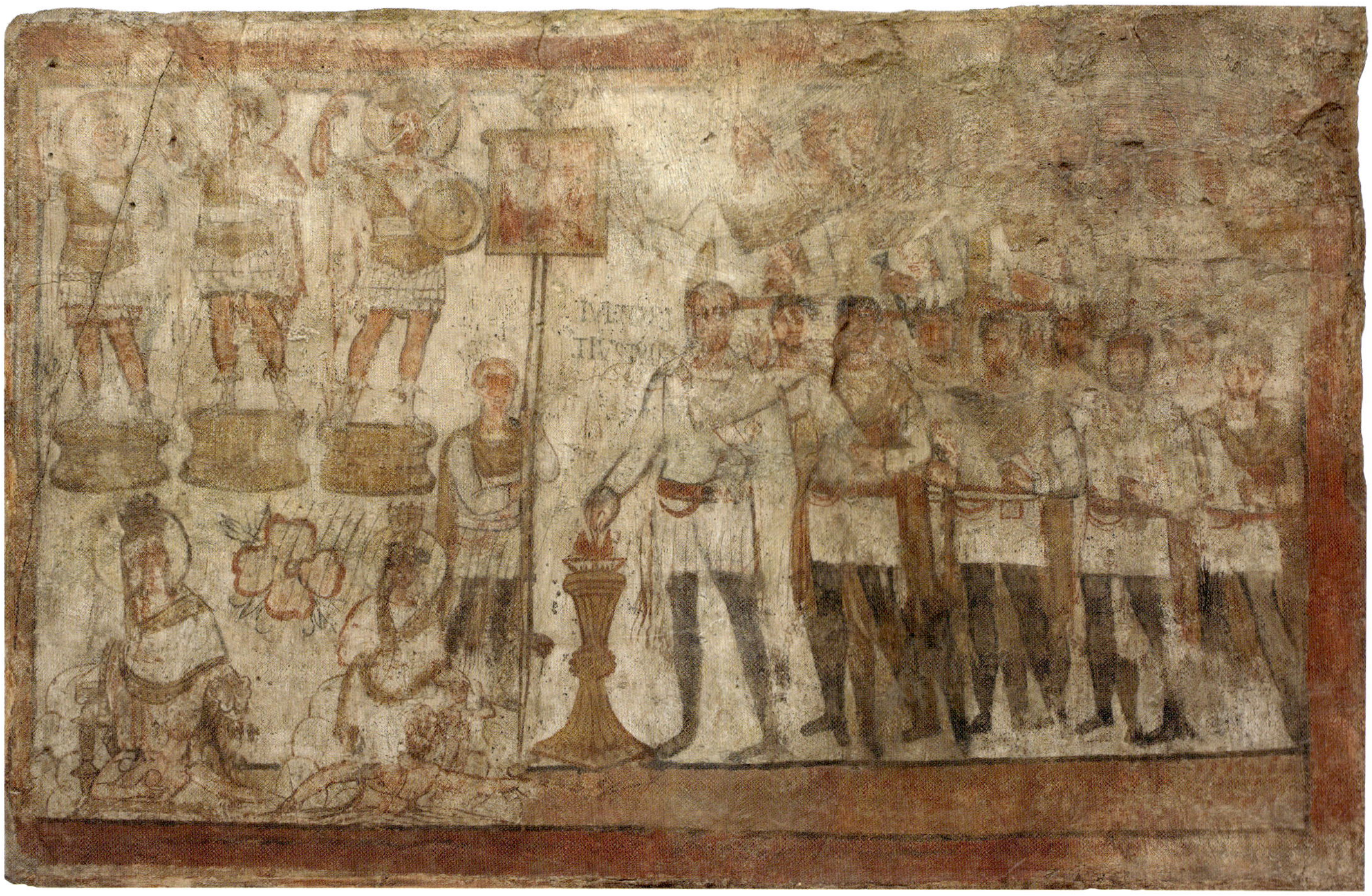

FIGURE 7.4
Julius Terentius performing a sacrifice, painted plaster from the Temple of Bel, Dura Europos, ca. 238 CE. Yale University Art Gallery, New Haven.

the Romans, would have been directly in the line of sight of any visitor approaching the imperial cult chamber. They might even have been left deliberately visible as a statement of continuity from one tradition to another, between Egyptian and Roman cult practices. The reliefs on the doorjambs show Amenhotep III entering the chamber while offering incense and pouring libations to an image of the god Amun, who faces outward, as though emerging from within (see figures I.11 and 3.5). As the visitor stepped onto the raised floor and into the space of the imperial cult chamber to pay homage to the image of the Roman emperors, probably with incense or libations (or both), he thus in a sense reiterated the actions of the virtual image of the pharaoh preserved on the outer walls. Again, though it is impossible to know just how legible these pharaonic reliefs may have been to a Roman audience, the thematic concordance between the iconography of the surviving Egyptian scenes and that of the Roman decorations is certainly suggestive.

The visitor has now arrived in the imperial cult chamber, a space in which the pharaonic decoration was completely replaced with the frescoes entirely in the Roman style, though nuanced by their Egyptian context and strategic manipulation of Roman iconography to emphasize the divine character of Diocletian (see chapter 6). In addition to the plastering over of the pharaonic reliefs in this room, the Roman modifications included the construction of a four-columned architectural canopy (*ciborium*) designed to frame and focus attention on the images of the Roman emperors within the room, as well as the altar or throne it sheltered.[63] Only two of the four columns topped with Corinthian capitals are in situ today.[64] Like the painted images of the emperors enthroned on a *suppedaneum* on either side of the niche, the ciborium serves to delimit the space within from the rest of the room and, by extension, to frame the person inside. This notion becomes all the more vivid when we imagine the experience within the imperial cult chamber. The ciborium in front of the niche would have been quite large and imposing within the space of the room, even more so than it appears in plan (see figures 3.8). Its position prevents ordinary people from getting too close to the image of the emperors in the niche or to whoever or whatever sat beneath the canopy. One can imagine, then, the emperor, or perhaps the *dux* of the Thebaid presiding over an official military audience, sitting in splendid isolation in the confines of the protected space, while an audience crowded around the sacred boundary of the throne.

More often, however, the actual presence of the emperors was not required, as the images in the niche meant that they were present by proxy. Depending on the occasion, once in the imperial cult chamber proper, the viewer would commence various honorific actions appropriate for veneration of the emperor, such as pouring libations or burning incense, like those pictured in a circa 239 painting from the Temple of Bel (the Syrian avatar of Zeus-Jupiter) in Dura Europos, which illustrates the Roman tribune and commander of the Cohors XX Palmyrenorum performing an official sacrifice in front of the military standards (figure 7.4).[65] These rites, honoring the images of the emperors or the legionary standards, which in Luxor would have been displayed in the imperial cult chamber or one of the adjacent small rooms, could be performed on a large or reduced scale. They were universal rites, performed by all residents of the empire regardless of their personal faith. Only the Christians and Jews refused to participate in them, but before the official acceptance of Christianity such resistance was not widespread. Imperial rites were considered vital for the maintenance of social order within the legion, and high-ranking officials performed them as well as, and perhaps even alongside, the lowliest foot soldier.

Implicit in the language describing the types of rituals performed in spaces such as the imperial cult chamber is the notion that ritual is performative. A ritual, in other words, represents above all a physical action or event, and it is through action or performance that a ritual is believed effective. The one who performs the ritual, therefore, embodies and concretizes the action, making a major medium of ritual the movement of the body.[66] Another key aspect of ritual practice is that it is spatially constructed and sustained. In other words, the space in which the ritual is enacted fundamentally defines or colludes with the ritual action. Thus, the images decorating such spaces are as intimately connected with the ritual experience of the viewer as the space itself. The viewer in the space of the imperial cult chamber would thus transition from audience member to protagonist in the great drama that was the late Roman courtly bureaucracy. The visitors' actions were made all the more powerful by the fact that within the space of the chamber they were surrounded by other, painted participants in the honorifics directed at the emperor, perpetually arriving to perform those rites enacted in reality below.

LATE ANTIQUE PANEGYRICS AND THE IMPERIAL ADVENTUS

Besides the role the Luxor paintings play in the experience of viewing, their significance can be realized through an examination of a body of textual evidence, which until now has not been considered in conjunction with the architectural remains of Diocletian's sojourn in Egypt. Although the careful placement of the imperial cult chamber and its painted program at the center of Luxor Temple probably came about because of the political events surrounding Diocletian's visit to Egypt at the end of the third century, the images themselves, formally and iconographically, were canonically Roman, conceived and executed by artists attached to the imperial court, and they do not relate, beyond their particular context, to Egypt. As discussed in chapter 6, the individual vignettes making up the program of images in the imperial cult chamber constituted a type of "stock footage" of imperial statecraft. What has not yet been noted, however, is that these Roman imperial tableaux were in use throughout the empire in conjunction with textual and auditory means of disseminating imperial ideology. The subject matter of the Luxor frescoes, echoed in other media, strongly suggests that a type of complicity between image and experience seen in other parts of the empire might have been intended here. And, inasmuch as the Romans appropriated and reworked an environment perfectly suited to ceremony and controlled viewing experiences, they were effective. Outside the confines of Luxor Temple, however, accompanying evidence connected to Diocletian's visit to Egypt indicates a less than successful reception for such a complex propagandistic assemblage. The following evaluation delves deeper into the Luxor paintings' thematic content to estimate the degree to which Diocletian's political agenda in Egypt might be considered a success or a failure.

Also discussed in chapter 6, the east and north walls of the Luxor imperial cult chamber probably illustrate a procession connected to an imperial adventus, a subject more commonly known as a literary trope because of its frequent appearance in the corpus of late antique literature. Scholarship of the past few decades has brought to light the close correlation among art, text, and ritual that existed in this period.[67] Because of such studies, we can learn a great deal about the significance of the Luxor imperial cult chamber by looking at texts related to adventus from other parts of the empire. In particular, the late antique panegyrics of the Gallic school describe in detail the imperial ceremonies of the late antique court, and they are thus an extremely useful tool for this study of Egypt, if only to understand what the *intended* effect of these paintings may

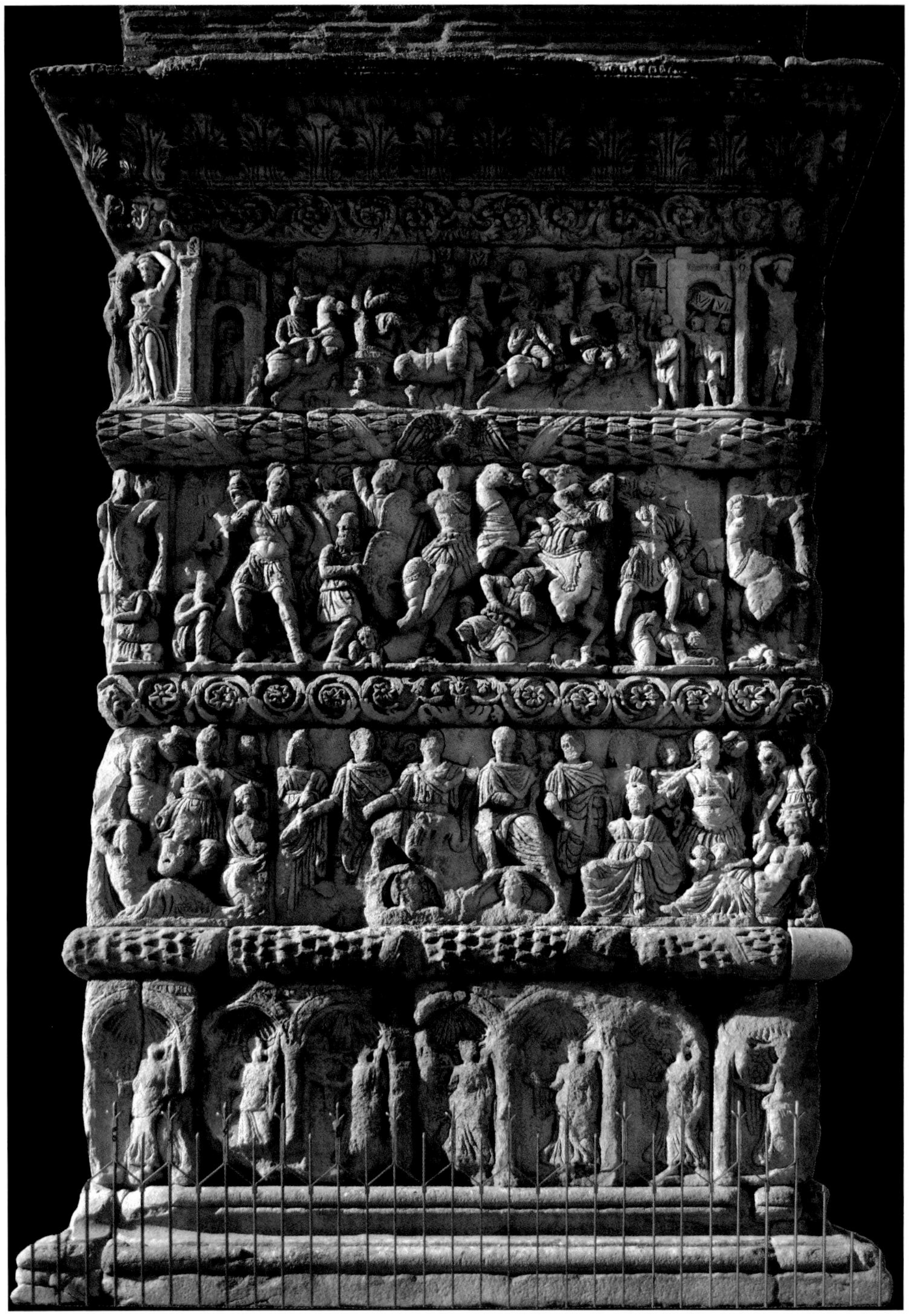

FIGURE 7.5
Arch of Galerius, Thessaloniki, southwest pillar of a quadrifonal arch, ca. 298–303.

have been. Whether they were *received* as intended is altogether another issue.

The term *panegyric,* a speech praising an important place or person, has its origins in Greek rhetoric of the fourth century BCE.[68] In Latin, speeches of praise were usually called *laudes,* but by the late empire the word *panegyricus* had become the accepted term to describe a *laudatio* of an individual, usually the emperor.[69] A substantial corpus of such literature specifically dedicated to the emperor survives from late antiquity; known as the XII *Panegyrici Latini,* it was compiled in Gaul at the end of the fourth century.[70] Eleven of the twelve speeches date from between 289 and 389, and though they are mostly unattributed, we can be reasonably certain that they are records of actual ceremonies performed in the presence of the emperor in various capitals of the Western Empire.[71]

Along with these texts, a substantial number of artifacts attest to the vast ceremoniousness of the late antique court and correlate with the verbal descriptions of those ceremonies in the panegyrics. Starting in the mid-second century, the iconographic vocabulary on imperial public monuments began to be reduced to the representation of a few traditional and frequently performed rites that were closely associated with the deeds of the emperor. The regularity with which these formally scripted rituals were performed allowed them to be referenced artistically as essentialized and universalized symbols of imperial virtue.[72] The adventus was particularly well suited to representation in the visual arts because it was a ceremony that was enabled by the peripatetic late antique court; the emperor and his entourage were constantly "arriving" in places, and the memory of each arrival needed to be imprinted in the minds of local populations throughout the empire. As a result, the adventus is often pictured on late antique monuments. Near-contemporary parallels to the Luxor example include the adventus of Galerius on his Arch in Thessaloniki (figure 7.5) and Constantine's adventus in Rome on the east face of the Arch of Constantine (figure 7.6).

The great spectacle of imperial arrival embodied the "splendid theater" of Gibbon's late antiquity.[73] Yet the formal interplay described in the panegyrics between the court and its audience during the ceremony was more than just scripted obsequiousness. Sabine MacCormack fittingly describes the adventus as a "double faced ceremony," one that stressed both the moment when the traveling emperor arrived and mixed with his subjects on familiar terms, and the moment when the emperor's numinous presence granted symbolic security to the city.[74] The ceremony of adventus thus captured a moment in which the language of ceremonial actions was shared between subject and ruler and was therefore universalized into a cosmic and imperial, not merely a transitory, urban event.

As the Panegyric of Maximian (circa 289), given at the court of Trier on the occasion of Rome's birthday, confirms, for example, the appeal to sight and vision is explicit in the wording of the panegyrics and suggests involvement on the part of the listener in bestowing authority on the person described: "*We saw you,* Caesar, on the very same day taking up vows on behalf of the State and incurring the debt of them being answered. . . . *We saw you,* Caesar, on the same day both in the most splendid garb of peace and in magnificent

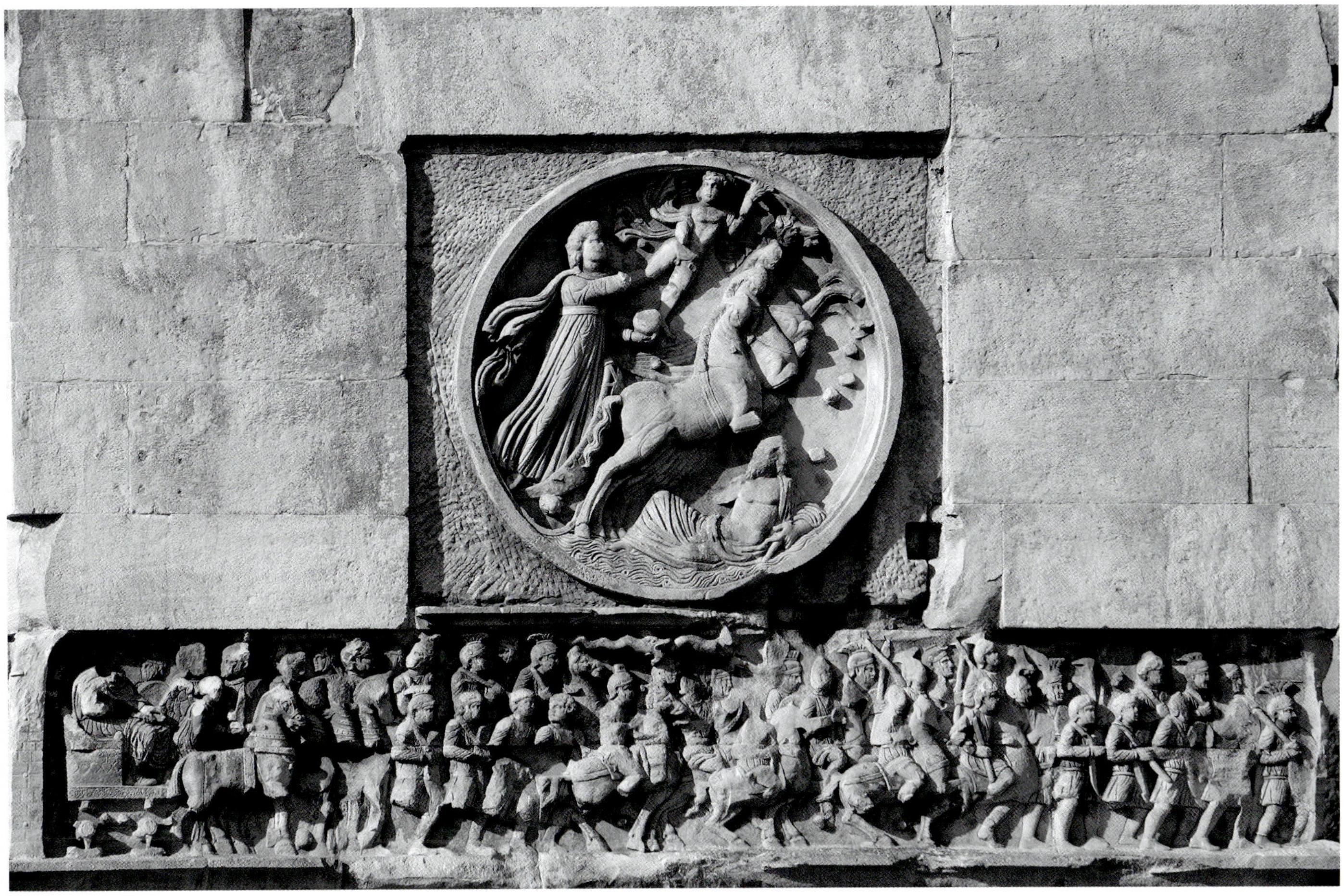

FIGURE 7.6
East face of the Arch of Constantine, Rome, ca. 315; frieze depicting Constantine's entry into Rome (adventus) after his victory against Maxentius at the Milvian Bridge.

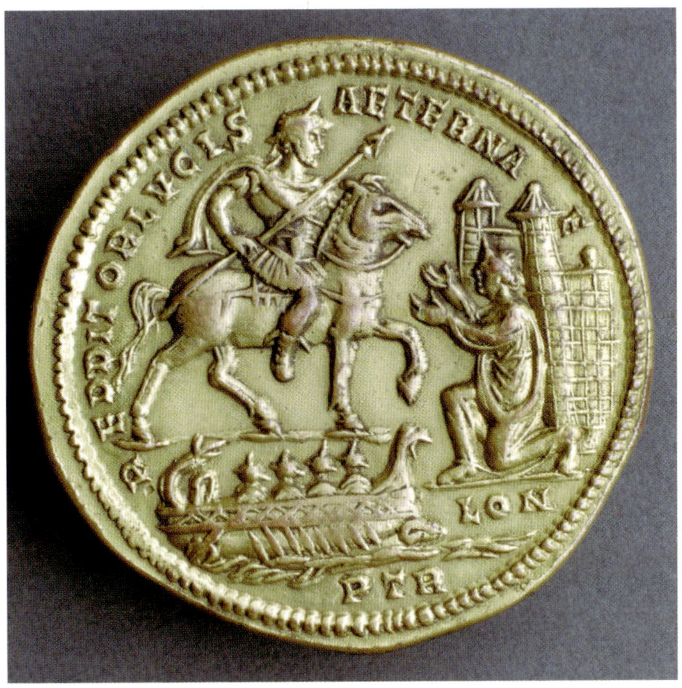

FIGURE 7.7
Obverse of the gold Arras Medallion, minted at Trier after 296; part of a horde discovered at Beaurains near Arras in 1922, now in the Bibliothèque Nationale, Paris.

accouterments of war [author's italics]."[75] Seeing, according to the principles of classical philosophy and science, was an active sense; the eye was understood to make haptic contact with the visible world. In other words, casting one's eyes on an object was equivalent to touching it.[76] In the panegyrics the literary evocation of the instant when the audience "saw" and thus "touched" the figure of the emperor describes a fundamentally important moment of contact between the community and the arriving emperor. It was a moment expressing the ideal of consensus on which the tetrarchic power rested, when the presence of an audience granted legitimacy, by means of the active process of vision, to whomever the panegyric was addressed.

Furthermore, the main techniques of the Gallic orators were to speak by allusion, implication, symbol, and comparison as well as to present facts and events as images or tableaux.[77] The Gallic orator's "osmosis between sound and vision"[78] drew on distinguished traditions of Roman rhetoric, referring to early classical ideas regarding harmony among the arts, encapsulated by Horace's often cited analogy, *ut pictura poesis* ("as is painting, so is poetry").[79] These descriptions (of events or of works of art), called *ekphrases,* which were first perceived through the sense of hearing, were designed to appeal to all the senses, especially the eyes. But they were more than generalized mental pictures; the panegyrics can be matched with existing works of imperial art or iconography that would have been familiar to the listener.[80]

This nexus between art and text is illustrated by the Panegyric of Constantius Chlorus, delivered presumably at Trier

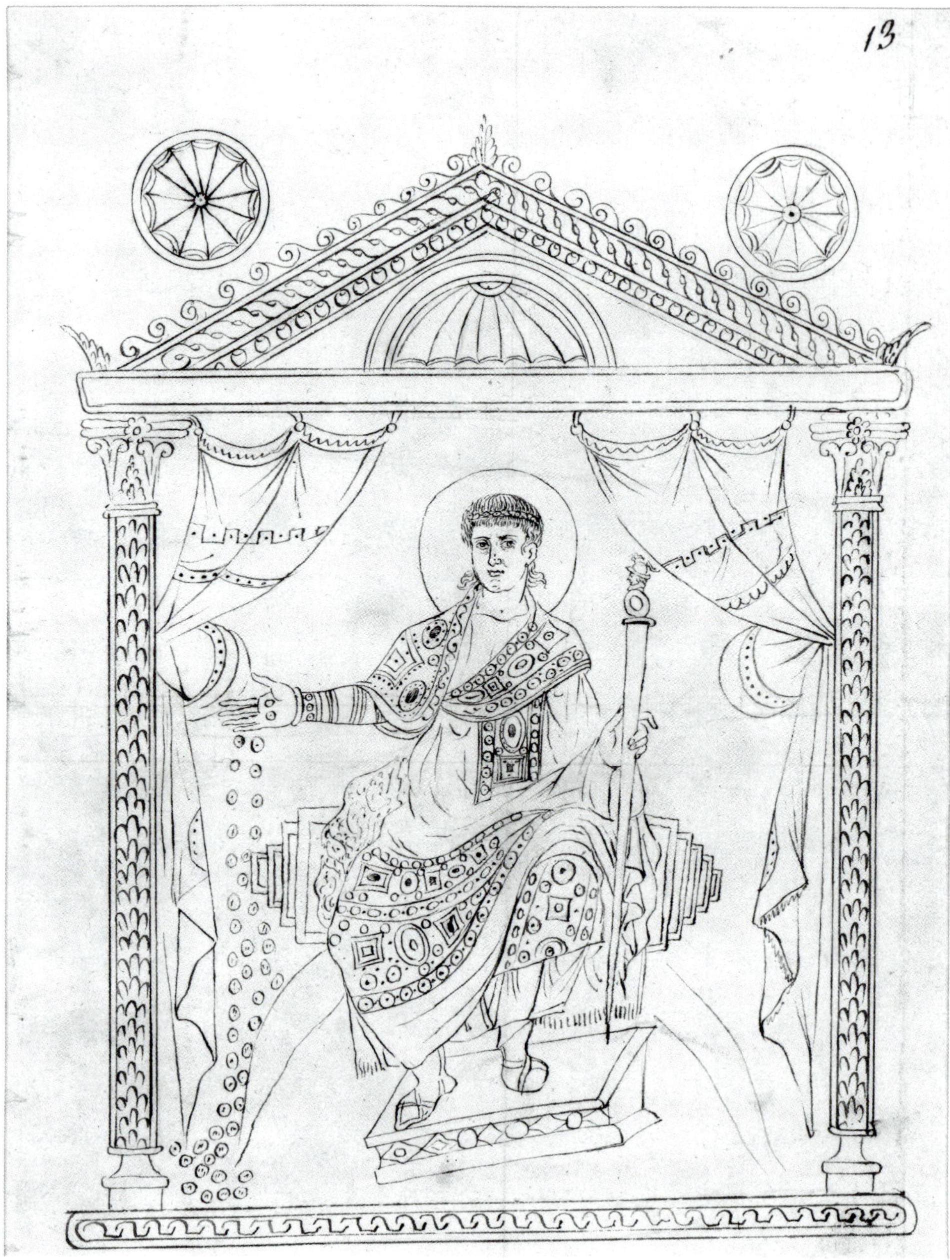

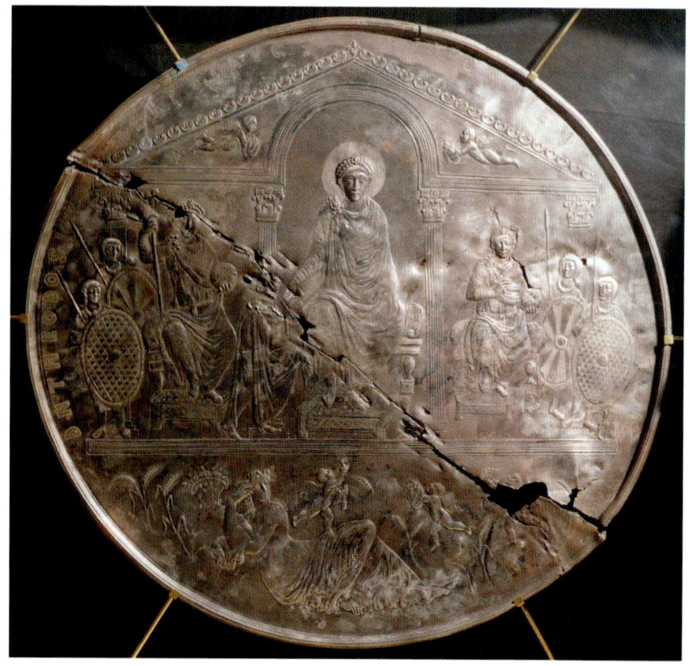

FIGURE 7.8
(left) Manuscript page depicting Constantius II, from the Codex-Calendar of 354 (copy ca. 1620). Biblioteca Apostolica Vaticana, Vatican City, Rome.

FIGURE 7.9
(right) Silver Missorium of Theodosius I and his sons, ca. 387–388, diameter 74 cm. Real Académia de la Historia, Madrid.

in 296, in honor of the restoration of Britain to the Roman Empire.[81] A gold solidus called the Arras Medallion, minted at the same time, commemorates the event and offers a condensed version of the scene described in section 19.1–3 of the panegyric, in which the emperor disembarks from his ship onto the riverbank of London and is met by an exuberant and grateful crowd (figure 7.7).[82] The obverse of this medallion shows a laureate Constantius Chlorus, while the reverse illustrates the triumphant emperor on horseback and a Roman warship approaching the gates of a personified London, who kneels in thanks. This scene is surrounded by the legend *redditor lucis aeternae* (restorer of eternal light), which most certainly recalls line 19.3 of the panegyric, *vera imperii luce recreate* (restored to life by the true light of empire).

This collaboration between art and rhetoric is further facilitated by the imperial building programs of the late empire. Because panegyrics were integral to imperial ceremony, they needed fittingly grand architectural frameworks for their performance. In late antique basilicas, such as the Aula Palatina of Constantine at Trier and the Basilica of Maxentius and Constantine at Rome, as well as in the numerous small-town reception chambers that must once have existed, design elements such as exedrae and apses were added specifically to confine and highlight the important ceremonial activity enacted within. As at Luxor, these architectural framing devices signaled a numinous space. Moreover, the manuscript page from the Codex-Calendar of 354 (figure 7.8) and the Missorium of Theodosius (figure 7.9), discussed in chapter 6, illustrate that this late antique visual convention of framing the image of an emperor within an architectural space such as a canopy or archway extended even to the minor arts. This visual trope served both to draw attention to the emperor and to set him apart from the rest of the figures in the scene. In art as well as in reality, proximity to the emperor or his image in such spaces no doubt signaled rank.

The performative nature of these speeches meant that their success relied on the participation of the listeners. The panegyrics were therefore not an elite body of literature comprehensible and meaningful only to the upper echelons of late antique society. While the rhetors themselves may have been among the elite, their audience was wholly familiar with the formulae of their trade. The rhetors' ekphrastic descriptions and turns of phrase were culled from an ancient store of knowledge accessible to everyone in their milieu. This ceremonial character of late Roman life provided the backdrop against which art and literature converged in western Gaul. Both media were facets of late Roman culture expressing itself in ways appealing to both the eyes and the ears. And it is this polyvalent method of perception that emerged as one of the most lasting aspects of postclassical civilization, especially in the Christian liturgy as well as Byzantine court ceremonials.[83] Both art and text had equal roles as "players" in a common drama. One could not function without the other. The panegyrics achieved significance only because of the context in which they were delivered, within the vast architectural trappings of the imperial court that the listener then "glimpsed" through brief descriptions in the text.

INTENTION VERSUS RECEPTION AT LUXOR

The collaboration between art and text in the tetrarchic period presented a coherent message of imperial power comprehensible to Roman audiences in close proximity to the imperial courts. Nevertheless, it is unclear to what extent this propagandistic visual and literary language would have been intelligible and acceptable in a setting such as Luxor, where there was an equally strong history of local visual idioms and cultural expressions. It is tempting to argue that the adventus depicted at Luxor is directly comparable to the textual description of this ceremony in the panegyrics, since stylistically and iconographically the paintings correspond to other known examples of tetrarchic-era art. Yet though we may say that these images and the panegyrics were both conceived as what can be called "templates of intent" originating directly from the imperial court, this particular provincial manifestation of tetrarchic propaganda might not have been palatable in its venue of reception.

The message of the Luxor adventus, as conceived by the Roman architects, artists, and engineers of the complex, was a standard proclamation about the nature of the imperial office. The mobile nature of the emperor and his *comitatus* (courtly entourage) made necessary the strategy of imperial omnipresence,[84] hence the need to promulgate the types of symbolic visual tableaux describing an all-seeing emperor (looking down on the world from his throne), such as the one described in the Panegyric of Maximian and Constantine (307 CE): "It becomes you, father, to *survey from your pinnacle of command* the world you share, and with celestial nod decide the fate of human affairs, to announce the auspices for wars which have to be waged, and to impose the terms when peace is to be concluded [author's italics]."[85] Since the emperor could not be everywhere at once, his image came to stand in for his actual presence; representations of his person were understood as equivalent to his physical body, and thus they were expected to be revered as such.[86] The illustration of a scene of adventus at Luxor, coupled with an image of the enthroned emperors presiding over their subjects (figure 7.10), can thus be interpreted as perpetuating the presence of the emperor and disseminating a particular message about the omnipresent nature of tetrarchic rule, in much the same way as an oration in Gaul would have advanced an imperial agenda to listeners there. And such images were presumed to create loyalty through participation and consensus among their audiences, who themselves physically progressed through the pharaonic temple to encounter and pay tribute to the images.

Like the settings described in the panegyrics, the figures of the four Tetrarchs in the niche of the imperial cult chamber and the painted representation of an adventus procession generated an elaborate architectural setting befitting the requirements of court ceremonials. The Roman architects who reworked Luxor Temple re-created an appropriately dramatic atmosphere for display of the emperor's presence, and they also controlled, through strategic placement of curtains and doors, the moment of encounter between image and audience. Though no panegyric exists describing any actual adventus ceremony in Luxor Temple, the paintings of the ceremony act as proxy for the rite and also broadcast in perpetuity the same message of an all-seeing emperor as promoted by the panegyrics.[87]

A further convention of the panegyrics was for the orator to manipulate opinion regarding past imperial actions to make future policies clear to listeners. The Panegyric of 291, for example, compares a routine visit to Milan by Diocletian to Hannibal's famed crossing of the Alps during the Second Punic War.[88] We see such comparisons particularly in the case of a speech given in the aftermath of a war because panegyrists needed to make sure the point of the war was properly understood.[89] In the case of Luxor, the imperial cult chamber and its decorations thus acted as a perpetual reminder to viewers of the consequences of Egypt's most recent revolt against Roman rule. The images of the emperors might have been perceived as being akin to the emperors' watchful eyes, communicating to the inhabitants of Egypt that they should not challenge authority because the emperors see all. Additionally, the appropriation of a temple dedicated in pharaonic times to the cult of the divine king provided a visual juxtaposition of traditions that invited comparison of the Roman present with the Egyptian past. In other words, the numinous identity of the Roman emperor was reinforced by the

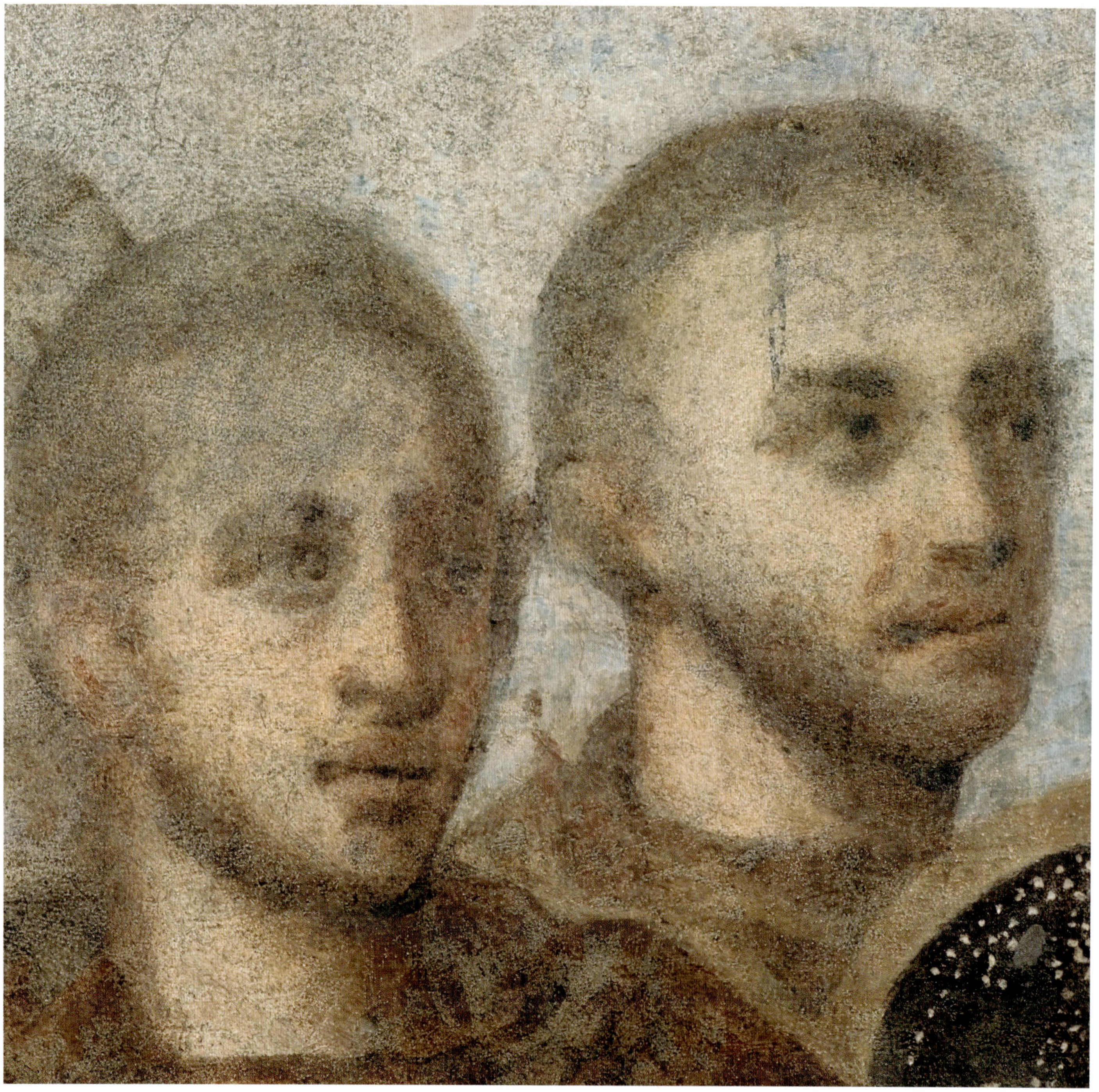

FIGURE 7.10
South wall, east end detail: the rapt faces of the emperors' adoring subjects.

placement of his image in a site already associated with the numinous. Therefore, while there is no evidence that a panegyric was performed on the occasion of Diocletian's arrival in Luxor, the close affinity between the paintings' iconography and imagery that can be connected with actual ceremonial performances in other parts of the empire certainly allows for the possibility. Hence, the adventus at Luxor can be considered a type of visual record, or a visual panegyric, recording an idealized historical moment of consensus between emperor and audience.

The question remains, however: Was the propagandistic message encoded into the Luxor frescoes received as intended? Would the average viewer in the provinces have understood or acknowledged the symbolic importance of the adventus? Or was there just a fundamental disjuncture between official art and its audience? Despite a widespread

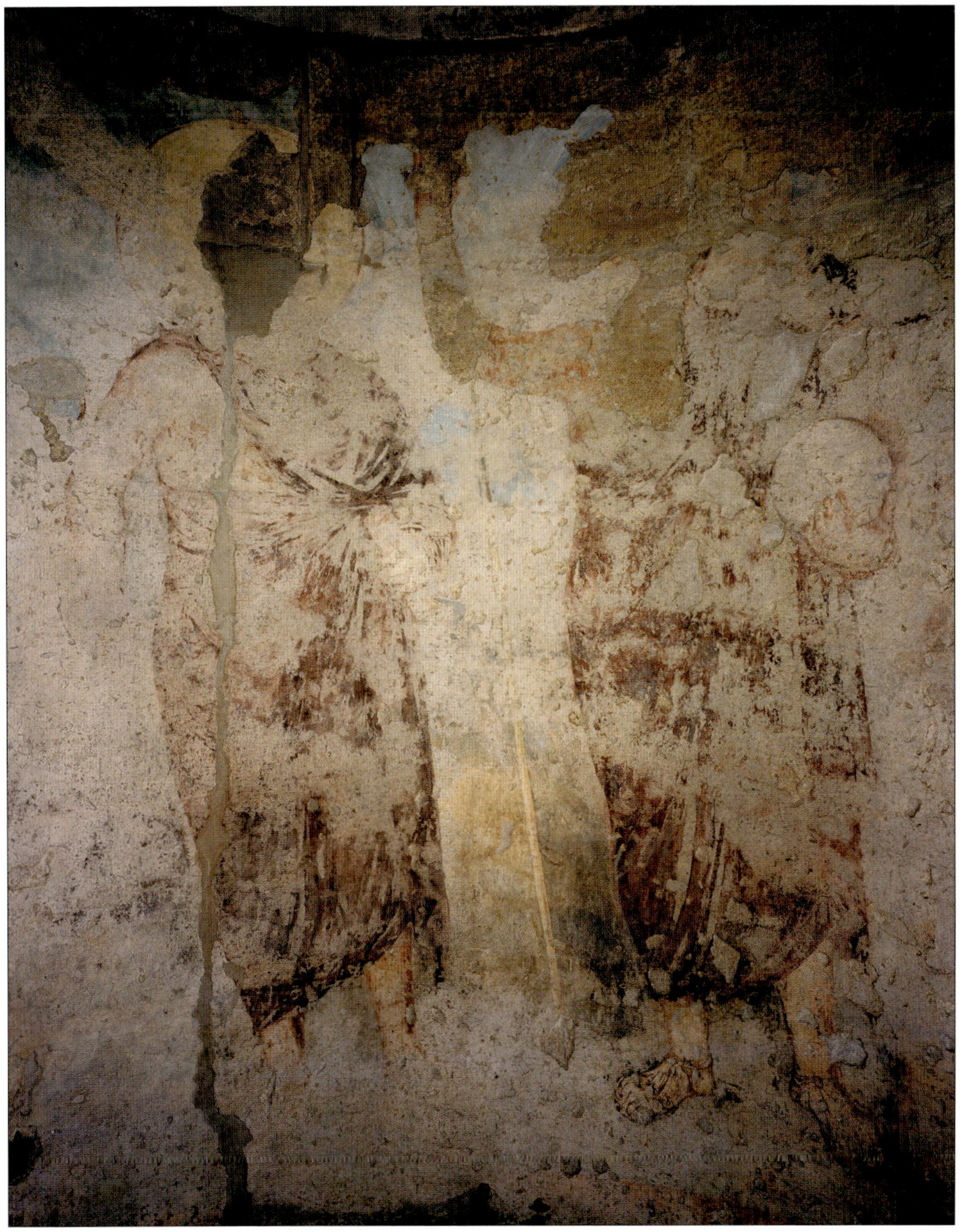

FIGURE 7.11
South wall niche: Diocletian (right) and Galerius (left).

effort on the part of image makers in late antiquity to promote a unified vision of imperial power, to which the paintings bear witness, it is extremely difficult to assess the effectiveness of this purpose outside the cities of the late Roman imperial court. Certainly, the soldiers of Diocletian's legions stationed at the Luxor camp would have been privy to the meaning of Roman iconography, as would the hellenized bourgeoisie of the local populations. They might even have realized just how far the unique context of the temple, formally dedicated to Amun, allowed for the pushing of iconographic boundaries in the representation of Diocletian's divine qualities (figure 7.11). But did the portrait of the emperor actually inspire loyalty among a wider audience, namely, a local Egyptian population that had, in fact, recently protested Roman rule?

In addition to the Luxor paintings, a slightly earlier hexameter poem dating to 285, discovered among the cache of papyri recovered from Oxyrhynchos and possibly connected with the temple of Jupiter Capitolinus, discussed above, confirms the existence of concurrent literary traditions in Egypt and Gaul; the poem's restoration motifs are similar to those found in the panegyrics.[90] Because it also predates the Egyptian revolts of the 290s, the text may be evidence of an attempt at disseminating tetrarchic ideology that was less than potent in actuality. The poem praises Diocletian's rule and paints a picture of a strong persona seeking to bring swift order to the empire:

> Capitoline Zeus took pity at last on the human race and gave the lordship of all the earth and the sea to godlike king Diocletian. He extinguished the memory of former griefs for any still suffering in grim bonds in a lightless place. Now a father sees his child, a wife her husband, a brother his brother released, as if coming into the light of the sun a second time from Hades. Gladly Diogenes, saver of cities, received the favor of the good king and swiftly dispatched to the cities the joyful forgetfulness of griefs. The whole land takes delight in its joy as at the light of a golden age, and the iron, drawn back from the slaughter of men, lies bloodlessly in the scabbard. You too have rejoiced to announce the royal gift to all, governor of the seven Nomes, and the Nile has praised your mildness earlier still, when you governed the towns on Nilotic Thebes with care and righteousness.[91]

This poem was probably circulated at the very beginning of Diocletian's reign and certainly exaggerates the fruitfulness and swiftness of his reforms in Egypt. Indeed, Diocletian's personal intervention in the province's politics twelve years later suggests such texts were not particularly successful in inspiring widespread loyalty to the Roman state.

From the occasion of Diocletian's visit to Egypt, a corpus of papyri from Panopolis (Akhmim) in the Thebaid provides another perspective on Roman rule, one unambiguously contrary to the tone set by the panegyrics and the Oxyrhynchos poem. A series of letters written by the *strategos* of this city allow a glimpse into the life of a mid-level administrator in late antique Egypt.[92] The letters, of which excerpts from two are transcribed below, are concerned with provisioning for a forthcoming visit to Panopolis by Diocletian in September of 298. They paint a picture of an inefficient bureaucracy intensely busy at the local level but experiencing only occasional intervention by the higher levels of provincial government:[93]

> From the strategos of the nome of Panopolis
> to the president:
>
> With regards to the supplies of the annona ordered to be stored up in various places in preparation for the auspiciously impending visit of our ruler the emperor Diocletian, the senior Augustus, I have both a first and a second time instructed you with all speed to select receivers and overseers of provisions for the most noble soldiers who will enter the city, in order that no more delay may occur in regard to this most honorable duty. But since up to the present nothing requisite has been achieved by you, now for the third time I enjoin you to take the appropriate measures with regard to this honorable visitation, and also carry into execution the orders of Aurelius Isidorus, the procurator of the Lower Thebaid. This letter is written by the clerk Leon, and signed by me.[94]

> From the strategos of the nome of Panopolis
> to the procurator:
>
> Upon your orders, my lord, that the ships of the treasury requisitioned from the Upper Thebaid should be repaired and refitted from the treasury funds for the service of the auspiciously impending visit of our ruler the emperor Diocletian, the ever-victorious senior Augustus, I have commanded the president of the city, Aurelius Plutogenes also called Rhodinus, to select a surveyor, so that the supervisions of the aforesaid ships may be carried out honestly and for the profit of the most sacred treasury; and also to select an overseer of the same ships, to receive the money from the public bank and account for the expenditure incurred, so that by all means the true amount expended may be known to you in your diligence. But he, in contempt for this most honorable duty, had the audacity to reply that the city ought not to be troubled. How, then, is it possible, when this man shows such contempt for me in my mediocrity, for the repairs of the ships to be carried out and provision for their refitting to be made? And not only this, but there is the appointment of receivers and overseers of the supplies of the annona which have been ordered to be reviewed in different localities in readiness for those who are expected to arrive with our ruler Diocletian, the senior Augustus.[95]

From these letters one senses that at the end of the third century, corruption was endemic and the financial and administrative hierarchies of the Roman fiscal system were bewildering to all involved.[96] The Panopolis papyri therefore illustrate more pragmatic perspectives on the occasion of the emperor's arrival than those disseminated by the official bards and by extension the images celebrating his visit preserved within the walls of the Luxor fort. While the tone of the panegyrics and their ekphrases of ceremonial settings imply that all towns were genuinely pleased to receive an emperor, the formulaic language and exasperated tone of the Panopolis letters are perhaps more realistic examples of a community's response to an emperor's impending visit. It was an event that would have put a serious burden on local taxpayers as well as tax collectors, in Egypt as in other parts of the empire. Yet at the same time it should be noted that the bureaucrats' responses, as chronicled in the Panopolis papyri, do not question the *necessity* for the elaborate ceremonials.

LUXOR AFTER DIOCLETIAN

The imagined adventus at Luxor and, indeed, almost all the other "stock" imperial-themed images found on public monuments in late antiquity were both historical and atemporal. The images captured a specific ceremonial performance of a courtly rite and simultaneously re-created it to imply its continued performance in perpetuity. We know that these formalized scenes maintained their popularity at least through the sixth century in other parts of the empire; the adventus continued to be pictured on numerous public monuments and to be used as a means of propaganda on widely circulating minor arts such as coins, medallions, and ivory diptychs.[97] But as for the painted adventus at Luxor, there is no direct evidence regarding the potency of its message. A statue base bearing an inscription of Constantine, dating somewhere between 310 and 325, still in situ in the central passage of the Amenhotep III portico directly in front of the imperial cult chamber, suggests a continued use for the chamber as a site of imperial veneration, at least through the end of Constantine's reign (see figure 2.6).[98]

This implies that in the early fourth century at least, Diocletian's successors continued to recognize the symbolic implications of the temple as a nexus of imperial authority.

In contrast, the only other textual evidence referring directly to the imperial cult chamber at Luxor, the fifth-century acts of the Martyrs Chanatomus, Sophronius, and Dalcina, is decidedly anti-imperial.[99] The text tells the story of several Christian martyrs who probably were killed during the persecutions under Diocletian and his successors (circa 303–311), among whom was Sophronius, a soldier of the Theban garrison. A man named Arianus is said to have arrived, some ten years after the beginning of the persecutions, in the "old temple of Ammon." Seeing smoke rising, Arianus asks whence it came and is told that it is a place "where the people were assembled in a room reserved for the worship of the divine idols and the genius of Caesar, and the smoke that climbs up in the air stems from the sacrifices that they are offering."[100] This account may corroborate the continued existence and functioning of an imperial cult chamber into the early fourth century, but we can be far from certain of this historical actuality, given the late date of the text and its rather suspect provenance. Moreover, the temple is mentioned only in passing to highlight a non-Christian activity in progress. Such texts, contrasting pagan rites with those of the Christian faith, are common in late antiquity and prone to exaggeration. The fact that they are the majority of texts to survive consequently presents an unbalanced view of the religious climate of the period, and thus they provide very little insight into how the ordinary soldier or resident of late Roman Thebes might have felt about the Roman imperial presence in Luxor Temple in the fourth or fifth century.

CONCLUSION

The descriptions of late Roman ceremonials in the panegyrics offer a glimpse of late Roman history through late Roman eyes. We can see how developments in politics and religion were first perceived and communicated by contemporaries.[101] In Egypt, however, and undoubtedly in other parts of the empire, the discrepancy between, on the one hand, the visual display of triumph and consensus encoded in the painted adventus and the imperial images in the niche and, on the other, the peevish reaction of a petulant local bureaucrat charged with procuring supplies for the emperor's impending visit signals a much wider gulf between reality and appearances than the panegyrics would have us believe. From the panegyrics and the visual evocation of the adventus ceremony at Luxor it is, therefore, possible to extrapolate the motivations and desires of the imperial propaganda machine for which both were created. The Luxor paintings and the texts both describe a constructed reality, what the imperial court wanted its contemporaries to think about the emperor. But whereas the Gallic panegyrics and the Luxor frescoes record, at least in part, the active participation of a supposedly enthusiastic crowd, history records no receptive audience for the Luxor adventus, leaving us to wonder if the intended message of the paintings fell on deaf ears.

APPENDIX

John Gardner Wilkinson's Documentation of the Imperial Cult Chamber and the Frescoes

MICHAEL JONES

THE WATERCOLOR SKETCHES BY SIR JOHN GARDNER Wilkinson are the most definitive record known of the imperial cult chamber and its frescoes. No other documentation has been traced showing the condition of the imperial cult chamber in such detail so soon after its excavation early in 1854. The excavator was almost certainly Victor Gustave Maunier (also known as V. Galli Maunier), whom Wilkinson mentions as "M. Monier" in a note on page 26v in this sketchbook, providing a valuable clue for reconstructing the archaeological history of the site (see chapter 4). Wilkinson made the sketches on the spot during his last visit to Thebes, in January 1856, and as so much was afterwards eroded or destroyed they have preserved on paper much of what has since been irretrievably lost from the walls. These sketches and notes are thus of the highest importance, as is shown in chapter 6 of this volume. The only other early color depiction yet found is the amateur watercolor sketch by General George de Sausmarez, painted on a journey through Egypt in March 1855 (see figure 4.6).

Wilkinson's sketches first appeared in the scholarly literature in 1953, when Ugo Monneret de Villard recognized their value and published them in his reappraisal of the imperial cult chamber, albeit in black and white.[1] Subsequently, selections of the watercolors have appeared in numerous scholarly and popular publications.[2]

This particular sketchbook is only a small part of the enormous archive of drawings, notes, letters, and other papers making up the collection of Wilkinson's papers now preserved at the Bodleian Library, Oxford. Wilkinson never published the material in this sketchbook, and, for many years following his death in 1875, it remained unnoticed among his manuscripts at Calke Abbey in Derbyshire, England. Fifty years later, F. Llewellyn Griffith borrowed fifty-six volumes of these documents and took them to Oxford to help with the work on the *Topographical Bibliography of Ancient Egyptian Hieroglyphic Texts, Reliefs, and Paintings* by Bertha Porter and Rosalind Moss. The sketchbook containing these watercolors of the imperial cult chamber at Luxor was not among this material and remained at Calke Abbey.[3] In 1981 all the Wilkinson manuscripts were reunited, and since 1985 they have been available for study at the Bodleian Library.[4]

The sketchbook containing the watercolors of the imperial cult chamber at Luxor is catalogued as:

Sketchbook, 1852–1856

Shelfmark: MS. Wilkinson dep. d. 34

Extent: 40 leaves

Binding: half red calf, embossed paper over boards.

Scope and content: Sketchbook, 1852–1856, in or near Farden, Wooler, Rowton Lynn, Hartside, Berwick, and Brinkburn (Northumberland), Richmond (N.R. Yorks.) and Blackwater (East Sussex), and in or near Idfou [Sohag?], Negadeh [Nag' el-Deir], Deyr Maribuktar [Deir Mari Buqtur], Luxor, Coptos [Qift], Walud Amr (?) and elsewhere in Upper Egypt, including prehistoric camps, churches, ruins, architectural details and frescoes.[5]

The watercolors of the imperial cult chamber cover six double pages in the sketchbook. Each page has two numbering systems. The Luxor sequence begins on pages 51 and 52 circled and continues to 62 circled. Circled numbers may have been Wilkinson's own system. The second sequence is the Bodleian Library cataloguing system, which treats each double page as verso–recto, starting with 25v–26r (equal to circled 51 and 52) and continuing to 30v–31r, although the last page, 62 circled, is also numbered 32. The pages are reproduced here in figures A.1 to A.7 as they appear in the open sketchbook. Figure A.7 presents all the notes that Wilkinson wrote beside and among the sketches. The Bodleian catalogue system of verso–recto numbering is used throughout this book.

The notes document Wilkinson's thoughts about the imperial cult chamber and the frescoes as he was working, except possibly in one instance, on page 26v, where the note referring to Taunton Museum seems to have been added after Wilkinson's return to England, while he was reviewing other material. In addition to these insights, Wilkinson's skillful renderings of what he saw communicate the impression made on him by the brightly preserved colors and the fresh appearance of the paintings when they were first uncovered. His drawing of the niche—with its accurate depiction of the masonry and stance of the granite columns—demonstrates his skill as a draftsman. Two drawings, on pages 28v and 29v, seem to have been left as preliminary pencil sketches or outlines within otherwise finished color copies, and they may indicate that Wilkinson intended to copy more; but because of the sunstroke he suffered while at Luxor, he was obliged to leave his work incomplete. There is no indication that Wilkinson ever copied the surviving dado frescoes on the west wall. The preserved height of most of this wall in Wilkinson's time, as today, extended only to the top of the decorative border separating the imitation opus sectile patterns from the lowest register of figurative paintings on the other walls (see figure 5.14). A pencil sketch of part of an opus sectile pattern in the upper part of page 26v may be an unfinished copy of all that survived on the west wall, but unfortunately it cannot be identified.

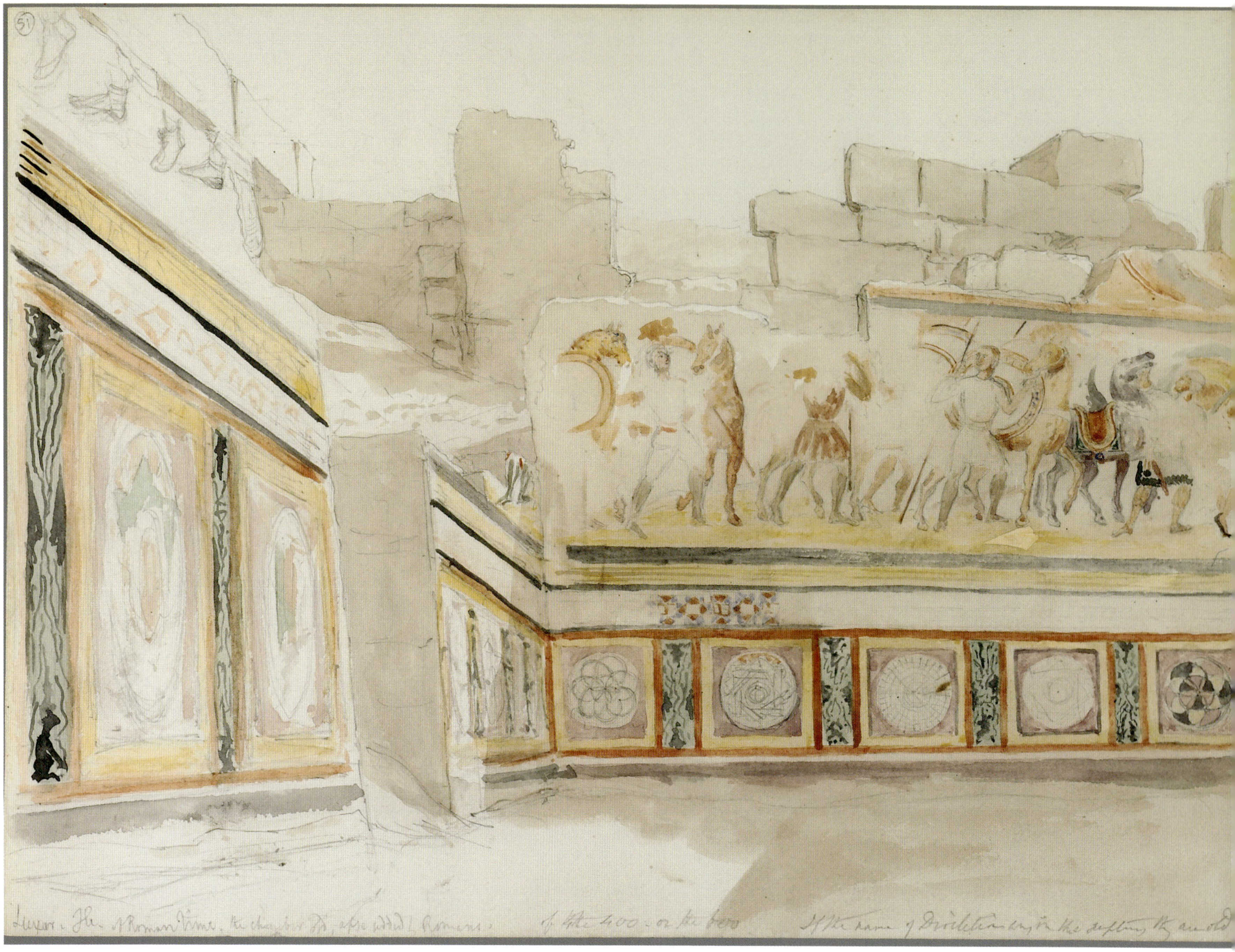

FIGURE A.1: PAGES 25V AND 26R

This is a view of the interior of the imperial cult chamber from inside the northwest corner. It shows the two halves of the north wall, with the entrance in the center; the whole of the east wall, with the doorway leading into the east side rooms; and the south wall, with the niche and the two granite columns. At the top left, the architraves and column capitals in the Amenhotep III portico are indicated in pencil outline. Debris still fills the spaces between the columns and spills through the doorway into the room. A small building, which also appears in Devéria's 1859 photograph, is shown in outline on the mounds above the east wall of the room (see figure 4.10). The imitation opus sectile dado is shown in a fine state of preservation on all the walls. The magnificent scene of soldiers and horses on the east wall is almost intact, and the baseline of the second, mostly missing, register of paintings runs along most of the length of the wall. On the north wall there is a group of legs outlined in pencil on the western section, at upper left, and a pair of legs near the far corner of the eastern section. Below the latter, a letter A is a cross-reference to the detailed copy of this small section on page 27r. The upper parts of the east and south walls are shown as bare

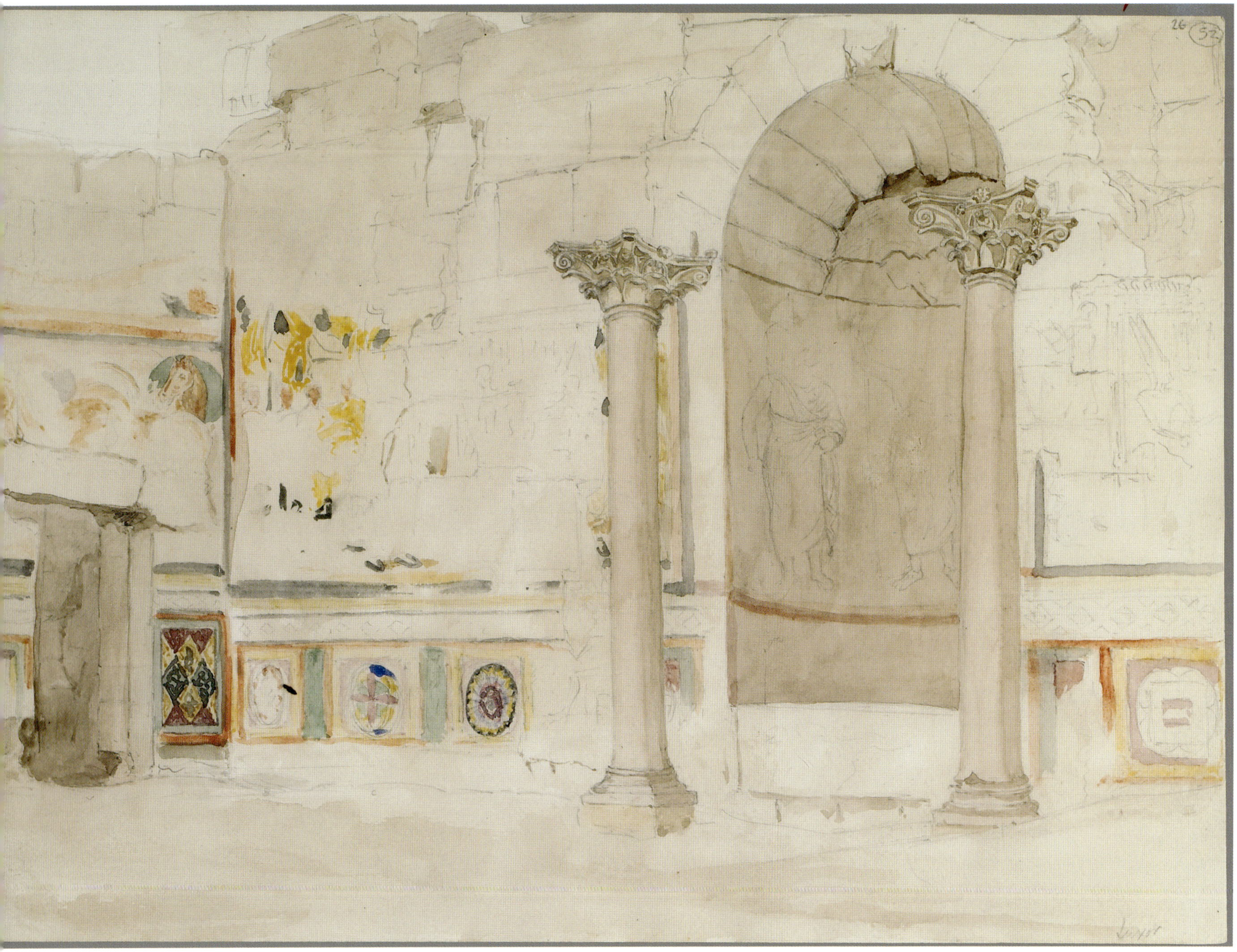

masonry, the blocks outlined. This emphasizes the upper edge of the surviving frescoes and may indicate the ground level in the room before it was excavated. The base of the western (right) granite column beside the niche appears to be partly buried.

At the bottom of page 25v Wilkinson wrote: "Luxor. H[all] of Roman time, the chamber and apse added by Romans, of the 400 or the 600. If the name of Diocletian was in the i[nscr]iptions they are older." A note at the bottom right corner of page 26r reads, "Luxor."

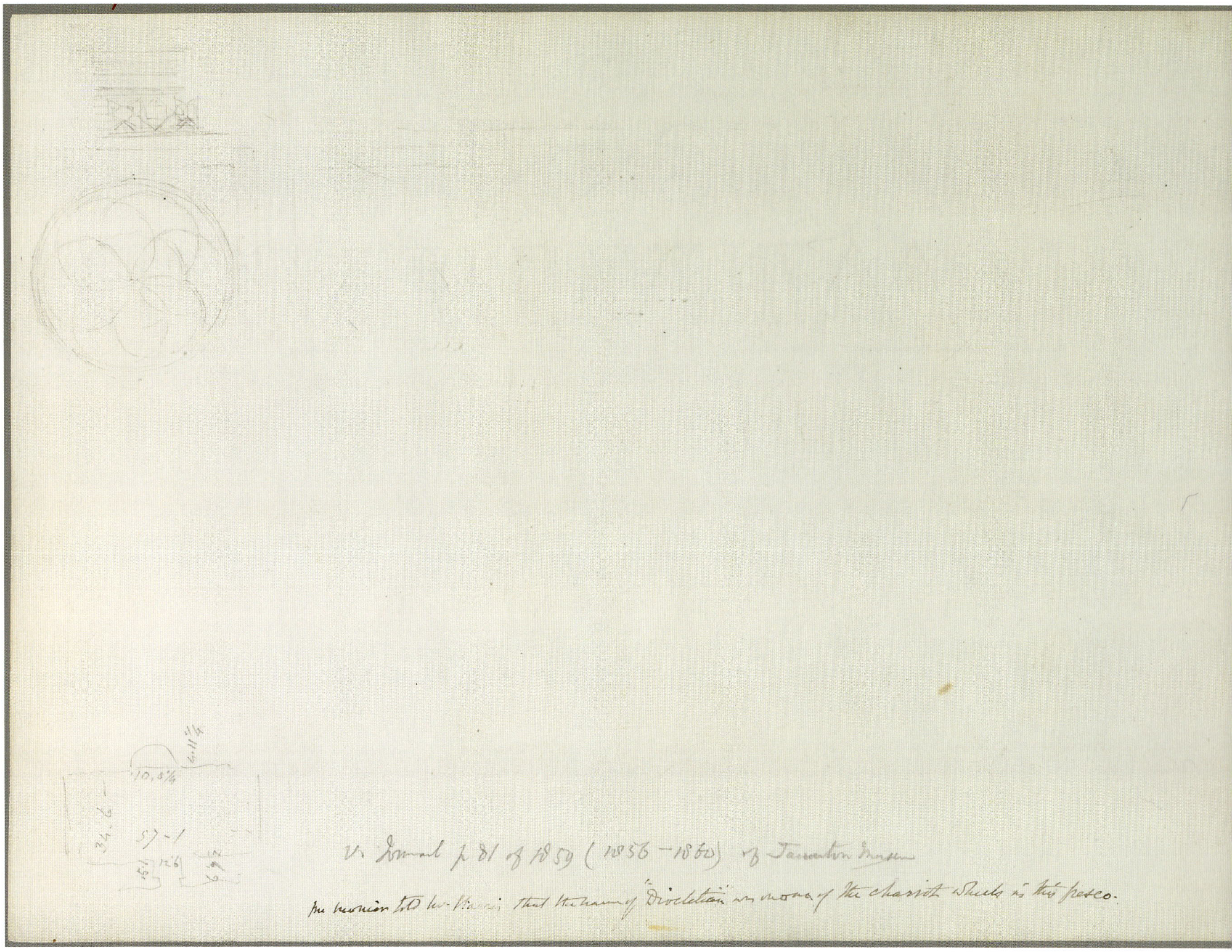

FIGURE A.2: PAGES 26V AND 27R

On the left (page 26v) pencil sketches show one of the circular patterns from the imitation opus sectile dado and above it a drawing of the geometric frieze that separates the dado from the figurative scenes above. At lower left is a rough pencil-sketch plan of the imperial cult chamber with dimensions in feet and inches.

There are two lines of notes at the bottom edge of page 26v. The upper one, in pencil, reads, “V. Journal p 81 of 1859 (1856–1860) of Taunton Museum.” The lower one, in black ink, reads, “M. Monier told Mr. Harris that the name of ‘Diocletian’ was on one of the chariot wheels in this fresco.”

There are two separate color sketches on page 27r. At the right side of the page is the pair of legs at the eastern end of the eastern section of the north wall, in the northeast corner of the imperial cult chamber, marked *A* on page 25v and identified here by a note, “over A.” In the center of the page a vertical line indicates the eastern edge of the apse (the word “apse” is in pencil at the bottom of this line). To the left are the two standing figures, now almost completely destroyed, beside the niche on the eastern section of the south wall.

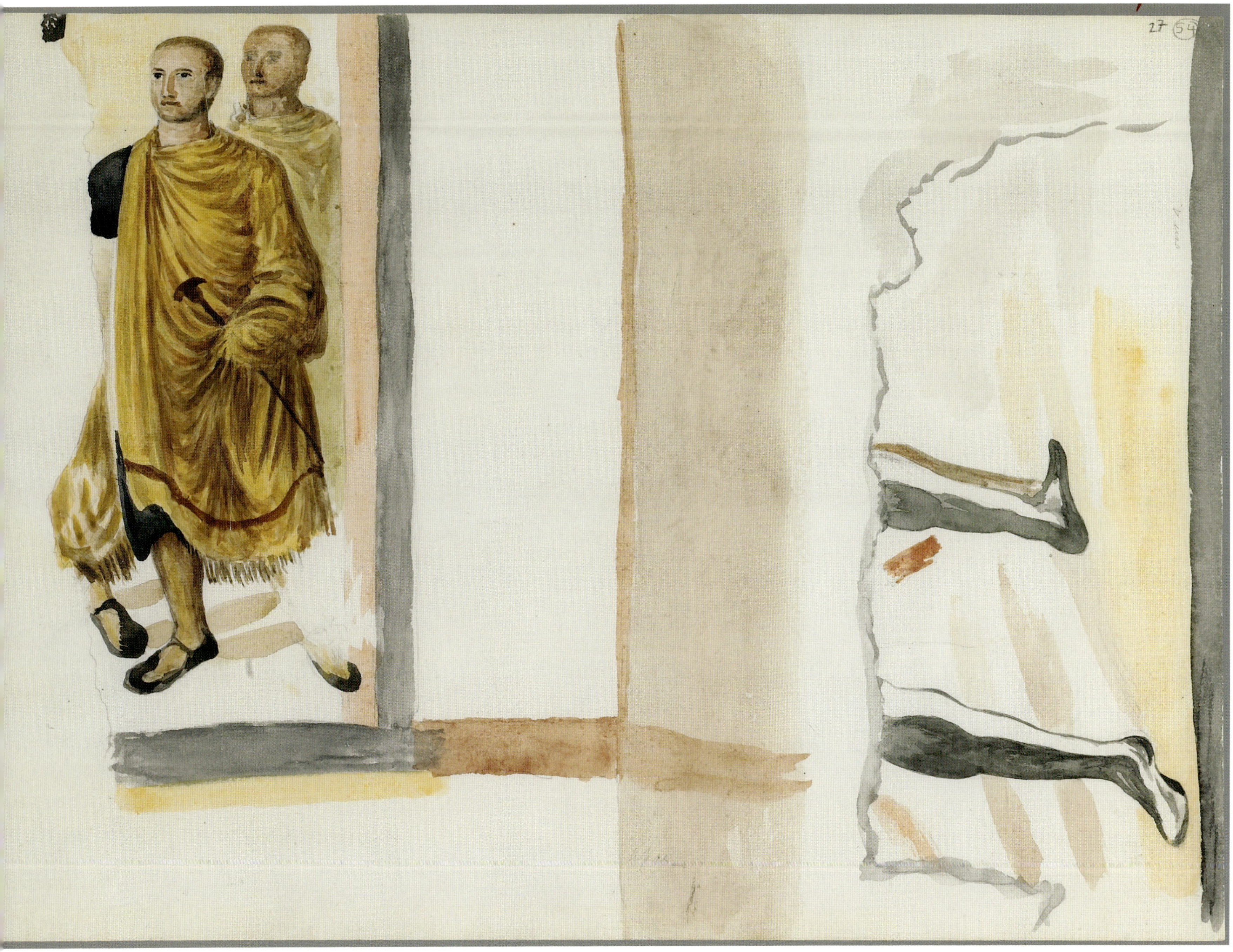

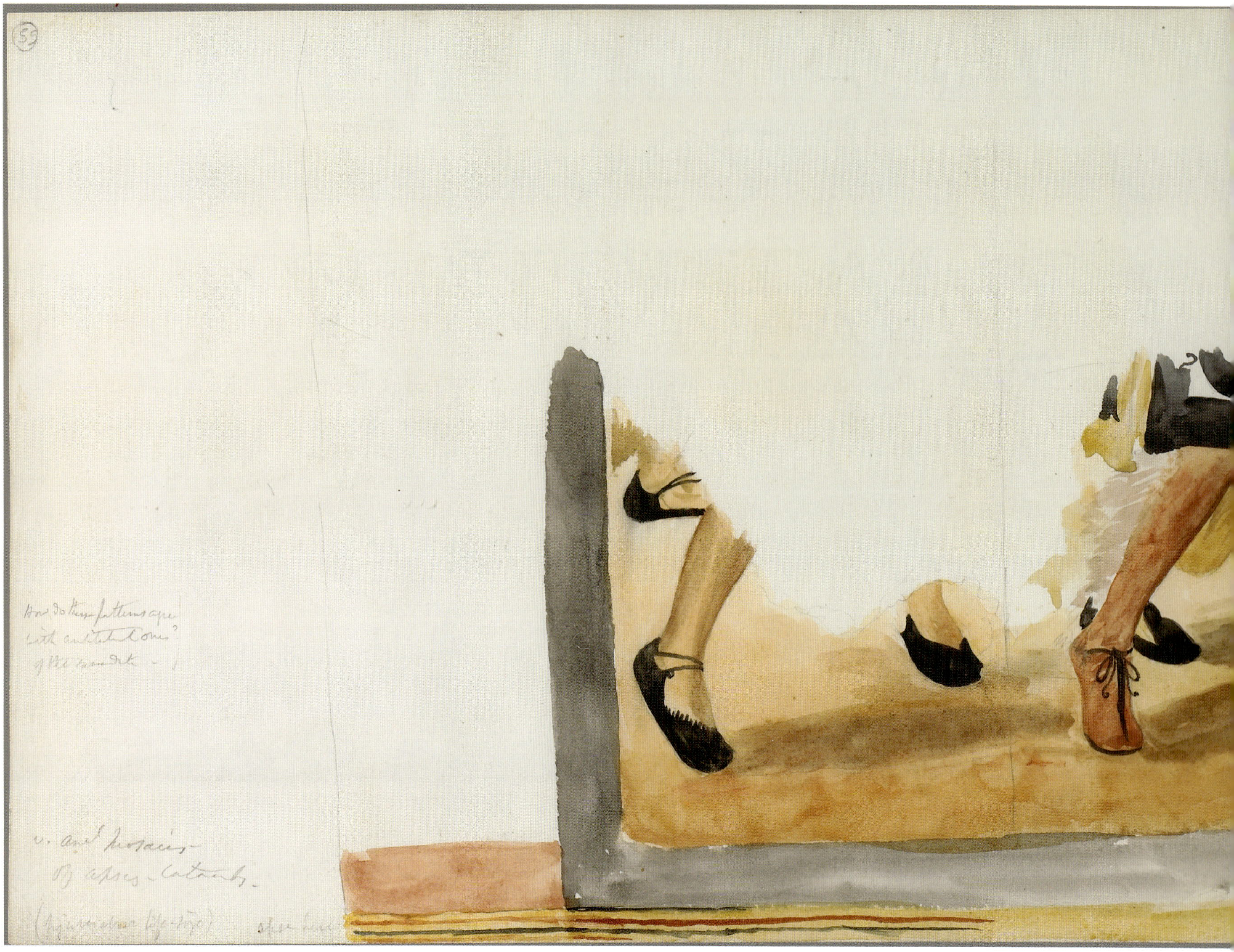

FIGURE A.3: PAGES 27V AND 28R

A drawing covering most of the double page shows the preserved lower parts of the group of figures on the south wall west of the niche. Today only the central portion of the group on page 28r is preserved (see figures 6.23 and 6.24).

Three pencil notes are written, one above the other, at the lower left corner of page 27v:

> Upper: How do these patterns agree with architectural ones? of the same date.
>
> Middle: v. anc[ient] mosaics—of apses—catacombs.
>
> Lower: (figures above life-size)

The edge of the niche is indicated by a note, "apse here." written in pencil at the bottom of page 27v against the left end of the yellow, red, and black-striped border.

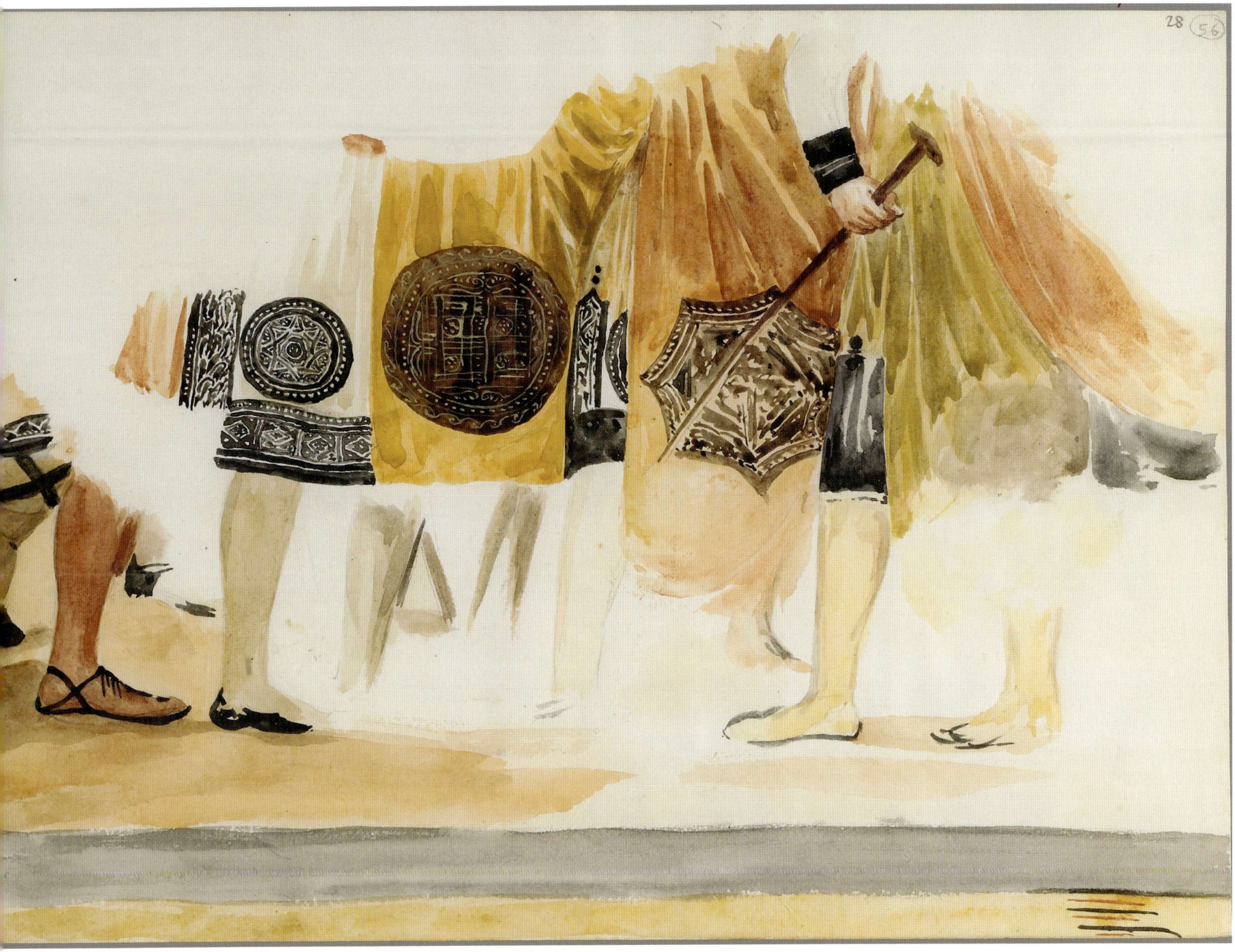
28 (56)

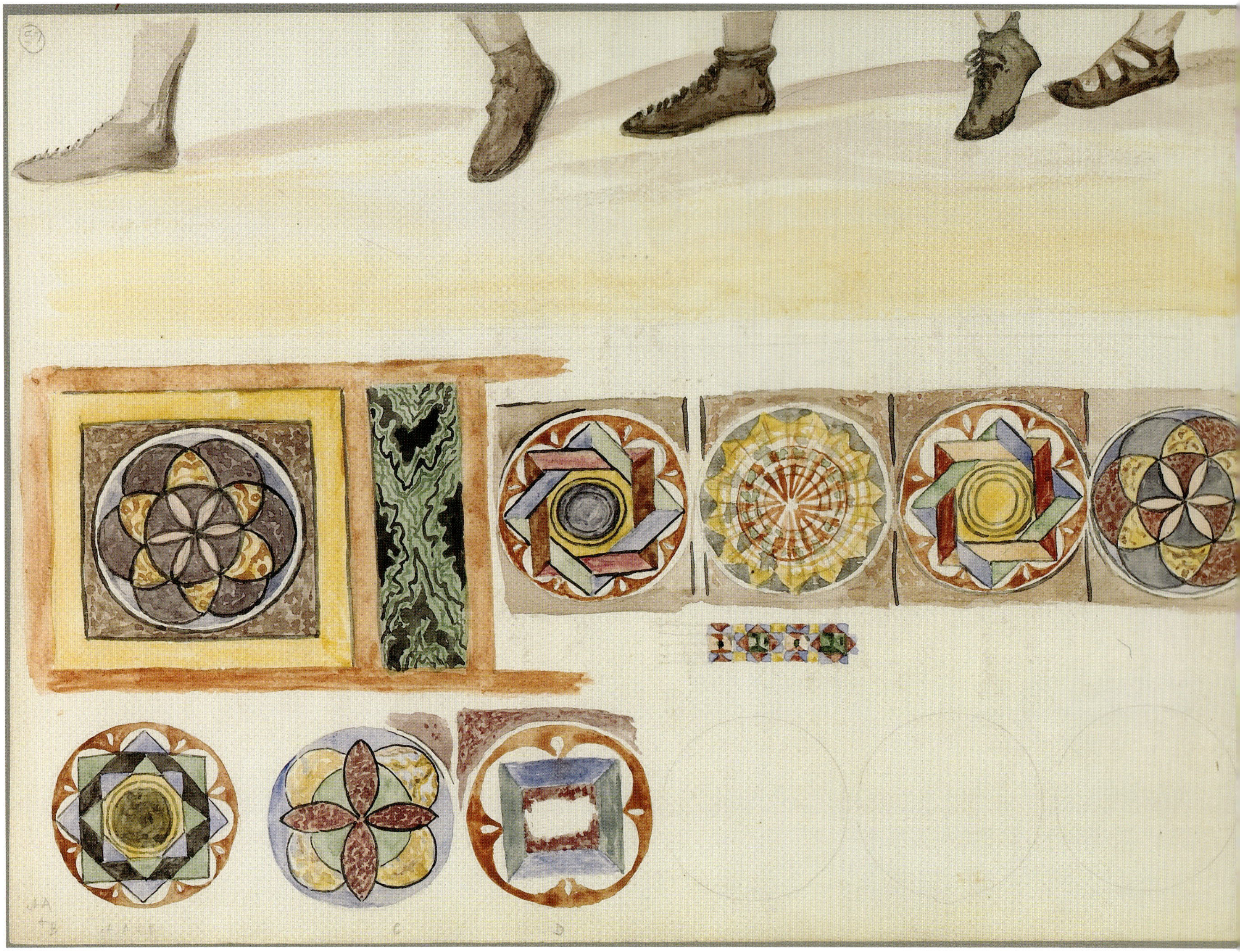

FIGURE A.4: PAGES 28V AND 29R

At the top of the left-hand page are the feet and lower legs of the only surviving figurative paintings on the western section of the north wall, west of the entrance (see page 25v, upper left). Details of footwear are clearly depicted.

Below are two rows of patterns from the painted imitation opus sectile dado. The finished examples are labeled in pencil A, B, C, and D. Three pencil circles with no details added and the incomplete colored detail in the third pattern from left seem to indicate that this illustration was left unfinished. A small section of the geometric border that runs along the top of the dado separating it from the figurative images above is also included. Today the dado is so severely damaged that no single design is preserved intact, which makes this drawing an especially important record.

On the right-hand page, 29r, the two emperor figures in the eastern half of the niche are shown, and the faint form of the erased figure, third from the left, is indicated by light color washes. Wilkinson has noted "Apse" in pencil at the lower left corner of the page, and at the lower right corner he indicated the match line in pencil, where the fourth figure joins these with the words "in AP[se]" (see page 30r).

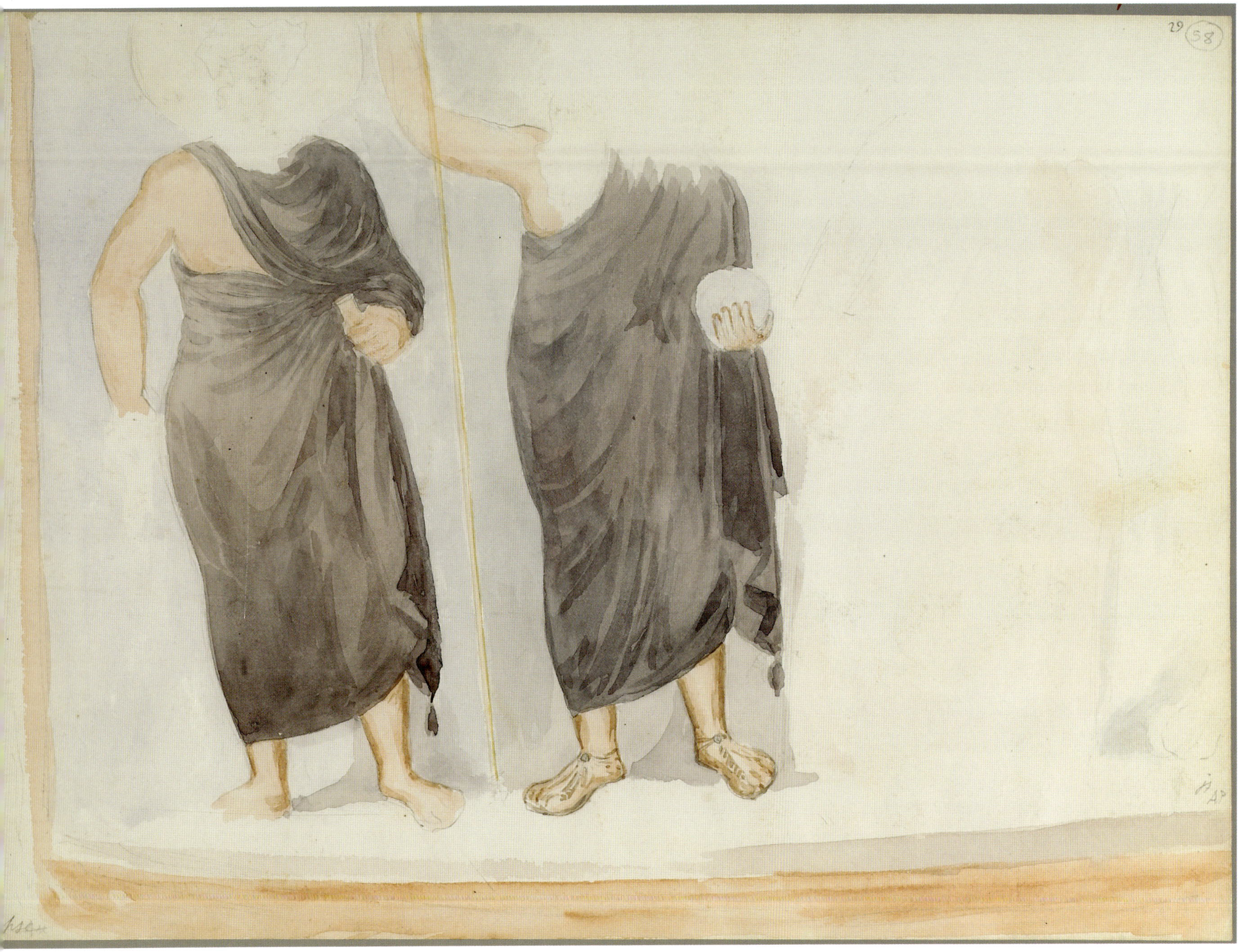

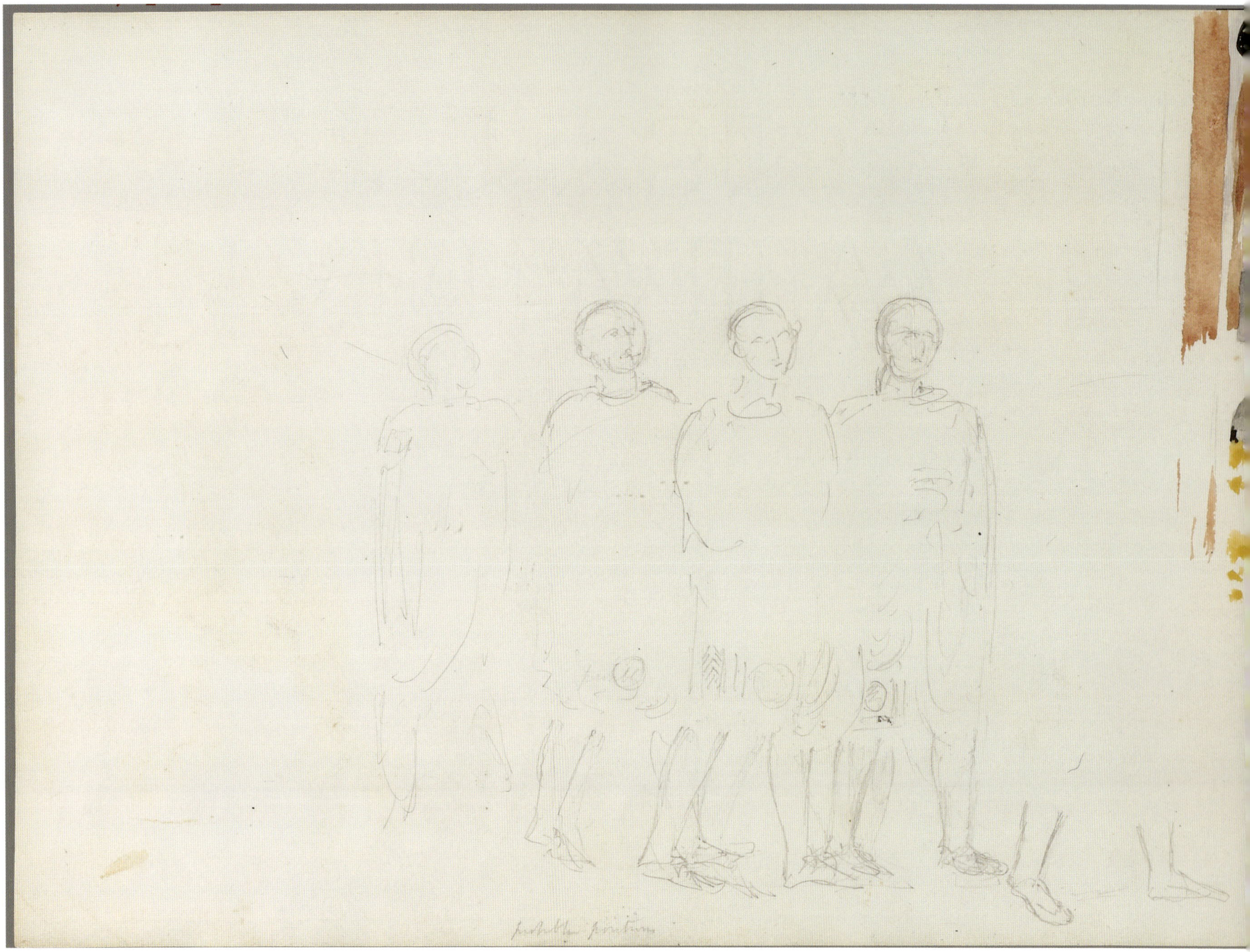

FIGURE A.5: PAGES 29V AND 30R

Most of this double page is devoted to the groups of standing figures on the south wall east of the niche. On page 29v, four standing figures and the lower legs of a fifth are roughly sketched in pencil, skillfully suggesting their stance and positions relative to one another. Wilkinson wrote "probable positions" below these figures. On the opposite page, 30r, a colored sketch shows the lower section of the figure group in the upper eastern end of the south wall. The heads of the upper group are missing where they were covered by later layers of plaster wash (see chapters 5 and 6), and the lower part is shown as already eroded. Under the group of standing figures at lower left of this page is a note in pencil: "Luxor (left of apse)." Beside the foot at the right of this group is a note: "this foot sh[oul]d be rather lower."

At the right of the page Wilkinson has depicted the emperor figure (first from the right) inside the western side of the niche. A note below his right foot says "in AP[se]." In the upper right corner, beside the left shoulder of the emperor, Wilkinson shows a rectangular frame containing a tall cross. This is now known to have been a misinterpreted

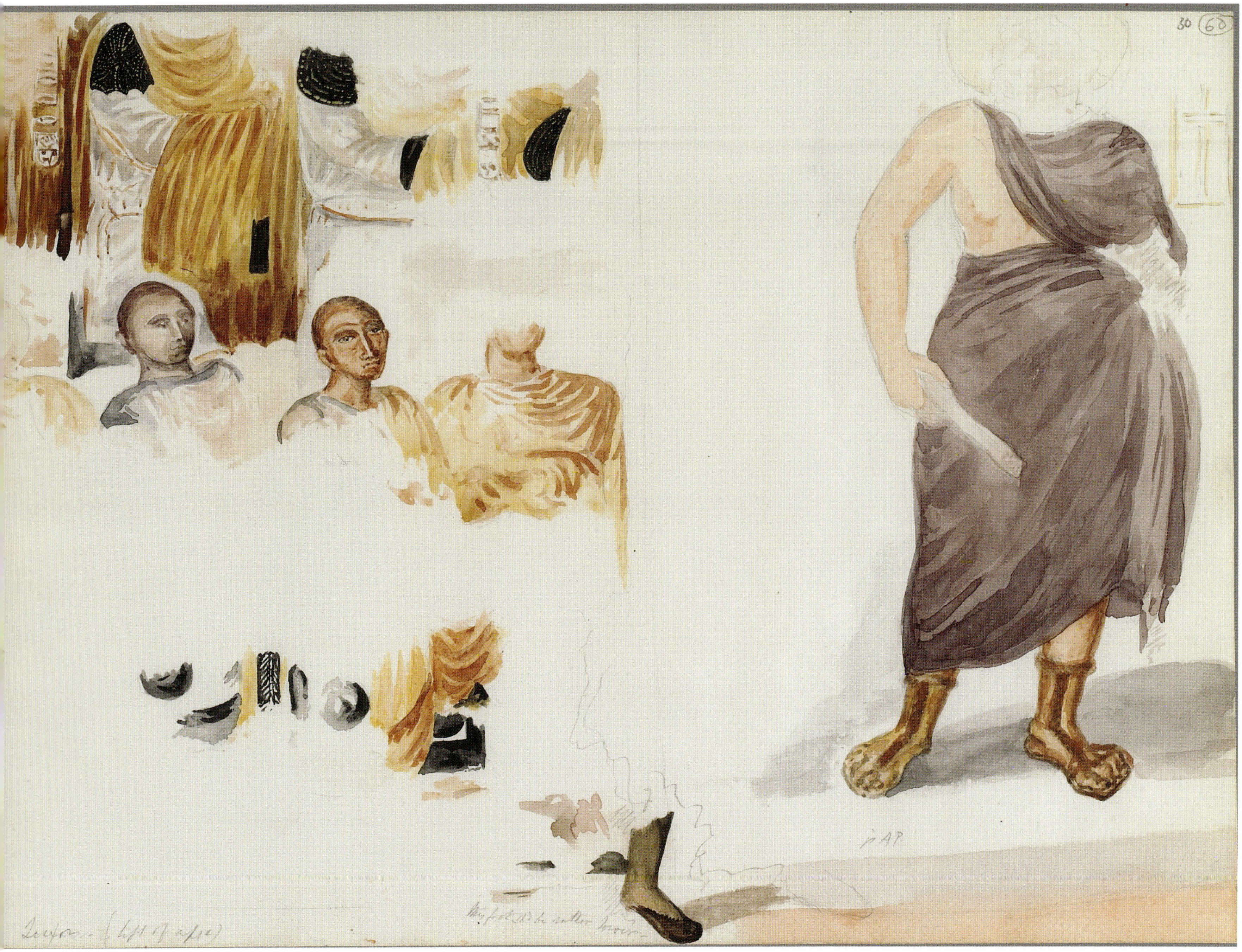

symbol, a mistake that may have led to, or supported the identification of the imperial cult chamber as an early Christian church and consequent imaginative speculations about the subjects in the frescoes (see chapter 4).

FIGURE A.6: PAGES 30V AND 31R

Page 30v, on the left, is blank. On the right, a dynamic color sketch shows a detail from the scene on the east wall. (See page 25v for its position on the wall.) Details of the horses, and in one case the saddle and outline of the bridle on the horse's rearing head, are shown. The soldier to the left of the composition holds what appears to be a lance and carries a round shield on his back. Other shields are shown in partial outline above and to his left. The word "Luxor" is at the bottom right corner of the page.

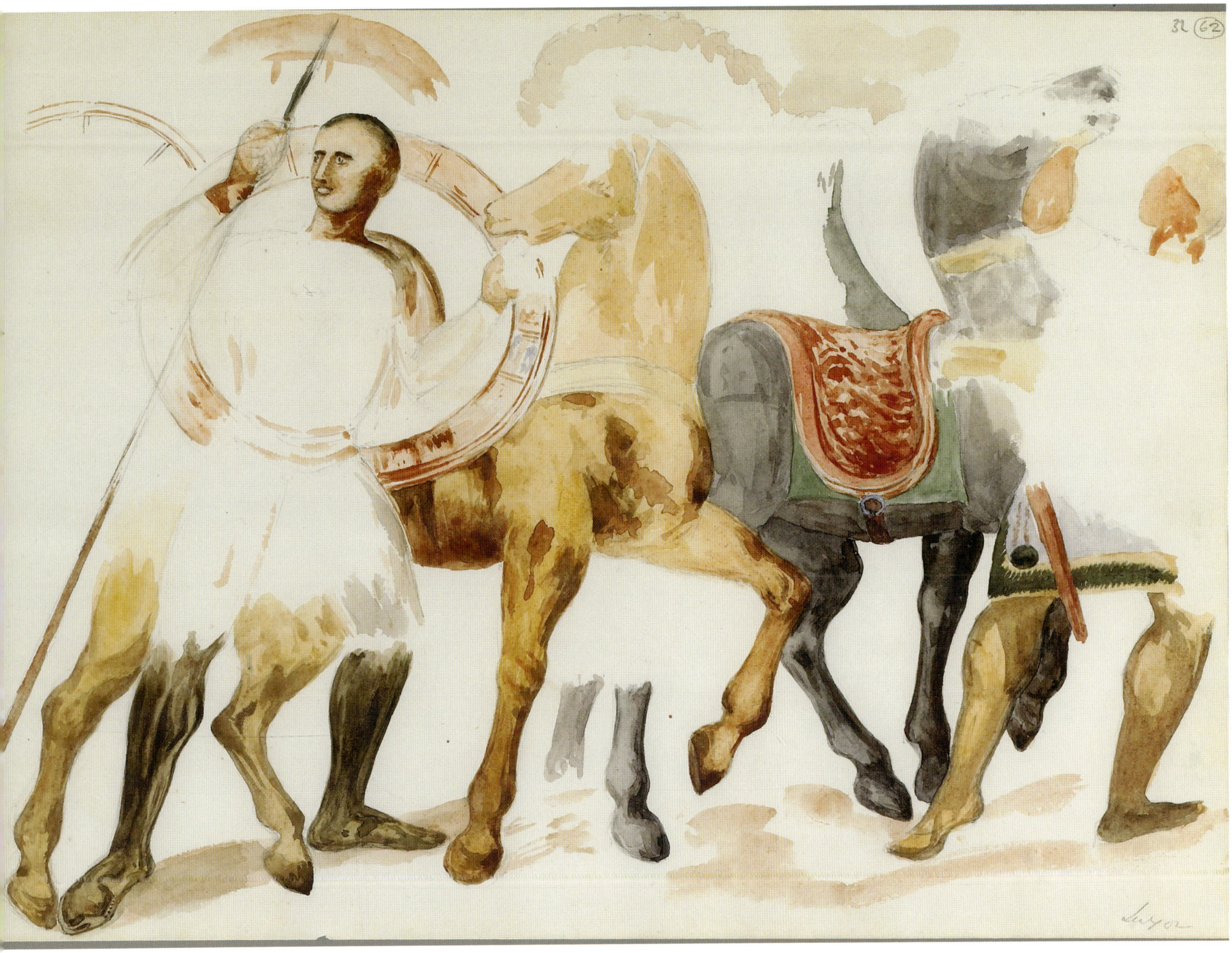
32 (62)
Luxor

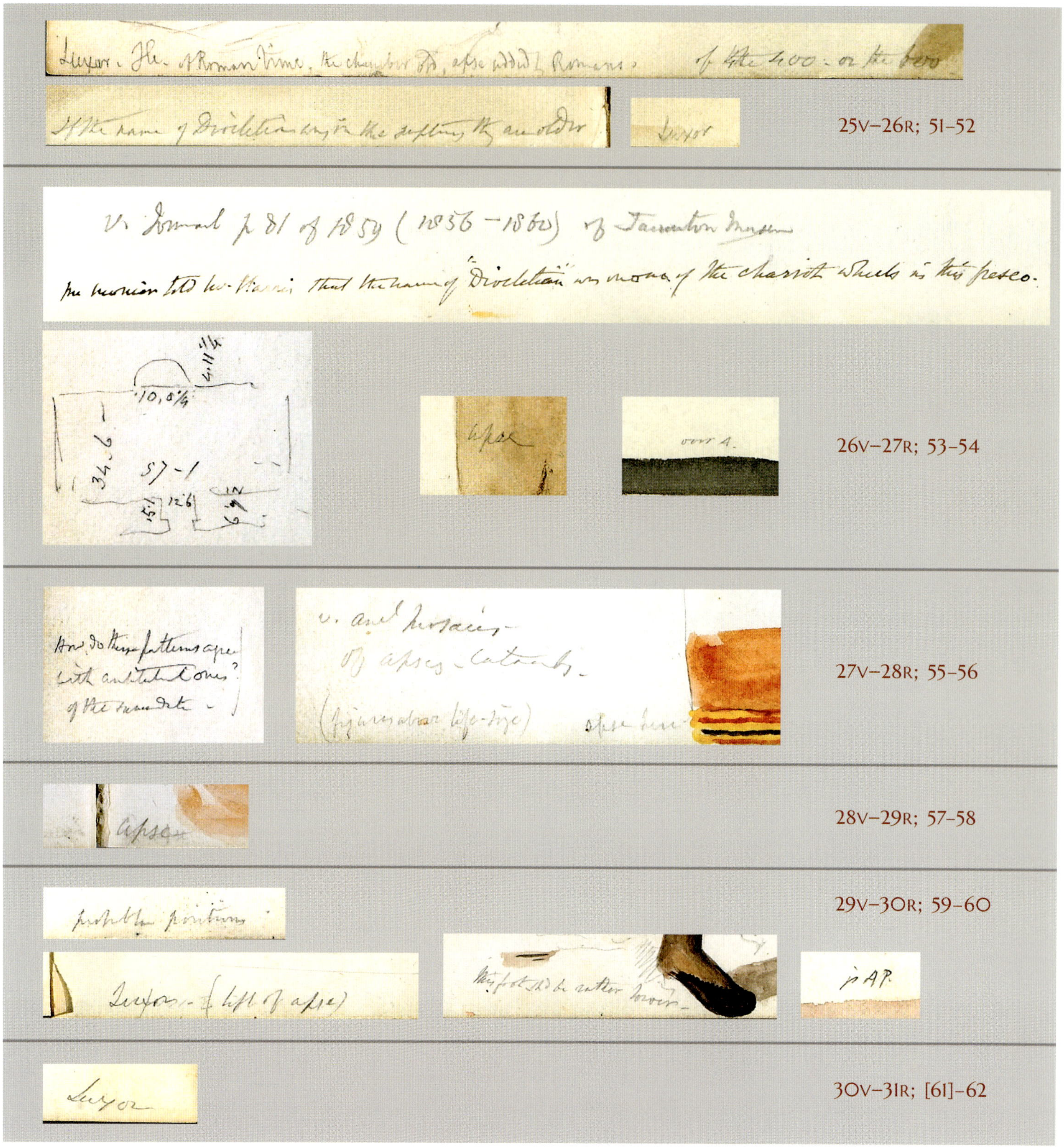

FIGURE A.7
The notes written by Wilkinson beside the sketches have been collected here and enlarged for legibility, each one with its original sketchbook page number.

CHRONOLOGY

20 November 284	Diocletian is proclaimed Augustus.
285	The Dyarchy (rule of two) is created.
21 July 285	Diocletian appoints Maximian Caesar.
1 April 286	Diocletian appoints Maximian Augustus of the West while maintaining control over the East.
ca. 288	Diocletian and Maximian adopt imperial *signa:* Diocletian *Jovius* and Maximian *Herculius.*
293	The Tetrarchy (rule of four) is created; Galerius crushes revolts at Busiris and Coptos.
1 March 293	Galerius is appointed Caesar in the East; Constantius Chlorus is appointed Caesar in the West.
294	Reform of the mints occurs.
297–298	Egypt rebels under Achilleus and Domitius Domitianus; Diocletian besieges Alexandria and defeats the rebels.
298	Galerius defeats the Persians.
301	Currency is reformed; Edict on Maximum Prices is issued.
February 303	The "Great" Persecution begins.
1 May 305	Diocletian and Maximian retire from office; Galerius (East) and Constantius Chlorus (West) are elevated to Augusti; Maximianus Daia is appointed Caesar in the East; Severus is appointed Caesar in the West.
July 306	Constantius Chlorus dies; his son Constantine is proclaimed Augustus of the West by the army at York. Galerius instead promotes Severus to Augustus and recognizes Constantine only as Caesar.
October 306	Maximian's son Maxentius is proclaimed emperor at Rome; Maximian comes out of retirement to join his son.
307	Severus attacks Maxentius in Italy but is defeated and killed; Constantine marries Maximian's daughter (Maxentius's sister) Fausta in Gaul; Galerius invades Italy but is forced to retreat; Maxentius and Constantine are both proclaimed Augusti (though not recognized as such by Galerius).

308	Maximian attempts to depose Maxentius and is forced to leave Italy.
November 308	Maximian meets Galerius, Maximinus Daia, and Diocletian at Carnuntum to sort out succession issues; Licinius is proclaimed Augustus in the West; Constantine and Maximinus protest Licinius's elevation to Augustus and are given the titles *filii augustorum* by Galerius in an attempt at appeasement; Maximian abdicates again.
310	Maximian is executed or is forced to commit suicide in Gaul; Constantine is recognized as Augustus in the West but only as *filius augustorum* in the East; Maximinus Daia is proclaimed Augustus by troops but is recognized only as Caesar or *filius augustorum* by Galerius and Licinius.
311	Galerius issues the Edict of Toleration; the "Great" Persecution ends.
Late April or early May 311	Galerius dies; Maximinus Daia is recognized as Augustus in the East alongside Licinius; Constantine is recognized as Augustus in the West.
3 December 311	Diocletian dies.
28 October 312	Constantine defeats Maxentius at the Battle of Milvian Bridge; Maxentius is killed in the melee.
February 313	Constantine and Licinius meet in Milan and grant official toleration to Christians throughout the Roman Empire.
July	Maximinus Daia dies, leaving only Licinius as Augustus of the East and Constantine Augustus of the West.
18 September 324	Licinius is defeated at the Battle of Chrysopolis, and he subsequently abdicates and is put to death (spring 325); Constantine assumes sole imperial authority.
22 May 337	Constantine dies.

ABBREVIATIONS

Citations of papyri and ostraca (prefixed with *P.* or *O.*) conform to the standards in the "Checklist of Editions of Greek, Latin, Demotic, and Coptic Papyri, Ostraca and Tablets," which also gives their published sources. This can be found online at http://library.duke.edu/rubenstein/scriptorium/papyrus/texts/clist.html

AAAH
Acta ad Archaeologiam et Artium Historiam

AE
L'année épigraphique. Paris: Presses Universitaires de France, 1888–

AJA
American Journal of Archaeology

AJP
American Journal of Philology

Amm. Marc.
Ammianus Marcellinus, trans. J. C. Rolfe. 3 vols. (Loeb Classical Library). Cambridge: Harvard University Press, 1935–1939

ANRW
Aufstieg und Niedergang der römischen Welt

ARCE
American Research Center in Egypt

ASAE
Annals du service des antiquités de l'Égypte

Aur. Vict. *Caes.*
Aurelius Victor, *De Caesaribus,* trans. H. W. Bird. Liverpool: Liverpool University Press, 1994

Barb. Lat.
Codex Vaticanus Barberini latinus 2154

BASP
Bulletin of the Society of American Papyrologists

BdÉ
Bibliothèque d'Étude

BGU
Aegyptische Urkunden aus den Königlichen [later Staatlichen] Museen zu Berlin, Griechische Urkunden. Berlin, 1895–

BICS
Bulletin of the Institute of Classical Studies

BIÉ
Bulletin de l'Institut Égyptien

BIFAO
Bulletin de l'Institut Français d'Archéologie Orientale

BSAC
Bulletin de la Société d'Archéologie Copte

CAH
Cambridge Ancient History, vol. 12, ed. A. K. Bowman, P. Garnsey, and A. Cameron. Cambridge: Cambridge University Press, 2005

CÉ
Chronique d'Égypte

Chronica Minora I
Chronica Minora Saec. IV. V. VI. VII, vol. 1, ed. T. Mommsen. Berlin, 1892 (= MGH AA IX)

CIL
Corpus Inscriptionum Latinarum, vol. III, suppl. 2, ed. T. Mommsen, O. Hirschfeld, and A. Domascewski. Berolini: apud G. Reimerum, 1902

CPR
Corpus Papyrorum Raineri (Vienna)

CR
Classical Review

De Cer
Constantine Porphyrogenitus. De ceremoniis aulae Byzantinae. Ed. and trans. J. J. Reiske. 2 vols. Bonn: Weber, 1829–1830

EMC
Echos du Monde Classique

Euseb. *Hist. eccl.*
Eusebius, *The History of the Church,* trans. G. A. Williamson. London: Penguin, 1965

Euseb. *Vit. Const.*
Eusebius, *The Life of Constantine,* trans. A. Cameron and S. G. Hall. Oxford: Oxford University Press, 1999

Eutr.
Eutropius, *Breviarium,* trans. H. W. Bird. Liverpool: Liverpool University Press, 1993

FIFAO
Fouilles de l'Institute Français d'Archéologie Orientale

Hom. *Il.*
Homer, *The Iliad,* trans. R. Lattimore. Chicago: University of Chicago Press, 1951

Hor. *Ars P.*
Horace, *Ars Poetica,* trans. R. H. Fairclough. Cambridge: Harvard University Press, 1978

IFAO
Institut Français d'Archéologie Orientale

IGRR
É. Bernand, *Inscriptions grecques d'Égypte et de Nubie: Répertoire bibliographique des IGRR.* Paris: Belles Lettres, 1983

ILS
Inscriptiones latinae selectae

JARCE
Journal of the American Research Center in Egypt

Jerome, *Chron.*
Jerome, *A Translation of Jerome's Chronicon with Historical Commentary,* trans. M. D. Donalson. Lewiston, N.Y.: Edward Mellen Press, 1996

JEA
Journal of Egyptian Archaeology

JNES
Journal of Near Eastern Studies

JRA
Journal of Roman Archaeology

JRS
Journal of Roman Studies

JSAH
Journal of the Society of Architectural Historians

LÄ
Lexikon der Ägyptologie, ed. W. Helck and E. Otto. Wiesbaden: Otto Harrassowitz, 1980

Lactant. *De mort. pers.*
Lactantius, *De mortibus persecutorum,* ed. J. L. Creed. Oxford: Oxford University Press, 1984

LIMC
Lexicon iconographicum mythologiae classicae, ed. J. Boardman et al. 8 vols. Munich: Artemis Verlag, 1981–1997

LSA
"Last Statues of Antiquity," online database, http://laststatues.classics.ox.ac.uk

MAAR
Memoires of the American Academy in Rome

MDAIK
Mitteilungen des Deutschen Archäologischen Instituts Abteilung Kairo

MDAI(R)v
Mitteilungen des Deutschen Archaologischen Instituts (Rom.)

MEFRA
Les Mélanges de l'École Française de Rome: Antiquité

MGH AA
Monumenta Germaniae Historiae, Auctores Antiquissimi

Mos. et Rom. Legum collatio
Mosaicarum et Romanarum legume collatio, ed. M. Hyamson. Oxford: Oxford University Press, 1913

MIFAO
Mémoires de l'Institute Français d'Archéologie Orientale

Not. Dig.
Notitia Dignitatum, or, Register of Dignitaries, trans. W. Fairley. Philadelphia: University of Pennsylvania, Department of History, 1900

O. Amst.
Ostraka in Amsterdam Collections, ed. R. S. Bagnall, P. J. Sijpesteijn, and K. A. Worp. Zutphen: Terra, 1976

O. Bodl.
Greek Ostraca in the Bodleian Library at Oxford and Various Other Collections, vol. 2, *Ostraca of the Roman and Byzantine Periods,* ed. J. G. Tait and C. Préaux. London: Egypt Exploration Society, 1955

O. Flor.
The Florida Ostraka: Documents from the Roman Army in Upper Egypt, ed. R. S. Bagnall. Durham, N.C.: Duke University, 1976

OGIS
É. Bernand, *Inscriptions grecques d'Égypte et de Nubie: Répertoire bibliographique des OGIS.* Paris: Belles Lettres, 1982

O. Ont. Mus.
Ostraka in the Royal Ontario Museum, vol. 2, ed. R. S. Bagnall and A. E. Samuel. Toronto: A. M. Hakkert, 1976

O. Stras. II
Thèbes et ses taxes: Recherches sur la fiscalité en Égypte romaine, ostraca de Strasbourg II, ed. P. Heilporn. Paris: De Boccard, 2009

Pan. Lat.
In Praise of Later Roman Emperors: The Panegyrici Latini, ed. C. E. V. Nixon and B. S. Rodgers. Berkeley: University of California Press, 1994

P. Beatty Panop.
Papyri from Panopolis in the Chester Beatty Library, Dublin, ed. T. C. Skeat. Dublin: Hodges, Figgis, 1964

PBSR
Papers of the British School at Rome

PCPS
Proceedings of the Cambridge Philological Society

PLRE
Prosopography of the Later Roman Empire, vol. 1, *260–395,* ed. A. H. M. Jones et al. Cambridge: Cambridge University Press, 1971

P. Mich.
Michigan Papyri

P. Oslo
Papyri Osloenses, Oslo

P. Oxy.
The Oxyrhnchus Papyri, ed. and trans. B. P. Grenfell and A. S. Hunt. London: Egypt Exploration Society, 1898–

Proc. *Hist. Arc.*
Procopius, *Secret History,* trans. R. Atwater. Ann Arbor: University of Michigan Press, 1961

RIA
Rivista dell'Istituto Nazionale di Archeologia e Storia dell'Arte

RIC Vb
The Roman Imperial Coinage, vol. 5, pt. 2, *Valerian to the Reform of Diocletian [Probus to Amandus],* ed. P. H. Webb, H. Mattingly, and E. A. Sydenham. London: Spink and Son, 1933

RIC VI
The Roman Imperial Coinage, vol. 6, *From Diocletian's Reform (A.D. 294) to the Death of Maximinus (A.D. 313),* ed. C. H. V. Sutherland. London: Spink and Son, 1967

RIC VII
The Roman Imperial Coinage, vol. 7, *Constantine and Licinius, A.D. 313–337,* ed. C. H. V. Sutherland, R. A. G. Carson, and P. Bruun. London: Spink and Son, 1966

Ritt. XII
E. Ritterling, "Legio: Bestand, Verteilung und kriegerische Betätigung der Legionen des stehenden Heeres von Augustus bis Diocletian." In *Paulys Realencyclopädie der classischen Altertumswissenschaft* (RE). Vol. 12:1–2 col. 1211–1829. Stuttgart: J. B. Metzler, 1924.

RQA
Römische Quartalschrift für christliche Altertumskunde und für Kirchengeschichte

RT
Recueil de Travaux Relatifs à la Philologie et l'Archéologie Égyptiennes et Assyriennes

SB
Sammelbuch griechischer Urkunden aus Aegypten, 1915–

SCA
Supreme Council of Antiquities, Egypt

WO
Griechische Ostraka aus Aegypten und Nubien, ed. U. Wilcken. Leipzig: Gieseke & Devrient, 1899

YCS
Yale Classical Studies

ZPE
Zeitschrift für Papyrologie und Epigraphik

NOTES

Introduction

1 Porter and Moss 1972, 320–321, V. First antechamber.

2 Luxor is the modern name for the settlements that occupy the site of the ancient city of Thebes, as it was known in Greek literary sources—not to be confused with the *Thebaid* or *Thebais,* which are terms used to describe the region. The city was known as Diospolis Magna ("city of the great god") in official documents during the Greco-Roman period because of the association of the Egyptian god Amun with Zeus. By the Roman era, the territory that made up Thebes was an agglomeration of settlements on both the east and west banks of the Nile, unified culturally but not administratively; each bank belonged to a different *nome,* or province; Łatjar 2012, 175.

3 On Luxor Temple, see Barguet 1980, 1103–1107; Murnane 2001, 309–312.

4 El-Saghir et al. 1986, 5–19.

5 Thompson 1981, 9–11; De la Torre and Lean 1997, 5–14; Palumbo 2000, 3–12.

6 Monneret de Villard 1953, building on important studies by Legrain 1917, Daressy 1920, and Lacau 1934.

7 Deckers 1973 and 1979; Kalavrezou-Maxeiner 1975; El-Saghir et al. 1986.

8 On the Opet Festival, Luxor Temple, and the divine ruler, see Bell 1985.

9 Kemp 2006, 264–276, particularly 270–273 for Luxor and the Opet Festival.

10 Egyptian regnal years before 664 BCE are approximate. The system here follows Baines and Málek 1992, 36–37. Von Beckerath 1997, 190–191, proposes another chronology.

11 Klotz 2012b, 324–327.

12 El-Saghir et al. 1986, 5–19, 42, 53, 55.

13 Ramesses II was known in the Roman tradition as Ozymandias from the rendering of an inscription at the Ramesseum (Memnonium) in Diodorus Siculus, *Bibliotheca historica,* 1.47.4. Diocletian erected two obelisks of Apries from Sais at the Iseum in Rome on the site now occupied by the church of Santa Maria Sopra Minerva: Ciampini 2004, 151–155 and fig. 17. Egyptian sculpture was displayed in Diocletian's palace at Split.

14 Dijkstra 2012, 239–247.

15 Sheehan 2010, 59–61, 63. The preexisting Trajanic riverfront determined the southwest fortification walls at Old Cairo. A comparison is possible at Luxor where the stone embankment mentioned by Lane 2000, 303 (shown in Denon's plan; Denon 1990, pl. 47 (lower) and pl. 48 (lower); and appearing in nineteenth-century photographs) may be an earlier riverside wall incorporated into the tetrarchic fortification. For similar stone embankments at Karnak, see Boraik 2010.

16 Habachi 1951, 453–469 and plan 1.

17 The statue was found in two parts—the upper when house foundations were dug in 1900–1901 and the lower in the 1930s in the same area while it was still covered by the town. Black granite standing statues of Khnum and Sekhmet, two unspecified black granite statue fragments, and a red granite stand or altar fragment were found with the lower part of the Osirid figure; Carter 1900, 191.

18 Grossmann 2002a, 34, 454.

19 For example, Karelyn 2013. Note, however, that the artistic license taken with the reconstruction of the paintings is problematic. Many details have been added that are not supported by the visual evidence presented in chapt. 6, such as the bushy beards on the tetrarchs and the five columns represented behind the enthroned tetrarchs on the south wall. These are fanciful iconographic details that would subtly alter the meaning of the images if they were in fact accurate.

20 Kopytoff 1986; Brand 1994, esp. 2–11.

21 Fowler 1992; Caple 2000; Mason and Avrami 2000, 13–26; Demas 2000, 27–54; Mathers et al. 2005; Jones 2008; Bendix 2009, 253–269.

22 Viñas 2009; Brandi 2005, 98.

23 Most 2009.

24 Trant 1997, 12.

25 Urry 2002, 129–130.

26 These topics are discussed in Avrami, Mason, and de la Torre 2000. For many of the issues involved in heritage packaged for tourism that apply to Luxor, see Kirshenblatt-Gimblett 1998.

27 Berger 1977, 13.

Chapter 1

1 I would like to thank my colleagues from Fairfield University, Bob Epstein, Angela Harkins, and Elizabeth Petrino, for their extensive comments and suggestions. Citations of papyri and ostraca herein conform to the standards in the "Checklist of Editions of Greek, Latin, Demotic, and Coptic Papyri, Ostraca and Tablets" found online at http://scriptorium.lib.duke.edu/papyrus/texts/clist.html.

2 Łajtar 2006, 100, 243, text no. 161.

3 For Amenhotep and Imhotep, see ibid., 46–48, and Łajtar 2008.

4 Łajtar 2006, text no. 164.

5 Ibid., text no. 168. For Amenhotep as the "great god" and Amenhotep and Imhotep together as the "Lords," see ibid., 100.

6 Ibid., 101, writes of "an already abandoned temple, which was still in a good state of preservation, but lacked an owner." He admits this theory is only an inclination. For scribes, see ibid., 95.

7 Milne 1924, 81.

8 This took place in 297/298 CE. See Bowman 1978 for the consensus against the 296/297 dating of Schwartz 1975 and 1977; see also Bowman 2005a, 82.

9 Barnes 1976a; Bowman 1978; Bowman 1984; Rea et al. 1985; Bowman 2005b. On the identification of Quseir al-Qadim with Myos Hormos, see Peacock and Blue 2006.

10 Paniskos's correspondence to his family in Philadelphia during his time in Coptos is in *P. Mich.* 3.214–221; see remarks in Baynes 1948 and Schwarz 1968.

11 Bowman 1976, 159–160, and Bowman 1978, 29.

12 For the settlement of the frontier, see Bowman 1978, 29–30; for Diocletian's inscription at Aswan, see *SB* 5.8393.

13 Bowman 1976, 161, and Bowman 1978, 28.

14 Bowman 1978 and Bowman 2005b, 317. On Luxor Temple, see El-Saghir et al. 1986. It should be noted, however, that some of Diocletian's forts in Egypt predate the revolts of the 290s, such as Qaret el-Tub in Bahariya Oasis. On this site see Charlier et al. 2012.

15 Grossmann et al. 1994, 272; Sheehan 2010.

16 Mustafa and Jaritz 1984–1985, 30; Mackensen 2009.

17 Schwartz and Wild 1950, 70–71.

18 The meaning and appropriateness of the term *romanization* are subject to scholarly debate; see Mattingly 2011. Here it is simply used to designate the late Roman building endeavors at Thebes, as distinct from previous Roman interventions in the area.

19 See, most recently, Heilporn 2009 (*O. Stras. II*) for nearly one hundred ostraca, largely related to tax issues.

20 Lewis 1937, 63–64.

21 Montserrat and Meskell 1997, 183.

22 Riggs 2000, 139.

23 Lewis 1937, 63–64.

24 Worp 1990, 243–244. For a less linguistically limited sample, consider the "Index des trapézites et signataires des reçus de taxes bancaires" in Bogaert 1984, 291–294, which includes Pamonthes and Psenmonthes, another name which, like Pamonthes, is based on the name of the Theban god Montu. See most recently the prosopography of *praktores argurikôn* in Heilporn 2009, with an interesting mix of Egyptian and Greek names.

25 *O. Ont. Mus.* 2:124; *WO* 567; *O. Bodl.* 2:622.

26 For example, *O. Ont. Mus.* 2:100; *O. Bodl.* 2:630; *WO* 568.

27 Hopkins 1980, 101.

28 Bagnall 1977, 75–77.

29 Clarysse 1984a, 1024, 1025.

30 For Galatians, see Kennedy 1985, 157; for Palmyrenes, see Speidel 1984, 222 (a dipinto at the temple of Hatshepsut at Deir el-Bahri). On epigraphic evidence for traders from India, see Salomon 1991, 731–736, and Sidebotham 1986, 55–56.

31 For the *skopelarioi* and their civilian role, see *O. Flor.* For the watchtower system in Roman Egypt, see Jones 1996, focusing on Abu Rawash, and Zitterkopf and Sidebotham 1989, focusing on eastern desert routes from Coptos.

32 Bagnall 1977, 71.

33 *O. Amst.* 10 intro.

34 Samuel et al. 1971, 23–24.

35 Łajtar 2006, 82–84.

36 Robichon and Varille 1940, v–vi.

37 Frankfurter 1998, 72. Ritual burials of Buchis bulls are attested until 340 CE; Grenier 1983.

38 Clarysse 1984b, 26; a list of Buchis names is at 30–35.

39 See Ruffini 2006 for further discussion of localizing Egyptian onomastics in a later period.

40 Bataille 1952, 285.

41 Ibid., 297.

42 Bataille 1951 and Bataille 1952, respectively.

43 Bataille 1951, 327.

44 Pausanias, *Description of Greece* 1.9.3.

45 See particularly remarks at Clarysse 1984b, 25.

46 The Heidelberger Gesamtverzeichnis (www.rzuser.uni-heidelberg.de/~gvo/gvz.html, accessed April 2010) shows over 2.8 times as many texts from first-century CE Egypt (4079) as from first-century BCE Egypt (1452); more than a quarter of the former group come from the Fayyum alone (1099, compared to 350 from the previous century), and 469 come from the Oxyrhynchite nome, compared to 68 from the previous century.

47 Bagnall 1977, with an appendix (77–82) listing all such texts then known.

48 Ibid., 77.

49 Bagnall 1977, 74. The Diospolite or Theban nome, or subprovince, was some 284 square kilometers; Bagnall 1993, 334.

50 See Bagnall and Frier 1994, 68, for the average village household of 3.43 for conjugal families, the most common type. Contrast Rathbone 1990, 130, who uses a multiplier of 3.1.

51 This description of Roman Jeme follows Wilfong 2002, 3–4.

52 Hölscher 1954, 36–38.

53 Hom. *Il.* 9.381–383.

54 "Une ville-musée"; Bataille 1951, 346.

55 Strabo, *Geography* 17.1.46.

56 Ibid.

57 See Bowersock 1984 for a survey of this literary evidence and a discussion of the colossus generally.

58 Bernand and Bernand 1960.

59 Ibid., 215–216.

60 Bowersock 1984, 24–25, 27.

61 Ibid., 31–32, proposes Zenobia and her son Vaballathus (ruled Egypt 269–274).

62 Rutherford 2003, 171.

63 Bataille 1951, 351.

64 Tait 1995 and De Haro Sanchez 2008.

65 Tait 1995, 174, citing Bataille 1938, Bataille 1951, and Geraci 1971, although noting that "there has been very little comment on this matter." Ritner 1998, 16, points out that the "last significant temple construction in Egypt" took place in the mid-second century, in the reign of Antoninus Pius. On temple building in the Roman era, see Minas-Nerpel 2012.

66 Heilporn 2008.

67 Bataille 1951, 337.

68 Bataille 1952, 296.

69 Łajtar 2006, 36–37.

70 Ibid., texts 112, 117, 118, 123.

71 Ibid., texts 199, 201.

72 Ibid., 82: Montu names are the most common; Montu's cult was highly popular on the west bank in this period.

73 Ibid., 83–85.

74 Ibid., 95, texts 157, 160–164, 166–169, 172–173.

75 Ibid., 96–99.

76 Riad 1968. But as Wagner wrote, by which criteria were the twenty-one chosen? El-Saghir et al. 1986, 101.

77 Wagner in El-Saghir et al. 1986; Bingen 1986.

78 Riad 1968, 283, no. 2, and 287, no. 10 = El-Saghir et al. 1986, 107, no. 15, and 109, no. 20.

79 Riad 1968, 288, no. 12.

80 For a brief introduction to the Feast of the Valley, see Graefe 1986.

81 On Theban-area funerary remains, see Dunand and Lichtenberg 1995, 3235–3237.

82 Bataille 1951, 346.

83 Montserrat and Meskell 1997, 187.

84 Riggs 2000, 139.

85 Ibid., 139–140.

86 The coffin is the British Museum, EA 6705.

87 Kákosy 1995, 63, and 32 for the hypothesis that the archive comes from the reused Nineteenth-Dynasty Theban tomb; Porter and Moss 1960, 49–50, plan on 44.

88 Reported in Bataille and Bruyère 1936 and Bataille and Bruyère 1938; see Dunand and Lichtenberg 1995 for a bibliography for the controversy regarding the family's date, and Montserrat and Meskell 1997, 188-192, for a detailed discussion of the family.

89 Montserrat and Meskell 1997, 189–190.

90 Riggs 2005, 226; Romano et al. 1979, 186, cat. no. 290, fig. 154 and pl. 15.

91 Although there "may have been another visit . . . by Diocletian later in his reign . . . this was the last securely attested visit by a Roman emperor to Egypt." Bowman 2005b, 316.

92 For Aurel. Reginus, see *PLRE* 1:762; Lacau 1934, 29–33, figs. 8–9; *AE* 1934, no. 9; El-Saghir et al. 1986, 11–12, 122; LSA 2625–2626. For Valerius Euethius 2, see *PLRE* 1:291; Lacau 1934, 33–35, fig. 12; *AE* 1934, no. 10; Riad 1968, 291–294, pl. IV, no. 22; LSA 2629, 2631. For Aurel. Maximinus 10, see *PLRE* 1:579; Lacau 1934, 20–29, figs. 3–4; *AE* 1934, nos. 7–8; El-Saghir et al. 1986, 11–12, 122; LSA 2621–2624.

93 Lacau 1934, 22; without emendation by Wagner in El-Saghir et al. 1986, 122.

94 Riad 1968, 292; El-Saghir et al. 1986, 122.

Chapter 2

1 For details on the archaeological investigations of the Roman remains at Luxor Temple, see Legrain 1917, Habachi 1951, and El-Saghir et al. 1986.

2 Contrast these with the more functional aspects of the Roman renovations, such as the fortification walls, gateways, and streets.

3 See Klotz 2012b, 378.

4 Breccia 1911, 50–51, no. 69.

5 Riad 1968, 294; el-Saghir et al. 1986, 121, no. 52, fig. 70.

6 Lesquier 1918, 200.

7 Redon 2009, 415–417, following the interpretation (Vandorpe 1995, 219) that the toponyme Ὠφιῆον (Ophieon) used in the ostraca refers specifically to Luxor Temple. Interestingly, recent excavations outside Karnak Temple have revealed a complex of Ptolemaic and Roman baths there (Boraik and El-Masekh, 2012; Boraik 2013) that may or may not be related.

8 Golvin 1981.

9 Klotz 2012b, 325.

10 On decline see Golvin 1981, 128; on continuity see Klotz 2012b, 326.

11 For a survey of primary sources related to the Tetrarchy see Rees 2004.

12 On the date of this revolt, see Barnes 1976a; Bowman 1978; Bowman 1984; Rea et al. 1985; Bowman 2005b. The uprising is not mentioned in the papyrological sources, but is briefly noted in Jerome, *Chron.* 226. In addition, a papyrus (*P. Oxy.* 43) from Oxyrhynchos, dated to 295, implies an imperial expedition to Egypt, perhaps the direct result of the revolt, consisting of several legions normally stationed in Moesia (*IV Flavia, VII Claudia,* and *XI Claudia*). Barnes (1976a, 181–182) and Bowman (1978, 27) note, however, that the text does not signal the presence of Galerius specifically but mentions only the "protector of the emperor(s)."

13 Euseb, *Hist eccl.* 8, 17, 3–5 reports the titles in Galerius's titulature only in 311. Barnes 1976a, 181–182.

14 El-Saghir et al. 1986, 120, no. 50, fig. 68; Speidel and Pavkovic 1989, 151–154.

15 *Not. Dig.* XXXI, 32; Ritt XII, 1356, 1452. It has been postulated that the Luxor camp was in fact designed to house two legions because of the unusual division of the grid plan by the pharaonic temple; El-Saghir et al. 1986, 23-24. This theory has also fed the notion that a second legion, the *legio I Maximiana* (named after Galerius Valerius Maximianus) was billeted alongside the *legio II Constantia* at Luxor (Speidel and Pavkovic 1989, 154), but there is no evidence at all to support this hypothesis.

16 Speidel and Pavkovic 1989, 154.

17 On the two Arches of Galerius in Thessaloniki, see Pond Rothman 1975 and 1977; Kleiner 1992, 418–425. For Galerius's building program in Gamzigrad, see Srejović 1993 and Srejović and Vasić 1993.

18 Or at least, as Barnes (1976a, 182) notes, not celebrated as an official victory over external enemies.

19 Eutr. 9.23. Reference to the rebellion is also made in *Pan. Lat.* 9.21.2. On the date of this revolt and the evidence for Diocletian's subsequent activities in Egypt, see Thomas 1976; Barnes 1976a and 1996; Bowman 2005b. An earlier date of 296 for this uprising was advanced by Schwartz (1975 and 1977), but this idea has been largely discarded.

20 On Diocletian's economic and administrative reforms and Egypt's reaction to them, see Adams 2004.

21 For example, *P. Oxy.* 1416; Proc. *Hist. Arc.* i.19.29; *P. Beatty Panop.* 1.53–59, 1.167–179, 1.221–224, 1.249–251, 1.264–271, 1.332–337.

22 Legrain 1917, 69–75, figs. 1 and 2; Legrain 1918, 241–260; Lacau 1934, 29–35, figs. 7–10; El-Saghir et al. 1986, 11–12, 20–21, 122, pls. XVIII–XIX; *AE* 1934, nos. 9–10; LSA 2625–2628.

23 On this second visit, see Bowman 1976, 160, and Barnes 1976a, 181. The evidence is not without issue. A slightly "confused compilation of evidence," as Bowman puts it (1976, 160), which goes under the name Barbarus Scaligeri, notes that Diocletian was in Egypt when Peter the Bishop was martyred (*Chronica Minora* I, 354). Procopius (Proc. *Hist. Arc.* 26.35) also refers to the fact that Diocletian organized a distribution of free corn in Alexandria, but when this happened is unclear. Finally, Diocletian issued a rescript concerning the Manichees from Alexandria on 31 March (*Mos. et Rom. Legum collatio* 15.3) that Barnes (1976a, 181) says can only have been in 302.

24 El-Saghir et al. 1986, 21.

25 Lacau 1934, 33–35, fig. 12; *AE* 1934, no. 10; Riad 1968, 291–294, pl. IV, no. 22; LSA 2629, 2631.

26 Lacau 1934, 20–29, figs. 3–4; *AE* 1934, nos. 7–8; El-Saghir et al. 1986, 11–12, 122; LSA 2621–2624.

27 For Valerius Rometalca, see PLRE I, 770. On the statue base in the Luxor Temple block yard, see Lacau 1934, 38–39, fig. 15, no. IV B; LSA 2630. For the lost statue base, see Lacau 1934, 40–42; CIL III, suppl. 2, 12050; Botti 1900, 255, no. 13; Breccia 1911, no. 91; LSA 1179. For the in situ statue base, see Lacau 1934, 35–48, no. IV A; CIL III, suppl. 2, 12073; LSA 1180.

28 Euseb. *Vit. Const.* 2.19.2; Barnes 1982, 24, 24n14.

29 Lacau 1934, 45. These inscriptions may in fact relate to an intended visit to Egypt by Constantine in the wake of his victory over Licinius (as attested by *P. Oxy.* 1261, 1626, according to Barnes 1982, 76n124). It is not known whether this visit actually took place.

30 The custom of obliterating disgraced rulers' names and images is not unique to the Roman era. Pharaonic practices, however, took several forms, and, though it is impossible to be sure of all the motives involved in the ancient Egyptian context, the destruction of names and images was not simply an expression of damnatio memoriae. Among the well-documented examples are the posthumous treatment of Hatshepsut's names and images, summarized by Dorman 2005, 267–269, Arnold 2005, 270–276, and Roth 2005, 277–281. On the removal of Hatshepsut, Akhenaten, and his immediate successors, together with some earlier rulers from the Ramesside ritual king lists and thus from the cycles of festivals and offerings, see Kitchen 1975, 178–179; 1993a, 153–156; 1993b, 119. On Psamtek II's replacement of Twenty-fifth-Dynasty kings' names with his own, see Yoyotte 1951, 215–239. Some elite tombs at Thebes were broken up in what seems to have been attacks aimed at their owners but often for unknown reasons; Säve Söderbergh 1957, 33–49 and pls. XXX–LXXI.

31 Lactantius (*Mort. Pers.* 42) reports that Constantine ordered statues of Maximian destroyed together with those of Diocletian, and the horror of seeing this disgrace caused Diocletian such grief that he promptly died.

32 Barnes 1973, 34–35; Barnes 1982, 33–34; Varner 2004, 214–215.

33 For example, RIC VII, 180, 252 (Trier), 310–311 (Arles), 395 (Rome), 429–430 (Aquileia), 503 (Siscia).

34 Euseb. *Hist. eccl.* 9.11.2. Very few portraits can be successfully attributed to Maximinus (Varner 2004, 220–221), which might attest to the success of the damnatio issued against him. An inscription from Tlos in Lycia with Maximinus's name chipped away at least indicates the wide geographical dissemination of these edicts of condemnation. See Barnes 1976b, 277–279.

35 Moormann 2011, 146, following Kolb 2001.

36 For the Tetrarchs enthroned on the Arch of Galerius, see Pond Rothman 1975.

37 This is perhaps suggested by the reconfiguration of a monument to the First Tetrarchy in front of the Temple of Hadrian at Ephesus. Three statue bases with inscriptions remain in situ, but the one that would have honored Maximian is missing and was replaced later by an inscription (and presumably a statue) honoring Theodosius. Kalavrezou-Maxeiner 1975, 247.

38 *P. Beatty Panop.* I (Skeat 1964); Fairley 1900, 18. For a concise discussion of the sources related to Diocletian's presence in the Thebaid, see Adams 2004.

39 Of the Latin inscriptions found at Luxor, only one makes reference to a legion, but in this case it is a legion associated with Galerius rather than Diocletian and may have been billeted in the vicinity of Luxor Temple in 293 (note 14, above). Unfortunately, the findspot of this inscription is unknown, so it is impossible to ascertain how it relates to the later Diocletianic renovations.

40 The west tetrastyle's dedicant is the *praeses* (governor) Aurelius Reginus (PLRE I, 762, Aurel. Reginus; Lallemand 1964, 250), whose dates of office are fixed by the latest date known for his predecessor, 30 January 300, and the earliest known for his successor, 305/306, Rea 1981, 282. The east tetrastyle instead is dedicated by the *dux* Aurelius Maximinus (PLRE I, 579, Aurel. Maximinus 10). This is one of the earliest known mentions of the title *dux*, a military office created during the tetrarchic reorganization of the province and one that illustrates a new principle of separating civilian and military authority in Egypt; Sidebotham et al. 1991, 571–622; Elton 2006, 193–205.

41 For a summary of what we know of the Theban region in late antiquity, see Łatjar 2012 and Vandorpe 1995.

42 Hom. *Il.* 9.381–383.

43 On the dynamics among temples, priests, pharaohs, and the cult of Amun in the New Kingdom, see Kemp 2006, 248–281.

44 Vandorpe 1995, 208; Łatjar 2012, 173.

45 Pausanias, *Description of Greece* 1.9.3.

46 Bagnall and Rathbone 2004, 185.

47 For a concise summary of the debate, see Dijkstra 2011. Dijkstra interestingly points out in particular the biases in the Christian literary evidence. These sources portray Egyptian temples as alive and powerful far into late antiquity so as to make all the more dramatic the narrative of Christianity's triumph over paganism, yet archaeological evidence attests to more practical and less ideological reasons for the abandonment of traditional cults. This more pragmatic approach to the question of when and how traditional cults were transformed in late antiquity is supported by the work of Roger Bagnall (see 1993, 2003, and 2008), who argues that the economic and administrative changes imposed on Egypt by Roman rule were the major factors in the late antique collapse of temple bureaucracies.

48 For a thorough treatment of the subject of the survival of vernacular cult practices in late antiquity, see Frankfurter 1998. The essays in Hahn et al. 2008 examine specifically the transformative effects of Christianity on local cults.

49 For example, see Dijkstra 2011, 403. It is not unusual to see the employment of this standard explanation for the Roman modifications to Luxor Temple in essays like this one that are otherwise nuanced and sophisticated examinations of the evidence attesting to the transformation of temples in late antique Egypt.

50 On Tell el-Herr (Magdolum), see Valbelle and Correz-Maratray 2000; on Qasr Qarun (Dionysias), see Schwartz and Wild 1950, Carrié 1974; on Babylon, see Sheehan 2010; on Nag el-Hagar, see Wareth and Pierre 1992, Mackensen 2009; and on Abu Shaar, see Sidebotham 1994. For the recently recorded fort at Qaret el-Tub in Bahariyah Oasis, see Charlier et al. 2012.

51 Reddé 2004 gives an overview of these sacella (also called *aedes principiorum*) in Egypt.

52 See Liversidge 1983, for example, for surveys of wall paintings from military sites in Roman Britain. Of course, the elaborateness of the Luxor decorative program may seem unique today simply because of the accident of their survival. We cannot assume that nothing comparable ever existed, but this does not discount the distinctiveness of the Luxor paintings in their specific geographical and historical context.

53 On *signa* and the cult of the standards, see Ando 2000, 259–269.

54 In contrast to the architecturally hybridized ceremonial space of the imperial cult chamber at Luxor Temple, at Nag al-Hagar, for example, recent excavations have brought to light the functional sectors of the camp, which are purely Roman in form, such as the administrative headquarters (*principia*) of the fort and an impressive complex interpreted as a palace (*palatium*) that might have been constructed for Diocletian's visit to Upper Egypt in 298 and thereafter used by the provincial governor (*praeses*) or the military commander (*dux*) of the Thebaid; Mackensen 2009, 309. Mackensen notes that a regimental shrine would probably have been in the area of the principia, though it is of far humbler scale than its counterpart at Luxor.

55 Bell 1985, 280.

56 Abd el-Raziq 1984.

57 Bagnall 1993, 268.

58 For further technical specifications, see El-Saghir et al. 1986, 5–19.

59 For a comprehensive study of four-columned honorific monuments in the Roman East and North Africa, see Thiel 2002 and 2006.

60 Bailey 1996, 161–165.

61 Thiel 2006, 277–286.

62 It does not take eight years to build a fortification wall such as the one at Luxor, as noted, for example, in El-Saghir et al. 1986, 21.

63 The same can be said about the Latin inscriptions attesting continued patronage of the site in the form of dedicatory statues; see notes 25–27, above.

64 Surveys of Greco-Roman architecture in Egypt include Bailey 1990 and 2012; McKenzie 2007.

65 For a bibliography on the debate about whether the streets with the tetrastyles at Luxor were also colonnaded, see Wareth and Pierre 1992, 195n47.

66 MacDonald 1986, 5.

67 For example, there were colonnaded avenues leading to the shrines of the military standards at Qasr Qarun (Dionysias), Tell el-Herr (Magdolum), and Abu Shaar. For a bibliography, see note 50, above.

68 Building in the classical style in Egypt was not a new trend in the Roman period; under the Ptolemies many Egyptian cities were elaborated with buildings distinctive to a Greek way of life. But the Ptolemies and later the Romans in the early imperial period also patronized architecture in the Egyptian style at the same time. Roman patronage of Egyptian-style architecture, on the other hand, seems to have slowed considerably starting in the second century CE. McKenzie 2007, 171.

69 For an overview, see ibid., 151–165. On Oxyrhynchos, see the recent collection of essays in Bowman 2007. On Antinoopolis, see Pintaudi 2008. Note also that excavations at the site have recently begun anew under the auspices of the Antinoopolis Foundation; www.antinoupolis.org.

70 The name "City of Hermes" comes from the city's ancient association with the Egyptian god Thoth, with whom Hermes was conflated in the Greco-Roman period. For the British Museum excavations conducted there between 1980 and 1990, see Bailey 1991.

71 These buildings are mentioned as being "repaired at great cost" in the papyrological archives of the town council from 263/264. Alston 2002, 240; Bailey 2012, 196.

72 Bailey 2012, 193–194. Evidence suggests that the Komasterion was in use until the fourth century, at which time Christianity probably made the building redundant.

73 Bailey 2012, 198.

74 On the possibility that the Romans created a new processional way specifically for the Amun cult, see chapt. 3.

75 Split into two zones during the Ptolemaic period, Thebes was divided into more than six in the Roman period; Bagnall and Rathbone 2004, 188.

76 The name "City of Zeus" derives from the New Kingdom "City of Amun," thus attesting to the association of the highest god in the Greco-Roman pantheon with his pharaonic counterpart; Vandorpe 1995, 218.

77 Vandorpe 1995, 220; Łatjar 2012, 179.

78 For an introduction to the topic of social memory, see Fentress and Wickham 1992 and Connerton 1989. For the material manifestations of memory, see Alcock 2001 and 2002.

79 Alcock 2002, 51–73.

80 Ibid., 2.

81 On Pausanias, see Alcock et al. 2001 and Elsner and Rutherford 2005.

82 For Diocletian's camp at Palmyra in general, see Gawlikowski 1984; on the Temple of Allat in particular, see Gawlikowski 2006 and 2008.

83 Gawlikowski 2006, 532–533.

84 For the use of the term *memory politics,* see Alcock 2002, 17.

Chapter 3

1 For Diocletianic forts outside Egypt, see Gregory 1995–1997. For a bibliography on Egyptian comparanda, see chapt. 2, note 50. For information regarding the dimensions of Luxor Temple, we have relied on the architectural drawings in Hanen 1991, plan version no. 1.

2 A more complete explanation of James Heidel's drawings and architectural reconstruction of tetrarchic Roman Luxor Temple will appear in the forthcoming Oriental Institute of the University of Chicago's epigraphic publication of the Luxor Temple imperial cult chamber.

3 Lacau 1934, plan I.

4 For a discussion of previous scholarship concerning this chamber that includes evidence supporting the reconstructions described and depicted in this chapter, see Tőrők 2005, 139–152. See also Gregory 1995–1997, vol. 3, fig. E1.7, a–d, for reconstruction drawings of the *principia* at Palmyra by Gawlikowski. This reconstruction of the contemporaneous Palmyra *principia* features many elements found in the reconstruction drawings in this chapter.

5 Features of the reconstruction discussed in the text are noted with a number in parentheses, e.g., "(01)." This same number will locate the feature for the reader in all the drawings where it appears.

6 See van Siclen 1990. Granite paving stones from the dismantled porch can still be seen in front of the Ramesses II pylons.

7 See Arnold 1991, 183–210 esp. 200–201, *True Stone Vaults.*

8 See El-Saghir et al. 1986, fig. 32, for the capital. Personal observation by the authors for the column shafts.

9 On second- and third-century Corinthian capitals in Egypt, see McKenzie 2007, 223–228.

10 Cf. the roughly contemporary Basilica of Constantine at Trier, Germany, ca. 310 CE. Its wooden-truss roof was almost exactly coeval with the roof of the imperial cult chamber at Luxor Temple, spanned twenty-six meters, and was intact before it was destroyed during World War II.

11 Cf. the clerestory in the Flavian Palace triclinium, as reconstructed by Gibson et al. 1994.

12 See Wilson Jones 2000, 45–46, for a concise discussion of Vitruvius's basilica. Vitruvius never mentions coffering in the basilica he designed and built, but this does not necessarily mean that it was not present.

13 Thanks to Michael Jones for the reference to St. Catherine's Monastery.

14 During the Oriental Institute's work in the Luxor Temple block yard in the late 1970s, at least two large, wadded-up sheets of ancient lead were noted in the block yard; personal observation by Ray Johnson. See Forsyth and Weitzman 1973, 8, for dating St. Catherine's roof; for photographs of the trusses and wood decking from inside the attic, ibid., pl. LXXXII and LXXXIII; for photos of the lead apse roof from the exterior, ibid., pl. XXXV, and Galey 1980, fig. 13. Also see Galey 1980, fig. 112, for an eighteenth- or nineteenth-century painting showing the lead roof; and for a discussion of the roof assembly, Galey 1980, 187n7.

15 A "foot graffito" is an incised outline of the foot or sandal of a worshipper, with or without an accompanying inscription, found on the roofs of Egyptian stone temples. These private, unofficial gestures are votive offerings left by priests and laity; they are often the only extant monument of these lower-status individuals; see Jacquet-Gordon 2003.

16 Such a light-well cutout, with the wider end of the "funnel" at the top, was a typical means for lighting the interior spaces of pharaonic stone temples.

17 It is possible that the doors were covered with bronze sheets like those in the Pantheon in Rome and two chapels in St. Catherine's Monastery; Forsyth and Weitzman 1973, pls. XCIV and XCV. In stone temples of the New Kingdom, temple doors might be single or double leaf, but the doorway here (15) had two door leaves in its Amenhotep III incarnation; both jambs were repaired by the tetrarchic Romans, which indicates that both jambs had fractured from heat caused by earlier burning of the original wood doors.

18 Perhaps the Twenty-fifth Dynasty.

19 Cf. the central axis beneath the portico of the Pantheon in Rome; MacDonald 1976, fig. 3.

20 By several, including Golvin in El-Saghir et al., 1986, 16. The two platforms Golvin shows west of the central axis are no longer there.

21 Sandstone was used for the monumental column drums of the two Luxor Temple tetrastyles, east and west.

22 For bibliography on this issue see chapt. 2, notes 47 and 48, and Tőrők 2005, 146.

23 Barguet 1980, 1103.

24 According to the Egyptian sense of cyclical time and annual renewal, the sun god grows old and must be reborn annually, assisted by the king, who reenacts his coronation at the conclusion of the rites. See Holland and Urban 1994, preface; also Klotz 2012b, 386; Bell 1985.

25 Arnold 1999, 143–273.

26 For the Greek association of Zeus with Amun/Ammon, see Herodotus, *The Histories,* book 2, particularly 42.4–5; also Peacock 2000, 437–438.

27 Later the Supreme Council of Antiquities (SCA), and now the Ministry of State for Antiquities (MSA).

28 El-Saghir 1991, 2–20.

29 Figure 3.14 is based on personal observations by Ray Johnson, in addition to published and unpublished photographs from the time of the discovery.

30 El-Saghir 1991, 21–27. Luxor Museum 838;

31 El-Saghir 1991, 31–34. Luxor Museum 836. Iwnet was a goddess of nearby Armant.

32 El-Saghir 1991, 28–31. Luxor Museum 835.

33 El-Saghir 1991, 35–40. Luxor Museum 837.

34 Personal observation by Ray Johnson.

35 Johnson 1998. This statue represents the king as the creator god Atum; it is in his fourth-decade "deification style."

36 El-Saghir 1991, 58–61. Luxor Museum 833. The dyad is late Eighteenth Dynasty in date, from the reign of either Tutankhamun or Ay; see Holland and Urban 1998, 72–73, pl. 222.

37 El-Saghir 1991, 18–20 and fig. 38. Deposits of buried sculpture are a common phenomenon in Egypt and throughout the Roman world. For a review of Egyptian and Nubian deposits, see Bonnet and Valbelle 2006, 172–182.

38 El-Saghir 1991, 4, fig. 3, top.

39 Reddé in el-Saghir et al. 1986, 81, no. 8.

40 For the Amenhotep III and Ramesses III–inscribed blocks from the sanctuary shrines reused in the southern gates, particularly the east gate, see Reddé in El-Saghir et al. 1986, 74–84.

41 Jorgensen 1998, 94–95. The statue was acquired by the museum at the sale of the Sabatier Collection in 1890. Cf. Legrain 1890, 1 (no. 1); personal communication from Tine Bagh, Carlsberg Scholar, Egyptian Art Department, Ny Carlsberg Glyptotek. Sabatier was the French consul-general in Egypt from 1852 and was allowed to excavate by the

viceroy, so he might actually have uncovered the sculptures himself during excavations. Personal communication from Kim Ryholt at the University of Copenhagen.

42 Our thanks to Christian Greco for this reference. See Legrain 1914, 9–13, and Tőrők 2005, 147; also El-Saghir et al. 1986, 21–23.

43 "For the second time" may indicate that he was appointed as doctor of the cohort for a second period of service, but Wagner has his doubts about this. Thanks to Christian Greco for the reference, and for his translation here; see Wagner in El-Saghir et al. 1986, 115, no. 37; also Tőrők 2005, 147. For a facsimile drawing of the graffito, see Holland and Urban 1998, pl. 209.

44 The first-century historian Strabo mentions an earthquake around 27 BCE that probably brought down the colonnade hall roof as well as the hypostyle hall roof at Karnak, necessitating the repair of both halls as well as the northern Memnon Colossus that was possibly restored by Septimius Severus; see Strabo, *Geography*, 17.1.46; also Golvin 1987, for Roman restorations to the hypostyle hall at Karnak. For Egyptian earthquakes, see also Mazza 1998.

45 The church beneath the Abu al-Hajjaj Mosque in the northeastern quadrant was identified in 1960; see Muhammed 1968, 260–261, pls. LXVI–LXXVI. Note the niche pictured in pl. LXX, found inside the southern wall of the church. Talatat quarried in the medieval period from the same pylons was excavated by IFAO at Medamud in the Christian levels; see Cottevieille-Giraudet 1936. There is no evidence for the use of Karnak Temple as a quarry until after the time of the Tetrarchy. A block published by Reddé as a talatat fragment built into the east gate was misidentified by him; Reddé in el-Saghir et al. 1986, 79, no. 26.

46 Clearing in the 1980s, personal observation by Ray Johnson. Daressy 1920, 170–171.

47 El-Saghir et al. 1986, 25–31, figs. 21 and 23.

48 The original stone roof had partly collapsed by the time of the Tetrarchy, and repairs appear to have been constructed of brick and wood. See Dorman 1994, pls. 129 (view from west) and 197 (bottom), for the arcs cut through the Tutankhamun/Horemheb architrave inscription when the vaulting was repaired.

49 The reduced size of the doorway may have been intended to limit access to the imperial part of the complex for security reasons.

50 For a discussion of the history of this chamber and the conversion of the false door at its southern end to a doorway and then back to a solid wall, see Murnane 1985, 137–148, including an elevation drawing of the Greek-style doorframe, 139, fig. 1. Note should be made that the doorway between the barque sanctuary and the barque sanctuary antechamber was not blocked in the Roman period, contra Murnane 1985, 145–146 (also fig. 3 on 147), who misinterpreted remarks of Daressy 1893, 7. There is no evidence that the doorway was ever blocked.

51 Modifications such as the rebuilt entryway and colonnaded approach are more appropriate for a cult place than for storerooms.

52 Personal observation by James Heidel.

53 See Darnell 2010. See also Bell 1985, 289–290; and Murnane 1999.

54 Hallof 2011.

55 Personal communication from the excavators, Mansour Boraik and Salah El-Masekh. Boraik and El-Masekh 2012; Boraik 2013.

56 Boraik 2010.

57 See Azim 1980. The removal of the obelisks is firmly dated by coins.

58 Van Siclen 2005. The villa is dated by Constantine-period coins and ceramics, and therefore the building itself may predate the reign of Constantine. David Klotz believes that both Luxor and Karnak temples continued to function as active Amun cult places during the Tetrarchy, noting that when Constantine removed the two obelisks from Karnak, the walls to the south that were demolished to move the obelisks to the river were never rebuilt. This, he suggests, marks the waning power of the priesthood but not the cessation of the cult. Klotz 2008, 543–554; Klotz 2012b, 379–380. See also Tőrők 2005, 146–147.

59 Klotz 2008, 554.

60 The second, ninth, and tenth pylons were quarried for the small-sized Akhenaten-period talatat blocks that had been reused by Pharaoh Horemheb as interior fill. These blocks occur in reuse contexts in Christian Byzantine occupation levels from as far north as Medamud, the settlement area around Luxor Temple, and southward to Tod. All texts on the Akhenaten talatat blocks refer to Akhenaten's Karnak structures.

61 The head of Jupiter and the nimbus-framed heads of the emperors and their Caesars were attacked in later antiquity, but within the painted outlines, which left a silhouette.

62 Bell 1985, 274.

63 Tőrők 2005, 146.

Chapter 4

1 Ten months after the invention of photography was announced in 1839, Horace Vernet and Frédéric Goupil-Fesquet began making daguerreotypes in Egypt. They were followed by Pierre Gustave Joly de Lotbinière and Joseph-Philibert Girault de Prangey into the 1840s: Vaczek and Buckland 1981, 35; Lyons et al. 2005, 9.

2 Urry 2002, 129–130; Schwartz and Ryan 2003, 1–9; Gregory 2003, 195–225.

3 Merewether 1997, 25–26. Numerous publications document nineteenth-century photography in Egypt, the motivations of photographers, and the reception of their work, and many Internet resources display their images. See, generally, Howe 1993; Osman 1997a and 1997b; Lyons et al. 2005; Nassar et al. 2010. On particular photographers and their work see Du Camp 1852, nos. 43–49; Howe 1992 (Félix Teynard); Nichol 2004 (Francis Frith); Osman 1997b, 6–11 (Robert Murray); Busi and Piacentini 2008 (Antonio Beato).

4 For Sheikh Yussef Abu al-Hajjaj al-Uqsuri, his mulid, and possible connections with the Opet Festival, see Wicket 2009.

5 Grossmann 1973, Abb. 1, 172n41, 179–180, and Taf. LXXV b; Grossmann 2002a, 35, 454.

6 The first detailed description of Luxor Temple dates from the visit of two French Capuchin monks in 1668; Sauneron 1983, 137–138. Claude Sicard explicitly identified the ruins at Karnak and Luxor as ancient Thebes and describes the ruins at Luxor ca. 1720–1721; Sicard 1982a, 138–140; 1982b, 228; 1982c, 148–157.

7 Pococke 1743, 1:106–109, pl. XL; Norden 1757, 2:43–46, pls. CII, CIII, CIV, and CV. Norden was in Luxor 11–13 December 1737. Pococke sailed from Karnak to Luxor on 17 January 1738. As the Gregorian calendar was not adopted in Britain until 1752, both accounts use Julian calendar dates; Pococke 1743, 13. Norden's sketch plan of Luxor Temple dated 4 February 1738 was completed after his departure; Buhl 1993, 103, 112.

8 Buhl 1993, 103–114, pls. 62, 63, 64, 65r, 65v, 66, 67r, 67v, 68r, 69r, and 70.

9 Norden 1757, 2:pl. CIV.

10 Description 1812, pls. 1, 5, and 9.

11 Pococke 1743, 1:pl. XL; Description, pls. 6–9. Some localized excavation provided information for these reconstructions, as shown in pl. 13 in Description 1812 of the colossi before the Ramesses II pylon.

12 Pococke 1743, 1:108–109.

13 Description 1812, pls. 1–4. Also compare Denon 1990, pls. 49.2, 47 (lower), and 48 (lower).

14 The granite columns with capitals stand 5.40 meters above the present floor level, the arch of the niche is 7.07 meters above the floor, and the preserved height of the wall above the niche is 8.67 meters.

15 Jacobi and Conti 1998, 47.

16 Nestor L'Hôte (in Luxor 1828–1830) based his plan on the Napoleonic map; http://gallica.bnf.fr/ark:/12148/btv1b55000580w/f10.item (accessed 12 October 2014).

17 See Jasanoff 2006, 241–306, esp. 293–296, for the dispute, tinged with nationalism, between Joseph Bonomi and Jean-François Champollion over French appropriation of the Luxor obelisk and detachment of reliefs in the tomb of Sety I in the Valley of the Kings. Hay wrote to the Keeper of Antiquities at the British Museum in 1836: "I do earnestly beg to call your attention to a love he [d'Athanasi] acquired under Mr. Salt for destroying Tombs under a false idea of preserving them, by attempting to cut the paintings off the Walls"; quoted in Usick and Parkinson 2008, 10.

18 Thompson 2010, 158–176.

19 Lane 2000, 296–303, figs. 76–78.

20 Lane 2000, 302.

21 Robert Hay was in Luxor 1824–1828 and 1829–1834.

22 British Library Additional Manuscript 29,827: Robert Hay, Egyptian Collection, vol. 16, Thebes, Luxor, 4 verso.

23 Hay's sketches of Luxor and the temple (ibid., 17–21, 24, 30) include several from the Nile (west) side showing the French ship *Le Luxor,* sent to transport the western obelisk. The low level of the Nile indicates early summer. The obelisk had been loaded aboard on 25 December 1831, and the ship remained at Luxor until it could be floated off on high water on 25 August 1832. Lebas 1839, 89–90, 144.

24 The origin of the yellow wash is not confirmed. A photograph by Wilhelm Hammerschmidt, active in Egypt in the 1860s and 1870s, shows white paint on the upper parts of all the columns of the Amenhotep III portico facing the imperial cult chamber. This is now yellow and possibly corresponds to the similar surface in the imperial cult chamber.

25 Lepsius 1849, 1:pl. 84.

26 General George de Sausmarez (1814–1890). The watercolor, reproduced here by permission, © V&A Images/Victoria and Albert Museum, London, SD 912 21, is part of the Searight Collection in the Victoria and Albert Museum. Thanks to Helen Whitehouse for first pointing out this watercolor. See Whitehouse 2010, 1010–1011, and Lloyd 2010, pl. 27.

27 Wilkinson 1835, 169.

28 I have interpreted "i[?]ptions," unclear in Wilkinson's handwriting, as an abbreviated i[nscri]ptions. Monneret de Villard read "sculptures" (Monneret de Villard 1953, 90), contra Wilkinson's note that "chariot wheels" bearing the emperor's name were in the frescoes.

29 Victor Gustave Maunier (d. 1874), also known as V. Galli Maunier, resided in Luxor 1840–1865; Bierbrier 2012, 363.

30 Brugsch 1992, 190–192.

31 Le Guen 2001, 19; "La photographie en Égypte: Travaux de M. Maunier," *La Lumière,* 1 April 1854, 50.

32 Wilkinson 1835, 169.

33 Prime 1857, 215.

34 Removal of Roman plaster layers later in the nineteenth century is discussed below.

35 Thompson 1992a, 199.

36 Wilkinson 1835, 169.

37 Monneret de Villard 1953.

38 Thompson 1992a, 199–202.

39 Murray 1873, 438–439.

40 Ebers 1879, 269; Von Bissing 1926, 181.

41 Coptic inscriptions are rare in Luxor Temple. An example recording a date is on the facade of the Amenhotep III and Tutankhamun colonnade hall; Dorman 1994, 19, 21, fig. 6.

42 By the Coptic calendar, "Era of Martyrs" (*Anno Martyrum*; AM) or "Diocletian Era," starts in Diocletian's accession year, 284 CE; Blackburn and Holford-Strevens 2003, 767. The Red Monastery graffito is number NEB.s.i-1 in Dilley's catalogue of inscriptions at the Red Monastery. Thanks to Paul Dilley for helpful suggestions on this graffito and comments on Wilkinson's report of the name of Diocletian.

43 See "John Beasly Greene," www.getty.edu/art/gettyguide/artMakerDetails?maker=1877&page=1 (accessed 29 January 2012). Ninety-four of Greene's images were published in Blanquart-Evrard 1854.

44 By midcentury the temple was filling up with houses and pigeon towers. Florence Nightingale's letter dated 19 February 1850 is typical and explains the apparent reticence to venture among the ruins: "We have been anchored for three weeks within a hundred yards of Luxor; and I have been up to the temple but once, it is such an odious place." The same letter describes her visit to the barque shrine of Alexander the Great and the "Divine Birth" rooms east of it, but it omits the imperial cult chamber; Nightingale 1987, 144. The Reverend Samuel Manning gives another graphic description that hints at the Victorian visitor's desired experience of ruined temples. On Luxor Temple: "the effect is grotesque, and detracts sorely from their impressiveness. The silence and sense of loneliness, which elsewhere give such a weird solemnity to the ruins, are here dispelled by the miserable hovels which cluster round the stately columns, and the swarms of beggars clamorously demanding backsheesh"; Manning 1887, 118–119.

45 Both images are in the collection of the Musée d'Orsay, Paris; reproduced here by permission. The east wall: "Peintures romaines à Luqsor. T. Devéria phot. 1859." (PHO 1986 131 262) négatif papier, Paris, Musée d'Orsay. The niche: "Louxor" (PHO 1986 131 266) négatif papier, Paris, Musée d'Orsay. Although undated, the negative of the niche was almost certainly taken at the same time.

46 The French House was a nineteenth-century Luxor landmark, but in a letter dated 20 December 1867 Lucie Duff Gordon records its partial collapse some nine days previously; Duff Gordon 1983, 371–372. Amelia Edwards remarked in 1874 that it was ruined and partly inaccessible; Edwards 1891, 451, 454, and notes 44 and 45. The house was removed in 1885.

47 Wilson 1883, 209.

48 Bernhard Fiedler (1816–1904) was an Austrian Orientalist painter. The engraving was reproduced in Ebers 1879, 265, and Rappoport 1903, 237.

49 A photograph sold by d.raines on eBay (http://www.ebay.com/itm/Egypt-Luxor-Temple-Ruin-1870-s-large-albumen-/201149095293) on 17 August 2014 shows the unexcavated archaeological deposits filling the portico of Amenhotep III, the nineteenth-century houses built on the mounds between the columns, and, most significantly, the north wall of the imperial cult chamber with the plaster preserving the painted feet recorded by Wilkinson in January 1856. Though undated, the photograph must predate the clearing work that started in 1885 and was probably made soon after the excavation of the imperial cult chamber around 1860–1870.

50 Daressy 1893, VIII; Lane 2000, 302.

51 Edwards 1891, 141.

52 Lowenthal 1998.

53 See Poole 1882, 47–48, for a contemporary comment.

54 Daressy 1893, V.

55 In 1884 the *Journal des Débats* and the *Times* of London launched a subscription, raising 19,000 francs for sequestration of houses and land; Kozloff and Bryan 1992, 17, figs. 1.4, 1. 5. To boost the available budget, a tax of one Egyptian pound was levied in 1887 on every visitor to ancient monuments: Grébaut 1890, 331. After the houses had been demolished, "the place was handed over to the *sebakhin* who went down many meters to the base of the mounds." Grébaut 1890, 328. On sebakh and sebakhin, see Bailey 1999.

56 Daressy 1894, 49, CV.

57 Daressy 1893, VIII. Documented flooding in the Theban temples has a long history. On seasonal flooding at Karnak in the ninth and eighth centuries BCE, see von Beckerath 1966. A hieratic text at Luxor dated Year 3 of Osorkon III records flooding in the Theban temples; Porter and Moss 1972, 317 (98), and Ritner 2009, 415–421. On flooding at Luxor under Tiberius, see Habachi 1975, 249–251. On Ptolemaic relief blocks reused in the quayside wall at Luxor, see Legrain 1918, 253. Groundwater and salts remain alarming today.

58 This restructuring of Luxor and its surroundings has continued to the present day; there are direct consequences for the people and for the conservation and preservation of the ancient heritage in their midst; Meskell 2003, 149–153; Van der Spek 2011, 35–38, citing Mitchell 1998 and 2001; Abu-Lughod 1998, 162; Gamblin 2004. On the recent project to demolish sections of Luxor to expose buried remains, see Abraham and Bakr 1999. On salvage archaeological work carried out in response to proposed destruction of sites beside Luxor Temple, see Kamal and Tavares 2010, 5–9.

59 Weigall 1907, 113–115. The clearance history in and around the temple from 1881 to 1960 is summarized and referenced in El-Saghir et al. 1986, 3–4.

60 Grébaut 1890, 329–330.

61 See remarks in Daressy 1893, IV. A plan produced for the Ministry of Public Works and published in 1887 seems to show the imperial cult chamber before the excavation of the eastern and western side rooms. Grand Bey 1888, pl. VIII.

62 Grébaut 1890, 334.

63 Daressy 1893, 59.

64 Legrain 1917, 54; Daressy 1920, 163.

65 Daressy 1920, 163.

66 Père Michel Jullien (1827–1911) was a Jesuit priest and the founder of the Collège de la Sainte Famille in Cairo; Mayeur-Jaouen 1992.

67 Munier 1940, 163; Mayeur-Jaouen 1992, 237.

68 Georg 1930, 26. But Wilkinson had long since affirmed that "the colours are much damaged by exposure, and the frescoes can hardly be distinguished"; Murray 1873, 438.

69 Gayet 1894, 55–56; Monneret de Villard 1953, 90.

70 William Prime may have been alluding to plaster removal soon after the imperial cult chamber was first excavated in 1853–1854. Rees's comment, 2004, 46, referencing Kalavrezou-Maxeiner 1975, that Wilkinson removed Roman plaster is implausible.

71 Baedeker 1892, 114–115.

72 Murray 1907, 390; Murray 1931. The Christian interpretation persisted long after it had been refuted; Porter and Moss 1972, 320; Buhl 1993, 104.

73 Clarke 1912, 190.

74 Legrain 1917, 248. Legrain, however, had recently published a photograph of the imperial cult chamber captioned "Partie romaine du temple de Louqsor"; Legrain 1914, pl. I.

75 Daressy 1920, 162–163.

76 Von Bissing 1926, 181–188; Georg 1930, 26–28.

77 For Apa Jeremias, see Quibell 1909, pls. VIII–XIII, 1; Quibell 1912, pls. V, VII, XII, XXII–XXVI. For Bawit, see Clédat 1904, vols. 1 and 2; Clédat 1916, vol. 2, pt. 1; Bénazeth and Rutschowscaya 1999.

78 Doxiadis 1995; Corcoran 1995.

79 Von Bissing 1926, 186.

80 Raulwing and Gertzen 2013, 101.

81 Lacau 1934, 45–46.

82 Stevenson Smith 1952, 43.

83 Daressy 1920, 162–163.

84 Epigraphic Survey, Luxor, Chevrier Archive *98524/256*47.

85 Leclant 1951, 456–457.

86 Ibid., 457; Leclant 1965, Texte 137–139 (with bibliography) and pl. LXXX; Deckers 1979, 611, abb. 5, and 616, abb. 10. Leclant suggested that the Shabako kiosk originally stood before the Ramesses II pylon at Luxor, like the Kushite kiosks at Karnak in front of the Montu Temple and the eastern approach to the temple of Amun-Ra. See also van Siclen 1990. The column drums are now displayed in the open-air museum east of the barque shrine room of the temple. Other blocks naming Shabako were reused in the gateways of the tetrarchic enclosure, together with others, from New Kingdom to Ptolemaic-period monuments; El-Saghir et al. 1986, 37–98 and figs. 36–40.

87 Leclant 1951, pls. XLVIII and XLIX, fig. 7; Leclant 1965, pl. LXXX.

88 Leclant 1951, 456: "the pavement was roughly arranged with a filling of earth."

89 Deckers 1979, 611, abb. 5, and 616, abb. 10. A Corinthian capital and a granite column fragment of the same design and proportions as those still in situ in the imperial cult chamber were found west of the Amenhotep III and Tutankhamun colonnade, which suggests possible reuse of the second pair in a later church here. See El-Saghir et al. 1986, 29n2 and fig. 32, for the capital. On the churches west of the temple, see Grossmann 2002a, 34–35, pl. 71, and Grossmann 1973, 167-181 and pls. LXXIII–LXXVa.

90 Thanks to W. Raymond Johnson for sharing his own photographs of this excavation.

91 The doorway was made during "improvements" supervised by Labib Habachi; personal communication from Lanny Bell.

92 Thanks to W. Raymond Johnson for his insights into these two reused Eighteenth-Dynasty blocks and to James Heidel, who recognized their provenance in the niche.

93 Nanda 2001, 71.

94 El-Saghir et al. 1986, 17, mistakenly suggests a premodern alteration: "in a second phase, probably post-military, a door was cut through the bottom of the niche."

95 Monneret de Villard 1953.

96 Ibid., 94–95.

97 Ibid., pl. XXVIIIa and XXIXa. See also Legrain 1914, pl. I, for the steps at the beginning of the twentieth century.

98 Monneret de Villard 1953, 90.

99 Ebers 1879, 269.

100 Dorigo 1971, 282.

101 Deckers 1973; Deckers 1979; Kalavrezou-Maxeiner 1975.

102 Meyer-Graft 1979.

103 Ibid., 620.

104 For example, Ebers 1879, 269; Daressy 1893, 59.

105 Thomas 2010, 1040–1042.

106 Since Deckers's and Kalavrezou-Maxeiner's publications, numerous works on Roman Egypt have addressed the imperial cult chamber and its frescoes; the most recent and in depth is McFadden 2007, 98–176.

107 Legrain 1914, pl. I.

108 Census figures for Luxor were 126,160 inhabitants in 1986, 153,758 in 1996, and 202,232 in 2006; http://www.citypopulation.de/php/egypt-admin.php?adm1id=29 (accessed 13 October 2014).

109 Rashed 1994 discusses the preservation of the historical environment of Luxor and attitudes to public participation, ownership, and responsibility for action in one of the first comprehensive studies of heritage management issues at Luxor. Much of it remains relevant today, after twenty years.

110 Groundwater investigations have produced several studies: Ismail 2003; Ismail et al. 2005; Ahmed 2009. In 2006 a groundwater-lowering project was initiated at Luxor Temple, funded by the United States Agency for International Development (USAID), designed and managed by Sweco ("About Sweco," www.swecogroup.com/Sweco-group/About-Sweco/ [accessed 4 August 2012]), and implemented by the National Organization for Potable Water and Sanitary Drainage (NOPWASD). Following engineering works, ARCE conducted a program monitoring the effects of this project on standing architectural remains and a training project for SCA conservators. Atmospheric conditions have been studied but not yet addressed. For an atmospheric pollution survey by the Egyptian Environmental Affairs Agency (EEAA) in 2005, see "Air Pollution," www.eeaa.gov.eg/english/reports/SOE2006En/1-air/01-air%20pollution/01-air%20pollution.pdf (accessed 4 August 2012).

111 Brandi 2005, 55: "If a work of art is not seen as a *whole,* it must be considered as a sum of its parts."

Chapter 5

1 The team for the preliminary season was Luigi De Cesaris, Alberto Sucato, and Maria Cristina Tomassetti. The team of conservators over the four-year period was Olivia Mosso, Cristina Caldi, Riccardo Remigio, Federico Ratti, Francesca Gheraldi, Alessandra Zampa, and Pilar Grazioli.

2 The two large vertical breaks clearly visible in the niche mark the junction of the Roman stonework with the preexisting masonry.

3 El-Saghir et al. 1986.

4 The term *pontata* is used to define an area of fresco painting that usually corresponds to the area available from the scaffold floor and can be recognized in horizontal joints in the intonaco plaster.

5 Poggi 2007. See also the scientific analyses below. We would like to extend our thanks to the geologist Dr. Poggi for his invaluable contribution to the project and for bringing his equipment to Egypt to analyze microsamples in situ.

6 Mora et al. 1999, 122.

7 This is demonstrated by the numerous drips of black and red on the second layer of plaster, visible where the third layer has fallen away. These must have dropped from above when the frescoes, or at least their upper frames, were being painted. The black stripe that separates the opus sectile patterns from the upper bands of decoration was painted once on the second layer of plaster and repainted and completed on the third.

8 This technique would explain why the Romans did not chisel off the pharaonic reliefs before applying the arricco but, rather, kept them, knowing that they would help promote a good bond between the plaster and the substrate.

9 Poggi 2007. See also the section headed "Scientific Investigations and Analyses," below.

10 *Egyptian blue* and *blue frit* are terms for a synthetic pigment, a calcium-copper-tetrasilicate known as cuprorivaite ($CaCuSi_4O_{10}$), used in Egypt from the Fourth Dynasty through the Roman period. In the Roman period it was sometimes mixed with other pigments, such as green earth, or "green frit," to produce other hues. Green frit, also called Egyptian green, is composed of similar materials in slightly different proportions, producing cupro-wollastonite ($[Ca,Cu]_3Si_3O_9$). See García-Moreno et al. 2013, 104; Lee and Quirke, 2000, 108–10; Eastaugh et al., 2004, 136 and 176.

11 "Shot" fabric is a textile (usually silk) woven with one color in the warp and another in the weft. In silk this produces an iridescent appearance that changes color in different lighting.

12 The poor state of the frescoes contributed to the incorrect interpretation that they were religious subjects decorating a church; see the discussion in chap. 4.

13 Poggi 2007. See also the section headed "Scientific Investigations and Analyses," below.

14 Meyer-Graft 1979.

15 Poggi 2007. See also the section headed "Scientific Investigations and Analyses," below.

16 At this low concentration, the resin penetrates the paint layer, consolidating it without covering or saturating it. This is important for maintaining the natural micro-porosity of the material without preventing the necessary exchange of air (and the moisture contained in it) with the atmosphere.

17 Our experience at other sites in Egypt and of traditional Egyptian and Coptic techniques have shown that it is still easy to find building materials from sources identical to those used

in antiquity. It is often necessary, however, to process the raw materials using techniques no longer commonly employed by local workmen—for example, slaking lime and preparing the straw to add to the mix of certain plaster types.

18 This stone probably originates from Gebel el-Silsila. On sandstone and its sources, see Aston, Harrell, and Shaw 2000, 54–56.

19 Ancient texts describe various procedures for bleaching straw, including boiling, leaching in a potash bath, and rinsing. In our case, a number of washes and rinses under running water proved adequate.

20 See note 10.

21 In one of the samples, analysis of the surface revealed the presence of polysaccharides.

Chapter 6

1 Recently excavated wall paintings from a house at the site of ancient Kysis in Kharga Oasis are currently the only other known example of the true fresco technique in Egypt; see Gehad et al. 2013. Dating to the late third and early fourth centuries, these paintings depict (from the waist down) three roughly life-size figures tentatively identified as an emperor and perhaps two military deities. In terms of theme and technique, therefore, the Kysis paintings are superficially similar to the Luxor paintings and may likewise be connected to late Roman military activities in Kharga. But the higher artistic quality and more complicated iconography as well as context of the Luxor frescoes preclude a direct comparison.

2 The only other surviving imperial paintings that are roughly comparable in style are the megalographic figures from the so-called *domus Faustae* in Rome, dating to the early Constantinian era. On these see McFadden 2013.

3 Deckers 1973 and 1979; Kalavrezou-Maxeiner 1975. Both these authors built on the work of Monneret du Villard 1953. More recent summary discussions include Brenk 2010, 43–45; Deckers 2007; Elsner 1995, 157–190; Tőrők 2005, 139–153.

4 A small sketch on page 26v of Wilkinson's notebook gives the dimensions of the room, 56.1 × 34.6 feet (slightly contradicted by Monneret du Villard's dimensions, 17.45 × 10.5 meters, as quoted in Kalavrezou-Maxeiner 1975, 230nn11–12).

5 Major studies of the relationship between art and imperial ideology include Brilliant 1963; Hannestad 1988; L'Orange 1971; Kolb 2001.

6 On the juxtaposition of styles as part of the "semantic system" of Roman art, see Hölscher 2004. On ancient Greek and Roman attitudes toward style, see Elsner 2007, 49–66.

7 Johannes Deckers speculates that the figural composition of the south wall would have been approximately 7.5 meters high and 6.2 meters wide on either side of the niche, a total of about 93 square meters of surface space; Deckers 1979, 624.

8 On the state of research into the Greco-Roman funerary arts in Egypt, see Riggs 2002.

9 The combination of these different modes of representation raises interesting questions about the relationship between art and identity, summarized concisely in Riggs 2005, 1–40.

10 Ibid., 242.

11 For an introduction to the visual culture of Greco-Roman Egypt, see Whitehouse 2010. The use of classical styles and visual idioms in Egypt during the Roman era is of course a more nuanced phenomenon than is possible to survey in the context of this chapter; it was concerned mainly with the imperial image. And the situation becomes even more complex in late antiquity, for example, with the appearance of new Christian narratives and cast of characters, but, in the interest of succinctness, the Christian comparanda are not addressed here.

12 At least, this is true for Upper Egypt. The visual culture of Alexandria is not as well understood in comparison. See McKenzie 2007 for a recent survey of Alexandrian evidence.

13 For a thorough discussion of Roman imperial patronage of Egyptian temples in Thebes, see Klotz 2012b and Minas-Nerpel 2012. Between the reigns of Augustus and Antoninus Pius, Roman emperors made architectural and epigraphic contributions in Egyptian style to at least fourteen different temples in the Theban area alone (Klotz 2008, 11). On hieroglyphic inscriptions of Roman emperors after Antoninus Pius in Upper Egypt, see Porter and Moss 1991, 108–109 (Marcus Aurelius at Denderah); 117, 114 (Marcus Aurelius and Decius at Esna); 254–255 (Lucius Verus, Marcus Aurelius, and Commodus at Philae). Commodus, Marcus Aurelius, and Diocletian are also named in stelae from Buchis bull burials at the Armant Bucheum; Mond and Myers 1934a, 18–19; Mond and Myers 1934b, pls. XLV–XLVII. The last known hieroglyphic inscription from Armant mentioning the Roman emperor dates to 340, and though made during the reign of Constantius II, it is dated to the regnal year 59 of Diocletian, the last great pagan emperor; Grenier 1983.

14 An exception to this rule is figure 1.5, a relief from 295 picturing Diocletian as pharaoh making an offering to the Buchis bull (see chap. 1).

15 Heinen 1991.

16 The tondo of Septimius Severus is probably related in particular to the production of cult images rather than funerary portraits. A substantial corpus of painted panels depicting deities popular in the Greco-Roman period is surveyed in Rondot 2013.

17 Very little in the way of mural painting survives from Roman Egypt in general, and what does is mostly domestic in context (Karanis in the Fayyum, Amheida and Kellis in Dakhla Oasis) or funerary (Kom el-Shuqafa in Alexandria, the necropolis of Hermopolis Magna). See Whitehouse 2010 for an overview of Roman painting in Egypt.

18 The image of a figure mounted on a rearing horse actually works better visually than would figures walking beside their horses, as the doorway to the east side rooms interrupts the composition at this point.

19 For example, see Stauffer 1995, cats. 31 and 43. For a detailed discussion of Roman military dress, see Sumner 2009, 41–70 (on tunic decoration) and 185–186 (on *toubia*).

20 Kalavrezou-Maxeiner 1975, 233.

21 Soldiers pictured in the Piazza Armerina Great Hunt mosaics cited below wear them (see fig. 6.18), but so do high-ranking servants in elite households, as depicted in a fourth-century tomb from Silistra, Bulgaria, and a fourth-century house on the Caelian Hill in Rome; Dunbabin 2003, figs. 3, 25.

22 On the insignia of the *Notitia Dignitatum*, see Berger 1981.

23 Alföldi 1935, 65; Sumner 2009, 191–205.

24 Kalavrezou-Maxeiner 1975, 233; Deckers 1979, 627.

25 Monneret du Villard, 91. *Cosmatesque* is a style of medieval polychrome floor design that used stone spoliated from Roman monuments and is named after the twelfth- and thirteenth-century workshop of the Cosmati brothers in Rome that supposedly pioneered the technique. Cosmatesque designs generally employed much smaller pieces of marble and more intricately tessellated designs than late antique examples of polychrome floors, so the use of the term in the context of this chapter is simply to conveniently distinguish the style of the upper frieze of the geometric register from that of the larger imitation opus sectile panels below.

26 Von Bissing 1926, color plate. Reportedly, Monneret de Villard also drew this section of plaster, but he did not publish these drawings; Monneret de Villard 1953, 91.

27 It should be noted that the first roundel on the left side of Wilkinson's panorama (page 25v) has seven circles instead of six, as does the first roundel on page 28v. It is difficult to know, given this discrepancy, which drawing most accurately records the in situ design.

28 Note the resemblance of some of the roundel designs at Luxor to later iterations of painted opus sectile in Egypt, such as the interlocking square motif, also found at Bawit; Bolman 2006, pl. 13.

29 For information about the status of this technique, see Dunbabin 1999, 254–268.

30 On the use of colored marble decoration in the Roman Empire, see De Nuccio and Ungaro 2002.

31 Notable late antique examples from Rome include the Roman houses underneath the Church of Ss. Giovanni e Paolo (Brenk 1995) and Santa Maria Maggiore (Mols and Moormann 2010).

32 For a concise introduction to the vast bibliography on painting in the Bay of Naples and the four Pompeian styles, see Stewart 2004, 74–92.

33 Roberts 1989, 66–122.

34 On the Red Monastery, late antique aesthetics, and the "painted skins" of early Byzantine church interiors, see Bolman 2006 and 2010. Conservation work at the Red Monastery was carried out by ARCE and funded by USAID from 2002 to 2014; "Red Monastery, Sohag," www.arce.org/conservation/featuredconservation/u1 (accessed 20 January 2014).

35 On the evolution of stock themes in Roman imperial art, see Brilliant 1963, 105–211.

36 Stewart 2004, 112.

37 Alföldi 1934, 93–95; Brilliant 1963, 174; Kalavrezou-Maxeiner 1975, 240.

38 Kalavrezou-Maxeiner 1975, 242–243, argues that the paintings at Luxor depict an Egyptian version of the adventus ceremony, a Ptolemaic and Roman ritual derived from pharaonic practices known as the *komasia* in papyri of the third and fourth centuries CE. The komasia was an occasion when sacred images were carried out of the temples to greet visiting dignitaries. She bases this hypothesis on her reconstruction of an element on the south wall as the base of a cult statue rather than of a throne, as is more likely. As I argue later in this chapter, the style and iconography of the remaining fresco fragments do not suggest any unusual thematic content outside what is known of late Roman imperial art. Kalavrezou-Maxeiner's interpretation, however, is an important prolegomenon to the study of these images, as she was among the first to point out the peculiar Egyptian context for these canonically Roman paintings.

39 Monneret de Villard 1953, 92, notes that the eighteenth- and nineteenth-century graphic record indicates that the perimeter wall to the north and west of the imperial cult chamber was already destroyed to its present height in Wilkinson's day (see figs. 4.5 and 4.13).

40 An additional note right above this one, also in pencil but presumably added later, reads, "v. [vide] Journal p. 81 of 1859 (1856–1860) Taunton Museum." The reference is to an excavation report discussing a Roman belt buckle found in Britain similar to those depicted at Luxor; Kalavrezou-Maxeiner 1975, 238n46.

41 Ibid., 238.

42 Deckers 1979, 624–628.

43 Kalavrezou-Maxeiner 1975, 233.

44 See chap. 4 of this volume.

45 Deckers 2007, 98.

46 Generally, the more important a figure in Roman state art, the more hierarchical and formal its representation. In images of imperial procession, for example the Triumph panel on the Severan Arch at Leptis Magna, Septimius Severus is isolated from the other figures by his size, height, and frontality (on this arch, see Kleiner 1992, 340–343). This "gradual emancipation of the imperial personage from the group situation" is fully articulated in the art of the Antonine period (Brilliant 1963, 146).

47 The *paludamentum* (in Greek, *chlamys*) was the cloak of a senior officer. It is sometimes confused with the more functional *sagum* commonly worn by ordinary soldiers but also on some occasions by all ranks.

48 On *paragaudae,* see Sumner 2009, 66.

49 On embroidered garments in late antiquity, see Thomas 2002.

50 A concise discussion of this issue is found in Stewart 2004, 111–121. On the historiography of Roman art, see Elsner 2002.

51 For a summary discussion of art and imperial policy in late antiquity, see Elsner 1998, 53–87. On the fourth-century ruler image versus those of the early empire, see Hannestad 2001.

52 Monneret de Villard 1953, 93.

53 Meyer-Graft 1979.

54 This is evinced by the concordance between iconographies of monumental projects like the Luxor paintings and those of the minor arts of late antique courts. Distributing gifts (imperial *largitio*) of elite objects made of precious materials, such as silver, ivory, and vellum, and exhibiting the emperor's image or the portraits of officials in the imperial government were also important means of circulating ideology in the late empire. On ivory diptychs, see Delbrück 1929. For silver, see Leader-Newby 2004.

55 On this manuscript (Romanus I ms. Barb. Lat. 2154 fol. 13, inv. 231.549, Palazzo Corsini, Rome), see Salzman 1990, specifically 34–35 for an image of Constantius II; Elsner 1998, 84–86. On the Missorium, see Kiilerich 1993, 19–26.

56 Compare the *liberalitas* panel on the northwest face of the Arch of Constantine, Rome (ca. 315). Constantine, in the aftermath of his successful campaigns against the usurper

Maxentius, sits majestically enthroned on a podium dispensing coins to adoring subjects arrayed hieratically around the frontal and static imperial figure. On this monument generally, see Kleiner 1992, 444–455; for contextualization of the arch, see Marlowe 2006.

57 Kiilerich 1993, 23. For more on the symbolism of the arcuated lintel, see Brown 1942; L'Orange 1982, 35–36.

58 *Amm. Marc.* 16.10.6–10.

59 On the relationship between the imperial image and Christian art, see Jensen 2005 and Deckers 2007. For an argument that downplays the indebtedness of Christian art to imperial iconography, see Mathews 1999, particularly 92–114.

60 The position is confirmed by Sausmarez's 1855 watercolor of the south wall.

61 Kalavrezou-Maxeiner 1975, 236, notes that the emperor Galerius is depicted wearing a similarly fringed cloak in the sacrifice scene on the south pier, east face, of the arch of Galerius in Thessaloniki.

62 Ibid.

63 The identification with Maximian is now out of favor, although the villa is believed to have belonged to a wealthy aristocratic patron connected with the imperial court during the early decades of the fourth century; Pensabene 2010.

64 On this monument, see L'Orange 1938; Kähler 1964.

65 The ritual gesture of covering one's hands (*manus velatae*) is commonly depicted in images of religious veneration in the Roman world. The earliest mention of the performance of this act directed toward the emperor rather than a deity dates from the time of the emperor Julianus, who reigned briefly in 193 CE; Alföldi 1934, 33–35. Christian art absorbed the idea that what is touched by the emperor (or deity) cannot also be touched by human hands; Deckers 1979, 650.

66 Eutr. 26; Lactant. *De mort. pers.* 18.9; *Pan. Lat.* 11.11.1–3.

67 Proskynesis was an act common in the Persian courts, and Kolb 1987 argues that Diocletian's reforms as a whole seem to have favored a style of governance inspired by an eastern-style monarchy. Ancient sources concur: Eutr. 26; Aur. Vict. *Caes.* 39; Kalavrezou-Maxeiner 1975, 235.

68 Deckers 2007.

69 Deckers 1979, 635, suggested that a second belt would have to be pictured if two emperors were seated on the throne base, but there is no trace of this today. It should be mentioned, however, that since the recent cleaning, the object looks more like a purse clasp than a belt buckle to me.

70 On the sacred nature of military standards, see Ando 2000, 259–277.

71 Before the recent conservation, it was assumed that one of the figures in the upper row carried the vexillum with veiled hands, but it is now clear that the standard has a particularly long pole that reaches all the way to the bottom row of figures.

72 Presumably, had the other three bases of the four-columned monument survived, we would have seen each of the other Tetrarchs sacrificing in turn on his respective base.

73 For a complete discussion of the arch's program, see Pond Rothman 1977. Note also the comparison between the Luxor Tetrarchs and the arch in Rees 1993.

74 For the particular meaning of *pietas* on the Arch of Galerius see MacCormack 1981, 23; on this specific panel, see Pond Rothman 1975.

75 For example, Beato's first niche photograph (see fig. 4.11) can be compared with his later photograph featuring local musicians (fig. 4.18), in which the sections of plaster just to the east and west of the niche are missing.

76 This is confirmed by a detail in Wilkinson's panorama drawing, barely noticeable in previous reproductions of the watercolors. On page 26r (see fig. A.1), two sets of feet moving in a westerly direction are sketched in very light pencil directly to the west of the niche. These feet directly correspond with those on the far left of pages 27v and 28r (see fig. A.2) and allowed Kalavrezou-Maxeiner and Deckers to securely locate the vignette within the room.

77 Rees 1993, 186.

78 See, for example, Ling 1991, 192–194. Notable exceptions to this rule are the studies of Elsner 1995 and Török 2005.

79 On the difficulties of pinpointing precisely a late antique style and the causes of late antique aesthetic developments, see Huskinson 2005.

80 On the history of the apse as a place for sacred images, see Brenk 2010, 31–50.

81 Lactant. *De mort. pers.* 42.1–2; Euseb. *Vit. Const.* 1.47. On why this figure is most likely Maximian and not Maximinus Daia, who was also subject to a *damnatio memoriae* in the tetrarchic period, see chap. 2.

82 On the tetrarchic image, see Rees 1993; Walden 1990; Ellingsen 2003.

83 General histories of Diocletian and the Tetrarchy in English include Barnes 1982; Williams 1985; Corcoran 1996; Rees 2004; in German, see Kuhoff 2001 and the essays collected in Demandt et al. 2004.

84 Kleiner 1992, 400–403.

85 More naturalistic portraits of individual Tetrarchs exist in media other than porphyry but do not seem to have been part of group portrait displays. See, for example, Weitzman 1973, fig. 2, cat. 6. In sculpture, an individual representation, lacking the need for similitude, could appear more classical.

86 For more on this subject see Nock 1947; Mattingly 1952; Kolb 2004; Rees 2005.

87 This was a naming choice that might have been intended to emphasize Diocletian's superiority, since Jupiter was the father of Hercules; Rees 2005, 55.

88 Nixon and Rodgers 1994, 48–50; on Roman medallions generally, see Gnecchi 1992 and Toynbee 1944.

89 Coin legends referring to Jupiter from the tetrarchic era generally read, "IOVI CONS[ERVATORI AUG]," which roughly translates as "Jupiter the pres[erver of the Augustus]," and would have been accompanied by an image of Jupiter and Diocletian, or Diocletian on the obverse and Jupiter on the reverse. The images are not conflated, as seems to be the case at Luxor. See *RIC Vb* and *RIC VI* for this numismatic evidence.

90 Rees 2005.

91 Surviving paintings connected to the imperial cult from the late empire are rare. Of the few other known examples, one of them is from Gaul and another is from the late second or early third century: Le Clos de la Lombarde, Triclinium de la maison à Portiques (Narbonne) and Nizy-le-Comte (Aisne). Both are from the "public" rooms of domestic contexts, which makes direct comparison with Luxor difficult. See Sabrié and Sabrié 1999.

92 Moormann 2011, 144–145, fig. 70; Brenk 2010, 42.

93 It is possible that the erased figure of Maximian was originally depicted with attributes of Hercules, particularly the lion skin (as seen on medallions of the era—see British Museum aureus minted in Trier: Bardill 2012, fig. 71), but this does not negate the primacy of Diocletian-Jupiter in the composition.

94 Alföldi 1935, 117.

95 *LIMC* 8:421–470.

96 For example, all four Tetrarchs carry the globus in the group portraits preserved on two porphyry columns now in the Vatican Library in Rome; Kleiner 1992, 403–404, figs. 368, 369.

97 Tőrők 2005, 148–152, and Noel 2003 argue that Diocletian's connection to Jupiter is manifested in his retirement palace at Split. There the physical juxtaposition of Diocletian's mausoleum and the temple of Jupiter highlights a special relationship between god and man, and the decorations evoke a theme of eternal triumph.

98 While the laurel branch is also an attribute of the god Apollo, there is no evidence that either of the Caesars was ever associated with this deity during the First Tetrarchy. In the iconography of the early years of Constantine's rise to power, he does claim association with Sol-Apollo, but only after 310, when he is elevated to the status of Augustus (see Bardill 2012, 81–89). Given the subordinate status of the figure holding the laurel branch, the possibility that this figure could be Constantine depicted as Sol-Apollo seems remote.

99 Deckers did not commit to this being Jupiter (1979, 644) and instead speculated that it may be an allegorical figure, such as a Nike (1973, 20).

100 It should be noted that they are not barefoot, another convention for the depiction of deities. What we thus have is an iconographic compromise of sorts. For more on the meaning of the costume of the Tetrarchs in the niche, see Deckers 1973, 21–22.

101 For the use of the nimbus in Sasanian Iran vis-à-vis Rome, see Canepa 2009. Numismatic employment of the nimbus before the tetrarchic period is very rare. Known exceptions include the reverses of *aurei* and *sestertii* minted under Antoninus Pius; see Bastien 1992–1994, 170, vol. 1; Ahlqvist 2001, 208.

102 On the radiate crown in general, see Bergmann 1998.

103 A gold medallion, ca. 297, minted in Trier (also known as the Lyon Lead Medallion or the Mainz Medallion), depicts Diocletian and Maximian nimbate and enthroned (Alföldi 1935, 144; Bastien 1989, 7; Bastien 1992–1994, 1:171–172). In addition, gold multiples of Constantius Chlorus, ca. 305, minted in Trier (from the Arras hoard), illustrate two nimbate Tetrarchs sacrificing in front of a temple (Bastien and Metzger 1977, 394; Toynbee 1944, pl. VIII, 7; Bastien 1992–1994, 1:172). *Pan. Lat.* 10.3.2, dedicated to Maximian, ca. 289, speaks of "that light which surrounds your [Maximian's] divine head with a shining orb" (*illa lux diuinum uerticem claro orbe complectens*).

104 Deckers 1979, 650.

105 L'Orange and Unger 1984, pl. 32a–b; Bardill 2012, fig. 81.

106 *RIC VII,* Ticcinum nos. 37, 38, 41, 59, Siscia no. 25; Bastien 1992–1994, 1:174–175. These coins are particularly unusual in that they depict frontal rather than profile portraits of Constantine.

107 Bardill 2012, 97–98; on the Arch of Constantine, and Sol and Constantine, see Marlowe 2006.

108 For the adoption of the nimbus in Christian iconography, see Ahlquist 2001.

109 For more on how the Luxor program is the forerunner of programmatic church decoration, not just in terms of iconography but also in terms of format and spatial arrangement of images, see Deckers 1983 and 2007. See also Brenk 2010 on the transition from pagan to Christian apse imagery.

110 On Wilkinson and the Christian interpretation of the niche, see chap. 4.

111 On the persecutions, see Millar 1973.

112 For Christian appropriation of pagan temples, see Hahn et al. 2008.

113 Grossmann 1995, 193; 2002a, 448–454; 2002b.

114 The Roman fort at Abu Shaar became a Christian settlement after its abandonment by the military, and its sacellum was converted into a church; Sidebotham 1994, 137–139.

Chapter 7

1 Art historians have long sought to understand not just what images *mean* (iconographic studies) in their particular historical context but also what they make the viewer *do*. Seminal studies on the performative aspects of art and viewer response include Freedberg 1989; Belting 1994; Nelson 2000. On the "agency" of images, and how the agency of artists, patrons, and viewers can be inferred from images in the Roman world in particular, see Stewart 2006 and 2007.

2 Elsner 2007, 29–49.

3 Major studies of the imperial cult include Scott Ryberg 1955; Bickerman and den Boer 1973; Fishwick 1988–2004 (in the West); Price 1984 (in the East); Small 1996; Gradel 2002.

4 On the distinction between imperial "cult" and "worship," see Gradel 2002.

5 It was not easy to become a god in the Roman world. A deceased emperor could not be considered divus without an elaborate *consecratio* ceremony enacted by his successor. See MacCormack 1981, 93–144.

6 Gradel 2002, 349–364.

7 Bickerman 1973, 9.

8 Ando 2000.

9 On the distinction between these terms in the early empire, see Fishwick 1969 and Gradel 2002, 234–250. For the late antique understanding of the emperor's genius, see MacCormack 1975b.

10 Stewart 2006, 244.

11 Stewart 2007, 170.

12 On Christian responses to the imperial image, see Jensen 2005, 51–59. It seems Byzantine emperors were in no hurry to do away with the imperial cult; Momigliano 1986, 191–192.

13 Kruse 1934, 12–18; Ando 2000, 228–232.

14 Belting 1994, 102–107. A notable example from the Byzantine Book of Ceremonies (De Cer, 1.87) describes the reception of the laurel-wreathed portrait of the Western Roman emperor Anthemius in Constantinople in 467.

15 Gradel 2002, 29.

16 As Greg Woolf fittingly puts it, "Understanding the place of ruler cult in the Roman Empire depends crucially on understanding the Empire as a mosaic of notionally autono-

mous religious systems. The worship of the emperors was ordered separately within each of these systems"; Woolf 2008, 249.

17 Price 1984, 11.

18 Alföldy 1996, 255.

19 The Roman grammarian Sextus Pompeius Festus states, "To be religious is not merely to hold the sanctity of the gods in great respect, but also to be dutifully obliging (*officiosus*) towards men" (quoted in Gradel 2002, 4). On Romans' conception of *religio,* see also Ando 2008.

20 Gradel 2002, 5–6.

21 For foundational texts on this topic, see Geertz 1966 and Harvey 2005.

22 In a letter to a pagan priest, Julian the Apostate (r. 355–360) advocates the veneration of cult statues because, like images of emperors, they are privileged objects but not the actual gods or emperors themselves (Julian, *Letter to a Priest* 293C–D, 294C). The very fact that Julian is cautioning against the notion that the images stand in for the actual presence of the emperor signals that this notion was still very much alive in the fourth century, in spite of popular Christian critiques of idolatry. Stewart 2006, 245.

23 Alföldi 1970, 66; Pekáry 1985, 116–129.

24 On the imperial cult in Egypt, see Blumenthal 1913; Dunand 1983; Dundas 1993; Huzar 1995; Herklotz 2007; Pfeiffer 2012.

25 Dunand and Zivie-Coche 2004, 253.

26 Elsner 1995, 171.

27 On the cult of Isis, see Bommas 2012, for Mithras in Egypt and other imported cults, see Tallet and Zivie-Coche 2012; for Christianity, see Choat 2012.

28 For example, Blumenthal 1913 (rupture) and Dunand 1983 (continuity).

29 Blumenthal 1913 and Dunand 1983 (cult was purely a local initiative); Dundas 1993 (Roman authorities in the province took an active role in maintaining the cult, but the cult was not governed directly from Rome); Pfeiffer 2012 (imperial cult in Egypt was instituted from Rome).

30 These terms are somewhat interchangeable. *Kaisareion* (or *caesareum*) is from the Latin *Caesar, sebasteion* is from the Greek translation of Augustus, and *hadrianeion* refers to buildings of the imperial cult dating from the reign of the emperor Hadrian, for whom Egypt had special symbolic meaning owing to the untimely death of his lover, Antinous, who drowned in the Nile near the city Antinoopolis, later named for him in commemoration.

31 Pfeiffer 2012, 86–87; McKenzie 2007, 177–178.

32 Sources for each building are cited in Glare 1993, 158–159; Dundas 1993, 135–177.

33 Pfeiffer 2012, 95; Dundas 1993, 127–132.

34 *CPR* 1.20 (250) and *P. Oxy.* 17.2130 (267) describe the placement of legal petitions at the feet of imperial images; the former is cited in Price 1984, 193, and the latter in Stewart 2006, 245.

35 Pfeiffer (2012, 88–91, figs. 6.1–6.3) argues that this architectural feature connects the temple to an imperial initiative directed from Rome and represents a clear break from the Ptolemaic model of ruler cult.

36 McKenzie 2007, 167–168, figs. 286–289.

37 This is a similar concept to Ptolemaic rulers' status of *synnaoi theoi* or "associated gods" in temples organized along Egyptian lines.

38 Wilcken 1885.

39 Jupiter Capitolinus was *the* most important state god in the Roman world; the center of his cult was on the Capitoline hill in the city of Rome. On Siwa see Kuhlmann 1988.

40 BGU 2.362. The text records that during certain festivals the cult statues in the temple were crowned and anointed with oil, and it also refers to a colossal statue of Caracalla in the temple precinct.

41 For a more comprehensive discussion of BGU 2.362, see Glare 1993, 142–154, and Dundas 1993, 295.

42 The text does not refer to the name of the god carried in procession, but generally the Greek terms *andrias* or *eikones* are used for statues of the living emperor, so *xoanon* here is taken to mean the cult statue of Jupiter Capitolinus, though there are significant variations in the use patterns of these words. On the terminology for sacred images, see Price 1984, 176–177.

43 *P. Oxy.* 12.1449 (213–217). Another komastes is referred to as carrying the bust of "Probus Augustus and his approaching Victory" in *P. Mich.* 11 (282). See also *P. Oslo* 3.94 (second–third century), *P. Oxy.* 38.2855 (291), and *P. Oxy.* 10.1265 (336).

44 Heinen 1991 argues that the emperor's images referred to here are not statues but painted portrait tondos like that of Septimius Severus and his family now in Berlin (see fig. 6.2).

45 Price 1984, 189–190; Huzar 1995, 3112.

46 For a survey of reliefs of the Roman emperor in Egyptian style, see O'Neill 2011 (early empire only). For representations of the Roman emperor in Theban temples specifically, see Klotz 2012b.

47 Glare 1993, 154.

48 The purpose of these modifications to the southeastern side of Luxor Temple is unclear. The renovated rooms may have been used for Roman administrative purposes, but the more provocative and tempting hypothesis, advanced in chapt. 3, is that this part of the temple was reworked to accommodate an abridged yet still vital form of the traditional pharaonic Amun cult. See also Klotz 2008, 546–551.

49 On the use of Latin in Egypt, see Evans 2012 and also chapt. 2, of this volume.

50 Alston 1995; Southern and Dixon 1996; Haensch 2012. A Syrian is documented as stationed at Coptos in the third century from a dedicatory inscription dating to 216 CE found there, which honors the Palmyrene god Hierabolus (*OGIS* 639 = *IGRR* I.1169). The inscription is in Greek, despite the archer who made the dedication having a Syrian name and serving in the Roman army. How then can we unravel this soldier's ethnic identity?

51 The portal leading from the Amenhotep III and Tutankhamun colonnade hall into the court of Amenhotep III was also narrowed with Roman jambs; El-Saghir et al. 1986, 16, and chap. 3 of this volume. Concurrently, a new door in the southeast corner of the colonnade hall was opened, leading to the eastern side of the camp, perhaps to redirect processional traffic toward the Amun sanctuary, behind the imperial cult chamber (see chap. 3).

52 Bell 1985, 259.

53 Ibid., 260.

54 Ibid., 256. The Egyptian king was not literally considered a god on earth and worshipped directly as such. Rather, the institution of kingship was considered divine and could be absorbed by the ka of the living king and contained in statues of the reigning pharaoh; Dundas 1993, 296–306.

55 Dundas 1993, 232.

56 On hieroglyphs in Roman Egypt, see Klotz 2012a.

57 On the colonnade hall see, Holland and Urban 1994 and 1998.

58 El-Saghir et al. 1986, 16.

59 For the collection of known examples, see Delbrück 1932.

60 Illustrating the particular association between Diocletian and porphyry is a curious story in the *Passio Sanctorum Quatuor Coronatorum auctore Porphyrio* (from the *Acta Sanctorum Novembris*), which describes how Diocletian, "admirer of art" (*dilectatus in artem*), sent a group of sculptors from Pannonia to Mons Porphyrites to work porphyry, but the Christian carvers refused to produce pagan images, so the emperor had them executed. Text reproduced in Delbrück 1932, xviii–xix.

61 On Abu Sha'ar, see Sidebotham 1994.

62 Greco-Roman Museum, Alexandria, inv. 5934; Delbrück 1932, 96–98, pls. 40–41; Kiss 2007, 188. This statue was previously identified as Constantine because it is more naturalistically modeled than examples from the tetrarchic era (Tőrők 2005, 186). The drapery of the painted Luxor Tetrarchs, rendered with such plasticity, suggests we cannot assume that images of the Tetrarchs were always stylized in the way the Venice Tetrarchs are. Considerable variation, depending on workshops, is possible, and a reevaluation of traditional methods for dating sculpture from this period on the basis of style alone is overdue.

63 See the ivory diptych panels of the empress Ariadne in Museo Nazionale in Florence and the Kunsthistorisches Museum in Vienna (Weitzmann 1973, cat. 25). It should be noted that Deckers cautions that a four-columned structure could not be verified archaeologically (Deckers 1979, 615–616), though Monneret de Villard claimed to have found the missing columns on the west side of the temple; Monneret de Villard 1953, 88. See also chap. 3.

64 The question of what was placed beneath the Luxor ciborium is still debated. The scale of a large cult statue, such as the one in Alexandria mentioned above, would have obscured the images of the emperors painted in the niche, and also would have been redundant, as the painted images themselves act as cult images (on whether cult images could be two-dimensional, see Brenk 2010, 44). An altar would have been for sacrifices to the *dii militares* or the *genius legionis,* or the emperor himself, but altars were more often in the open air (for an exception, see El-Saghir et al. 1986, 29). The most likely proposition is a throne, as in an imperial audience hall; Kalavrezou-Maxeiner 1975, 231.

65 On this painting see Dirven 2007 and Heyn 2011. The three figures in military dress standing on plinths to the proper right of the tribune were once believed to represent statues of the emperors Gordian II, Balbinus, and Pupienus, but scholarly consensus now leans toward their identification as cult statues of Palmyrene gods.

66 Barasch 2003, 44. See also Corbeill 2004.

67 On art and ceremony in particular, see MacCormack 1972, 1975a, 1981, 2012. On the panegyrics more generally, see Rees 2002 and 2012.

68 For a concise discussion of the origin of the genre, see Rees 2012, 3–4.

69 MacCormack 1975a, 143. Latin panegyrics were also related to the tradition of funerary orations, *laudatio funebris.*

70 This collection was discovered in Mainz, Germany, in the fifteenth century. It was possibly compiled by the rhetor Pacatus, the author of the last speech of 389 dedicated to Theodosius. For a translation, see Nixon and Rodgers 1994.

71 The twelfth speech, by Pliny, dated to 100, is a *gratiarum actio* dedicated to Trajan, thanking him for his consulship. This speech was probably used as a rhetorical guidebook for the other speeches.

72 MacCormack 2012, 241.

73 The continued practice of this ceremony throughout late antiquity is evident from the description by Ahmad Ibn Yahya al-Baladhuri (d. ca. 892 CE) of how the Byzantine people in Syria organized themselves to welcome their new rulers, the Arabs, ca. 634. Cited in MacCormack 1981, 22.

74 Ibid., 18.

75 *Pan. Lat.* 10.6.3–4.

76 Nelson 2000.

77 MacCormack 1975a, 185.

78 MacCormack 1981, 10.

79 Hor. *Ars P.* 361.

80 MacCormack 1975a, 178.

81 *Pan. Lat.* 8.19.1–3. "And so it was fitting that, as soon as you stepped onto that shore, a long-desired avenger and liberator, a triumphal crowd poured forth to meet Your Majesty, and Britons exultant with joy came forward with their wives and children, venerating not you alone, whom they gazed at as one who had descended from heaven, but even the sails and oars of that ship which had conveyed your divinity, and prepared to feel your weight upon their prostrate bodies as you disembarked. Nor is it any wonder if they were carried away by such joy after so many years of miserable captivity; after the violation of their wives, after the shameful enslavement of their children, they were free at last, at last Romans, at last restored to life by the true light of empire."

82 On this medallion see Toynbee 1944, 182–183, 195, and pl. VIII, 4.

83 MacCormack 1981, 1–14.

84 Rees 2004, 28.

85 *Pan. Lat.* 7.14.1.

86 Ellingsen 2003, 39.

87 The fact that the adventus ceremony was performed in Upper Egypt, if not Luxor specifically, is attested by Dioscoros of Aphrodito, who composed several panegyric-like poems describing the arrival of high-ranking officials in the Thebaid, including one describing the arrival of an imperial portrait of Justin II (r. 565–574) at Arsinoe (Antinoopolis). On these texts see Fournet 1999, 264–269, 409–417; MacCoull 1984; and MacCoull 1988, 72–76, 91–96, 107–108, 134–136.

88 *Pan. Lat.* 11.9.4–10.3.

89 MacCormack 1975a, 163–164.

90 Adams 2004, 86. The passage from the panegyric, composed in honor of Rome's birthday, reads, "In truth, O most sacred Emperor, one might justifiably call you and your brother the founders of the Roman Empire, for you are, what is almost the same thing, its restorers, and although this is the birthday of this City, which marks the origin of the Roman people, it is the first day of your rule, which marks the beginning of its salvation." *Pan. Lat.* 10.1.5.

91 *P. Oxy.* 63.4352.

92 The strategos was the immediate point of contact in the administrative hierarchy between the procurator for the Egyptian province and citizens of the nome. He was normally appointed from a different nome and held his position for approximately three years; Rees 2004, 34.

93 Ibid., 35.

94 *P. Beatty Panop.* 1.53–59 (13 September 298).

95 Ibid., 1.167–179 (15 September 298).

96 Rees 2004, 36.

97 On adventus post-Constantine, see MacCormack 1981, 33–61.

98 Lacau and Deckers report traces of at least three statue bases dating to the time of Constantine erected in the intercolumnia of the Amenhotep III portico, but only one remains in situ; Lacau 1934, 36; Deckers 1979, 607–608nn19, 20.

99 Legrain 1914, 2–17; El-Saghir et al. 1986, 21–23.

100 My translation of the French, itself translated from a lost Arabic manuscript printed in Legrain 1914, 15.

101 MacCormack 1981, 13.

Appendix

1 Monneret de Villard 1953, 90–94, pls. XXX–XXXII.

2 Baines and Málek 2000, 87; Bowman 1986, 54–55; Kalavrezou-Maxeiner 1975, figs. I–IV and 6–14.

3 Monneret de Villard 1953, 90.

4 Thompson 1992a, 227–228, gives a summary of the fortunes of the manuscripts and of the different cataloguing systems found in earlier publications, including his own referencing devised because no comprehensive catalogue existed at the time of his research. See also Thompson 1992b, 273–274.

5 The Wilkinson manuscripts catalogue is available at www.bodley.ox.ac.uk/dept/scwmss/wmss/online/1500-1900/wilkinson/wilkinson.html (accessed 1 September 2012).

BIBLIOGRAPHY

Abd el-Raziq, M. 1984. *Die Darstellungen und Texte des Sanktuars Alexanders des Grossen im Tempel von Luxor.* Mainz am Rhein: Philipp von Zabern.

Abraham G., and A. Bakr. 1999. *Comprehensive Development Plan for the City of Luxor, Egypt.* Cambridge, Mass.: Abt Associates.

Abu-Lughod, L. 1998. "Television and the Virtues of Education." In *Directions of Change in Rural Egypt,* ed. N. Hopkins and K. Westergaard, 147–165. Cairo: American University in Cairo Press.

Adams, C. E. P. 2004. "Transition and Change in Diocletian's Egypt: Province and Empire in the Late Third Century." In *Approaching Late Antiquity: The Transition from Early to Late Empire,* ed. S. Swain and M. Edwards, 82–108. Oxford: Oxford University Press.

Ahlqvist, A. 2001. "Cristo e l'imperatore romano: I valori simbolici del nimbo." *AAAH* 15:207–227.

Ahmed, A. A. 2009. "Deterioration of Pharaonic Monuments in Upper Egypt." *Journal of Engineering Science* 37, no. 1:161–177.

Alcock, S. 2001. "The Reconfiguration of Memory in the Eastern Roman Empire." In *Empires: Perspectives from Archaeology and History*, ed. S. Alcock et al., 323–350. Cambridge: Cambridge University Press.

———. 2002. *Archaeologies of the Greek Past: Landscape, Monuments and Memories.* Cambridge: Cambridge University Press.

Alcock, S., J. F. Cherry, and J. Elsner. 2001. *Pausanias: Travel and Memory in Roman Greece.* Oxford: Oxford University Press.

Alföldi, A. 1934. "Die Ausgestaltung des monarchischen Zeremoniells am römischen Kaiserhofe." *MDAI(R)* 49:1–118.

———. 1935. "Insignien und Tracht der römischen Kaiser." *MDAI(R)* 50:1–171.

———. 1970. *Die monarchische Repräsentation im römischen Kaiserreiche.* Darmstadt: Wissenschaftliche Buchgesellschaft.

Alföldy, G. 1996. "Subject and Ruler, Subjects and Methods: An Attempt at a Conclusion." In *Subject and Ruler: The Cult of the Ruling Power in Classical Antiquity*, ed. A. Small, 254–261. Ann Arbor: *JRA* Suppl. Series 17.

Alston, R. 1995. *Soldier and Society in Roman Egypt.* New York: Routledge.

Alston, R. 2002. *The City in Roman and Byzantine Egypt.* New York: Routledge.

Ando, C. 2000. *Imperial Ideology and Provincial Loyalty in the Roman Empire.* Berkeley: University of California Press.

———. 2008. *The Matter of the Gods: Religion and the Roman Empire.* Berkeley: University of California Press.

Arnheim, M. 1975. "The Imperial Cult." *CR* 25, no. 2:273–275.

Arnold, D. 1991. *Building in Egypt: Pharaonic Stone Masonry.* Oxford: Oxford University Press.

———. 1999. *Temples of the Last Pharaohs.* Oxford: Oxford University Press.

Aston, B., J. Harrell, and I. Shaw. 2000. "Stone." In *Ancient Egyptian Materials and Technology,* ed. P. T. Nicholson and I. Shaw, 5–77. Cambridge: Cambridge University Press.

Arnold, D. 2005. "The Destruction of the Statues of Hatshepsut from Deir el-Bahri." In *Hatshepsut: From Queen to Pharaoh,* ed. C. H. Roehrig, 270–276. New York: Metropolitan Museum of Art.

Aufrère, S., J.-C. Golvin, and J.-C. Goyon. 1991. *L'Égypte restituée: Sites et temples de l'haute Égypte (1650 av. J.-C.–300 ap. J.-C.).* Paris: Éditions France.

Avrami, E., R. Mason, and M. de la Torre. 2000. *Values and Heritage Conservation.* Los Angeles: Getty Conservation Institute.

Azim, M. 1980. "La fouille de la cour du VIIIe pylône." *Cahiers de Karnak* 6:91–129.

Azim, M., and J.-Cl. Golvin. 1982 "Étude technique de l'abattage de l'obélisque ouest du VIIe pylône de Karnak." *Cahiers de Karnak* 7:167–180.

Baedeker, K., ed. 1892. *Egypt: Handbook for Travellers, Part Second: Upper Egypt, with Nubia as Far as the Second Cataract and the Western Oases.* Leipzig: Karl Baedeker.

Baer, N. S., and F. Snickars, eds. 2001. *Rational Decision-Making in the Preservation of Cultural Heritage.* Berlin: Dahlem University Press.

Bagnall, R. S. 1977. "Army and Police in Roman Upper Egypt." *JARCE* 14:67–86.

———. 1993. *Egypt in Late Antiquity.* Princeton: Princeton University Press.

———. 2003. *Later Roman Egypt: Society, Religion, Economy and Administration.* Burlington, Vt.: Ashgate.

———. 2008. "Models and Evidence in the Study of Religion in Late Roman Egypt." In *From Temple to Church: Destruction and Renewal of Local Cultic Topography in Late Antiquity,* ed. J. Hahn, S. Emmel, and U. Gotter, 23–42. Boston: Brill.

Bagnall, R. S., and B. W. Frier. 1994. *The Demography of Roman Egypt.* Cambridge: Cambridge University Press.

Bagnall, R. S., and D. W. Rathbone, eds. 2004. *Egypt from Alexander to the Early Christians: An Archaeological and Historical Guide.* Los Angeles: J. Paul Getty Museum.

Bailey, D. M. 1990. "Classical Architecture in Roman Egypt." In *Architecture and Architectural Sculpture in the Roman Empire,* ed. M. Henig, 121–137. Oxford: Oxford University Press.

———. 1991. *British Museum Expedition to Middle Egypt: Excavations at El-Asmunein, IV. Hermopolis Magna: Buildings of the Roman Period.* London: British Museum Press.

———. 1996. "Honorific Columns, Cranes, and the Tuna Epitaph." In *Archaeological Research in Roman Egypt: Proceedings of the Seventeenth Classical Colloquium of the Department of Greek and Roman Antiquities, British Museum, 1–4 December, 1993,* 155–169. Ann Arbor: *JRA* Suppl. Series 19.

———. 1999. "Sebakh, Sherds and Survey." *JEA* 85:211–218.

———. 2012. "Classical Architecture." In Riggs 2012, 189–205.

Baines, J. 1997. "Temples as Symbols, Guarantors and Participants in Egyptian Civilization." In *The Temple in Ancient Egypt: New Discoveries and Recent Research*, ed. S. Quirke. London: British Museum Press.

Baines, J., and J. Málek. 1992. *Atlas of Ancient Egypt.* Oxford: Equinox.

Barasch, M. 2003. "*Elevatio:* The Depiction of a Ritual Gesture." *Artibus et Historiae* 24:43–56.

Bardill, J. 2012. *Constantine, Divine Emperor of the Christian Golden Age.* Cambridge: Cambridge University Press.

Barguet, P. 1980. "Luxor." *LÄ* 3:1103–1107.

Barnard, H., and K. Duistermaat, eds. 2012. *The History of the Peoples of the Eastern Desert.* Los Angeles: Cotsen Institute of Archaeology Press.

Barnes, T. D. 1973. "Lactantius and Constantine." *JRS* 63:29–46.

———. 1976a. "Imperial Campaigns, A.D. 285–311." *Phoenix* 30:174–193.

———. 1976b. "Three Imperial Edicts." *ZPE* 21:275–281.

———. 1982. *The New Empire of Diocletian and Constantine.* Cambridge: Harvard University Press.

———. 1996. "Emperors, Panegyrics, Prefects, Provinces and Palaces (284–317)." *JRA* 9:532–52.

Bastien, P. 1989. *Le monnayage de l'atelier de Lyon: Supplément. Le médaillon de plomb de Lyon.* Wetteren: Éditions Numismatique Romaine.

———. 1992–1994. *Le buste monétaire des empereurs romains.* 3 vols. Wetteren: Éditions Numismatique Romaine.

Bastien, P., and C. Metzger. 1977. *Le trésor de Beaurains (dit d'Arras).* Wetteren: Éditions Numismatique Romaine.

Bataille, A. 1938. "Une stèle grecque de Deir el Bahari." *ASAE* 38:63–67.

———. 1951. "Thèbes gréco-romaine." *CÉ* 26:325–353.

———. 1952. *Les Memnonia.* Cairo: IFAO.

Bataille, A., and B. Bruyère. 1936. "Une tombe gréco-romaine de Deir el Médineh." *BIFAO* 36:145–174.

———. 1938. "Une tombe Gréco-Romaine de Deir el Médineh." *BIFAO* 38:73–107.

Baynes, N. H. 1948. Review of *Dioclétien et la Tétrarchie. I. Guerres et Réformes (284–300)* by W. Seston. *JRS* 38:109–113.

Beard, M., J. North, and S. Price, eds. 1998. *Religions of Rome.* 2 vols. New York: Cambridge University Press.

Bell, L. 1985. "Luxor Temple and the Cult of the Royal Ka." *JNES* 44, no. 4:251–294.

Belting, H. 1994. *Likeness and Presence: A History of the Image before the Age of Art.* Chicago: Chicago University Press.

Bénazeth, D., and M.-H. Rutschowscaya, eds. 1999. *Jean Clédat: Le monastère et la nécropole de Baouît. MIFAO* 111. Cairo: IFAO.

Bendix, R. 2009. "Heritage between Economy and Politics: An Assessment from the Perspective of Cultural Anthropology." In Smith and Akagawa 2009, 253–269.

Benjamin, I. 1990. *The Limits of Empire: The Roman Army in the East.* Oxford: Oxford University Press.

Berger, J. 1977. *Ways of Seeing.* New York: Penguin Books.

Berger, P. 1981. *The Insignia of the Notitia Dignitatum.* New York: Garland.

Bergmann, M. 1998. *Die Strahlen der Herrscher: Theomorphes Herrscherbild un politische Symbolik im Hellenismus und in der römischen Kaiserzeit.* Mainz am Rhein: Philipp von Zabern.

Bernand, A., and E. Bernand. 1960. *Les inscriptions grecques et latines du Colosse de Memnon.* Cairo: IFAO.

Bickerman, E. 1973. "Consecratio." In Bickerman and den Boer 1973, 1–25.

Bickerman, E. J., and W. den Boer, eds. 1973. *Le culte des souverains dans l'empire romain.* Geneva: Fondation Hardt.

Bierbrier, M. J. 2012. *Who Was Who in Egyptology.* 4th ed. London: Egypt Exploration Society.

Bingen, J. 1986. "Épigraphie grecque: Les proscynèmes de Louqsor." *CÉ* 61:330–334.

Blackburn, B., and L. Holford-Stevens. 2003. *The Oxford Companion to the Year: An Exploration of Calendar Customs and Time-Reckoning.* Oxford: Oxford University Press.

Blanquart-Evrard, D. 1854. *Le Nil: Monuments; paysage; explorations; photographiques.* Lille: Imprimerie Photographique de Blanquart-Evrard.

Bloom, J. M. 1984. "Five Fatimid Minarets in Upper Egypt." *JSAH* 43:162–167.

Blumenthal, F. 1913. "Der ägyptische Kaiserkult." *Archiv für Papyrusforschung* 5:317–345.

Bogaert, R. 1984. "Banques et banquiers à Thèbes à l'époque romaine." *ZPE* 57:241–296.

Bolman, E. 2006. "Late Antique Aesthetics, *Chromophobia* and the Red Monastery, Sohag, Egypt." *Eastern Christian Art* 3:1–24.

———. 2010. "Painted Skins: The Illusions and Realities of Architectural Polychromy, Sinai and Egypt." In *Approaching the Holy Mountain: Art and Liturgy at St. Catherine's Monastery in the Sinai,* ed. S. E. J. Gerstel and R. S. Nelson, 119–142. Turnhout: Brepols.

Bommas, M. 2012. "Isis, Osiris, and Serapis." In Riggs 2012, 419–435.

Bonnet, C., and D. Valbelle. 2006. *The Nubian Pharaohs: Black Kings on the Nile.* Cairo: American University in Cairo Press.

Boraik, M. 2010. "Excavations of the Quays and the Embankment in Front of Karnak Temples: Preliminary Report." *Cahiers de Karnak* 13:65–78.

———. 2013. "A Roman Bath at Karnak Temples: A Preliminary Report." *Cahiers de Karnak* 14:33–46.

Boraik, M., and S. El-Masekh. 2012. "A Roman Bath at Karnak: A Preliminary Report." *Ancient Egypt Magazine* 12, no. 6, issue 72:34–48.

Botti, G., 1900. *Catalogue des monuments exposés au Musée Gréco-Romain d'Alexandrie.* Alexandria: A Mourès.

Bowersock, G. W. 1984. "The Miracle of Memnon." *BASP* 21:21–34.

Bowman, A. K. 1976. "Papyri and Roman Imperial History, 1960–1975." *JRS* 66:153–173.

———. 1978. "The Military Occupation of Upper Egypt in the Reign of Diocletian." *BASP* 15:25–38.

———. 1984. "Two Notes: I. The Revolt of Busiris and Coptos. II. Market Taxes at Oxyrhynchus." *BASP* 21:33–38.

———. 1986. *Egypt after the Pharaohs: 332 BC–AD 642.* London: British Museum Press.

———. 2005a. "Diocletian and the First Tetrarchy, A.D. 284–305." *CAH* 12:67–89.

———. 2005b. "Egypt from Septimius Severus to the Death of Constantine." *CAH* 12:313–326.

———. 2007. *Oxyrhynchus: A City and Its Texts.* London: Egypt Exploration Society.

Brand, S. 1994. *How Buildings Learn: What Happens after They're Built.* Harmondsworth: Viking Penguin.

Brandi, C. 2005. *Theory of Restoration.* Trans. C. Rockwell. Rome: Nardini Editore.

Breccia, E. 1911. *Iscrizioni greche ed latine.* Cairo: IFAO.

Brenk, B. 1995. "Microstoria sotto la chiesa dei SS. Giovanni e Paolo: La cristianizzazione di una casa privata." *RIA* 18:169–205.

———. 2010. *The Apse, the Image and the Icon: An Historical Perspective of the Apse as a Space for Images.* Wiesbaden: Reichert Verlag.

Brilliant, R. 1963. *Gesture and Rank in Roman Art.* New Haven: Yale University Press.

Brown, D. F. 1942. "The Arcuated Lintel and Its Symbolic Interpretation in Late Antique Art." *AJA* 46:389–399.

Brugsch, H. K. 1992. *My Life and My Travels.* Trans. G. Laughead Jr. and S. Panarity. Originally published as *Mein Leben und mein Wandern.* 1894. Berlin: Zweite Auflage. www.vlib.us/brugsch/chapter3.html (accessed 20 July 2012).

Buhl, M.-L. 1993. *Les dessins archéologiques et topographiques de l'Égypte ancienne faits par F. L. Norden, 1737–1738, et conservés à l'Académie Royale des Sciences et des Lettres de Danemark.* Copenhagen: Kongelige Danske Videnskabernes Selskab.

Busi, C., and P. Piacentini. 2008. *Il fotografo dei faraoni: Antonio Beato in Egitto, 1860–1900.* Bologna: Pendragon.

Canepa, M. 2009. *The Two Eyes of the Earth: Art and Ritual of Kingship between Rome and Sasanian Iran.* Berkeley: University of California Press.

Cannadine, D., and S. Price, eds. 1987. *Rituals of Royalty: Power and Ceremonial in Traditional Society.* Cambridge: Cambridge University Press.

Caple, C. 2000. *Conservation Skills: Judgement, Method and Decision Making.* New York: Routledge.

Carrié, J.-M. 1974. "Les Castra Dionysiados et l'évolution de l'architecture militaire romaine tardive." *MEFRA* 86:819–850.

Carter, H. 1900. "Rapport sur un découvert à Louxor." *ASAE* 1:191.

Charlier, F., F. Colin, L. Delvaux, et al. 2012. *Bahariya I. Le fort romain de Qaret el-Toub I.* Cairo: IFAO.

Choat, M. 2012. "Christianity." In Riggs 2012, 474–493.

Ciampini, E. M. 2004. *Gli obelischi inscritti di Roma.* Rome: Libreria della Stato.

Clarke, S. 1912. *Christian Antiquities in the Nile Valley: A Contribution towards the Study of the Ancient Churches.* Oxford: Clarendon Press.

Clarysse, W. 1984a. "A Roman Army Unit Near Thebes." *Atti del XVII Congresso Internazionale di Papirologia* 3:1021–1026.

———. 1984b. "Theban Personal Names and the Cult of Bouchis." In *Grammata Demotika: Festschrift für Erich Lüddeckens,* ed. H.-J. Thissen and K.-T. Zauzich, 25–39. Würzburg: Zauzich.

Clédat, J. 1904. *Le monastère et la nécropole de Baouît. MIFAO* 12, 1 and 2. Cairo: IFAO.

———. 1916. *Le monastère et la nécropole de Baouît. MIFAO* 39, no. 2, pt. 1. Cairo: IFAO.

Connerton, P. 1989. *How Societies Remember.* Cambridge: Cambridge University Press.

Corbeill, A. 2004 *Nature Embodied: Gesture in Ancient Rome.* Princeton: Princeton University Press.

Corcoran, L. H. 1995. *Portrait Mummies from Roman Egypt (I–IV Centuries A.D.).* Chicago: Oriental Institute of the University of Chicago.

Corcoran, S. 1996. *The Empire of the Tetrarchs—Imperial Pronouncements and Government, AD 284–324.* Oxford: Clarendon Press.

———. 2006. "The Titulature of the Third Tetrarchy." *BICS* 49:231–240.

Cottevieille-Giraudet, R. 1936. *Rapport sur les fouilles de Médamoud (1932): Les reliefs d'Aménophis IV Akhenaton FIFAO* 13. Cairo: IFAO.

Cuvigny, H., ed. 2003. *La route de Myos Hormos: L'armée Romaine dans le désert oriental d'Égypte. Praesidia du désert de Bérénice I. FIFAO* 48. Cairo: IFAO.

Daressy, G. 1893. *Notice explicative des ruines du Temple de Louxor.* Cairo: Imprimerie Nationale.

———. 1894. "Notes et remarques." *RT* 16:42–60.

———. 1920. "Notes sur Louxor de la période romaine et copte." *ASAE* 19:159–175.

Darnell, J. C. 2010. "Opet Festival." In *UCLA Encyclopedia of Egyptology (UEE).* http://escholarship.org/uc/item/4739r3fr#page-2

De Blois, L. 2006. "Emperorship in a Period of Crises: Changes in Emperor Worship, Imperial Ideology and Perceptions of Imperial Authority in the Roman Empire in the Third Century A.D." In *The Impact of Imperial Rome on Religions, Rituals and Religious Life in the Roman Empire. Proceedings of the Fifth Workshop of the International Network Impact of Empire (200 B.C.–A.D. 476), Münster, June 30–July 4, 2004,* ed. L. de Blois, P. Funke, and J. Hahn, 268–279. Leiden: Brill.

Deckers, J. G. 1973. "Die Wandmalerei des tetrarchischen Lager heiligtums im Ammon-Tempel von Luxor." *Römische Quartalschrift für christliche Altertumskunde und Kirchengeschichte* 68:1–34.

———. 1979. "Die Wandmalerei im Kaiserkultraum von Luxor." *Jahrbuch des Kaiserlich Deutschen Archäologischen Instituts* 94:600–652.

———. 1983. "Constantin und Christus: Das Bildprogramm in Kaiserkulträumen und Kirchen." In *Spätantike und frühes Christentum: Ausstellung Liebighaus Museum alter Plastik,* ed. H. Beck, 267–283. Frankfurt am Main: Liebieghaus.

———. 2007. "Constantine the Great and Early Christian Art." In *Picturing the Bible: The Earliest Christians on Art,* ed. J. Spier, 87–111. New Haven: Yale University Press.

De Haro Sanchez, M. 2008. "Les papyrus iatromagiques grecs et la région thébaine." *Papyrologica Buxellensia* 34:96–102.

De Jong, J. 2006. "Emperors in Egypt: The Representation and Perception of Roman Imperial Power in Greek Papyrus Texts from Egypt, A.D. 193–284." Ph.D. diss., Radboud Universiteit Nijmegen.

De la Torre, M., and M. M. Lean. 1997. "The Archaeological Heritage of the Mediterranean Region." In *The Conservation of Archaeological Sites in the Mediterranean Region,* ed. M. de la Torre, 5–14. Los Angeles: Getty Conservation Institute.

Delbrück, R. 1929. *Die Consulardiptychen und verwandte Denkmäler.* Berlin: W. de Gruyter.

———. 1932. *Antike porphyrwerke.* Berlin: W. de Gruyter.

Demandt, A., A. Goltz, and H. Schlange-Schöningen, eds. 2004. *Diokletian und die Tetrarchie: Aspekte einer Zeitenwende.* Berlin: Walter de Gruyter.

Demas, M. 2000. "Planning for Conservation and Management of Archaeological Sites: A Values-Based Approach." In Teutonico and Palumbo 2000, 27–54.

Denon, V. 1990. *Voyage dans la Basse et la Haute Égypte pendant les campaignes du Général Bonaparte.* Cairo: IFAO.

De Nuccio, M., and L. Ungaro, eds. 2002. *I marmi colorati della Roma imperial.* Venice: Marsilio.

Description. 1812. *Description de l'Égypte, ou recueil des observations et des recherches qui ont été faites en Égypte pendant l'expédition de l'armée française,* vols. 1–5, *Antiquités.* Paris: Imprimerie Imperial.

De Villard, M. 1953. "The Temple of the Imperial Cult at Luxor." *Archaeologia* 95:96–97.

Dijkstra, J. H. F. 2011. "The Fate of the Temples in Late Antique Egypt." In *The Archaeology of Late Antique Paganism,* ed. L. Lavan and M. Mulryan, 389–438. Leiden: Brill.

———. 2012. "Blemmyes, Noubades and the Eastern Desert in Late Antiquity." In H. Barnard and K. Duistermaat 2012, 239–247.

Dirven, L. 2004. "Religious Competition and the Decoration of Sanctuaries: The Case of Dura Europos." *Eastern Christian Art* 1:1–20.

———. 2007. "The Julius Terentius Fresco and the Roman Imperial Cult." *Mediterraneo Antico* 10, nos. 1–2:115–127.

Dorigo, W. 1971. *Late Roman Painting: A Study of Pictorial Records, 30 BC–AD 500.* Trans. J. Clough and J. Warrington. London: J. M. Dent.

Dorman, P. F. 1994. "Epigraphic Survey." In *Oriental Institute 1993–1994 Annual Report,* ed. W. M. Sumner, 16–26. Chicago: The Oriental Institute. http://oi.uchicago.edu/about/annual-reports/oriental-institute-1993-1994-annual-report

———. 2005. "The Proscription of Hatshepsut." In *Hatshepsut: From Queen to Pharaoh*, ed. C. H. Roehrig, 267–269. New York: Metropolitan Museum of Art.

Doxiadis, E. 1995. *The Mysterious Fayum Portraits: Faces from Ancient Egypt.* London: Thames and Hudson.

Du Camp, M. 1852. *Égypte, Nubie, Palestine et Syrie: Dessins photographique recueillis pendant les années 1849, 1850 et 1851.* Paris: Gide et J. Baudry.

Duff Gordon, L., et al. 1983. *Letters from Egypt.* London: Virago.

Dunand, F. 1983. "Culte royal et culte impérial en Égypte: Continuités et ruptures." In *Das römisch-byzantinischen Ägypten: Akten des internationalen Symposions 26–30, September 1978 in Trier,* ed. G. Grimm, H. Heinen, and E. Winter, 47–56. Mainz am Rhein: Philipp von Zabern.

Dunand, F., and R. Lichtenberg. 1995. "Pratiques et croyances funéraires en Egypte Romaine." *ANRW* II 18, no. 5:3216–3315.

Dunand, F., and C. Zivie-Coche. 2004. *Gods and Men in Egypt, 3000 BCE to 395 CE.* Ithaca: Cornell University Press.

Dunbabin, K. 1999. *Mosaics of the Greek and Roman World.* Cambridge: Cambridge University Press.

———. 2003. "The Waiting Servant in Later Roman Art." *AJP* 124:443–468.

Dundas, G. S. 1993. "Pharaoh, Basileus and Imperator: The Roman Imperial Cult in Egypt." Ph.D. diss., University of California, Los Angeles.

Eastaugh, N., V. Walsh, T. Chaplin, and R. Siddall. 2004. *The Pigment Compendium: A Dictionary of Historical Pigments.* Boston: Elsevier Butterworth-Heinemann.

Ebers, G. 1879. *Egypt: Descriptive, Historical and Picturesque,* vol. 2. Trans. Clara Bell. London: Cassel.

Edwards, A. B. 1891. *A Thousand Miles up the Nile.* 2nd ed. New York: Routledge.

El Bialy, M., and A. von Kienlin. 2008. "Report on the Third Season of the Egyptian-Swiss Joint Mission at Nag el-Hagar." *ASAE* 82:61–66.

El-Saghir, M. 1991. *The Discovery of the Statuary Cachette of Luxor Temple.* Mainz am Rhein: Philipp von Zabern.

El-Saghir, M., J.-C. Golvin, M. Reddé, E. Hegazy, and G. Wagner. 1986. *Le camp romain de Louqsor. MIFAO* 83. Cairo: IFAO.

Ellingsen, G. 2003. "Some Functions of Imperial Images in Tetrarchic Politics." *Symbolae Osloenses* 78, no. 1:30–44.

Elsner, J. 1995. *Art and the Roman Viewer: The Transformation of Art from the Pagan World to Christianity.* New York: Cambridge University Press.

———. 1998. *Imperial Rome and Christian Triumph.* Oxford: Oxford University Press.

———. 2000a. "Between Mimesis and Divine Power: Visuality in the Greco-Roman World." In *Visuality before and beyond the Renaissance: Seeing as Others Saw,* ed. R. S. Nelson, 45–70. Cambridge: Cambridge University Press.

———. 2000b. "From the Culture of Spolia to the Cult of Relics: The Arch of Constantine and the Genesis of Late Antique Forms." *PBSR* 68:149–185.

———. 2002. "The Birth of Late Antiquity: Riegl and Strzygowski in 1901." *Art History* 25, no. 3:358–379.

———. 2007. *Roman Eyes: Visuality and Subjectivity in Art and Text.* Princeton: Princeton University Press.

Elsner, J., and I. Rutherford, eds. 2005. *Pilgrimage in Graeco-Roman and Early Christian Antiquity: Seeing the Gods.* Oxford: Oxford University Press.

Elton, H. 2006. "The Transformation of Government under Diocletian and Constantine." In *A Companion to the Roman Empire,* ed. D. S. Potter, 193–205. Malden, Mass.: Blackwell.

Evans, T. V. 2012. "Latin in Egypt." In Riggs 2012, 516–526.

Fentress, J., and C. Wickham. 1992. *Social Memory.* Oxford: Blackwell.

Fishwick, D. 1969. "Genius and Numen." *Harvard Theological Review* 62, no. 3:356–367.

———. 1988–2004. *The Imperial Cult in the Latin West: Studies in the Ruler Cult of the Western Province of the Roman Empire.* 3 vols. Leiden: Brill.

Forsyth, G. H., and K. Weitzmann. 1973. *The Monastery of Saint Catherine at Mount Sinai: The Church and Fortress of Justinian.* Ann Arbor: University of Michigan Press.

Fournet, J.-L. 1999. Hellénisme dans l'Égypt du VIe siècle. Cairo: IFAO.

Fowden, G. 1986. *The Egyptian Hermes.* Cambridge: Cambridge University Press.

———. 2000. "Religious Traditions Great and Small in Roman Egypt." *JRA* 13:789–792.

Fowler, P. J. 1992. *The Past in Contemporary Society: Then and Now.* London: Routledge.

Frankfurter, D. 1998. *Religion in Roman Egypt: Assimilation and Resistance.* Princeton: Princeton University Press.

Freedberg, D. 1989. *The Power of Images: Studies in the History and Theory of Response.* Chicago: University of Chicago Press.

Gabelmann, H. 1984. *Antike Audienz- und Tribunalszenen.* Darmstadt: Wissenschaftliche Buchgesellschaft.

Galey, J. 1980. *Sinai and the Monastery of St. Catherine.* Givatayim, Israel: Massada.

Gamblin, S. 2004. "Luxor: A Tale of Two Cities." In *Upper Egypt: Identity and Change,* ed. N. Hopkins and R. Saad, 267–284. Cairo: American University in Cairo Press.

García-Moreno, R., et al. 2013. "Archaeometry Research on the Wall Paintings in the Tomb of Menna." In *The Tomb Chapel of Menna (TT 69): The Art, Culture, and Science of Painting in an Egyptian Tomb,* ed. M. Hartwig, 93–111. Cairo: American University in Cairo Press.

Gawlikowski, M. 1984. *Les principia de Diocletien: "Temple des Enseignes."* Varsovie: PWN–Editions Scientifiques de Pologne.

———. 2006. "Palmyra: Excavations in the Allat Sanctuary, 2005–2006." *PAM* 18:531–541.

———. 2008. "The Statues of the Sanctuary of Allat in Palmyra." In *The Sculptural Environment of the Roman Near East,* ed. Y. Z. Eliav, E. A. Friedland, and S. Herbert, 397–413. Leuven: Peeters.

Gayet, A. 1894. *Le Temple de Louxor:* Premier fascicule: "Constructions de Amenophis III." Paris: Ernest Leroux.

Geertz, C. 1966. "Religion as a Cultural System." In *Anthropological Approaches to the Study of Religion,* ed. M. Banton, 1–47. London: Tavistock.

Gehad, B., M. Wuttmann, H. Whitehouse, M. Foad, and S. Marchand. 2013. "Wall-Paintings in a Roman House at Ancient Kysis, Kharga Oasis." *BIFAO* 113:157–182.

Georg, J. 1930. *Neue Streifzüge durch die Kirchen und Klöster Ägyptens.* Leipzig: B. G. Teubner.

Geraci, G. 1971. "Ricerche sul proskynema." *Aegyptus* 51:3–211.

Gibson, S., J. DeLaine, and A. Claridge. 1994. "The Triclinium of the Domus Flavia: A New Reconstruction." *PBSR* 62:67–99.

Glare, P. 1993. "The Temples of Egypt: The Impact of Rome." Ph.D. diss., University of Cambridge.

Gnecchi, F. 1912. *I medaglioni romani.* 3 vols. Rome: Arnaldo Forni.

Golvin, J.-C. 1981. "Le petit Sarapieion romain de Louqsor." *BIFAO* 81:115–148.

———. 1987. "La restauration antique du passage du IIIe pylone." *Cahiers de Karnak* 8:189–206.

Gradel, I. 2002. *Emperor Worship and Roman Religion.* Oxford: Oxford University Press.

Graefe, E. 1986. "Talfest." *LÄ* 6:187–189.

Grand Bey. 1888. *Rapport sur les temples Égyptiens addressé à S. E. le ministre des travaux publiques.* Cairo: Imprimerie Nationale.

Grébaut, M. E. 1890. "Fouilles de Louqsor." *BIÉ* 327–337. Cairo: Imprimerie Centrale Jules Barbier.

Gregory, D. 2003. "Emperors of the Gaze: Photographic Practices and Productions of Space in Egypt, 1839–1914." In J. M. Schwartz and J. R. Ryan, *Picturing Place: Photography and the Geographical Imagination,* 195–225. London: I. B. Taurus: 2003.

Gregory, S. 1995–1997. *Roman Military Architecture on the Eastern Frontier.* 3 vols. Amsterdam: A. M. Hakkert.

Grenier, J.-C. 1983. "La stèle funéraire du dernier taureau Bouchis." *BIFAO* 83:197–208.

Grossmann, P. 1973. "Eine vergessene frühchristliche Kirche beim Luxor-Tempel." *MDAIK* 29:167–181 and pls. LXXIII–LXXVa.

———. 1995. "Tempel als Ort des Konflikts in christlicher Zeit." In *Le temple, lieu de conflit: Actes du colloque de Cartigny 1991,* ed. P. Borgeaud et al., 181–201. Leuven: Peeters.

———. 2002a. *Christliche Architektur in Ägypten.* Leiden: Brill.

———. 2002b. "Frühchristliche Kirchen im Gebiet des Ammon-Tempels von Luqsur." *RQA* 97:17–39.

Grossmann, P., C. Le Quesne, and P. Sheehan. 1994. "Zur Römischen Festung von Babylon—Alt-Kairo." *Archäologischer Anzeiger* 1:271–287.

Habachi, L. 1951. "Clearance of the Area to the East of Luxor Temple and Discovery of Some Objects." *ASAE* 51:447–469.

———. 1975. "Two More Stelae of King Tiberius Unearthed in the Eastern Side of Luxor Temple." In *Miscellanea in Honorem Josephi Vergote. Orientalia Lovaniensia Periodica 6/7,* ed. P. Naster, H. de Meulenaere, and J. Quaegebeur, 247–252. Leuven: Department Oriëntalistiek.

Haensch, R. 2012. "The Roman Army in Egypt." In Riggs 2012, 68–83.

Hahn, J., S. Emmel, and U. Gotter, eds. 2008. *From Temple to Church: Destruction and Renewal of Local Cultic Topography in Late Antiquity.* Leiden: Brill.

Hallof, J. 2011. "Esna." In *UCLA Encyclopedia of Egyptology (UEE).* http://digital2.library.ucla.edu/viewItem.do?ark=21198/zz002b2xv3.

Hanen, C. 1991. "Archéologie et vie urbaine." Thesis, École d'Architecture de Paris.

Hannestad, N. 1988. *Roman Art and Imperial Policy.* Aarhaus: Aarhaus University Press.

———. 2001. "The Ruler Image of the Fourth Century: Innovation or Tradition." *AAAH* 15:93–107.

Harvey, G., ed. 2005. *Ritual and Religious Belief: A Reader.* New York: Routledge.

Heilporn, P. 2008. "À la recherche du clergé thébain à l'époque romaine." *Papyrologica Bruxellensia* 34:125–136.

———. 2009. *Thèbes et ses taxes: Recherches sur la fiscalité en Égypte romaine (Ostraca de Strasbourg II).* Paris: De Boccard.

Heinen, H. 1991. "Herrscherkult im römischen Ägypten und Damnatio Memoriae Getas: Überlegungen zum Berliner Severertondo und zu Papyrus Oxryhynchus XII 1449." *MDAI(R)* 98:263–298.

Helck, W., and E. Otto, eds. 1980. *Lexikon der Ägyptologie III.* Wiesbaden: Otto Harrassowitz.

Herklotz, F. 2007. *Prinzeps und Pharao: Der Kult des Augustus in Ägypten.* Frankfurt: Antike.

Heyn, M. K. 2011. "The Terentius Frieze in Context." In *Dura Europos: Crossroads of Antiquity,* ed. L. R. Brody and G. L. Hoffman, 221–233. Chicago: University of Chicago Press.

Hobson, D. 1988. "Towards a Broader Context of the Study of Greco-Roman Egypt." *EMC* 32:353–363.

Holland, T. A., and T. G. Urban, eds. 1994. *Reliefs and Inscriptions at Luxor Temple,* vol. 1, *The Festival Procession of Opet in the Colonnade Hall,* Plates 1–128. Chicago: Oriental Institute of the University of Chicago.

———. 1998. *Reliefs and Inscriptions at Luxor Temple,* vol. 2, *The Façade, Portals, Upper Register Scenes, Columns, Marginalia, and Statuary in the Colonnade Hall.* Plates 129–227. Chicago: Oriental Institute of the University of Chicago.

Hölscher, T. 2004. *The Language of Images in Roman Art.* Cambridge: Cambridge University Press.

Hölscher, U. 1954. *The Excavation of Medinet Habu V.* Chicago: University of Chicago Press.

Hopkins, K. 1980. "Taxes and Trade in the Roman Empire (200 B.C.–A.D. 400)." *JRS* 70:101–125.

Howe, K. S. 1992. *Félix Teynard: Calotypes of Egypt. A Catalogue Raisonné.* New York: Hans P. Kraus Jr.

———. 1993. *Excursions along the Nile: The Photographic Discovery of Ancient Egypt.* Santa Barbara: Santa Barbara Museum of Art.

Huskinson, J. 2005. "Art and Architecture, A.D. 193–337." *CAH* 12: 672–702.

Huzar, E. G. 1995. "Emperor Worship in Julio-Claudian Egypt." *ANRW* II.18, no. 5:3092–3143.

Ismail, A. M. A. 2003. "Geophysical, Hydrological and Archaeological Investigation in the East Bank Area of Luxor—Southern Egypt." Ph.D. diss., University of Missouri, Rolla. AAT 3115167: Dissertation Abstracts International. Volume 64-12, section B, p. 5982.

Ismail, A. M., N. L. Anderson, and D. Rogers. 2005. "Hydrogeophysical Investigation at Luxor—Southern Egypt." *Journal of Environmental and Engineering Geophysics* 10, no. 1:35–49.

Jacobi, D., and T. Conti, eds. 1998. *Pascal Coste: Toutes les Égyptes.* Exhib. cat. Marseilles: Bibliothèque Municipale.

Jacquet-Gordon, H. 2003. *The Graffiti on the Khonsu Temple Roof at Karnak: A Manifestation of Personal Piety.* Chicago: University of Chicago Press.

Janowitz, N. 2002. *Icons of Power: Ritual Practices in Late Antiquity.* University Park: Pennsylvania State University Press.

Jasanoff, M. 2006. *Edge of Empire: Conquest and Collecting in the East, 1750–1850.* New York: HarperPerennial.

Jensen, R. M. 2005. *Face to Face: Portraits of the Divine in Early Christianity.* Minneapolis: Augsburg Fortress.

Johnson, J. H., ed. 1992. *Life in a Multi-Cultural Society: Egypt from Cambyses to Constantine and Beyond.* Chicago: Oriental Institute of the University of Chicago.

Johnson, W. R. 1998. "Monuments and Monumental Art under Amenhotep III: Evolution and Meaning." In *Amenhotep III: Perspectives on His Reign,* ed. D. B. O'Connor and E. H. Cline, 86–94. Ann Arbor: University of Michigan Press.

Jones, M. 1996. "A Roman Station at Abu Rawash." *MDAIK* 52:251–262.

———. 2008. "Monument and Site Conservation." In *Egyptology Today,* ed. R. H. Wilkinson, 98–120. Cambridge: Cambridge University Press.

Jorgensen, M. S. 1998. *Catalogue: Egypt II (1550–1080 B.C.: Ny Carlsberg Glyptotek.* Copenhagen: Ny Carlsberg Glyptotek.

Kähler, H. 1964. *Das Fünfsäulendenkmal für die tetrarchen auf dem Forum Romanum:* Monumenta Artis Romanae 3. Cologne: Verlag M. Dumont Schauberg.

Kákosy, L. 1995. "The Soter Tomb in Thebes." In Vleeming 1995, 61–68.

Kalavrezou-Maxeiner, I. 1975. "The Imperial Chamber at Luxor." *Dumbarton Oaks Papers* 29:225–251.

Kamal, M., and A. Tavares. 2010. "Rising to the Call: Salvage Archaeology Field School—2." In *Empowering the Present, Saving the Past.* Boston: Ancient Egypt Research Associates.

Karelyn, D. A. 2013. "Khram kul'ta rımskogo ımperatora v Diokletianovskoy kreposti: Sovremmenoye i komp'yuternaya rekonstruktsiya" (The cult sanctuary of the Roman emperor Diocletian in the fortress: The current state and a computer reconstruction) in Russian, www.xlegio.ru/fortification/roman-luxor/ (accessed 23 April 2014).

Kemp, B. J. 2006. *Ancient Egypt: Anatomy of a Civilization.* 2nd ed. New York: Routledge.

Kennedy, D. 1985. "The Composition of a Military Work Party in Roman Egypt (ILS 2483: Coptos)." *JEA* 71:156–160.

Kiernan, P. 2003. "Imperial Representation under Diocletian and the Tetrarchy (A.D. 284–305)." M.A. thesis: University of Cincinnati.

Kiilerich, B. 1993. *Late Fourth Century Classicism in the Plastic Arts: Studies in the So-Called Theodosian Renaissance.* Odense: Odense University Press.

Kirshenblatt-Gimblett, B. 1998. *Destination Culture: Tourism, Museums, and Heritage.* Berkeley: University of California Press.

Kiss, Z. 2007. "Alexandria in the Fourth to Seventh Centuries." In *Egypt in the Byzantine World, 300–700,* ed. R. Bagnall, 187–207. Cambridge: Cambridge University Press.

Kitchen. K. A. 1975. *Ramesside Inscriptions: Historical and Biographical.* Vol. 1. Oxford: Blackwell.

———. 1993a. *Ramesside Inscriptions Translated and Annotated: Translations,* vol. 1, *Ramesses I, Sethos I and Contemporaries.* Oxford: Blackwell.

———. 1993b. *Ramesside Inscriptions Translated and Annotated: Notes and Comments,* vol. 1, *Ramesses I, Sethos I and Contemporaries.* Oxford: Blackwell.

———. 2001. "King Lists." In *The Oxford Encyclopedia of Ancient Egypt,* vol. 2, ed. D. B. Redford, 234–238. Oxford: Oxford University Press.

Kleiner, D. 1992. *Roman Sculpture.* New Haven: Yale University Press.

Klotz, D. 2008. "Kneph: The Religion of Roman Thebes." Ph.D. diss., Yale University.

———. 2012a. "Egyptian Hieroglyphs." In Riggs 2012, 563–581.

———. 2012b. *Caesar in the City of Amun: Egyptian Temple Construction and Theology in Roman Thebes.* Turnhout: Brepols.

Kolb, F. 1987. *Diocletian und die Erste Tetrarchie.* Berlin: Walter de Gruyter.

———. 2001. *Herrscherideologie in der Spätantike.* Berlin: Akademie Verlag.

———. 2004. "*Praesens Deus:* Kaiser und Gott unter der Tetrarchie." In *Diokletian und die Tetrarchie: Aspekte einer Zeitenwende,* ed. A. Demandt, A. Goltz, and H. Schlange-Schöningen, 27–38. Berlin: Walter de Gruyter.

Kopytoff, I. 1986. "The Cultural Biography of Things: Commoditization as Process." In *The Social Life of Things: Commodities in Cultural Perspective,* ed. A. Appadurai, 64–91. Cambridge: Cambridge University Press.

Kozloff, A. P., and B. M. Bryan. 1992. *Egypt's Dazzling Sun: Amenhotep III and His World.* Cleveland: Cleveland Museum of Art.

Kruse, H. 1934. *Studien zur offiziellen Geltung des Kaiserbildes im römischen Reiche.* Paderborn: Ferdinand Schöningh.

Kuhlmann, K. P. 1988. *Das Ammoneion: Archäologie, Geschichte und Kultpraxis des Orakels von Siwa.* Mainz am Rhein: Philipp von Zabern.

Kuhoff, W. 2001. *Diokletian und die Epoche der Tetrarchie.* Frankfurt: Peter Lang.

Lacau, P. 1934. "Inscriptions latines du temple de Louxor." *ASAE* 34:17–46.

Lallemand, J. 1964. *L'administration civile de l'Égypte de l'avènement de Dioclétien à la creation du diocèse (284–382): Contribution à l'étude des rapports entre l'Égypte et l'Empire à la fin du IIIe et au IVe siècle.* Brussels: Mémoires de l'Académie Royale de Belgique.

Lane, E. W. 2000. *Description of Egypt.* Ed. J. Thompson. Cairo: American University in Cairo Press.

Łajtar, A. 2006. "Deir el-Bahari in the Hellenistic and Roman Periods: A Study of an Egyptian Temple Based on Greek Sources." *Journal of Juristic Papyrology. Supplement 4.*

———. 2008 "The Cult of Amenhotep Son of Hapu and Imhotep in Deir el-Bahari in the Hellenistic and Roman Periods." *Papyrologica Bruxellensia* 34:113–123.

———. 2012. "The Theban Region under the Roman Empire." In Riggs 2012, 171–189.

Leadbetter, W. 2000. "Galerius and the Revolt of the Thebaid in 293/4." *Antichthon* 34:82–94.

Leader-Newby, R. 2004. *Silver and Society in Late Antiquity: Functions and Meanings of Silver Plate in the Fourth to Seventh Centuries.* Aldershot, U.K.: Ashgate.

Lebas, M. A. 1839. *L'obelisque de Luxor: Histoire de sa translation à Paris.* Paris: Carilian-Goenry et V. Dalmont.

Leclant, J. 1951. "Fouilles et travaux en Égypte, 1950–1951." *Orientalia NS* 20, 453–475. http://www.egyptologues.net/orientalia/pdf/Orientalia_20_1951_453-475.pdf

———. 1965. *Recherches sur les monuments Thébains de la XXVe dynastie dite Éthiopienne.* 2 vols. Cairo: IFAO.

Lee, L., and S. Quirke. 2000. "Painting Materials." In *Ancient Egyptian Materials and Technology,* ed. P. T. Nicholson and I. Shaw, 104–120. Cambridge: Cambridge University Press.

Legrain. G. 1890. *Catalogue de feu M. R. Sabatier.* Paris: Imprimerie Alcan-Lévy.

———. 1914. *Louqsour sans les pharaons.* Paris: Vromant & Co.

———. 1917. "Rapport sur les nouveaux travaux exécutés à Louqsor à l'ouest du temple d'Amon (Octobre 1916–Mars 1917)." *ASAE* 17:49–75.

———. 1918. "Fouilles et recherches au forum de Louxor." *BIÉ* 11:241–260.

Le Guen, N. 2001. "L'Égypte et ses premiers photographes: Études des différents techniques et du matériel utilisés de 1839 à 1869." *Mémoires de DEA en Histoire des Techniques.* http://nileg.free.fr/doc/Memoire1_Cm.pdf (accessed 19 July 2012).

Lepsius, C. R. 1849. *Denkmaeler aus Aegypten und Aethiopien.* I. Berlin: Nicolaische Buckhandlung.

Lesquier, J. M. 1918. *L'armée romaine d'Egypt d'Auguste à Dioclétien.* Cairo: IFAO.

Lewis, N. 1937. "ΜΕΡΙΣΜΟΣ ΑΝΑΚΕΧΩΡΗΚΟΤΩΝ: An Aspect of the Roman Oppression in Egypt." *JEA* 23, no. 1:63–75.

———. 1983. *Life in Egypt under Roman Rule.* Oxford: Clarendon Press.

———. 1984. "The Romanity of Roman Egypt: A Growing Consensus." In *Proceedings of the 17th International Congress of Papyrology,* 1077–1084. Naples: Centro internazionale per lo studio dei papiri ercolanesi.

Ling, R. 1991. *Roman Painting.* New York: Cambridge University Press, 1991.

Liversidge, J. 1983. "Wall Painting from Military Sites in Roman Britain." In *La peinture murale romaine dans les provinces de l'Empire: Journées d'étude de Paris 23–25 septembre 1982,* ed. A. Barbet, 141–157. Oxford: BAR International Series 165.

Lloyd, A., ed. 2010. *A Companion to Ancient Egypt.* Vol. 2. Oxford: Wiley-Blackwell.

L'Orange, H. P. 1933. *Studien zur Geschichte des spätantiken Porträts.* Cambridge: Harvard University Press.

———. 1938. "Ein tetrarchisches Ehrendenkmal auf dem Forum Romanum." *Römische Mitteilungen* 53:1–34.

———. 1971. *Art Forms and Civic Life in the Late Roman Empire.* Princeton: Princeton University Press.

———. 1982. *Studies on the Iconography of Cosmic Kingship in the Ancient World.* New Rochelle, N.Y.: Caratzas Brothers.

L'Orange, H. P., and R. Unger. 1984. *Das spätantike Herrscherbild von Diokletian bis zu den Konstantin-Söhnen, 284–361 n. Chr.* Das Römische Herrscherbild. III. Abteilung 4. Berlin: Mann.

Lowenthal, D. 1998. *The Heritage Crusade and the Spoils of History.* Cambridge: Cambridge University Press.

Lyons, C. L., et al. 2005. *Antiquity and Photography: Early Views of Ancient Mediterranean Sites.* Los Angeles: J. Paul Getty Trust.

MacCormack, S. 1972. "Change and Continuity in Late Antiquity: The Ceremony of Adventus." *Historia* 21:721–752.

———. 1975a. "Latin Prose Panegyric." In *Empire and Aftermath: Silver Latin II,* ed. T. A. Dorey, 143–205. London: Routledge.

———. 1975b. "Roma, Constantinopolis, the Emperor, and His Genius." *Classical Quarterly* 25, no. 1:131–150.

———. 1981. *Art and Ceremony in Late Antiquity.* Berkeley: University of California Press.

———. 2012. "Imagery in Panegyric." In *Latin Panegyric,* ed. R. Rees, 240–250. New York: Oxford University Press.

MacCoull, L. 1984. "The Panegyric of Justin II by Dioscorus of Aphrodito." *Byzantion* 54:575–585.

———. 1988. *Dioscoros of Aphrodito: His Work and His World.* Berkeley: University of California Press.

MacDonald, W. 1976. *The Pantheon.* Cambridge: Harvard University Press.

———. 1986. *The Architecture of the Roman Empire,* vol. 2, *An Urban Appraisal.* New Haven: Yale University Press.

Mackensen, M. 2009. "The Tetrarchic Fort at Nag al-Hagar in the Province of Thebaïs: Preliminary Report (2005–8)." *JRA,* 22:286–311.

Mackensen, M., and M. El-Bialy. 2006. "The Late Roman Fort at Nag el-Hagar Near Kom Ombo in the Province of Thebaïs (Upper Egypt): Report on the First Season of the Egyptian-Swiss Joint Mission." *MDAIK* 62:161–195.

Manning, S. 1887. *The Land of the Pharaohs, Including a Sketch of Sinai.* London: Religious Tract Society.

Marlowe, E. 2006. "Framing the Sun: The Arch of Constantine and the Roman Cityscape." *Art Bulletin* 88, no. 2:223–242.

Mason, R., and E. Avrami. 2000. "Heritage Values and Challenges of Conservation Planning." In Teutonico and Palumbo 2000, 13–26.

Mathers, C., T. Darvill, and B. J. Little. 2005. *Heritage of Value, Archaeology of Renown.* Gainesville: University Press of Florida.

Mathews, T. 1999. *The Clash of Gods: A Reinterpretation of Early Christian Art.* Princeton: Princeton University Press.

———. 2001. "The Emperor and the Icon." *AAAH* 15:163–179.

Mattingly, D. 1997. *Dialogs in Roman Imperialism: Power, Discourse, and Discrepant Experience in the Roman Empire. JRA* Suppl. Series 23.

———. 2004. "Being Roman: Expressing Identity in a Provincial Setting." *JRA* 17:5–25.

———. 2011. *Imperialism, Power, and Identity: Experiencing the Roman Empire.* Princeton: Princeton University Press.

Mattingly, H. 1952. "Jovius and Herculius." *Harvard Theological Review* 45:131–134.

Mayeur-Jaouen, C. 1992. "Un jésuite français en Égypte: Le père Jullien." In *Itinéraires d'Égypte: Mélanges offerts au père Maurice Martin S.J.*, ed. C. Décobert, 213–247. Cairo: IFAO.

Mazza, R. 1998. "The Supposed Egyptian Earthquakes of 184 and 95 BC: Critical Review and Some Lines of Research in Historical Seismology Using Greek Papyri from Egypt." *Annali di Geofisica* 41, no. 1:121–125.

McFadden, S. 2007. "Courtly Places and Sacred Spaces: The Social and Political Significance of Monumental Wall Paintings in Late Antiquity." Ph.D. diss., University of Pennsylvania. http://repository.upenn.edu/dissertations/AAI3292052/ (accessed 10 May 2012).

———. 2013. "A Constantinian Image Program in Rome Rediscovered: The Late Antique Megalographia from the So-Called *domus Faustae.*" *MAAR* 58:82–114.

McKenzie, J. 2007. *The Architecture of Alexandria and Egypt, c. 300 B.C. to A.D. 700.* New Haven: Yale University Press.

Merewether, C. 1997. "Traces of Loss." In *Irresistible Decay: Ruins Reclaimed,* ed. M. S. Roth, C. Lyons, and C. Merewether, 25–40. Los Angeles: Getty Research Institute for the History of Art and the Humanities.

Meskell, L. 2003. "Pharaonic Legacies: Postcolonialism, Heritage, and Hyperreality." In *The Politics of Archaeology and Identity in a Global Context,* ed. S. Kane. Boston: Archaeological Institute of America.

Meyer-Graft, R. 1979. "Zur Technik der Wandmalerei und ihrer Reinigung." In Deckers 1979, 617–620.

Millar, F. 1973. "The Imperial Cult and the Persecutions." In *Le culte des souverains dans l'Empire romain,* ed. W. den Boer, 145–165. Geneva: Fondation Hardt.

Milne, J. G. 1924. "Aemilianus the 'Tyrant.'" *JEA* 10, no. 2:80–82.

Minas-Nerpel, M. 2012. "Egyptian Temples of the Roman Period." In Riggs 2012, 362–382.

Mitchell, T. 1998. "The Heritage of Violence." Paper presented at the sixth biennial conference of the International Association for the Study of Traditional Environments, "Manufacturing Heritage/Consuming Tradition," Cairo, 15 December 1998.

———. 2001. "Making the Nation: The Politics of Heritage in Egypt." In *Consuming Tradition, Manufacturing Heritage: Global Norms and Urban Forms in the Age of Tourism,* ed. Nezar al-Sayyad, 212–239. London: Routledge.

Mols, S. T. A. M., and E. M. Moormann. 2010. "L'edificio romano sotto S. Maria Maggiore a Roma e le sue pitture: Proposta per una nuova lettura." *Römische Mitteilungen* 116:469–506.

Momigliano, A. 1986. "How Emperors Became Gods." *American Scholar* 55:181–193.

Mond, R., and O. H. Myers. 1934a. *The Bucheum,* vol. 2, *The Inscriptions.* London: Egypt Exploration Society.

———. 1934b. *The Bucheum,* vol. 3, *The Plates.* London: Egypt Exploration Society.

Monneret de Villard, U. 1953. "The Temple of the Imperial Cult at Luxor." *Archaeologia* 95:85–105 and pl. XXXIV.

Montserrat, D., and L. Meskell. 1997. "Mortuary Archaeology and Religious Landscape at Graeco-Roman Deir el-Medina." *JEA* 83:179–197.

Moormann, E. M. 2011. *Divine Interiors: Mural Paintings in Greek and Roman Sanctuaries.* Amsterdam: Amsterdam University Press.

Mora, P., L. Mora, and P. Philippot, 1999. *Conservation of Wall Paintings.* Rome and London: Butterworths.

Most, G. W. 2009. "On Fragments." In *The Fragment: An Incomplete History,* ed. W. Tronzo, 9–19. Los Angeles: Getty Research Institute.

Muhammed, M., and Abdel Qader. 1968. "Preliminary Report on the Excavations Carried out in the Temple of Luxor, Seasons 1958–1959 and 1959–1960." *ASAE* 60:227–279.

Munier, H. 1940. "Les monuments coptes d'après les explorations du Père Michel Jullien." *BSAC* 6:141–168.

Murnane, W. J. 1985. "False Doors and Cult Practices inside Luxor Temple." *Mélanges Gamal eddin Mokhtar, BdÉ* 97, no. 2:135–148.

———. 1999. "Temple of Luxor." In *Encyclopedia of the Archaeology of Ancient Egypt,* ed. K. A. Bard and S. B. Shubart, 449–453. New York: Taylor and Francis.

———. 2001. "Luxor." In *The Oxford Encyclopedia of Ancient Egypt,* ed. D. B. Redford, 309–312. Oxford: Oxford University Press.

Murray, J. 1873. *Murray's Handbook Egypt: A Handbook for Travellers in Egypt.* 4th ed. London: John Murray.

———. 1907. *Murray's Handbook Egypt: A Handbook for Travellers in Egypt.* 11th ed. London: E. Stanford.

Mustafa, M. el-D., and H. Jaritz. 1984–1985. "A Roman Fortress at Nag' el-Hagar. First Preliminary Report." *ASAE* 70:21–31.

Nanda, R. 2001. "Group Report: Values and Society." In Baer and Snickars 2001, 61–80.

Nassar, I., P. Almárcegui, and C. Worswick. 2010. *Gardens of Sand: Nineteenth-Century Photographs of Egypt, Arabia, Turkey, and the Levant.* Cairo: American University in Cairo Press.

Nelson, R. S. 2000. "To Say and to See: Ekphrasis and Vision in Byzantium." In *Visuality before and beyond the Renaissance: Seeing as Others Saw,* ed. R. S. Nelson, 143–169. Cambridge: Cambridge University Press.

Nichol, D. R. 2004. *Francis Frith in Egypt and Palestine: A Victorian Photographer Abroad.* Princeton: Princeton University Press.

Nicholson, C., and O. Nicholson. 1989. "Lactantius, Hermes Trismegistus and Constantinian Obelisks." *Journal of Hellenic Studies* 109:198–200.

Nightingale, F. 1987. *Letters from Egypt: A Journey on the Nile, 1849–1850,* ed. A. Sattin. London: Parkway Publishing.

Nixon, C. E. V. 1983. "Latin Panegyrics in the Tetrarchic and Constantinian Period." In *History and Historians in Late Antiquity,* ed. B. Croke and E. M. Emmett, 88–99. New York: Pergamon Press.

———. 1990. "The Use of the Past by the Gallic Panegyrists." In *Reading the Past in Late Antiquity,* ed. G. Clarke, 1–36. Rushcutters Bay: Australian National University Press.

Nixon, C. E. V., and B. S. Rodgers, eds. 1994. *In Praise of Later Roman Emperors: The Panegyrici Latini.* Berkeley: University of California Press.

Nock, A. D. 1947. "The Emperor's Divine Comes." *JRS* 37:102–116.

Noel, J. M. 2003. "Ritual, Religion, and the Law: Transformations in Architecture under the Tetrarchy." In *Confrontations in Late Antiquity: Imperial Presentation and Regional Adaptation,* ed. L. J. Hall, 129–147. Cambridge: Orchard Academic.

Norden, F. L. 1757. *Travels in Egypt and Nubia.* 2 vols. London: Lockyer Davis and Charles Ryemer.

O'Neill, S. J. 2011. "The Emperor as Pharaoh: Provincial Dynamics and Visual Representations of Imperial Authority in Roman Egypt, 30 B.C.–A.D. 69." Ph.D. diss., University of Cincinnati.

Osman, C. 1997a. *Egypt Caught in Time.* Cairo: American University in Cairo Press.

———. 1997b. "Robert Murray of Edinburgh (1822–1893): The Discovery of Neglected Calotypes of Egypt." *Photoresearcher* 6.5–11. http://www.donau-uni.ac.at/imperia/md/content/studium/kultur/zbw/eshph/photoresearcher/photoresearcher_no6.pdf

Palumbo, G. 2000. "Threats and Challenges to the Archaeological Heritage in the Mediterranean." In Teutonico and Palumbo 2000, 3–12. Los Angeles: Getty Conservation Institute.

Peacock, D. 2000. "The Roman Period." In *The Oxford History of Ancient Egypt,* ed. I. Shaw, 437–438. Oxford: Oxford University Press.

Peacock, D., and L. Blue. 2006. *Myos Hormos—Quseir al-Qadim, Roman and Islamic Ports on the Red Sea,* vol. 1, *The Survey and Report on the Excavations.* Oxford: Oxbow.

Pekáry, T. 1985. *Das römische Kaiserbildnis in Staat, Kult und Gesellschaft: Dargestellt anhand der Schriftquellen.* Berlin: Mann Verlag.

Pensabene, P. 2010. "Villa del Casale e il territorio di Piazza Armerina tra tardoantico e medioevo le nuove recherché del 2004–2009." In *Piazza Armerina: Villa del Casale el la Sicilia tra tardoantico e medioevo,* ed. P. Pensabene, 1–33. Rome: L'Erma di Bretschneider.

Pfeiffer, S. 2012. "The Imperial Cult in Egypt." In Riggs 2012, 83–102.

Pintaudi, R. 2008. *Antinoupolis,* vol. 1. Florence: Istituto Papirologico G. Vitelli.

Pococke, R. 1743. *A Description of the East and Some Other Countries,* vol. 1. London: W. Boyer.

Poggi, D. 2007. "Conservation of the Roman Wall Paintings in Luxor Temple: Study of Constituent Materials and Techniques Employed for the Realization of the Different Pictorial Phases." Unpublished internal document, Artelab s.r.l. Cairo: ARCE, Egyptian Antiquities Conservation Project Archive.

Pond Rothman, M. S. 1975. "The Panel of the Emperors Enthroned on the Arch of Galerius." *Byzantine Studies Tempe* 2, no. 1:19–40.

———. 1977. "The Thematic Organization of the Panel Reliefs on the Arch of Galerius." *AJA* 81, no. 4:427–454.

Poole, R. S. 1882. *The Cities of Egypt.* London: Smith, Elder.

Porter, B., and R. L. B. Moss. 1960. *Topographical Bibliography of Ancient Egyptian Hieroglyphic Texts, Reliefs, and Paintings,* vol. 1, *The Theban Necropolis,* part 1, *Private Tombs.* 2nd ed. Oxford: Clarendon Press.

———. 1972. *Topographical Bibliography of Ancient Egyptian Hieroglyphic Texts, Reliefs, and Paintings,* vol. 2, *Theban Temples.* 2nd ed. Oxford: Clarendon Press.

———. 1991. *Topographical Bibliography of Ancient Egyptian Hieroglyphic Texts, Reliefs, and Paintings,* vol. 6, *Upper Egypt: Chief Temples.* Oxford: Griffith Institute.

Price, S. 1984. *Ritual and Power: The Roman Imperial Cult in Asia Minor.* Cambridge: Cambridge University Press.

Prime, W. C. 1857. *Boat Life in Egypt and Nubia.* New York: Harper & Brothers.

Quibell, J. E. 1909. *Excavations at Saqqara (1907–1908).* Cairo: IFAO.

———. 1912. *Excavations at Saqqara (1908–9, 1909–10): The Monastery of Apa Jeremias.* Cairo: IFAO.

Rappoport, A. S. 1903. *History of Egypt from 330 B.C. to the Present Time,* vol. 9, pt. B. London: Grolier Society.

Rashed, A. 1994. "Public Participation in the Preservation of Historical Environments: A Case Study of Luxor City, Egypt." Ph.D. diss., University of York, U.K., Institute of Advanced Architectural Studies.

Rathbone, D. W. 1990. "Villages, Land and Population in Graeco-Roman Egypt." *PCPS* 36:103–142.

Raulwing, P., and T. L. Gertzen. 2013. "Friedrich Wilhelm Freiherr von Bissing im Blickpunkt ägyptologischer und zeithistorischer Forschungen: Die Jahr 1914 bis 1926." In *Egyptology from the First World War to the Third Reich: Ideology, Scholarship and Individual Biographies,* ed. T. Schneider and P. Raulwing, 34–119. Leiden: Brill.

Rea, J. R. 1981. "Aurelius Reginus, Praeses Thebaidos." *CPR* 7, no. 21, *ZPE* 41:281–282.

Rea, J. R., R. P. Salomans, and K. A. Worp. 1985. "A Ration-Warrant for an Adiutor Memoriae." *YCS* 28:101–113.

Reddé, M. 1995. "Dioclétian et les fortifications militaries de l'Antiquité tardive: Quelques considerations de méthode." *Antiquité Tardive 3:91–124.*

———. 2004. "Réflexions critiques sur les chapelles militaries (aedes principiorum). *JRA* 17:442–463.

Redon, B. 2009. "L'armée et les bains en Égypte hellénistique et romaine." *BIFAO* 109, 407–450.

Rees, R. 1993. "Images and Image: A Re-examination of Tetrarchic Iconography." *Greece and Rome* 40:181–200.

———. 2002. *Layers of Loyalty in Latin Panegyrics, AD 289–307.* Oxford: Oxford University Press.

———. 2004. *Diocletian and the Tetrarchy.* Edinburgh: Edinburgh University Press.

———. 2005. "The Emperors' New Name: Diocletian Jovius and Maximian Herculius." In *Herakles and Hercules: Exploring a Graeco-Roman Divinity,* ed. L. Rawlings and H. Bowden, 223–239. Swansea: Classical Press of Wales.

———, ed. 2012. *Latin Panegyric.* Oxford: Oxford University Press.

Riad, H. 1968. "Quelques inscriptions grecques et latines du temple de Louxor." *ASAE* 60:281–295.

Riggs, C. 2000. "Roman Period Mummy Masks from Deir el-Bahri." *JEA* 86:121–144.

———. 2002. "Facing the Dead: Recent Research on the Funerary Art of Ptolemaic and Roman Egypt." *AJA* 106:85–101.

———. 2005. *The Beautiful Burial in Roman Egypt: Art, Identity and Funerary Religion.* Oxford: Oxford University Press.

———, ed. 2012. *The Oxford Handbook of Roman Egypt.* Oxford: Oxford University Press.

Ritner, R. K. 1998. "Egypt under Roman Rule: The Legacy of Ancient Egypt." In *The Cambridge History of Egypt,* ed. C. F. Petry, 1–33. Cambridge: Cambridge University Press.

———. 2009. *The Libyan Anarchy: Inscriptions from Egypt's Third Intermediate Period.* Atlanta: Society for Biblical Literature.

Roberts, M. 1989. *The Jeweled Style: Poetry and Poetics in Late Antiquity.* Ithaca: Cornell University Press.

Robichon, C., and A. Varille. 1940. *Description sommaire du temple primitive de Médamoud.* Cairo: IFAO.

Romano, J. F., K. Parlasca, M. Rogers, and B. V. Bothmer. 1979. *The Luxor Museum of Ancient Egyptian Art: Catalogue.* Cairo: ARCE.

Rondot, V. 2013. *Derniers visages des dieux d'Egypte: Iconographies, panthéons et cultes dans le Fayoum hellénisé des IIe–IIIe siècles de notre ère.* Paris: PUPS (La Sorbonne).

Roth, A. M. 2005. "Erasing a Reign." In *Hatshepsut: From Queen to Pharaoh*, ed. C. H. Roehrig, 277–281. New York: Metropolitan Museum of Art.

Ruffini, G. 2006. "The Commonality of Rare Names in Byzantine Egypt." *ZPE* 158:213–225.

Rutherford, I. 2003. "Pilgrimage in Graeco-Roman Egypt: New Perspectives on Graffito from the Memnonion at Abydos." In *Ancient Perspectives on Egypt,* ed. R. Matthews and C. Roemer, 171–190. London: UCL Press.

Sabrié, M., and R. Sabrié. 1999. "Les manifestations du culte impérial à travers la peinture." *Revue Archéologique de Narbonnaise* 32:57–63.

Salomon, R. 1991. "Epigraphic Remains of Indian Traders in Egypt." *Journal of the American Oriental Society*, 111, no. 4:731–736.

Salzman, M. 1990. *On Roman Time: The Codex-Calendar of 354 and the Rhythms of Urban Life in Late Antiquity.* Berkeley: University of California Press.

Samuel, A. E., W. K. Hastings, A. K. Bowman, and R. S. Bagnall. 1971. *Death and Taxes: Ostraka in the Royal Ontario Museum*. Toronto: A. M. Hakkert.

Sauneron, S. 1983. *Villes et légendes d'Égypte.* 2nd ed. Cairo: IFAO.

Säve Söderbergh, T. 1957. *Private Tombs at Thebes,* vol. 1, *Four Eighteenth Dynasty Tombs.* Oxford: Oxford University Press.

Schwartz, J. 1968. "Autour du dossier de Paniskos (P. Mich. 214–221)." *Aegyptus* 48:110–115.

———. 1975. *L. Domitius Domitianus (Étude numismatique et papyrologique).* Brussels: Fondation Égyptologique Reine Élisabeth.

———. 1977. "L. Domitius Domitianus." *ZPE* 25:217–220.

Schwarz, J., and H. Wild. 1950. *Fouilles Franco-Suisses. Rapports I: Qasr-Qarun/Dionysias 1948.* Cairo: IFAO.

Scott Ryberg, I. 1955. "Rites of the State Religion in Roman Art." MAAR 22:1–227.

Severin, H. 1998. "Zur Skulptur und Malerei der spätantiken und frühmittelalterlichen Zeit in Ägypten." In *Ägypten in spätantik-christlicher Zeit*, ed. M. Krause. Wiesbaden: Dr. Ludwig Reichert Verlag.

Sheehan, P. 1996. "The Roman Fortress of Babylon in Old Cairo." In *Archaeological Research in Roman Egypt,* ed. D. M. Bailey, 95–98. Ann Arbor: Journal of Roman Archaeology, Suppl. Series 19.

———. 2010. *Babylon of Egypt: The Archaeology of Old Cairo and the Origins of the City.* Cairo: American University in Cairo Press.

Sicard, C. 1982a. *Oeuvres,* vol. 1, *Lettres et relations inédits.* Ed. M. Martin. Cairo: IFAO.

———. 1982b. *Oeuvres*, vol. 2, *Relations et mémoires imprimés.* Ed. M. Martin. Cairo: IFAO.

———. *Oeuvres,* vol. 3, *Parallèle géographique de l'ancienne Égypte et de l'Égypte moderne.* Ed. S. Sauneron and M. Martin. Cairo: IFAO.

Sidebotham, S. E. 1986. *Roman Economic Policy in the Erythra Thalassa.* Leiden: Brill.

———. 1994. "Preliminary Report on the 1990–1991 Seasons of Fieldwork at 'Abu Sha'ar (Red Sea Coast)." *JARCE* 31:133–158.

Sidebotham, S. E., R. E. Zitterkopf, and J. A. Riley. 1991. "Survey of the 'Abu Sha'ar—Nile Road." *AJA* 95:571–622.

Skeat, T. C. 1964. *Papyri from Panopolis in the Chester Beatty Library.* Dublin: Hodges, Figgis.

Small, A., ed. 1996. *Subject and Ruler: The Cult of the Ruling Power in Classical Antiquity.* Ann Arbor: *JRA*, Suppl. Series 17.

Smith, J. Z. 1987. *To Take Place: Towards Theory in Ritual.* Chicago: University of Chicago Press.

Smith, L., and N. Akagawa. 2009. *Intangible Heritage.* New York: Routledge.

Southern, P., and K. R. Dixon. 1996. *The Late Roman Army.* London: B. T. Batsford.

Speidel, M. P. 1984. "Palmyrenian Irregulars at Koptos." *BASP* 21:221–224.

Speidel, M. P., and M. F. Pavkovic. 1989. "Legion II Flavia Constantia at Luxor." *AJP* 110:151–154.

Srejović, D. 1993. "The Representations of Tetrarchs in Romuliana." *Antiquité Tardive* 2:143–152.

Srejović, D., and Č. Vasić. 1993. "Emperor Galerius's Buildings in Romuliana (Gamzigrad, Eastern Serbia)." *Antiquité Tardive* 2:123–141.

Stauffer, A., ed. 1995. *Textiles of Late Antiquity.* New York: Metropolitan Museum of Art.

Stevenson Smith, W. 1952. "Archaeological News: The Near East, 1950–1951: Egypt." *AJA* 56:39–50.

Stewart, P. 2004. *Roman Art.* New York: Cambridge University Press.

———. 2006. "The Image of the Roman Emperor." In *Presence: The Inherence of the Prototype within Images and Other Objects,* ed. R. Maniura and R. Shepherd, 243–259. Aldershot, U.K.: Ashgate.

———. 2007. "Gell's Idols and Roman Cult." In *Art's Agency and Art History,* ed. R. Osborne and J. Tanner, 158–179. Oxford: Blackwell.

Sumner, G. 2009. *Roman Military Dress.* Stroud, U.K.: History Press.

Tait, W. J. 1995. "Theban Magic." In Vleeming 1995, 169–182.

Tallet, G., and C. Zivie-Coche. 2012. "Imported Cults." In Riggs 2012, 436–456.

Teutonico, J. M., and G. Palumbo, eds. 2000. *Management Planning for Archaeological Sites.* Los Angeles: Getty Conservation Institute.

Thiel, W. 2002. "Tetrakionia: Überlegungen zu einem Denkmaltypus tetrarchischer Zeit im Osten des Römischen Reiches." *Antiquité Tardive* 10:299–326.

———. 2006. "Die 'Pompeius-Säule' in Alexandria und die Viersäulenmonumente Ägyptens: Überlegungen zur tetrarchischen Repräsentationskultur in Nordafrika." In *Die Tetrarchie: Ein neues Regierungssystem und seine mediale Präsentation*, ed. D. Boschung and W. Eck, 249–322. Wiesbaden: Reichert Verlag.

Thier, C. 1995. Civils et militaires dans les temples: Occupation illicite et expulsion. *BIFAO* 95:493–516.

Thomas, D. J. 1976. "The Date of the Revolt of L. Domitius Domitianus." *ZPE* 22:253–279.

Thomas, T. 2002. "The Medium Matters: Reading the Remains of a Late Antique Textile." In *Reading Medieval Images: The Art Historian and the Object,* ed. E. Sears and T. Thomas, 38–49. Ann Arbor: University of Michigan Press.

———. 2010. "Egyptian Art of Late Antiquity." In Lloyd 2010, 1032–1063.

Thompson, J. 1992a. *Sir John Gardner Wilkinson and His Circle.* Austin: University of Texas Press.

———. 1992b. "The Sir John Gardner Wilkinson Papers: An Update." *JEA* 78:273–274.

———. 2010. *Edward William Lane, 1801–1876: The Life of the Pioneering Egyptologist and Orientalist.* Cairo: American University in Cairo Press.

Thompson, M. W. 1981. *Ruins: Their Preservation and Display.* London: British Museum Publications.

Tőrők, L. 2005. *Transfigurations of Hellenism: Aspects of Late Antique Art in Egypt,* A.D. *250–700.* Leiden: Brill.

Toynbee, J. M. C. 1944. *Roman Medallions.* Rev. ed. New York: American Numismatic Society.

Trant, C. 1997. "Art, Landscape and the Past: An Artist's View." In *The Cultural Life of Images,* ed. B. L. Molyneaux, 11–21. New York: Routledge.

Ulrich, R. B. 2007. *Roman Woodworking.* New Haven: Yale University Press.

Urry, J. 2002. *The Tourist Gaze.* London: Sage.

Usick, P., and R. Parkinson. 2008. "The History of the Nebamun Wall Paintings: An Archival Investigation." In *The Nebamun Wall Paintings: Conservation, Scientific Analyses and Display at the British Museum,* ed. A. Middleton and K. Uprichard, 5–15. London: Archetype Publications.

Vaczek, L., and G. Buckland. 1981. *Travelers in Ancient Lands: A Portrait of the Middle East, 1839–1919.* Boston: New York Graphic Society.

Valbelle, D., and J.-Y. Carrez-Maratray, eds. 2000. *Le camp romain du Bas-Empire à Tell el-Herr: Mission Franco-Égyptienne de Tell el-Herr (Nord Sinai).* Paris: Errance.

Vandersleyen, C. 1962. *Chronologie des préfets d'Égypte de 284 à 395.* Brussels: Latomus.

Van der Spek, K. 2011. *The Modern Neighbors of Tutankhamun: History, Life, and Work in the Villages of the Theban West Bank.* Cairo: American University in Cairo Press.

Vandorpe, K. 1995. "City of Many a Gate, Harbour for Many a Rebel." In Vleeming 1995, 203–241.

Van Siclen, C. C. 1990. "A Kiosk(?) of Shabako at Luxor Temple." *Varia Aegyptiaca* 6:177–183.

———. 2005. "La cour du IXe pylône à Karnak." *Bulletin de la Société Française d'Égyptologie* 163:27–46.

———. 2006. "Soundings South of the Eighth Pylon at Karnak, 1999–2000." *ASAE* 79:187–193.

Varner, E. 2004. *Mutilation and Transformation:* Damnatio Memoriae *and Roman Imperial Portraiture.* Leiden: Brill.

Viñas, S. M. 2009. "Minimal Intervention Revisited." In *Conservation Principles, Dilemmas and Uncomfortable Truths,* ed. A. Richmond and A. Bracker, 47–59. Oxford: Butterworth-Heinemann.

Vleeming, S. P., ed. 1995. *Hundred-Gated Thebes: Acts of a Colloquium on Thebes and the Theban Area in the Graeco-Roman Period.* Leiden: Brill.

Von Beckerath, J. 1966. "The Nile Level Records at Karnak and Their Importance for the History of the Libyan Period." *JARCE* 5:43–55.

———. 1997. *Chronologie des pharaonischen Ägypten: Die Zeitbestimmung der ägyptischen Geschichte von der Vorzeit bis 332 v. Chr.* Mainz am Rhein: Philipp von Zabern.

Von Bissing, F. W. 1926. "Altchristliche Wandmalereien aus Ägypten." In *Festschrift zum Sechzigsten Geburtstag von Paul Clemen*, 181–188. Düsseldorf: L. Schwann.

Walden, C. 1990. "The Tetrarchic Image." *Oxford Journal of Archaeology* 9, no. 2:221–235.

Wareth, U. A., and Z. Pierre. 1992. "Nag al-Hagar: A Roman Fortress with a Palace of the Late Roman Empire. Second Preliminary Report." *BIFAO* 92:185–210.

Weigall, A. E.-P. 1907. "Report on Work Done in the Temple of Luxor in 1905–1906." *ASAE* 8:113–115.

Weitzmann, K., ed. 1973. *Age of Spirituality: Late Antique and Early Christian Art, Third to Seventh Century.* New York: Metropolitan Museum of Art.

Whitby, M., ed. 1998. *The Propaganda of Power: The Role of Panegyric in Late Antiquity.* Boston: Brill.

Whitehouse, H. 1998. "Roman in Life, Egyptian in Death: The Painted Tomb of Petosiris in the Dakhleh Oasis." In *Life on the Fringe: Living in the Southern Egyptian Deserts during the Roman and Early-Byzantine Periods,* ed. O. Kaper, 253–267. Leiden: Research School CNWS, Leiden University.

———. 2010. "Mosaics and Paintings in Graeco-Roman Egypt." In Lloyd 2010, 1008–1031.

Wickett, E. 2009. "Archaeological Memory, the Leitmotifs of Ancient Egyptian Festival Tradition, and Cultural Legacy in the Festival Tradition of Luxor: The *Mulid* of Sidi Abu'l Hajjaj al-Uqsori and the Ancient Egyptian 'Feast of Opet.'" *JARCE* 45:403–426.

Wilcken, U. 1885. "Arsinoitische Tempelrechnungen." *Hermes* 20:430–476.

Wilfong, T. 2002. *Women of Jeme: Lives in a Coptic Town in Late Antique Egypt.* Ann Arbor: University of Michigan Press.

Wilkinson, J. G. 1835. *Topography of Thebes and General View of Egypt.* London: John Murray.

Williams, S. 1985. *Diocletian and the Roman Recovery.* New York: Methuen.

Wilson, C. W. 1883. *Picturesque Palestine, Sinai and Egypt,* vol. 4. London: J. S. Virtue.

Wilson Jones, M. 2000. *Principles of Roman Architecture.* New Haven: Yale University Press.

———. 2002. "Genesis and Mimesis: The Design of the Arch of Constantine in Rome." *JSAH* 59:50–77.

Woolf, G. 2008. "Divinity and Power in Ancient Rome." In *Religion and Power: Divine Kingship in the Ancient World and Beyond,* ed. N. Brisch, 243–260. Chicago: University of Chicago Press.

Worp, K. A. 1990. "Observations on Demotic Tax Receipts from the Theban Region in Roman Times." *ZPE* 80:243–252.

Yegul, F. 1982. "A Study in Architectural Iconography: Kaisersaal and the Imperial Cult." *Art Bulletin* 64, no. 1:7–31.

Yoyotte, J. 1951. "Le Martelage des noms royaux éthiopiens par Psammétique II." *Revue d'Égyptologie* 8:215–239.

Zitterkopf, R. E., and S. E. Sidebotham. 1989. "Stations and Towers on the Quseir-Nile Road." *JEA* 75:155–189.

CONTRIBUTORS

Luigi De Cesaris
Master Conservator and Restorer and former teacher at the Istituto Centrale del Restauro, Rome. Director of the conservation project. (De Cesaris S.r.l. Enterprise.)

James B. Heidel
Architect, Archaeological Mission of the Epigraphic Survey, Oriental Institute, University of Chicago, Luxor, Egypt.

W. Raymond Johnson
Director, Epigraphic Survey, Oriental Institute, University of Chicago, USA and Egypt.

Michael Jones
Associate Director, Egyptian Antiquities Conservation Project, American Research Center in Egypt, Cairo, Egypt.

Susanna McFadden
Assistant Professor, Department of Art History & Music, Fordham University, New York, New York, USA.

Emiliano Ricchi
Head Conservator and Restorer. (De Cesaris S.r.l. Enterprise).

Giovanni Ruffini
Associate Professor, Departments of Classical Studies and History, Fairfield University, Fairfield, Connecticut, USA.

Alberto Sucato
Head Conservator and Restorer. (De Cesaris S.r.l. Enterprise.)

INDEX

Illustration references, indexed using figure numbers, *are found at the ends of entries, following all page references.*

PICTURE CREDITS

Frontispiece Photo Y. Kobylecky: ARCE

Introduction

Figure I.1 Photo A. and A. Vescovo: ARCE
I.2 Photo M. Jones: ARCE
I.3 Photo A. and A. Vescovo: ARCE
I.4 Photo M. Jones: ARCE
I.5 Photo M. Jones: ARCE
I.6 M. Jones Collection (Wide World Photo 873992)
I.7 Photo M. Jones; superimposed outline J. Dobrowolski
I.8 Photo M. Jones. Reproduced courtesy of the Ministry of State for Antiquities, Luxor Museum: Reg. no. 38
I.9 Photo M. Jones: ARCE
I.10 M. Jones Collection
I.11 Photo M. Jones: ARCE

Chapter 1

Figure 1.1 Map J. Dobrowolski
1.2 Map J. Dobrowolski
1.3 Photo Rajan Patel; superimposed outline J. Dobrowolski
1.4 M. Jones Collection, Acme photo no. 224695
1.5 Courtesy the Egypt Exploration Society
1.6 Reproduced courtesy of the Ministry of State for Antiquities, Luxor Museum: Reg. no. J.194, Q.1512

Chapter 2

Figure 2.1 Plan J. Dobrowolski
2.2 Photo M. Jones: ARCE
2.3 Photo Sameh Abdel Mohsen. Courtesy of the Egyptian Museum, Cairo: JE 10176, CG 727
2.4 Photo A. and A. Vescovo: ARCE
2.5 Photo A. and A. Vescovo: ARCE
2.6 Photo A. and A. Vescovo: ARCE
2.7 ARCE
2.8 Photo M. Jones: ARCE

Chapter 3

Figure 3.1 Photo A. and A. Vescovo: ARCE
3.2 Photo J. Heidel
3.3 After Gregory 1995–1997, vol. 3, E1.5 (left) and F1.3.a (right)
3.4 Drawing J. Heidel
3.5 Photo M. Jones: ARCE
3.6 Photo J. Heidel
3.7 Photo M. Jones: ARCE
3.8 Drawing J. Heidel
3.9 Drawing J. Heidel
3.10 Drawing J. Heidel
3.11 Drawing J. Heidel
3.12 Drawing J. Heidel
3.13 Drawing J. Heidel
3.14 Drawing W. R. Johnson
3.15 Photo A. and A. Vescovo: ARCE
3.16 Photo W. R. Johnson
3.17 Photo Ole Haupt. Ny Carlsberg Glyptotek, Copenhagen: AEIN 33
3.18 Photo M. Jones: ARCE
3.19 Photo M. Jones: ARCE
3.20 Photo W. R. Johnson
3.21 Photo W. R. Johnson
3.22 Photo A. and A. Vescovo: ARCE
3.23 Photo A. and A. Vescovo: ARCE
3.24 Photo A. and A. Vescovo: ARCE

Chapter 4

Figure 4.1 © National Trust Images. Courtesy of the Bodleian Libraries, Oxford. MS. Wilkinson, dep. d. 34, page 26r (52)

4.2 M. Jones Collection; superimposed outline J. Dobrowolski

4.3 Courtesy of the Chicago House Photographic Archives, Epigraphic Survey, Oriental Institute, University of Chicago, Archive 0112

4.4 Drawing J. Dobrowolski (after Norden in Buhl 1993, pl. 62, and Pocock 1743 pl. XL)

4.5 ARCE

4.6 © V&A Images, Victoria and Albert Museum, London: SD 912 21

4.7 © National Trust Images. Courtesy of the Bodleian Library, Oxford. MS. Wilkinson, dep. d. 34, page 27r (54)

4.8 © National Trust Images. Courtesy of the Bodleian Library, Oxford. MS. Wilkinson, dep. d. 34, page 25v (51)

4.9 © Réunion des Musées Nationaux. Courtesy of the Musée d'Orsay, Paris: PHO 1986 131 266.

4.10 © Réunion des Musées Nationaux. Courtesy of the Musée d'Orsay, Paris: PHO 1986 131 262

4.11 Photo A. Beato. Courtesy of the Chicago House Photographic Archives, Epigraphic Survey, Oriental Institute, University of Chicago, Archive 994

4.12 M. Jones Collection

4.13 M. Jones Collection

4.14 Photo A. Beato. Courtesy of the Chicago House Photographic Archives, Epigraphic Survey, Oriental Institute, University of Chicago, Archive 13458

4.15 M. Jones Collection

4.16 M. Jones Collection. Epigraphic Survey, Photographic Archive P. 98

4.17 M. Jones Collection. Stereo image 9760, Keystone View Company

4.18 Photo A. Beato. Reproduced with permission of Patrick Montgomery, Archives Farms, Inc.

4.19 M. Jones Collection, Gaddis, Luxor

4.20 Chevrier Archive *97097/115*07. Courtesy of the Chicago House Photographic Archives, Epigraphic Survey, Oriental Institute, University of Chicago

4.21 M. Jones Collection, Associated Press photo

4.22 Photo W. R. Johnson

4.23 Photo Y. Kobylecky: ARCE

4.24 Photo M. Jones: ARCE

4.25 Photo Y. Kobylecky: ARCE

4.26 Photo Y. Kobylecky: ARCE

4.27 Photo Y. Kobylecky: ARCE

4.28 Photo M. Jones: ARCE

Chapter 5

Figure 5.1 Photo M. Jones: ARCE

5.2 Drawing S. Tagliacozzi, M. Gorini, and M. Marchese

5.3 Photo M. C. Tomassetti

5.4 Photo M. C. Tomassetti

5.5 Photos M. C. Tomassetti

5.6 Photo Y. Kobylecky: ARCE

5.7 Photo M. C. Tomassetti

5.8 Photo A. and A. Vescovo: ARCE

5.9 Photo Y. Kobylecky: ARCE

5.10 Photo A. and A. Vescovo: ARCE

5.11 Photo M. Jones: ARCE

5.12 Photo M. C. Tomassetti

5.13 Photos M. C. Tomassetti

5.14 Photo A. and A. Vescovo: ARCE

5.15 Photo Y. Kobylecky: ARCE

5.16 Photo A. and A. Vescovo: ARCE

5.17 Drawing S. Tagliacozzi, M. Gorini, and M. Marchese

5.18 Photo M. C. Tomassetti

5.19 Drawing S. Tagliacozzi, M. Gorini, and M. Marchese

5.20 Drawing S. Tagliacozzi, M. Gorini, and M. Marchese

5.21 Photo Artelab s.r.l.

5.22 Photos Artelab s.r.l.

5.23 Photo Artelab s.r.l.

5.24 Photos Artelab s.r.l.

5.25 Photo A. and A. Vescovo: ARCE

5.26 Photo Artelab s.r.l.

Chapter 6

Figure 6.1 Photo A. and A. Vescovo: ARCE

6.2 Photo Bpk, Berlin/Staatliche Museen, Berlin/ Johannes Laurentius/Art Resource, N.Y.

6.3 Photo A. and A. Vescovo: ARCE

6.4 Photo A. and A. Vescovo: ARCE

6.5 Photo A. and A. Vescovo: ARCE

6.6 © National Trust Images. Courtesy of the Bodleian Library, Oxford. MS. Wilkinson, dep. d. 34, page 31r (62)

6.7 Photo Y. Kobylecky: ARCE

6.8 Photo A. Vescovo

6.9 Courtesy of the Bodleian Libraries, Oxford: MS. Canon. Misc. 378, folio 094, recto

6.10 Photo A. and A. Vescovo: ARCE

6.11 From von Bissing 1926

6.12 Reproduced by permission of Johannes Deckers

6.13 Photo Y. Kobylecky: ARCE
6.14 Photo Y. Kobylecky: ARCE
6.15 Photo A. Vescovo: ARCE
6.16 Photo Y. Kobylecky: ARCE
6.17 Photo Y. Kobylecky: ARCE
6.18 Photo S. McFadden
6.19 Photo A. Vescovo
6.20 Reproduced by permission of Johannes Deckers
6.21 Photo Y. Kobylecky: ARCE
6.22 Photo A. Vescovo
6.23 Photo Y. Kobylecky: ARCE
6.24 Photo Y. Kobylecky: ARCE
6.25 Photo Y. Kobylecky: ARCE
6.26 Photo S. McFadden
6.27 Photo Y. Kobylecky: ARCE
6.28 Photo Y. Kobylecky: ARCE
6.29 Photo Y. Kobylecky: ARCE
6.30 Photo A. Vescovo
6.31 Photo Y. Kobylecky: ARCE
6.32 Photo S. McFadden

Chapter 7

Figure 7.1 Photo A. and A. Vescovo: ARCE
7.2 Photo S. McFadden
7.3 Photo A. and A. Vescovo: ARCE
7.4 Yale University Art Gallery 1931.386
7.5 Photo D. Diffendale
7.6 Photo A. Vescovo
7.7 HIP/Art Resource, N.Y.
7.8 Biblioteca Apostolica Vaticana, Romanus I, MS Barb. Lat. 2154, fol. 13. Foto Marburg/Art Resource, N.Y.
7.9 Real Académia de la Historia, Madrid, Spain Scala/Art Resource, N.Y.
7.10 Photo Y. Kobylecky: ARCE
7.11 Photo Y. Kobylecky: ARCE

Appendix

Figure A.1 © National Trust Images. Courtesy of the Bodleian Library, Oxford. MS. Wilkinson, dep. d. 34, pages 25v (51) and 26r (52); 26v (53) and 27r (54)
A.2 © National Trust Images. Courtesy of the Bodleian Library, Oxford. MS. Wilkinson, dep. d. 34, pages 27v (55) and 28r (56); 28v (57) and 29r (58)
A.3 © National Trust Images. Courtesy of the Bodleian Library, Oxford. MS. Wilkinson, dep. d. 34, pages 29v (59) and 30r (60); 30v (61, blank) and 31r (62)
A.4 © National Trust Images. Courtesy of the Bodleian Library, Oxford. MS. Wilkinson